Library of
Davidson College

Virginia Historical Society
Documents

Volume 14

The Official Papers of
Francis Fauquier
Lieutenant Governor of Virginia
1758–1768

The Official Papers of
FRANCIS FAUQUIER
Lieutenant Governor of Virginia
1758–1768

EDITED BY GEORGE REESE

VOLUME I
1758–1760

Published for
The Virginia Historical Society

The University Press of Virginia
Charlottesville

Published with the assistance
of a grant from
the Old Dominion Foundation
to the Virginia Historical Society

THE UNIVERSITY PRESS OF VIRGINIA
Copyright © 1980 by the Virginia Historical Society

First published 1980

Frontispiece: Francis Fauquier. Attributed to Benjamin
Wilson, 1757. Courtesy of the Thomas Coram Foundation
for Children, London, England

Library of Congress Cataloging in Publication Data
Virginia (Colony). Lieutenant Governor, 1758–1768
  (Fauquier)
  The official papers of Francis Fauquier, Lieutenant
Governor of Virginia, 1758–1768.

  (Virginia Historical Society documents; v. 14)
  Includes index.
  CONTENTS: v. 1. 1758–1760.
  1. Virginia—Politics and government—Colonial
period, ca. 1600–1775—Sources. 2. Fauquier,
Francis, 1704?–1768. I. Reese, George Henkle.
II. Title. III. Series: Virginia Historical
Society, Richmond. Documents; v. 14
F229.V528 1980   975.5'02'0924   80-19866
ISBN 0-8139-0856-6

Printed in the United States of America

Contents

Acknowledgments	xix
Editorial Method	xxi
Abbreviations and Short Titles	xxvii
Repositories	xxxi
Introduction	xxxv

1758

Commission to Fauquier, 10 February	1
From John Clevland, 14 March	2
From James Abercromby, 15 March	3
James Abercromby to Major General James Abercromby, 12 March	6
Memorial to the Treasury, ca. 15 March	7
Petition of Robert Hunter Morris, ca. 11 February	9
Warrant for Nathaniel Blakiston, 23 August 1716	10
Order in Council, 1 April	11
Warrant for Robert Carter, 7 April	12
From James Abercromby, 26 April	13
To John St. Clair, 6 June	14
To John Forbes, 8 June	19
To William Henry Lyttelton, 8 June	20
To Major General James Abercromby, 10 June	21
Address to Francis Fauquier and Reply, 10 June	22
To the Board of Trade, 11 June	23
To William Pitt, 11 June	25
Address to Francis Fauquier and Reply, 12 June	27
From William Byrd, *14 June* (Abstract)	28
To William Henry Lyttelton, 16 June	28
From George Washington, 17 June	30
Orders for George Washington, 13 June	32
To Horatio Sharpe, 18 June	33
To William Byrd, 19 June	34
From George Washington, 19 June	35
From James Abercromby, 23 June	37
Memorial of London Merchants, ca. 21 June	38

To George Washington, 25 June	41
To the Board of Trade, 28 June	43
From Horatio Sharpe, 3 July	46
From John Forbes, 8 July	47
Major General James Abercromby to the Marquis de Vaudreuil, 26 June	48
General Order from Major General James Abercromby, 25 June	49
From John Forbes, *10 July*	50
From George Washington, 10 July	50
From Horatio Sharpe, 12 July	51
To John Forbes, 20 July	52
To George Washington, 20 July	52
From James Abercromby, 20 July	53
From William Byrd, *21 July* (Abstract)	55
To the Board of Trade, 24 July	55
To William Prentis, 27 July	56
From Edward Boscawen, *ca. 27 July*	56
From William Henry Lyttelton, *ca. August* (Abstract)	56
From William Byrd, *3 August* (Abstract)	57
From George Washington, 5 August	57
From John Forbes, 16 August	59
To William Byrd, 17 August	60
To John Clevland, 25 August	62
To the Admiralty, 25 August	63
From William Henry Lyttelton, *28 August*	64
From William Denny, *30 August* (Abstract)	64
From Christopher Smith, *ca. September*	65
From George Washington, 2 September	65
To the Earl of Loudoun, 10 September	69
To William Denny, *ca. 11 September* (Abstract)	70
From James Abercromby, 12 September	70
To George Washington, 16 September	72
From William Pitt, 18 September	73
To the Board of Trade, 23 September	74
To John Clevland, 23 September	78
From George Washington, 25 September	79
From William Henry Lyttelton, *26 September* (Abstract)	80
From George Washington, 28 September	81
From Robert Winn, *ca. October* (Abstract)	82
From John Forbes, *1 October* (Abstract)	83

Contents ix

From Charles Smith, *ca. 2 October*	83
To William Henry Lyttelton, 5 October	84
From James Abercromby, 5 October	85
To George Washington, 7 October	86
To George Washington, *7 October*	88
From John Forbes, *9 October* (Abstract)	88
To William Henry Lyttelton, 13 October	89
Council Journal, 12 October	91
To John Forbes, *19 October*	92
From William Byrd, *21 October* (Abstract)	93
From John Forbes, *22 October* (Abstract)	94
Warrant for James Robert, 27 October	94
From George Washington, 30 October	96
From John Buchanan, *ca. November*	97
From William Ramsay, *ca. November* (Abstract)	97
From William Henry Lyttelton, *1 November* (Abstract)	98
Proclamation, *ca. 3 November*	98
To John Forbes, *ca. 4 November*	99
To George Washington, 4 November	99
From John Forbes, 5 November	101
From George Washington, 5 November	104
To William Byrd, 12 November	104
To John Buchanan, 14 November	105
From James Abercromby, 17 November	106
To John Forbes, 19 November	107
To the Earl of Loudoun, 20 November	109
To George Washington, 22 November	113
From William Denny, *22 November*	113
From John Forbes, *26 November* (Abstract)	114
From William Byrd, *28 November*	114
From George Washington, 28 November	115
From George Washington, 2 December	117
To George Washington, *3 December*	119
From William Henry Lyttelton, *7 December* (Abstract)	119
Journal of the Council of South Carolina, 8-16 November	120
From William Byrd, *9 December* (Abstract)	127
From William Pitt, 9 December	128
From George Washington, 9 December	130
From William Henry Lyttelton, 12 December	131
From Jeffery Amherst, 13 December	133
Proclamation, *ca. 14 December*	134

To William Henry Lyttelton, 14 December	134
From Christopher Gist, *27 December* (Abstract)	135
From James Abercromby, 28 December	135
From William Byrd, *29 December*	137
From William Pitt, 29 December	138

1759

Petition of John Catlet, ca. 1759	140
To the Bishop of London, ca. 1759	142
To the Board of Trade, 5 January	143
From John Pownall, 5 January	149
The Board of Trade to Robert Dinwiddie, 3 July 1754	149
The Board of Trade to Robert Dinwiddie, 18 April 1755	152
From John Forbes, *11 January* (Abstract)	154
From the Board of Trade, 18 January	155
From John Pownall, 19 January	156
Order in Council, 11 January	157
To William Henry Lyttelton, *ca. 23 January*	158
To William Byrd, 23 January	158
From William Pitt, 23 January	160
To Jeffery Amherst, 24 January	161
To John Forbes, 24 January	162
From William Henry Lyttelton, *26 January*	163
From Robert Wood, 26 January	163
Orders for Mourning, 22 January	164
To the Board of Trade, 30 January	164
From James Abercromby, 31 January	167
Order in Council, 2 February	168
The Board of Trade to the King, 18 January	169
From William Pitt, 5 February	170
To George Washington, 7 February	171
Additional Instruction, 9 February	172
James Abercromby to John Blair, 10 February	173
From Jeffery Amherst, 11 February	175
From Jeffery Amherst, 16 February	175
To Arthur Dobbs, *ca. 17 February*	177
To William Denny, 17 February	177
To William Henry Lyttelton, 27 February	177
From Horatio Sharpe, *ca. March*	179

From James Abercromby, *ca. 1 March*	179
To Jeffery Amherst, 2 March	179
To William Byrd, 2 March	180
To Horatio Sharpe, 9 March	180
To Jeffery Amherst, 11 March	181
To Jeffery Amherst, 11 March	183
To Jeffery Amherst, 11 March	184
From Richard Coytmore, *ca. 15 March* (Abstract)	184
From the Little Carpenter, *15 March* (Abstract)	185
To Jeffery Amherst, 17 March	186
From Jeffery Amherst, 18 March	187
To Horatio Sharpe, 19 March	188
From James Abercromby, 21 March	189
From Jeffery Amherst, 22 March	191
From William Byrd, *22 March* (Abstract)	192
From William Byrd, *25 March*	193
From William Byrd, *26 March* (Abstract)	193
From John Blagg, *27 March*	193
From Jeffery Amherst, 28 March	193
From Jeffery Amherst, 30 March	195
From Jeffery Amherst, 30 March	196
To Arthur Dobbs, *31 March*	197
To William Henry Lyttelton, *31 March*	198
From Jeffery Amherst, 31 March	198
From John Stanwix, *2 April*	198
To Jeffery Amherst, 3 April	199
To William Pitt, 3 April	200
From Beverley Robinson, *6 April* (Abstract)	201
To William Henry Lyttelton, 7 April	202
To Jeffery Amherst, 8 April	202
To the Board of Trade, 10 April	204
To the Board of Trade, 14 April	207
Address to the Assembly, 14 April	210
Order in Council, 14 April	211
To William Pitt, 16 April	212
To Horatio Sharpe, 18 April	213
From Jeffery Amherst, 22 April	213
From William Henry Lyttelton, *27 April* (Abstract)	214
From John Stanwix, *28 April* (Abstract)	215
To the Board of Trade, 9 May	215
From Horatio Sharpe, 18 May	216

From Samuel Davies, *30 May* (Abstract)	217
From John Stanwix, *30 May*	217
From William Byrd, *4 June* (Abstract)	218
From William Henry Lyttelton, *7 June* (Abstract)	218
To the Board of Trade, 9 June	218
To William Henry Lyttelton, 19 June	220
Philip Grymes to William Henry Lyttelton, 13 June	221
To the Board of Trade, 23 June	221
To the Earl of Loudoun, 13 July	223
To the Board of Trade, 14 July	224
From the Lords of the Admiralty, 20 July	226
From James Abercromby, 26 July	226
From Jeffery Amherst, 27 July	229
To the Board of Trade, 2 August	230
From Jeffery Amherst, 8 August	231
Order in Council, 10 August	232
From Jeffery Amherst, 14 August	234
From William Byrd, 15 August	234
From William Henry Lyttelton, *15 August* (Abstract)	235
Richard Coytmore to William Henry Lyttelton, 3 August 1759	235
To Jeffery Amherst, 18 August	238
From William Byrd, *23 August* (Abstract)	239
From Henry Bouquet, 25 August	239
Order in Council, 29 August	241
To the Board of Trade, 30 August	242
To William Henry Lyttelton, 5 September	243
To Henry Bouquet, 11 September	245
To Richard Smith, 14 September	246
From Jeffery Amherst, 14 September	247
To Jeffery Amherst, 16 September	248
Additional Instruction, 21 September	249
To James Abercromby, *29 September*	250
From Adam Stephen, *ca. October*	250
From William Henry Lyttelton, *1 October*	250
From John Stanwix, 4 October	251
From Jeffery Amherst, 7 October	251
To the Board of Trade, 13 October	252
To John Clevland, *13 October*	254
From William Henry Lyttelton, *16 October*	254
To William Henry Lyttelton, 21 October	254

Contents xiii

From Jeffery Amherst, 22 October	255
To Adam Stephen, 24 October	256
From Jeffery Amherst, 25 October	257
From William Henry Lyttelton, *25 October* (Abstract)	257
From William Byrd, *29 October*	258
From Adam Stephen, 29 October	258
From John Mercer, *ca. November*	259
To John Stanwix, *ca. 1 November*	263
From Arthur Dobbs, *ca. 1 November*	263
To Jeffery Amherst, 10 November	263
To William Henry Lyttelton, 11 November	264
From the Board of Trade, 13 November	265
Proclamation, 23 October	265
From Jeffery Amherst, 16 November	266
Jacob Van Braam to Jeffery Amherst, 9 November	267
From the Board of Trade, 20 November	269
To William Henry Lyttelton, 22 November	269
To William Byrd, *ca. 24 November*	270
To John Stanwix, 24 November	271
To Jeffery Amherst, 25 November	272
Warrant for David Bowman, 26 November	274
From William Peachey, *28 November* (Abstract)	275
To the Board of Trade, 1 December	275
To John Stanwix, 1 December	278
From John Stanwix, *1 December*	279
From William Peachey, *4 December*	279
From John Stanwix, *5 December*	279
From John St. Clair, *8 December* (Abstract)	280
From Lord Colville, *9 December* (Abstract)	280
Memorial to the Treasury, *ca. 12 December*	280
To James Abercromby, *14 December*	281
To the Board of Trade, 17 December	281
From Jeffery Amherst, 21 December	284
From James Abercromby, 22 December	285
Opinion of the Attorney General, 24 December	288
To John Stanwix, 24 December	289
From Jeffery Amherst, 27 December	290
From William Henry Lyttelton, *27 December*	291
Treaty with the Cherokees, 26 December	292
Appendix A: Account of 2/ per Hogshead Revenue, 25 April–25 October 1758	295

Appendix B: Account of Quitrents, 1757 — 299
Appendix C: Account of 2/ per Hogshead Revenue,
    25 October 1758–25 April 1759 — 303

1760

Petition of James Pittillo, ca. 1760 — 305
To Beverley Robinson, *ca. January* — 306
From John Stanwix, 6 January — 306
From William Pitt, 7 January — 308
To Jeffery Amherst, 17 January — 310
From Robert Stobo, *ca. February* — 311
From William Henry Lyttelton, *2 February* (Abstract) — 311
    Richard Coytmore to William Henry Lyttelton,
    23 January — 312
To William Henry Lyttelton, 4 February — 317
From Peter Wyche, *5 February* — 318
From Jeffery Amherst, 9 February — 318
From William Byrd, *11 February* — 319
From Jeffery Amherst, 14 February — 320
From James Abercromby, 15 February — 321
From Jeffery Amherst, 15 February — 322
From Jeffery Amherst, 21 February — 323
To Jeffery Amherst, 23 February — 325
From William Byrd, *ca. March* — 326
Proclamation, *ca. 5 March* — 326
Proclamation, *ca. 5 March* — 326
To Jeffery Amherst, 5 March — 326
To Jeffery Amherst, 5 March — 327
To John Stanwix, *8 March* — 330
From John Clevland, 12 March — 330
To the Board of Trade, 13 March — 331
To William Pitt, 14 March — 334
From Jeffery Amherst, 17 March — 334
From Samuel Martin, *19 March* (Abstract) — 335
From James Abercromby, 20 March — 336
To John Stanwix, 22 March — 337
From Thomas Pownall, *24 March* (Abstract) — 338
From Abraham Maury, *28 March* (Abstract) — 339
From William Byrd, *30 March* (Abstract) — 339
From Jeffery Amherst, 31 March — 339

Contents xv

To Andrew Lewis, *ca. April*	340
To Abraham Maury, *ca. April* (Abstract)	340
From Thomas Bullitt, *ca. April* (Abstract)	341
From Jeffery Amherst, 1 April	341
From Jeffery Amherst, 1 April	342
To Jeffery Amherst, 5 April	342
Order in Council, 5 April	343
Order in Council, 5 April	344
Proclamation, *ca. 11 April*	345
To Horatio Sharpe, 12 April	345
From William Bull, *12 April* (Abstract)	346
From James Abercromby, 14 April	346
From Jeffery Amherst, 20 April	348
To Peter Wyche, 22 April	348
From Arthur Dobbs, *24 April* (Abstract)	350
From Jeffery Amherst, 28 April	350
From William Bull, *28 April* (Abstract)	351
From Thomas Walker, *29 April* (Abstract)	351
To William Bull, *ca. May*	351
To Arthur Dobbs, *ca. May*	351
To John Stanwix, *ca. 3 May*	352
To Jeffery Amherst, 3 May	352
To James Hamilton, 7 May	352
From Robert Monckton, 7 May	354
To Jeffery Amherst, 8 May	354
From James Abercromby, 10 May	355
Agent's Account, ca. 8 May	356
To the Board of Trade, 12 May	358
To the Treasury, 12 May	360
To Jeffery Amherst, 18 May	360
From Robert Monckton, *18 May* (Abstract)	361
From Robert Monckton, *19 May*	361
To William Byrd, *20 May*	361
Order in Council, 20 May	361
Order in Council, 20 May	363
To County Lieutenants, *ca. 24 May*	364
To William Bull, 24 May	365
To Robert Monckton, 24 May	366
To Horatio Sharpe, 26 May	367
From James Hamilton, *27 May* (Abstract)	367
From Jeffery Amherst, 28 May	368

From Arthur Dobbs, *28 May* (Abstract)	368
From William Byrd, *29 May* (Abstract)	368
From William Bull, *31 May* (Abstract)	369
From Landon Carter, *ca. June*	369
From William Preston, *ca. June*	369
From Horatio Sharpe, *ca. June*	370
From James Abercromby, 1 June	370
To the Board of Trade, 2 June	371
From Arthur Dobbs, *8 June* (Abstract)	373
Proclamation, *ca. 12 June*	373
To William Byrd, *ca. 12 June* (Abstract)	374
To Robert Monckton, 12 June	374
From the Board of Trade, 13 June	375
The Board of Trade to the King, 16 May	377
Mathew Lamb to the Board of Trade, 15 May	379
To Horatio Sharpe, 14 June	380
To James Abercromby, *22 June*	381
To William Preston, 24 June	381
To James Abercromby, *ca. 25 June*	382
To Samuel Martin, *ca. 25 June*	383
To the Board of Trade, 30 June	383
To Landon Carter, 30 June	386
From William Bull, *ca. July*	386
From William Byrd, *ca. July*	387
From John Chiswell, *ca. July*	387
From Horatio Sharpe, *ca. July*	387
From James Abercromby, 3 July	387
Agent's Account, ca. 3 July	389
From William Byrd, *4 July* (Abstract)	389
To Commanding Officers, *ca. 8 July*	390
To the Board of Trade, 11 July	390
From William Byrd, *11 July* (Abstract)	391
To William Byrd, *24 July* (Abstract)	392
From William Bull, *26 July*	392
To Richard Bland, 28 July	392
To Horatio Sharpe, 28 July	394
From Jeffery Amherst, 28 July	394
From William Byrd, *August*	395
From Cadwallader Colden, 4 August	395
From William Byrd, *ca. 20 August* (Abstract)	396
Articles of Capitulation, 7 August	397

From Robert Monckton, 21 August	398
To Jeffery Amherst, 22 August	398
From William Pitt, 23 August	399
Petition of St. Andrew's Parish, ca. 25 August	400
From Jeffery Amherst, 26 August	401
To Cadwallader Colden, 31 August	402
To the Board of Trade, 1 September	403
To James Abercromby, *2 September*	406
From Jeffery Amherst, 9 September	407
To Robert Monckton, 10 September	408
From William Byrd, *10 September*	409
Andrew Lewis to William Byrd, 9 September	409
To William Bull, *ca. 16 September* (Abstract)	410
To William Byrd, *ca. 16 September* (Abstract)	410
To the Board of Trade, 17 September	411
From William Byrd, *19 September* (Abstract)	412
William Byrd to the Cherokees, 16 September	413
Articles of Peace, 17 September	414
From William Bull, *21 September* (Abstract)	415
From William Byrd, *24 September*	415
From James Abercromby, 1 October	416
To Jeffery Amherst, 5 October	418
From Robert Monckton, *16 October*	418
To Adam Stephen, *ca. 17 October*	419
To William Byrd, *17 October*	419
To Robert Monckton, 17 October	419
From John Pownall, 18 October	420
To Robert Monckton, 27 October	420
From Robert Monckton, *27 October*	421
To William Pitt, 28 October	421
From John Pownall, 29 October	423
From Robert Monckton, *30 October* (Abstract)	423
To James Abercromby, *31 October*	424
From the Board of Trade, 31 October	424
From the Privy Council, 31 October	425
Proclamation of George III, 29 October	426
Warrant for Use of Seal, 28 October	427
Proclamation, 27 October	427
Additional Instruction, 31 October	429
Order in Council, 27 October	430
To Edward Montagu, *ca. November* (Abstract)	430

From William Byrd, *3 November* (Abstract)	431
To James Abercromby, *6 November*	431
To Jeffery Amherst, 7 November	432
To Robert Monckton, 12 November	433
To William Byrd, *13 November*	433
To William Byrd, *14 November*	434
From William Bull, *16 November* (Abstract)	434
From William Byrd, *22 November* (Abstract)	434
To James Abercromby, *23 November*	435
From Arthur Dobbs, *25 November* (Abstract)	435
From the Board of Trade, 28 November	436
From James Abercromby, 1 December	436
From William Byrd, *3 December* (Abstract)	438
To Jeffery Amherst, 5 December	438
To the Board of Trade, 6 December	439
To William Byrd, 10 December	442
To Jeffery Amherst, 15 December	443
To the Board of Trade, 15 December	444
From William Pitt, 17 December	446
From Robert Monckton, *18 December* (Abstract)	448
From James Abercromby, 25 December	448
From Jeffery Amherst, 28 December	449
Appendix A: Account of Quitrents, 1758	451
Appendix B: Account of 2/ per Hogshead Revenue, 25 April-25 October 1759	455
Appendix C: Account of 2/ per Hogshead Revenue, 25 October 1759-25 April 1760	457

Acknowledgments

I acknowledge gratefully the permission I have received from owners and custodians to include in this present collection papers in their hands; I am particularly obliged to Her Majesty's Stationery Office for permission to publish papers in the Public Record Office. The Tracy W. McGregor Library, University of Virginia, has provided the facsimile of Francis Fauquier's signature on the cover.

Many people and institutions, too many to be named individually, have given me indispensable help. I have a special debt of gratitude to the Research Department of the Colonial Williamsburg Foundation for providing copies of text and supplying an expert reference service over a period of some ten years. I owe much to the staff of the Manuscript Department in the William L. Clements Library for their generous gift of time in answering many questions and their vigorous pursuit of elusive letters and enclosures.

I am very thankful for the people who did most of the clerical work and an important part of the research required by this undertaking: Joan Carl, Nora Lea Reefe, Kathy Flippo, and above all Sally Henkel, who carried out much of the final revision and prepared the index. Their skill and intelligence, their patient industry, and their unflagging good temper have been a comfort.

Editorial Method

The aim of this collection is to bring together the official papers of Francis Fauquier during the decade when he was lieutenant governor of Virginia, or, more precisely, from 10 February 1758, the date of his first commission, through 12 May 1768, the date by which the earl of Hillsborough, secretary of state responsible for the colonies, had certainly learned of Fauquier's death.

The collection comprises all known official correspondence to and from Fauquier. It includes papers not specifically addressed such as proclamations, as well as all enclosures except some printed pieces (for which the reader is referred to a printed text), manuscript acts of assembly, and journals of the council and the House of Burgesses, all of which have been printed. The naval officers' returns, which seldom can be identified with any certainty, are also omitted, but they are tentatively identified whenever it is possible, and the manuscripts are cited by their designation in the Public Record Office. Finally, whenever several very similar enclosures accompany one covering letter, one representative enclosure is printed; the others are listed in a note indicating the particulars in which they differ from the representative enclosure.

Papers known only because they are mentioned in the correspondence, or in the journals of the council or the House of Burgesses, or elsewhere are included in the form of entries giving whatever abstract of the contents has been found or is thought to be a reasonable conjecture.

The collection does not include formal documents essentially unvarying, such as commissions, patents for land, or ships' registers, on which the governor's signature is simply a certification.

It must be supposed that much of Fauquier's correspondence and other papers has been lost. Aside from the numerous letters and papers known only by some reference to them, there was probably a considerable amount of correspondence with people in Virginia or elsewhere in America and with the Treasury and perhaps other offices in England that has disappeared without leaving any trace. In the normal way, the executive journals of the council would refer to Fauquier's official letters and papers of any but a routine nature and often supply a summary. However, those journals for the period between 15 September 1763 and 8 September 1767 are missing, except for extracts from the entries for six or eight days in the years 1763–65; the minutes, a preliminary draft of the journals, for fifteen days in the years 1764–67 have survived, but they probably omit much or most of the information in the journal entries. Issues of the *Virginia Gazette*, in which printed proclamations and other official pronouncements by Fauquier often appeared, are missing from the beginning of 1758 until March 1766, except for a single issue from each of the years 1759, 1761, 1762, 1764, and 1765.

William Gordon, in *The History of the Rise, Progress, and Establishment, of the Independence of the United States of America* . . . (London, 1788), 1:136, asserted that toward the end of 1759 or the beginning of 1760 William Pitt suggested in a letter to Fauquier that after the war the government might tax the colonies in order to raise a revenue from them; and in reply Fauquier gave his opinion that such taxation would cause a great disturbance and hoped his answer might deter Pitt from carrying out his plan. These letters have not been found, and it may be doubted that such an exchange took place: as early as 1757 Pitt was firmly opposed to plans to tax the colonies; he seems to have been constant in his opposition to taxation without representation; moreover, if he were concerned to gauge colonial opposition to taxation, he would surely have canvassed the opinion of all the colonial governors, and no indication of such a general inquiry has been found.

Correspondence from Fauquier is commonly in his own hand, though a clerk or secretary wrote some of his letters and Fauquier only signed them; some of his letters survive only as copies made by or for the persons to whom they were addressed. Ordinarily, the text printed here is that of a receiver's copy in Fauquier's hand, but a secretary's copy with Fauquier's signature is preferred if it provides a more complete or legible text.

No original correspondence to Fauquier has been found, except for a couple of petitions originating in Virginia and the royal warrant of 22 May 1767 appointing George William Fairfax to the council, so that correspondence to Fauquier is commonly in copies retained by the writers or, in some instances, in copies made by the writer or another person to be sent to someone else for his information. As a result, many pieces addressed to Fauquier, notably many orders in council, are not actually known to have been received, for they are nowhere acknowledged or otherwise mentioned.

An occasional paper, either to or from Fauquier, exists only in print, any manuscript version having disappeared.

Copies of papers other than the copies printed here are not mentioned

Editorial Method xxiii

unless they contribute emendations or provide information on the item not found in its text. All copies, however, have been carefully collated with the text chosen for printing.

The cardinal principle of this collection has been to avoid all but the indispensable editorial intervention. Accordingly, the text is printed in a form as nearly like that of the original as is practicable (with exceptions in transcription as noted), although a date in brackets is inserted in the upper right corner above the text if there was none there. Nothing has been added to the text of the papers but brackets (usually enclosing letters or words), periods at ends of paragraphs, and reference numbers for notes. The editor has tried to use as few notes as possible, and to keep those few both short and objective.

The papers are arranged in order of date, with papers sent by Fauquier preceding those sent to him, and with papers in each group arranged in alphabetical order by the names of senders or recipients. If the sender of a paper is not exactly identified (as is true, for example, of orders in council), the paper precedes those of the same date sent by specified persons.

Undated papers are placed before dated ones. A paper which can be referred only to some year precedes dated papers of that year, a paper which can be dated only as of about a certain month precedes dated papers of that month, and one which can be dated only as of approximately a stated day precedes dated papers of that day.

Enclosures follow the papers with which they were sent. If a paper has more than one enclosure, they are arranged in whatever order is suggested by the covering paper or by the enclosures themselves; otherwise, enclosures are arranged in some arbitrary order. However, the accounts of quitrents and of the revenue of two shillings per hogshead on tobacco are collected in appendixes following papers of the year in which the accounts were transmitted.

A paper in a foreign language is printed in its normal place in an English translation, with the original text put in an appendix following other papers of the year.

Each item is followed by a bibliographical note, not numbered, describing the item as printed or as some variety of manuscript, stating where the manuscript is found and citing its archival reference, and including other information not provided by the text. Papers are in the Public Record Office, London, if no location is indicated. The bibliographical note is usually followed by numbered notes providing identifications, explanations, or references to other sources of information.

Papers are described by these designations:

ALS Autograph letter signed, one wholly in the hand of the signer
ADS Autograph document signed, something not a letter, wholly in the hand of the signer
LS Letter signed, one in a hand or hands not the signer's
DS Document signed, one in a hand or hands not the signer's
Copy A manuscript copy, made from an original of any of the varieties described above
MS A manuscript not accurately or certainly described by any of the designations above
Printed A text deriving from a printed text

Superscript letters are brought down to the line. Abbreviated or contracted words (but not the contracted verb forms still in common use or those now obsolete forms where an apostrophe replaces *l* in the modal auxiliaries and *e* in the verb-ending *-ed*) are expanded without comment, except that names of months and days, titles, ordinal numerals, weights and measures, and any short forms still in current usage, or readily understood, are left unchanged.

The *p* with a crossed descender is rendered as *per*, long *s* as short *s*, and thorn as *th*.

Spelling is unchanged, except that a single letter evidently left out by mistake is inserted silently and the ligatures of *o* and *a* with *e* are rendered as separate letters.

Capitalization is retained. If it is not clear whether a letter was meant as a capital or a small letter, the editor has tried to follow the writer's normal practice.

Punctuation is that of the manuscript, except that a virgule in the salutation of a letter is replaced by a comma; an omitted period is supplied at the end of a paragraph; and quotation marks are retained only at the beginning and end of quoted text. The placing of an omitted mark of quotation or parenthesis is the subject of a note.

Insertions by the writer are included in the text without comment, and matter deleted by the writer is omitted without comment unless it is judged to have interest or significance, when it may be retained in brackets with an explanatory note, or else quoted in a note.

Words or letters supplied from another copy of the text and conjectural readings are in brackets.

Occasional manuscript text in unusually large or ornate letters, as well as italic, boldface, or blackletter type in printed documents, is transcribed as ordinary roman.

Editorial Method

The arrangement of text in the original is usually preserved, but some changes have been made for the sake of economy or to facilitate printing. The complimentary close of a letter is run into the last paragraph of the letter. The arrangement of accounts and lists is often simplified or compressed, but the substance is never altered. Only radical changes in arrangement are noticed.

A gap due to illegible text or loss of text through damage is indicated by a blank space inside brackets.

Endorsements and other annotations providing information not in the papers proper are quoted or paraphrased in notes, but others are ignored.

Adherence to the policy of following without comment the writer's insertions and deletions in his drafts or copies ought to achieve the text of the receiver's copy. However, this is not necessarily true, and it is almost certainly not true of letters in George Washington's letter books, in which the copies were altered long after the letters were sent off and received. The editor has transcribed those copies in their altered form because the deleted words are generally altogether obliterated; his impression is that the changes were usually attempts at a more elegant style or a softer statement and do not alter the essential meaning of the text.

James Abercromby's letter book requires special comment. His handwriting is difficult to read, and very often the editor has had to transcribe a word as what it ought to be according to sense or idiom or grammar. A secretary turned out manuscripts of exemplary neatness and legibility, but these Abercromby often altered with deletions or insertions of remarkable slovenliness, of the sort he put into his holograph manuscripts. Whether a letter is in Abercromby's hand or in some secretary's hand, if Abercromby made any revisions it is often hard to decipher the alterations and equally hard to decide where they are to be made. A fair number of Abercromby's letters are represented by a bare summary of what was to be written (or, rarely, perhaps of what had been written). Something like the text of one letter to Fauquier in Abercromby's letter book has been discovered in a separate document, which may be a copy, or even the receiver's copy, but in any event is markedly different from the letter-book manuscript, even though obviously written on the same topics. The editor decided that the contents of Abercromby's letter book had best be designated simply as MS, since it seemed impossible to describe them safely as copies or drafts.

All transcriptions have been made from photographic copies of the originals.

The present collection will be issued in several volumes; the index will appear in the last volume.

Abbreviations and Short Titles

Acts P.C.   *Acts of the Privy Council of England. Colonial Series*. London, 1908–12; rept. Nendeln, Liechtenstein, 1966.
Alberts.   Robert C. Alberts. *The Most Extraordinary Adventures of Major Robert Stobo*. Boston, 1965.
Alden.   John Richard Alden. *John Stuart and the Southern Frontier: A Study of Indian Relations, War, Trade, and Land Problems in the Southern Wilderness, 1754–1775*. Ann Arbor, Mich., and London, 1944.
Black.   Henry Campbell Black. *Black's Law Dictionary: Definitions of the Terms and Phrases of American and English Jurisprudence, Ancient and Modern*. Rev. 4th ed. St. Paul, 1968.
Boston Gaz.   *Boston Gazette*.
Bouquet.   Sylvester K. Stevens and Donald H. Kent, eds. *The Papers of Col. Henry Bouquet*. Harrisburg, Pa., 1940–.
Bristol.   Roger P. Bristol. *Supplement to Charles Evans' American Bibliography*. Charlottesville, Va., 1970.
Brydon.   George M. Brydon. *Virginia's Mother Church and the Political Conditions under Which It Grew*. Richmond and Philadelphia, 1947–52.
BTJ.   *Journal of the Commissioners for Trade and Plantations* . . . London, 1920–38.
Chamberlayne.   C. G. Chamberlayne, ed. *The Vestry Book of Petsworth Parish, Gloucester County, Virginia, 1677–1793*. Richmond, 1933.
Colden.   *The Letters and Papers of Cadwallader Colden. Collections of the New-York Historical Society*. New York, 1918–37.
Crane.   Verner Winslow Crane. *The Southern Frontier, 1670–1732*. Philadelphia, 1929.
CSP.   *Calendar of State Papers, Colonial Series* . . . London, 1860–19—.
Dinwiddie.   R. A. Brock, ed. *The Official Records of Robert Dinwiddie, Lieutenant-Governor of the Colony of Virginia, 1751–1758*. Richmond, 1883–84.
EJC.   H. R. McIlwaine et al., eds. *Executive Journals of the Council of Colonial Virginia, 1680–1775*. Richmond, 1925–66.
Evans.   Charles Evans. *American Bibliography* . . . Chicago, 1903–59.
Fitzpatrick.   John C. Fitzpatrick, ed. *The Writings of George Washington from the Original Manuscript Sources, 1745–1799*. Washington, D.C., 1931–44.
Flippin.   Percy Scott Flippin. *The Royal Government in Virginia, 1624–1775*. New York, 1919.

Forbes. Alfred Procter James, ed. *Writings of General John Forbes Relating to His Service in North America.* 1938; rept. New York, 1971.

Foreman. Carolyn Thomas Foreman. *Indians Abroad, 1493–1938.* Norman, Okla., 1943.

Franklin. Leonard W. Labaree, ed. *The Papers of Benjamin Franklin.* New Haven, 1966—.

Freeman. Douglas Southall Freeman. *George Washington, a Biography.* New York, 1948–57.

Gage. Clarence Edwin Carter, ed. *The Correspondence of General Thomas Gage.* New Haven and London, 1931–33.

GM. *The Gentleman's Magazine.* London.

Gipson. Lawrence Henry Gipson. *The British Empire before the American Revolution.* New York, 1966–70.

Hamilton. Stanislaus Murray Hamilton, ed. *Letters to Washington and Accompanying Papers.* Boston and New York, 1898–1902.

Hening. William Waller Hening, ed. *The Statutes at Large: Being a Collection of All the Laws of Virginia, from the First Session of the Legislature, in the Year 1619.* Richmond, Philadelphia, and New York, 1819–23; rept. Charlottesville, Va., 1969.

James. Alfred P. James. *The Ohio Company: Its Inner History.* Pittsburgh, 1959.

JHB. H. R. McIlwaine and John P. Kennedy, eds. *Journals of the House of Burgesses of Virginia, 1619–1776.* Richmond, 1905–15.

JHC. *Journals of the House of Commons.* London.

Johnson. The Papers of Sir William Johnson. Albany, 1921–65.

Koontz. Louis Knott Koontz. *The Virginia Frontier, 1754–1763.* Baltimore, 1925.

Labaree [1]. Leonard Woods Labaree. *Royal Government in America: A Study of the British Colonial System Before 1783.* 1958; rept. New York, 1964.

Labaree [2]. Leonard Woods Labaree, ed. *Royal Instructions to British Colonial Governors, 1670–1776.* 1935; rept. New York, 1967.

LJC. H. R. McIlwaine, ed. *Legislative Journals of the Council of Colonial Virginia, 1680–1773.* Richmond, 1918–19.

Lon. Gaz. London Gazette. London.

Md. Arch. *Archives of Maryland.* Baltimore, 1883–19—.

Md. Gaz. *Maryland Gazette.* Annapolis.

Meade. Robert Douthat Meade. *Patrick Henry, Patriot in the Making.* Philadelphia, 1957.

MHSC. *Collections of the Massachusetts Historical Society.*

Abbreviations and Short Titles

Morton.   Richard Lee Morton. *Colonial Virginia.* Chapel Hill, N.C., 1960.

Mulkearn.   Lois Mulkearn, ed. *George Mercer Papers Relating to the Ohio Company of Virginia.* Pittsburgh, 1954.

Namier.   Sir Lewis Bernstein Namier and John Brooke. *The House of Commons, 1754–1790.* New York, 1964.

O'Callaghan [1].   E. B. O'Callaghan. *The Documentary History of the State of New-York.* Albany, 1849–51.

O'Callaghan [2].   E. B. O'Callaghan and Berthold Fernow, eds. *Documents Relative to the Colonial History of the State of New-York.* Albany, 1853–87.

Pa. Arch. [1].   *Pennsylvania Archives.* 1st series. Philadelphia, 1852–56.

Pa. Arch. [2].   *Pennsylvania Archives: Second Series.* Harrisburg, Pa., 1879–90.

Pa. Gaz.   *Pennsylvania Gazette.* Philadelphia.

Pargellis.   Stanley McCrory Pargellis, ed. *Military Affairs in North America, 1748–1765: Selected Documents from the Cumberland Papers in Windsor Castle.* 1964; rept. Hamden, Conn., 1969.

Parl. Hist.   *Parliamentary History of England from the Earliest Period to the Year 1803.* London, 1806–20.

P.C. Pa.   *Minutes of the Provincial Council of Pennsylvania.* Philadelphia, Harrisburg, Pa., 1852.

Perry.   William Stevens Perry, ed. *Historical Collections Relating to the American Colonial Church.* Hartford, 1870–78.

Pitt.   Gertrude Selwyn Kimball, ed. *Correspondence of William Pitt.* New York, 1906.

S.C. Gaz.   *South-Carolina Gazette.* Charleston.

S.C. Records.   William L. McDowell, Jr., ed. *Colonial Records of South Carolina: Documents Relating to Indian Affairs, 1754–1765.* Columbia, S.C., 1970.

Smith.   Joseph Henry Smith. *Appeals to the Privy Council from the American Plantations.* New York, 1950.

Statutes.   Owen Ruffhead, ed. *The Statutes at Large, from Magna Carta, to the End of the Last Parliament, 1761.* London, 1763–1800.

THM.   *Tennessee Historical Magazine.*

Thomas.   Peter David Garner Thomas. *British Politics and the Stamp Act Crisis.* Oxford and New York, 1975.

Timberlake.   *The Memoirs of Lieutenant Henry Timberlake.* London, 1765; rept. Johnson City, Tenn., 1927, with notes and introduction by Samuel Cole Williams; the latter rept. New York, 1971.

Tyler.   Lyon Gardiner Tyler, ed. *Encyclopedia of Virginia Biography*. New York, 1915.

Va. Gaz.   *Virginia Gazette*. Williamsburg.

Va. Gaz. P.D.   *Virginia Gazette*. Williamsburg: Purdie and Dixon.

Va. Gaz. Rind.   *Virginia Gazette*. Williamsburg: Rind.

VMHB.   *The Virginia Magazine of History and Biography*.

VSP.   William P. Palmer et al., eds. *Calendar of Virginia State Papers and Other Manuscripts.* . . . Richmond, 1875–93.

WMQ.   *William and Mary Quarterly*.

Wyndham.   Hon. Mrs. Maud Mary Lyttelton Wyndham. *Chronicles of the Eighteenth Century, Founded on the Correspondence of Sir Thomas Lyttelton and His Family*. Boston, 1924.

Repositories

Ballindalloch Castle, Banffshire, Scotland
    Ballindalloch Castle Muniments
Bodleian Library, Oxford, England
    MS North
British Library, London, England
    Add. Mss.
    Stowe
Chicago Historical Society Library, Chicago
William L. Clements Library, Ann Arbor, Mich.
    Amherst Papers
    Gage Papers
    Lyttelton Papers
Colonial Williamsburg Foundation, Williamsburg, Va.
County Record Office, Stafford, England
    Dartmouth Papers
Darlington Memorial Library, University of Pittsburgh, Pittsburgh
    George Mercer Papers
Hall of Records of Maryland, Annapolis
    Council Proceedings, 1753–1767
    Executive Papers
    Governor's Letter Book
    Sharpe Letter Book
Harvard University Library, Cambridge, Mass.
    Governor Tryon's North Carolina Papers
Historical Society of Pennsylvania, Philadelphia
House of Lords Record Office, London, England
    Main Papers
Henry E. Huntington Library and Art Gallery, San Marino, Calif.
    Brock Collection
    Loudoun Papers
Kent Archives Office, Maidstone, Kent, England, by permission of Kent
    County Council
Lambeth Palace Library, London, England
    Fulham Palace Papers

Library of Congress, Washington, D.C.
  George Washington Papers
  Peter Force Papers
Maine Historical Society, Portland, Maine
  Fogg Autograph Collection
Maryland Historical Society, Baltimore
  Sharpe Papers
Massachusetts Historical Society, Boston
  Parkman Collection
Morristown National Historical Park, Morristown, N.J.
New-York Historical Society, New York
  Cadwallader Colden Papers
New York Public Library, New York
  Astor, Lenox and Tilden Foundations, Manuscript Division, Emmet Papers
Pennsylvania Historical and Museum Commission, Harrisburg, Pa.
  Records of the Provincial Council of Pennsylvania, Executive Correspondence, 1682–1776
Public Archives of Canada, Ottawa
Public Record Office, London, England
  Adm.   Admiralty
  A.O.   Exchequer and Audit Department
  C.   Chancery
  C.O.   Colonial Office
  H.C.A.   High Court of Admiralty
  M.P.G.   Maps and Plans
  P.C.   Privy Council
  P.R.O.   Public Record Office (gifts, deposits, transcripts)
  Prob.   Probate
  S.P.   State Paper Office
  T.   Treasury
  W.O.   War Office
Rhode Island Historical Society, Providence, R.I.
  Obadiah Brown Papers
Royal Society of Arts, London, England
  Guard Book
Scottish Record Office, Edinburgh, Scotland
  Dalhousie Muniments, by permission of the Right Honorable the Earl of Dalhousie, Brechin Castle, Brechin, Angus
State Historical Society of Wisconsin, Madison, Wis.
  Draper Manuscripts

Repositories

University of Virginia Library, Charlottesville, Va.
  Manuscripts Department, Page-Walker Papers
University of Virginia, Charlottesville, Va., Tracy W. McGregor
  Library
Virginia Historical Society, Richmond
Virginia State Library, Richmond
  Colonial Papers
  James Abercromby Letter Book
West Sussex Record Office, Chichester, England
  Petworth House Archives, by permission of the Right Honorable the
    Lord Egremont and the County Archivist of West Sussex

Introduction

Francis Fauquier was the second child of John Francis Fauquier, a French Huguenot immigrant naturalized in 1698, and his wife Elizabeth, the daughter of Francis Chamberlaine, citizen and grocer of London. He was born after 26 March 1703 and was baptized in the church of St. Andrew Undershaft in London on Sunday, 11 July 1703.[1] His elder sister Mary was born in 1702; his brother Samuel was born in 1704 and died in 1705; his younger sister Elizabeth was born in 1706, and his brother William in 1708.[2] No more is known of the Fauquier children until they were young adults, but one may suppose that their early years were comfortable and that they were members of a congenial and close-knit family.[3]

About 1696 John Francis Fauquier became financial agent to Thomas Neale, master worker of the mint, and apparently Neale's deputy for mint affairs as well. John Francis continued as deputy master under Isaac Newton, successor to Neale in 1699; from about 1716 he took on a share of Newton's duties, including the major responsibility for the copper coinage of George I, and remained in office until his death in 1726.[4] He had been elected a director of the Bank of England in 1716, and so continued until he died. His will left more than £62,000 in specific bequests (nearly all of it to his children) and the residue of his estate to his wife; Francis Fauquier inherited £5,000 in capital stock of the Bank of England, £5,000 in capital stock of the South Sea Company, and £15,000 in joint stock of South Sea annuities.

Francis Fauquier's earliest recorded action was the disposal of his capital stock of the Bank of England. He transferred it in sums of £1,000 to five persons, two of whom may be identified as London merchants, during the period 12 August 1729–4 June 1730.[5] Why he disposed of the stock is not known, but he may have needed money for the household he was establishing at about that time.

In 1730 William Hogarth painted a conversation piece known as *The Wollaston Family*, in which appear Francis Fauquier and his wife, his brother William Fauquier, his two sisters, and their husbands, for whom the painting is named.[6] Elizabeth had married William Wollaston in April 1728, and in the following November Mary married Francis Wollaston, William Wollaston's younger brother. Francis Fauquier married Catherine Dalston, a daughter of Sir Charles Dalston, Bart., but the date of the marriage has not been discovered. By the beginning of 1733 Francis

Fauquier and his wife had a son, Francis,[7] and their second son, William, was born in 1733.

We have no intimation of what Fauquier did for a livelihood, if he did anything, although some of his activities suggest an interest in finance or economics.[8] He was elected one of the thirty directors of the South Sea Company for three consecutive terms, from February 1748 until February 1757, and appointed to the committees on shipping, accounts, and lawsuits and trusts. The directorship provided a stipend of £150 a year but, according to the company's charter, required the holding of at least £3,000 in capital stock.[9]

In 1751 Fauquier was elected a governor of the Foundling Hospital in London, and was twice elected to its general committee, the select committee of governors that acted as a board of managers. The range of Fauquier's activities on the committee has not been explored, but in June 1754 he was deputed to call on George Frederick Handel to discuss arrangements for performances of Handel's music given for the benefit of the hospital; perhaps the portrait of Fauquier painted in 1757 and attributed to Benjamin Wilson, now owned by the Thomas Coram Foundation for Children (successor to the Foundling Hospital), is a mark of Fauquier's eminence as a governor of the hospital.[10]

In November 1752 Fauquier was proposed for membership in the Royal Society of London, as "A Gentleman of great merit, well versed in Philosophical & Mathematical inquiries, and a great promoter of usefull Learning, & the Advancement of Natural Knowledge," and in February 1753 he was elected a Fellow of the society. His only active participation in the society's proceedings seems to be an account of a hailstorm over Williamsburg; he must have had some contacts with other Fellows, however, since he owned presentation copies of David Hartley's *Observations on Man* and Stephen Hales's *Treatise on Ventilators*.[11]

Five years later, shortly before his departure for Virginia, Fauquier was elected a corresponding member of the Society for the Encouragement of Arts, Manufactures, and Commerce, commonly called the Society of Arts (now the Royal Society of Arts) in London; corresponding members were men distinguished in various ways or men who had rendered services to the society and were usually foreigners or resident abroad. Fauquier had very little time to take part in the society's activities before he left England, but in Virginia he promised to forward its patronage of applied science.[12]

Fauquier's appointment as lieutenant governor of Virginia was announced in January 1758, and his commission was issued in February. The circumstances of Fauquier's being chosen as lieutenant governor are not known, but he and others gave credit to the earl of Halifax, president of the Board of Trade, for the appointment. In March 1758 James Abercromby, Virginia's agent in London, intimated Halifax's hand in the choice when he referred to Fauquier as "a Gentleman of whose Capacity and Abilitys the King and his Ministers (and none more so than the Earl of Hallifax) have very high regard." Early in 1764 Fauquier alluded to "the great Obligations" which Halifax had laid him under, and later in that year William Robinson, the commissary in Virginia of the bishop of London, wrote that Fauquier had declared the clergy were arrant fools when they turned politicians, "giving for an Instance of it, that they had sent a Complaint to the Board of Trade the Head of which was my Lord Halifax, his particular Friend who had procured him the Government." In 1765 Fauquier described Halifax as "my friend and patron, the Earl of Halifax." Fauquier's final acknowledgment of his debt to Halifax was made in his will, where he directed that a diamond ring be purchased for Halifax; he went on to describe Halifax as his "much esteemed and respected Patron," and the ring as a token of his gratitude for the many favors Halifax had conferred on him, ending with the hope that Halifax would wear the ring "in remembrance of a Man who never one Moment forgot the great Obligations he had to his Lordship."[13]

At about the time of his appointment as lieutenant governor of Virginia, Fauquier executed a deed of trust by which he disposed of his estate in Great Britain. Such a deed was not necessarily recorded, as a will was, and Fauquier's deed of trust, with whatever light it may have shed on his financial position and personal relationships, is known only through his mention of it in his will executed in Virginia. However, it seems likely that the four men in England specified in that will as proper arbiters in any dispute over settlement of Fauquier's estate were the trustees named in the deed of trust and men whom he thought of as his intimates. Two of them certainly were, his brother William Fauquier and his brother-in-law Francis Wollaston. The third was James Burrow (1701–1782), a legal reporter and master of the crown office from 1733 until his death, a Fellow of the Royal Society and of the Society of Arts, and one of the men who recommended Fauquier for election to the Royal Society. The fourth was Gabriel Hanger (1697–1773), created Baron Coleraine of Coleraine in 1762, who spent his youth in the Bengal establishment of the East India Company, returned to England in 1725, and was a member of Parliament for Maidstone 1753–61 and for Bridgwater 1763–68.

We have only random details of Fauquier's history before his appointment to Virginia, and although his public actions as governor are generally a matter of record, very little is known of his private life in Virginia, where he arrived in June 1758. His wife and their elder son, Francis, accompanied him to Virginia, where they stayed until they sailed for England toward the end of May 1766. The younger son, William, came to Virginia on a visit, perhaps as early as 1763 and probably by June 1764 (when the muster rolls of his regiment reported him as absent on leave), and remained until April 1765. It appears that Fauquier's intimates in Virginia, aside from his own family, were the four men whom he named as executors of his will, in which he mentioned them with affection and directed the purchase of a diamond ring for each as a remembrance: these were Robert Carter, William Nelson, Peyton Randolph, and George Wythe.[14]

During the last years of his life, from about the middle of 1760 or earlier, Fauquier suffered attacks of illness. In the spring of 1767 he was disabled for weeks. By midsummer he was said to have made a good recovery, but by the end of February 1768 he was so ill that his life was despaired of. He died on 3 March 1768 and was buried on 8 March in the north aisle of Bruton Parish Church in Williamsburg. The *Virginia Gazette* of Purdie and Dixon for 3 March published a brief notice of Fauquier's death which assessed his administration as having been "much to his own honour, and the ease and satisfaction of the inhabitants." Of his character, the notice added: "He was a Gentleman of a most amiable disposition, generous, just and mild; and possessed, in an eminent degree, of all the social virtues." The *Virginia Gazette* of Rind for the same date printed a much fuller obituary notice, with these judgments on Fauquier's public and private character: "As a faithful Representative of his Sovereign; he was vigilant in Government, moderate in Power, exemplary in Religion, and merciful where the Rigour of Justice could by any means be dispensed with. In the Exercise of his less public Virtues; he was warm in his Attachments, punctual in his Engagements, munificent to Indigence, and in his domestick Connexions truly paternal." A week later, both newspapers gave accounts of Fauquier's funeral, reporting that the president of the council (the acting governor), the speaker, the attorney general, the treasurer, some unidentified members of the council, and principal gentlemen of Williamsburg and the neighborhood attended the funeral, and that the militia of Williamsburg were present to render a military salute. The *Virginia Gazette* of Rind added a eulogy in the form of an epitaph, applauding Fauquier's public life, praising his private character, and admiring the manner in which he had borne the sufferings of his illness, "and submitted to the relentless hand of death with a fortitude and resignation known to but few in the evening hours of departing life."

Introduction xxxix

Soon after Fauquier's burial several men of his acquaintance voiced their praises of the late governor. Robert Carter wrote of him that "during his administration every royal order, which his Sovereign caused to be transmitted here was spiritously and diligently enforced," and that he had acted in his office "with grace, and dignity." John Blair, president of the council, who became acting governor when Fauquier died, described him as "a most punctually diligent Man."[15] James Horrocks, rector of Bruton Parish and president of the College of William and Mary, made this comment:

On the 3th. Inst. we receiv'd no small Misfortune in the Death of our late Governor, not only a sensible Loss to his particular Friends, amongst whom I had the Honor to be numbered, but in my humble Opinion to this Country in general. According to my Judgement, his Administration was conducted with so fair & even a hand between the Prerogative & Authority of our Mother Country, & the Rights & Priveleges of America, that I think he highly merited the Esteem & Affection of the People here, tho' they seem'd unwilling to allow them to him in those Times of Difficulty & Confusion occasion'd by the Stamp Act & the Repeal of it.[16]

With allowances for the conventions of obituary notices and the prejudices of residents of America and friends of the late governor, these comments on him sound reasonable and accurate, although it appears that Carter was unaware of or chose to overlook the several occasions when Fauquier was rebuked for passing laws without the suspending clause required by royal instructions.

The very few known comments on Fauquier made during his tenure of office were most often favorable and not very informative: Robert Dinwiddie described him as a good-natured gentleman, of good sense, and with influence (Dinwiddie's term was "interest") in London, while Brigadier Robert Burton, lieutenant governor of Trois Rivières, considered Fauquier "a sensible good Man."[17] However, Commissary William Robinson on two occasions reported Fauquier's disregard for the practice of the Church of England. In 1761 he wrote to an unknown correspondent, probably a bishop, that Fauquier had asked the rector of Bruton Parish to omit the Athanasian Creed from the service and, when the rector refused, asked to be excused for sitting down while the creed was being read. Also, Robinson added, Fauquier had told another clergyman that he thought the clergyman ought not to refuse parents as sureties for their children at baptism. In 1764 Robinson repeated his report, with embellishments, to the bishop of London, writing that when the rector of Bruton had refused to omit the Athanasian Creed, Fauquier asked to be excused from paying any regard to that part of the service; and that when the other minister had said he could do nothing so contrary to the laws of the church as to let parents stand as sureties for their own children at baptism, Fauquier rejoined that the laws of the church meant nothing, for he, the governor, thought it right that parents be allowed as sureties.[18] Although there is no way to disprove Robinson's report, it is hard to credit his allegation of Fauquier's parading his authority as governor to oppose church practice about sponsors in baptism; as for the creed, one may suspect that Robinson, being on far from amiable terms with Fauquier, was not unwilling to impute to him a disrespect for the creed, or less than orthodox views of the Trinity, perhaps anti-Trinitarianism and a tendency to deism.[19] Whatever he may have thought of deism, Fauquier's references in his correspondence to the church point to respectful conformity with the religious establishment, while the wording of his will is what one would expect of an orthodox Christian.

Three men who published comments on Fauquier long after his death, or two of them at least, have contributed most to an image of him which has taken form over the years: that of a polished and erudite man, a good musician, something of a thinker or philosopher, an able governor, with no fault except a passion for gambling. The first to remark on Fauquier was John Daly Burk, the author of a *History of Virginia*, in the third volume of which, published in 1805, he described Fauquier as "an excellent judge of merit" and "in the habit of pronouncing the retreat of Loyal Hanning equal to anything of its kind in history"; Burk referred to the engagement (reported in George Washington's letters of 25 and 28 September 1758 to Fauquier) near Fort Duquesne in which the French and their Indian allies routed a body of British regular and provincial troops; a small party of men guarding the baggage fought back vigorously and covered the retreat of the survivors. Burk went on to describe Fauquier as "generous, liberal, elegant in his manners and acquirements," a man whose "example left an impression of taste, refinement and erudition on the character of the colony," and "the ornament and delight of Virginia." To Fauquier he attributed the single fault of a passion for gambling, which led him to lose the whole of his patrimony in one night of playing cards with Captain George Anson, lately returned from his voyage around the globe, who was so taken with Fauquier that "he procured for him the government of Virginia." Burk alleged, moreover, that Fauquier had made gambling fashionable in Virginia.[20]

Burk, a native of Ireland, came to America in 1796, so that one assumes he collected his information in conversations held about thirty years or more after Fauquier's death. It is clear that Fauquier was acquainted with

Introduction

Anson, to whom he dedicated his treatise on taxation and whom he mentioned in his correspondence as a friend; it is possible that Anson, first lord of the Admiralty from June 1757, suggested Fauquier's name to Halifax. The rest of Burk's tale is implausible. Anson completed his circumnavigation of the earth in 1744, more than a dozen years before Fauquier's appointment. Fauquier had disposed of a considerable part of his patrimony, in the strict sense, years before Anson's voyage, and he retained part of it at least for years afterwards. He may have lost money at cards, but there is no reason to suppose he was ruined. It is altogether unlikely that he had any effect on the prevalence of gambling in Virginia, where the General Assembly passed the first of a series of laws against gambling as early as 1619 and Governor Dinwiddie in 1752 exhorted the General Assembly to discourage gaming, which, he said, was pretty general in the country and much practiced among the lower classes, "very apt to follow the Examples of their Superiors."

Not long after the publication of Burk's remarks, probably around 1808, John Page recalled in an autobiographical memoir that in his student days at the College of William and Mary, Thomas Dawson, the president, and Page's beloved professor William Small had brought him to the attention of Governor Fauquier, whom he described as "highly enlightened."[21] A similar reminiscence occurs in what is probably the most familiar and influential comment on Fauquier, that of Page's college contemporary and friend Thomas Jefferson.

Jefferson made his observations on Fauquier first in his letter of 15 January 1815 to L. H. Girardin, then repeated them in a somewhat different version in his autobiography, which be began to write in January 1821. The sense of the two accounts is that Dr. William Small obtained George Wythe's patronage for Jefferson, and Small and Wythe together brought him to the attention of Fauquier, whom Jefferson judged to be the ablest man who ever served as governor of Virginia. Small, Wythe, and Fauquier were inseparable companions, according to Jefferson, and he joined them frequently at Fauquier's table, where he derived much instruction from their good sense and rational and philosophical conversation. Jefferson added that Fauquier was musical, a good performer, and included Jefferson and two or three other amateurs in his weekly concerts. Jefferson's recollection of the circumstances of Fauquier's dinners was faulty, for he wrote to Girardin that they were held after the governor's family returned to England, while in the autobiography he gave 1762 as the date of Small's return to England. In fact, Mrs. Fauquier and her son sailed for home in May 1766, and Small went home in the fall of 1764. On the other hand, the interest in music, with skill to play it, is the one quality which Jefferson or anyone else attributed to Fauquier having any solid corroboration: the inventory of Fauquier's estate lists among his effects two violins, a tenor violin or viola, two violoncellos, nine bows, strings, two French horn mouthpieces; his will left to his son William, in addition to his musical instruments, all his "musick Books" in Virginia and in England.[22]

In 1837 George Tucker in his life of Jefferson published what sounds like some of Burk's observations on Fauquier combined with part of Jefferson's reminiscences on the governor and additions evidently provided by Tucker himself and John Randolph of Roanoke. Tucker followed Jefferson's account of his debt to Small for an introduction to Fauquier, going on to attribute to Fauquier "talents, highly improved by cultivation," and "the most engaging exterior and manners." Tucker suggested that Jefferson acquired at Fauquier's table both his admirable manners and a taste for the elegancies of life, then, evidently quoting John Randolph of Roanoke, he gave Fauquier the character of "a follower of Shaftesbury and Bolingbroke, in morals and religion," who made their tenets fashionable in Virginia. Finally, Tucker repeated Burk's allegation of Fauquier's passionate devotion to gambling.[23]

The reference to Shaftesbury and Bolingbroke was perhaps misstated, for Fauquier could hardly have followed both men in morals and religion. Shaftesbury was by reputation anticlerical, heterodox and skeptical in religion, a deist, yet he was at the same time respectful of religion, a regular churchgoer and communicant, a man of lofty character and high principles, generous and benevolent. Bolingbroke too is said to have been anticlerical, a freethinker, perhaps a deist, but he was notoriously indifferent to orthodox belief, a hard drinker, a dissolute and immoral libertine. However, Tucker's further observations suggest that he may have meant in fact to ascribe to Shaftesbury and Bolingbroke only the "fearless and independent spirit, impatient of dictation and contemning authority," thought to have been imparted by Fauquier to Jefferson, in all of whose speculations that spirit was to be seen. In any event, nothing known of Fauquier's character suggests that he was especially like Shaftesbury, let alone Bolingbroke, in intellectual outlook, manners, or morals or that he had anything to do with making their tenets fashionable in Virginia.

Fauquier himself gave a glimpse of his character in his will, when he directed that the physicians or surgeons attending him in his last illness might perform an autopsy on his body, if he might thereby be useful to his fellow creatures. Furthermore, he evinced his concern for his slaves, a part of his estate which he found disagreeable but necessary for him in

Introduction xliii

his situation.[24] He directed that his slaves should be allowed to choose their own masters and that the women and their children should not be separated. The slaves were to have six months to choose their masters, with Fauquier's estate maintaining them during that period. They were to be sold for 75 percent of their market value to the masters of their choice, or, if they had made no choice, to Fauquier's executors, or else to any person who had a favorable opinion of Fauquier and would remember that his slaves had had kind treatment; in an extremity, but not otherwise, the slaves were to be sold at the best price that could be got for them.[25]

Finally, the inventory of the governor's estate includes objects perhaps indicating hobbies, perhaps serving more utilitarian interests. He left a small collection of optical instruments, consisting of a microscope, a telescope, a spyglass (either another telescope or some kind of reading glass), a camera obscura, and a solar microscope, a variety of magic lantern using sunlight for illumination. He had also a number of instruments, most of them presumably surveyor's tools: a perambulator, or wheel for measuring distances, pushed along the ground by hand; a measuring wheel, which may have been a perambulator, or a circumferentor (a sighting device), or perhaps a pedometer or an odometer; a level, a quadrant, a plumb; and a brass circular dial, not identified, although it may have been a compass. Obviously for diversion were cards and card tables, a backgammon table, chessmen and board, materials for painting and drawing, gold medals (presumably a collection of commemorative medals and perhaps coins), carvings in ivory, and impressions of copperplates (assumed to have been engravings or etchings).

The events and problems of Fauquier's administration have been so carefully recorded and so exhaustively investigated that anything more than a brief recapitulation of the major ones seems superfluous. Even before he left England, Fauquier received instructions from the Board of Trade to see to it that the two offices of treasurer of Virginia and speaker of the House of Burgesses, lower house of the provincial legislature, should be divided and no longer held (as they had long been held) by the same person. In his letters from Virginia, Fauquier declared that he could not try to divide the offices without endangering his good relations with the burgesses; in spite of repeated complaints from the board, the two offices remained in the hands of John Robinson, with Fauquier's acquiescence, until Robinson's death in 1766.

When Fauquier arrived in Virginia in June 1758, the French and Indian War was in progress, with the French in the ascendant. Later in 1758 the British began to get the upper hand. The surrender of Montreal in September 1760 in effect brought the war in North America to an end, although hostilities did not cease officially until late in 1762; the final treaty of peace was concluded in February 1763.

Trouble with the southern Indians began long before victory over the French could be foreseen. The Cherokees had been alienated from the British interest as early as the spring of 1758, when they engaged in several skirmishes with settlers on the frontiers of Virginia. In January 1760 they attacked the frontier regions of South Carolina and Georgia and besieged Fort Loudoun in the Cherokee country, in what is now eastern Tennessee. Open warfare with the Cherokees came to a halt late in 1761, yet relations between Virginia and the Cherokees remained unhappy, marked by occasional overt hostilities such as the killing of a party of Cherokees in May 1765 by frontiersmen of Augusta County. In the spring of 1763, during the uneasy truce with the Cherokees, the revolt of the northern Indians known as Pontiac's War broke out and continued into the summer of 1764, with the frontier settlements of Virginia suffering attacks by northern Indians.

No major fighting between British and Virginian troops and the French and Indians took place in the older settled regions of Virginia, nor did Cherokees or northern Indians press their sporadic raids beyond the border settlements. Nevertheless, Virginia carried the burden of finding money to clothe, feed, and pay the troops raised by the colony during the struggle against the French and subsequent defensive or punitive measures against the Indians. The General Assembly could find no practicable way of raising funds for provincial defense except emissions of paper money, or treasury notes; the emissions, although they served their purpose, annoyed and alarmed the British government and British merchants, fearful that debts in sterling money would be paid off in current money, or colonial paper. The Board of Trade was outspokenly dissatisfied with Fauquier's handling of its instructions to arrive at some solution of the problem of paper money acceptable to British merchants.

The Stamp Act was doubtless the most explosive issue of Fauquier's administration; another irritant was the second of the Two Penny Acts, authorizing the payment of debts in money rather than in tobacco, and its consequences. In violation of his instructions, Fauquier signed the act of 1758 without a clause to suspend its operation until the king had approved it. He thus incurred a rebuke from the board, with a command to obey his instructions thenceforward, upon pain of being recalled. The Parsons' Cause resulted from resentment of clergy of the established church at the effect of the Two Penny Act upon their stipends; the suits brought by clergy against vestries tended to alienate laymen from the

Introduction

church, the king's disallowance of the Two Penny Act displeased Virginians in general, and the official rebuke directed to Fauquier, especially the manner in which it was delivered, bred hostility between Fauquier and leaders of the clerical party.

Chronic problems of Fauquier's term of office were pressure for grants of western land, illegal settlements on those lands, intractable settlers, the inveterate hostility of Virginia frontiersmen toward all Indians, and finally the question of a boundary with the Cherokees.

Except when he urged upon the Board of Trade, without success, the need for defining the boundaries of Pennsylvania and Virginia in the west, Fauquier seems to have found no occasion to initiate action in a measure of government. However, he presumably conceived and certainly recommended to the General Assembly his humanitarian plan for establishing a hospital to care for the insane. The House of Burgesses resolved that a hospital should be erected, directed that a bill be prepared for that purpose, then dropped the matter.[26]

If the scanty evidence is reliable, the people of Virginia in general approved of Fauquier's administration; the House of Burgesses tendered him a substantial token of their approval in a gift of £1,000. In England, on the contrary, Fauquier's conduct provoked suggestions that he was gullible, too much guided by the council, and too eager to please the burgesses. On several occasions the Board of Trade administered sharp rebukes for Fauquier's disregard of his instructions (as in his passing acts of assembly without the suspending clause called for by the character of those acts), threatening once at least to recall him.

Whatever the quality of his administration, however, Fauquier's official papers are of substantial importance through their content, their variety, and above all because they mirror the preoccupations of the governor of one of the largest, most populous, wealthiest, and most influential of the colonies in North America during the critical decade of 1758–68, spanning the last five years of government by king, Privy Council, and Board of Trade and the first five years of the new order marked by increasing intervention of Parliament in colonial government.

---

1. Francis Fauquier signed his will on 26 Mar. 1767, in the sixty-fourth year of his age; for the registered copy see Prob. 11/973, p. 480. The Book of Common Prayer admonished parents not to defer the baptism of a child longer than the first or second Sunday after its birth, unless with good reason; if Fauquier's parents were mindful of the prayer book (and no good reason delayed his baptism), he was born late in June or early in July. His baptism is recorded in the register of St. Andrew Undershaft (Corporation of London, Guildhall Library, Ms. 4107/3).

2. The most useful account of the various Fauquiers and their relations is that by G. Woods Wollaston, "The Family of Fauquier," *Proceedings of the Huguenot Society of London* 13(1927): 340-55. However, it contains some errors, especially in the family tree.

3. It appears likely that John Francis Fauquier was a man of good financial position by the time his children were born, and his wife had inherited a share of her father's substantial estate as early as 1695. The scanty evidence indicates that Francis Fauquier was on confidential terms with his brother and brothers-in-law throughout their lives.

4. Letter of R. Carnot, Librarian and Curator of the Royal Mint, to the editor 1 Aug. 1969.

5. Letter of the secretary of the Bank of England to the editor, 6 Feb. 1967.

6. See George H. Reese, "Portraits of Governor Francis Fauquier," *VMHB* 76(1968): 2-10. Since the publication of that article, the editor has received further information on the miniature once said to be a portrait of Francis Fauquier and on the Wilson portrait. In a letter of 5 Oct. 1973 to the editor, Graham Hood, Director of Collections, Colonial Williamsburg Foundation, stated that he had examined the miniature and found it signed with the initials "J S," presumably for John Smart, and dated 1761, so that it cannot be a portrait of Governor Fauquier. In a letter of 13 June 1978, J. G. B. Swinley, Director and Secretary of the Thomas Coram Foundation, informed the editor that the Wilson portrait is now attributed to Benjamin Wilson, although it was recorded by the Foundling Hospital as the work of Richard Wilson.

7. On 29 Jan. 1733, Francis Fauquier received the freedom of Ipswich, having one son, Francis. The circumstances of his becoming a freeman are not known, but may have had some political motive, perhaps involving his brother-in-law William Wollaston, who was elected member of Parliament for Ipswich in a byelection on that same day and held the seat until 1741.

8. In 1755 Fauquier wrote *An Essay on Ways and Means for Raising Money for the Support of the Present War, without Increasing the Public Debts*, published in 1756. And two of the four personal papers of Fauquier's known to survive are evidence of loans he made. The Virginia Historical Society has a bond (MSS 1 D2856 a 12), dated in 1731, for a loan of £1,500 at 5 percent interest to James Seamer, Jr. In the French Archives Nationales is a receipt (T.741), dated in 1748, for a bond for a loan of £371.12.0 at 5 percent. The particulars are confusing, but what was involved was apparently a payment made or to be made by Fauquier and Simon Fanshawe to the singer Domenica Casarini, with the earl of Middlesex (later duke of Dorset) as security. It is perhaps relevant that Middlesex was extremely generous in supporting opera in London, that Casarini was at some time married to Gaetano Latilla, and that Latilla's comic opera *Don Calascione* (later called *La finta giardiniera*) was performed in London in Feb. 1749 and later; the cast of the performances was not listed.

9. The records of the South Sea Company are in the British Library, Add. Mss. 25,494-581; notes of Fauquier's appointments are in the court minutes, vols. 20–22. Fauquier may have retained all of the £5,000 in capital stock he inherited for its voting strength, since that amount entitled the holder to three votes at the election of governors and directors.

10. The committee minutes regarding the visit to Handel are quoted in O. E. Deutsch, *Handel, a Documentary Biography* (New York, 1954), pp. 752-53. For the portrait, see n. 6 above.

11. The recommendation of Fauquier, with the names of thirteen subscribers, is printed in Raymond Phineas Stearns, "Colonial Fellows of the Royal Society of London," *WMQ*, 3d ser., 3(1946): 242–43. The account of the storm, paraphrased in a letter from Fauquier's brother William, was read to the society on 9 Nov. 1758 and printed in the society's *Philosophical Transactions* 50(1758): 746. The Hartley book is mentioned in a letter from Francis Fauquier, Jr., to Robert Carter, 31 May 1770

Introduction xlvii

(Colonial Williamsburg Foundation); the Hales book, with an inscription in an unknown hand, is in the Virginia State Library.

12. See Robert Leroy Hilldrup, "A Campaign to Promote the Prosperity of Colonial Virginia," *VMHB* 67(1959): 410–28. It is not evident that Fauquier proposed the passage of "An Act for encouraging Acts and Manufactures," passed in the General Assembly of Virginia in 1759 and fostering the same aims as the society in London, but he spoke of the act with approval in his address of prorogation in Apr. 1759, and his name led the list of subscribers to a fund to advance the intentions of the act set up in 1760. The basic act and a further amending act are in Hening, 7: 288–90, 563–70; Fauquier's remarks on the first act are in *JHB, 1758–1761*, p. 129.

13. James Abercromby to John Blair, 3 Mar. 1758, Virginia State Library, James Abercromby Letter Book, pp. 69–70; Francis Fauquier to the earl of Halifax, 30 Jan. 1764, C.O.5/1345, ff. 56–57; William Robinson to the bishop of London, Lambeth Palace Library, Fulham Palace Papers, XIV, 27–40; Francis Fauquier to Henry Seymour Conway, 9 Oct. 1765, C.O.5/1345, ff. 95–96.

14. The letter book of Robert Carter (Colonial Williamsburg Foundation) and that of William Nelson (Virginia Theological Seminary, Alexandria) give us a few glimpses of Fauquier's connections with the two men: Mrs. Fauquier was godmother to Carter's daughter Ann Tasker Carter; Fauquier and Carter were joined in various financial and business matters; Fauquier endured his long illness in 1767 at Nelson's house in Yorktown. Fauquier's esteem for Wythe is manifest in his attempts to procure Wythe's appointment as attorney general, but no indication of his friendship with Randolph has been found except for what is in Fauquier's will.

15. See Robert Carter's letters of 9 Mar. 1768 to Thomas Bladen and to Jeffery Amherst, Colonial Williamsburg Foundation, Robert Carter Letter Book, and John Blair to the earl of Shelburne, 21 Mar. 1768, C.O.5/1346, ff. 7–8.

16. James Horrocks to the bishop of London, 29 Mar. 1768, Lambeth Palace Library, Fulham Palace Papers, XIV, 137–40. The closing observation in Horrocks's statement is supported by the remark of a French traveler in 1765 that he had gone on 4 June to Fauquier's celebration of the king's birthday expecting to see a great deal of company but found no more than a dozen people there and left before supper; see "The Journal of a French Traveller in the Colonies, 1765," *American Historical Review* 26(1921): 741–46.

17. See Robert Dinwiddie to Thomas Dawson, 14 Mar. 1758, in Louis Knott Koontz, ed., *Robert Dinwiddie Correspondence* (Berkeley and Los Angeles, 1951), pp. 1453–56; Dinwiddie to Richard Corbin, Nov. 1758, in *Dinwiddie* 2: 723; and Ralph Burton to Jeffery Amherst, 11 Sept. 1763, W.O.34/6, ff. 336–38.

18. For Robinson's two letters, one of 3 Nov. 1761 to "My Lord," and one of 17 Aug. 1764 to the bishop of London, see Lambeth Palace Library, Fulham Palace Papers, XIV, 5–6, 27–40. The rectors of Bruton Parish during Fauquier's administration were Thomas Dawson, rector 1743–59, William Yates, rector 1759–64, and James Horrocks, rector 1764–71. The Book of Common Prayer directed that the Athanasian Creed should be said or sung at morning prayer, by the minister and people standing, on thirteen feasts. (The creed, still in the English book, has never been in the American book.) Canon 29 of the Canons of 1604 directed that no parent should be admitted to answer as godfather for his own child; it appears from commentaries on the prayer book that the canon was interpreted to mean that parents of both sexes were forbidden to stand as sponsors to their children.

19. In the middle of the eighteenth century the bishop of London received at least two reports of omission of the Athanasian Creed, one of them explicitly construing the omission as the sign of deism. In 1752 Alexander Adams, minister of Stepney Parish in Maryland, complained that some of the younger clergy in that colony omitted reading the creed; in the same year John Blair, of the council in Virginia, writing to

oppose the appointment of William Stith as the bishop's commissary in Virginia, charged Stith with being anti-Trinitarian because he omitted the creed from his services. These letters are abstracted in William Wilson Manross, comp., *The Fulham Papers in the Lambeth Palace Library* (Oxford, 1965), pp. 45, 197. The creed has been objected to because of its obscurity in expression and its threatening tone. Objection was not uncommon: in 1749 the vicar of Alconbury, John Jones, published his *Disquisitions*, a set of proposals for revision of the Book of Common Prayer which would have omitted the Athanasian Creed; there followed a number of unofficial schemes for revision drawn up by others, of whom all the Church of England authors would have omitted the creed.

20. John Daly Burk, *The History of Virginia, From Its First Settlement to the Present Day* (Petersburg, Va., 1804–16), 3:233, 333–34.

21. John Page (1743–1808) entered the grammar school at William and Mary in 1756 and attended the college in 1761–63, being about a year behind his great friend Thomas Jefferson. Page's memoir, thought to have been written about 1808, is printed in the *Virginia Historical Register* 3 (1850): 142–51.

22. The letter and autobiography are printed in Andrew A. Lipscomb and Albert Ellery Bergh, eds., *The Writings of Thomas Jefferson* (Washington, D.C., 1903–4) 1: 1–64, 14: 231–32. The inventory of Fauquier's estate and accounts of the sale of his effects are in York County Records, Wills and Inventories, no. 22, 1771–83, pp. 8–103, Virginia State Library.

23. George Tucker, *The Life of Thomas Jefferson* (Philadelphia, 1837), 1: 41–42. Tucker (1775–1861) was a professor at the University of Virginia when he published his book.

24. Fauquier had voiced something like an idea of the brotherhood of man, or human dignity, in a letter of 5 Oct. 1760 to Amherst when he expressed regret that Virginia and the Carolinas had not treated Indians with such justice and humanity as Amherst had shown them; he went on to observe, "White, Red, or Black; polished or unpolished Men are Men." Nevertheless, it would have been hard for him to free his slaves even if he had wished to do so, for an act of Oct. 1748 (Hening, 6: 104–12) declared that no slave should be set free except as a reward for meritorious services, of which governor and council were to be the judges.

25. The inventory of the governor's estate listed seventeen slaves, six men, six women, five children, all valued at £785. They were bought by nine men, none of whom was an executor, and brought a total of £587.10.0, very nearly three-quarters of their appraised value (a deduction of £7.10.0 was made for the death of one of the children).

26. Fauquier broached the plan for a hospital in his speech to the General Assembly on 6 Nov. 1766, and two weeks later the burgesses took their steps to realize the plan. However, Fauquier reminded the General Assembly in his speech of 11 Apr. 1767 that nothing further had been done about the hospital, observing that he would again recommend it to them at their next meeting, but his death intervened (*JHB, 1766–1769*, pp. 12, 33, 131).

The Official Papers of
Francis Fauquier
Lieutenant Governor of Virginia
1758–1768

1758

Commission to Fauquier

George R. [St. James's, 10 February 1758]

George the Second, by the Grace of God, of Great Britain, France & Ireland, King, Defender of the Faith &ca. To Our Trusty & Welbeloved Francis Fauquier Esqr. Greeting: We reposing especial Trust & confidence, in your Loyalty, Courage & Prudence, do, by these Presents[1] constitute & appoint you to be Our Lieutenant Governor of Our Colony & Dominion of Virginia in America in the room of Robert Dinwiddie Esqr.,[2] To have, hold, & enjoy the said Place & Office, during Our Pleasure, with all Rights, Privileges, Profits Perquisites & advantages to the same belonging or appertaining, And further, in Case of the Death or Absence of Our Captain General & Governor in Chief in & over Our said Colony of Virginia now & for the Time being,[3] We do hereby authorize & impower you to execute & perform all & singular the Powers & Directions contained in Our Commission to Our said Captain General & Governor in Chief,[4] according to such Instructions as are already sent or hereafter shall from Time to Time be sent unto him,[5] or as you shall receive from Us, & from Our said Captain General & Governor in Chief of Our said Colony of Virginia, now & for the Time being; And all & singular Our Officers, Ministers, & loving Subjects of Our said Colony & Dominion, & all others whom it may concern, are hereby commanded to take due Notice hereof, & to give a ready obedience accordingly. Given at Our Court of St. James's the 10th Day of Febry 1758, in the Thirty First Year of Our Reign.

By His Majesty's Command.
Holdernesse[6]

Copy: C.O. 324/38, pp. 496–97.

1. The commission was the instrument by which a governor or lieutenant governor was invested with his authority, and the reading of the document in the colony where he was appointed marked the beginning of his administration. Fauquier's commission was read before the council on 5 June 1758 (see *EJC* 6:100; see also Labaree [1] and Labaree [2]. It was evidently the practice to keep a copy of the commission (or perhaps the original commission) to the governor of Virginia in the archives of the colony; see Fauquier's comment on this practice in his letter to Amherst of 5 Mar. 1760 and his remark on the derivation of his own authority from the commission to the governor in chief.

2. Robert Dinwiddie (1693–1770) was lieutenant governor of Virginia 1751–58. See Louis Knott Koontz, *Robert Dinwiddie: His Career in American Colonial Government and Westward Expansion* (Glendale, Calif., 1941).

3. John Campbell (1705–1782), fourth earl of Loudoun, was governor of Virginia 1756–59, although it does not appear that he was ever in Virginia. See S. M. Pargellis, *Lord Loudoun in North America* (New Haven, 1933).

4. Loudoun's commission as governor, dated 8 Mar. 1756, is in C.66/3651, no. 19. Except for a few verbal differences of no consequence, it is the same, mutatis mutandis, as that given to James Glen of South Carolina, in Labaree [2], 2:816–25.

5. The instructions to a governor comprised a set of general instructions for his guidance and another set of instructions regarding the laws on trade and navigation, usually called the trade instructions. The instructions were secret orders and were not published or as a rule revealed even to the council, although separate articles of the instructions might be divulged to the council in executive session or quoted in addresses to the legislature. See Labaree [1] and [2]. The general instructions to Loudoun, submitted on 17 Mar. 1756 and approved the next day, are in C.O.5/1367, ff. 90–144. They are very like those of 1771 to Lord Dunmore, in *MHSC*, 4th ser., 10 (1871): 630–66, except that arts. 13, 14, 25, and the last sentence of art. 34 of the Dunmore instructions are not in those to Loudoun and arts. 13, 39–52, 65–67, 74–75, 95–97, 103, and 107 of the instructions to Loudoun are not in those to Dunmore. See Labaree [2], arts. 62, 154, 414, 416, 420, 464–66, 473, 539, 552, 553, 672, 733, 902, 985, and 992. Loudoun's trade instructions have not been found, but they were submitted and approved along with the general instructions, and the representation (C.O.5/1367, f. 89) submitted with them stated that they were "conformable to the instructions . . . for the like purposes to other Governors on the Continent of North America." Evidently Loudoun's trade instructions were essentially the same as those of 1761 to Benning Wentworth of New Hampshire, in C.O.5/942, pp. 163–252, and *The Laws of New Hampshire* 3 (Bristol, N.H., 1915): 281–305. All extant sets of trade instructions are much alike except for the first article, enumerating the principal laws relating to the plantation trade, which grew in length as new laws were passed, and then was reduced to a few lines.

6. Robert D'Arcy (1718–1778), fourth earl of Holdernesse, was secretary of state for the Southern Department (the official responsible for colonial affairs) 1751–61, except for a brief period in 1757.

From John Clevland

Sir   14 March 1758

I[1] send this to acquaint you that before you can be appointed Vice Admiral[2] of Virginia His Majesty's Pleasure must be signified by a Secretary of State, to the Lords of the Admiralty.[3] I am &c

                                                                J C

Fauquier Esqr.

Copy: Adm.2/1056, p. 54.

1. It is assumed that the initials after the letter are those of John Clevland (ca. 1707–1763), who was secretary to the Admiralty from 1751 until his death. See Namier.

2. A commission as vice admiral conveyed jurisdiction over all admiralty or maritime affairs within a colony; the powers which it granted were judicial rather than naval. It was prepared by the Admiralty at the request of the Board of Trade or of a secretary of state and issued under the great seal of the Admiralty (see Labaree [1]). This letter was perhaps a reply to Fauquier's request for a vice admiral's commission. There is no indication that Fauquier ever received such a commission, and in his letter of 5 Mar. 1760 to Amherst, Fauquier stated that he was acting under Lord Loudoun's commission, which was still in force because it had not been revoked by Amherst's "patent under the Great Seal," his commission as governor. Loudoun's commission as vice admiral, dated 15 Mar. 1756, is in H.C.A.50/11, ff. 10–16, 106, the model commission being one granted to the governor of Bermuda, on ff. 10–16, with a list of changes to be made in the commission to Loudoun following on f. 106. The commission to Loudoun is the same in all essentials as that granted to the governor of Massachusetts on 12 Feb. 1760, in *Publications of the Colonial Society of Massachusetts* 2 (Boston, 1913): 257–66.

3. The Lords Commissioners for Executing the Office of Lord High Admiral were a group of men appointed to administer the navy in the place of a lord high admiral. In the eighteenth century such commissioners were responsible for naval administration from 1709 onwards.

From James Abercromby

Sir   March 15th 1758

Inclosed you have the following papers for perusal, First my Letter to General Abercromby relative to the money granted last Session of Parliament, what I[1] have said thereon to him as Commander in Chief of his Majestys Forces,[2] will lead you into the necessary Correspondence on this Subject.

2nd Copie   My Memorial to the Lords of the Treasury in the Case of the application for an aid out of the Quitrents,[3] to the Tobacco Revenue which comes recommended to me from the President & Council of Virginia, to which I shall give my utmost attention in Concurrence with Governor Dinwiddy as directed so to do.

3rd Copie   Of Governor Morriss's Petition to Parliament for an exclusive Right to make Salt in North America,[4] which Petition the Agent for South Carolina,[5] and myself for Virginia, together with the Merchants of these Provinces have under Consideration, in order to form an opposition thereto, at least to have put it off 'til the Provinces are apprised of the Nature of the Application, and are heard thereon.

4th Copie   Of the Establishment granted to Mathew Blackiston heretofore Agent for Virginia,[6] whereby the Council of Virginia, will see the Encouragment some former Agents have Received on the Service of that Government, and should the Governor and Council of Virginia, think proper to remonstrate to My Lords for Trade, the great Increase and Multiplicity of Affairs relative to Government, attending the Duty of the Agent, by throwing in some personal Weight into the Scale, I should hope to succeed, at a proper time, for pressing the matter, and the rather, since where the nomination of Agents is with their Lordships as in Georgia, and Nova Scotia, they allow £300 per Annum as Salarys, besides Extras for Contingencys. But in the Interim, I have submitted it to the Consideration of the Gentlemen of the Council, that as the Articles for Coach hire, and for Christmas Gratuitys, to Offices, and to the Servants of the Ministers of State, are very heavy, and Standing Annual Charges upon the Agent, And as all other American Agents, and Solicitors of every nature are allowed for their Contingent Expences, I have therefore desired the permission of the Council to make an Annual Charge, Including Coach or Chair hire, Christmas Gratuitys Postage Pen Ink and Paper, and all other Petty Disbursments £50 per Annum which I hope will be thought reasonable, by you and the Gentlemen of the Council, which shall be remitted, whenever the Establishment on the Quitrents takes place.[7]

I have these five years past carryd through a very great variety of Business for the Assembly of Virginia, recommended to me by the Governor and Council and without the least allowance from the Assembly, for so doing, the success whereof has amply testified my Zeal in their service, Added to my trouble, I have been greatly out of Pocket, the Gentlemen of the Council sensible of Success have thereupon undertaken to recommend me to the Assembly,[8] and herein let me beg your Concurrence, I have stated my Account to the Assembly to the President Mr Blair for what is passd,[9] and in time to come, It will be equally agreeable to me if so to the Assembly, to make me an Annual & certain Allowance for their Service, otherwise to charge them occasionally for Business done for them, to either propositions I shall acquiesse as they shall think fit, wishing you and your Family a very good voyage, and happy arrival. I am &c.

Governor Fauquier at Portsmouth.

Copy: Virginia State Library, James Abercromby Letter Book, pp. 84–86. In a clerk's hand. Communicated to the council 15 June 1758; abstract in *EJC* 6: 102–3.

1. James Abercromby (1707–1775) was agent for Virginia 1754–59 and agent for the governor and council of Virginia 1759–74; he was also deputy auditor general of the plantations 1757–65. See Namier; see also Ella Lonn, *The Colonial Agents of the Southern Colonies* (Chapel Hill, N.C., 1945) and Michael G. Kammen, *A Rope of Sand: The Colonial Agents, British Politics, and the American Revolution* (Ithaca, N.Y., 1968).
2. Major General James Abercromby (1706–1781) assumed the supreme command

15 March 1758

of British forces in North America in Mar. 1758. The letter that Abercromby enclosed was no doubt that of 12 Mar. 1758, which follows.

3. This enclosure is assumed to have been a copy of the memorial that follows. The proposal of a transfer of funds from the quitrents to the tobacco revenue was put forward by President John Blair, on behalf of the council of Virginia, in a letter to Abercromby dated 23 Dec. 1757 and carried to London by Governor Dinwiddie; Blair's letter has not been found, but two letters from Abercromby of 3 and 5 Mar. 1757 (pp. 68–71 of his letter book) indicate what it was about. At the time of this correspondence the members of the council in Virginia were the president, John Blair (1687–1771); William Nelson (1711–1772); Thomas Nelson (1716–1787); Peter Randolph (1713?–1767); Philip Grymes (d. 1761); Richard Corbin (1708–1787?); Philip Ludwell (1716–1767); Rev. Thomas Dawson (d. 1760); William Byrd III (1728–1777); Philip Ludwell Lee (1727–1775); and John Tayloe (1721–1779). Robert Carter (1728–1804) had been proposed for the twelfth seat on the council, but his warrant was not issued until 7 Apr. 1758, and he was not sworn in until 18 Oct. of that year.

4. Robert Hunter Morris (ca. 1700–1764) was governor of New Jersey 1754–56. The House of Lords Record Office reports that apparently no copy of Morris's petition was presented to the Lords and that no copy of the petition presented to the Commons has survived. However, a summary of the petition is in *JHC* for 11 Feb. 1758, the day when it was presented, and that summary follows. On 2 Mar. 1758 the petition was referred to a committee of the Commons, but there is no record of any further action upon it.

5. James Wright (1716–1785) was agent for South Carolina 1757–60, lieutenant governor of that colony 1760–61, and its governor 1762–76. He and Abercromby attended the Board of Trade on 16 Mar. 1758 to offer objections to Morris's petition.

6. Abercromby meant Col. Nathaniel Blakiston, governor of Maryland 1698–1701 and then agent for that colony; Blakiston was appointed agent for Virginia in 1705 and evidently served in that capacity until 1721 or 1722. What Abercromby meant by Blakiston's "Establishment" is not certain, but he probably referred to the warrant that follows.

7. On 3 Mar. 1758 Abercromby wrote to President Blair to say (among much else) that he was submitting accounts of charges to the council and to the assembly, and he made special mention of the standing expenses of coach and chair hire (at least £40 per annum) and Christmas gratuities (25 guineas). Abercromby remarked that this letter was to be delivered by Fauquier, then of course still in England. On 8 Mar. Abercromby wrote again to Blair, inviting his attention to some enclosed accounts, and particularly to items of coach hire and Christmas gratuities. He mentioned a proposal that the agent should have an allowance of £50 per annum for contingent expenses and added that it would be appropriate that this allowance to the agent of governor and council (like those to other officers of government) should be made from the quitrents. It is not clear whether this was a separate letter or an addition to that of 3 Mar. If it was a separate letter, it no doubt was entrusted to Fauquier. The two letters, or parts of one letter, are on pp. 69–70 and 72–73 of Abercromby's letter book.

8. Abercromby's letter of 3 Mar. 1758 suggests that the council's approval and support were conveyed in a letter from Blair of 23 Dec. 1757 (brought over by Dinwiddie), which has not been found.

9. There are two accounts with Abercromby's communications described in n. 7. One is dated 8 Mar. 1758 and is a bill to the governor and council for contingent expenses incurred in the period Jan. 1753–Jan. 1758: it states one charge of 3 guineas for copies of papers, refers in general terms to coach and chair hire and to Christmas gratuities, and requests an allowance from the governor and council of £50 a year for contingent expenses. The other account is undated, but is for the period of Jan. 1753–Jan. 1758, and is addressed to the assembly: it lists several items of money spent

and charges for services rendered, coming to £196.7.6. The two accounts are on pp. 74, 81–82 of Abercromby's letter book. See Abercromby's letter of 28 Dec. 1758 to Fauquier for what may be further reference to the account to the assembly.

Enclosure: James Abercromby to Major General James Abercromby

Sir,   Craven street March 12th 1758

This will come to you forewarded by Governor Dobbs in behalf of North Carolina,[1] to let you know, that upon Enquiry I do find that the £50,000 which was granted by Parliament last Session, to the Provinces of North, South Carolina and Virginia,[2] remains still in the Treasury and there is to remain, until such time, as you as Commander in Chief of the Kings Forces in America, have ascertaind the respective Provincial Proportions due, and have notified the same to the Lords of the Treasury.

And in order to enable you so to do it becomes necessary for these provinces herein concerned, to lay before you, if not already done (to the Earl of Loudon) their respective Claims, from the several Aids granted by their General Assemblys for Military Services, if this shall be thought the Rule to follow in the Distribution of the mony, but this must be finally left to the Orders of Government here, after that you have reported your oppinion thereon to my Lords Commissioners of the Treasury, and to the Secretary of State, for as the Case appears to me in the Channel of Office, I do not apprehend that you can draw for, or apply, this money, till the proportions are fix'd, and finally approvd at home; and the sooner this is done, the better with regard to the Provinces concerned therein, and this I have signified to the Governments for whom I am Concerned.

To Maj. Gen. Abercromby.

Copy: Virginia State Library, James Abercromby Letter Book, p. 80. In a clerk's hand. A copy of this letter was enclosed in Abercromby's letter to Fauquier of 15 Mar. 1758.

1. Arthur Dobbs (1689–1765) was governor of North Carolina 1754–65. The letter was brought over by Fauquier. On 5 June he showed it to the council, which ordered the preparation of a letter to General Abercromby. See *EJC* 6:100–101.

2. On 16 May 1757 this message was presented to the House of Commons: "His Majesty, being desirous that his faithful Subjects in his Provinces of North and South Carolina and Virginia, in America, should receive a proper Recompence for such Services, as, with the Approbation of the Commander in Chief of his Forces in America, they respectively shall have performed, or shall perform, either by putting the said Provinces in a State of Defence, or by acting with Vigour against the Enemy,

recommends it to this House to take the same into their Consideration, and to enable his Majesty to give them a proper Recompence for such Services." On 19 May the Commons resolved "That a Sum, not exceeding Fifty thousand Pounds, be granted to his Majesty, upon Account, to be paid to such Persons, and in such Manner, and by such Proportions, as his Majesty, shall direct, for the Use and Relief of his Majesty's Subjects in his several Provinces of North and South Carolina and Virginia, in America" (*JHC*, 27:894, 901).

Enclosure: Memorial to the Treasury

[ca. 15 March 1758]

To the Right Honble The Lords Commissioners of His Majesty's Treasury.[1]

The Memorial of the Lieutenant Governor and Council of his Majesty's Province of Virginia.

Sheweth

That from the Extraordinary Exigencys of Government, and from many of the Inhabitants being obliged to quit their Settlements, and from various other Causes and Calamitys of War, the Staple Produce of Tobacco for three years last past, has been greatly reduced, and thereby the Public Revenue of 2 shillings per Hogshead on Tobacco,[2] granted in perpetuity, by the Laws of Virginia for the Public Support of Government has fallen short, and in fact from the 25th of last October, is in Arrear to the Receiver General the sum of £488.9.10 Sterling, and by the 25 of April next, it is justly apprehended that the deficiency therein will be greater, and so on successively, from time to time, while the Province continues in a State of War.[3]

In this Situation, the Governor and Council of Virginia, having greatly at heart the Welfare of the Province, and the preservation of his Majestys Dominions, think themselves in duty bound, to Remonstrate to your Lordships hereupon, the many inconveniencys, that may ensue, from the deficiency of this Fund, whereupon rests, not only, the ordinary Establishments, but many unforseen Extraordinary Exigencys of Government, more especially in time of Danger; And to move your Lordships That the Deficiency, which has already happened, in the Tobacco Revenue, ammounting as aforesaid, to the sum of £488.9.10, and such as may hereafter necessarily arise, for the Extraordinary services of Government, Incurred, by the Lieutenant Governour and his Majestys Council of Virginia, may be made up, to the Revenue of 2/ per Hogshead out of the Revenue of Quitrents,[4] and this Proposition, it is hoped, will appear to Your Lordships the more just and reasonable, in so far as that, the Revenue of 2/ per Hogshead on Tobacco, when in good Circumstances, has occasionally from time to time, been applyd, by the Governour and Council, in Aid of the Quitrents, and by way of Contingent Charges, for Deficiencys in the Quitrent mony, and for other special Services of Government, usually provided for, out of the Quitrents, which sums, so given in Aid of the Quitrents, do, on the whole, from October 1744 to June 1756 amount to £3079.4.3 as by the Accounts transmitted by the Officers of the Revenue, to his Majesty's Auditor General of the Plantations, will more particularly appear.

And whereas the Fund of 2/ pr Hhd is now totally exhausted, and likely to continue in a declining State, during the War, It is from thence submitted to your Lordships Consideration, as essentially necessary, for the good of His Majesty's Service & Government, that the said sum of £3079.4.3 be now replaced, to the said Tobacco Fund, out of the Quitrents, so as to answer public Emergencys, and to which the same shall be accordingly applyd, by the Governor and Council, and duly accounted for, in Aid of such deficiencys, as may hereafter occasionally arise in the Tobacco Revenue during the War.

All which is most humbly submitted.

       Jas. Abercromby Agent for Virginia
       by order of the Leut. Governor & Council

DS: T.1/389, ff. 110–11. Both the signature and the rest of the subscription are in Abercromby's hand. The tentative date is that of Abercromby's letter of 15 Mar. 1758 to Fauquier, in which a copy of this memorial presumably was enclosed. An endorsement is "Send for Mr. Abercromby. Q. How much hath been lent from the Tobacco duty to the quitt rents, and when. This article to be particularly referred to the Auditor Genl. of the Plantations who is the proper officer." It is not clear when the memorial was presented to the Treasury, but it had been submitted before 26 Apr. 1758, according to Abercromby's letter to Fauquier of that date.

 1. These commissioners were appointed to administer the Treasury, in the place of a lord high treasurer.

 2. This revenue was derived from a tax of 2s. on each hogshead of tobacco exported from Virginia, and from several minor sources; it was the principal income of the colony, and most of it was spent for support of the provincial government. For details, see notes to app. A, 1759.

 3. The 2s. per hogshead account had shown a substantial surplus of receipts over disbursements for a number of years, until the account for the six months ending 25 Apr. 1756 showed a credit balance of less than £94, and the account for the next six months, to 25 Oct. 1756, showed a credit balance of a little under £14. The next account, to 25 Apr. 1757, showed a deficit of about £1,283; the account for 25 Apr.–25 Oct. 1757 is missing, but the next account indicates that there was a deficit of £488.9.10 as of 25 Oct. 1757. The accounts demonstrate that the deficits did continue until the statement for 25 Apr.–25 Oct. 1761 once more noted a surplus of receipts over disbursements.

4. The revenue of quitrents consisted for the most part of an annual rent of 1s. for every 50 acres of land; as a rule most of the revenue was remitted to England for the use of the crown. For details, see notes to app. B, 1759.

Enclosure: Petition of Robert Hunter Morris

[ca. 11 February 1758]

A Petition of Robert Hunter Morris Esquire, was presented to the House, and read; alleging, That no Salt is at present made in the British Colonies in North America; but that the said Colonies depend upon a precarious Supply from Foreigners of that Commodity; and that the Petitioner, from a personal Knowledge of the Situation and Circumstances of many Parts of North America, from an Enquiry into the Causes of the Miscarriages of former Attempts, and from many Years Enquiry and Observation into, and an Acquaintance with, the Manner of making Salt, as practised in several Parts of Europe, is well convinced, that good Marine Salt may be made in his Majesty's Colonies in North America, in Quantities sufficient for their own Use and Consumption, and at a moderate Price; and further alleging, that the carrying from hence proper Men and Materials, and the erecting necessary Works, for the making of Salt, will be attended with a very large Expence and great Hazard; but the Petitioner is willing to undertake the same at his own Risque and Charge, provided he can be secured in the Enjoyment of the Profits which may arise therefrom (in Case it succeeds), for such a Term of Years as may seem to the House a proper and adequate Compensation for so great an Undertaking; and that the Petitioner conceives no Loss or Inconvenience can possibly attend the giving such an Encouragement, as every Method by which the Colonies are at present supplied will be left open; and that the Encouragement proposed can only arise from the Success of the Undertaking; but that, if, by this Means, they are brought to supply themselves with Salt, of their own making, it will render many considerable Branches of Trade more certain and beneficial: And therefore praying the House to take the Premises into their Consideration, and to grant the Petitioner such Assistance therein as to them shall seem proper.

Ordered, That the said Petition do lie upon the Table.

Printed: *JHC*, 11 Feb. 1758. A copy of the petition here abstracted was enclosed in Abercromby's letter to Fauquier of 15 Mar. 1758. See n. 4 to that letter.

Enclosure: Warrant for Nathaniel Blakiston

[Hampton Court, 23 August 1716]
By his Royal Highness the Prince Guardian of the Kingdom.
George P: C: R:[1]

These are to authorize and Require you out of his Majesty's Revenues arising by Quitrents in Virginia to Cause payment to be made to Nathaniel Blackiston Esqr: Agent for the said Colony or to his assigns of the yearly Sum of £200 which his Majesty is greaciously pleased to allow him as addition to his Salary of 100 per annum in consideration of the Extraordinary Services by him performed to his Majesty the same to commence from midsummer now last past and to be paid him Quarterly during his Majesty's pleasure and this shall be as well to you for so doing as to all others concerned in making the said payments or allowing thereof upon account a Sufficient Warrant Given at the Court at hampton Court the 23d day of August 1716 in the 3d year of his Majesty's Reign.

By his Royal Highness's Command
R: Walpole
Wm: St: Quintin
R: Edgcumbe[2]

[To] the Rt Honble: Geo: Earl of orkeney[3] Govr: of his Majestys Colony of Virginia [or] the Govr: Deputy Govr: & Recr: Genl: [the]re for the time being and all other [his] Majestys Officers herin concerned.

Copy: C.O.5/1329, f. 159. Part of the address is concealed in the gutter, and the bracketed words or letters are suggested as what is concealed. The text is that of a copy of the warrant which Abercromby submitted as one of several attachments to his undated memorial to the Board of Trade (C.O.5/1329, ff. 152–55), read on 21 Nov. 1759, in which he asked to be confirmed in his appointment as agent for Virginia and to receive either an addition to his salary or whatever salary the board considered him entitled to, with a further allowance for his expenses. A copy of this warrant was enclosed in Abercromby's letter to Fauquier of 15 Mar. 1758.

1. In July 1716 George Augustus (1683–1760), Prince of Wales and later George II, was named guardian of the kingdom, or guardian of the realm, to act as regent during the absence of his father, George I, in Hanover. Presumably the initials after his name stand for *Princeps, Custos Regni*.

2. These three men were lords of the Treasury: Robert Walpole (1676–1745), first lord and chancellor of the Exchequer (knighted in 1725, created first earl of Orford in 1742); Sir William St. Quintin, Bt., (1660?–1723); and Richard Edgcumbe (1680–1758), created first Baron Edgcumbe in 1742.

3. George Hamilton (1666–1737), earl of Orkney, was governor of Virginia from 1710 until his death.

1 April 1758

Order in Council

[St. James's, 1 April 1758]
At the Court at St. James's the 1st of April 1758
Present
The Kings most Excellent Majesty in Council.

Whereas by Commission under the Great Seal of Great Britain, the Governor Council and Assembly of His Majestys Colony of Virginia, are Authorized and empowered to make Constitute and Ordain Laws Statutes and Ordinances for the Publick Peace Welfare and good Government of the said Colony, which Laws Statutes and Ordinances are to be, as near as conveniently may be, agreable to the Laws and Statutes of this Kingdom, and to be transmitted for His Majestys Royal Approbation or Disallowance. And whereas in pursuance of the said Powers An Act was passed in the said Colony in May 1759 which hath been transmitted, Entituled as follows Vizt

An Act for Settling the Titles and Bounds of Lands and for preventing unlawful Hunting and Ranging.[1]

Which Act, together with a Representation from the Lords Commissioners for Trade and Plantations thereupon, having been referred to the Consideration of a Committee of the Lords of His Majestys most Honourable Privy Council for Plantation Affairs, The said Lords of the Committee did this day report their Opinion to His Majesty, that the said Act was proper to be approved. His Majesty in Council taking the same into Consideration, was graciously pleased to declare His Approbation of the said Act, and pursuant to His Majestys Royal Pleasure thereupon expressed, the said Act is hereby confirmed, finally Enacted, and Ratified accordingly. Whereof the Governor, Lieutenant Governor, or Commander in Chief of His Majestys said Colony of Virginia for the time being, and all others whom it may concern, are to take Notice and Govern themselves accordingly.

A true Copy
W: Sharpe[2]

Copy: C.O.5/1329, ff. 183–84. The order was read in the council of Virginia on 17 Oct. 1761 and ordered to be registered in the secretary's office. See *EJC* 6:198.

1. The act (Hening, 5:408–31) was not passed in May 1759 but in May 1749. The act had a remarkable history. By May 1750 the Board of Trade had referred the act to Matthew Lamb, its legal adviser, and in May 1751 ordered it sent to the Treasury for review. By Apr. 1752 the Treasury had returned the act without any opinion, and the board ordered it sent to Horatio Walpole, auditor general of the plantations. The auditor's report was not read until 22 Feb. 1758, when the board considered the act

and ordered a representation prepared for the king; on 1 Apr. 1758 the order in council confirming the act was drawn up. Whether the board did not receive the order or simply overlooked it is not clear, but by July 1760 the board had received this copy of the order. On 10 Mar. 1761 the board read a memorial from Edward Montagu, the Virginia agent, who prayed the board to request the king's confirmation of the act. The secretary to the board informed it that the act had been referred to the auditor general in 1752, but he had made no report on it; the board then ordered the act referred to the present auditor. About this time someone seems to have remembered that the act had been confirmed in 1758, and the order in council was sent off to Virginia.

2. The attestation appears to have the autograph signature of William Sharpe (d. 1767), clerk in extraordinary of the Privy Council from about 1723 until 1762, when he became clerk in ordinary. He was one of the brothers of Gov. Horatio Sharpe of Maryland.

Warrant for Robert Carter

G[eorge] R. [St. James's, 7 April 1758]

Right Trusty and Right Wellbeloved Cousin, We Greet you well. We being well satisfied of the Loyalty Integrity and Ability of Our Trusty and Wellbeloved Robert Carter Esqr.,[1] have thought fit hereby to signify to you Our Will and Pleasure, that forthwith upon the Receipt of these Presents,[2] you swear and Admit him, the said Robert Carter, to be of Our Council in Our Colony of Virginia in America, in the room of Wm. Fairfax Esqr. deceased.[3] And for so doing this shall be your Warrant. And so We bid you farewell. Given at Our Court at St. James's the [seventh] day of [April] 1758 in the thirty first Year of Our Reign.

By His Majesty's Command.

To Our Right Trusty and Right Welbeloved Cousin John Earl of Loudoun, Our Capt. General and Governor in Chief of Our Colony and Dominion of Virginia in America; or in his Absence to Our Trusty and Wellbeloved Francis Fauquier Esqr. Our Lieutenant Governor or to the Commander in Chief of Our Said Colony for the time being.

Copy: C.O.324/51, p. 122. This draft of the warrant is dated only Mar. 1758. The sign manual is supplied in the usual form, and the date of the actual warrant is supplied from a memorandum of the warrant in C.O.324/38, p. 500.

1. Robert Carter III (1728–1804), of Nomini Hall.
2. This letter was read on 18 Oct. 1758, when Carter took the oaths and was admitted to the council; he continued as a member until the Revolution.
3. William Fairfax (1691–1757) was admitted to the council in 1744 and had been the senior member and president for several years before his death. He was acting governor for a brief period in the spring of 1757 while Dinwiddie attended a conference with Loudoun in Philadelphia.

26 April 1758

From James Abercromby

Craven street April 26 1758

I lay hold of this opportunity from Bristol[1] to inform you, that after a very hard strugle before the Committee of the house of Commons, who had under their Consideration the Petition of Hunter Morriss Esqr for the sole previlege of making Salt in North America, the Merchants for Virginia and Maryland in conjunction with the Agents for Virginia and the Carolinas, have prevailed in their opposition to this Petition, & the Petition is accordingly dismissed, after five hearings thereon, we have been the more strenuous in our opposition before the Committee, from the Extraordinary trouble and Expence, that must have attended an Opposition in the house, had Mr Morriss gained his point for bringing in a Bill for the purposes set forth in his Petition.

The Petition before the Treasury for an Aid to the Tobacco Revenue out of the Quitrents has not as yet been taken into Consideration, the hurry of Business in money matters depending before Parliament for Home, as well as Foreign Subsidys, allows no time for other matters, but from this Delay, I shall avail myself of Mr Dinwiddy's assistance on his return from Bath,[2] which place he purposes to leave as next week, having found some benefit from the Waters.

The public Newspapers collected together for your use, being too bulky by Post to Bristol, I shall hereby take notice of the most matterial Events; a Convention between England and Prussia to act conjunctly against France, and make no seperate peace, in Consideration whereof, we give 2 Millions to the King of Prussia, payable by equal proportions in the space of three years, if the War shall so long continue, and this Exclusive of paying the Army of Hanoverians &c now under the King of Prussias direction.[3]

The Capture of the Foudrouyant of 84 Guns and the Orpheus of 64 going under the Command of Monsr. Dequesne now in England at Northampton, to reinforce Monsr Declue at Carthagena, this proves a very great Disappointment to the French who are still block'd up at Carthagena,[4] add to this Sir Ed. Hawkes having about 15 Days ago drove on shore five Ships of the Line near Rochfort with many Transports having 3000 men ready to embark therein for America, the mud was soft where those Ships run ashore, however having thrown their Guns & Stores overboard, their intended Expedition becomes frustrated, whether they do or do not get off.[5] Upon the whole our affairs in Europe, as well as in America by Genl Abercrombys Letters of the 17th March have a better Aspect than heretofore.[6] I wish you Success on your Frontiers & with

Compliments I hope you and your Lady find the Country agreeable after the fatigue of your Voyage. I am &c.

To Gov. Fauquier by Bristol.

Copy: Virginia State Library, James Abercromby Letter Book, pp. 97–99. In a clerk's hand, except for "by Bristol" in Abercromby's hand in the address.

1. A town in Gloucestershire, Bristol was a major port and a center of North American trade and shipping.
2. Bath, a resort in Somerset, was the most fashionable spa in England from the early part of the century. The warm springs were valued for their curative properties.
3. The convention between the king of England and the king of Prussia, signed 11 Apr. 1758, in fact provided that the parties should not conclude any treaty of peace unless both agreed to it and that England should pay Prussia a subsidy of approximately £670,000. The text of the convention is in *JHC* 28:188.
4. Six French warships under the command of Admiral Duquesne were ordered to the relief of Admiral de la Clue, whose division, bound for North America and the West Indies, had been driven into the Spanish port of Cartagena and blockaded there. On 28 Feb. 1758 Admiral Osborn intercepted the French force and captured the *Foudroyant*, Duquesne's flagship, and the *Orphée*. Duquesne was taken prisoner and brought to England; the *Annual Register* reported that he arrived in London on 8 May, and the *Gentleman's Magazine* reported that he set out from Northampton on 21 Oct. on his way to France on parole, "perhaps to facilitate a peace."
5. On 5 Apr. 1758 Adm. Sir Edward Hawke intercepted off the French port of Rochefort a large French convoy bound for America, five men-of-war, six or seven frigates, and about forty merchantmen with 3,000 troops aboard; most of the French vessels were driven ashore. The French salvaged some of the ships but lost a quantity of guns and gear they had jettisoned, and their dispatch of supplies to America was thwarted.
6. General Abercromby's letters have not been identified.

To John St. Clair

Sir,[1]   Wmsburgh June 6th 1758

His Majesty having been graciously pleased to appoint me to succeed the Honble Robert Dinwiddie Esqr. in the Administration of the Government here, your Letter of June 1st for his Majesty's Service, to Mr. President Blair,[2] was therefore brought to me yesterday, the day of my Arrival to this place. On opening it, I was concern'd to find some heavy Charges on Mr. Blair's Administration; and therefore thought proper (as I could not possibly be yet acquainted with past Transactions) to lay it before the Council this morning.[3]

Your first paragraph acknowledges the receipt of his of May 25th,[4] and charges your being at a Loss how to answer it, seeing the little regard he paid to what was required by Brigadier General Forbes;[5] or your self; whom I find he has deputed to act in his absince.

Mr. Presidents Copy of that Letter was read, and the Council were convinced that he had done all in his power, consistent with their Advice, & his duty to protect the Fronteers, to furnish the Regiment with Arms,[6] tho' an unexpected Demand upon us. And on his finding the want of Blankets, had sent to several distant places to purchase them, the accommadating such Numbers of Indians at Winchester[7] having drained us hereabouts, The demand on us for Tents and Kettles came it seems two days after by Col. Washington;[8] and tho: The General was to have furnished these as well as arms; by Mr. Secretary Pitt's Letter[9] yet this too is complied with I find; and the councel look on the President as forward to make every stretch for the Service; as, for Dispatch, he took down all the arms here & sent all off before the Councill met,[10] relying on what he should purchase for our own use; tho this ought to have been proposed in Council first. This is what I learn as to your general Charge. Your next relates to the Situation, of the first Rigiment as wanting one Hundred men & not by the fault of Col; Washington. as to this the President informs me that he had drawn on the Treasury for the Recruting Service till the Treasurer[11] informed him he had paid out all that was appropriated for that Service & could issue no more. Soon after this it seems Came Col; Washington's demand for a large Sum to Recruit his Regiment; which he theirfore could not send him But had the Recruiting officers that were then out succeeded according to what was Expected from them; we should have had enough he said for both Regiments.

In your next you Complain of your being left with 9 Companys of the 2d Regiment without Arms Cloathing or Blankets, many Sick & no Surgeon nor one kettle to make broth for them. To this the President says if you had delayed your complaint till Col. Washingtons return (who: only waited for the Council) you would have found he had done all he could to Remove those Complaints; & what Col: Washington hoped you would have thought Satisfactory and he thinks it hard to have the want of arms charged on him, when we expected them & Tents &ca. to have been furnished as proposed to Us and that therefore he had no fund for it. As to Blankets he says they were directed to be furnished in another way as he has wrote to you but on finding they were not provided he immediatly applied to purchase them as already mention'd. By the want of Clothing he supposes you mean that of a Uniform for the Cloths they had were thot sufficent for the Campaign; and Brigdr. General Forbes to save time dispences with uniformity alltogether. as to the want of a Surgeon the President confisses it with great concern. He tells me he had sent a Commission to a Gentleman well Recommended to him. & given Commissions to two others to be his two mates but unfortunatly Mr.

Johnston the Surgeon had returned his Commission & Mr. Wallace his first mate he finds is discharged by Col Byrd,[12] for some failing He has been in Expectation of Doctr. John Walker of King William & of a Gentleman from Richmond that Mr. Finnie wrote to,[13] but neither are come The difficulty it seems is that those that are fit for it are generally in such good business they will not quit it for so short a service which is a Difficulty I fear hard to get over as we cannot compel them. What you say of the scalping the men and then leaving them in the Road seems very blamable; but many of the Cherokees discover'd their inclinations to leave us before this happen'd it seems and many of them had left us or this had not happen'd.[14] So all their desertion he thinks cannot be imputed to that Scuffle But what Ever Effects it had How can Mr. Blair be charged with them: He has order'd a Strict Enquiry to be made; before which no punishment can be Legally inflicted; He has given Orders that the Militia sent to protect the Frontiers from those Crueltys they had Comitted should use no violence if possible to be avoided but endeavour to pacify their Rage.

But if they should prove obstinatly bent on Mischief, and could not be prevailed on to attend the General,[15] he thought it could not be inconsistant with any Orders you may have, to desire your assistance in that case to prevent their murdering our people, by disarming them or Otherwise. He mentions there I perceive several Inducements to a pacification: the Goods just expected (& which are since arrived) and the Garrison for their fort which would be sent with the goods, as they desire. By Col. Byrd's Letter I find the Little Carpenter is coming with 200 men to assist the General.[16] and I hope will not be diverted from it by this Scuffle with some of his Nation as they were the Aggressors by their own confission; but that by his Intrest with them they will be pacified. It seems the act of Assembly, past in July last, directs one of the Companys of Col. Washingtons Regiment to be sent to garrison the Fort they then built in the Cherokee Nation, which Company was to consist of 100 Men;[17] but as the General can ill spare them at this time, and as I find all possible Stretches are made to favour the Grand Design you are upon (for the Success of which we shall, by the Presidents appointment of a General Fast, to morrow implore the Blessing of Heaven) I am willing to defer the Execution of that Clause (so long hitherto postponed) to a more favourable Oppertunity. The President has issued his Orders, by advice of Council, for the Militia from several Countys, to garrison the Forts in Stead of the Regulars,[18] and if any Extraordinary delays have happen'd he is sorry for it, as he heartily wishes to promote the Service; & hopes his Endeavours & good degree of success will evince his attachment. And

6 June 1758

as to Establishing Post Horses it was not askt he says till after the Assembly broke up. and as no such Establishment was in General Bradocks time, so no provision was made for it, & as he could not do it without a Fund. He therefor desired the General would enable him. Thus Sir I have by the assistance of the President & Council consider'd the several particulars of your Letter.

Your Zeal for the Service is admitted as a good appolegy for that Degree of warmth which appears in it and our only endeavour is to give your Honour all possible satisfaction in every point. This coming just at my admission I can only add that in my future administration, General Forbes your Self and every one acting by his appointment, may depend on my best Assistance for carrying on the great work his Majesty has sent you to Execute I assure you it gave much greater pleasure to hear the arms were to be usefully employed than it would have done to have found them as mere ornaments in my Hall. tho' for the Safity of the Colony they ought to be Replaced there or in the Magzine of this Capital. I hope you will Excuse my begging the Favour of you to forward my Letter to General Forbes[19] when you have an Occation to send to him as it was the shortest Conveyance I could find and believe me to be with great Esteem. Sir Your very Humble Servant

Fran: Fauquier

To Sir Jno. St. Clair Bart.

LS: University of Virginia, Tracy W. McGregor Library. Superscription in Fauquier's hand.

1. Col. Sir John St. Clair, Bart. (d. 1767), was deputy quartermaster general in America 1754–67. See Charles R. Hildeburn, "Sir John St. Clair, Baronet," *Pennsylvania Magazine of History and Biography* 9 (1885): 1–14.

2. A copy of this letter, evidently sent by St. Clair to Forbes, dated 31 May 1758, is in the Tracy W. McGregor Library.

3. The council journal for 6 June 1758 cites the date of the letter as 1 June 1758 and notes that Fauquier had asked Blair to "take upon himself the Trouble of answering it, as it was directed to him, and he was best acquainted with the Proceedings which occasioned it." No reply signed by Blair has been traced, and it may be that Blair drafted this present letter for Fauquier's signature.

4. Blair's letter of 25 May 1758 to St. Clair is in the Tracy W. McGregor Library.

5. Brigadier, or Brigadier General, John Forbes (1710–1759) was in command of the expedition against Fort Duquesne, and from the end of April till the beginning of July 1758 he was in Philadelphia waiting for troops and stores.

6. Perhaps Fauquier referred to the First Virginia Regiment, raised in 1754 and under the command of George Washington. However, it is more likely he referred to the Second Virginia Regiment, under the command of William Byrd. The new regiment was authorized by "An Act for augmenting the forces in the pay of this Colony to two thousand men; and for other purposes therein mentioned" (Hening, 7:163-69), passed during the General Assembly's session of 30 Mar.–12 Apr. 1758. The act authorized the appropriation of £32,000 for support of the new troops, of Rangers

previously authorized, and of Indian allies, as well as for Indian goods and bounties for scalps or for captives. See *JHB, 1752–1755, 1756–1758*, pp. 493–506.

7. In Frederick County, Va., at the northern end of the Shenandoah Valley, Winchester was settled about 1744 and was still a frontier outpost. A number of Indian auxiliaries had already arrived there, and many more were expected.

8. George Washington had been appointed colonel and commander in chief of all Virginia forces in 1755. He had arrived in Williamsburg on 27 or 28 May 1758.

9. Fauquier no doubt meant General Abercromby, the commander in chief in North America; Mr. Pitt's letter was that of 30 Dec. 1757 from William Pitt (1708–1778), secretary of state, to the governors of the southern colonies (*Pitt* 1:140–43).

10. On 2 June 1758 Blair informed the council that he had sent off to Winchester all the arms from the magazine in Williamsburg and all those in the Governor's House.

11. John Robinson (1704–1766) was treasurer of Virginia.

12. The surgeon was Robert Johnston, and his two mates were presumably the Henry DuVal Mauger whose petition for compensation was rejected by the House of Burgesses in 1764 and Michael Wallace or Wallis (1719–1767), a surgeon of Falmouth, across the Rappahannock River from Fredericksburg.

13. Walker was perhaps the Dr. John Walker who died at Hanover Town, just across the Pamunkey River from King William County, in 1774. The gentleman from Richmond, not identified, was perhaps of Richmond County on the Rappahannock River or of the town of Richmond in Henrico County. Mr. Finnie was no doubt Maj. Alexander Finnie, adjutant of the middle district of Virginia, who died in York County about the beginning of May 1769.

14. The incident referred to was an attack by inhabitants of Bedford County on some Cherokee Indians: the inhabitants scalped some of the Indians and left them in the road, as St. Clair reported, so that other Indians coming to join the British forces might see them; St. Clair said the result of this affair was that all the Cherokees had gone or were going home, except those with Byrd. The Cherokees were a powerful tribe of Indians of the Iroquoian family who in historic times lived in the southern Appalachians. At the outbreak of the French and Indian War they were disposed to be friendly to the British, and parties of them joined the British as auxiliaries, but they were increasingly alienated and by 1759 were generally hostile to the British.

15. Here and below this refers to Forbes.

16. Byrd's letter of 21 May 1758 to this effect is abstracted in *EJC* 6:95–96. The Little Carpenter, or Attakullakulla (ca. 1700–ca. 1780), was a noted chief of the Cherokees, on various occasions a spokesman and negotiator for them, and reputedly the second in authority among the tribe.

17. The eleventh article of "An Act for granting an aid to his majesty for the better protection of this colony, and for other purposes therein mentioned" (Hening, 7:69–87) directed that one of the companies then in the pay of the colony and a surgeon were to be sent to garrison the fort. The act was passed on 8 June 1757, not in July. The fort was one built by Andrew Lewis about the middle of 1756 on the north bank of the Little Tennessee River, a mile above the Cherokee town of Chotee, near the site of the fort built later in the same year by South Carolina and called Fort Loudoun. The Virginia fort is sometimes called Fort Loudoun on the Holston or the Fort at Chotee.

18. On 2 May 1758 the council advised Blair to "order out half the Number of the Militia from the adjacent Counties to garrison the Forts, which the Virginia Forces there station'd consisted of."

19. The letter of 8 June 1758.

8 June 1758

To John Forbes

Sir Williamsburgh June 8th 1758

I take the Opportunity of an Express which is going to Sir John St. Clair in Relation to the Arming the new raised Virginia Regiment[1] to notify to you my Arrival here, honoured with his Majestie's Commission by which he has been graciously pleased to appoint me to succeed to the Honble. Robt. Dinwiddie Esqr. as Lieutenant Governor of this his Majesties Colony and Dominion of Virginia: And at the same Time of assuring you that I shall with the greatest Readiness embrace every Opportunity that may offer it self for the carrying on any Correspondence between us that you may favour me with, or judge necessary for the Service of his Majesty and the Benefit of his Colonies in America.

It was an unspeakable Pleasure to me on my Arrival to find this Colony so zealously resolved to support the Common Cause, as to omit no Opportunity of exerting themselves on the Occasion; as an Instance of which I cannot omit the almost incredible Dispatch used in raising a second Regiment compleat for the Defence thereof. I shall on my Part do all in my Power to promote a Continuance of the same Spirit which so nobly appears amongst us at present. With the greatest Regard I am, Sir, Your obedient Humble Servant,

Fran: Fauquier

Since I wrote this I received your Letter to the President[2] by Coll. Hunter.[3] It gives me great Satisfaction that the Zeal of this Colony meets with your Approbation, which it shall be my Endeavours to merit a Continuance of.

To the Honble. Brigr. Genl. Forbes.

ALS: Scottish Record Office, Dalhousie Muniments GD 45/2/80/1.

1. The Second Virginia Regiment.
2. The letter from Forbes to John Blair, president of the council, has not been exactly identified, but it was probably one from Philadelphia dated 31 May 1758, in which Forbes wrote that he had sent tents, camp kettles, and canteens for the new regiment, as well as goods for the Indians, and would provide silver armplates and breastplates. A copy of this letter is in the Tracy W. McGregor Library at the University of Virginia; it was communicated to the council on 15 June 1758 and is abstracted in *EJC* 6:102.
3. This is possibly Col. John Hunter, of Little England, near Hampton in Elizabeth City County, where he was colonel of militia; he apparently was a substantial merchant who sold out in 1766 to Capel & Osgood Hanbury & Richard Goslin, of London, and removed to London with his family. As early as 1752 and as late as 1763 he seems to have been active as an agent for the providing of food, clothing, and arms, and the executive journals of the council for 17, 21, and 23 Dec. 1762 refer to John Hunter as

"Agent Victualler" and allude to the terms of his contract (*EJC* 6:245–46 and passim, and *Dinwiddie*, passim). The various scanty and confusing references may concern more than one man of the name of John Hunter.

To William Henry Lyttelton

Sir   Williamsburgh June 8th 1758

I take the earliest Opportunity of notifying to your Excellency[1] my Arrival here,[2] honoured with his Majesties Commission by which he has been graciously pleased to appoint me to succeed to the Honble. Robt. Dinwiddie Esqr. as Lieutenant Governor of this his Majesties Colony and Dominion of Virginia: and at the same Time of assuring you that I shall with the greatest Readiness embrace every Opportunity that may offer it self for the carrying on any Correspondence you may favour me with, and judge necessary for the Service of his Majesty and the Benefit of his Colonies in America.

The Honour I have of being acquainted with Lord Lyttelton,[3] and your other Brothers,[4] gives me Room to hope that our Intercourse may become more frequent than our public Characters might otherwise demand. This I shall on my part endeavour to cultivate, as a thing sincerely desired by, Sir, Your Excellency's most Obedient Humble Servant,

                                                            Fran: Fauquier

To his Excellency W. Henry Lyttelton Esqr.

ALS: William L. Clements Library, Lyttelton Papers.

1. William Henry Lyttelton (1724–1808) was governor of South Carolina 1755–60. See Wyndham.

2. Fauquier sailed from England with Mrs. Fauquier and their elder son, Francis, 1 Apr. 1758 on the *Wilson*, a merchant vessel of 400 tons commanded by Judson Coolidge, and arrived in Virginia on 5 June. The *Pa. Gaz.* for 6 July 1758 gives an account (under the dateline of Williamsburg, 9 June) of the arrival of H.M.S. *Chesterfield*, Capt. Julian Legge commanding, with the convoy that included the *Wilson*. Captain Legge's letters to the Admiralty of 2 Apr. and 4 June 1758, with particulars of the convoy and his passage, are in Adm. 1/2047, sec. 14.

3. George Lyttelton (1709–1773), created first Baron Lyttelton of Frankley in 1756, was a Whig politician, a man of letters, and a friend and patron of literary people; Henry Fielding dedicated *Tom Jones* to him. See Wyndham.

4. The other brothers were Charles Lyttelton (1714–1768), clergyman and antiquary, Fellow of the Royal Society, chaplain to the king (1747) and dean of Exeter (1748); and Richard Lyttelton (1718–1770), a soldier who rose to the rank of lieutenant general, married the duchess of Bridgwater in 1745, and was made Knight of the Bath in 1753. An illegitimate half brother of Governor Lyttelton was Thomas Smith (1707?–1762), who was the flag officer appointed to preside at the court martial of

Admiral Byng in 1756, and became Admiral of the Blue in 1757. Charles Lyttelton, Thomas Smith, and Richard Lyttelton are among the principal figures in Mrs. Wyndham's *Chronicles*.

To Major General James Abercromby

Sir   Williamsburgh June the 10th 1758

I take the earliest opportunity of notifieing to you my Arrival here honoured with His Majesty's Commission by which he has been Graciously placed to appoint Me to Succeed to the Honble. Robt. Dinvidie Esqr. as Lieutenant Governour of this His Majesty's colonie and Dominion of Virginia and at the same time of Asureing you that I shall with the greatest Readiness Embrace every opportunity that may offer itself for the carrieing on any Corespandance you may favour me with, or Judge necessary for the service of His Majesty, and the benefit of His Colonies in America, ACompanying this, I have the pleasure to forward to you A Letter from Mrs. Abercromby to whom I paid my Respects before I Left England, and can with Equal Truth and Satisfaction Asure you I left her and all your Family weel.

Mr. Abercromby our Agent to whom I was Oblidged for my Introduction to your Lady Likewis committed some Dispatches to my care which you will also receive with this, He communicated one to me which relates to the Disposition of the £50,000 Granted by Parliament for this and the Neighbouring Colonies;[1] which is in the Treasury till a Report is made from the Commander in Chief to which that Board will pay great Regard in the proportioning the several Sums to the Respective Colonies, you will Receive a Letter Wrote in counsel Here upon that head,[2] not doubting but that their Zeal for the publick Service, and the great Sums they have actually raised in Support of the common cause will be Deem'd to Merit a large Share thereof. But as my late Arrival since the Transacting these Affairs, makes me not so much Master thereof as I could wish I must refer you to that Letter.

I have only to add that you may depend upon me that no one Shall be found more assiduous and Active to serve his Majesty by assisting as far as is in my Power, the Plan of Operations for this Continent, than I hope you will find me, who am with great Esteem and Regard, Sir, Your Most obedient Humble Servant,

                                             Fran: Fauquir

Copy: W.O.34/37, f. 8.

1. A copy of the letter of 12 Mar. 1758 from Abercromby to General Abercromby was enclosed in the former's letter of 15 Mar. to Fauquier. On 5 June Fauquier communicated it to the council, which ordered the preparation of a letter to General Abercromby. See *EJC* 6:100–101.

2. This letter from the council to General Abercromby of about 19 June 1758, written in accordance with the council's order of 5 June, was signed by President Blair on 19 June and evidently carried by the courier who delivered Fauquier's letter of 10 June to the general. The council wrote that it had applied to Loudoun on 14 Dec. 1757 for a share of the £50,000 granted by Parliament and had submitted a memorandum on the total of £207,600 raised by Virginia for defense; it now renewed its application and laid before the general "An Account of the Money rais'd for His Majesty's Service in the Colony of Virginia reciting the respective Acts of Assembly," probably the memorandum previously sent to Loudoun; it pointed out that to the £207,600 ought to be added at least £2,500 for the 400,000 lbs. of tobacco paid to the militia. See *EJC* 6:105–6. The council's letter to the general and the memorandum are in the Huntington Library, Abercromby Papers AB 975 and AB 344.

Address to Francis Fauquier and Reply

[Williamsburg, 10 June 1758]

To the Honourable Francis Fauquier, Esq. His Majesty's Lieutenant-Governor, and Commander in Chief, of the Colony and Dominion of Virginia, The humble Address of the Mayor, Recorder, Aldermen, and Common-Council, of the City of Williamsburg.[1]

Sir

We his Majesty's most dutiful and loyal Subjects, the Mayor, Recorder, Aldermen, and Common-Council, of the City of Williamsburg, humbly beg Leave to approach your Honour with our sincerest Congratulations upon your safe and happy Arrival with your Family into this Colony; and we do most heartily welcome you to the Seat of your Government.

This City having been particularly honoured with the Residence of many of your worthy Predecessors, hath thought herself peculiarly happy, under their Patronage, in the free Exercise and Enjoyment of her Rights and Privileges;[2] and we flatter ourselves that you, Sir, will be pleased to receive her into your Favour, and afford her your kind Protection. On our Parts, permit us to assure your Honour, that we shall always study, so far as it may be in our Power, to make your Administration agreeable and delightful to you, and that we shall ever esteem that a lucky Incident, which affords us an Opportunity of rendering to your Honour any acceptable Service.

11 June 1758

To which his Honour was pleased to return the following Answer.
Gentlemen,
I return you my sincere Thanks for your Congratulations on my safe Arrival in this Dominion, of which his Majesty has done me the Honour to appoint me his Lieutenant-Governor, and for the Assurances you give me of your Endeavours to make my Administration agreeable to me; and, that it may be so to myself, it shall be my Study to render it easy to you, by making Justice and Equity the Rule of my Conduct to the People his Majesty has committed to my Charge, and by having a due Attention to the Rights and Privileges of the City of Williamsburg, which may safely rely on my constant Protection.

Printed: *Pa. Gaz.* for 6 July 1758, in an account of Fauquier's arrival and the attendant ceremonies. The section of the account with the address and reply is dated 16 June 1758, and the address is said to have been presented "Last Saturday," which would have been 10 June 1758.

1. The charter of 28 July 1722, by which Williamsburg was incorporated, provided that the corporation should consist of "a Mayor, one Person learned in the Law, stiled and bearing the Office of Recorder of the said City, six Aldermen, and twelve other Persons to be Common Council Men of the said City." There is no known record of the identity of the members of the corporation at this time. See Rutherfoord Goodwin, *A Brief & True Report Concerning Williamsburg in Virginia* (Richmond, 1935), pp. 350–57.

2. The charter conferred specific rights and privileges, among which were rights as a legal body, the use of a seal, the exercise of executive authority, the licence to hold markets and fairs, and the power to institute a hustings court. Modifications of the rights and privileges, particularly with respect to courts of law, militia service, and markets, had been effected by acts of assembly passed in 1723–57; see Hening, vols. 4–7: passim.

To the Board of Trade

My Lords[1]   Wmsburgh June 11th 1758

I have the Honour to acquaint your Lordships that on my Arrival here on the 5th instant I found this Colony very zealous in his Majesties Service, and very Strenuous to support the Common Cause: and in order thereto, have lately raised a second Regiment of 1000 Men under the Command of Coll. Byrd, which with the first Regiment of the same Number formerly raised and commanded by Coll. Washington are both now at Winchester ready to proceed on their March to Fort Cumberland the general Rendezvous appointed by Brigr. Genl. Forbes for his Majesties Forces under his Command. I ought to have excepted one Company of Coll. Washington's who are at present on the Frontiers on Account of a Scuffle between some of the Cherokee Indians,[2] and some of our People whose patience was worn out, by repeated Insults and Robberies committed on them, and at last took up Arms in their Defence. However I hope this affair is quite settled, and the Cherokees appeased by the Care of Coll. Byrd. They own themselves to be the Aggressors, and we are informed 250 of them are at Winchester determined to join his Majesties Troops and more are expected to come with a famous Warriour among them called the Little Carpenter.

I find no papers have been sent from hence since the Departure of Governor Dinwiddie, and I hope your Lordships will consider the very short Time I have been on Shore and excuse my not sending them with this. I propose to order the Servants of his Majesty in their respective Offices to prepare them as soon as possible, that I may transmit them to your Lordships agreeably to my Instructions which on all Occasions I shall use my Endeavours to execute with the greatest punctuality.[3]

The affair your Lordships recommended to me in regard to the Treasurership being annexed to the Speakers place,[4] I am afraid will meet with great Difficulty, as it has been a Custom of so long standing and the present Gentleman so popular & so sure of the Chair.[5] But I cannot with propriety say any thing on this Head as I have hardly stir'd in it yet.

A Ship just ready to sail for Glasgow has given me an Opportunity of writing to your Lordships I would not lose.[6] I shall do my self the Honour to send a Duplicate of this by the first Mail that sails from New York for England. I am with the greatest Respect, my Lords, Your Lordships most Obedient & devoted Humble Servant,

Fran: Fauquier

The Rt. Honble the Lords of Trade & Plantations

ALS: C.O.5/1329, ff. 75–76. Endorsed as read 12 Dec. 1758.

1. A body of eight regular commissioners who were charged with several duties, among which was the supervision of colonial affairs, the board is known by the names of Board of Trade and Plantations, Lords Commissioners of Trade and Plantations, and simply Lords of Trade; it was commonly addressed as "My Lords" and "Your Lordships." For accounts of the board, see Oliver Morton Dickerson, *American Colonial Government, 1696–1765* (Cleveland, 1912) and Arthur Herbert Basye, *The Lords Commissioners of Trade and Plantations, Commonly Known as the Board of Trade, 1748–1782* (New Haven, 1925). The proceedings of the board, in abstract, for the period down to Apr. 1704 are in *CSP*, and the proceedings in full for Apr. 1704 and afterwards are in the fourteen volumes of *BTJ*. At the date of this letter the board was made up of these members, appointed by a commission dated 13 Dec. 1756: George Dunk, earl of Halifax, the president, and Andrew Stone, James Oswald, Thomas Pelham, Soame Jenyns, Richard Rigby, William Gerard Hamilton, and William Sloper. The *Dictionary of National Biography* has sketches of all of these men except for Sloper, of whom a brief account is given in Namier, 3:444–45.

2. The "Scuffle" to which Fauquier referred was apparently a series of three engagements between parties of Cherokees and the militia of Halifax and Bedford counties in May 1758. See *EJC* 6:94, 102.

3. Arts. 27–30 of the instructions to Loudoun (C.O. 5/1367, ff. 103–4) directed him to transmit authentic copies of all laws, statutes, and ordinances within three months of their enactment and also send copies of orders and journals of the council and copies of journals and other proceedings of the General Assembly.

4. The treasurer of Virginia was an officer of the colony who, after 1691, was appointed by the House of Burgesses. The duties of the treasurer were to receive revenues from duties on liquors, servants, and slaves imported and any special levy raised by act of assembly and to borrow money on the authority of the assembly. From 1699 to 1766 the office of treasurer was held by the speaker of the House of Burgesses, the presiding officer of that house who was elected at the beginning of each new assembly. See Percy Scott Flippin, *The Financial Administration of the Colony of Virginia* (Baltimore, 1915) and *The Royal Government in Virginia, 1624–1775* (New York, 1919). The recommendation of the board to Fauquier in the matter of the treasurer's office was most immediately inspired, it appears, by Robert Dinwiddie. *BTJ*, 7 Mar. 1758, records his attendance at the board: "Mr. Dinwiddie, late Lieutenant Governor of Virginia, attending without was called in; and their lordships had some conversation with him upon several points relative to the state of that colony. After which he stated to their lordships the improper practice, which the House of Burgesses there has of late years fallen into, by nominating their Speaker to be Treasurer of the country duties and revenue, and the inconveniences resulting from such practice, and proposed that some directions should be given to the Lieutenant Governor now going out, upon this point; Mr. Dinwiddie being withdrawn, their lordships ordered the Secretary to desire the favour of Lieutenant Governor Fauquier's attendance at the Board on Thursday next at twelve o'clock." *BTJ*, 9 Mar., continues the story: "Mr. Fauquier, Lieutenant Governor of Virginia, attending, as desired, was called in; and their lordships having acquainted him with the representation made to them by the late Lieutenant Governor of the impropriety of the offices of Speaker of the House of Burgesses and Treasurer being united in the same person, it was recommended to him to use the most prudent endeavours, and to take all such measures, as he should judge consistent with the good of his Majesty's service to put a stop to a practice, which appeared to them to be highly improper, liable to great inconveniences, and prejudicial to his Majesty's service."

5. John Robinson was speaker of the House of Burgesses and treasurer of the colony of Virginia from 1738 until his death in 1766.

6. This ship was presumably the *Girzie*, Captain Dunlopp (or Dunlop), which sailed from Virginia on 12 June 1758, according to Fauquier's letter of 28 June 1758 to the Board of Trade.

To William Pitt

Sir,[1]   Wmsburgh June 11th 1758

I have the honour to Inform you that on my Arrival here on the 5th Instant, I found that the Colony in Obedience to his Majesty's Commands Signify'd in your Letter of the 30th Decr. 1757,[2] and received here on the 14th March 1758 had Raised a Second Regiment of 1000 Men under the Command of Colo. Byrd,³ which with the other Regiment of 1000 under Colo. Washington are now both at Winchester (one Company excepted which are sent to defend the Frontiers against some stragling Indians) ready to proceed on their March to meet the rest of His Majesty's Forces at Fort Cumberland,⁴ the General Rendezvous appointed by Brigadier Genl. Forbes. Having the opportunity of a Ship just ready to sail for Glasgow,⁵ I would not lose it, to give you the earliest Information in my power, and shall do my self the honour to send a Duplicate of this with any thing new that may happen by the first Pacquet that sails from New York.⁶ I am with the greatest Respect Your most Obedient Humble Servant,

Fran: Fauquier

I have nothing to add to the foregoing Letter but that the provincial Troops have been in Motion some Time, and I hope by this, the Army is formed that is to march to Fort du Quesne,⁷ and that I am with the most profound Respect, Sir, Your most Obedient & most Humble Servant.

Fran: Fauquier

June 30th 1758 / To the Rt. Honble. Wm. Pitt.

LS: C.O.5/18, ff. 452–53. Postscript and signature are in Fauquier's hand. Endorsed as a duplicate and as received 11 Aug. [1758].

1. Pitt was secretary of state, with supreme direction of the war and of foreign affairs, and remained in office until 1761.
2. This circular letter to the governors of Pennsylvania, Maryland, Virginia, North Carolina, and South Carolina urged the raising of bodies of men who would march to a rendezvous appointed by Brigadier General Forbes, join British forces under his command, and begin offensive operations by the first of May 1758 or as soon thereafter as possible. The text of the letter is in *Pitt* 1:140–43; it is essentially the same as Pitt's circular letter of 9 Dec. 1758 below.
3. William Byrd III, of Westover (1728–1777), was colonel of the Second Virginia Regiment 1757–62.
4. Built 1754 near the junction of Will's Creek and the Potomac River and named for William Augustus, duke of Cumberland (1721–1765), son of George II and at that time captain general of British land forces, the fort stood where Cumberland, Md., now is, at a natural gateway through the Appalachian Mountains to the Ohio Valley. Fort Cumberland was about 45 mi. northwest of Winchester and served as the base of operations for Braddock's disastrous expedition of 1755 against Fort Duquesne. See Koontz, pp. 111–48, and the map of the Virginia frontier in 1756 in Frederick Bittle Kegley, *Kegley's Virginia Frontier* (Roanoke, Va., 1938), facing p. 244.
5. Presumably the *Girzie*; see Fauquier's letter of 11 June 1758 to the Board of Trade, n. 6.
6. It was a practice of the time to send two or more copies of an official letter or document by different vessels, as a safeguard against loss by shipwreck, enemy action, or simple negligence.
7. Built 1754 at the junction of the Allegheny and Monongahela rivers, where they come together to form the Ohio River, and named for Michel-Ange Du Quesne,

marquis de Menneville (1702–1778), who was then governor of New France, the fort stood where Pittsburgh, Pa., now is, about 85 mi. to the northwest of Fort Cumberland. It replaced a fort built by order of Governor Dinwiddie and captured by the French, and the strategic position of Fort Duquesne made it a major objective of the British.

Address to Francis Fauquier and Reply

[Williamsburg, 12 June 1758]

To the Honourable Francis Fauquier, Esq. His Majesty's Lieutenant-Governor, and Commander in Chief, of the Colony and Dominion of Virginia, The humble Address of the President and Masters of the College of William and Mary.[1]

Sir,

We his Majesty's most dutiful and loyal Subjects, the President and Masters of the College of William and Mary, wait upon your Honour to testify our firm Attachment to our most gracious Sovereign, and all due Respect to your Honour, as appointed by his Majesty Governor of this Dominion.

We heartily congratulate your Honour upon your safe Arrival, and humbly beg Leave to embrace this Opportunity to recommend the College, Church and Clergy,[2] to your Patronage and Protection.

Permit us, Sir, to assure your Honour, that, in grateful Return, we shall always endeavour, both by Example and Doctrine, to promote the Happiness and Tranquility of your Government, and constantly offer up our fervent Prayers to the Great Governor of the Universe, that he would be graciously pleased to confer his Blessings upon your Labours, in the Discharge of the arduous Duties of your important Station.

To which his Honour was pleased to return the following Answer.

Mr. President, and the Masters of the College of William and Mary, Gentlemen,

Nothing can be more acceptable to me than your Professions of Attachment to his Majesty and his Government, and on that Account, of Respect to me; for this first Specimen of which, I return you my sincere Thanks.

The Cause of Religion shall always be uppermost in my Thoughts, as that is the Cement of Government; and as the Church and Clergy in general, so the College in particular, may always claim my Patronage.

I hope your Prayers to the Divine Majesty, for which I stand greatly obliged to you, will prevail on Him to confer his Blessing on my Endeavours to make the People easy and happy under my Administration.

Printed: *Pa. Gaz.* for 6 July 1758, in an account of Fauquier's arrival and the attendant ceremonies. The section of the account with the address and reply is dated 16 June [1758], and the address was said to have been presented "On Monday last," which would have been 12 June 1758.

1. At this time the president of the College of William and Mary in Virginia, at Williamsburg, was the Reverend Thomas Dawson, and it is probable that the only masters in residence were the Reverend Goronwy Owen and Emmanuel Jones, Jr. See Tyler; and Edward Lewis Goodwin, *The Colonial Church in Virginia* (Milwaukee and London, 1927).
2. The address refers to the Church of England and its clergy. The college was founded largely for the training of clergymen and was linked in many ways with the church. The governor had specific duties with respect to the church; see arts. 84–92 of the instructions to Lord Loudoun, C.O. 5/1367, ff. 131–34. See also Brydon.

From William Byrd

[Winchester, 14 June 1758]

This letter has not been found, but it was communicated to the council on 19 June 1758 and is abstracted in *EJC* 6:105–7:

The Governor communicated to the Board, a Letter from Col. Byrd, dated Winchester, June 14th, signifying the second Virginia Regiment is in great Confusion, the Officers being nettled at their recruiting Accounts being refused, and the Men complaining of being naked; the Gentlemen unanimously agreeing, not to accept of their Commissions, unless the necessary Expences charged by them, are allowed;—that Captain Posey was sent recruiting about twenty four Days since, with Orders to return to the Rendezvous in ten Days; that no other Advice has been received of him, than that he has been to Williamsburg, tho' he had positive Orders not to go there—that he shall put him under an Arrest when he returns, and that probably he will be broke, in which Case he shall appoint Mr. Thomas Cocke to his Company till his Honor's Pleasure be known.

Capt. John Posey was the second captain, and Thomas Cocke was the captain lieutenant of the Second Virginia Regiment. A captain lieutenant was a military officer commanding a company or troop who had a captain's rank but a lieutenant's pay.

To William Henry Lyttelton

Sir   Wmsburgh June 16th 1758

I don't doubt but your Excellency has heard of some unhappy Broils that have happen'd on our Frontiers, between some of our People, and some of the Cherokee Indians, in their return home from Winchester,[1] which we apprehended might be attended with very bad Consequences, at this Time, as it might entirely change the Disposition that Nation seem to be in towards us at present. However by the Care of Coll. Byrd and other Gentlemen I hope they are tolerably well appeased and those of them who are with his Majesties Troops at Winchester now, will be influenced to remain with them during the Expedition to Fort Du Quesne. Presents and all other Measures to reconcile them have been made use of: And a Strict Enquiry has been order'd to be taken by Coll. Read and Coll. Talbot on the Spot, the whole Narrative of which is, with this sent to your Excellency to make a proper Use of it to the Chiefs of that Nation,[2] with whom you are more acquainted, and over whom you have more Influence than any other Person.[3] We imagine these Cherokees are the worst of that people, who are Straglers and do not follow any noted Warriour among them.

We rely on your Excellencies prudence and Zeal for his Majesties Service that you will do all in your Power to prevent, if possible, these unlucky Encounters, doing any Harm to the common Cause, or obstructing the projected Designs. I have not had this Narrative transcribed because I thought there was no Time to be lost in the transmitting it to your Excellency, therefore beg the Favour you would return it to, Sir, Your Excellency's most Obedient & most Humble Servant,

Fran: Fauquier

P.S. I forgot to mention the Cherokees themselves own they were the Aggressors, tho' they breath Revenge.

To his Excellency Wm. Hen. Lyttelton Esqr.

ALS: William L. Clements Library, Lyttelton Papers.

1. The "unhappy Broils" were evidently the same disturbances to which Fauquier referred in his letter of 11 June 1758 to the Board of Trade.
2. On 15 June, Fauquier communicated to the council a letter from Clement Read (1707–1763) of Lunenburg County enclosing a report of engagements between militia of Halifax and Bedford counties and parties of Indians, with the substance of sworn depositions taken 1 June by Read and Matthew Talbot (d. 1758) of Bedford County; the council advised that the report should be sent to Lyttelton, with the request that he use "his Influence and Power over the Cherokees towards obtaining a Reconciliation." See *EJC* 6:102, 108, and passim for the transmittal of Read's report and subsequent correspondence and meetings with the Cherokees. A copy of the report was entered in the Indian Books of the Council of South Carolina, and is printed in *S.C. Records*, pp. 463–70. The depositions, taken at Mays' Ferry on Staunton River in Halifax County on 1 June, concern three engagements between militia of Bedford and Halifax counties and several parties of Indians, and a number of robberies by the Indians. Hamilton, 2:307–16, has correspondence of Read, Talbot, and others containing details of these troubles with the Cherokees.

3. For Lyttelton's dealings with the Cherokees and their relations in general with the English, see Alden. The Cherokee lands lay just to the northwest of South Carolina; the extensive commercial relations of the Cherokees were largely with traders from that colony; and indeed South Carolina asserted that it had jurisdiction over Cherokee country.

From George Washington

Honble. Sir [Fort Loudoun,[1] 17 June 1758]

Although but a poor hand at Compliments permit me, nevertheless to offer your Honour my congratulations on your appointment; and safe arrival to a Government which His Majesty has been pleasd to entrust to your Administration; and to assure you, that It is my sincere wish that that Administration may be crowned with pleasure to yourself & with ease & satisfaction to the People.

I flatter'd myself with the hope of seeing your Honour in Williamsburg, when I was down, but the business that carried me there was of too Urgent a Nature to admit of delay, after I had got it accomplishd. Mr. President Blair has, no doubt, informd you of the nature of that business—of the State of the Troops here, and generally of the situation of Affairs in this Quarter; I will not, therefore, trouble your Honour with a repetition of them; but shall Enclose you a Copy of the last Orders I have received which I am preparing to execute with the greatest exactness. Sir John St. Clair set out from hence for Connegocheague[2] the 11th Instt. to which place I accompanied him in consequence of a Summon's from Colo. Bouquet.[3] He proceeded on to Carlyle,[4] and I returned to this Post; where at present I have the Honour to Command.

I shall transmit your Honour, so soon as I leave this place (I cant well do it before, as alterations are continually happening while the Troops remain here) an exact return of our Stores, agreable to the Presidents Orders. Inclosd is a return of the Strength of the first Regiment.[5] I have directed one to be made out & sent to you of the 2d Also.

When I was down, the President was pleased to promise me 5 blank Commissions to compleat my Regiment with Officers; by mistake I received one less than I applied for, and must therefore beg the favour of your Honour to send me the deficient one; or, that you would be pleasd to take the Trouble yourself, of appointing Mr. Jno. Lawson (who is the oldest Ensign, in my Regiment) to be Lieutenant in Lieutt. Colo. Stephen's[6] Company, where there is a Vacancy. This would have been done before, had not the above mistake prevented it.

I enclose your Honour the Pay Rolls of Captn. Rutherford's Company of Rangers,[7] and beg the favour of you to send the money to Mr. Thos. Rutherford of this place, who will pay the men in behalf of his Brother; who, being in an ill state of health, got leave to visit Doctr. Brown of Maryland,[8] and is not yet returned.

When I was in Williamsburg last, I endeavourd to make Mr. President Blair and the Council, sensible of the great want of Cloaths for the first Regiment; and how necessary it was to send to England for a Supply. they declind doing any thing in the matter at that time, because the Funds granted by the late Act of Assembly were almost exhausted. But I hope it will not escape your Honours notice if an Assembly shoud soon be calld. Field equipgje[9] of all kinds will also be wanting, and will come better & cheaper from England than they can be bought in this Country: Colo. Byrd is apprehensive he sh[all] want Cloaths for his Men, if we shoud be late taking the Field; but his redress must be immediate or useless, as that Rejiment by Law will be disch[arged] the first Day of December next. I have the Honour to subscribe myself with great Respect Your Honours most Obedient Humble Servant

Go: Washington

Fort Loudoun 17th June 1758 / To the Honble. Francis Fauquir Govr. of Va.

Copy: Library of Congress, George Washington Papers, 6:5–6. In Washington's hand, with deletions and insertions. This transcription respects all deletions and insertions indicated. The missing letters supplied in brackets are evidently worn off at the margin.

1. Fort Loudoun was built at Winchester, Va., by George Washington in 1756–57 and was named for the earl of Loudoun, at that time commander in chief in North America as well as governor of Virginia.

2. Conococheague was a settlement at the mouth of Conococheague Creek, in Maryland, on the north side of the Potomac River some 7 mi. southwest of Hagerstown and about 35 mi. to the northeast of Winchester and Fort Loudoun. It was a trading post of some importance and the site of a blockhouse.

3. Henry Bouquet (1719–1765) of the Royal American Regiment was second in command of the expedition against Fort Duquesne under General Forbes.

4. Carlisle, Pa.

5. This return has not been found or identified.

6. Adam Stephen (ca. 1724–1791); see Freeman, 1:345–46.

7. Robert Rutherford. The Rangers were companies of 100 men each, with their officers, raised by order of the General Assembly for the protection of the frontiers. The payrolls referred to have not been found or identified.

8. Dr. Gustavus Brown of Port Tobacco, Md.

9. The manuscript seems to have "equipgje," but "equipage" must be what was meant.

Enclosure: Orders for George Washington

[Conococheague, 13 June 1758]

Orders, for Colonel Washington commanding the Troops of the Colony of Virginia.

As you will receive near 700 Arms for the 2d Virginia Regiment from Williamsburg, you are to take into your Store at Winchester the Maryland Arms which were deliverd to the 2d Regiment, these Arms are to be deliverd to Govr. Sharpe on his Order.[1]

The same proportion of Tools that the 1st Company of Artificers had, to be deliverd to the 2d Company, with an addition of 12 Pick Axe's and 12 Spades or Shovels. The half of the Sand Bags at Winchester to be sent to Connogochieg, and the other half will serve to carry up to Fort Cumberland the Corn that may be got about Winchester and the South Branch.[2]

Five Companies of the first Virginia Regiment to begin their March for Fort Cumberland the 24th of June, with the 2d Company of Artificers of the 2d Regiment. Colo. Byrd with as many Companies as are ready of his Regiment to March the 26th and the rest of that Regiment to follow with Lieutt. Colo. Mercer[3] so soon as they can be got ready.

One Company of the 2d Regiment to be station'd at Job Pearsalls[4] on the South Branch & Edwards's[5] till all the Convoys of Provisions have passd and then to Join.

Whatever Escorts are requird by Mr. Commissary Walker[6] are to be furnishd to him; he is to lay in Provisions for 1800 Men for Six Weeks at Fort Cumberland from the day of their arrival, and victual them on their March. The Officers are only to draw single Rations of Provisions for themselves as the General has no more.

Captn. Stewarts[7] Troop of Light Horse are to March up to Fort Cumberland. 30 Barrels of Powder and 100 Boxes of Shott to be carried from Fort Loudoun with 8 Whip Saws to Fort Cumberland. Given under my Hand at Conegocheague this 13th day of June 1758.

John St. Clair

DS: Library of Congress, George Washington Papers, ser. 4, f. 994. This transcription respects all insertions and deletions indicated. It is assumed that these were the orders of which Washington sent a copy to Fauquier in his letter of 17 June 1758.

1. Horatio Sharpe (1718–1790) was governor of Maryland 1753–69.
2. The south branch of the Potomac River runs from Highland County, Va., northeast through West Virginia and joins the north branch of the Potomac about 15 mi. southeast of Cumberland, Md.

3. George Mercer (1733–1784), of the Second Virginia Regiment; see Tyler, 1:289.

4. Job Pearsall built a stockade fort called Fort Pearsall at the point where the road to the west from Fort Loudoun crossed the south branch and where Romney in Hampshire County, W.Va., now stands. It was about 35 mi. northwest of Fort Loudoun.

5. Fort Edwards was a stockade defense on or near the spot where the village of Capon Bridge now stands, on the Cacapon River in Hampshire County, W.Va. The fort was roughly halfway between Fort Loudoun and Fort Pearsall.

6. Dr. Thomas Walker (1715–1794) was appointed commissary general of Virginia troops in 1755.

7. Robert Stewart, of the First Virginia Regiment.

To Horatio Sharpe

Sir   Wmsburgh June 18th 1758

I did my self the Honour of writing to you by Captn. Coolidge[1] of the Wilson, on board of whom I took my Passage for this Government, and who was to proceed immediately for Patuxsen River;[2] and with my own I committed to his Care a Letter from Dr. Gregory Sharpe,[3] which he charged me with in England. For fear that should not have come to your Hands I take the Opportunity of an Express I am sending to General Abercrombie to notify to you my Arrival here, honoured with his Majesties Commission of Lieutenant Governor of his Colony and Dominion of Virginia: and to assure that I shall with the greatest Pleasure lay hold of every Opportunity of corresponding with you, which his Majesties Service or the Advantage of his American Colonies may require. I am Your Excellency's most Obedient Humble Servant.

Fran: Fauquier

To his Excellency Horatio Sharpe Esqr.

ALS: Hall of Records of Maryland, Executive Papers, folder 102.

1. Judson Coolidge of the merchant ship *Wilson;* see Fauquier's letter of 8 June 1758 to Lyttelton, n. 2. Fauquier's letter sent by Coolidge has not been traced, but Sharpe acknowledged it in his letter of 3 July 1758 to Fauquier.

2. The Patuxent River in Maryland empties into the Chesapeake Bay.

3. Gregory Sharpe (1713–1771), a brother of Governor Sharpe, was a lawyer, clergyman, and classical and oriental scholar. He was chaplain to Frederick, Prince of Wales; Fellow of the Royal Society in 1754; and a prebendary of Salisbury Cathedral from 1757.

To William Byrd

Sir,   Wmsburgh, June 19th 1758

I received the favour of your Letter by Mr. Munford[1] by whom I send this in Answer thereto. I am extremely obliged to You for your Congratulations on the safe Arrival of my self and my Family in this Dominion of which his Majesty has been graciously pleased to appoint me his Lieutenant Governor.

The Contents of your Letter being of great Importance and requiring an immediate Answer, I summon'd a Council to meet this Morning; by whose Advice, after duely weighing every Part, I give you our Determination which I hope will be satisfactory in every Particular.

In the first place it was agreed to submit the recruiting Accounts[2] of the Officers to your Self and the Field Officers of your Corps, and you are desired to examine and audit the same, and whatever shall be found reasonable by you will be allowed, of which You may assure the Gentlemen, tho' the Money raised by the Assembly for paying &ct. of the 2d Regiment is so far exhausted, that it cannot be immediately repaid them before the Assembly meets. This I hope will entirely remove all Cause of Uneasiness from the part of the Officers: as I shall most earnestly recommend this point to the Assembly on their Meeting.

As for the private Men, they have this Day orderd the French prize Cloaths to be purchased of Coll. Hunter,[3] and to be immediately forwarded to the Army where it is hoped they may arrive in 7 or 8 Days. This Cloathing is sufficient but for 800 Men, therefore it is desired that you distribute them amongst those who are most in Need of them, stopping 2d a Day out of their Pay as was practised in the first Regiment and as it is imagined, that at least 200 of your Regiment have Cloaths sufficient for this Campaign, their pay will go on without any Stoppage. By this Step I hope the Desertion and all Complaints of the men will be entirely stop'd.

I ought to mention that there are but 200 Shirts made but there is Cloth and Thread to make up the rest, as well as Materials for the Leggings.

The Officers Bonds will be sent up, to be deposited in your Hands, and to be deliver'd by You, when you shall find the Conditions have been complied with.

In Case of Captn. Posey's being broke, Mr. Cockes being appointed to succeed to that vacant commission is approved of;[4] and He may have the Commission accordingly. And in that Case, the Blank Commission herewith sent to you, may be fill'd up with the Name of either Mr. Lightfoot

19 June 1758

or Mr. Munford,[5] as upon an Enquiry and Examination You shall find best intitled to it, by having first brought in their Complement of Men to Winchester, the Rule originally laid down and most religiously observed in distributing these Commissions.

The calling Mr. Cocke, Mr. Lightfoot, and Mr. Munford all Captain Lieutenants arose from a Mistake in the Gentlemen who were not well-versed in Military Affairs, and supposed the Lieutenants of the three Companies belonging to the three Field Officers, had all a Title to be rank'd as Captains Leiutenants.[6]

Thus Sir We hope we have settled all Matters to yours and the Regiments Satisfaction. I am sure nothing shall ever be wanting on my Part to give all reasonable Content to every Man engaged in his Majesties Service to the utmost of my power.

I sincerely wish You all Success in the approaching Campaign, and to add to the Success hope to thank you all personally on your Return. I am Your Very Humble Servant

Fran: Fauquier

To Coll. Byrd.

ALS: State Historical Society of Wisconsin, Draper Manuscripts 4 ZZ 41.

1. This was probably Robert Munford, a lieutenant in Byrd's regiment, the Second Virginia. The letter from Byrd was that dated Winchester, 14 June 1758.
2. Officers were authorized to pay a reward of £10 to each man who enlisted and to recover the amount of these rewards as well as their necessary expenses.
3. These were captured French uniforms, the source of which has not been traced. See Fauquier's letter to Washington of 25 June 1758 for further reference to them.
4. Thomas Cocke, a captain lieutenant, was next in rank after Posey. A footnote in *JHB, 1758–1761*, p. 261, identifies the former as William Cocke, but he is called Thomas in *EJC* 6:99, 106.
5. John Lightfoot and Robert Munford were lieutenants in Byrd's regiment.
6. Fauquier referred to a list of the officers of the Second Virginia Regiment (*EJC* 6:99) where Cocke, Lightfoot, and Munford are all ranked as captain lieutenant.

From George Washington

Honble. Sir   [Fort Loudoun, 19 June 1758]

The Letter herewith Inclosd,[1] woud have been sent according to the date, but I have been waiting till now for Captn. Rutherfords Pay Roll, his Company being much dispersed on the Ranging Service.

This day the Prince William Militia are to March for the South Branch, to relieve two Companies of my Regiment, agreeably to Orders. Inclosd is a return of their present Strength.² I shoud think myself difficient in duty were I to pass over in Silence the conduct, and State of this Company from their first coming out—about the 20th Ulto—until the present moment.

One hundred Militia, were Orderd from Prince William County (but at what time I cant exactly say) by Mr. President Blair. instead of that number, 73 only came; and every one of them unprovided with Arms or Ammunition, as the Law directs;³ by which means they were not only useless, but really burthensome to the Country, as they were eating its Provisions & had their Pay running on. This matter was represented to Colo. Henry Lee, Lieutenant of that County,⁴ by Sir Jno. St. Clair then Commanding Officer here. The Consequence of this representation was, that about the first of this Instt.; near 100 Arms were sent up by his order out of which number Scarce 5 were Serviceable; and not more than 30 coud possibly be made to Fire. This was also represented to Coll. Lee, who after expressing his Concern for it, said, the County expected Arms from England, every day, and has taken no farther notice of the matter since that I have yet heard. I immediately set Smiths to repairing their Arms, and have, with the Assistance of 35 old Muskets which I causd to be deliverd out of the Store here, got this Company, which ought to have consisted of 100 Men (thô there is but 68) at last compleated.

'Till this time, they have been a dead expence to the Publick, and no Service to the Inhabitants. This Sir, is a true statement of Facts, and really merits reprehension; for if such behaviour is sufferd to escape unnoticed, the most destructive Consequences may accrue. In the present case, if the Troops had Marchd agreeable to the Orders I at first received, the Companies on the South Branch woud have been drawn off, and the Inhabitants thereby left destitute of support, or must have come of with them, which it seems they were determined to do. This I understand actually did happen in Augusta County when Majr. Lewis came from thence,⁵ by the negligence, I suppose, of the County Lieutenants. I am with due respect your Honours most Obedient Humble [Servant]

Go: Washington

Fort Loudoun 19th June 1758 / To the Honble. Governor Farquier.

Copy: Library of Congress, George Washington Papers, 6:12 a-b. Draft in Washington's hand, with deletions and insertions. This transcription respects all deletions and insertions indicated. Probably the word "Servant" in the complimentary close has been worn off at the margin.

1. The letter has not been identified, but it probably was Washington's letter of 17 June 1758, which was to enclose Rutherford's payroll.

2. 'At this time Prince William County included what is now Fauquier County, and

thus reached from the Potomac River to the Blue Ridge, and to Frederick County, which included today's Shenandoah, Warren, and Clarke counties. The return of the Prince William militia has not been traced.

3. "An Act for the better regulating and disciplining the Militia" (Hening, 7:93–106), passed in Apr. 1757, stated that each man enlisted in the militia should have a firelock, bayonet, cartridge box, powder, and ball; and that if he could not afford these himself, they were to be procured from Great Britain and paid for by the county.

4. Henry Lee (1729–1787), of Leesylvania in Prince William County, was the father of Light-Horse Harry Lee. The county lieutenant was the official appointed to supervise the regulating and disciplining of the county militia.

5. At this time Augusta County included all of Virginia west of the Blue Ridge and southwest of Frederick County. Andrew Lewis (1720–1781) was an officer in the First Virginia Regiment.

From James Abercromby

Sir,   London June 23rd 1758

Inclosed, I lay before you, Copie of the Memorial presented by the Merchants of London relative to the Paper Money Bill, another of the same nature, is presented to the Lords for Trade by the Merchants of Bristol, and one is expected from Liverpool, to that presented by the London Merchants no other answer is given as yet, than, that their Lordships, shall take it under Consideration when the affairs of Virginia come in Course before them.[1]

The Memorial some time since, presented to the Lords of the Treasury for Aid, out of the Quitrents to make good the Deficiencys of the Tobacco Revenue, lays still in suspence, and no reference made thereof to the Auditor General of the Plantations, by Examination of the Books in the Auditor General's Office, I have found Precedents, in our favour, which shall be pointed out to the Auditor General, when the Case comes before him.

No Provincial matters requiring my Animadversion, for Public Events, since you left us, I refer you to the Newspapers now transmitted that of the 21st inst. will shew you, our Proceedings in France, and at Senegal, with both of which Events the City of London are vastly pleased, whether our Troops are now gone to Granville, or elsewhere is a Secret.[2]

You will be pleased to communicate so much of this, as concerns the Gentlemen of the Council to be informed of, I remain on all occasions, Sir, yours &c.

To Govr. Fauquier.

Copy: Virginia State Library, James Abercromby Letter Book, pp. 102–3. In a clerk's hand.

1. The memorial of the London merchants follows. A memorial of the Bristol merchants to the same effect (C.O.5/1329, f. 57) was apparently submitted about the same time as the London memorial, for both memorials were read at the board on 21 June 1758. There is no evidence that the memorial expected from Liverpool was ever submitted. The result of the two memorials was an additional instruction of 9 Feb. 1759 requiring the governor of Virginia to act as the memorials had requested; the instruction (C.O.5/1367, ff. 178–80) is printed below under its proper date.

2. The newspapers Abercromby sent have not been identified. The proceedings in France referred to must have been the operations of an amphibious force in the English Channel throughout June, intended to create a diversion in behalf of the king of Prussia. The fleet anchored off St. Malo and landed a force of soldiers which did a great amount of damage but did not attack St. Malo itself. Then the fleet sailed to Le Havre, found the French too well prepared for attack, and so moved back to Cherbourg, but was forced by foul weather, sickness, and a failure of supplies to return to England at the end of June. At the date of this letter, the fleet was evidently thought to be in the Bay of St. Malo, where Granville lies across the bay about 25 mi. from St. Malo. The proceedings in Senegal refer to an attack on French settlements in West Africa: a squadron arrived at the mouth of the Senegal River in late April and at the beginning of May captured Fort Louis and various stations further up the river, thus cutting off the supply of slaves to the French West Indies.

Enclosure: Memorial of London Merchants

[ca. 21 June 1758]

To the Right Honourable the Lords Commissioners for Trade & Plantations

The Memorial of the Merchants of London in behalf of themselves & others trading to & interested in the Province of Virginia

Humbly Sheweth

That the General Assembly of Virginia have lately passed an Act whereby their Provincial Treasurer is authorised for the purposes therein mentioned to Issue Paper Notes to the amount of Eighty thousand pounds which said Paper Notes so issued & rated at Proclamation money by the said Act of Assembly are thereby declared to be a lawfull tender in payment of any debt or demand whatever (except his Majesties Quit rents.)[1]

That your Memorialists having large Sums of money now due to them in the said Province in the course of Trade with the inhabitants thereof by actual Loan of sterling money in specie, by bills of Exchange drawn payable in Sterling, & by goods & merchandises purchased in Great Britain for their Account & paid for in Sterling money before the issuing such Paper Notes, Your Memorialists beg leave hereupon to remonstrate to your Lordships the very great injury that will arise to the trading interest of these Kingdoms & more particularly to your Memorialists from the said Virginia Act as it now stands, not only by reason that it does affect all kind of debts actually due & owing to the Merchants of these Kingdoms in Sterling money before the passing of the said Act, but moreover the very nature of their trade is inverted from a certain to an incertain value, & so far your Memorialists doe conceive the said Act to be oppressive & injurious, by reason that it does ex Post facto extend to debts actually due & owing before the passing of the said Act, & that it does depreciate the value of such debts owing in Sterling money of certain & fixed value, & subject them to be discharged in Paper Notes of a local, incertain & fluctuating value, at the same time that no proviso is made by the said Act for making payments in such Paper Notes ad valorem of Sterling according to the difference of Exchange between such Paper & Sterling when payment is made, which provision on the Principles of Law & Equity ought to have been made.

So far therefore as your Memorialists will be very great sufferers from the defects in the said Act as it now stands, as well as from a certain clause in one other Act heretofore passed in the said Province in 1748 intitled an Act declaring the Law concerning Executions, & for relief of insolvent debtors, whereby Executions for Sterling debts shall be levied in Current money at the rate of 25 per Cent advance on Sterling for a difference of Exchange & not otherwise,[2] which Act remains in force tho' the Exchange is risen from 25 to 45 per Cent; Your Memorialists do therefore humbly offer to Your Lordships Consideration, an Expedient which your Memorialists apprehend may fully answer the end proposed by them, by guarding against the injuries that have & will arise from the said Acts in respect to your Memorialists properties, & the trade of these Kingdoms, & at the same time no way defeat the operation of the said Acts with regard to the Military or Provincial services thereby intended: Which expedient is that the Governor of Virginia be instructed by his Majesty to urge to the Assembly the passing another Act for explaining & amending the said Acts now in question, & thereby provide that all debts due & owing before the passing the said Acts shall remain & stand payable in Sterling money only, & that all debts that have been heretofore contracted, or that may hereafter be contracted in the course of our Trade or otherwise between his Majesties subjects in Great Britain & Virginia, if not otherwise expressly stipulated, shall be deemed sterling debts & made payable according to Sterling or lawfull money of Great Britain, that then, & in such case, such Paper Notes so issued, or that may hereafter be issued, or any other species of Current money not being Sterling money, shall not be deemed a lawfull tender in payment of any such debt, bargain or contract so entred into payable in Sterling or lawfull money of Great Britain, unless the person or persons to whom such is tendered in Paper Notes or other species of Current money, shall think proper to accept thereof in such paper notes, if the [same shall] be offered him with the difference of Exchange, between such Paper Notes or other species of Current money, & Sterling money at the time when such Paper Notes or other species of Current money shall be so offered in payment of Sterling debts; And that the Person or persons so accepting of payment in Paper Notes according to the difference of Exchange between Sterling & Paper money & such other species of Current money, shall be deemed & held as fully paid & satisfied for his or their debts to all intents & purposes as if such payment had been made in Sterling or lawfull money of Great Britain anything in the said Act or in any other Act to the contrary notwithstanding.

To an amendment of this nature your Memorialists conceive the Assembly in Virginia can make no objection, in so far as the same is bona fide founded on principles of common justice & the Laws of this Kingdom, & more particularly agreeable to the Act of the 6th year of her late Majesty Queen Ann whereby foreign silver coin is made current in the Plantations, but in due proportion as the intrinsic value thereof is to Sterling; And at the same time it is thereby provided that such species of silver coin so made current shall not affect contracts or bargains made prior to the said Act; And it is thereby further provided that nothing in the said Act shall be construed to compell any person or persons whatsoever to receive in payment any of the said species of such foreign silver coin as the same is rated in the Act;[3] so far therefore the amendment proposed by your Memorialists to the Act of the Virginia Assembly coincides with Equity & with the Laws of England; & with the regard that is at all times due to the trading interests of these Kingdoms, & with the Justice that is due to your Memorialists in this particular case.

From such considerations your Memorialists humbly hope for your Lordships interposition with his Majesty for an instruction to the Governor of Virginia for the purposes aforesaid; And that your Lordships will be pleased to suspend judgment upon the Virginia Act for establishing Paper Currency by way of approbation thereof as it now stands, till such time as the sense of the Assembly of that Province is had upon the amendment proposed thereto.

     Jno Stewart   John Buchanan
     Bosworth & Griffith James Russell
     Matthius Gale   Will: Montgomery
     Antho: Bacon   Saml. Waterman
     Robt Cary & Co   W Bowden
     John Bell   James Buchanan & Co:
     J Hanbury & Co   Thos: Flowerdewe
     John Philpot   Sydenham & Hodgson
     Edwd Athawes   Lyonel & Samuel Lyde
     John Maynard

DS: C.O.5/1329, f. 56. Autograph signatures of or on behalf of the subscribers. Undated, but endorsed as read 21 June 1758. The two words in square brackets are largely obliterated by a tear in the fold, but are undoubtedly correct. A copy of the memorial was enclosed in Abercromby's letter of 23 June 1758 to Fauquier.

1. The twenty-third and twenty-ninth clauses of "An Act for granting an aid to his majesty for the better protection of this colony, and for other purposes therein mentioned" (Hening, 7:69–87), passed in Apr. 1757, contained the provisions objected to here.

2. The twenty-ninth clause of "An Act declaring the law concerning Executions; and for relief of Insolvent debtors" (Hening, 5:526–40), passed in Oct. 1748, contained the provision objected to here.

3. This act of Parliament was 6 Anne, cap. 30, "An Act for ascertaining the Rates of foreign Coins in her Majesty's Plantations in America" (*Statutes* 4:324–25).

To George Washington

Sir   Wmsburgh June 25th 1758

Your Congratulations and kind wishes expressed in your Letter of the 17th which I received yesterday with one of the 19th, do me the greater Honour, as you profess yourself a Gentleman not addicted to Compliments.

I have received from Mr. President Blair and all the Gentlemen of the Council, all the Information I could wish for; but still as I cannot be Master of the State of Affairs, I must desire Gentlemen will be indulgent where I am wrong.

I have inclosed to you the blank Commission as you desire and don't doubt but you will fill it with Justice, and Advantage to his Majesties Service.

The Money granted by the Assembly for the first Regiment is more than expended by £2000 and upwards, so that the Affair of your Cloathing must be postponed till the next Assembly; which as Money will be wanting I fear must meet at the Return of the Writs, tho an unseasonable and disagreeable Time to the Members.[1] All the Money for the 2d Regiment not being expended, We in Council last Monday bought Coll. Hunters prize french Regimentals which we suppose will reach the Regiment before this can reach you; the Messenger from you having met them at Fredericsburgh in his Way hither.[2] He likewise met at Kg. William Court-House 29 Nottoway and Tuscarora Indians going to Join the Army.[3] We had no guns for them so the General must supply them. I promised those that should behave well and signalize themselves should be rewarded with a breast plate. Brass seems to content them.

I am extremely sensible of all you say in your Letter of the 19th relative to the bad Condition of the Militia, and wish I knew how to redress it, however I will use my Endeavours personally, and will recommend the same to the approaching Assembly at their opening.[4] In some Counties they have been mutinous (for so I must term it) and refus'd to go when drafted out, unless they might pick and chuse their own Officers; whether this proceeds from any influence of the Officers over the Men, or from the Caprice and Licentiousness of the Men themselves I know not; but this I know if complied with there is an End of all Discipline. I have order'd the Names of all such Refusers to be sent up that they may be prosecuted according to Law, and I can do no more, for to send fresh Orders not to be obeyed is still weakening the Hands, and looseing the Reins of Government.

I have received the pay Rolls of Captn. Rutherfords Company of Rangers and will provide for the payment of them as you desire. I have likewise received the Returns from the two Virginia Regiments. I grieve to see so many sick Men and wish they were compleat to a Man, to secure the Conquest of fort du Quesne, in which I wish you all possible Success, to obtain which you will oblige me to assure the General and Commander in Chief and all under him that nothing shall be wanting on my Part who am with great Regard, Sir, Your very Humble Servant

Fran: Fauquier

To Coll. Washington.

ALS: Library of Congress, George Washington Papers, ser. 4.

1. On 15 June 1758 the council advised that the current assembly be dissolved and writs be issued as of that day for election of new burgesses and made returnable 27 July; on 20 July, however, the council advised Fauquier to prorogue the assembly to the second Thursday in September. The assembly accordingly met on 14 Sept., when

Fauquier in his opening address requested a fresh supply of money for the war. See *EJC* 6:103, 107, and *JHB, 1758–1761*, p. 4.

2. These "prize french Regimentals" were the uniforms, "the French prize Cloaths," of which Fauquier wrote in his letter of 19 June 1758 to Byrd. Fredericksburg is in Spotsylvania County, at the head of navigation on the Rappahannock River, and roughly halfway between Winchester and Virginia port towns of the lower Chesapeake Bay, where Hunter probably carried on his business.

3. King William Court House is in east central King William County near the Mattaponi River. The Nottoways were Indians of an Iroquoian tribe living along the Nottoway River in southern Virginia. They spoke a language closely akin to that of the Tuscaroras, members of a confederation by that time widely scattered; these Tuscaroras must have lived in the upper part of North Carolina near the Virginia border.

4. In his address at the opening of the assembly Fauquier urged a revisal of the militia law and offered to produce his correspondence on the militia (*JHB, 1758–1761*, pp. 4–5).

To the Board of Trade

My Lords,   Wmsburgh June 28th 1758

I did my self the Honour to write to your honourable Board, by the Girzie Captn. Dunlopp, who sail'd from hence the 12th instant, a Duplicate of which I shall send with the present Dispatches by Captn. Clarke of the Ludlow Castle[1] who is to sail for England in a few Days with the Trade under his Convoy.

In the former Letter I just mention'd the Affair,[2] relating to the Speaker and Treasurer being united in one Person, which was recommended to me before my Departure from England. I have since that sounded many of the principal People of this Country, and find more Difficulties arise daily: And they have alledg'd several Reasons which appear to me to have great weight and which I shall leave to your Lordships Judgment.

In the first place it is a known Fact, that Mr. Robinson the late Speaker (for I have dissolved the Assembly and call'd a new one, according to the usual Custom) and Treasurer, is the most popular Man in the Country: beloved by the Gentlemen, and the Idol of the people; so that he is absolutely sure of the Chair as long as he pleases to fill it.

It is an establish'd Custom at least of long Date, tho' not from the beginning of the Colony, that the Assembly have elected their own Treasurer for all Monies by them raised for any publick Service: to be accountable to them, for the Disbursement of it. The Assemblies of this Colony have been extremely generous on the present Occasion, and have actually raised very great Sums of Money, more perhaps than would have been necessary, if managed with proper Oeconomy; but as it is, not sufficient for the Services actually enter'd upon, so that the Assembly must meet at the Return of the Writs, and more Money must be demanded; Not a penny of which will be granted as I am informed if Mr. Robinson is not to be Treasurer. This is a Thing of great immediate Consequence; but were not that the urgent Case at present, (if I am not grossly imposed upon,) The Assembly would resent any slight they thought was put upon Mr. Robinson, and would obstruct all public Business, and entirely break up the Harmony that at present subsists between two of the Legislative Bodies, and I am in great Hopes I may add the Third.

Before the Treasurership was annexed to the Chair as it seems to be at present; there was an Allowance from the Country of 40,000 Weight of Tobacco, for the Speaker of the Assembly which has not taken place; and the Treasury has been given him in Lieu of it. In Times of Peace the Treasury is worth communibus Annis about £300 a year, which is thought not too much here for a Place of that Dignity. Now indeed it is worth about £1000.

These Considerations had Weight with me, not only to postpone it till after this Session was over, the Money raised and the present Turn served; but for fear my Transactions might come to Mr. Robinson's Ears (of which there was no Doubt), and he might take Umbrage at it and a Jealousy might arise, which might be detrimental to his Majesties Service: I went directly to himself (as your Lordships may remember you gave me Leave so to do) and in the frankest Manner talk'd to him of it. He said it was an Old Grudge of the late Governor's begun upon the Affair of the Pistole Fee,[3] and I find was apprized of his having push'd it with your Lordships; at which he seem'd a good deal dissatisfyed, and at the same Time was highly pleased with the open Manner in which I dealt with Him. And I am told by those who know his Character that I have attach'd him to me in the strongest Manner, by the Openness of my Behaviour.

In this I have concealed nothing from your Lordships and hope my Conduct herein will meet with your approbation, as I acted to the best of my Abilities for his Majesties Service, in this critical Conjuncture. And your Lordships must acknowledge the Affair was of a delicate Nature, and wanted the Touch of a more masterly Hand than my own.

With this your Lordships will receive the Two Acts pass'd in the late short Assembly, with the Journals of the Council and House of Burgesses.[4] And Mr. President Blair proposes to send to your Lordships, in the same Box, the Half yearly Accounts of the two Shillings per Hhd. Duty on Tobacco, to the making up thereof in April last; and all other

Transactions done by Him during his presidentship after Mr. Dinwiddies departure, and before my Arrival, He will give you a full Account of in a Letter for that Purpose.[5]

I have no public News to add, only that all our provincial Troops are in motion, and that we hope by this, The Forces of this Colony, Pensylvania, and Carolina (Maryland have not sent a Man) have join'd his Majesties Britannic Forces under General Forbes, and that the Army is formed that is to march to the Attack of Fort du Quesne of the Surrender of which I hope soon to give your Lordships a satisfactory Account. I have the Honour to be with the greatest Respect Your Lordships most Obliged & most Obedient Humble Servant

Fran: Fauquier

ALS: C.O.5/1329, ff. 77–79. Endorsed as read 12 Dec. 1758. Not addressed, but endorsed as "to the Board."

1. Capt. Edward Clark was commander of H.M.S. *Ludlow Castle*.
2. See Fauquier's letter of 11 June 1758 to the board, and in particular nn. 2 and 3.
3. Dinwiddie and the burgesses carried on a dispute over his imposing a tax of one pistole for sealing each patent for land. The pistole fee was a fee of one pistole, a Spanish gold coin worth something between 16s. 6d. and 18s. sterling, which Dinwiddie proposed to charge for the signing and sealing of each patent for land. The proposal drew protesting petitions to the House of Burgesses from the counties of Henrico, Chesterfield, Cumberland, Albemarle, Amelia, and Dinwiddie and was the occasion of petitions from the House of Burgesses to Dinwiddie and to the king objecting to the fee, while the council of Virginia and the authorities in Great Britain upheld Dinwiddie. A general survey of the dispute is found in chap. 18, "The Pistole Fee Controversy," Morton, 2:621–34. The addresses and resolutions of the House of Burgesses and Dinwiddie's replies are in *JHB, 1752–1755, 1756–1758*, pp. 132, 136, 141, 143–44, 154–55, 166–69; the proceedings of the council in the business are noted in *EJC* 5:421–22, 455–57.
4. The two acts, passed during the General Assembly's session of 30 Mar.–12 Apr. 1758, were "An Act for augmenting the forces in the pay of this Colony to two thousand men; and for other purposes therein mentioned" and "An Act for preventing mutiny and desertion." See Hening, 7:163–70 for the text of the acts; the manuscript copies that Fauquier sent are perhaps those in C.O.5/1398, ff. 70–74. The council journal was presumably the manuscript copy of the journal of the council in assembly in C.O.5/1429, ff. 139–43, endorsed as read 12 Dec. 1758. The journal of the House of Burgesses was the manuscript copy in C.O.5/1434, ff. 52–68, endorsed as received with Fauquier's letter of 28 June 1758 and read 12 Dec. 1758.
5. Blair's letter, of 20 June 1758, comments at length on Virginia's raising men and money for the war, on Virginia's claim to a share of the £50,000 voted by Parliament for Virginia and the Carolinas, on the absolute necessity of issuing paper money, and on the deficit of the tobacco revenue and hopes of a relief from the quitrents. Blair sent with his letter the account of the revenue of 2s. per hogshead on tobacco for 25 Oct. 1757–25 Apr. 1758, which showed a deficit of £986.1.11 (C.O.5/1329, ff. 70–74).

From Horatio Sharpe

Sir   Fort Frederick[1] the 3d of July 1758.

Being favoured with Your Letter advising me of Your safe Arrival in Your Government[2] I embrace the first Opportunity that has offered since I received it to congratulate You thereupon & to wish you an easy & happy Administration: permit me to return You Thanks at the same time for forwarding my Brother's Letter which affords me the greater Satisfaction as it informs me that the Doctor has been some time honoured with Your Acquaintance & with the Friendship of Your Family. As I am persuaded that a friendly Correspondence between the Governors of these Colonies is in the present State of Affairs highly expedient Your Declaration on that head is very agreeable to me as I shall on all Occasions endeavour to shew by writing freely to You as often as I may have any thing to communicate which might concern either of these Colonies or which it might be agreeable to You to be advised of. By a Letter which I lately received from Carlyle I find that neither the General, the Artillery nor the Highland Battalion[3] had got thither the 28th of last Month, Colo. Bouquet with Six Companies of Your Troops & some of the Pensylvania Forces was opening a new Road from F. Lyttleton to Ray's Town & thence to the Forks of the Yogyogany[4] which was likely to prove a very laborious & difficult Task. A small Detachment of the Royal American Regiment[5] & two Companies of the Delaware Troops are come hither with Sixty Waggon Load of Musquet Ball & Artillery Stores, which are if it is possible to be sent to Fort Cumberland by Water I sent off about Twenty Tun of them Yesterday Morning but am afraid the Waters of Potowmack will be too much fallen before the Canoes return for them to make another Trip. We are told by a Party of Cherokees that were lately in Sight of Fort Du Quesne that the Number of the Enemy at that place does not exceed four or five hundred, Most of whom go over the Ohio every Day to work on a Fort that is begun at the Distance of about half a Mile beyond the River,[6] I am likewise told by a Gentleman at Carlyle that the French at & in the Neighbourhood of Venango are much alarmed at no Provisions being sent this Year as usual from Niagara.[7] As I shall find Myself obliged to remain here the greatest part of the Summer to encourage or compel the Militia (that I have contrary to the Advice of our Lower House of Assembly ordered out for the Protection of the Frontier Inhabitants) to do their Duty You will be pleased to send any Letters that You may think proper to favour me with during that time to Winchester whence if they are directed to the Care of the Commanding

Officer at Fort Loudoun they will find a speedy Conveyance I should be much obliged to You for having the inclosed Letters put on board the first Vessel that sails for London from Your Government.

To the Honble. Francis Fauquier Esqr.

Copy: Hall of Records of Maryland, Sharpe Letter Book, III, 188–89. The seven words following "Conveyance," at the end of the letter, seem to be struck through but are retained as necessary to make sense.

1. Fort Frederick was near the Potomac River on the site of the present town of Hancock, in western Maryland, and about 30 mi. east of Fort Cumberland.
2. This was evidently the letter Fauquier mentioned in his letter of 18 June 1758 to Sharpe.
3. Forbes was supposed to have about forty artillerymen from the Royal Regiment of Artillery, with the appropriate train; and thirteen companies of Montgomery's Highlanders, over a thousand men.
4. Fort Lyttelton was on or near Aughwick Creek, in what is now Fulton County in Pennsylvania, about 18 mi. north of the Maryland line. Rays Town was on the Raystown branch of the Juniata River, at the place where Bouquet had begun the construction of Fort Bedford; the town of Bedford now occupies the site, in the center of Bedford County, Pa. It was about 35 mi. from Fort Lyttelton to Rays Town. The Youghiogheny River flows about 135 mi. from Preston County, W.Va., to join the Monongahela River at McKeesport.
5. The Royal American Regiment (later the Sixtieth Foot, and the King's Royal Rifle Corps) was raised in Pennsylvania in 1756 largely of German and Swiss immigrants; it was the first regular regiment raised for the specific task of fighting a colonial war. Forbes was supposed to have 350 men from this regiment.
6. No other reference to this report has been found, except that in his letter of 24 July 1758 to the Board of Trade, Fauquier mentioned a very similar story, which he said Washington had got from some deserters.
7. Venango was a settlement at the junction of French Creek and the Allegheny River in northwestern Pennsylvania where the city of Franklin now stands, and it was the site of Fort Machault, built by the French in 1754, enlarged in 1758, and abandoned in 1759. Niagara was a powerful fortress on the east bank of the Niagara River, at its mouth on Lake Ontario, first built in 1725 but largely reconstructed and improved in 1756–57.

From John Forbes

Sir   Head Quarters at Carlisle July the 8th 1758

I have received from General Abercromby an Extract of a Letter to the Govr. General of Canada[1] in relation to the Capitulation of fort Wm. Henry,[2] which Extract I send your Excellency inclosed with General Abercrombys order in consequence of it. I am with great Regard Your Excellencys Most obedient humble Servant

                                                 Jo Forbes

PS / please to forward the Inclosed

LS: University of Virginia, Tracy W. McGregor Library. Although the letter has what looks like the autograph signature of Forbes, it is a draft or copy of a circular letter; a list of persons to whom the letter was to be sent, following the text, includes the governors of Pennsylvania, Maryland, Virginia, the two Carolinas, and Georgia, but the name of William Denny of Pennsylvania is crossed through. The letter to Fauquier presumably used the address of "The Honble." and "your Honor," as did that to Governor Sharpe of Maryland (Maryland Historical Society, Portfolio 4, Papers and Letters, no. 36). That version of the letter has the postscript as "Please forward the Inclosed by Express."

1. Pierre François de Rigaud (1698–1765), marquis de Vaudreuil-Cavagnal, was the last French governor of Canada, 1755–60.
2. Fort William Henry, at the southern end of Lake George in northeastern New York, capitulated to the French on 9 Aug. 1757.

Enclosure: Major General James Abercromby to the Marquis de Vaudreuil

Sir, [Fort Edward, 26 June 1758]

I have the honour of Your Excellency's Letter of the 4th of June, with sundry Enclosures in relation to the Capitulation of Fort William Henry made the 9th of August last: Without entering into a Discussion of Particulars, Give me leave to acquaint Your Excellency that a Breach of that Capitulation on the part of the Forces of the King your Master, immediately after the Surrender of that Fortress,[1] was so notorious, contrary to the good Faith which subsists amongst all Nations, that in Honour & Justice to the King my Master, who has entrusted me with the Command of His Troops in North America, I think myself obliged to look upon that Capitulation as null & void, which I have signified to all His Majestys Governours & Commanders by Sea & Land in North-America.

I persuade myself, that upon due Consideration, Your Excellency will be convinced of the Justice of my Proceedings in respect to the Capitulation, & that nothing can induce you so far to lay aside Humanity, as to offer the least Violence on the Person of any of His Majesty's Subjects, Civil or Military, comprehended in that Capitulation, that may unfortunately fall into your Hands; as I must myself be obliged, as well as all His Majestys other Commanders, both by Sea & Land, to make Retaliation on all Subjects of His Most Christian Majesty, that are now Prisoners amongst us, or who may hereafter fall into Our hands. Allow me further to acquaint Your Excellency that I am determin'd to carry on the War with all possible Humanity, agreeable to the Intentions of the King my Master, & nothing shall engage me to pursue contrary Measures, but a Failure in that Respect on the part of the Troops of the King your Master.

Copy: University of Virginia, Tracy W. McGregor Library. Headed "Extract of a Letter from His Excellency Major General Abercromby Commander in Chief of all His Majesty's Forces in North America, To His Excellency The Marquis de Vaudreuil, Governour-General of Canada, bearing date at Fort-Edward June 26 1758." A copy of the extract was enclosed in the circular letter of 8 July 1758 from Forbes to Fauquier.

1. The Indian allies of the French massacred or carried off into captivity a number of people from Fort William Henry, although the French had promised them safe-conduct.

Enclosure: General Order from Major General James Abercromby

Fort-Edward, June 25th 1758

The Enemy having become Masters of Fort William Henry by virtue of a Capitulation made upon the 9th of August last; which Capitulation they immediately broke in a most notorious & flagrant manner, by murdering, pillaging, & Captivating many of His Majesty's good Subjects, in Violation of the said Capitulation, as well as of the Law of Nations. Upon these Considerations, & in honour & Justice to His Majesty's Arms, Major General Abercromby hereby declares the said Capitulation null & void, & that all Officers & Soldiers serving the 9th of August last at Fort William Henry, are hereby empowered & commanded to serve in the same manner as if no such Capitulation had ever been made. All which Major-General Abercromby has notified to the Governour General of Canada, signifying to him at the same time, that if any of His Majesty's Subjects supposed to be comprehended in the said Capitulation may fall into the Enemy's hands, & any Violence follow thereupon, that he will retaliate on the Persons of the French Prisoners now in His hands, as well as on all such as shall be taken hereafter by Sea or Land.

The above to be published at the Head of every Corps in His Majesty's Service in North America.

Copy: University of Virginia, Tracy W. McGregor Library. A copy of this order was enclosed in the circular letter of 8 July 1758 from Forbes to Fauquier.

From John Forbes

[10 July 1758]

This letter has not been found, but Fauquier acknowledged it in his letter of 20 July 1758 to Forbes. Forbes's letter was probably his reply to Fauquier's letter of 8 June 1758.

From George Washington

Honble. Sir.   Camp at Fort Cumberland, 10th July 175[8]

Your favour of the 25th past, I had the Honour to receive yesterday. I am obligd to you for the blank Commission you sent me, your honour may depend, I shall have regard to strict Justice in disposing of it.

I Marchd from Winchester the 24th Ulto. according to Orders, and Incampd at this place the 2d Inst; Colo. Byrd follow'd the 26th and arrivd here 4 days after me. before I left Winchester I appointed Lieutt. Smith of my Regiment[1] and 30 Invalids to remain at Fort Loudoun to take care of our Stores; and I orderd him to continue the minor at Work in the Well, and to proceed in covering the Barracks till your honour shoud be pleasd to direct him further in those matters. The Work woud have sustaind considerable damage if these small, but essential parts of it, were neglected. I left Mr. Smith £25 for this purpose, which he is to account for.

Inclosd is an account of the Stores left at Winchester;[2] the Arms are not Included; because they were then repairing at the Armourers. I have however directed Mr. Smith to transmit your Honour an Account of them by this Express. I have also Inclosd an Account of the Tools deliverd out of our Stores, to the Artificer's of Colo. Byrds Regiment, by Order of Sir Jno. St. Clair; and have directed Mr. Ramsay[3] (Contractor for supplying the Troops of Virginia with Provisions) to render your Honour an exact account of all the Provisions that has been expended, of his purchasing, since the time of Sir John St. Clairs first arrival at Winchester; that you may be able to settle that matter on the part of Virginia; it being imagind, we are entitled to Provisions from the Crown, since that time.

A Letter from Colo. Bouquet of the 6th which I have just receivd Contains this Paragraph.

"The Cuttawbas[4] under the Command of Captn. Johnne[5] are gone to Winchester; they have behav'd in the most shameful manner, and run away as a parcell of thieves rather than Warriors without seeing me; they have never killd a deer, and there is the strongest suspicians that the Scalp they pretend to have taken, was an old one.

"I think it woud be very necessary to send a message to their Nation to complain of their Conduct, and know at once if they are Friends or Enemies. if you approve of it, I shoud be obligd to you to propose the thing to the Governor of Virginia: I write to General Forbes on the subject."

We have no advice of the General, and the greatest uncertainty when we shall move from this place. I am with all due respect Your Honours Most Obedient & Most Humble Servant

Go: Washington

To the Honble. Governor Fauquier

Copy: Library of Congress, George Washington Papers, 6:30–31. Draft in Washington's hand, with deletions and insertions. This transcription respects all deletions and insertions indicated. The last digit of the year date is lost at the margin.

1. Lt. Charles Smith. Washington's orders to him, dated 24 June 1758, are in Fitzpatrick, 2:222–23.
2. This account and the others mentioned have not been found.
3. William Ramsay.
4. The Catawbas, settled in the Carolinas, were the most important of the eastern Siouan tribes and had been the most important and populous tribe in the region except for the Cherokees. They were usually friendly toward the English but were constantly at war with other Indian tribes, including the Cherokees. By the middle of the eighteenth century their numbers were much reduced by warfare, disease, and debauchery.
5. This is probably the Catawba chief referred to also as Captain Johny, Captain John, or Capt. John Thomson. He has also been identified as Captain Johnny or Jemmy Bullen.

From Horatio Sharpe

Sir   Fort Frederick the 12th of July 1758.

As I am told that the Ludlow Castle has not yet left Virginia tho all the Vessels that belong to this Province sailed some Weeks ago for the Place of Rendezvous I take the Liberty to inclose You a few Letters which I should be glad to have sent by this Convoy hoping that You will be so kind as to give Orders for their being put on Board any of the Vessels that are bound to London. Since I did Myself the honour to write to You the 3d Inst. I have been favoured with Your Letter of the 18th of June, for which be pleased to accept my Acknowledgments. I hear that General Forbes arrived at Carlyle last Tuesday Sen'night, & I have Reason to think that the Artillery & the Highland Battalion are there also by this time. The two Companies from N. Carolina consisting of 110 Men came hither Yesterday from Winchester to assist in making a Road that the General has ordered to be laid out thro this Province to Fort Cumberland.

To Governor Fauquier.

Copy: Hall of Records of Maryland, Sharpe Letter Book, III, 192–93.

To John Forbes

Sir   Wmsburgh July 20th 1758

Your Favour of the 10th was deliver'd to me on the 18th. I am much obliged to you for all your good Wishes, and kind Expressions in it, and will endeavour to merit your good Opinion by doing all in my power to assist his Majisties Forces in all their operations.

All possible Care is taken that the Cherokees and all other Indians are civilly and kindly treated in their Passage thro' our back Settlements, but their behaviour on some Occasions has been so extremely provoking, viz by stealing Horses, forcibly taking all provisions out of the poor Inhabitants Houses, even cutting their Beds to pieces for the Sake of carrying off the Ticks, and supporting these Outrages by Arms, That the people could not at last submit to it, and some Skirmishes ensued which I can not wonder att. and hope we shall hear no more of them, Tho' the people dread every thing from them in their Return, for which Reason I beg the Favour of you to let none return at the End of the campaign without proper Escorts.

I sincerely wish you all the Success you can desire and am with great Esteem Sir Your most Obedient Humble Servant

                                                           Fran: Fauquier

Brigr. Genl. Forbes

ALS: University of Virginia, Tracy W. McGregor Library.

To George Washington

Sir   Wmsburgh July 20th 1758

I received your Favour of the 10th on the 18th with an inclosed Account of the Stores left at Winchester, and of the Tools deliver'd for the use of the 2d Regiment: but had no Account from Mr. Smith of the Arms, nor from Mr. Ramsay of the Provisions issued for the Subsistance of the Men since Sir John St. Clair's Arrival at Winchester, when I apprehended our Men were to be provided for out of the Stores belonging to the Crown.

In Relation to Coll. Bouquet's Paragraph about the Catawba's I am not much surprized for I have never entertain'd any high Opinion of the Friendship of any Indians, nor form'd any great Expectations from their Service. As for sending any Messenger to them as he proposes I apprehend it will be too late to under take any Thing of that Sort for the Benefit of this Campaign, and according to their Behaviour in it, We shall be better able to know what to say to them at the End of it. All that is now to be done seems to me to be this, to keep those in good Humour who still remain with you, lest They should do Mischief to the Inhabitants in their Return home (as some have done) if they leave you in an ill Humour. But as you have already wrote to General Forbes on this Subject I shall readily acquiesce in any Measure you shall agree to be proper.[1]

I beg you would assure the General and Sir John St. Clair of my Respect to them, and of my Readiness on all Occasions to assist his Majesties Forces in all their Operations, in which I sincerely wish you all imaginary Success and am with great Regard, Sir, Your very Humble Servant

Fran: Fauquier

Coll. Washington

ALS: Library of Congress, George Washington Papers, ser. 4.

1. Fauquier must have misread Washington's letter, which indicates that Bouquet, not Washington, was writing to Forbes about the misconduct of the Catawbas. Bouquet referred to the subject in his letter of 11 July 1758 to Forbes (British Library, Add. Mss. 21652, f. 53; printed in *Bouquet* 2:175–83). Bouquet then said more or less what he had written to Washington about the Catawbas.

From James Abercromby

July 20th 1758

Tell him of the hearing of the Merchants on the Paper Money, that the Lords for Trade seem disposd to grant their Publick [hearing] on the Paper Money Act.[1] That notwithstanding Mr Dinwiddies Representations & mine on the Aid out of the Quit Rents nothing done thereon before the Adjournment of the Treasury that the Lords of Treasury had referrd Messrs Randolphs & Byrds Case to the Board of Trade who probably was to refer the same to the Auditor General[2] but it must rest til their meeting in October Tell him the News with News Papers by Mr Hanburys Ship.

MS: Virginia State Library, James Abercromby Letter Book, p. 104. This is evidently an abstract, or notes for a letter. It is in Abercromby's hand and extremely hard to decipher, and this transcription must be used with caution. The word in brackets has been supplied to complete the sense.

1. The journal of the Board of Trade records that on 5 July 1758 it considered the memorials of the merchants of London and Bristol complaining of the act to establish a paper currency and make it legal tender; the board heard what Robert Dinwiddie, Abercromby, and the principal merchants of London had to say upon the matter and ordered the preparation of a representation to the king. The representation was approved the next day, although it was not signed until 12 July. It remarks that the act of 1748 on executions was confirmed, no objection having been made to it, and adds that the board believes the courts in Virginia decree as damages "the whole Amount of the debt according to the actual Value of it in sterling money," in actions of debt where all the parties appear in court; however, it thinks that in cases of executorship, where minors are concerned, the courts would have to adhere to the letter of the law, and thus "the Parties must be greatly injured." As for the act of 1757 and paper currency, such a thing is a novelty in Virginia, and seems the less necessary since there is a staple commodity of trade. Dinwiddie justified his assent to the act on the grounds that the silver and gold in the colony had for the most part been collected and sent up north to pay the king's forces and the thousand men on the frontiers in the pay of the colony could be paid only by the issuing of bills of credit; the act had evidently been carried into execution, and it would be difficult and inconvenient to repeal it. The board concluded by proposing an instruction recommending that the Virginia assembly pass an act to amend the two objectionable acts, so as to provide that all debts contracted before the passage of the acts must be paid in sterling money, while debts contracted after the passage of the acts may be payable in bills of credit, with the creditor's agreement, but only at the actual rate of exchange between the bills and sterling money, and not at the nominal value of the bills. The memorial of the London merchants appears above as an enclosure in Abercromby's letter of 23 June 1758 to Fauquier; the text of the board's representation is in C.O.5/1367, ff. 165–70; the resulting instruction of 9 Feb. 1759 is below under its proper date.

2. On 4 July 1758 Samuel Martin, secretary to the Treasury, sent to the Board of Trade a memorial from William Byrd and Peter Randolph upon which the Treasury desired the opinion of the board (C.O.5/1329, ff. 58–66). The undated memorial from Byrd and Randolph to the Treasury represents that by Dinwiddie's commission of 23 Dec. 1755 they had been appointed commissioners to negotiate a treaty with the Cherokees and Catawbas; that the governor and council had approved their statement of expenses and ordered that an application be made to the Treasury for their reimbursement; the memorialists cited a royal warrant of 1744 for £1620.2.11 to pay the expenses of a treaty with the Six Nations and repeated their request for reimbursement, as they had had no allowance; they appended a number of extracts from the journal of the council concerning their mission and the earlier mission to the Six Nations. It is not clear whether the board at this point referred the memorial to the auditor general: John Pownall, secretary to the Board of Trade, wrote to Martin on 14 July that the Board of Trade had considered the memorial from Byrd and Randolph, but it had no knowledge of the facts in the case, and the demand alleged to have been made and allowed in 1744 was never under its consideration; the board could give no opinion in the matter (C.O.5/1367, f. 170).

24 July 1758

From William Byrd

[Fort Cumberland, 21 July 1758]

This letter has not been found, but it was communicated to the council on 17 Aug. 1758 and is mentioned in *EJC* 6:107–8:

The Governor communicated to the Board two Letters from Colo. Byrd at Fort Cumberland, the one dated July 21st informing, that General Forbes had thought proper to divide his Army into three Brigades, the British, Pensylvanian, and Virginian; that the two first have their Majors appointed at 10s per Day, and recommending Captain Abraham Bosomworth of His Majesty's 60th Regiment as a proper Person to do that Duty in their Brigade, they being at present without that necessary Officer: Upon which the Council were of Opinion that the said Request could not at present be complied with as no Provision had been made by the Assembly for such an Officer.

To the Board of Trade

My Lords   Wmsburgh July 24th 1758

Tho' I have nothing very material to inform your Lordships of, I would not omit the Opportunity of a Ship sailing for England, to acquaint you that by the last Advices I received from Coll. Washington, he tells me that by some Deserters he has learn'd that the Garrison at fort du Quesne does not consist of above 4 or 500 Men at most, which daily go over the Ohio to work at a new Fort the French are building about half a Mile on the other Side that River.[1] From which Circumstance and the bad Condition they are in, it is not impossible but that if they hear bad News from their Northward Settlements, they may abandon Fort du Quesne and the Country on this Side the River and retire into the Fort they are building on the other Side.

I shall defer sending all public papers till the Departure of Captn. Legge in his Majesties Ship the Chesterfield, which he has appointed for the 10th of September. The Assembly is to meet on the 14th of the same Month. I have the Honour to be, My Lords, Your Lordships most obliged & obedient Humble Servant

                                                   Fran: Fauquier

The right honble. the Lords of Trade.

ALS: C.O.5/1329, ff. 80–81. Endorsed as read 12 Dec. 1758.

1. There is no trace of a communication from Washington to Fauquier with this report on Fort Duquesne and the new fort being built across the Ohio River from Fort Duquesne. No other reference to this intelligence has been traced, except that Horatio Sharpe's letter of 3 July 1758 to Fauquier passed on a nearly identical report from a party of Cherokees.

To [William] Prentis

Sir [Williamsburg, 27 July 1758]

Pay to Thos. Withers[1] Thirty Pounds in Cash, who is going Express to Adml. Boscawen[2] at Louisbourgh.[3]

Fran: Fauquier

To Mr. Prentis[4] / July 27th 1758 / N.B. this is to be repaid by the Province of South Carolina.

ALS: William L. Clements Library, Lyttelton Papers. Endorsed with a signed receipt by Withers, 27 July 1758, and with what looks like a note of the expenses of his errand to Boscawen.

1. Thomas Withers is not exactly identified, but must have been a courier or messenger. On this occasion he was evidently engaged to forward a dispatch from Governor Lyttelton; it is likely that Fauquier referred to this mission and this messenger in his letter of 5 Oct. 1758 to Lyttelton.
2. Edward Boscawen (1711–1761) in Feb. 1758 was named Admiral of the Blue and commander in chief of the fleet at the siege of Louisburg. See the *Dictionary of National Biography*.
3. Louisburg, or Louisbourg, on Cape Breton Island, was the site of a powerful French fortress guarding the entrance to the Gulf of St. Lawrence. It was besieged by General Amherst and Admiral Boscawen at the beginning of June 1758 and surrendered on 26 July, opening the sea route to Quebec.
4. This is probably William Prentis (1701?–1765), a prominent merchant of Williamsburg on several occasions involved in business dealings with the government.

From Edward Boscawen

[*Namur*, Louisburg Harbor, ca. 27 July 1758]

This letter has not been found, but Fauquier informed the General Assembly on 18 Sept. 1758 that he had the night before received an authentic account from Admiral Boscawen of the success of His Majesty's arms against Louisburg; it is assumed that Boscawen sent out a circular letter immediately after the French surrendered on 26 July. See *JHB, 1758–1761*, p. 10.

From William Henry Lyttelton

[ca. August 1758]

This letter has not been found. It was communicated to the council on 17 Aug. 1758; it is abstracted in *EJC* 6:108:

His Honor likewise communicated a Letter from Governor Lyttelton, informing he had dispatched a Messenger to the Cherokees with Letters to the Commandants of the

Forts there, relating to the late Engagements of the Militia of Halifax and Bedford with several Parties of Indians, belonging to that Nation, in their March thro' those Counties; and wishes they may be productive of good Effects; inclosing a Copy thereof, and Col. Read's Report.

The letters to the commandants have not been identified. At this time Halifax and Bedford were frontier counties, extending to the Blue Ridge: Halifax then included approximately the present-day Halifax, Pittsylvania, Henry, and Patrick counties; Bedford included approximately the present-day Bedford, Campbell, and Franklin counties. Colonel Read was no doubt Clement Read, and his report was what Fauquier had sent to Lyttelton in his letter of 16 June 1758 with the request that it should be returned.

From William Byrd

[Fort Cumberland, 3 August 1758]

This letter has not been found, but it was communicated to the council on 17 Aug. 1758 and is mentioned in *EJC* 6:108:

> The other Letter dated August 3d advising that the Road they are to march is not yet determin'd; that he fears a new Road is intended to be cut over the Laurel-Mountains, in which Case no Benefit can be expected from the Forces this Year; inclosing a Copy of the Forage and Bat-Money Account, and a Return of the 2d Regiment.

The account and return have not been identified.

From George Washington

Honble. Sir   Fort Cumberld Camp 5th August 1758

Your favour of the 20th Ulto. I was honourd with the day before yesterday. I am sorry to find that Mr. Smith has not sent you a return of the Arms, nor Mr. Ramsay a return of the Provisions. I will write to both those Gentlemen to know the reason. Inclosd is a return of the first Regiment.[1]

I have delayed till now—purposely—(since my last of the 10th Ulto.) to give your honour any account of our movements; hoping to be furnishd with something agreeable; being disappointed in this, I am sorry to inform you that we are still Incampd here, and have little prospect of decamping, unless a fatal Resolution takes place of opening a New Road from Rays Town to Fort Duquesne[2]—in this event—I have no doubt but the Virginia Troops will be honourd with a full share of the Labour; as they have already been in opening a Communication from hence to Rays Town; and doing the principal part of the Work at that place.

I am just returnd from a Conference held with Colo. Bouquet on this occasion. The General lying indisposd at Carlyle. In this conference I urgd, in the most forcible terms I was Master of, the advancd Season as an argument against new discoveries. I pressd also—the difficulties of cutting a Road over these Mountains—known to me from experience—the length of time it must require to do it—the little time left for that Service—the moral certainty of its obstructing Our March beyond what the advanced season will admit—and the probable miscarriage of the Expedition from that cause. and lastly. I endeavourd to represent the distressd Condition the Colonies woud be reducd to, consequent thereupon. In fine, I said, every thing the importance of the subject suggested to me to avert a measure that seemd to forebode the manifest Ruin of the Expedition, for this is the light in which it presents itself to my mind! I pray heaven my Fears may not be realised. but the thoughts of opening a Road 100 Miles over Mountains almost inaccessable, at this advanced Season, when there is already a good Road made, a Road universally confess[d] to be the best that either is, or can be found anywhere thr[o] these Mountains, prognosticates something not quite favourable.

I have now drawn up a Representation of real Facts to be presented to the General, in which I think, the advantag[es] of going the old Road, and the moral certainty of failing in the new are so clearly demonstrated, that it must strike every unbiass'[d] Mind.[3]

The small Pox getting among the Troops, is another unpromising Circumstance. An Officer and two Men of my Regiment are now down with it at Rays Town. from this short narrative of our Affairs your honour may draw conclusions: you may depend the statement is true, free from exagerations, and flowing from a Mind deeply affected at the prospect before Us. I hope, as I once before said, that I see matters in too strong a point of view; and, that my Apprehensions for the Consequence of opening a new Road are Groun[d]less. I am with all due Respect Your Honours most Obedient Humble Servant

Go: Washington

P.S. I was this moment presented with a Letter from Colo. Bouquet telling me, that the General had directed the other Road to be opend;[4] I expect therefore to be Orderd that way immediately. Order's are not yet arrivd.

Go: Wn.

To Governor Fauquier

Copy: Library of Congress, George Washington Papers, 6:51–52. Draft in Washington's hand, with deletions and insertions. This transcription respects all deletions and insertions indicated. Letters in brackets have been lost at the margin. This letter was communicated to the council 17 Aug. 1758.

1. This return has not been traced.
2. Rays Town was on or near several important trails between the Ohio and Susquehanna; it was about 30 mi. northeast of Fort Cumberland and about 85 mi. southeast of Fort Duquesne (or 100 mi. by Washington's reckoning).
3. The representation Washington prepared is in his letter to Bouquet of 2 Aug. 1758; in another letter of the same date to Maj. Francis Halkett, Forbes's aide-de-camp, Washington made it clear that the representation was intended to be transmitted to Forbes. The two letters are in Fitzpatrick, 2:252–61, and are followed on pp. 263–64 by an informative note on the prospect of a new road, which Washington opposed. See Gipson, vol. 7, chap. 9, for an extended account of the expedition against Fort Duquesne.
4. The letter is presumably one in *Bouquet* 2:343, where the date is conjectured to be ca. 9 Aug. 1758: the letter reports receipt of a letter from Forbes "with express Orders to begin to open the road from this place across the Allegheny Mountains." The draft copy of the letter in the British Library, Add. Mss. 21641, f. 54, is undated, but it must be the letter of 3 Aug. to Washington that Bouquet referred to in his letter to Washington of 4 Aug. (*Bouquet* 2:315–16).

From John Forbes

Sir   [Shippensburg, 16 August 1758]

I had the favour of yours from Williamsburgh some days ago, but have been so bad of a Flux that I could not acknowledge the receipt of yours sooner.[1]

I am sorry to tell you, that our Cherokee Indians have behaved like a parcell of Scoundrells and have now left us to go home. They have been particularly talked too, with regard to their behaviour in the Countrys they are to pass through and not withstanding their Infamous behaviour wee have given thim presents to carry home, in order to purchase their good behaviour towards the Inhabitants of Virginia and Maryland where they pass. But as there is no truth in them, nor no trust to be given, I thought it necessary to give you this trouble, that you may give suitable directions, not only to the safe passage of the Indians but likewise for the protiction of your back Inhabitants. I should have Gladly sent escorts along with them, but the many different posts that I must occupy at present, leaves me scarce any men at all behind. Colo Byrds Indians left him some days ago and I hear that 50 from Raestown came to Fort Loudoun last night,[2] to demand their presents and if they were refused; to take them by force, this last I have prevented by sending 300 Highlanders there, But I can not promise that they will not committ violence, where they dare do it.

I thank you for your good wishes of Success. but Genll Abercrombys repulse,[3] and the Defection of those Indian's are two very unhappy circumstances at this criticall period. Nor can I well foresee what bad effects it may produce, in order to guard against them I am with great regard Sir Your Most obedient &c &c

J F

I beg pardon for giving you the trouble of forwarding the enclosed to Govr. Dobbs, but have no other Certain method of sending either to him, or Govr Littleton but by your Channell. I ought to acquaint you likewise that after a variety of Intrigue and manadgment I have at last brought about a Convention of most of the Indian Nations friends & foes to meet all the Governors at East town in pensylvania about the 10th of Septr.[4] There to settle and finish all Complaints, and if possible by doing the Indians justice to make them our Friends, which from their demands I do think easily Done, as it would be a great stroke, so make no doubt of your being invited there.
Govr. Fauquier

Copy: University of Virginia, Tracy W. McGregor Library. A few corrections suggest that this is a draft copy. Date and place of writing are supplied from an endorsement.

1. Forbes arrived on the evening of 12 Aug. 1758 at Shippensburg, in Cumberland and Franklin counties in southern Pennsylvania, after he had been ill for several weeks. This letter apparently was the reply to Fauquier's letter of 20 July 1758.

2. Rays Town was about 35 mi. west and north from Fort Loudoun; this Fort Loudoun in Pennsylvania was built in 1756 on the west branch of Conococheague Creek, about 115 mi. southeast of Fort Duquesne.

3. In July 1758 General Abercromby attacked Fort Carillon (which the English called Ticonderoga), built in 1755 by the French to command the route between Lake Champlain and Lake George. Although Abercromby had a force of more than 15,000 men, he suffered a crushing defeat by Montcalm, who had only 3,600 men.

4. This was the conference to be held at Easton.

To William Byrd

Sir   Williamsburgh Augst 17th 1758

I received your two Letters of the 21st July and 3d instant by Jenkins[1] who arrived here on the 15th and am so far from thinking you troublesome for your frequent writing, that I am always desirous to hear from the Army; for I think the better I am informed of the posture of Affairs, the better able I shall be to be serviceable to this Colony which is the utmost of my Wishes. I am sorry to find by yours and Coll. Washington's Letters, that We have so little Room to expect great Matters this Year. I have by Jenkins wrote to him my Sentiments at large on this Head to which I beg Leave to refer you,[2] and I desire you will join with him in representing the Case of the Virginia Regiments, and the Temper of the Assembly who have with so remarkable Alacrity raised these Men, for the important Service of the Reduction of Fort du Quesne which they so much depended on being performed or at least attempted this Year, that they enlisted the Men till December only, and God only knows whether they may be prevail'd on to do as much the next Year. My Endeavours shall not be wanting to induce them to it. But perhaps all this is too late to ward off the Attempt to cut a new Road, which if already determined upon, seems to determine the Fate of that Fort for this Year at least. I don't doubt but that Coll. Washington and your self will do all in your power to set this in its true light to your Commanding Officers. All I can add to what I have already wrote to Col. Washington is, that I write these Letters by Advice of Council which I summoned to meet this morning to consider of your Letters, and may be supposed to well know the state of this Country, of which I must be in great Measure ignorant.

It was the Opinion of the Council that we had it not in our power to comply with your Request in relation to a Brigade-Major; the Act of Assembly is so particular, as even to mention the Number of Officers to command the Regiment,[3] and we cannot add one for whose Subsistence there is no provision by the Act. But as the Assembly will sit certainly on the 14 of September, If such an Officer is absolutely necessary, I don't doubt but they will readily come into it, as they have so generously done in all Measures for the public Service.

I have seen nor heard nothing of Humphries since I sent him up, but hope you will be able to provide your self with a Doctor (a Surgeon I fear you will not much want) for I really can not find any Body to send up to assist your Men;[4] your Account of whom is the only comfortable Part of your Letter. I desire to have an exact Account of all the Indians who have been with you, and of all who remain with you at this Day distinguishing their Nations, for I am very apt to believe, the Service they do us is very inadequate to the Expence they occasion.

I shall never think it a trouble to correspond with the Gentlemen who have Command in the Army, on the Contrary I desire to hear every Step on all Occasions particularly so now before the Assembly meets, and the more free you are in giving your Sentiments (as far as you care trust them which shall never transpire beyond the Limits you shall prescribe to them) the greater pleasure you will give to, Sir, Your sincere Humble Servant

Fran: Fauquier

P.S. I will pay your Draught to Mr. Cunningham when presented, and the Money due to your Sutler, I am glad Capt. Fields Demand will not be soon made as the Treasury is low.[5]

Coll. Byrd

ALS: State Historical Society of Wisconsin, Draper Manuscripts 4 ZZ 42.

1. William Jenkins was an express, or courier.
2. This letter has not been traced, but it must have been the letter of 17 Aug. 1758 from Fauquier that Washington acknowledged in his letter of 2 Sept. 1758 to the governor.
3. "An Act for augmenting the forces in the pay of this Colony to two thousand men; and for other purposes therein mentioned" (Hening, 7:168), passed in Apr. 1758, authorized "a colonel, lieutenant-colonel, major, seven captains, twenty lieutenants, and ten ensigns" to command the regiment which the act provided for. A brigade major was a staff officer, attached to a brigade, who assisted the brigadier in command and acted as the channel for the issuing of orders and transmitting of reports and correspondence.
4. Humphries is not identified, but the context suggests he was a physician or surgeon; the weekly return of the Second Virginia Regiment dated 19 July 1758 includes the note "Dr. Humphries resign'd" (Library of Congress, George Washington Papers). The act cited in n. 3 above authorized one surgeon and two surgeon's mates for the regiment.
5. Mr. Cunningham was probably William Cunningham, a merchant of Falmouth, who had previously furnished food or supplies for the Virginia troops. The sutler has not been identified. Capt. John Field, first captain of the regiment, was killed at the Battle of Point Pleasant on 10 Oct. 1774.

To John Clevland

Sir Wmsburgh Augst 25th [1758]

I shall be obliged to you if you wil lay the inclosed petition of the Council and Merchants of this Colony,[1] before their Lordships, on the first Board Day,[2] and deliver the inclosed Letter to Lord Anson.[3] We are impatient to hear of his Success.[4] I am, Sir, Your very Humble Servant.

Fran: Fauquier

John Cleveland Esqr.

ALS: Adm.1/3818.

1. See the next letter.
2. The Board of Admiralty were the Lords Commissioners of the Admiralty, and members of the board were addressed as "My Lords" or "Your Lordships."

3. George Anson (1697–1762), created Baron Anson of Soberton in 1746, was an admiral and in 1758 was first lord of the Admiralty. This letter to Anson has not been found, but on 17 Aug. Fauquier had promised the council that he would write to Lord Anson to request protection for the coast of Virginia; see *EJC* 6:108.

4. In the summer of 1758 Anson was in command of the main fleet off Brest, covering the operations of a small squadron and landing force directed against St. Malo and Brest.

To the Admiralty

My Lords,   Wmsburgh Augst 25th 1758

I am sollicited by the Gentlemen of the Council and the Mercantile Part of this Colony, to represent to your Lordships, That the Trade of this Colony and Maryland in Tobacco, is a very considerable Branch of Trade, and produces a very great Revenue to his Majesty. That this Colony in particular having lately applyed it self to the Cultivation of Indico, a very valuable Commodity, with which the Merchants of England had used to be supplyed by the French, apprehend the protection of their Trade becomes daily more important. That during the Interval between one Convoy sailing to England with the Trade, and the Return of another from thence, and during any Cruize of any of his Majesties Ships while upon this Station, in quest of any privateer &ct The Trade is exposed to the Depredations of the Enemy. That in Case a Rupture should happen with the Court of Madrid, (which is much apprehended here) The Trade would be still more exposed, as they have experienced in the late War; Privateers of that Nation having carried off Ships out of the very Bay of Chesapeak with Impunity.

Upon these Considerations They hope your Lordships will indulge them with ordering two Ships of War of what Force your Lordships think proper, to protect their Trade; that in the Absence of one, whether by a Cruize or otherwise, They may be always sure of the Protection of the other, either within the Bay, or at the Entrance of the Capes.[1] It being impossible for the most active and vigilant Man, to protect the Trade and drive off the Enemy without the Capes at the same Time.

All this is submitted to your Lordships to do therein as you shall see convenient by, My Lords, Your Lordships most Obedient Servant
                                                           Fran: Fauquier

The Lords of Admiralty.

ALS: Adm. 1/3818. Evidently enclosed in the letter of the same date to John Clevland. A second copy of this letter, and apparently filed with it, is in another hand than

Fauquier's, although the complimentary close, signature, and address are all in Fauquier's hand.

1. The entrance to the Chesapeake Bay is between Cape Charles on the north and Cape Henry on the south.

From William Henry Lyttelton

[28 August 1758]

This letter has not been found, but Fauquier communicated it to the council on 13 Dec. 1758. It is mentioned in *EJC* 6:123, but it appears that the abstract given there relates only to a letter of 1 Nov. 1758 from Lyttelton. It is possible that Lyttelton's letter of 28 Aug. was an acknowledgment of an unrecorded letter to him from Fauquier of ca. 17 Aug. which replied to Lyttelton's letter of ca. Aug. 1758 returning Read's report.

From William Denny

[Philadelphia, 30 August 1758]

This letter has not been found, but it is mentioned in *EJC* 6:109:

The Governor was pleased to communicate to the Board a letter from Governor Denny, dated Philadelphia August 30th advising he had received a Letter from Mr. Croghan, the Deputy of Sir William Johnson, then at Easton, acquainting him that about Twenty Indian Messengers, who left Wyomink at different Times, informed him, that the upper Nations were gathering there, in order to proceed to hold a Treaty in that Province; that at the Request of General Forbes, who had been instrumental in bringing about this Meeting, he had writ to the Governors of the Middle Provinces, and also to Sir William Johnson, desiring their Assistance at the Conferences proposed to be held the middle of September, and hoped for the Pleasure of seeing his Honor there.

William Denny (1709–1765) was lieutenant governor of Pennsylvania 1756–59. Sir William Johnson (1715–1774) was superintendent for the northern Indians from 1755. George Croghan (d. 1782) was a highly influential Indian trader and frequently acted as Pennsylvania's agent in Indian negotiations. He became Johnson's deputy in 1756. Croghan was at Easton in eastern Pennsylvania, on the Delaware River, and the Indian messengers he mentioned probably came from the Wyoming Valley in northeastern central Pennsylvania, along the Susquehannah River.

From Christopher Smith

[ca. September 1758]

This letter has not been found. Fauquier communicated it to the council on 11 Sept. 1758, and it is mentioned in *EJC* 6:109 as enclosing a letter from Colonel Vanmeter which reported that the Prince William militia stationed on the branch had no ammunition. Neither Smith nor Vanmeter has been identified.

From George Washington

Honble Sir   Camp at Fort Cumberland Sepr 2d 1758

Your favour of the 17th Ulto.[1] I had the honour to receive the 30th following. If you are surpriz'd to find us Still Incamp'd at this place I shall only remark that your Surprise cannot well exceed my own.

In my last I inform'd your Honour that a Resolution was taken to open a new Road from Rays Town to Fort Duquesne, 'twas instantly begun and since that time from one to two Thousand Men have wrought on it continually—they had by the last accounts I received cut it to the foot of Laurill Hill[2] about 35 Miles and I suppose by this time 1500 Men have taken Posts at Loyall Hanning[3] about 10 Miles further, where I understand another Fort is to be built to deposite our Provisions in.

What time it will require to Build a Fort at Loyall Hanning and after that is accomplish'd, what further time is necessary to cut the Road thro' very rugged Grounds to Fort Du Quesne (Grounds of which the Enemy are actually possest & know every advantageous Post to harrass & dispute with us in) I say what time is required for the completion of all this, I must leave to time that faithfull expositor of Events to reveal—not caring even to guess at it myself.

The first Division of the Artillery has past the Allegany Hill[4] and I suppose may by now be got up with the advancd working Party, the 2d Division I beleive may be March'd by this, and they talk of putting all the Troops in motion immediat'ly.

We have not in our Stores at Rays Town two Months Provisions for the Army; and if the best Judges are to be credited, the nipping Frosts will soon destroy the Herbage on the Mountains, and then, tho' the Communication is not quite stop'd, the Subsistence for horses is render'd very difficult till Snows and hard Frost prevents all intercourse with the Ohio and these sets in early in November.

The Road from Reas Town to Carlyle from whence the Provisions and Stores chiefly come is perhaps worse than any other upon the Continent—infinit'ly worse than any part of the Road from hence to Fort Duquesne along General Braddocks Road,[5] and has already worn out the greatest part of the horses that have been imploy'd in Transporting the Provisions—the Carriage of which only, it is said and from good authority, I have it, stands the Crown upwards of 40/ every hundred weight.

We have certain advices that the French the 13th Ulto. had received no new Reinforcements at Fort Duquesne from Canada and that their Totall strength at that Garrison could not exceed 800 Men Indians Included. This Intelligence is brought by two Officers of the first Virginia Regiment viz Chew & Allan[6] who at different times and in different Partys since the aforesaid 13th have been to Fort Duquesne and there lain wait in view of the Fort observing the works and strength for several days there accounts agree exactly and have given great satisfaction to the Commanding Officer at Reas town,[7] from whence they were sent being corroborated also by Indian Intelligence a Party of Cherrokees having been out there & some Delawares[8] just come in. What a Golden opportunity have we lost!—but this is past—irrecoverably gone I fear.

A Party of our Troops 75 in number is now 40 miles advanc'd way-laying the Road—from whom I hope a Prisoner, if the Enemy should be passing or repassing—I sent out also the day before yesterday a Serjeant & 5 Men to Fort Duquesne for Intelligence—they will be back in fourteen days.

I can give your Honour no satisfactory account of the General. He lay ill at Carlyle a long time of a Flux, from thence getting a little strength he mov'd to Shippensbourg[9] where his Disorder return'd & where I am told he now is. By a Letter received from him the other day he hopes soon to be at Rays Town where he desires to see Colo. Byrd and myself[10]—but alas! the Expedition must either stand or fall by the present Plan.

In the conference I had with Colo. Bouquet and of which I gave your Honour an account in my last I did among other things to avert the resolve of opening a new Road, represent the great Expence the Coloney of Virginia had been at to support the war, the Charge of raising a 2d Regiment at so short a Notice; the time limited for the Service of it; and the Cruelty therefore of risking the Success of an Expedition upon such precarious Measures when so much depended on it; and our inability to do more. I then exprest my apprehensions of the Southern Indians in case of a miscarriage, and the increase of French strength in new Alliances; & after this I demonstrated very clearly or endeavourd so to do the time it would take us to proceed on the old Road; and at how much easier expence, even if we were oblig'd to get all our Provisions and Stores from Pensylvania—and no occasion for this surely—In fine I urg'd every thing then I could do now; and repeated it by Letter Copies of which I have now to shew—if required; but urg'd in vain, the Pensylvanians whose Interest present and future it was to conduct the Expedition thro' their Government, and along that way, because it secures their Frontiers at present, and the Trade hereafter, a Chain of Forts being Erected, had prejudic'd the General absolutely against this Road; made him believe we were the partial people and determin'd him at all Events to pursue that Rout, so that their Sentiments are already fully known on this matter; and to them as Instigators, may be attributed the great misfortune of this miscarriage; for I think *now* nothing but a miracle can procure Success.

The Contractor[11] has Orders to lay in at Loyall Hanning for 4000 Men the Winter from whence it is imagin'd that our Expedition for this Campaign will end there. shoud we serve to make up the Number of Troops which Garrison that place our Frontiers will thereby not only be expos'd but the Soldiers for want of Cloathing & proper conveniencies must absolutely perish; few of them having a whole Coat to their backs and many none at all; this is a matter I have fully and repeatedly written about these 12 Months past: I hope it will now merit the Assembly's notice.

A Major of Brigade to the Virginia Troops is an Officer absolutely necessary, while there is more than one Regiment; the General has repeatedly urg'd this matter; and Colo. Byrd who once Recommended another Gentleman that is now found to be too deeply engag'd in Indian Affairs,[12] Joins me in proposing Capt. Robt. Stewart for this Office; a Gentleman whose assiduity and Military Capacity is second to none in our Service; we beg the favour therefore of a Commission for him, & that your Honour wou'd be pleas'd to have the Date of it Blank in Order that he may take Rank before some other Majors of Brigade to which his longer Services entitles him.

The First Virginia Regiment have August's Pay due to them and no money in the Pay Master's[13] hands—this he will inform your Honour off more particularly, as desired.

Capt. Bullen[14] and Capt. French two Catawbas much esteem'd for their Bravery and steady attachment to our Interest, were kill'd about ten days ago on their way from Winchester to this Camp by the Enemy we got very early notice of it at this place (it happening within 3 Miles) and sent out several Partys to pursue which they did fruitlessly.

I have wrote to Mr. Gist[15] who had the Direction of Indian Affairs to make out such a Return as your Honour requires and forward it to you—he is now at Rays Town. Inclos'd is a Return of my Regiment[16] I beleive it is exact but as six of the Companys are upon the new Road I can not absolutely say what alterations have happened therein since my last advices.

Thus Sir, I have given your Honour a full and impartial account of the present posture of our affairs here of which any use may be made you think proper. I may be blam'd possibly for expressing my Sentiments so freely, but never can be asham'd of urging the Truth, and none but obvious Facts are Stated here. The General I dare say, from his good Character, can account fully and no doubt satisfactorily for these Delays that surprize all that Judge from appearances only, but I really cannot.

Colo. Byrd being very unwell has desired me to offer his Compliments to your Honour an excuse (which is Sickness) for his not writing. I am with all due Respect Your Honours Most Obedient & most humble Servant

Go: Washington

P.S. Upon Second thoughts I have transmitted Copies of some of the Letter's I wrote to Colonel Bouquet (who Commands in the Generals absence) upon the Posture of our Affairs; particularly my Sentiments of the New Road.[17] It will give your Honour some trouble in reading them; but it will at the same time shew, that nothing in my power has been wanting to bring this Expedition to a speedy, and I hoped to a happy conclusion. As I well foresaw that every delay still subjected Us to further difficulties, and the chance of encountering a French Reinforcement; which very clearly appear's they had not receivd the Middle of August, long before which, might we have been there had the old Road been timely adopted as above I am &ca.

Go: Washington

To Governor Fauquier.

Copy: Library of Congress, George Washington Papers, 6:70–74. Draft in a clerk's hand, with deletions and insertions, but with postscript and signature apparently in Washington's hand. This transcription respects all deletions and insertions indicated.

1. This letter has not been found. See Fauquier to Byrd of 17 Aug. 1758, nn. 3 and 4, for the tenor of Fauquier's letter.

2. Laurel Hill is a ridge in the Alleghenies about 55 mi. long, running southwest to northeast in Pennsylvania from south Fayette County to west central Cambria County.

3. Now Loyalhanna, this was an Indian settlement on Loyalhanna Creek, about halfway between Rays Town and Fort Duquesne, and the site of Fort Ligonier, a stockade fort built in 1758 and named for Sir John Ligonier (1680–1770), the commander in chief.

4. Also known as Allegany Mountain, this ridge of the Alleghenies runs parallel to and about 20 mi. southeast of Laurel Hill.

5. In 1755 Gen. Edward Braddock had a road cut from Fort Cumberland toward Fort Duquesne, running from Cumberland northwest to Fort Necessity, then north, then northeast, and finally northwest again to Fort Duquesne.

6. Ens. Coleby Chew and Ens. John Allen.

7. Col. Henry Bouquet.

8. Delawares was a name given by the English to a confederation of tribes of Algonquian stock (called by themselves Lenape or Lenni Lenape) who lived in the basin of the Delaware River. By the middle of the eighteenth century they had moved westward in Pennsylvania and into what is now Ohio.

9. Shippensburg is about 21 mi. southwest of Carlisle and about 48 mi. east of Rays Town.

10. Perhaps the letter was one of 19 Aug. 1758 from Forbes to Byrd, to which Washington referred in his letter of 28 Aug. to Bouquet (Fitzpatrick, 2:276).

11. Not identified.

12. This was evidently Capt. Abraham Bosomworth of the Sixtieth Regiment. See Byrd's letter of 21 July 1758 to Fauquier.

13. Alexander Boyd.

14. This Catawba was also known as Captain Johnny, it seems; see Washington to Fauquier, 10 July 1758, n. 5.

15. Christopher Gist (ca. 1706–1759) was deputy agent for southern Indian affairs.

16. Not traced.

17. The enclosures are not present, and it is impossible to guess which letters from Washington to Bouquet were enclosed. From 3 July 1758, the date of Washington's first letter to Bouquet, until 2 Sept., the date of the last letter from Washington to Bouquet that could have been sent with this letter to Fauquier, Washington sent Bouquet twenty-two letters. The originals are all in the British Library, Add. Mss. 21641, ff. 2–56, two of them in a clerk's hand but signed by Washington, all the rest holographs. The letters are all printed in Fitzpatrick, 2:226–86, but Fitzpatrick's text is from copies kept by Washington and differs from that of the originals.

To the Earl of Loudoun

My Lord,   Wmsburgh Sepr 10th 1758

His Majesty having been graciously pleased to appoint me his Lieutenant Governor of the Colony and Dominion of Virginia; I find by his Instructions to your Lordship, I am to account with your Lordship for half of the Salary and perquisites of Government.[1] I have accordingly open'd a Book in which I keep that Account regularly, and shall be obliged to your Lordship to inform me, whom you will think proper to depute here to settle that Account with me, and authorize to receive your Lordships Moiety, and it shall be punctually paid to your Lordships Order, from Time to Time as I receive it. I am, my Lord, with great Regard, Your Lordship's most Obedient Humble Servant.

                                                             Fran: Fauquier

The Earl of Loudoun.

ALS: The Huntington Library, San Marino, Calif., HM, Loudoun Papers, LO 5913. Endorsed as received 18 Oct. 1758.

1. Art. 110 of Loudoun's general instructions fixed his salary at £2,000 per annum, payable quarterly from the revenue of 2s. per hogshead on tobacco; Art. 113 of those instructions directed that during Loudoun's absence from Virginia one full moiety of the salary and all perquisites and emoluments should be paid to the lieutenant governor or the president of the council acting as commander in chief (C.O. 5/1367, ff. 142–43). In practice, the salary was paid semiannually, about 25 Apr. and 25 Oct., to the lieutenant governor or commander in chief, who then remitted the governor's share of the salary, perquisites, and emoluments to him in accordance with whatever arrangement they had agreed on.

To William Denny

[ca. 11 September 1758]

This letter has not been found. It was sent in reply to Denny's letter of 30 Aug. 1758, and it may have been written several days earlier than the conjectural date, perhaps as early as 5 Sept. Fauquier's answer is mentioned in *EJC* 6:109 under date of 11 Sept. 1758:

The Governor told the Council he had answer'd Mr. Denny's Letter, and excused himself from attending the said Treaty, on Account of the General Assembly meeting here the 14th of this Instant, and should be glad of their Opinion if any Step could be taken by him to promote that Service. Upon which it was the Opinion of the Council that Nothing could be done by his Honor at this Juncture, unless to represent to Mr. Denny the base Conduct of the Indians in marching thro' this Country, and request him to press in the strongest Terms the Indian Chiefs to use the most effectual Measures towards restraining their young Men from committing hereafter any Violencies on our Inhabitants, and to prevent as far as possible the fatal Consequences of their extravagant Behaviour.

From James Abercromby

London September 12th 1758

I have your favour of the 26th June,[1] & rejoice on your safe arrival after so agreeable a Voyage.

I hope you may find an Administration, and every other Circumstance of Life to your's & Mrs. Fauquier's best wishes.

I do not doubt of General Abercromby's disposition to serve your Province, so far as lies in his Power, and the Council have done well to lay their Claim before him.[2]

I shall repeat my Application for an Aid out of the Quitrents to the

Tobacco Revenue with the Alteration of the Deficiencys being now become greater, and the liklyhood of their becoming more and more so, during the War, & this I took Care to suggest to the Treasury in my Original Memorial on this head.³

Since my last Govr Dinwiddy & myself have had a long Conference, with the Secretary of the Treasury Mr. Martin, who has this matter before him, the chief purport of our Application to him was to get the Memorial refer'd to the Auditor General, because through this Channel, I shall be better able, to give it a favourable turn, from the Precedents I have with some difficulty met with by searching the Books in the Auditors Office, you may assure the Council that nothing shall be wanting on my part to procure Redress.

I am sorry that the Council have other Ideas of the Tendency of Mr Morriss's application for a temporary Monopoly of Salt, than what I, and every other Agent for the American Colonys, and the Trading Interest of this Kingdom conceived,⁴ could I have foreseen this, I had saved myself an immense trouble and some Expence, however it shall be a Caution to me for the future to act by particular instructions only and the rather since from what is insinuated by you that the Council do not seem inclined to give me Credit for Extraordinary trouble and Expence, and as little to be hoped for from the House of Burgesses.

The Lords for Trade being under their long adjournment,⁵ since the Merchants appeared before them, on their Memorial against the Paper Currency Law, their Lordships have hitherto come to no final Official Measures in this Case.

Public affairs abroad have for the present a tollerable good appearance, and should they continue so, I should not be surprised to see overtures of Peace from France, the Victory obtained by the King of Prussia over the Russians, was of the most obstinate kind therein was added Rage and Resentment to Valour on both sides.⁶ My Compliments to your Lady concludes me with thanks for the tender of your good offices in what concerns me, which shall on my part at all times be acknowledg'd by Sir &c.

Govr. Fauquier

Copy: Virginia State Library, James Abercromby Letter Book, pp. 104–6. In a clerk's hand.

1. Not traced.
2. See Fauquier to General Abercromby, 10 June 1758, n. 2.
3. Abercromby's renewed application was perhaps a representation presented about 23 July 1759 (T.1/389, ff. 107–11). His original memorial was presumably that of about 15 Mar. 1758, enclosed in his letter of that date to Fauquier.

4. There is no record of what the council thought about Governor Morris's petition.

5. The Board of Trade did not meet between 3 Aug. and 11 Oct., according to its journal.

6. On 25 Aug., Frederick the Great had attacked the Russians under William Fermor at Zorndorf in Brandenburg (now Sarbinowo in Poland). There is some question as to how complete Frederick's victory was, but the battle was the bloodiest of the war; the Prussians suffered 13,500 casualties and the Russians 42,000 (of whom 21,000 were killed).

To George Washington

Sir   Willmsburgh Sepr 16th 1758

I am obliged to you for the particular Account you have sent me of the State of our Affairs which I received by Jenkins on the 9th with Mr. Gists Letter (by which it appears he is not very sollicitous to make such a Return) and a Copy of your Correspondence with Coll. Bouquet: All which tend to corroborate the Opinion we had before entertain'd of your Zeal for the Service of this Colony. I have not returned Coll. Bouquet's Letter, as the Assembly which are now convened may perhaps call for it: but it shall be returned to you whenever you desire it.[1]

Since it is determined to go by Loyal hanning, I hope the Difficulties attending that Road are not so great as apprehended; that the Army may reach Fort du Quesne this year, otherwise I much fear whether the Ardor this Colony has shown to support the War will continue for another Year, the Flame being a little stifled by the inactivity of this Campaign. But one glorious stroke will reanimate us. My Interest here can yet be of no Consideration, yet I will use my Endeavours with the Assembly that our Troops may not be weaken'd for another year but I much doubt of my Success.

The Treasury is exhausted and I cannot yet say what the Assembly will do to replenish it. Arrears must undoubtedly be paid; and you may be assured the first Money that comes there shall be applyed to the Payment of the Army, that they may not have any Room for Discontent from that Quarter.

I have directed the Letters I have received from you and Coll. Byrd to be laid before the Assembly as you will see by my Speech which I send you herewith,[2] and must wait their pleasure in Relation to the Major of Brigade as I have it not in my power to issue such a Commission the Number of Officers being limited by the last Act of Assembly by which the second Regiment was raised. I shall always recommend it to them, to let you have every thing that is necessary for the Service.

18 September 1758 73

I have detained Jenkins till the House of Burgesses had taken the Affair of the Regiments into Consideration and voted their Subsistance,³ for all the Money before granted was exhausted. I hope your Men are not uneasy but it was impossible for me to provide for their pay before. Mr. Boyd may have £5000 when ever he pleases to come or send for it as I have wrote to him this Day.

We are impatient to have frequent News from your Quarter in the present Situation of Affairs. I am, Sir, with great Esteem Your Very Humble Servant.

Fran: Fauquier

Sepr. 29th / Coll. Washington

ALS: Library of Congress, George Washington Papers, ser. 4.

1. Bouquet's letter has not been identified. There is no indication that Washington had enclosed or forwarded to Fauquier any letter from Bouquet, and no such letter can be recognized among those which Fauquier laid before the burgesses on 19 and 20 Sept. See *JHB, 1758–1761*, pp. 5, 11, 12, 14, for references to correspondence referred to the House of Burgesses.

2. Fauquier's speech to the General Assembly on 15 Sept. is in *JHB, 1758–1761*, pp. 4–5. What he sent to Washington may have been either a manuscript copy of the speech or a printed copy of the speech with the addresses of the two houses of assembly (Evans 8277). Fauquier's speech did not in fact identify the authors of the correspondence, on a revisal of the militia law, which he said he was prepared to lay before the assembly; but on 19 Sept. Fauquier sent to the burgesses several letters from General Forbes, Colonel Washington, Colonel Byrd, and Colonel Mercer which were identified as those mentioned in his speech. See *JHB, 1758–1761*, pp. 11–12.

3. On 26 Sept. the burgesses resolved that a sum not to exceed £20,000 should be raised to provide arrears of pay due to the forces in the pay of the colony and their pay until 1 Dec. It was not until 10 Oct. that the burgesses passed "An Act for the defence of the Frontiers of this Colony, and for other purposes therein mentioned" (Hening, 7:171–79), which authorized the raising of the money; the council signified its concurrence on 11 Oct., and Fauquier assented to the act on 12 Oct.

From William Pitt

Sir, Whitehall 18th Septr 1758

The King having judged proper, that Major General Abercromby, should return to England; and His Majesty having been pleased to appoint Major General Amherst to be Commander in Chief of the King's Forces in North America, with the same Powers and Authorities;¹ I am commanded to signify to You His Majesty's Pleasure, that You do apply to, and Correspond with, Major General Amherst, on all matters relating to The King's Service, and that You do obey such Orders, as You shall receive from him, in the same manner, as You have been directed to do with regard to the several former Commanders in Chief in North America;[2] and You will, from Time to Time, give Major General Amherst all the Assistance and Lights in Your Power; in all Matters relative to the Command, with which the King has Honored him.

I am particularly to signify to You His Majesty's Pleasure, that in Case Major General Amherst, or the Commander in Chief of His Majesty's Forces, shall, at any Time, apply to You to lay an Embargo on all Ships within Your Province You do strictly Comply with the said Request, for so long a time as the Commander in Chief shall desire.[3] I am &ca.

W. Pitt.

Copy: C.O.5/213, pp. 157–58. Circular to governors in North America; annotations indicate it was sent "by Capt. Amherst [William, younger brother and aide to General Amherst] in a Sloop, & Duplicates at same time by New York Packet." Fauquier communicated this letter to the council on 19 Jan. 1759, when it had its first recorded meeting since that of 13 Dec. 1758. It is probably the letter laid before the House of Burgesses when it convened on 22 Feb. 1759 (*JHB, 1758–1761*, p. 56).

1. Abercromby apparently got notice of his recall in another letter from Pitt of 18 Sept. 1758. Maj. Gen. Jeffery Amherst (1717–1797) had distinguished himself as army commander at the siege and capture of Louisburg in June and July.

2. See *JHB, 1752–1758*, and *EJC*, vol. 6, passim under Edward Braddock, William Shirley, Loudoun, and Abercromby for notices of their appointments as commander in chief and their various requests or orders directed to Virginia. Most commonly the commanders ordered men and money, and occasionally artillery, provisions, and other supplies.

3. There was considerable precedent for an embargo of some description. In Mar. 1755 and Sept. 1756 Dinwiddie banned the export of foodstuffs from Virginia, in obedience to the king's command to keep provisions from the French. In Mar. 1757 Loudoun ordered a complete embargo on shipping. Pitt's letter of Dec. 1758, appointing Abercromby as commander in chief, authorized the imposition of a complete embargo whenever the commander in chief required it, and in Mar. 1758 Abercromby ordered an embargo on all ships in North America. See *EJC* 6:29, 83, 84, 587, 597–98.

To the Board of Trade

My Lords   Wmsburgh Sepr 23d 1758

I herewith send your Lordships the Duplicates of the Acts of last Sessions of Assembly, with the Journals of the Council and House of Burgesses, all of which I did my self the Honour to send by his Majesties Ship Ludlow Castle, Captn. Clarke.[1] With this pacquet your Lordships will also receive the Accounts of the Naval Officers, which are all the public Papers which have yet been delivered to me.[2] Mr. President Blair informs me, he had sent all Accounts of Quit-Rents and Tobacco Duties made up to the 25th April last with their Duplicates.³

In looking over the Papers left by the last Lieutenant Governor Mr. Dinwiddie, I cannot find your Lordships Letter of Directions in Relation to the pistole Fee, of which He suffered no Copy to be taken in this Colony. There are now as I am inform'd 1360 patents lying in the Office not taken up, by which his Majesties Revenue of Quit-Rents suffers above £1000 a Year.

Being extremely desirous to keep peace and Harmony in this Country (of which I have at present a most pleasing Prospect) and that his Majesties Revenue should not suffer under my Administration of Affairs here; I have made a Declaration in Council that I would be willing to acquiesce in every thing that should be thought reasonable to procure both these Advantages. This Affair has formerly raised a great Flame in this Country which is not yet quite subsided, and as I am endeavouring to quench it entirely, that the Assemblies may be the easier prevailed upon to give what is necessary in Support of his Majesties just Rights, I hope your Lordships on these Considerations will give Directions that I may be furnish'd with a Copy of the said Letter.⁴

By some Captures lately made by Captn. Legge in his Majesties Ship Chesterfield it appears plainly that a regular Trade is carryed on between Rhode Island, and the French West India Islands by means of Ships who carry a few prisoners as Cartel Ships, and under protection of a Flag of Truce supply the French with provisions.⁵ The Rhode Island Men knowing there were 60 french prisoners at Boston, sent four Ships from Providence to Boston at their own Expence, and put fifteen on board each Ship by which they skreen'd four Cargoes of provisions &ct. to port au Prince one of these fell into Captn. Legge's Hands.⁶ on Board a french prize he found a Letter containing this paragraph. "Nous sommes tous les Jours a la Veille de manquer, sans le Secours de nos Ennemis nous serons obligez de vivre comme vous nous l'annoncez avec ce que nous fournit la Colonie. La Condition est dure, et l'on n'y resisteroit pas; nous sçavons bien qu'il est impossible au Commerce de France de nous secourir, tout est abandonne et la Cour ne pense pas a nous."⁷

In another Letter taken on board the same Ship there are these paragraphs. "Il n'y a rien a faire en parlementaire nous allons cependant de faire en sorte de Tasté de ce Commerce sous la Protection de nos puissances. En peu nous contons envoyer le frere de notre Sieur Rousseau a Jamaique de quel Endroit Il vous ecrira par Londres s'il fait quelques Affaires."

"Vous ferez bien de ne nous faire aucun Envoye par Navires hollandois ny françois, une bonne affaire sous le pavillon Espagnol seroit bonne a faire, s'il reste encore neutre. Il n'y a pas d'apparences qu'il prenne Partie pour vous."[8]

One of these Ships which was a regular Cartel between Port au Prince and Jamaica is since brought in. the Captain is furnish'd with passports from both the English and French Governor He is loaded up to the Hatches and was taken by a privateer as soon as he was out of Port, and brought in here as lawful prize.[9]

The Council and Merchants have requested the Board of Admiralty thro' me to grant them some Vessel of Force to remain on this Station to protect their Trade in the Absence of the Men of War who come and go as Convoys. The putting a Stop if possible to this illicit Trade may perhaps be an additional Motive to their Lordships to grant their Request.

By the last Accounts I had from the Army designed to act against Fort du Quesne, I find they have determined not to go by the old Road of General Bradock, but to cut a new one from Rays Town over the Laurell Hills, and that the Advanced Guard was imagined to be at Loyal Hanning a post on a Creek to the westward of the Hills about 50 Miles from Fort du Quesne on the 2d of this Month; of which Date were my Letters. This Inactivity as it is here call'd, and the long Delay before they set forward, has raised a Doubt whether the Attack can be attempted this year which has so much soured some of the Members of the Assembly that they are unwilling to grant any more Money towards carrying on the Expedition; however I hope when the Time comes they will be brought to do what is ask'd of them; and for this purpose I am endeavouring to gain their Confidence by all Means in my Power. The Step I took in Regard to the Speaker, has done me much Service as it has given him and all his Friends a great Opinion of the Openness of my Conduct. I am if possible more and more convinced that it will always be impracticable to separate the Offices of Speaker and Treasurer during the Life of Mr. Robinson, perhaps even after his Decease. I gave your Lordships a full Account of my Proceedings in that Affair, which I hope you will not disapprove.

By the latter part of the Address of the House of Burgesses which I herewith transmit to your Lordships, you may observe the Temper of the House, and that paragraph was agreed on as a Medium between granting and refusing the whole.[10] But I am yet told, if I do nothing to create a Misunderstanding between us, I may obtain whatever I can in reason desire for next Summers Campaign, if another Campaign should be necessary. The Assembly which will not sit long now, are to meet early in the Spring for that purpose.

I must now humbly intreat your Lordships that you would excuse the

Liberty I take in sending my Speech and the Addresses of both Houses in print.[11] But Captn. Legges departure happening in the Time of the Assembly, and my deferring writing to the last, in Expectation of some Resolves the House of Burgesses might make of which I might inform your Lordships did not give me Time to have them transcribed.

I am afraid I have taken up too much of your Lordships Time in being too particular and minute and am with great Respect, My Lords, Your Lordships most obliged Obedient & devoted Servant.

Fran: Fauquier

The Lords Commissioners of Trade & Plantations.

ALS: C.O.5/1329, ff. 82-85. Endorsed as received 13 Nov. and read 12 Dec. 1758.

1. Fauquier had sent copies of the acts and journals with his letter of 28 June 1758. It does not appear that a duplicate set of these has survived.
2. The Board of Trade journal for 12 Dec. 1758 describes these only as "Naval Office lists from January to July, 1758," and it is impossible to identify them. They may have been the lists from the South Potomack district for 5 Jan.–5 Apr. and for 5 Apr.–5 July 1758 and a list from James River upper district for 5 Apr.–5 July 1758, all of which are in C.O.5/1447, ff. 85–86, 99.
3. Blair's letter to the board of 20 June enclosed only the account of the 2s. per hogshead revenue for 25 Oct. 1757–25 Apr. 1758 (C.O.5/1329, ff. 70–74). There is no indication that Blair sent any other accounts at this period. While the quitrent account for 1756 and the 2s. account for Apr.–Oct. 1757 are missing, they were certified by Dinwiddie on 5 and 11 Nov. 1757, and since he apparently did not send them to England he may have carried them home when he sailed in Jan. 1758.
4. At the board's instructions, John Pownall sent Fauquier copies of the board's letters to Dinwiddie of 3 July 1754 and 18 Apr. 1755 on the question of fees for patents. See Pownall's letter of 5 Jan. 1759 with the two enclosures.
5. Capt. Julian Legge's ship *Chesterfield* was a frigate of forty guns. A cartel ship (or ship of truce) was one commissioned in time of war to exchange the prisoners of two hostile powers or to carry proposals from one power to the other. On 24 Aug. 1758 Legge wrote from Virginia to John Clevland at the Admiralty to report that he had brought in two brigantines: a French one from Port au Prince bound for New York and loaded with sugar, molasses, and rum and an English one from Rhode Island bound for Port au Prince and heavily loaded with provisions and other necessaries. Legge pointed out that both ships were certainly engaged in illicit trade, although they sailed under flags of truce, and the French brigantine had six prisoners aboard. He added that the two vessels had been libeled in the admiralty court in Virginia and would doubtless be condemned. On 22 Nov., Legge, back in England, wrote to Clevland to report that the French brigantine, the *Union*, had been condemned as a capture "to the Ship," while the English brigantine, the *Prudent Hannah*, had been condemned as a seizure to the king, the governor, and himself; a copy of the proceedings against the *Prudent Hannah* is in the Rhode Island Historical Society, Obadiah Brown Papers. This letter comments on the iniquitous trade carried on from Rhode Island with the enemy under flags of truce and notes that the cargo of the *Union* was meant to be traded in Rhode Island or New York for provisions. Legge enclosed with his second letter the copies of two letters mentioned below, which he took on the *Union*. Legge's letters with the enclosures are in Adm.1/2047.
6. Legge's letter of 22 Nov. 1758 (Adm.1/2047) notes that the vessel he took (the

Prudent Hannah, presumably) informed him that three or four other vessels of her size were loading in Rhode Island with provisions for Hispaniola. Fauquier may have got the other information from Legge or from the proceedings of the admiralty court.

7. This excerpt is from a letter of 13 June 1758 from Pavayeau Rousseau & Co., at Port au Prince, to Messrs. Portier frères, at Nantes (Adm.1/2047). A couple of phrases in the French are not altogether clear but the meaning seems to be this: "Every day we are on the point of running out of something; without the help of our enemies we shall have to live (as you prophesy) on what the colony supplies us with. Those are harsh terms, and people would not put up with them. We know very well that French trade cannot help us, all is lost, and the Court does not give a thought to us."

8. These two excerpts are from a letter of 13 June 1758 from Pavayeau Rousseau & Co. to Mons. Charles Chancerel, at Nantes (Adm.1/2047). A free translation of the two paragraphs would be this:

"There is nothing to be done with cartel ships. However, we are going to handle things so as to try our hand at this business under the protection of our authorities. I mean to say we expect to send our Sieur Rousseau's brother to Jamaica. He will write to you from there by way of London, if he gets some business done."

"You will be well advised not to send us any shipment by Dutch or French ships. It would be good to do a nice bit of business under the Spanish flag, if Spain stays neutral. There is no sign that Spain is going to take your side." In Legge's copy, the last word of the second excerpt is *nous*, so the last words of the translation should be "our side."

9. This capture is probably the one mentioned by Legge in his letter of 22 Nov. 1758 (Adm.1/2047), when he wrote that after his seizures had been made, a privateer sent in another vessel, evidently sailing under a flag of truce, and that this capture had also been condemned.

10. The burgesses regretted that aggravated poverty prevented their supporting the common cause as generously as before, but they undertook to do anything in their power for the good of His Majesty and the colony. See the text of the address in *JHB, 1758–1761*, pp. 8–9.

11. Fauquier sent the text of his speech to the assembly, the addresses from the burgesses and the council, and his replies, printed by William Hunter (Evans 8277, Bristol B2003-4), now in C.O.5/1329, ff. 86–89. The text can be found in *JHB, 1758–1761*, pp. 4–5, 8–10, and *LJC* 3:1190–91. Fauquier interpreted art. 30 of Loudoun's instructions (C.O.5/1367, f. 104) as requiring manuscript copies of journals and proceedings of the assembly to be sent to the Board of Trade.

To John Clevland

Sir   Wmsburgh Sepr 23rd 1758

I some time since transmitted to you a Memorial to be laid before the Lords Commissioners of the Admiralty of which I now enclose to you a Duplicate.[1] I am, Sir, Your most Obedient Humble Servant.

                                                         Fran: Fauquier

John Cleveland Esqr.

ALS: Adm. 1/3818.

1. See Fauquier's letter of 25 Aug. 1758 to Clevland, with the letter of the same date from Fauquier to the Admiralty that it enclosed. Both copies of the letter to the Admiralty are now attached to Fauquier's letter of 25 Aug. to Clevland.

From George Washington

Honble. Sir [Camp at Raystown, 25 September 1758]

I think it incumbent upon me to give you the following account, altho' it is with very great concern I am furnished with the occasion.

The 12th instant Major Grant,[1] of the Highland-Battalion, with a chosen Detachment of 800 Men, marched from our advanced Post, at Loyal-Hannan, for Fort du Quesne, what to do there (unless to meet the fate he did) I can not certainly inform you: however, to get intelligence and annoy the Enemy, was the ostensible plan.[2] On the 13th in the night, they arrived near that place, formed upon the Hill in two columns, and sent a Party to the Fort to make discoveries, which they accomplished accordingly, and burned a Log-house not far from the walls without interruption: Stimulated by this success, the Major kept his post and disposition until day, then detached Major Lewis,[3] and part of his command 2 miles back to their Baggage-guard, and sent an Engineer with a covering party in full view of the fort, to take a plan of the works, at the same time causing the Revilé to beat in several different places.

The enemy hereupon sallied out, and an obstinate Engagement began, for the particulars of which I beg leave to refer your Honor to the enclosed letters and returns of the Regiment.[4] Major Lewis it is said met his fate in bravely advancing to sustain Maj. Grant. Our Officers and men have acquired very great applause for their gallant Behaviour during the action. I had the honor to be publickly complimented yesterday by the General on the occasion. The Havock that was made of them is a demonstrable Proof of their obstinate defence; having 6 officers killed, and a 7th wounded, out of 8.[5] Major Lewis, who chearfully went upon this Enterprize (when he found there was no dissuading Colonel Bouquet from the attempt) frequently there and afterwards upon the march, desired his friends to remember, that he had opposed the undertaking to the utmost. He is a great loss to the Regiment and is universally lamented. Captn. Bullett's behaviour is matter of great admiration:[6] and Capt. Walter Stewart, the other surviving officer, distinguished himself greatly while he was able to act—he was left in the Field, but made his escape afterwards.

What may be the consequence of this affair, I will not take upon me to decide; but this I may venture to declare, that our affairs in general appear with a greater gloom than ever; and I see no probability of opening the Road this Campaign: How then can we expect a favourable issue to the Expedition? I have used my best endeavours to supply my men with the necessaries they want: 70 Blankets I got from the General, upon the promise to return them again: I therefore hope your Honor will direct that number to be sent to Winchester for his use. I must also beg the favour of having blank-commissions sent to me—it will take near a dozen for the promotions and vacancies: I must fill up the vacancies with the volunteers I have, and some of the best Sergeants. I marched to this Camp the 21st instant, by order of the General. Having little else of moment to relate; I beg leave to assure your Honour that I am Your most obedient, & most humble Servant,

G:W.

Camp, at Raystown, the 25th Septembr 1758 / To The Honorable Govr. Fauquier

Copy: Library of Congress, George Washington Papers, 5:139–41.

1. James Grant (1720–1806), of the Seventy-seventh or Montgomery Highlanders, often called the Highland Regiment, was taken prisoner in the engagement that Washington describes.
2. See Freeman, 2:340–46, for a synthesis of accounts of the engagements. The reports of the affair sent to Forbes by Grant and Bouquet are in *Bouquet* 2:499–505, 513–22. The objects of the operation were to make a reconnaissance of Fort Duquesne and, if circumstances were favorable, to make a night attack on the Indians thought to be camped around the fort.
3. Maj. Andrew Lewis was in charge of the advanced companies of the First Virginia Regiment.
4. The letters have not been traced. The return is probably the list of killed, wounded, and missing for the First Virginia Regiment, still in the Washington Papers at the Library of Congress.
5. It was at first supposed that from the First Virginia Regiment, Maj. Andrew Lewis, Lt. James Baker, Lt. John Campbell, Ens. John Allen, Ens. Colby Chew, and Ens. Thomas Gist had all been killed, Capt. Walter Stewart had been wounded, and only Capt. Thomas Bullitt was free and unscathed. It soon transpired that Major Lewis was taken prisoner.
6. Captain Bullitt and his detachment of about fifty men who guarded the baggage, horses, and provisions had attacked the French with great vigor and suffered heavy losses.

From William Henry Lyttelton

[26 September 1758]

This letter has not been found, but Fauquier acknowledged it in his letter of 13 Oct. 1758 to Lyttelton. It was probably one of the letters that Fauquier communicated to the council on 12 Oct. 1758, mentioned in *EJC* 6:112. On that day Fauquier brought in some unidentified letters with the report that Cherokees of the Middle and Lower Towns were taking up the hatchet against Virginia to revenge the killing of some of their people, and he brought in also a letter of 26 Sept. 1758 from Lyttelton which is mentioned in *EJC* 6:112:

Also a Letter from Governor Lyttelton to the Head Men and Warriors dated the 26th of Septemr. pressing them to make up the Matter in an amicable Manner, and pointing out to them the fatal Consequencies of a Rupture.

Lyttelton's letter of 26 Sept. 1758 to the Cherokees must have been enclosed in this letter of the same date to Fauquier. The letter to the Cherokees is in the minutes of the conferences with the Cherokees that Lyttelton sent to Fauquier in his letter of 7 Dec. 1758. It is likely that the unidentified letters communicated to the council on 12 Oct. included some others (or part of others) to and from Lyttelton: a letter of 16 Sept. from James Beamer, a trader at Estatoe, and one of 18 Sept. from Ens. Lachlan McIntosh, commanding at Fort Prince George, both received by Lyttelton on 25 Sept.; they informed him that Indians lately arrived from Virginia had brought news of fresh attacks on Cherokees in Bedford County, with Beamer writing that thirty Cherokees had been killed in Virginia during the summer, and McIntosh reporting that forty Indians had already set off for Virginia and thirty more were to follow them within three days. These two letters have not been found, but Lyttelton included their salient points in his letter of 2 Oct. 1758 to the Board of Trade, in C.O.5/376, ff. 55–58, largely concerned with the relations of Virginia and the Cherokees. The unidentified letters probably included also a letter of 28 July to Lyttelton from Old Hop and the Upper Cherokee headmen (with a postscript asking that it be passed on to the governor of Virginia) and a letter of 29 July to Lyttelton from the Little Carpenter. These two conciliatory messages from the Cherokees were evoked by Lyttelton's instructions to the commanding officers at Fort Loudoun and Fort Prince George (sent out about 4 July when Lyttelton received Fauquier's letter of 16 June) to do what they could to placate the Cherokees. Copies of these two messages and of Lyttelton's message to the Middle and Lower Cherokees of 26 Sept. were enclosed in his letter of 2 Oct. to the Board of Trade cited above, and are in C.O.5/376, ff. 60–64.

From George Washington

Honble. Sir [Camp at Raystown, 28 September 1758]

I forgot to notice in my last, of the 25th instant, that a Flag of truce was sent to Fort du Quesne by Colo. Bouquet. It is now returned, and we learn with certainty (tho' few things have yet transpired) that Major Grant with two other Highland officers, and Major Lewis, with two officers of the Royal Americans, and one belonging to Pennsylvania, together with 2 Sergeants and 30 private men, were made prisoners in the late action, and sent immediately to Montreal.[1] From all the accounts I have yet been able to collect, it appears very clear, that this was either a very ill-concerted or very ill-executed plan: perhaps *both:* but it seems to be generally acknowledged, that Major Grant exceeded his orders in some particulars; and that no disposition was made for engaging.

The troops were divided, which caused the Front to give way, and put the whole into confusion, except the Virginians, commanded by Captn. Bullett, who were (in the hands of Providence!) a means of preventing *all* of our People from sharing one common fate.

This mistake, I fear, may be productive of bad consequences to the common Cause!

The promoters of opening a new road, either do believe (or would fain have it thought so) that there is time enough to accomplish our Plan this season: But others who judge freer from prejudice, are of a quite contrary opinion, as the Road is not yet opened half way, and not 20 days provision for the troops got the length of this place, which can not be attributed to a juster cause than the badness of the *road;* altho' many other reasons are assigned for it. We find that the frosts have already changed the face of nature, among these mountains. We know there is not more than a month left for Enterprize: we know also, that a number of Horses can not subsist after that time, on a Road stripped of its herbage, and very few there are who apprehend that our affairs can be brought to a favourable issue by that period, nor do I see how it is possible, if every thing else answered, that men half-naked can live in Tents much longer. I am Hon. Sir, Your most obedient, and most humble Servant.

G:W.

Camp, at Raystown, the 28th Sept. 1758 / To the Honorable, Governor Fauquier

Copy: Library of Congress, George Washington Papers, 5:141–43.

1. The seven officers are identified in a list sent (probably to Bouquet) by François-Marie Le Marchand, sieur de Ligneris (or Lignery), commandant of Fort Duquesne (*Bouquet* 2:534–35). One of the prisoners was in fact at Detroit with the Hurons, because Ligneris had not been able to retrieve him.

From Robert Winn

[ca. October 1758]

This letter has not been found. Fauquier communicated it to the council on 24 Oct. 1758, and it is mentioned in *EJC* 6:114:

The Governor communicated to the Board, and desired their Advice upon, a Letter he received this Morning from Captain Winn, signifying that some of Capt. Talbot's Company, who were of the Party that put the Cherokees to Flight, by which a large Booty of Goods and Horses were left behind, had opposed him in the Execution of the Orders he received from his Honor, to deposit the Goods in Mr. Mackey's Store at Warwick; and inclosing a Paper containing the Names of the principal Persons concerned—It was the Advice of the Council that his Honor would issue his Warrant to the Sheriff for apprehending the said Persons, so that they may be proceeded against according to Law; that he'd repeat his Orders to Capt. Winn, safely to conduct the Goods to Warwick, and to apply to the County Lieutenant for more Force, if he apprehends his Men, and Capt. Anderson with his Company will not be sufficient to protect him; and that he would be pleas'd also to write to Col. Calloway, the County-Lieutenant to be aiding and assisting to Capt. Winn in that Service by all Means in his Power.

Neither Captain Winn, who wrote the letter, nor any of the people mentioned in it has been identified, except Colonel Calloway, who was Col. William Callaway, county lieutenant of Bedford County. However, the writer was perhaps Capt. Robert Winn or Wynn, of the Bedford County militia, and Captain Talbot was perhaps Capt. Matthew Talbot, also of the Bedford militia (or possibly Charles or James, two other sons of Col. Matthew Talbot of Bedford County). Mr. Mackey sounds like a trader or merchant, and Warwick was presumably Warwick's Fort (also known as Hog's Fort, Byrd's Fort, and Fort Dinwiddie) on the Jackson River about 5 mi. from Warm Springs in what is now Bath County.

From John Forbes

[Camp at Rays Town, 1 October 1758]

This letter has not been found, but it was communicated to the council on 18 Oct. 1758 and is mentioned in *EJC* 6:113:

The Governor communicated to the Board a Letter from General Forbes dated Camp at Ray's Town Octor. 1st recommending that the Virginia Light Troop should be put upon the same Footing with that they raised and supported in Campaign 1755, inclosing a Copy of its Establishment, and hoping his Honor will have no Difficulty in getting his Assembly to defray all their necessary Charges, an Account whereof he has order'd Captain Stuart to transmit to him.

Captain Stuart was Capt. Robert Stewart.

From Charles Smith

[Fort Loudoun, ca. 2 October 1758]

This letter has not been found, but on 4 Oct. 1758 Fauquier sent to the House of Burgesses a letter from Smith, received on 3 Oct., which seems to have reported the explosion of a magazine at Fort Cumberland (see *JHB, 1758–1761,* p. 37); and in his letter of 7 Oct. 1758 to Washington, Fauquier refers to an account of the explosion evidently sent to him on 2 Oct. by Smith.

To William Henry Lyttelton

Sir   Wmsburgh Octr. 5th. 1758

    The united Societies of New-England & of Scotland for the propagation of Christian Knowledge[1] have thought proper to send Mr. Richardson to the upper Chirokee Nations to the Assistance of Mr. Martin,[2] and have furnish'd him with a set of Instructions for his Conduct, which have been approved of by my self in Council here. As his going down to Charles Town to wait on your Excellency would have been attended with great Loss of Time, and Expence to the Society They hope you will excuse that Omission, and have applyed to me for a Letter of Recommendation to the Commandants of the Forts in that Country; which out of a Desire of promoting so good a work I have complyed with, and hope your Excellency will not think I have made any Infringement of your Right thereby; as they only Contain my Wish that the Commandants would give him a Friendly Reception till your Pleasure is known therein.

    Admiral Boscawen tells me he answered your Dispatch which I forwarded,[3] by a Frigate to your self immediately. The Expence has been Sixty three pounds which is paid by Mr. Grymes his Majesties Receiver general,[4] and your Excellency may remit it to him here, or to his Office in London as will best suit your Conveniency. I think the Charge is high but the Messenger has been a great While out and was frequently forced to change his Manner of conveyance which increased the Expence. the Amount is of this Currency.[5]

    There have been some Skirmishes with the Cherokees in their passage from the Army thro' this Country. If these should provoke a Spirit of Revenge and you perceive any Mischief is brewing, Mr. Richardson will give you an impartial Account of the State of the Case. I am with the greatest Esteem Your Excellencys most Obedient Humble Servant

                                                   Fran: Fauquier

P.S. the Messenger who went to admiral Boscawen I find is going to Charles Town with some Express from the North, he may probably make some Demand on you as he is always encroaching, but the Above 63 pounds is designed as his full payment.

Governor Lyttelton.

ALS: William L. Clements Library, Lyttelton Papers.

1. These were the Company for Propagation of the Gospel in New England, seated in London and controlled by Anglicans, and the Society in Scotland for Propagating Christian Knowledge, seated in Edinburgh and controlled by Scotch Presbyterians, who were eager to win over the Indians to Christianity. The Society in Virginia for Managing the Missions and Schools among the Indians, largely at least a Presbyterian organization, undertook to select and supervise missionaries to the Indians.

2. The Reverend William Richardson, a Presbyterian, was employed by the Society in Virginia, who asked the council to approve and recommend him. On 4 Oct. the council advised Fauquier to provide Richardson with letters of recommendation to Lyttelton and the commanding officers of forts in the Cherokee towns; Richardson's instructions were read and approved (see *EJC* 6:110). Mr. Martin was the Reverend John Martin, a Presbyterian minister whom the society had employed as a missionary in 1757. For the activities of Martin and Richardson, see Samuel C. Williams, "An Account of the Presbyterian Mission to the Cherokees, 1757–1759," *THM*, 2d ser., 1 (1931): 125–38.

3. See Fauquier to William Prentis, 27 July 1758, on a payment to the express Thomas Withers, going to Admiral Boscawen, on behalf of South Carolina.

4. Philip Grymes was receiver general of Virginia.

5. That is, Virginia money.

From James Abercromby

Sir   London Oct 5th 1758

Since my letter of Septr. 12 nothing material has happend in the way of Office, and while Mr Martin of the Treasury, who has before him my several Memorials relative to the Quitrents giving an Aid of the Deficiencys of the Tobacco Duty, and for Reward to Messrs Byrd & Randolphs Services, while Mr Martin is in the Country all these Matters rest—in the mean time I have met with more Precedents in our favour from the Books in the Auditors Office, so that when these Memorials come referrd to the Auditor General I shall be able to form a very favourable Report to the Treasury in both Cases and [   ].

Hereupon let me observe that by thus Acting in a double capacity in the service of your Government I have the greater reason to expect their proper Encouragment, but as Mr President Blairs letter to me tells me,[1] that my chief hopes must rest on the Governors & Councils Assistance in obtaining for me a Warrant on the Quitrents for 200 per annum as Mr Blakiston heretofore Agent for Virginia had; this being the Case I must rely on your recommendation of this matter to the Council I have taken the liberty to point out to Mr Blair,[2] the manner of taking this Matter up in Council vizt by Representing the great increase of public Business, Acknowledging my Diligence and Zeal in the Public Service, and thereupon to recommend me to the Lords of the Treasury to Mr Secretary Pitt as Secretary of State for the Colonys, and to the Lords for Trade for the like Establishment of 200 per annum out of the Quitrents as Mr Blakiston had this being done, what may be further wanted will with my personal Interest, & Solicitation in which by Mr Pitts means I do not doubt of Success at the Treasury where the Stress of the Case lays, but as these are the three Channels of my Business, as Agent it must come recommended to all of them, In this and in no other way do I see any hopes of my making up for Contingencys that ought to be allowed and I do believe in every other Colony Agency are allowd for the Service beyond the Salary.

The news papers now sent, will inform you of the public situation of affairs Two Expeditions are preparing, their Destination not known, to Affrica, America, or Italy time will show,[3] General Abercromby takes his leave of America, and I can from very good Authority tell you, that he comes home in a situation entirely to the satisfaction of himself & his friends[4] my best Compliments to Mrs Fauquiere concludes me always very Sincerely Sir your most Obedient

Gov. Fauquiere

Copy: Virginia State Library, James Abercromby Letter Book, pp. 108–9. The brackets at the end of the first paragraph mark an apparent omission.

1. This must have been a letter of 24 June 1758 from Blair to Abercromby, not traced, to which Abercromby replied on 12 Sept. (Abercromby's letter book, pp. 106–7).

2. On 5 Oct. 1758 Abercromby wrote a letter to Blair in which he made the points about his remuneration that he here summarizes for Fauquier (Abercromby's letter book, pp. 110–11).

3. The newspapers have not been identified. One of the two expeditions that Abercromby mentions was probably a fresh attack on French possessions in West Africa: Commodore Augustus Keppel commanded an expedition which, after some delay, sailed on 11 Nov. 1758 from Cork and on 29 Dec. captured the fortified island of Gorée, a center of the slave trade off Dakar. The other expedition may have been the expedition against Quebec under Vice Adm. Charles Saunders and Maj. Gen. James Wolfe.

4. The writer would naturally have looked on General Abercromby's situation in the most favorable light, since the two men were friends, and not improbably kinsmen. Nevertheless, it is true that Major General Abercromby was promoted to the rank of lieutenant general on 31 Mar. 1759, and it would appear that the defeat at Ticonderoga was not a permanent disability for him.

To George Washington

Sir   Wmsburgh Octr 7th [1758]

I received your Dispatches containing the [dis]ag[ree]able Accounts of the Check we received before Fort du Quesn[e] as forwarded by Lieutt.

Smith from Fort Loudoun on [the] 2d instant and laid them immediately before the Hous[e] who are still debating, one Day resolving on one Sch[eme] the next on another in Relation to Military affairs but nothing is yet determined upon.[1]

Our Loss is great if we consider the brave Off[icers and] men who fell but if we think only of numbers [it is] inconsiderable, and can be of no great Consequ[ence] for by the Behaviour of your Men they show they a[re] not to be soon daunted. They have acted in the Ma[nner] that was expected from them, and in which I don't doubt they will continue to act, and so merit and meet the Applause of their Country.

I have order'd the Blankets up to Winchester to b[e] deliverd as soon as possible that you may repay the General those he furnish'd you with. And have sent up the blank Commissions you desired, and dont doub[t] but you will fill them up according to merit.

The same Messenger who brought yours brought also an [Accoun]t of the blowing up a Magazine at Fort-Cumberland [whi]ch surely was owing to Neglect somewhere; for I should think it highly improper that every Officer should have [fr]ee Admission into a Magazine, and suppose it is some [pa]rticular Officers Duty, whether Storekeeper or other[wi]se to go in; and fetch what is wanted from Magazines. [If] this is the Case at present I think Inquiry ought to [be m]ade where the Neglect lay, if it is not a Rule, I think [it oug]ht to be made one.[2]

[I am so]rry to give you any additional Trouble, but must [desire] you will give orders, that whoever is sent down to [me] with Expresses may be furnish'd with Money in ad[van]ce to proceed on his Journey, for want of which [D]avis a Soldier in your Regiment (I think) who brought [your] Dispatch to me came almost dead having lain [t]hree nights in the Woods almost without Sustenance. He having no Money, no House would receive him, or [s]upply him with common necessaries of Life. This can [be no] hardship on any Body as they are sure to have it [al]lowed and repaid.

I most sincerely wish you better and speedy Success being with great Esteem Your very Humble Servant

Fran: Fauquier

[P.S.] Davis applyed to Lieut. Smith [for M]oney and was refused at least his Desire was without Effect.[3]
[Col.] Washington.

ALS: Library of Congress, George Washington Papers, ser. 4. The letter has been damaged, with some loss of text, but the conjectural readings in brackets seem very likely.

1. The journal of the House of Burgesses does not support Fauquier's statement. The house sat on Sat. 30 Sept. 1758 as a committee of the whole to consider means of raising the £20,000 it had agreed to on 26 Sept.; it resolved to raise the money from a land and poll tax and ordered the preparation of a bill for the purpose. On Mon. 2 Oct. the bill had its first reading, and its second reading the following day. On Sat. 7 Oct. the house sat as a committee of the whole to consider the bill and ordered some unspecified amendments. The amended bill was agreed to on Mon. 9 Oct. and passed by the burgesses the same day; concurrence of the council was reported the next day, and Fauquier signed the bill on 12 Oct.

2. No enquiry into the accident has been traced. In an undated letter to Forbes, Sharpe wrote "Since my last I have had the Misfortune to lose Capt Spriggs & Mr Luckett my Adjutant by the blowing up of the lesser Magazine, the Fire it occasioned was soon got the better of & no Loss sustained except the Stores therein lodged" (*Md. Arch.*, 9:270). In the *Md. Gaz.* for 5 Oct. 1758 is an account of the accident which gives the date of the explosion as 27 Sept. and states that it took place when Captain Sprigg and Mr. Luckett were in the inward magazine searching for tent cloths to make better provision for the sick.

3. On 16 Nov. 1758 Charles Smith wrote from Fort Loudoun to answer Washington's letter of 30 Oct. which mentioned supplying expresses with money. Smith said he had always done that and added "I have convinced the Governer that what Davis told him was Entirely falce" (Hamilton, 3:127–28).

To George Washington

[Williamsburg, 7 October 1758]

This letter has not been found, but Washington acknowledged receipt of it in his letter of 30 Oct. 1758 to Fauquier. It was no doubt a letter enclosing the blank commissions referred to in Fauquier's surviving letter of 7 Oct. 1758 to Washington. On 25 Oct. Capt. Robert Stewart wrote to Washington from Rays Town, enclosing a letter from Fauquier just received from Winchester; Stewart remarked that the cover of the governor's letter had come to pieces, so that he could see it contained some commissions. Stewart's letter is in Hamilton, 3:123–24.

From John Forbes

[Camp at Rays Town, 9 October 1758]

This letter has not been found, but Fauquier communicated it to the council on 18 Oct. 1758, and it is mentioned in *EJC* 6:113–14:

Also a Letter dated the 9th Instant from the same Place, requesting his Honor's Advice in Case of Success against Fort Du Quesne, whether it ought to be preserved or destroy'd; and desiring to know what Part Virginia will act in supporting His Majesty's Rights to those Parts.

To William Henry Lyttelton

Sir   Wmsburgh Octr 13th 1758

Your Dispatch of the 26th ulto. forwarded by Governor Dobbs was brought to me yesterday. I immediately laid your Letter and all the papers before the Council, who together with my self are much obliged to you for your Information.[1]

As We do not in the least doubt your Assistance in the present unhappy situation of Affairs, it is necessary You should be informed of the true State of the Case, and the Cause of the Enmity now subsisting between our People and the Indians, with the Steps We propose to take to remove it, before more Blood is shed.

When the Indians went up to Winchester to join his Majesties Forces that were to be employed against Fort du Quesne, they were in general very quiet on their March tho We some times heard of Mischief done by some Indians but of what Nation we were ignorant. There were at Winchester once above 700 who all received their usual presents and all returned without doing us any Service. On their Return home loaded with their presents they were not contented with what they had got, but stole the Horses, Provisions, and whatever else they could lay their hands on, belonging to the poor Inhabitants settled near the Road they march'd. Some of our people submitted to all these Insults, and brought their Demands for the Losses they sustained, on the Country, who to encourage peace and Quietness regularly paid them, and these Demands began to amount to a Sum. Others of the Inhabitants had not so much Temper, and endeavoured to recover by Force what the Indians had taken by Force. And if the Indians were or thought themselves superior a Skirmish ensued, if inferior they fled, sometimes leaving their Baggage behind them.

The Indians on their March often practised this Devise, If they saw any arm'd Men able to oppose them they call'd themselves Cherokees and shook Hands as Brothers, if only Women, Children or an inferior Force were in View the same party would call themselves Shawnese, and immediately fall to plundering, killing and scalping. It is impossible to distinguish the Nations of Indians; and perhaps our Reward for Scalps may have done mischief therefore We have now repealed it.[2]

Human Nature cannot sit still and see their little all taken from them, by people purchased by presents to do what they returned without doing, neither perhaps is it politic to be quite so tame, for the Indians are too well convinced that in general the people are afraid of them, and commit many Outrages upon that Principle, as I apprehend.

You see Sir the Government has taken all possible Care to prevent these Inconveniences and restrain their People, by paying for the Goods stole by the Indians, by repealing the Scalping Law, by giving the most positive Orders to all Officers commanding parties of Militia, that they do not suffer their Men to molest Indians on their March and to take great Care they are not the Aggressors. All which Circumstances We hope you will take Care to have represented properly to the chiefs of the Cherokee Nation and to assure them, that what Mischief has been done, has not been by Direction, or Connivance of the Government, but from the resentment of the Sufferers by the Indians, who possibly may have some times transgressed beyond the Bounds set them: please likewise to assure them that We are willing and ready to make them all reasonable Satisfaction and Compensation, and that the last Booty they lost in a Skirmish is by my Orders deposited in a proper place to be return'd them if demanded and proved to be their property. But if nothing but Blood will satisfye them, they must take the Consequence, and they have had Opportunities of seeing our Strength, and the Forces the King of great Britain can march against them.

In order to do all in our Power to satisfye the Cherokee Nation, we propose sending a Messenger into the Country with Letters assuring them of our Intentions, and to invite some of their grave discreet Chiefs to Williamsburgh to settle these Disputes amicably. We propose also to send after the little Carpenter to discourse of this Matter with him and to perswade him to meet the other Chiefs if they can be prevailed upon to come to us.[3]

We beg the Favour of you to inform their Nation of our Friendly and peaceable Inclinations towards them, & of all our Intentions to give them all reasonable Satisfaction, and to assist us with your Influence over those Indians, and your Advice from Time to Time in what Manner it is best for us to proceed.[4] I am with the greatest Esteem, Sir, Your most Obedient Humble Servant

Fran: Fauquier

P.S. I also transmit to your Excellency the Minute of the Council for your further Information.

Governr. Lyttelton.

ALS: William L. Clements Library, Lyttelton Papers.

1. What Fauquier laid before the council was the letter to him from Lyttelton of 26 Sept. 1758, with a letter of the same date from Lyttelton to the Cherokees which is included in the minutes enclosed in Lyttelton's letter of 7 Dec. 1758 to Fauquier. See the note on Lyttelton's letter of 26 Sept. 1758 to Fauquier for speculation on the other papers laid before the council. The proceedings of the council of Virginia regarding

these communications are recorded in the journal for 12 Oct., a copy of which Fauquier enclosed for Lyttelton's information. It follows this letter.

2. The scalping law was "An Act for the more effectual preventing and repelling the hostile incursions of the Indians at enmity with the inhabitants of this colony" (Hening, 7:121–23), passed in the General Assembly of Apr. 1757, which authorized payment by the treasurer of the colony of bounties of £15 for every enemy Indian taken prisoner and £10 for every such Indian killed or destroyed, within the limits of Virginia, with an additional bounty of £30 for every Indian taken prisoner, killed, or destroyed, to be paid by the next succeeding session of the General Assembly. The law was repealed by "An Act for repealing an act, intituled, An Act for the more effectual preventing and repelling the hostile incursions of the Indians at enmity with the inhabitants of this colony" (Hening, 7:241), passed in the General Assembly of Sept. 1758.

The Shawnees were a warlike tribe of Algonquian stock, by this time congregated in the Ohio River Valley, and considered to be Virginia's nearest Indian neighbors to the northwest. They were hostile to the English colonists and frequently at war with the Virginians.

3. The messenger to the Cherokees was Richard Smith, at one time a trader from Virginia to the Overhill Cherokees and on several occasions a guide, agent, or interpreter with the Cherokees on behalf of South Carolina and Virginia. No letter to the Cherokees has been traced, but Smith's mission was obviously a success. On 19 Jan. 1759 Smith, the Little Carpenter, and fourteen other Cherokees were received by the governor and council, and they met again on 20 and 23 Jan. to exchange messages. See *EJC* 6:124–30 for the council record of the meetings.

4. On 14 Nov. 1758 the governor and council of South Carolina received a deputation of Cherokees sent to settle their dispute with the Virginians, and Lyttelton communicated to the Cherokees the points that Fauquier makes in this letter. Lyttelton sent a copy of the proceedings to the Board of Trade with his letter of 1 Dec. 1758 (C.O.5/376, ff. 65–70).

Enclosure: Council Journal

[12 October 1758]

At a Council held Octor. 12th 1758.
Present
The Governor

The Governor communicated some Letters advising him that several Parties of Indians belonging to the middle and lower Settlements of the Cherokee Nation had resolved upon taking up the Hatchet against Virginia to revenge the Loss of some of their People in the late Engagements here. Also a Letter from Govr. Lyttelton to the Head Men and Warriors dated the 26th of Septemr. pressing them to make up the Matter in an amicable Manner, and pointing out to them the fatal Consequences of a Rupture.

Upon which it was the Advice of the Council that his Honor would send for Richard Smith now at Winchester in the Service of this Government, and dispatch him as soon as possible with a Letter to the Chiefs of that Nation expressing our Concern for the unhappy Effects of the late Disturbances, assuring them that upon repeated Complaints received of Robberies and Murders committed on our Inhabitants, he had order'd out Parties of the Militia to their Protection with positive Commands to act upon the defensive only, and to avoid as far as possible doing any Injury to the Cherokees whom we esteem'd our Friends; that what has been done against them, was in Violation of those Commands, and ought to be imputed to the Rashness of a few disorderly Men, but by no means to be consider'd as any Act of the Government or regarded as a just Cause of War between the two Nations; that Endeavors have been used in vain to apprehend and punish the Offenders; promising them all possible Satisfaction if they will call back their Parties already gone out, and prevent the Effusion of more Blood; that the greatest Care will be taken to guard against any such Disorders for the Time to come, and that we are determin'd to do every Thing to recover and preserve a mutual good understanding and inviolable Friendship. His Honor was also advised to write to Govr. Lyttelton by Return of the Express thanking him for the Trouble he has already had in this Affair, to request he will still exert his Influence and Power to effect a Reconciliation, and to acquaint him what Steps we propose to persue towards that End.

Copy
N. Walthoe Cl. Con.[1]

Copy: William L. Clements Library, Lyttelton Papers. Enclosed in Fauquier's letter of 13 Oct. 1758 to Lyttelton.

1. Nathaniel Walthoe (ca. 1709–1770) was an emigrant from England who is said to have arrived in Virginia in 1740 or 1741, during Governor Gooch's absence from the colony. Walthoe was sworn in as clerk of the council on 21 Oct. 1743 and was appointed clerk of the General Assembly for the session of Sept. 1744. He held both posts until his death on 23 Aug. 1770.

To John Forbes

[19 October 1758]

This letter has not been found, but Forbes acknowledged receipt of it in his letter of 5 Nov. 1758 to Fauquier. Probably Fauquier's letter answered Forbes's letters of 1 and 9 Oct., in accordance with the council's advice given on 18 Oct., and printed in *EJC* 6:113–14. As to the letter of 1 Oct., "it was the Advice of the Council that his Honor would acquaint the General that his Letter of March last respecting the Troop of Light Horse, was refer'd to the Consideration of the Assembly then sitting, and that as the last Session was prorogued before the Receipt of this Letter, Nothing at present could be done in the Affair." And as to the letter of 9 Oct., "it was the Opinion of the Council, that the Question proposed by General Forbes in regard to Fort Du Quesne, was more proper to be answer'd by the Commander in Chief of His Majesty's Forces, than by his Honor; and it was their Advice he would inform the General that the Assembly has continued the Virginia Regiments to the 1st of Decemr.; and that it is not in his Power to promise what a future Assembly may be prevailed upon to do." Forbes's letter of March, referred to in the council's advice on his letter of 1 Oct., was probably one written from New York about 20 Mar. and sent to Governor Denny of Pennsylvania to be forwarded (cf. Forbes to Denny, [New York, 20 Mar. 1758], *Forbes*, pp. 58–59). That letter has not been found but is abstracted in *EJC* 6:85–86: it requested fifty men, mounted on serviceable horses, to form part of a troop of light horse. It was doubtless this letter which was laid before the burgesses on 5 Apr. and on the next day referred to the committee of the whole which was to consider a bill on defense, later enacted as "An Act for augmenting the forces in the pay of this Colony to two thousand men; and for other purposes therein mentioned." The house journal seems to suggest that the letter from Forbes and one from Abercromby had brought about some amendments in the bill, but the act has no mention of mounted troops. Cf. *JHB, 1756–1758*, pp. 501–2; Hening, 7:163–69.

From William Byrd

[Rays Town, 21 October 1758]

This letter has not been found, but Fauquier communicated it to the council on 1 Nov. 1758, and it is mentioned in *EJC* 6:116:

The Governor was pleased to communicate to the Board, a Letter from Col. Byrd dated Ray's Town Octor. 21st signifying they are at a Loss to know what is to be done with the Men after the 1st of Decemr.—that the last Division of the Army marches from thence with the General on the 23d and imagines they must sit down before Fort Du Quesne between the 20th and 30th of Novemr.—that he has laid out near £200 for under Waistcoats for his Men, the Weather being extremely cold, which he hopes the Assembly will allow.

This is doubtless the same letter that Fauquier mentioned in his speech and laid before the House of Burgesses on 9 Nov., when the assembly convened. See *JHB, 1758–1761*, pp. 49–50.

From John Forbes

[Rays Town Camp, 22 October 1758]

This letter has not been found, but Fauquier communicated it to the council on 4 Nov. 1758, and it is mentioned in *EJC* 6:117–18:

> The Governor communicated to the Board a Letter from General Forbes, dated Ray's Town Camp Octor. 22d signifying that the last Division was to march from thence the next Day—that whether they are successful or not, it is necessary to leave as large and extensive a Barrier as possible to cover the Dominion of Virginia—that the Number of King's Troops under his Command, does not exceed 1200 Men, the greatest Part of which he must send to the inhabited Parts of the Country to recruit, and fit themselves out for the ensuing Campaign—that he has writ to Mr. Denny to learn what Assistance he may receive from Pensylvania—that he has Nothing to expect from Maryland, being inform'd that they have abandon'd Fort-Cumberland and Frederick, the former of which, he thinks it will be necessary, for the Virginia Troops to garrison—subjoining a List of the Posts that are proposed to be kept up, with the Number of Men to each, leaving it to his Honor and the Assembly to judge of their Importance, and desiring to know how far they will contribute in Men and Expences for the supporting those Posts, and making the Soldiers Life comfortable in that severe Climate.

This is doubtless the same letter that was laid before the House of Burgesses on 9 Nov., when the assembly convened. See *JHB, 1758–1761*, p. 50.

Warrant for James Robert

George R. [Kensington, 27 October 1758]

Right Trusty and Right Welbeloved Cousin, We Greet you well. Whereas We have taken into Our Royal Consideration the Loyalty, Integrity & Ability of Our Trusty and Welbeloved James Robert Esqr.[1] We have thought fit hereby to authorize & require you forthwith to cause Letters Patent to be passed under Our Seal of Our Colony and Dominions of Virginia, constituting and appointing him the said James Robert Clerk of the Naval or Navy Office in the Upper District of James River in Our Colony aforesaid. To have, hold, exercise, and enjoy the same to him the said James Robert, by himself or his sufficient Deputy or Deputies during Our Pleasure, together with all and singular the Fees, Rights, Priveleges, Perquisites and Advantages to the said Office or Place belonging or appertaining, with a Proviso, that nothing in the said Letters Patent contained shall extend or be construed to extend to the Prejudice or Disadvantage of the Office of Our High Admiral of Great Britain, or of Our Admiralty of Our foreign Plantations for the time being or of any of the Rights, Priveleges, Jurisdictions, Powers and Authorities to the same in any wise appertaining. And for so doing this shall be your Warrant. And so We bid you farewell. Given at Our Court at Kensington the 27th day of October 1758 in the thirty second year of our Reign.

By His Majesty's Command
W. Pitt.

To Our Right Trusty and Right Wellbeloved Cousin John Earl of Loudoun, Our Capt. Genl. and Govr. in Chief of Our Colony & Dominion of Virginia in America: and in his Absence to Our Trusty and Wellbeloved Francis Fauquier Esqr. Our Lieutenant Govr. of Our said Colony; Or to the Commander in Chief of Our said Colony for the time being.

Copy: C.O.324/38, p. 504. The superscription is as given in another, undated copy of the warrant in C.O.324/51, pp. 129–30, because the dated copy above has for address a considerably abbreviated form.

1. Little is known about James Robert, except that he must have been and remained a resident of Great Britain. On 25 Oct. 1758 the Board of Trade agreed to write to Pitt, desiring that he would move the king to appoint James Robert naval officer of the upper district of James River in Virginia. Lewis Burwell, Jr., of Kingsmill (d. 1784) had been naval officer of the district since 14 Dec. 1743, and continued in the post, presumably as deputy to Robert. There is some information on Robert in the various files of loyalist papers in the Public Record Office. On 18 Mar. 1777 an order to the Treasury authorized the payment of £200 to James Robert, late naval officer of the Upper James district; in 1782 he was drawing an allowance of £100 per annum, but this was reduced to £30 in the next year on the grounds that he had held the office by proxy and had been paid £100 per annum (presumably by Burwell). See A.O.12/106, ff. 16–17; A.O.13/32; T.50/6–7.

The naval officer, or clerk of the navy office, was a civilian official whose principal occupation seems to have been the observance of the navigation acts, and especially the keeping of lists of vessels entering and departing from the district for which he was responsible, with prescribed information on the build and origin of the vessels, on their owners and masters, cargo, destination, and bonding. The trade instructions to the governor, and the attached forms, will demonstrate the kind of information required from the naval officers; see the commission of 10 Feb. 1758 to Fauquier, and n. 5. For many years these officers were appointed exclusively by the governor and council, but from about the middle of the eighteenth century a number of them were appointed by royal warrant, some of them Virginians and resident officials, but some of them British and absentee officials whose duties were performed by deputies.

Virginia was divided into six naval districts. The upper district of James River, to which Robert was appointed, consisted of the region above Lawnes Creek, which runs between Surry and Isle of Wight counties, and the port was Williamsburg. The lower district of James River comprised the region to the east of Lawnes Creek, and the port was Hampton. The port of the district of York River was Yorktown, and that of the district of Rappahannock River was Urbanna. The customshouse for the district of South Potomack was for many years (probably from about 1747, when Richard Lee was appointed naval officer, and perhaps earlier) at Lee Hall, until it was moved in 1773 to Hominy Hall; both places were estates on or near the Potomac River. The sixth district, on the Eastern Shore, was called the Port of Accomack; it is not quite clear whether the port was fixed at Accomack Court House.

From George Washington

Honble. Sir [Camp at Loyalhanna, 30 October 1758]

Colo. Byrd promised to apologize to you for my not writing by Jenkins; since which I have been honored with your second favour of the 7th instant,[1] both of which now lie before me for acknowledgment. My sudden march from Rays-town (the intent of which I presume you are already informed of) allowed me no time to furnish Mr. Boyd with proper estimates for drawing the Pay of our Regiment: and I was the less anxious on that head, as the officers equally with myself considered, that our affairs wou'd some how or other come to a conclusion before he could return and that it might be difficult and very unsafe for him to follow us. I am very much oblig'd to your Honor for the Commissions you were pleased to send. Be assured, Sir, the confidence which you have reposed in me, shall never be wilfully abused. I am not less oblig'd to your Honor for the favour of returning, so readily, the Blankets which I borrowed of the General. I am, however, sorry to inform you, that, upon reviewing the six companies of my Regiment at this place (which had been separated from me since my last) I found them deficient in the necessaries contained in the enclosed Return;[2] and, consequently, I am under an indispensable Duty of providing them (or more properly of endeavouring to do so; for I yet doubt very much the possibility of succeeding). Your Honor, therefore will not I hope be surprized, shou'd I draw on you for the amount, in case of success.

Govr. Sharpe, in Person, commanded a Garrison of Militia (from his Province) at Fort Cumberland, when the Magazine was blown up; and had, I believe his Store-Keeper included in the blast.[3] I have desired Mr. Smith to furnish any Express which he may have occasion to send your Honor, with money to bear their Expences. The want of three months, and the unavoidable expence that an officer is continually exposed to, while on Duty (rather than a doubt of repayment) was, I apprehend, the cause of Davis's distress. Mr. Smith might however, have borrowed money on such an extraordinary occasion.

My march to this Post, gave me an opportunity of forming a judgment of the Road; and I can truly say that it is undescribably bad: Had it not been for an accidental discovery of a new Passage, over the Laurel-hill, the Carriages must inevitably have stopped on the other side—this is a fact no body here takes upon him to deny!

The General and great part of the Troops, &c. being yet behind, and the weather growing very inclement, must, I apprehend, terminate our Expedition for this year, at this place. But as our Affairs are now drawing

November 1758 97

to a crisis, and a good or a bad conclusion of them will shortly ensue, I chuse to suspend my judgment, as well as a further account of the matter, to a future day; and conclude with that due deference and respect with which I am Your most obedient, and most humble Servant,

G:W.

Camp, at Loyalhannon, 30th October, 1758 / To Governor Fauquier.

Copy: Library of Congress, George Washington Papers, 5:147–49. Fauquier communicated this letter to the council on 13 Dec. 1758, and it is noted in *EJC* 6:121 only as enclosing a return of necessaries wanted by the First Virginia Regiment.

1. Only one letter of 7 Oct. 1758 from Fauquier to Washington has been found. Perhaps the blank commissions that Fauquier said, in his letter of 7 Oct., he had sent, were sent separately with a second letter dated 7 Oct.

2. The return is not present, but it must have been one dated Loyalhanna, 26 Oct. 1758, "A Return for Necessarys Wanting to Compleat the 1st Virginia Regt." (Library of Congress, George Washington Papers).

3. See Fauquier's letter of 7 Oct. 1758 to Washington, n. 2. Perhaps the storekeeper was Captain Spriggs.

From John Buchanan

[ca. November 1758]

This letter has not been found, but Fauquier acknowledged it in his reply of 14 Nov. 1758 to Buchanan. It apparently was concerned with the disposition of the Rangers in the frontier counties. Col. John Buchanan (d. 1769) was commissioned as lieutenant of Augusta County by Fauquier on 30 Sept. 1758; the commission is in the State Historical Society of Wisconsin, Draper Manuscripts 2 QQ 7.

From William Ramsay

[ca. November 1758]

This letter has not been found, but Fauquier communicated it to the council on 4 Nov. 1758, and it is abstracted in *EJC* 6:118:

The Governor also produced a Letter from Mr. Ramsay, signifying that ever since his Contract with the late Governor expired, he has continued to furnish the Militia in Garrison, Captain Rutherford's Company of Rangers, and the few Soldiers that are left in Frederick and Hampshire—that as he understands Part of the first Regiment or some Militia would be stationed there, he should be glad of his Honor's Instructions what Number of Men to provide for, and how long Provision may be made for them before 'tis too late—proposing to act as in his former Contract, with this Difference that he pay no Carriage that may be unforeseen, and have a further Allowance for Indians supported in Winchester, who can't be maintain'd for less than 10d. per Day.

Mr. Ramsay was William Ramsay, the commissary or contractor for supplying provisions to the Virginia troops. The terms of his contract, which ran till 1 Aug. 1758, are stated in *EJC* 6:67–68. The captain was Robert Rutherford.

From William Henry Lyttelton

[1 November 1758]

This letter has not been found, but Fauquier communicated it to the council on 13 Dec. 1758. It is mentioned in *EJC* 6:123. It appears that the abstract, which follows, refers only to this letter, and not to that of 28 Aug. also mentioned.

His Honor likewise communicated to the Board a Letter from Governor Lyttelton, dated August 28th and another dated Novemr. 1st inclosing the Answers of the upper and lower Cherokees to the Talks he sent them in Consequence of his Honor's Letter, and the Depositions concerning the Depredations in Virginia, and an Extract of a Letter from Ensign McIntosh, at Fort Prince-George, dated the 9th of Octor. by which he learns that he may soon expect a Deputation from the middle and lower Towns of the Cherokees, to consist of six of the most considerable Men; that when they arrive, he shall not fail to inform them of all those Matters, it is desired may be represented to them.

The answers of the Cherokees are assumed to have been their replies to Lyttelton's letter of 26 Sept., which is included in the journal enclosed in Lyttelton's letter of 7 Dec. 1758 to Fauquier. McIntosh's letter has not been traced. The Upper or Overhill Cherokee Towns lay along the lower reaches of the Little Tennessee River, and the Middle Cherokee Towns lay along the upper reaches of that river, to the southeast of the Overhill Towns. The Valley Towns were to the north of the Hiwassee River, and thus to the south of the Middle Towns. The Lower Towns were in the valleys of the Keowee and Tugaloo rivers, to the east of the Middle and Valley Towns. At this time the Valley Towns and the Overhill Towns were often not differentiated. Ens. Lachlan McIntosh (1725–1806) was in command at Fort Prince George, built in 1753 on the east side of the Keowee River, across the stream from Keowee, the principal Cherokee town of the region, and about 25 mi. south of the North Carolina line.

Proclamation

[ca. 3 November 1758]

On 2 Nov. 1758, it was ordered in council "That a Proclamation be issued immediately for apprehending William Ball of Lancaster County, who has been presented in the General Court by the Grand Jury for uttering Counterfiet Treasury Notes, knowing them to be forged, and that a Reward of £50 be offer'd therein to any Person who shall take, and conduct him to Williamsburg, so that he may be prosecuted according to Law." On the same page is noted an order for a new commission of the peace for Lancaster County, with William Ball to be left out of it. On 9 Nov. following, when the General Assembly met after prorogation, the House of Burgesses heard the information about Ball, who was a burgess for Lancaster County, and resolved that he should be expelled from the house and rendered incapable of ever sitting or voting in it. See *EJC* 6:116; *JHB, 1758–1761*, p. 50. No copy of the proclamation has been found, and the date is a conjecture. The man involved was William Ball of Millenbeck, St. Mary's White Chapel Parish, Lancaster County, a burgess for the county 1756–58 and one of its justices as early as 1749.

To John Forbes

[Williamsburg, ca. 4 November 1758]

This letter has not been found, but on 4 Nov. 1758 Fauquier read to the council a letter he had prepared to send by the return of the messenger to Forbes; see *EJC* 6:118. The letter was a reply to that of 22 Oct. 1758 from Forbes, presumably.

To George Washington

Sir   Wmsburgh Novr 4th 1758

By an Act of the last Assembly The Regiment under your Command was remanded back to Virginia to protect the Frontiers, and in that Case they were provided for; but if they were not permitted to return by the first of December Their pay from this Colony was to stop from that Day.[1] Some other saving schemes were obliged to be complyed with, for fear the whole should be given up.[2]

By a Letter I received from Coll. Byrd I find the Army will be in the Heat of Action, and the Fate of Fort du Quesne depending at that Time.[3] I have therefore summoned an Assembly to meet on Thursday the tenth instant in order to prolong the Time for both the Regiments to remain in the Field in Conjunction with the rest of his Majesties Forces. This is the only Step I could take to prevent the Ruin of the whole Expedition, and save the Colony from the Censure they would lie under as being the sole Cause of the Miscarriage of the whole; If the Fort should not be reduced by that Day.

I make no Doubt but that the Resolves of this Assembly will be favourable to our Wishes; as they have always proved themselves strenuous Asserters of his Majesties Rights. Whatever they are, you shall have them by Express as soon as they are known.

Mr. Turner[4] who brought me Letters from the Army carries five Thousand pounds up with him for the Payment of the Regiments. Whether this is sufficient I do not at all know, as I have had no Account either from Mr. Boyd, or Major Peachy[5] of what would be necessary: however it will serve to stop a present gap, and more shall be sent on the first Notice. But I desire you will give Orders to the paymasters to send down an Account of the Time to which the Forces are paid and what more will be wanting to compleat their pay to the first of December.

I long to see you returned Victorious, that I may have the pleasure of taking you by the Hand, and assuring you with what Truth and Regard I am, Sir, Your Very Humble Servant

Fran: Fauquier

P.S. As the Money of the new Emission that is signed is in too large Notes for the purpose of Payment of the Troops;[6] Captn. Turner will remain here till the Assembly meets, so I have sent this Letter by the Return of the last Messenger [who] came from the General.

F:F:

Coll. Washington

ALS: Library of Congress, George Washington Papers, ser. 4. The postscript is badly faded, and the word in brackets has been supplied.

1. The "Act . . . for . . . defence . . ." (Hening, 7:171–79) authorized expenditure of £15,000 for pay and subsistence of the First Virginia Regiment from 1 Dec. 1758 to 1 May 1759, during which time it was to serve in small parties or detachments of Rangers on the frontiers of Virginia. If the regiment was prevented by any authority from returning to Virginia after 1 Dec. 1758, or if after its return it was not used in the prescribed service, its pay and subsistence were to cease. On 11 Oct. the burgesses resolved to desire the governor to ask the commanding officer of the forces with which the regiment was serving to order it into the colony immediately after 1 Dec., because it was needed for the defense of the frontiers; on 12 Oct., in his closing address to the assembly, Fauquier assured the burgesses that he would take a proper opportunity to write to the commander in chief of His Majesty's forces in compliance with the address from the burgesses (*JHB, 1758–1761*, pp. 44, 45). Whether Fauquier did write to General Abercromby is uncertain. It is possible that he reminded General Forbes of the 1 Dec. deadline in a letter written 19 Oct., for Forbes wrote on 26 Nov. to Fauquier that he would send off the Virginia troops as soon as he could supply them with four days' provisions; the two letters have not been found, but the former is mentioned in Forbes's letter of 5 Nov. 1758, and the latter is abstracted in *EJC* 6:122.

2. These "other saving schemes" were probably the provisions of the act that elim-

inated chaplain, adjutant, quartermaster, and fort major from the First Regiment and allowed it only one colonel, who was not to have any allowances for his table expenses; and perhaps the clause of the act authorizing £4,000 for the maintenance of four companies of Rangers for frontier defense. On 12 Oct. the burgesses resolved to present an address to Fauquier stating the sense and desire of the house that no more than four companies of Rangers be stationed on the frontiers, the house not being willing to provide the pay of more than 400 men for that service; see *JHB, 1758–1761,* p. 44.

3. On 1 Nov. Fauquier communicated to the council the letter from Byrd of 21 Oct. 1758. As a consequence of the letter, the council advised that the assembly should be summoned to meet on Thursday 9, not 10, Nov. The letter has not been found, but it is abstracted in *EJC* 6:116.

4. Mr. Turner, or Captain Turner as the postscript styles him, has not been identified. He may have been George Turner, an Indian agent.

5. Alexander Boyd was paymaster of the First Virginia Regiment, and Maj. William Peachey was paymaster of the Second.

6. The act cited in n. 1 above gives the details of the emission. In summary, the emission of £56,625 was made in notes of £5, £3, £2, £1, 10s., 5s., 2s.6d., 1s.3d., and 1s. There were 126,750 notes to be signed, of which 120,000 were for £1 or less.

From John Forbes

Sir Loyal Hannon 5th Novemr 1758

I have the favour of yours of October the 19th,[1] and I am extreamly sorry that the Postoffices are so ill regulated on this Great Continent of North America, that one can never Depend on the certainty of a letter, unless it be sent by Express.

When I applyed to the Government of Virginia that part of the troops they were to raise for His Majestys Service in the protection of these Colonies might consist of a Body of light Horse whose services in the kind of war I must carry on is so vissibly and absolutely necessary was in consequence of what the Quarter Master General told me what the Colony of Virginia had done in Mr. Braddocks time without Reluctance or finding any difficulty in the cloathing and appointing them.[2]

I shall not here enter into any discussion about the Assembly's having complied with every thing that was demanded from them by Mr. Pitt's letter,[3] nor shall I medle with the Government's not being able to perform their promises in furnishing the Virginians with Arms, Tents, Blanketts &ca but I beg leave to observe that if the Colony were so good as readily to make up those defficiences in the Governments promise it never could have entered my thoughts that they would have made the smallest hesitation in mounting a few of their troops upon hackneys particularly being assured that those people mounted upon those Scrubs could be of Quadruple Service in this kind of War to any other Number of troops they could furnish me.

As to their Pay Sir and the difference you write me of fourpence per day in your letter these are things I never once thought off nor could I imagine that the Colony expected payment for any troops raised at the King's desire, or that of His Commanding Officer when the Service of them was so plainly evident and necessary and solely destined for the protection of those provinces.

But I take up your time about a triffle for what does this Great body of light horse consist off. why only betwixt 30 and 40 miserable scrubbs not one exceeding £7 price and the expences of their appointment you have already before you, and as to the four pence difference that you mention and desire me to pay in I beg to be excused from that Step as I know no promise of that kind I ever made nor should I think it very prudent in me to be defraying the pay of troops that His Majesty had Graciously condescended to ask from the Colony besides the seting a bad example to a neighbouring province who made no difficulty of mounting and equiping 100 of their soldiers upon the first requisition made by me and of paying the four pences extraordinary without any hesitation being sensible I did not impose upon them when I shewed them the Services I expected and have actually had from such a body of troops, I therefore hope that upon your representation of those things to the Assembly that they will see the Justness of my demands in the light I do and consequently provide for them accordingly.[4]

As to Fort Du Quesne the reasons you give for not giving your opinion in a publick capacity are extreamly Just, and those as a private Gentleman are intirely consonant with my own altho' God knows the difficultys I labour under, left intirely to myself to act as it shall seem most fitting to me in every particular relating to my Command in the Southern Provinces of America, Genll. Abercromby neither having instructions for me, nor as he is pleased to say any power over me. The Minister has never favoured me with any of His orders except those in the General Circular letter to the different provinces, of annoying the Enemy and protecting the frontiers.[5] The Army that I have the honour to Command composed of raw undisciplined troops, Officer and Soldier, newly raised and collected from all parts of the Globe, from the Highlands of Scotland, Germany &ca to South Carolina with this variety of minds gathered together of a sudden and supported with provisions thrô a desart of 200 Miles and by roads almost impracticable for Carriages makes the task that I am employed in not only extremely difficult in the execution but also extreamly precarious in the Success therefore you may very easily believe

5 November 1758

that I am willing to Grasp at every advice that can give me the smallest insight into the Situation of my own affairs.

I am now here with all the Army I can expect and all my Artillery ready to move to the Enemy directly but if abandoned by your troops and the Pennsylvanians by the first of December I do not know what a thousand new collected Highlanders [could do][6] in Garrisoning and protecting such a frontier, or how there would be a possibility of subsisting them during the winter.

I am extreamly sensible of your Goodness and your kind invitation to Williamsbourg as no mortal can stand more in need of Nursing and relaxation from thought than I do but I am so far embarked I must see the end of the Campaign. So hope you will think it necessary that I ought to have some troops along with me and consequently send your orders accordingly. I am, Sir, with great Esteem Your Most obedient humble Servant

J: F

Govr. Fauquier

Copy: Scottish Record Office, Dalhousie Muniments GD 45/2/80/2. Fauquier communicated this letter to the council on 13 Dec. 1758.

1. Fauquier's letter of 19 Oct. 1758 must have been one written in reply to the two letters from Forbes, written at Rays Town on 1 and 9 Oct.

2. Forbes evidently referred to the request in his letter of 20 Mar. 1758, for which see Fauquier's letter of 19 Oct. 1758 to Forbes. What the deputy quartermaster general, Sir John St. Clair, told Forbes is unknown, and there is no known record of exactly how Virginia's complement of mounted troops was raised. However, Braddock listed in the establishment agreed to by Dinwiddie one troop of horse rangers consisting of one captain, two subalterns, two sergeants, and thirty men; and a return of the troops at Will's Creek on 8 June 1755 includes among the Virginia troops Capt. Robert Stewart's troop of light horse with one captain, one lieutenant, one second lieutenant or cornet, two sergeants, and thirty-three men. Cf. Braddock to Robert Napier, Williamsburg, 17 Mar. 1755, and the troop return of 8 June 1755, in Pargellis, pp. 78, 88–89.

3. This was Pitt's circular letter of 30 Dec. 1757, urging the raising of men to serve under Forbes. See Fauquier's reply of 11 June 1758.

4. In the absence of Fauquier's letters it is impossible to follow Forbes's arguments in detail. Fauquier evidently had reminded Forbes of the lack of blankets, clothing, and tents (and perhaps other supplies) that Washington had to complain of. And Fauquier must have stated objections to the cost of mounting troopers and paying them fourpence a day more than foot soldiers got; see Fauquier's letter of 19 Nov. 1758 to Forbes.

5. Forbes confused two circular letters of 30 Dec. 1757 from Pitt to the northern governors and the southern governors on raising troops with Pitt's letter of the same date to General Abercromby issuing orders for the impending campaign: the latter included an order that Forbes was to be in command of whatever forces Abercromby left in the southern provinces and of any forces raised in those provinces, and that Forbes was to use them "on any such offensive Operations, as may be judged by Him

most expedient for annoying the Enemy, and most efficacious towards removing and repelling the Dangers that threaten the Frontiers of any of the Southern Colonies on the Continent of America" (*Pitt* 1:143–51).

6. Something, probably like the two words in brackets, was omitted from the copy.

From George Washington

Honble. Sir,   Camp-Loyal-hannon, the 5th November, 1758

Being unwilling to omit any opportunity that offers of writing to your Honor, I embrace the present, that serves the General. I have, however, very little to say, as I wrote fully on the 30th ultimo; and have received no letter from your Honor since the 7th of the same month. Our affairs, as I observed in my last, are drawing to a crisis. The General being arrived, and most of the artillery & troops, we expect to move on in a very few days, encountering every hardship, that an advanced season, want of clothes, and indeed (no great stock of Provisions) will expose us to. But it is no longer a time for pointing out difficulties, and I hope my next will run in a more agreeable strain. In the mean time I beg leave to assure your Honor that, with very great Respect, I am your most obedient, and most humble Servant,

G:W.

To the Honble. Govr. Fauquier

Copy: Library of Congress, George Washington Papers, 5:149–50.

To William Byrd

Sir   Wmsburgh Novr 12th 1758

I have now the pleasure to inform you that the Assembly which I summoned to meet on Thursday, broke up Yesterday after having pass'd an Act to impower me to keep the Regiments with the Kings Army till the first of January;[1] by which Time it is supposed the Fort will be taken or the Army retired from before it. I hope and believe there is no Doubt which of the two Events will take place. By the End of this Month or the beginning of next, I expect to be gratifyed with the agreeable News of its Surrender.

The Regiments under your Command can not by Law be compelled to stay with you, but what I before wrote to you, and what I have said of them in my Speech will, I flatter my self, induce them to stay till the End of December,[2] as their pay is provided for if they chuse it. But it must be their own Option. I am with great Esteem, Sir, Your Very Humble Servant

Fran: Fauquier

Coll. Byrd

ALS: State Historical Society of Wisconsin, Draper Manuscripts 4 ZZ 43. An accompanying fragment of a cover is addressed and franked in Fauquier's hand.

1. See *JHB, 1758–1761*, pp. 49–52, for the proceedings of the assembly 9–11 Nov. 1758, and Hening, 7:251–53, for "An Act to amend an act, intituled, An Act for the defence of the frontiers of this colony, and for other purposes therein mentioned."

2. Fauquier said, in his opening address, "I am very sensible that one of our Regiments cannot be continued beyond the first of December, without Breach of the public Faith, which I shall always deem too sacred to be touched; but I have great Reason to hope that Honor will supply the Place of Law, and that this Body of Virginians will be influenced by the first, to do that voluntarily, which the last cannot compel them to."

To John Buchanan

Sir　　　　　　　　　　　　　　　Williamsburgh Novr 14th 1758

I received your Letter by Serjt. Skillern[1] and am sorry you have been so ill. As for the Disposition of the Rangers, I cannot make alteration in the Plan agreed on here by the Burgesses, for the Frontier Counties, without causing great Confusion so all must conform to the Orders already issued, till the Return of the first Regiment, which will make an Alteration necessary, when I propose to disband every Man of the Militia.

Captn. Wade[2] has I fear brought himself into an ugly Scrape in relation to the Cherokees, therefore take Care what you do, and by no means offer to molest Cherokees who are innocently and lawfully hunting; for the Government will be very far from protecting you if they should be insulted and attacked. I am Your Humble Servant

Fran: Fauquier

Coll. Buchanan

ALS: State Historical Society of Wisconsin, Draper Manuscripts 2 QQ 11. Addressed on verso in a hand not Fauquier's and endorsed with the name of Sergeant Skillern, presumably the bearer.

1. This sergeant is not exactly identified, but (considering the uncommon name) perhaps was George Skillern of Augusta County. The letter that he carried from Buchanan to Fauquier, probably ca. Nov. 1758, has not been found, so what Buchanan had proposed about the disposition of the Rangers is unknown.

2. On 13 Dec., Capt. Robert Wade, of the Rangers, probably of Halifax County, appeared before the council to answer an accusation that he was concerned with the murder of some Cherokees, and the council decided that there was no foundation for a prosecution. The accusation may refer to the killing of four Indians in Augusta County in the preceding August by Wade and his Rangers; Wade described them as Shawnees and petitioned the House of Burgesses for payment of the bounty for their scalps. See *EJC* 6:91, 120, 124 and *JHB, 1758–1761*, pp. 31, 35.

From James Abercromby

Sir   London 17th Novr 1758

Since my last, notwithstanding the repeated and pressing applications made to the Treasury by Mr. Dinwiddie & myself, I have not been able hitherto to bring the Case of the Tobacco Revenue to a Hearing by the Lords of the Treasury, and from such Answers as we get from the Secretaries, it is hard to form any Judgment what may be the Event of our Sollicitation.

I now inclose for your Consideration Copy of a Letter I have lately received from General Abercromby relative to the Money granted by Parliament for the three Colonies:[1] from the fluctuating State of the Commanders in Chief of his Majesty's Forces, I am led to conclude that the most ready way to bring about a Distribution of this Money will be to submit the Matter to the Lords of the Treasury; if you are of this Opinion, it will be necessary to send me proper Instructions on this head, with proper Documents to establish your Right to a large Proportion of the Sum so granted by Parliament: from the Steps already taken by your Government with Genl. Abercromby,[2] your Instructions may be more pointed.

I shall only observe that as the Case may require a further Explanation by the House of Commons, the sooner my Instructions come, the better for your Service, and by the several Agents concerned concurring together in an Application to the Treasury for a Distribution,[3] the matter may be the sooner accommodated.

The Parcel of News Papers herewith sent will tell you the Publick Events, Altho' Peace has been for some Days the City Talk, I have no reason to believe it has any Foundation: for According to the present System, Peace must come from the American Continent, come what will of Other Continents, My best Wishes for yourself and Family concludes me always Sir yours &ca.

Govr. Fouquier.

19 November 1758   107

Copy: Virginia State Library, James Abercromby Letter Book, pp. 114–15. Fauquier communicated this letter to the council on 6 Apr. 1759; it is mentioned in *EJC* 6:678 simply as enclosing a letter from General Abercromby.

1. General Abercromby's letter has not been found. It was presumably written about two months before the date of this letter, and thus before General Abercromby had notice of his recall.
2. See Fauquier's letter of 10 June 1758 to General Abercromby.
3. The agent for South Carolina in the years 1757–60 was James Wright. The writer, James Abercromby, was, of course, the agent for Virginia, and apparently he acted as agent for North Carolina, at least in the business of this parliamentary grant, until the middle of 1759, even though (as he had informed the Board of Trade on 13 Apr.) his appointment as agent for North Carolina was terminated in Dec. 1757. When Abercromby referred to the several agents, he may have had in mind someone to be named by North Carolina as his successor.

To John Forbes

Sir   Wmsburgh Novr 19th 1758

I received the Favour of yours by Jenkins yesterday.[1] As you seem to approve of what I said as a private Man, in relation to the garrisoning Fort du Quesne; I am desirous of entering into such a Correspondence, and hope you will consider this whole Letter as wrote upon that Plan. I am the more inclined to this from a full Perswasion that it will be the most effectual Means of forwarding his Majesties Service; For I dare say as private Gentlemen We shall generally be of the same Opinion, both having the same Object in View; whereas if we write under our public Characters, We are both as I apprehend under some kind of Restraint. I am sure for my self I am obliged from Duty to express the Sentiments of this Colony, tho' they should not exactly tally with my Own.

I agree with you entirely that the Difference of Pay between the Horse and Foot Soldier is such a Trifle in the Numbers mounted as don't deserve to be at all dwelt upon. But then, there is a proper Time to endeavour to adjust these Trifles which often raises a ferment if not attended to.

This is not a proper Time on many Accounts. For this Colony having brought it self greatly in Debt, by doing all that was ask'd of them from home and having as yet received no fruits from this great Expence, had begun to reflect on the Situation of their Country, and try to save all Expences possible. Some young Members chose into the Assembly promised great Things to their Constituents, and set out on this principle; so that it was judged expedient by all sober minded Men not to mention many things, that the great One of keeping the Regiments in pay might not receive any Obstructions.

It is certain this Colony was promised to be discharged from all Expences but those of raising paying and cloathing the Regiments; It is as certain they have been a great deal of Money out of Pocket for such Necessaries as the Men wanted, which were to be paid from the Crown, and you know the Difficulty there is to get any such Accounts settled. The £50,000 given in Parliament the year before last for the Assistance of this and the contiguous Colonies lies still in the Treasury unappropriated, for want of the Report of the Commander in chief to ascertan the different proportions according to the different Services performed by the respective Colonies. These Delays have given some Disgust, and make the Gentlemen of the Colony cautious how they engage in any Expence which is not properly their own, and applicable to their own Colony only.

On these Considerations it is my Opinion, that all these Affairs had better be buried in Silence till the great Event is over, when Peoples Minds will have a more chearful Turn, and the present Gloom be dispersed. And at that Time I do not doubt but by your cooperating with me We may be able to adjust all Matters to the Satisfaction of all Parties. In Regard to this Colony putting a Garrison of 200 into Fort Cumberland as you desire; I can inform you of a Fact which possibly you may be ignorant of, but which I fear will defeat all such Schemes. This Colony did formerly garrison that Fort, but at a Conference with the Governors in Lord Loudouns Time, Governor Sharpe insisted on its being given up to Maryland, as it was scituated in that Colony not in this, and Governor Dinwiddie was obliged very much against the Grain of him self and this Colony to resign it. therefore I much fear it will be difficult to perswade them to meddle with it a second Time.[2]

However as it must be garrison'd, and if Maryland will not keep it, now they have taken it from us, and no other Method can be thought of, I will use my Endeavours to inculcate the Necessity of keeping it, tho' probably it will be without Success: but let the worst that can happen, I am already impower'd by the Assembly, to dispose of the first Regiment when it returns into Winter Quarters, as is most conducive to protect the Frontiers;[3] and I will, by that Power given me, keep as many Men as I conveniently can, near the south Side of Potowmack to be ready at hand if call'd upon. This is all I *can* do, and all that I can you may depend upon it I *will* do for his Majesties Service & the common Cause.

I can but say, I am a little surprized at the Commander in chief's having no Instructions what to do with important Posts when taken from the Enemy, and I truly feel for you in all your Difficulties.

I hope to receive an Answer from you wrote with the same Freedom as I have used towards you, and that you will be convinced there are public Reasons as well as my own private pleasure, why I should wish to see you here. being with great Regard, Sir, Your most Obedient Servant

Fran: Fauquier

P.S. I hope Captn. Turner reach'd the Army some Days before the first of December, as he left this Town on the 14th instant.

F: F:

Novr. 22d. / To Brigr. genl. Forbes.

ALS: Scottish Record Office, Dalhousie Muniments GD 45/2/80/3.

1. Fauquier evidently referred to Forbes's letter of 5 Nov. 1758, to which this letter clearly replies. In addition, Fauquier's fifth and sixth paragraphs in this letter answer points raised in the letter from Forbes to Fauquier of 22 Oct. 1758, which Fauquier must have received about 3 Nov. This letter of 22 Oct. from Forbes was laid before the burgesses on 9 Nov., along with Byrd's letter of 21 Oct. (for which see Fauquier to Washington of 4 Nov. 1758, especially n. 3), the immediate reason for this unforeseen session of the assembly.

2. In Mar. 1757, at Philadelphia, Lord Loudoun conferred with governors Dinwiddie of Virginia, Sharpe of Maryland, Denny of Pennsylvania, and Dobbs of North Carolina, to make plans for the defense of the southern colonies. Dinwiddie communicated the report of the conference to the council on 4 Apr. 1757 (see *EJC* 6:34–37); one decision of the conference was that 300 men raised by Maryland should be sent to garrison Fort Cumberland, where the garrison had been supplied in part by Maryland and in part by Virginia. Nothing has been found to substantiate Fauquier's picture of the attitudes of Sharpe, Dinwiddie, and Virginia towards this arrangement. A memorandum of 20 Mar. 1757 from Dinwiddie to Loudoun proposed that, of the 1,000 men to be raised by Virginia, 100 should be sent to Fort Cumberland, with 300 more to be sent there by Maryland (Huntington Library, Loudoun Papers, LO3111). The correspondence of Loudoun, Sharpe, and Dinwiddie suggests that the plan to send a Maryland garrison to Cumberland was Loudoun's, or that he was in favor of it; that Dinwiddie agreed to it without comment; and that Sharpe accepted it without objections, though he certainly knew that the Maryland assembly might persist in balking at the support of Fort Cumberland, as they had done before.

3. The act of assembly (Hening, 7:251–53) passed in the brief November session authorized the governor to continue both the regiments then in the pay of the colony, under their existing establishment and regulation, and to use them until 1 Jan. 1759 in such manner and on such service as he should judge best for His Majesty's interest and the safety of the colony, with the proviso that soldiers in the Second Regiment should not be obliged to continue in service later than 1 Dec. 1758.

To the Earl of Loudoun

My Lord Wmsburgh Novr 20th 1758

I wrote to your Lordship about three Months since,[1] to desire your Lordship would appoint some Agent here, with whom I might Account for the Moiety of the Salary and Emoluments of this Government agreably to his Majesty's Instructions.

I have since received the Honour of a Letter from your Lordship wrote before you could possibly have received my former Letter,[2] therefore am uncertain what Resolution your Lordship will come to in Relation to this Affair. As there is no Agreement subsisting I have kept a regular Account open of all the Monies I have received on Account of Government; which can be controuled by the Accounts of the Receiver General, the Naval Officers, the Secretarys Chief Clerk, and the Clerks of the County Courts.[3]

I have paid to Mr. President Blair £218.11.7 as the due Proportion of the Salary for 40 Days from the 25th of April to the 5th June the Day I was sworn in; so that there remains £781.8.5 between your Lordship and myself for the rest of the half Year, on Account of the Salary only.[4]

The President has taken his part of all the Emoluments as they have arisen from Time to Time; and as I apprehend has remitted to your Lordship your Right as by Agreement with Mr. Dinwiddie viz £180.19.2. If I was to remit to your Lordship now £634.0.10 to make that Sum £815 the half Years Amount as by Agreement now subsisting, it would be a great deal more than the half of what I have received as by my Books will plainly appear.[5]

As I shall always act with the greatest Candor to your Lordship I will frankly confess, that I am very far from supposing that my present Receipts are a sufficient Ground Work to make an Estimate upon; but on the other Hand by all the Intelligence I can get at, Mr. Dinwiddie paid too much which was owing to this cause Sir Wm. Gooch paid Lord Orkney £1300 when he came to England, Mr. Lee the then President, came to an Agreement with Sir Wm. to pay him £365 out of the Salary, which was to be continued if he could get Mr. Lee appointed Lieutenant Governor, or as long as he could keep the Government vacant. Upon the Appointment of Mr. Dinwiddie, Lord Albermarle took Advantage of this, and insisted on the Additional £365 which he said the Lieutenant Governor could well afford to pay, and if he would not accept of it on these Terms, the President would; upon which Mr. Dinwiddie immediately closed the Bargain.[6]

As the Country is advanced £1300 is certainly too little and £1630 your Lordships Terms certainly too much,[7] therefore if your Lordship pleases to come into an Agreement to take £1500 on the Exchange of London remitted every half Year by the first Ship that sails after the General Courts in April and October, the Times of Payment of the Salary, it shall be punctually complied with under any Penalty your Lordship shall desire. My Brother who will deliver this to your Lordship has full power from me to make any Agreement in my Name.[8] Perhaps my Lord the Amount may be upwards of £3000. I suppose it will, or I would not make such a Proposal, for I would not undertake to pay your Lordship the full Half, If I am to negotiate the Bills, and be saddled with any that shall come back protested, whereas the Instructions only demand that I should divide the whole as I receive it: And the Agency might possibly be as disadvantagious to your Lordship. So that this may be a mutual Conveniency and Advantage to both. I have taken up a great deal of your Lordships Time to make you perfect Master of the Affair, to prevent more time being waisted in Negotiations. Your Lordship will do herein as is most convenient to your self it being at present a Matter of the utmost Indifference to me whether I pay the Half to an Agent of your Lordship's here, or remit you £750 half Yearly to England. I will further add, that if I find the Income beyond my Expectations, or by any considerable Sum more than double I will make it up to 1500 Guineas but I don't propose it now being fully convinced that the Income will not bear it.

My Brother has £390.14.2½ in his hands to pay you as half of the remaining part of the half Years Salary or in part of the remittance by Agreement as your Lordship shall chuse.

I should have been extremely glad to have had the pleasure of meeting your Lordship either here or in England, and very glad your Lordship's Regard to Virginia has led you to recommend it to my Care to which I shall pay great Attention; and in Return give me leave to represent to your Lordship the ardent Desires of this Colony that you would be pleased to use your Endeavours that the £50,000 given by Parliament for the Benefit of this and the neighbouring Colonies, and now lodged in the Treasury, for the Report of the Commanding Officer in what Manner it ought to be proportion'd according to the Services done by each Colony: may be settled and adjusted. And they hope for your Lordships Interest and Favour in behalf of this Colony, which by the Share of the Burthen it has born they think has a Right to a great Share of that Sum. I am, My Lord, Your Lordship's most Obedient Humble Servant.

Fran: Fauquier

To the Earl of Loudoun.

LS: The Huntington Library, San Marino, Calif., HM, Loudoun Papers, LO 5965. Marked "Duplicate" and in a secretary's hand except for signature, address, and most of the complimentary close, which are in Fauquier's hand; presumed to be the copy which Fauquier mentioned in his letter of 13 July 1759 to Loudoun, q.v. Endorsed as received 12 Sept. 1759.

1. See Fauquier's letter of 10 Sept. 1758.
2. Loudoun's letter has not been found.
3. In addition to his salary of £2,000 a year, paid from the revenue of 2s. per hogshead on tobacco, the governor received a variable amount of money in fees. By act of assembly he received fees in Virginia money (current money or currency) of £1.15.0 for each license to keep a house of public entertainment (an ordinary) and of £1 for every marriage license. By custom, usage, or prescription he got fees in sterling money for each ship entered in the naval offices, £1.10.0 for each ship of 100 tons or over and £1 for each ship of under 100 tons; a fee of £1 currency for each testimonial issued from the secretary's office; a pistole for each patent for land he signed; and a pistole for swearing a person to the register of every vessel built or bought in the colony. See Fauquier's statements of fees paid to the governor, enclosed in his letter of 23 Nov. 1764 to the Board of Trade. Another statement enclosed in that letter, from the admiralty of Virginia, has Fauquier's note that he got a fee of £1.1.6 currency for signing a register and freedom, which appears to be another way of stating the fee of one pistole for a ship's register mentioned above. The salary and fees were divided equally between the governor in chief and the lieutenant governor or acting governor. The receiver general's accounts recorded the salary payments, the naval officers' accounts stated the fees for entering vessels, the secretary's chief clerk kept records of fees for testimonials, land patents, and ships' registers, and the clerks of the county courts kept records of fees for ordinary and marriage licenses.
4. On 6 Nov. Fauquier had signed a warrant for the £1,000 due to the governor as half a year's salary, for the period 25 Apr. to 25 Oct. Blair was bound to remit to Loudoun £109.5.9½, or a half of the salary for forty days, just as Fauquier was bound to give Loudoun one half of the remainder of £781.8.5.
5. Blair's remittance was effected by a bill of exchange, dated 10 Nov., drawn by Governor Fauquier on his brother William Fauquier, and payable to John Blair, who endorsed the bill as payable to Lord Loudoun. The actual bill is in the Huntington Library, Loudoun Papers, LO 5962. The amount of £180.19.2 probably represents a remittance of income (salary and fees) for forty days, at the rate of £1,665 a year, which was what was due to the governor in chief according to the agreement between Loudoun and Dinwiddie. Fauquier confused that agreement with one proposed by Loudoun and dealt with later in this letter.
6. William Gooch (1681–1751) was lieutenant governor of Virginia 1727–49, and acted in place of George Hamilton (1666–1737), earl of Orkney, governor of Virginia 1710–37, and in place of William Anne Keppel (1702–1754), earl of Albemarle, governor of Virginia 1737–54. Thomas Lee (1693–1750), president of the council, was acting governor 1749–50. The agreement between Dinwiddie and Albemarle was that Albemarle should have £1,665 sterling a year as his share of the salary and fees paid to the governor of Virginia. Dinwiddie offered to make the same arrangement with Loudoun, and Loudoun accepted the offer. See *Dinwiddie* 2:534–35, and the Huntington Library, Loudoun Papers, LO 2652.
7. The sum of £1,300 as half of the governor's income is no doubt that mentioned in the preceding paragraph as what Gooch paid Orkney. The sum of £1,630 was evidently proposed by Loudoun as a half share in his letter to Fauquier mentioned in the second paragraph of this letter.
8. William Fauquier (ca. 1708–1788) was associated with his elder brother Francis in a number of ways. William was elected a member of the Royal Society in 1746, and became a governor of the Foundling Hospital and a member of its general managing committee in the same year. He was made a director of the South Sea Company in 1757. William Fauquier was apparently a businessman of some kind and in 1758 he was appointed secretary to the comptrollers of army accounts. He appears to have acted as a business agent for his brother Francis on many occasions.

To George Washington

Sir   Wmsburgh Novr 22d 1758

Jenkins brought me yours of the 30th Octr. and 5th instant. I hope this will find you full of Joy, and all Difficulties removed that those represented you to be involved in. I hope Captn. Turner who left this Place on Tuesday the 14th, with the provision the Assembly made for impowering me to keep the Regiments a Month longer abroad, and £5000 for Pay of the Forces has reach'd the Army some Days before the first of December, that the Commander in chief, you, and the rest of the Forces might be fully apprized of the Determination of the Assembly before it was too late. I have nothing particular to add but my most hearty good wishes for your Success. being with great Regard, Sir, your Very Humble Servant

Fran: Fauquier

To Coll. Washington.

ALS: Library of Congress, George Washington Papers, ser. 4.

From William Denny

[Philadelphia, 22 November 1758]

This letter has not been found, but it is mentioned in *EJC* 6:123, as "inclosing the Minutes of the late Conferences at Easton," which must have been the printed minutes delivered to the speaker of the Pennsylvania assembly on 16 Nov. The proceedings are in *P.C. Pa.* 8:174–223, and the printed version sent to Fauquier is *Minutes of Conferences, Held at Easton, in October, 1758* . . . , Evans 8156. The conference opened on 7 Oct. 1758 and was concluded on 26 Oct. Pennsylvania was represented by Lt. Gov. William Denny and various members of the council and House of Representatives of Pennsylvania; New Jersey was represented by Gov. Francis Bernard and some commissioners for Indian affairs in New Jersey; also present were George Croghan, Sir William Johnson's deputy, interpreters, and private persons, principally Quakers. The Indians were representatives of the Six Nations and other tribes, notably the Delawares. Denny reported the results as a general peace, a promise by the Indians to return all captives, and an agreement by the Indians to try to win over the Indians settled on the Ohio from the French interest and bring them back into friendship with the English.

From John Forbes

[Fort Duquesne, now Pittsburgh, 26 November 1758]

This letter has not been found, but Fauquier communicated it to the council on 13 Dec. 1758, and it is abstracted in *EJC* 6:122:

A Letter from General Forbes, dated Fort Du Quesne, now Pittsburgh, the 26th of Novemr. signifying the signal Success of His Majesty's Troops over all his Enemies on the Ohio, by having obliged them to burn and abandon their Fort Du Quesne, which they effectuated on the 24th of that Month, and of which he took Possession with his Army the next Day; the Enemy having made their Escape down the River, Part in Boats, and Part by Land, to their Forts and Settlements on the Missisippi, being abandon'd, or at least not seconded by their Friends the Indians, whom he had previously engaged to act a neutral Part, and who now seem all willing and ready to embrace His Majesty's most gracious Protection—that he shall send off the Virginia Troops as soon as he can give them four Days Provisions, to set them on their March, and take Care that they want for Nothing till they come to our Frontiers—hoping the Colony of Virginia will contribute, with other adjoining Provinces to enable him to fix a proper Fort, and maintain a suitable Garrison for the Defence of the Country, to establish an equitable and just Traffick with the Indians, and to allow them proper hunting Boundaries—giving an Account of the infamous Behaviour of the Little Carpenter, who had deserted with nine or ten Followers; that he had order'd an Express to Ray's Town to disarm him and his Companions—that the rest of his Nation leave him the next Day, all well satisfied—that he shall be obliged to keep about Two Hundred of Col. Washington's Battalion, as a Part of the Troops necessary there this Winter—that he shall leave that Place in four or five Days after settling with the Head People of the Indians—adding a Postscript proposing that the Colony should build a Blockhouse and Saw-Mill upon Redstone Creek.

Presumably Forbes had in mind a site at or near the point where Redstone Creek empties into the Monongahela River, about 30 mi. southeast of Pittsburgh and about 60 mi. northwest of Cumberland in Maryland. There had been a post called Redstone Old Fort there or nearby, and in 1759 Col. James Burd of Pennsylvania erected Fort Burd there to defend the route from Fort Pitt to Fort Cumberland.

From William Byrd

[Fort Duquesne, 28 November 1758]

This letter has not been found, but Fauquier communicated it to the council on 13 Dec. 1758, and it is noted in *EJC* 6:122 as giving information of the success of His Majesty's troops against Fort Duquesne.

From George Washington

Honble. Sir [Camp at Fort Duquesne, 28 November 1758]

I have the pleasure to inform you, that Fort du Quesne, or the ground rather on which it stood, was possessed by His Majesty's troops on the 25th instant. The Enemy, after letting us get within a days march of the place, burned the fort, and ran away (by the light of it) at night, going down the Ohio by water, to the number of about 500 men, from our best information. The possession of this fort has been matter of great surprize to the whole Army, and we can not attribute it to more probable causes than those of weakness, want of Provisions, and desertion of their Indians: of these circumstances we were luckily informed, by three Prisoners who providentially fell into our hands at Loyal-Hannon, at a time when we despaired of proceeding; and a Council of War had determined that it was not advisable to advance beyond the place above-mentioned, this season: But the information above caused us to march on without Tents or Baggage, with a light train of artillery only; with which we have happily succeeded. It would be tedious, and I think unnecessary to relate every trivial circumstance that has happened since my last. To do this, if needful, shall be the employment of a leisure hour, when I have the pleasure to pay my respects to your Honor.

The General purposes to wait here a few days to settle matters with the Indians, and then all the Troops (except a sufficient Garrison which will I suppose be left here to secure the possession) will march to their respective Governments. I therefore give your honor this early notice of it, that your directions relative to those of Virginia, may meet me timely on the Road. I can not help premising in this place, the hardships the Troops have undergone and the naked condition they now are in; in order that you may judge if it is not necessary that they shou'd have some little recess from fatigue, and time to provide themselves with necessaries; for at present they are destitute of every comfort of life.

If I do not get your Orders to the contrary, I shall march the troops under my command directly to Winchester; from whence they may be disposed of, as you shall afterwards direct.

Genl. Forbes desires me to inform you, that he is prevented, by a multiplicity of different affairs, from writing to you so fully now,[1] as he would otherwise have done, and from enclosing you a copy of a letter which he has written to the commanding officer on the communication from hence to Winchester, &c. relative to the little Carpenters conduct (a Chief of the Cherokees).[2] But that, the purport of that letter was to desire, they would deprive him of the use of arms and ammunition; and escort him from one place to another, to prevent his doing any mischief to the Inhabitants, allowing him Provisions only. His behaviour, the General thought, rendered this measure necessary.

This fortunate, and indeed unexpected success of our Arms, will be attended with happy effects. The Delawares are suing for Peace; and I doubt not that other Tribes on the Ohio will follow their Example. A Trade free, open and upon equitable terms, is what they seem much to stickle for; and I do not know so effectual a way of rivetting them to our interest, as sending out Goods immediately to this place for that purpose: It will at the same time be a means of supplying the Garrison with such necessaries as may be wanted: and I think, those Colonies which are as greatly interested in the support of this place as Virginia is, should neglect no means in their power to establish & support a strong Garrison here. Our Business (wanting this) will be but half finished: while, on the other hand, we obtain a firm and lasting Peace, if this end is once accomplished.

Genl. Forbes is very assiduous in getting these matters settled upon a solid basis; and has great merit (which I hope will be rewarded) for the happy issue he has brought our Affairs to, infirm and worne down as he is.[3] At present I have nothing further to add, but the strongest assurances of my being Your Honors Most obedient, and most humble Servant

G:W.

Camp, at Ft. d'Quesne, the 28th November, 1758 / To Governor Fauquier.

Copy: Library of Congress, George Washington Papers, 5:159–62. Fauquier communicated the letter to the council on 13 Dec. 1758, and it is briefly mentioned in *EJC* 6:122.

1. Forbes had written at length to Fauquier from Fort Duquesne on 26 Nov. 1758 to announce the capture of the fort, as Washington and Byrd were to do on 28 Nov. The letters from Forbes and Byrd have disappeared, but both were communicated to the council on 13 Dec. and are mentioned in *EJC* 6:122.

2. Washington must have been referring to a letter of 19 Nov. 1758 from Forbes to Col. James Burd of the Pennsylvania troops, in command at Fort Ligonier or Loyalhanna, ordering measures to disarm the Little Carpenter and his fellow Cherokees and to take away their horses. This letter, somewhat damaged, is in *Forbes*, pp. 256–58.

3. Forbes had been for some time in bad health, and about 27 Nov. he suffered an acute attack of illness. He died in Philadelphia on 11 Mar. 1759.

From George Washington

Honble. Sir   [Loyalhanna, 2 December 1758]

The enclosed was wrote with intention to go by an Express of the Generals but his indisposition prevented that Express from setting out for three days afterwards;[1] and then, the General thought that my waiting upon your honor would be more elligible; as I could represent the situation of our Affairs in this Quarter more fully, than could well be done by letter.

This I accordingly attempted; but upon trial found it impracticable to proceed with despatch for want of Horses (now having near 200 miles to march before I can get a supply) those I at present have, being entirely knocked up. I shall notwithstanding endeavour to comply with the Generals request as I can not possibly be down till towards the 1st of next month (and the Bearer may much sooner).

The General has in his letters told you what Garrison he proposed to leave at Fort du Quesne:[2] but the want of Provisions rendered it impossible to leave more than 200 men in all there: These, without peculiar exertion, must, I fear, abandon the place, or perish. To prevent as far as possible either of these events happening, I have, by this conveyance, wrote a circular Letter to the back inhabitants of Virginia;[3] setting forth the great advantages of keeping that place, the improbability of doing it without their immediate assistance, that they may travel safely out while we hold that Post, and will be allowed good prices for such species of Provisions as they shall carry. Unless the most effectual measures are taken early in the Spring to reinforce the Garrison at Fort du Quesne, the place will inevitably be lost; and then our Frontiers will fall into the same distressed condition that they have been in for sometime past. For, I can very confidently assert, that we never can secure them properly, if we lose our footing on the Ohio: as we consequently lose the interest of the Indians. I therefore think that every necessary preparation should be making: not a moment should be lost in taking the most speedy and efficacious steps, in securing the infinite advantages which may be derived from our regaining possession of that important country.

That the preparative steps should immediately be taken for securing the communication from Virginia, by constructing a Post at Red-stone-creek,[4] which would greatly facilitate the supplying our Troops on the Ohio, where a formidable Garrison should be sent as soon as the season will admit of it. That a Trade with the Indians should be upon such terms, and transacted by men of such Principles as would at the same time turn out to the reciprocal advantage of the Colony and the Indians;

and which would effectually remove those bad impressions that the Indians received from the conduct of a set of rascally Fellows divested of all faith and honor: and give us such an early opportunity of establishing an Interest with them as would be productive of the most beneficial consequences, by getting a large share of the Fur-trade, not only of the Ohio indians, but, in time, of the numerous nations possessing the backs countries westward of it: and to prevent this advantageous commerce from suffering in its infancy by the sinister views of designing, selfish men; of the different Provinces, I humbly conceive it absolutely necessary, that Commissioners from each of the colonies be appointed, to regulate the mode of that Trade, and fix it on such a basis that, all the attempts of one Colony undermining another, and thereby weakening and diminishing the general system, might be frustrated: To effect which the General would (I fancy) chearfully give his aid.

Altho' none can entertain a higher Sense of the greate importance of maintaining a Post upon the Ohio than myself; yet under the unhappy circumstances that my Regiment is, I would by no means have agreed to leave any part of it there, had not the General given an express order for it. I endeavoured to shew that the Kings Troops *ought* to garrison it; but he told me, as he had no instructions from the Ministry relative thereto, he could not order it, and our men that are left there, are in such a miserable situation, having hardly rags to cover their nakedness, exposed to the inclemency of the weather in this rigorous season: that, unless provision is made by the country for supplying immediately, they must inevitably perish! And, if the First Virginia Regiment is to be kept up any longer, or any services are expected therefrom, they should forthwith be clothed; as they are, by their present shameful nakedness, the advanced season, and the inconceivable fatigues of an uncommonly long and laborious campaign, rendered totally incapable of any kind of Service: and sickness, death and desertion must, if not speedily supplied, greatly reduce its numbers; and, to replace them with equally good men will, perhaps, be found impossible.[5]

Colo. Byrd begs that the money for which he wrote may be sent by Express to Winchester;[6] as detaining his Regiment there, will encrease that demand, & add to the general Expence. With the greatest Respect I am, Hon Sir, &c.

G: W.

Loyal-Hannon, the 2d December, 1758 / To Governor Fauquier.

Copy: Library of Congress, George Washington Papers, 5:165–66. Fauquier communicated this letter to the council on 13 Dec. 1758, and it is abstracted in *EJC* 6:122–23.

1. The enclosure has not been precisely identified, but it was perhaps a letter from Forbes to Governor Lyttelton which Fauquier forwarded in his letter to Lyttelton of 14 Dec. 1758.

2. Forbes at first intended to keep 200 Virginians and an equal number of Pennsylvanians, and presumably the same number of Marylanders, at Duquesne. See Forbes to Denny, 26 Nov. 1758, in *Forbes*, pp. 264–65, and *EJC* 6:122.

3. This circular letter has not been found. A summary of it in *EJC* 6:122–23 repeats Washington's summary almost verbatim.

4. See Forbes's letter of 26 Nov. 1758 to Fauquier.

5. This letter was communicated on 13 Dec. to the council, which advised that the men should be furnished with everything mentioned in the return enclosed in Washington's letter of 30 Oct. 1758, with their pay stopped for the "common Cloathing"; that Christopher Gist should be instructed to supply anything suitable out of the Indian goods; and that Washington should order the rest to be provided from "the adjacent Stores." See *EJC* 6:123.

6. Byrd's letter has not been identified, although it was perhaps his letter of 21 Oct. mentioned in Fauquier's letter of 4 Nov. 1758.

To George Washington

[Williamsburg, 3 December 1758]

This letter has not been found, but Washington acknowledged receipt of it in his letter of 9 Dec. 1758 to Fauquier.

From William Henry Lyttelton

[7 December 1758]

This letter has not been found, but it is referred to in Lyttelton's letter of 12 Dec. 1758 to Fauquier, and Fauquier communicated it to the council on 23 Feb. 1759. It is abstracted in *EJC* 6:131:

His Honor was also pleas'd to communicate a Letter from Governor Lyttelton, dated the 7th of Decemr. inclosing a Copy of the Minutes of the Conferencies he had with the Cherokee Deputies who arrived at Charles Town the 7th of Novemr. and signifying he shall write to the Commanding Officers of the Forts, in the Cherokee Nation, that they may give all the Countenance in their Power to Mr. Richardson agreeably to his Honor's Request.

A copy of the minutes of conferences is just below. For the letter recommending Mr. Richardson, see Fauquier's letter of 5 Oct. 1758 to Lyttelton.

Enclosure: Journal of the Council of South Carolina

[Charles Town, 8–16 November 1758]
In the Council Chamber Mercurii 8th Die November 1758 A. M:
Present,
His Excellency the Governour.
Honble. Edward Fenwicke, Othniel Beale, Henry Middleton, Esqrs.[1]

His Excellency the Governour acquainted the Board that the Deputies from the Cherokee Nation for settling the Disputes and Differences which lately happened between some of the Indians of that Nation and some of the Inhabitants of Virginia were come to Charles Town, and that he had ordered them to attend: They were thereupon called in (to wit) Tiftoe of Hywassey, the Wolf and Man killer of Keowee, Conjurer Jamie, two Head Men from Tocksegway and eleven Warriours,[2] four Women and two Children, they shook Hands with his Excellency and the Council, and being all seated, Robert Bunion Interpreter to the Indians was called in,[3] and duly sworn well and truly to Interpret between his Excellency the Governour, and the Indians at the present or any future Conference with them on this Occasion.

His Excellency then desired the Interpreter to inform them, that by a Talk they had sent him, he was apprised of the Cause of their coming. That he was glad to see them, and bid them welcome. That he had given Orders for their being well entertained during their Stay here. That Friday next being the Anniversary day of the Great King George's Birth, they would have an Opportunity of seeing His Warriours under Arms, and of rejoycing and giving Thanks to the Great Spirit above for prolonging the Life of the King, the common Father of all His People, white and Red. That when that Day was passed, he would proceed to talk with them upon Business, and in the mean time if they had any thing to say concerning their Entertainment, desired them to speak.
Tiftoe: They would be obliged to his Excellency, if he would order them Bread, instead of Corn and Pumpkins.
Governour: It shall be done.
Tiftoe: They would consider of a Talk to be delivered in their own form, when his Excellency should be pleased to receive the same.
Governour: Very well.
They thereupon shook Hands, and withdrew.

In the Council Chamber. Martis 14 Die Novembris 1758: A.M.
Present,
His Excellency the Governour.

Honble. William Bull, George Saxby, James Michie,[4]
Othniel Beale & Henry Middleton, Esqrs.

His Excellency the Governour acquainted the Board, that he had appointed this Day for the Cherokee Indians now in Charles Town to attend. They were thereupon called in, when they shook Hands as usual, and being all seated his Excellency desired Robert Bunning their Interpreter to acquaint them, That when he saw them last, his intention was only to take them by the Hand, and to welcome them to Charles Town, but he now met them to Talk upon matters of Consequence (Vizt.) That sometime ago his Warriour Mr. McIntosh of Fort Prince George Keowee, and several other Persons in their Nation sent him Information, that many of the Cherokee Warriours had taken up the Hatchet, and were preparing to go to War against the People of Virginia, and that their reason for so doing was, that they had received Intelligence that divers of their People had been lately killed by some of the Inhabitants of that Colony. That as soon as he was made acquainted with their Proceedings, he sent a Talk to their Nation, which he would now repeat to them, and it was as follows:

Friends and Brothers.

The Warriour at Fort Prince George has sent me an account of some new Disturbances that have happened in Virginia, in which I am very sorry to hear that some of your People have been killed. I desire You will mark well the Words I now write to You, and lay them up in your Hearts.

The Fire that was kindled many Years ago by our Fathers and yours, has long burnt bright, between us, and the Chain of Friendship which the Great King George has fixed, is unsullied, and free from Stain, but that it may always remain so, You may remember how often it has been concluded in Publick Talks and solemn Treaties, that whenever it should happen, that a Red Man was killed by a White, it should not be a Cause of War between the two Nations, but the Red People should apply to the King's Governour for satisfaction; notwithstanding which I am now informed that bad Talks have been given in some of your Towns against the People of Virginia, and that some Parties have taken up the Hatchet and are gone to spill their Blood. Mark again what I say to You. I have sent a Messenger to the Governour of Virginia to inform him of these things, and am confident he will give you entire Satisfaction for whatsoever Injuries have been done to You; And as a further Mark of the desire I have to remove from You all cause of Complaint, I do hereby promise that if You will dispatch Runners to bring back those Parties that are gone out, so that they may return without having made the Path bloody, I will give Presents to the Relations of your People that have been slain, sufficient to hide the Bones of the dead men, and wipe away the Tears from the Eyes of their Friends. But if You shall refuse to make up the matter in an Amicable way and shall shed the Blood of the Virginians, Mark again what I say to You. The Armies of the Great King are strong and mighty: His Warriours are without number; well arm'd; well Cloathed; well fed and supplied with all the necessarys of War; But You are few, and soon will be in want of every thing, when once the Trade is withdrawn from You. The English are the only Nation that can furnish You, and are willing to continue to do it, if You do not prevent them by your own Faults; But if You do, you will remember my Words, and repent your Rashness when it is too late. The Governour of Virginia has given no Orders to his People to fall upon yours, but what they have done was their own private Act. I thank you Wawhatchee, and the Young Warriour of Estitoe for the particular Talk you sent to me.[5] I am your Friend and Brother.

Given at Charles Town 26th September 1758:

His Excellency then acquainted them that the Messenger he had sent to the Governour of Virginia had returned with a Letter from him, by which and several other Papers it plainly appeared that the Cherokees were the first Aggressours, and that the Devices and Practices used by them in their March through Virginia were as followth (Vizt.) When they met any armed Men able to oppose them they called themselves Cherokees and shook Hands as Brothers; On the contrary if an inferiour Force was in View, the same Party called themselves Shawenese, and immediately fell to plundering, killing and Scalping. That not-withstanding the Governour of Virginia had the greatest cause to resent their Conduct therein, he was still willing to pardon it, and as a Proof of his desire to preserve Peace between the two Nations, he had given Orders to the commanding Officers of his Militia not to suffer their Men to molest any Cherokees that should be on their March through his Province; and to take especial care not to be the first Aggressours; And least the poor Inhabitants who had grievously suffered in the loss of their Effects should fall on the Cherokees to take Satisfaction for the Injuries they had sustained, the Government of Virginia had made good all their damages, notwithstanding it amounted to a very considerable Sum. That as a further Instance of their Friendly Disposition towards the Cherokees, they had repealed an Act lately passed, publishing a Reward for the Scalps of all the French Indians that should be taken by any of their scouting Parties, least by their not being able to distinguish between the different Nations of Indians that shall hereafter pass thro' their Province further Mischief might happen.

That the Governour had even gone so far, as to order the last Booty taken in a Skirmish with them by some of his People, to be deposited in a proper Place that it might be delivered to them, if demanded, and proved to be their Property. And finally he intended to send one of his Beloved Men to their Nation to invite some of their Grave and prudent Sachems to come to Williamsburgh, where he would treat with them, that all differences might be accomodated between the Two Nations; but if notwithstanding all this, they still persisted in their evil designs and nothing but Blood would satisfy them, they must abide the Consequence, and they were not ignorant of the strength of the People of Virginia, and of the number of Warriours, the Great King George could march to act in Conjunction with them. These things his Excellency told them he was authorized to say to them in the name of his Brother the Governour of Virginia.

His Excellency then acquainted them that he had received a written Talk on the part of fourteen of the Cherokee Towns in answer to one he sent to them and that Tiftoe, and the other Head Men and Warriours now present having been nominated and appointed Deputies by those Towns for settling and adjusting certain matters referred to in the said Talk, he should consider them as the Mouth of their Countrymen, and would rely and depend on whatever they should say accordingly. He then desired them to acquaint him whether upon receiving his Talk they had complied with that part of it, which related to the sending Runners immediately from their Nation to bring back those Parties that were gone out to War against the Virginians:

Tiftoe: Answer'd, That on receipt of his Excellencys Talk Runners were immediately sent from the fourteen Towns, and in Consequence thereof forty of the Warriours who had gone for Virginia were returned before he left the Nation. That Runners had been sent likewise, after those who went from the Valleys who he supposed were also returned before now:

His Excellency then said, That he hoped all he had told them from the Governour of Virginia would sink deep into their Hearts, and that in their Answer they would say nothing, but what they were resolved strictly to perform, and his Excellency particularly desired to know, if he might acquaint the Governour of Virginia, that they would send some of their Chiefs to that Province as soon as the beloved Man should arrive from thence to invite them and added, that he was well pleased with their having sent Runners after those Parties who went out to War against the Virginians, and then desired they would acquaint him on what Day they proposed to make their Reply.

Tiftoe: Answer'd, That his Excellencys Talk contained matters of great

Importance, and he was therefore desirous to consider well of what he had to say in return, and when he had so done, he would acquaint his Excellency, and thereupon delivered a String of Wampum, adding that he was one of the Chiefs of the Cherokees who went to see the Great King George,[6] and that part of the said Wampum was an Emblem of the Great King, and the other part, that of their Nation, for their Mouths were as one, That his Excellency was the Great King's Representative, and whatever Talk was delivered by him, was the same as delivered by the Great King himself.

That the Path which was lately cloudy and Dark, was again become light and clear, and hoped it would continue so. That the Governour of Chotee was desirous to hear from his Excellency,[7] and his Beloved Men, therefore had deputed them to come hither as Representatives of the whole Nation to receive his Excellencys Talk. And then delivered another String of Wampum, and said, That his Heart when in the Nation was dead, but upon seeing his Excellency and hearing his Talk he was alive again. That he was fully convinced and Satisfied of the regard his Excellency had for their Nation; therefore desired to take him by the Hand. That upon his return he would communicate his Excellencys Talk, to the Nation, And thereupon shook Hands and withdrew.

In the Council Chamber. Iovis 16 Die Novembris 1758: A: M: Present
His Excellency the Governour.
Honble. William Bull, James Michie, Othl. Beale,
Henry Middleton, Esqrs.

The Board being informed that Tiftoe, and four of the Principal Head Men of the Cherokee Nation attended, with Robert Bunion their Interpreter. They were thereupon called in, when they shook Hands as usual and being all Seated, His Excellency desired the Interpreter to acquaint them, that he was ready to hear their Answer to his Talk delivered at the last Meeting:

Tiftoe: Thereupon said, that upon hearing of his Excellencys Talk, and that of the Governour of Virginia, he was very glad; that the care and concern expressed in those Talks for the good and welfare of their Nation, and spoke as with one Mouth greatly affected his Heart. That he would truly deliver them to the Governour of Chotee, and desired his Talk might be sent to the Governour of Virginia, assuring him, that when his Beloved Man whom he proposed to send to their Nation comes there, all their Hearts will rejoice at it, and that he would give notice to all the Towns to meet him, and he himself, and several others of their Nation will go with him to Williamsburgh, and hoped that would be a satisfac-

8–16 November 1758

tory Answer to the Governour of Virginia's Talk; He then took his Excellency by the Hand, and said it was the same as if he took the Governour of Virginia by the Hand.

His Excellency then asked them, if they were not truly sensible of the Great Goodness of the Governour of Virginia towards them in the part he had taken.

Tiftoe: Made answer, That the Governour of Virginia had shown his regard for them in what he had done.

Governour: Then said, that as they upon receipt of his Talk, and agreable to his desire expressed therein, had dispatched Runners to recall the Warriours who went against the People of Virginia, he would order some Presents to be delivered to them, as a Token of his approbation of their Behaviour on that Occasion, but for the future expected, that if any of their People should be killed by the white People of any of the Great King's Governments, they should not take Satisfaction themselves, by putting any white People to Death, but should acquaint him therewith, or any other of the Kings Governours who would always give them reasonable Satisfaction. That he did not mention this to them, thro' any Fear or Apprehension of any Thing they could do, but from a Principle of Compassion for them. That he supposed, they imagined he was ignorant of the Messages sent from them to the Creeks and Chickesaws, requesting those Nations to join them against the People of Virginia,[8] but that he was well acquainted with those Messages and the Answers also that had been made to them. That the Creeks had replyed that they were very well satisfied with the Behaviour of the English, and were so far from harbouring the least Thought of going to War against them, that they could not even be prevailed upon to say they would sit still, if their Brothers the English were attacked by the Cherokees. That the answer from the Chickesaws was not more favourable to the Cherokees, so he left them to judge, Whether if they had persisted in their purposes of going to War against the Virginians they would not soon have had cause to repent their Rashness, especially as all the King's Children upon this Continent were Brothers, and those in Virginia, North and South Carolina, and Georgia, would have fallen upon them, nor would they have had any supply of Ammunition, for he had given Orders that none should be sent to their Nation. And now before he recalled that Order he required their Promise in the Name of the Nation, that they would not for the future give cause of complaint to the English, nor violate the Treaties that had been made between the Great King George and them.

Tiftoe: Answer'd that they would.

Governour: Thereupon said, he would give Orders that Ammunition

and Goods should be sent to their Towns as usual; and desired to know if any of the Indians present had lost any of their Relations in Virginia.
Tiftoe: He lost his Nephew, but his Mouth never mentioned it.
Conjuror Jamie: He lost two Cousins.
Governour: Replied, That if they had continued to make War against the People of Virginia, they soon would have lost many more, but was glad they had seen their Error and come to a better way of thinking. That their sending Messages to the Creeks and Chickesaws to join them against the English was contrary to their Agreement with the white People, and when their Father the Great King heard of it he would be very angry, but might be induced to pardon it, if he heard that they had repented, and therefore he would venture to give them some of those Presents the Great King had entrusted him with for the use of his Children the Indians; but if they misbehaved again, and he did not resent it, the King would send another Governour that would; His Excellency added that the King was good and Mercifull to all who deserved his Favour, but well knew how to take Satisfaction from those who dipt their Hands in the Blood of His Subjects. And that if they imagined the Great King or His Warriours were afraid of them, or any Indians they were greatly mistaken. That the Presents were given to them, because they were looked upon as the King's Children, and that whilst he sat in that Chair as His Majestie's Representative, what he did he would never do from Fear, but from Motives of Love and Regard for them. That as they had been convinced of their late Error, and requested that all things might be accommodated, and had promised to go to Virginia, he hoped those Clouds which had made the Path darker between the English and them than ever he had known it since his Arrival in this Province would all disappear. That now the Sun shone brightly and the Room was clear and white, and the Feelings of his Heart were good and Friendly towards them: In Token of which his Excellency said he took them again by the Hand, and then dismist them.

Copy: C.O.5/376, ff. 67–70. Endorsed as received with Lyttleton's letter of 7 Dec. 1758 and as read 6 Feb. 1759. A copy of these minutes was enclosed in Lyttleton's letter to Fauquier of 7 Dec. 1758. The names of members of the council have been put in horizontal lines with commas, rather than in columns with brackets as in the manuscript; in the quasi-dialogue the names of speakers have been brought in from the margin, and series of dots after the names have been replaced by colons.

1. Edward Fenwicke (died before 1777) was sworn in as a member of the council for South Carolina in 1747; Othniel Beale (ca. 1688–1773), a merchant, was sworn in 1755; and Henry Middleton (1717–1784), the future president of the Continental Congress, was sworn in 1756.

2. The deputies were no doubt those whose visit was referred to in Lyttelton's letter

of 1 Nov. 1758 to Fauquier. Tiftoe (or Tisto) of Hywassey was from the Valley Town on the Hiwassee River, some miles to the southeast of Fort Loudoun in what is now Tennessee. The Wolf and Mankiller of Keowee were from the Lower Town on the Keowee River near Fort Prince George. The two headmen of Tocksegway were from the Lower Town of Tockswey, a settlement near Estatoe, on the Tugaloo River. Conjuror Jamie's town has not been identified.

3. The interpreter's name occurs later in this journal, and elsewhere, as Bunning.

4. William Bull, Jr. (1710–1791), a planter, was sworn in as a member of the council in 1748; in 1759 he was commissioned as lieutenant governor, and he was acting governor of South Carolina for much of the period 1760–75. George Saxby was sworn in as a member of the council in 1753; he was receiver general of the quitrents for the colony 1742–74, and was still alive as late as 1782. James Michie (d. about July 1760) was sworn as a member of the council in 1755 and was chief justice in 1759.

5. Wawhatchee was probably a chief or headman of the Lower Town of Keowee. The Young Warrior of Estatoe was also known as Salloue, or Saluy.

6. Tiftoe evidently had been one of the party of seven Cherokees taken to England in 1730 by Sir Alexander Cuming, when he was referred to as Tathtiowie or Tethtow. (However, in 1756 the Little Carpenter, one of the visitors in 1730, when he was known as Ouconecaw or Oukandekah, asserted that he was the only Cherokee then alive who had been in England and seen King George; see "Historical Relation of Facts Delivered by Ludovick Grant, Indian Trader, to His Excellency the Governor of South Carolina," *South Carolina Historical and Genealogical Magazine* 10 [1909]: 65.) There are accounts of this visit in Crane and in Foreman.

7. The governor of Chotee, an Overhill Town near the Little Tennessee, at this time was Old Hop (Conocortee or Caneecatee). These governors or emperors, as they were also styled, chiefs of Chotee, seem to have had a vague sort of primacy among the Cherokee chiefs.

8. In his letter of 2 Oct. 1758 to the Board of Trade, Lyttelton remarked that he had written to Mr. Atkin (the Indian agent, then on his way to the Creek nation) to communicate this passage from a letter of 16 Sept. from Mr. Beamer (the Indian trader) to Lyttelton: "There is now at this time Several Creek Indians in my Town (Eastertoe) and this day there are Runners sent off to that Nation & the Chickasaws with White beads & black ones & Pipes & Tobacco and a Talk to both Places which I cannot find out, but I am certain it is for no good by reason what Southern People is here encourages these People on." Lyttelton added the explanation "By which last Words Mr Beamer means that they encourage the Cherokees to go to War against the Virginians" (C.O.5/1376, ff. 55–58). The Creeks were neighbors of the Cherokees on the south, primarily in what is now Alabama and Georgia, a confederacy of tribes for the most part of Hokan-Siouan linguistic stock. The English, the French, and the Spanish had sympathizers among the Creeks, but the nation as a whole remained neutral. The Chickasaws were neighbors of the Cherokees on the west, in what is now northern Mississippi. They were of Hokan-Siouan linguistic stock, like the Creeks, but were constantly at war with the Creeks and hostile to the French, while they were steadfastly friendly toward the English.

From William Byrd

[9 December 1758]

This letter has not been found, but Fauquier acknowledged it in his letter of 23 Jan. 1759 to Byrd; it is doubtless one of the two letters that Fauquier communicated to the council on 19 Jan. 1759. The two letters are abstracted in *EJC* 6:126:

> His Honor communicated two Letters from Colo. Byrd, signifying he had order'd Lieutt. Colo. Mercer to wait on him with an Account of every Particular relating to the Regiment he commanded; and informing of his Intention of going to England in the Spring, unless his Country has a further Call for him, and that he shall wait in New York till the last of March for his Honor's Commands.

Perhaps the abstract down to the semicolon concerns this letter, and the rest of the abstract concerns Byrd's letter of 29 Dec. 1758 to Fauquier.

From William Pitt

Sir   Whitehall 9th Decr 1758

    His Majesty having Nothing so much at Heart, as to improve the Great & Important Advantages gained the last Campaign, as well as to repair the Disappointment at Tionderoge;[1] and, by the most vigorous and extensive Efforts, to avert, by the Blessing of God on His Arms, all Dangers, which may threaten North America from any future Irruptions of the French; and the King not doubting, that all His Faithfull and Brave Subjects there, will chearfully cooperate with, and second to the utmost, the large Expence, and extraordinary Succours, supplied by this Kingdom for their Preservation & Defence; And His Majesty considering, that the several Provinces from Pensylvania inclusive, to the Southward, are well able with proper Encouragements to furnish a Body of several Thousand Men, to join the King's Forces in those Parts, for some Offensive Operations against the Enemy; And His Majesty not judging it expedient to limit the Zeal & Ardor of any of His Provinces, by making a Repartition of the Forces to be raised by Each, respectively, for this most important Service; I am commanded to signify to You the King's Pleasure, that You do forthwith use Your utmost Endeavours & Influence with the Council & Assembly of Your Province to induce them to raise, with all possible Dispatch, within Your Government, at least as large a Body of Men, as they did for the last Campaign, and even as many more as the Number and Situation, of Its Inhabitants may allow. And forming the same into Regiments, as far as shall be found convenient, that You do direct them to hold Themselves in readiness, as early as may be, to march to the Rendezvous, at such Place or Places, as may be named for that Purpose, by the Commander in Chief of His Majesty's Forces in America, or by the Officer who shall be appointed to command the King's

Forces, in those Parts, in order to proceed from thence, in conjunction with a Body of His Majesty's British Forces, and under the Supreme Command of the Officer to be appointed as above, so as to be in a Situation to begin, by the First of May, if possible, or as soon after as shall be any way practicable such Offensive Operations, as shall be judged by the Commander of His Majesty's Forces in those Parts, most expedient for annoying the Enemy, & most efficacious towards removing & repelling the Dangers, that threaten the Frontiers of any of the Southern Colonies on the Continent of America; And the better to facilitate this important Service, The King is pleased to leave it to You to issue Commissions to such Gentlemen of Your Province, as You shall judge from their Weight & Credit with the People, and their Zeal for the Publick Service, may be best disposed and enabled to quicken and effectuate the speedy Levying of the greatest Number of Men; In the Disposition of which Commissions, I am persuaded You will have nothing in View, but the Good of the King's Service and a due Subordination of the whole, when joined, to His Majesty's Commander.

And all Officers of the Provincial Forces, as high as Colonels, inclusive, are to have Rank according to their several respective Commissions, agreable to the Regulations, contained in His Majesty's Warrant of the 30th of December last year.[2]

The King is further pleased to furnish all the Men, so raised as above, with Arms, Ammunition & Tents, as well as to order Provisions to be issued to the same, by His Majesty's Commissaries, in the same Proportion and Manner, as is done to the Rest of the King's Forces.

And a sufficient Train of Artillery will also be provided at His Majesty's Expence for the Operations of the Campaign: The whole therefore, that the King expects & requires from the several Provinces, is, the Levying, Cloathing, & Pay of the Men, And, on these Heads also, that no Encouragement may be wanting to the fullest Exertion of Your Force; His Majesty is farther most Graciously pleased to permit me to acquaint You, that strong Recommendations will be made to Parliament, in their Session next Year, to grant a proper Compensation for such Expences as above, according as the Active Vigour, and strenuous Efforts of the respective Provinces shall justly appear to merit.

It is His Majesty's Pleasure, that You do, with particular Diligence, immediately collect & put into the best Condition All the Arms issued last Campaign, which can be any ways render'd Serviceable, or that can be found within Your Government, in order that the same may be employed, as far as they will go in this Exigency. I am, at the same Time to acquaint You that a reasonable Supply of Arms, will be sent from

England to replace such as may have been lost, or have become unfit for future Service.

I am further to inform You, that similar Orders are sent by this Conveyance, to [Pensylvania, Maryland,] North Carolina, & South Carolina. The Northern Governments are also directed to raise Men in the same Manner, to be employed in such Offensive Operations, as the Circumstances and Situation of the Enemy's Possessions in those Parts may point out, which, it is hoped, will oblige them so to divide their Attention & Forces, as will render the several Attempts more easy & successfull.

It is unnecessary to add any Thing to animate Your Zeal in the Execution of His Majesty's Orders on this great occasion, where the future Safety and Welfare of America, and of Your own Province in particular, are at Stake; And the King doubts not, from Your known Fidelity & Attachment, that You will employ Yourself, with the utmost Application and Dispatch in this urgent & decisive Crisis. I am &ca.

Wm. Pitt.

Copy: C.O.5/213, pp. 363–74. Circular to Southern Governors, viz. those of Pennsylvania, Maryland, Virginia, and North and South Carolina; this version was that addressed to Pennsylvania, and the change of text appropriate for Virginia is indicated in brackets. Annotations indicate that the letter was sent by packet boat, a duplicate was sent by Admiralty vessel on 29 Dec., and a triplicate was sent by packet boat on 13 Jan. Other annotations provide alternative readings of the text that are disregarded here, since they were apparently intended to provide a draft form for the very similar letter from Pitt to the governors of 7 Jan. 1760.

1. This is one of the variant forms of Ticonderoga, where General Abercromby suffered a crushing defeat in July 1758.
2. Pitt's circular letters of 30 Dec. 1757, very much like this one, at this point read "And all Officers of the Provincial Forces, as high as Colonels inclusive, are to have Rank according to their several respective Commissions, in like manner, as is already given by His Majesty's Regulations, to the Captains of Provincial Troops in America" (*Pitt* 1:140–43).

From George Washington

Sir. Winchester, the 9th Dec. 1758

I arrived at this place last night, and was just setting out (tho' very much indisposed) for my own House, when I was honored with your obliging favour of the 3d instant.[1] My last letters would fully inform your Honor of the success of His Majesty's Arms under General Forbes, of the march of the Virginia Troops to Winchester, and the condition (the very *distressed condition*) the 1st Regiment is in. It is needless therefore, to recapitulate facts, or to trouble your Honor further on this head.

Reason, nay, common humanity itself points out that some respite should be granted to Troops returning from every toil and hardship that cold, hunger & fatigue can inflict: and I hope your honors sentiments correspond therein.

If I easily get the better of my present Disorder, I shall hope for the honor of kissing your hand, about the 25th instant. The want of almost every necessary for the journey, and, a still greater inducement if possible, the want of my Papers, requisite to a full and final settlement with the Country oblige me to take my own house in the way down.

Those matters which your honor has glanced at in your letters, have been fully communicated to me. That you had not the least share in causing it, I am equally well satisfied of;[2] and shall think myself *honored* with your Esteem: Being, with the greatest Respect, Your most obedient, and most oblig'd Humble Servant,

G:W.

To the Honble. Governor Fauquer.

Copy: Library of Congress, George Washington Papers, 5:166–67. Fauquier communicated this letter to the council on 5 Mar. 1759, and a brief abstract is in *EJC* 6:131–32.

1. No letter of 3 Dec. 1758 from Fauquier has been found.
2. There is no clue as to what matters Fauquier had "glanced at" in his letters, or as to what Fauquier had no part in causing. It seems likely that Fauquier's missing letter of 3 Dec. 1758 was the occasion of Washington's remark; and perhaps other letters from Fauquier to Washington have disappeared without a trace.

From William Henry Lyttelton

Charles Town, 12 December 1758

I send herewith a Publick Letter dated the 7th Inst. concerning my proceedings with the Cherokees[1] & letter for Mr. Davies.[2]

Mr. Martin the Missionary[3] has taken charge of the Packet in which this goes & will carry it himself to N. Carolina from whence he has promised to convey it to you by a safe hand. He assures me he shall return here in about a month & then set out after making some short stay for Virginia. If I can't find a better method of doing it sooner I shall send by him the sixty three pounds to Mr. Grymes & am much obliged to you & that Gentleman for what you did in the affair for which that money is due. Withers has never yet appeared here with any dispatches for any body that I can hear of but If he comes I shall remember your Caution.[4]

I have read with much pleasure your Pamphlet concerning a new mode of taxation which Mr. Michie brought me:[5] how they now find Funds to raise the Supplies in England in the old way, I am at a loss to discover, but by all the accounts I have had the Ministry have been under no Embarrassment in money matters. I have no late Letters from Europe & every thing here is quiet. I shall have great pleasure in taking every Opportunity to correspond with you & to assure you with how much truth I am &c.

P.S. I beg the favour of you to forward the inclosed Letters to General Amherst & Govr. Pownal[6] by the first good Opportunity & hope you will pardon my troubling you so often with Letters to be sent to other Places as the Post is so irregular I have ventured to assure Mr. Martin you woud pay any Express he may send to you from N. Carolina.
To Lt. Govr. Fauquier.

Copy: William L. Clements Library, Lyttelton Papers. Marked "P," evidently to indicate a private letter.

1. See the note on the letter of 7 Dec. 1758.
2. This is probably the Reverend Samuel Davies (1723–1761), of Hanover, a Presbyterian clergyman, head of the Society in Virginia for Managing the Missions and Schools among the Indians, and soon to be president of the College of New Jersey, or Princeton. It is likely that Davies was the author of the plan to Christianize the Cherokees.
3. John Martin, the missionary, had been Davies's pupil. See Fauquier's letter of 5 Oct. 1758 to Lyttelton.
4. Fauquier's letter of 5 Oct. 1758 to Lyttelton mentions the £63 and the questionable character of the courier Thomas Withers.
5. Mr. Michie was perhaps James Michie, appointed to the council of South Carolina in 1755. Fauquier's pamphlet was *An Essay on Ways and Means for Raising Money for the Support of the Present War, without Increasing the Public Debts. Inscribed to the Right Honourable George Lord Anson, First Lord Commissioner of the Admiralty, &c.*, published in London in 1756, with a second and slightly enlarged edition in the same year, and a third edition in 1757. It was reprinted in Baltimore in 1915 in a series of economic tracts edited by Jacob H. Hollander. The theme is a graduated tax on houses, ranging from 5s. to £4 per house. Hollander's introduction to the reprint indicates that there was nothing especially novel about Fauquier's suggestion, but it did get some notice on its first appearance. The *Gentleman's Magazine* 26(1756): 143–44, in its list of books published in March, devoted nearly a whole page to an abstract of the *Essay;* and on p. 256 of the same volume is a review of *Observations on Mr. Fauquier's Essay* . . ., stating objections to Fauquier's proposal.
6. Thomas Pownall (1722–1805), appointed governor of Massachusetts in 1757, was a distinguished student of colonial administration and was the younger brother of John Pownall, secretary to the Board of Trade.

From Jeffery Amherst

Sir,   New York, December 13th 1758

The King having been pleased to appoint me Commander in Chief of all His Majesty's Forces in North America; and having at the same Time signified to me His Royal Pleasure, that I shou'd correspond with, and apply to, all His Governors on the Continent, for their aid and Assistance, in carrying on the Services pointed out to me, I am, in Obedience to those Commands to acquaint You, that altho' I have not as yet any Particular Orders, relative to the Operations of the ensuing Campaign, I imagine they will require the same Number of Provincial Troops, that were voted by the respective Provinces and Colonies this Year; and it will likewise be necessary in Order to carry those Operations the more effectually into Execution, that those Troops shou'd be at the Place of Rendezvous as early in the Spring as possible; I wou'd therefore recommend it to You, if the Troops raised by Your Province for the Services of last Campaign are not already disbanded, that You wou'd move Your Assembly to continue them in their Pay during the Winter, which will not only be a great Saving in Point of Time but, by what I can understand, a great saving of Expence to the Province; Wherefore I shou'd hope, You will the more easily succeed in Your Application. But if it shou'd so happen, that before the Receipt of this Letter, those Troops had already been disbanded, in that Case I must desire that You will lose no time in using Your Influence with Your Assembly to move them to order new Levies, and to cause these to be provided with the usual Necessaries,[1] and to be ready by the Time the Season will admit their taking the Field.

Having also received His Majesty's Orders to recruit and compleat the regiments now serving on the Continent, I am likewise to begg Your Countenance & Protection to the Officers I shall have Occasion to send, as well as to those that have already been sent by my Predecessor on that Service, and that You will be aiding and assisting unto them in the Execution thereof. I am &ca

                              a true copy   Jeff Amherst

Copy: C.O.5/54, ff. 6–7. Circular to governors of New York, New Jersey, Connecticut, Rhode Island, Massachusetts Bay, New Hampshire, Pennsylvania, Maryland, and Virginia. Endorsed as received in Amherst's letter of 18 Dec. 1758. Marginal notes, and dots, indicate that "Colony" was to replace "Province" in an unspecified copy or some copies of the letter.

1. Fauquier communicated this letter to the council on 19 Jan. 1759, when it had its first recorded meeting since that of 13 Dec. 1758. The text of the letter, up to this

point, is abstracted in *EJC* 6:126. The letter is probably the one laid before the House of Burgesses when it convened on 22 Feb. 1759; see *JHB, 1758–1761*, p. 56.

Proclamation

[ca. 14 December 1758]

On 13 Dec. 1758 it was ordered "That a Proclamation issue for a general Thanksgiving for the Success of His Majesty's Arms, on Thursday the 11th of January next" (*EJC* 6:123). The immediate reason for the thanksgiving was the capture of Fort Duquesne. No copy of the proclamation has been found, and the date is a conjecture.

To William Henry Lyttelton

Sir   Wmsburgh Decr 14th 1758

I am desired by Brigr. Genl. Forbes to forward a Dispatch to you, which I suppose will inform you of his Success against Fort du Quesne and of the scandalous Behaviour of the Little Carpenter and some of his Men, and the Generals procedure thereon.[1]

I hope you have long received the Dispatches which Withers was to bring you, They came by the Packet from New York and were delivered to Withers at Philadelphia, as the usual Post Carrier was ill. Mr. Pitts Letter as I imagine by one I received by the same Conveyance was a Notification of Mr. Amherst's being appointed by his Majesty to succeed Mr. Abercrombie in the Command of his Forces in this Part of the World.[2] Withers left them I find in the Post House here and went no farther; he is so idle and drunken a Fellow, that I have discharged him. I am with great Esteem, Sir, Your most Obedient Humble Servant

Fran: Fauquier

to Governor Lyttelton.

ALS: William L. Clements Library, Lyttelton Papers. Endorsed as received 25 Jan. 1759.

1. This dispatch was evidently one of 26 Nov. 1758, and much like Forbes's letter of that date to Fauquier.
2. See Pitt's circular letter of 18 Sept. 1758.

From Christopher Gist

[Winchester, 27 December 1758]

This letter has not been found, but Fauquier communicated it to the council on 19 Jan. 1759, and it is mentioned in *EJC* 6:124–25:

The Governor acquainted the Council, that the Little Carpenter accompanied by Fourteen of the Cherokees, and Smith, the Interpreter, was come here, and desired a Conference, which he thought it necessary to summon them to attend and assist at; and communicated a Letter from Mr. Christopher Gist, Deputy Agent for Indian Affairs, dated Winchester Decemr. 27th signifying he could not put off the said Indians from going by Williamsburg, the Little Carpenter being unwilling to return Home, till he had settled all the Differences between his Nation and this Colony—that tho' he had not behaved well, and according to his Promise to the General, yet he is allowed by every Body to be a Man of Power in his own Nation—was of Opinion he should wait on his Honor, and had therefore sent Smith the Interpreter with him—that he should have come down himself, but had the General's Orders to meet him at Carlisle in Pensylvania, as soon as he had sent all the Indians from that Place, to receive his Directions respecting Indian Service for the ensuing Year.

Smith the interpreter was no doubt Richard Smith.

From James Abercromby

Sir   London Decr 28th 1758

I had the Honour to write you very lately & probably Mr. Gibson may bring this with my former Letters;[1] Since my last the Lords for Trade have had under their Consideration the Act passd in 1752 with a suspending Clause for erecting a Light House on Cape Henry, their Lordships thereupon desired my Attendance, and at the same Time that of the Agent for Maryland.[2]

However well disposed their Lordships appear to support the Measures proposed by this Act nevertheless from the Impropriety thereof by Carrying its Operation beyond the territorial Jurisdiction of Virginia (vizt) into Maryland, their Lordships cannot therefore advise His Majesty to assent thereto, inforce, or extend the Act to another Province.

Their Lordships have therefore been pleased to direct the Agents for these Governments to take the Opinion of the Merchants and Traders to Virginia and Maryland upon the Utility of a Light House so proposed, and if the Trading and Provincial Interests do concur together, their Lordships on the Principles of a general Utility are inclined to take it up as a Measure of Government in Parliament, in which Case 'tis to be supposed that the different Provinces as Parties concerned with the Trading Interest will mutually contribute to the necessary Expence.[3]

However much I am out of Pocket in Publick Services, more particularly so in my Parliamentary Solicitations, Witness the Cases of the Supply from Parliament and the Salt Bill, and on other occasions, in Business more immediately relative to the Assembly, and for all which I have not received the smallest Allowance from the House of Burgesses since the Commencement of my Agency, & for which my Bill of Expences are now before them:[4] that this Service may not suffer I shall nevertheless advance the Proportion of the Expence on Account of Virginia, if the Lords for Trade with the Approbation of the Merchants and the Agent for Maryland, think fit to take the Matter up in Parliament before I can Know the Pleasure of your Government hereon. I cannot conclude this without acquainting you that I have seen Copy of a Bill projected in the House of Burgesses (but rejected by the Council) for appointing Mr. Paris Agent for Virginia:[5] Upon the Face of this Bill, it carries with it its own Condemnation, for whatever Person should Act under the Authority of such a Bill must necessarily become An Agent for Faction in Place of Agent for Government, nor will the Liberality of the House of Burgesses by the Salary proposed for their Agent, establish the Rectitude of the arbitrary Principles of the Committees Authority, over such Agent. This Bill being rejected by the Council I shall take it for granted that I am at Liberty to correspond with the Governor without incurring Censure for so Doing.

Complements of the Season attend you & yours from me, who am on all Occasions with truth, Sir, Your most Obedient &ca.

The Honble. Govr. Fouquier.

Copy: Virginia State Library, James Abercromby Letter Book, pp. 119–21. In a clerk's hand. A marginal note in Abercromby's hand after the letter seems to say "NB by Mr Greeme."

1. There is no record of any letter from Abercromby to Fauquier between this one and that of 17 Nov. 1758. Mr. Gibson has not been identified.
2. The act was "An Act for erecting a Light-House at Cape-Henry" (Hening, 6:227–29). It provided for the erection, at the expense of the colony of Virginia, of a lighthouse at Cape Henry, on the south side of the entrance to Chesapeake Bay; and it provided further for a duty of 2d. per ton on each vessel clearing out of the bay, to be applied to reimbursing the cost of building the lighthouse and to its maintenance. On 24 Nov. 1757 the Board of Trade took the act into consideration and concluded that it might affect the interests of the proprietor of Maryland and the inhabitants of that colony; it therefore ordered a copy of the act to be sent to the proprietor's agent and invited his comments upon it. On 14 Dec. 1758 the board discussed the act with Robert Dinwiddie and afterwards agreed to call in the agents for Virginia and Maryland for further discussion of the act on 19 Dec. On that day the board heard what

was said about the act by Mr. Hamersley, in behalf of Lord Baltimore, the proprietor, and Caecilius Calvert and James Abercromby as agents for Maryland and Virginia; there was agreement that a lighthouse at the entrance to the Chesapeake would be of great value to the trade and shipping of both colonies, and the agents were asked to ascertain what British merchants trading to those colonies thought of the idea. However, as soon as the agents had withdrawn, the board ordered the preparation of a representation to the king, recommending the repeal of the act.

3. The essential objection to the act was that Maryland shipping would be taxed by Virginia, and thus Maryland would be made liable to the authority of Virginia. The act was repealed by an order in council of 2 Feb. 1759 (C.O.5/1329, ff. 186–87; *Acts P.C.* 4:401–2). Abercromby had informed the board on 9 Jan. 1759 that although the merchants approved of the idea of a lighthouse at Cape Henry, they objected to a tax on shipping and would not contribute in any way to the cost of the lighthouse (see C.O.5/1329, ff. 90–93).

4. A memorial (C.O.5/1329, ff. 152–55) from Abercromby, which the Board of Trade read on 21 Nov. 1759, indicates that this bill of expenses was an account for extraordinary charges of £196.7.0 which Abercromby had incurred in successful negotiations on behalf of Virginia, including his efforts in procuring Virginia's share of the grant from Parliament. On 29 Sept., Fauquier sent to the House of Burgesses a letter and an account from James Abercromby; neither letter nor account was identified, but the account was said to enclose an account of money spent by him and of services rendered by him as agent for Virginia. The burgesses disallowed the account on 2 Oct., on the grounds that Abercromby had not been appointed to act for Virginia except in one particular instance, for which he had received satisfaction (see *JHB, 1758–1761,* pp. 30, 34). It is possible that the letter and account which Fauquier sent to the burgesses were some which Abercromby had addressed to President Blair in March and entrusted to Fauquier. See Abercromby's letter of 15 Mar. 1758 to Fauquier, nn. 7–9.

5. The bill was passed by the House of Burgesses as "An Act for appointing an Agent," on 2 Oct. 1758; on the following day it was referred to the council, which ordered amendments to it on 7 Oct., then rejected it on 9 Oct. (see *JHB, 1758–1761,* pp. 21, 25, 31, 34; *LJC* 3:1193, 1195, 1196). The text of the bill has not been found. Mr. Paris, presumably, was Ferdinand John Paris, a solicitor, who often acted as agent for the colonial governments.

From William Byrd

[29 December 1758]

This letter has not been found, but Fauquier acknowledged it in his letter of 23 Jan. 1759 to Byrd; it is evidently one of the two letters that Fauquier communicated to the council on 19 Jan. 1759. See Byrd's letter of 9 Dec. 1758 to Fauquier for an abstract of the two letters.

From William Pitt

Sir,   Whitehall Decr 29th 1758

In transmitting to You the inclosed Duplicate of my Letter of the 9 Instt. I have the King's particular Commands to renew and enforce, in the strongest manner, the Necessity of a punctual Compliance with the Orders therein contained; And You will accordingly urge, in the most expressive Terms, to the Council and Assembly of Your Province,[1] the Importance of Their Exerting Themselves in the present critical and decisive Moment, in which their own Interests and Security are so nearly concerned, that It would seem superfluous to add the further Motives of their Duty to the King, and of the Gratitude They owe to this Country, for the very great Expence, and Succours, supplyed, for their immediate Defence, and for the future Safety of all their Rights and Possessions in America; And the Levying the Men, to be furnished by the several Provinces, without any Delay, and in such Time, that They may not fail to be at the Rendezvous, That shall be Appointed for Them, so as to be ready to commence the Operations by the 1st of May, is so essential, as well for preventing the Extraordinary Efforts, which, it is supposed, the Enemy is preparing to make, to stop the further Progress of His Majesty's Arms in America, as for pushing, with Success, the ensuing Campaign, that It is the King's Pleasure, that You do employ the utmost Diligence, and every Means in Your Power, to forward, and expedite this Service in the most effectual Manner, and to avoid any Disappointment happening from the Slowness of the Levies, or from the Men, who shall be raised, not proceeding, in due Time, to the Rendezvous. With regard to the Expences, incurred by Your Province, for the last Campaign, I am further to acquaint You, that as soon as the Agents of the respective Provinces, duely authorised, shall produce the necessary Documents, the Same will, without Delay, be recommended to Parliament, for a reasonable Compensation, agreable to the Gracious Assurances, which the King was pleased to allow me to give, in my Letter of the 30th December last Year.[2] I am &ca.

                                                                        W. Pitt

Copy: C.O.5/213, pp. 461–66. Circular to governors in North America, but marginal notes indicate that it was not to be sent to Georgia, Nova Scotia, and Newfoundland and that a section should be omitted from the version sent to Massachusetts. It is also noted that the letter was sent out by Admiralty vessel and that a duplicate was sent out by packet boat on 13 Jan.

   1. On 26 Mar. 1759 Fauquier commanded the attendance of the burgesses in the council chamber, where he sat with the council, and informed both houses of the

receipt of this letter, sent express by a warship; he delivered the letter to the speaker of the house and asked him to lay it before the burgesses, recommending it to their immediate consideration. The burgesses read the letter and ordered it referred to the committee of the whole, to which was committed a bill for completing the regiment in the pay of the colony to 1,000 men, to be continued in service until 1 Dec. 1759, and for raising the sum of £26,298.17.8 for recruiting and providing for those troops. On 29 Mar. the committee of the whole considered Pitt's letter and the bill and made unspecified amendments to the latter; on 30 Mar. the bill was considered again and further amended, and on 2 Apr. the burgesses passed the bill. See Fauquier's letter of 3 Apr. 1759 to Amherst; *LJC* 3:1210; and *JHB, 1758–1761*, pp. 108–13.

2. Pitt refers to the king's intimation that Parliament would be asked, in its session in the following year, to provide proper compensation for the expenses of the colonies. On this point, the wording of the letter of 30 Dec. 1757 was repeated in the letter of 9 Dec. 1758.

1759

Petition of John Catlet

[ca. 1759]

To the Honourable Francis Fauquier Esqr. Lieutenant Governor and Commander in Chief of the Colony and Dominion of Virginia

The humble Petition of John Catlet alias Harvey,

Your Petitioner truly sensible of the disadvantagious Light he must appear in to your Honor as loaded with the triple Guilt of Horse stealing Desertion and Forgery would not have Trespassed upon your Honors good Nature so far as even to have begged for Mercy was he not convinced in his own Breast that he appears at present a much greater Criminal than he really is. This he can no way so well evince as by giving a Short Abstract of his Life, your petitioner was born of honest and industrious parents in the County of Prince William where he married a Neighbours Daughter by whom he has a large Family of Children and always maintained an unsullied Character till the Year Seventeen hundred and fifty six having Occasion to go upon some business to North Carolina in his return from thence in Company with one Peter Lehen and Oswald Adams, he had the Misfortune to tire his Horse and was perswaded by his Companions to take the first Horse he met with which at first your Petitioner refused to do, but they threatning to leave him if he did not, and not caring to be left alone on a Road he was unacquainted with at length was so imprudent as to follow their Advice firmly resolved to leave the Horse he so took at the first publick House he came to and wait there till his own was Sufficiently refreshed to carry him Home, but the Owner pursuing him he was overtaken in a few Miles and together with his Companions sent down to Williamsburg where they were all three tried and condemned but some Circumstances appearing in favour of your petitioner his Honor the late Governor thô he would not Grant a formal pardon Suffered your Petitioner to go at large upon Condition he would inlist as a Soldier upon this to free himself from a nauseous Goal and the Sentence of Death which hung over him your petitioner received the enlisting Money but never was Sworn or regularly enlisted a Soldier for when he had Time to Consider that he was to leave all his Freinds to be Seperated from his Wife and a large Family of Children to whom he had no hopes of ever returning. for thô your petitioners Father was very Able and always intended to leave him a good Fortune both in Lands and Negroes at his Death and would have Spared no Expence to have procured a Discharge for him, Yet as the pardon was only nominal the Sentence of Death still hung over his head and might have been pulled down upon him by every person he Offended, when your petitioner considered these things the Mercy extended to him appeared more terrible to him than Death itself. and he chose rather to Run the Risque of Suffering an ignominious Death by living with his Wife and Children than to embrace that Mercy which was to deprive him of every Blessing which made life dear to him.

What Hardships your petitioner hath since endured are too tedious to enumerate but if your Honour can form to yourself an Idea of a wretched Outlaw whose Life was equally forfeited to Civil as well as Military Justice Seperated from the Society of his Friends and afraid of every Man he Met, Your Honors Humanity will Surely incline you to think that the punishment your petitioner hath already Suffered is more than adequate to the Offense he committed. With regard to the Crime upon which your petitioner was convicted he in the most Solemn manner protests his Innocence, assuring your Honour he did not know the Bills he had were Forged, and calls upon that God to whom the Secrets of all hearts are revealed and before whose awful Tribunal he fears he is Shortly to Appear to attest the Truth of his Assertions.

Your petitioner begs leave to remind your Honor that the proof of his knowing the Bills to be Forged was by no means positive but Supported by such Slight Circumstances of probability that your petitioner conscious of his Innocence well hoped that the Jury would have acquitted him, but as for the Discouragement of all Offenders of this Sort they have convicted upon Slighter Circumstances than usual in other Offences Your petitioner tho Innocent hath now no other Hopes no other Resource left him than those tender Sensations of Humanity which inform your Honours Breast and which he hopes will incline you to compassionate if not an unhappy Criminal, his aged Parents his helpless Wife and Innocent children Your petitioner begs leave to remind your Honor that it hath been an invariable Rule with all your Honors Predecessors to pardon the first Offender convicted under their Administration your petitioner in some measure looks upon himself as fortunate in this Circumstance of being the first convicted since your Honours Arrival as he flatters himself you will not think he hath offended so far beyond the reach of Mercy as to render it necessary that your Honours Administration and your petitioners Case should be the first Exception to that Rule and your petitioner Sincerely promises that if Mercy can be extended to him, so far from abusing your Honors Goodness he will by his future life and Behaviour Endeavour to set a more edifying Example than his death would Occasion.

Wherefore your petitioner humbly prays your Honour will grant him your most gracious pardon for the two Offences of which he is convicted and give him such a discharge from the Army as may Enable him without Fear to betake himself to an honest and industrious life by which he may become a Useful Member of that Society he has injured.

And Your petitioner shall ever pray.

MS: Virginia State Library, Colonial Papers, Folder 46, no. 4. The petition is endorsed as being of about 1762, but the grounds for the dating are unknown. A dating of ca. 1759 seems more plausible: if the petitioner was the first person convicted since Fauquier's arrival (a point on which Fauquier could hardly have been deceived), he was convicted in some court of 1758 or 1759, and not later than the General Court of Oct. 1759, for one Caesar Valentine was condemned to death in the General Court of Oct. 1759 and executed on 30 Nov. following. It seems likely that the petitioner would have begged for mercy as soon as he could, and it seems unlikely that he would have remained under sentence of death as late as 1762. The absence of information on the persons, crimes, and courts involved in the petition makes precise dating impossible.

To the Bishop of London

My Lord,[1] [Virginia 1759]

The bearer of this, Mr Alexander Rhonnald, who has been for many years schoolmaster at Hampton in this Colony,[2] humbly desires admission into holy orders. He is an entire stranger to us, but brought the enclosed certificates from three Clergymen, & two letters from Gentlemen,[3] whose testimonies may be depended upon. Mr Tabb too the Burgess for that County now in town,[4] a Man of worth and veracity, gives him an exceeding good character as to Life and conversation, & adds that he is a constant Churchman & never failing Communicant. If your Lordship shall be pleased to ordain and license him, he shall be presented to a living immediately upon his return there being now 3 or 4 Parishes on our Frontier, which haveing been Vacant above 12 months, the right of presentation to them in Course has devolved upon the Governor.[5] We are My Lord Your Lordship's most dutiful, and most obedient servants,

Fran: Fauquier
Thomas Dawson[6]

LS: Lambeth Palace Library, Fulham Palace Papers, XXIV, 88. Autograph signatures of Fauquier and Dawson. The date is supplied from an endorsement.

1. Thomas Sherlock (1678–1761) was bishop of London from 1748 until his death. The bishop of London was responsible for the administration of the church in the American colonies, and the governor of Virginia was forbidden to appoint to a parish any minister without a certificate from the bishop (see art. 86 of the instructions to Loudoun, C.O.5/1367, ff. 131–32). The clergy had to be ordained by a bishop, and since there were no bishops in America the ordination had to be performed in Britain. It was a common practice for the governor or the commissary, or both together, to send such a letter of recommendation as this to the bishop of London.

2. Little is known of Rhonnald, either before or after his ordination. It has been suggested that he was master of a charity school, the Eaton School, in Hampton.

3. These recommendations have not been found or identified.

4. John Tabb was a militia officer, justice of the peace and sheriff of Elizabeth City County, and one of the burgesses for the county from 1748 till 1761. He was presumably in Williamsburg for the General Assembly of 22 Feb.–14 Apr. 1759, and this letter may have been written during that period.

5. Rhonnald was licensed for Virginia on 25 Aug. 1759, but there is no known record of when or where he began his ministry in Virginia; in 1762 he was minister of Elizabeth River Parish in Norfolk County, and he perhaps remained there as the incumbent until 1773. The ruling on presentation to which the letter refers was fairly recent. In 1703 the attorney general in England had given the opinion that Virginia vestries had the right to appoint ministers of their own choosing, but that the right of appointment reverted to the governor if a vestry had not made an appointment within six months from the beginning of a vacancy. In 1748 the General Assembly passed "An Act for the support of the Clergy; and for the regular collecting and paying the parish levies" (Hening, 6:88–90), which provided that the sole right of presenting a minister to a parish should remain in the vestry for twelve months from the beginning of the vacancy.

6. Thomas Dawson (d. 1760), identified above as a member of the council, signed this letter as the commissary of the bishop of London, a post he held from 1752 until his death. He was also president of the College of William and Mary from 1755 till his death.

To the Board of Trade

My Lords,   Wmsburgh Janry 5th 1759

Inclosed in the Box with this your Lordships will receive the Acts and Journals of two Sessions of Assembly, The Accounts of the naval Officers from Lady Day to Michaelmas last past, the Receiver generals Accounts of the 2 sh. per Hhd. Duty on Tobacco from the 25th of April to the 25th of October 1758 and his Accounts of Quit-Rents for the year 1757.[1]

Your Lordships may be surprized at my mentioning two Sessions of Assembly, but you will observe that in the first Session, an Act was pass'd to recall the first Virginia Regiment home into Winter Quarters by the first of December;[2] if they were detained by any Power whatever they were not to be deemed to be any longer in the pay of this Colony. The second Regiment by the Terms of their enlisting were to be discharged by the same Day, as it was concluded the Service of this Campaign would by that Time be over. But by Letters I received from the Army I was informed,[3] that his Majesties Forces would be in Action before Fort du Quesne just at that Time; I therefore Summoned the Assembly to meet again to prolong the Time, and provide for the further Pay of the Regiments. What I said to them on their Meeting I have transmitted to your Lordships; and I must further add that they came into it so readily, that they met on the ninth of November pass'd a Bill to prolong the Time to the first of January,[4] which received my Assent and the Assembly was prorogued on the eleventh, the third Day from their Meeting. as appears from the Journals.

As my Instructions require me to give my Reasons for passing Bills of a public Nature, where the Reason is not apparent in the Preamble, I cannot omit mentioning two Acts which pass'd in the first Session.[5] One is the Act by which the price of Tobacco is fixed at 2d per pound for all Dues to be paid in that Staple, whether to Clergy or Laity. The last are well contented a few of the first very much otherwise, and applyed to me to stop it, while it was depending in the House of Burgesses, where they made no Opposition to it by petition or otherwise; they acted in the same passive Manner while it was before the Council; but have since used all their Endeavours to spirit up their Brethren to Contention. Those that came to me on this Errand urged one very strong Reason (indeed the only one of any weight) why I ought to refuse my Assent to the Bill, which was this, it was altering a Law that had received the Royal Assent, without a suspending Clause.[6] Perhaps my Lords I have done wrong in getting over this Difficulty, but my Reasons were these. As the Bill was a temporary Law to ease the people from a Burthen which the Country thought too great for them to bear, for one Year only; a suspending Clause would have been to all Intents and Purposes the same as rejecting it. A Bill of the same Nature in a like Time of Scarcity of Tobacco had been pass'd without such a Clause, in the late Governors Time and he incurred no Censure for having pass'd it.[7] The Country were intent upon it, and both the Council and House of Burgesses were almost unanimous in their passing it; And I conceived it would be a very wrong Step for me to take who was an entire Stranger to the Distresses of the Country, to set my Face against the whole Colony in refusing a Bill which I had a precedent for Passing. Whatever may be the Case now, I am perswaded that if I had refused it I must have despaired of ever gaining any Influence either in the Council or House of Burgesses. The Clergy are now become so warm about this Affair, that they have as it were compelled the Commissary to call a Convention of the Clergy, which notwithstanding the Efforts of the hot headed Leaders was so thinly attended that a third only of their Body appeared at it, at which they subscribed a Sum to send as an Agent to England to sollicit this Affair before the Privy Council, one Mr. Camm, who has made himself remarkable here, as being one of the late Masters turned out of the College for refusing to submit to the power of the Visitors; and for introducing Mr. Brunskill (a Clergyman deprived of his Living by the late Governor in Council, for his indecent and lascivious Conduct, and who was not only a Reproach to the Clergy but a Scandal to Human Nature) into his Pulpit to preach before two Members of the Council who had assisted in his Deprivation, and as far as in them lay in rendering him incapable of performing any Ecclesiastical Function. In short Mr. Camm is a Man of Abilities but a Turbulent Man who delights to live in a Flame. I hear he is to sollicit your Lordships in this Affair.[8]

The other Bill on which it is requisite, I should explain my self, is the Act which provides for the payment of the Regiments and the Militia employed for the Defence of the Frontiers: which is done by a new Emission of paper Currency; a Method which I have convinced the World I do not approve, and which has given an Alarm to the Merchants of great Britain; and yet I do not see how it was to be avoided, as the Country is obliged to be at this Expence: For I must declare that if all the Specie of any Kind, that I have seen since I came into the Colony were to be brought together and thrown into one Heap, it would not amount of £100 Sterling. So much is the Colony drain'd at present by Money sent to New York.[9]

If great Britain is obliged to borrow Money on Loans for the current Service, and either can not, or it is not thought expedient, She should raise the Money within the Year, how can it be expected from this Colony, And the Emissions of paper is a Means of borrowing Money without Int[erest] and a Tax is always laid by way of sinking Fund for the Redemption of every Emission. The Merchants of great Britain who are alarm'd at this, and have presented a Memorial against it, do not know the Law that is now in Force relating thereto otherwise there could be no Ground for their Fears.[10] They go upon a Supposition that the old Law takes place by which this Money is to be a Tender for Sterling Debts at £25 Pr. Cent. whereas Sterling Debts are by Law to be paid according to the Rate of Exchange at the Time of payment or Judgment obtained;

which is always fluctuating, and is settled twice a Year by the general Court; and at the last Court was settled at £35 Pr. Cent. So that unless they suppose that the supreme Court of Judicature here, should in Contempt of their Oath and Neglect of their Characters as private Men, make a false Rule of Court to regulate the Affair of Exchanges, in the Face of all Merchants and Traders who are always present at that Court; No body can be hurt as the Law now stands. Indeed the paper Money and Specie is by Law put upon the same Footing which is £25 Pr. Cent, a Guinea passing for £1.6.3, a Shilling for 1/3, but let the Value of paper Currency fall as much as they please by the frequent Emissions, Exchange will rise as fast, and they will obtain for a sterling Debt just as much of the paper Currency as will purchase a good Sterling Bill of Exchange, and then what Injury is done them; unless as I said before the whole Court combine in a bare faced Villany to defraud them; and if that is to be feared, they may as well fear they would give a wrong Judgment wherever their property comes in Question. They are certainly in the power of a supreme Court of Judicature, so is every Man in every Country, and how can they avoid it, and if they could, would they chuse it? But Mr. Abercrombie the Agent is furnished with a Letter in Answer to the Merchants Memorial, wrote by the Council and with the Advice of some of the principal Merchants here which will perhaps set this Matter in a clearer Light than I am capable of doing.[11]

As the giving a Reward for Indian Scalps, was found to produce bad Consequences, by setting our people on to kill Indians whether Friends or Enemies, for the Sake of the Reward; by which we much fear the Cherokee Nation are incensed against us; it was thought adviseable to repeal it.[12]

The abandoning Fort du Quesne by the French and their blowing up and destroying all the Buildings and Works as far as the Time would give them Leave, General Forbes being then within a Days March of the place, is, I imagine what your Lordships will be fully informed of, before this can reach England. The Manner of its Surrender to his Majesties Arms does not afford Matter for many particulars. We yet know nothing of the March of the French Garrison which it is said consisted of between 4 and 500, but by all Circumstances it is apprehended that wherever they are gone, they are in a miserable Condition. The General has garrison'd the place with provincial Troops, and not with those in the pay of Great Britain, which Step I fear will not be relished by this Assembly when they meet in February.

I am afraid I have been already too prolix, therefore after begging your Lordships would accept of my Congratulations on the present Turn of

5 January 1759 147

Affairs in his Majesties Favour on this Continent, I subscribe myself with all Respect and Regard to your Lordships Your Lordships most Obedient Humble Servant

Fran: Fauquier

The Lords Commissioners of Trade & Plantations.

ALS: C.O.5/1329, ff. 100–103. Endorsed as read 23 May 1759. The letters in brackets in the fifth paragraph are concealed in the binding.

1. The acts that Fauquier enclosed were those passed in the assembly sessions of 14 Sept.–12 Oct. 1758 and of 9–11 Nov. 1758 (Hening, 7:171–249, 251–53); the manuscript copies of the acts that Fauquier sent are evidently those in C.O.5/1398, ff. 1–16. The journals of those sessions enclosed comprised the manuscript journal of the House of Burgesses for 14 Sept.–12 Oct. 1758, now in C.O.5/1434, ff. 70–122, and probably the printed journal of the session of 9–11 Nov. 1758 (Evans 8276), for no manuscript copy has been discovered; the journals of the council in assembly for the two sessions were in the manuscript copy now in C.O.5/1429, ff. 145–56. The naval officers' returns (or accounts, or lists) were the returns submitted by the six naval officers reporting shipping information for various periods: often the period was a quarter, as from Michaelmas to Christmas, or from 5 Jan. to 5 Apr., but sometimes two quarters, as from Michaelmas to Lady Day. The returns listed shipping entered and shipping cleared on successive dates within the period, in either case giving for each entry the name of the vessel, the master's name, and the owner's name; the ship's build (e.g., sloop, schooner, or ship), tonnage, number of guns, number of crew, place and date of construction and of registration; the cargo, the place from which the vessel came or to which it was bound; and the date and place of giving the bonds required by law. Naval officers' returns are not printed here because of their bulk and the difficulty of setting their matter in type. The accounts of the naval officers with this letter must have been those now in C.O.5/1447: those for the port of Hampton (lower district of James River), ff. 74, 75, 77; for the district of York River, ff. 81–84; for the district of South Potomac, ff. 85–87; for the district of Rappahannock River, ff. 89–91; and for the upper district of James River, ff. 99–100. No returns from the Port of Accomack (Eastern Shore) have been found for the relevant period. For the account of 2s. per hogshead, see app. A for 1759, and for the account of quitrents, see app. B for 1759.
2. The act was "An Act for the defence of the Frontiers of this Colony, and for other purposes therein mentioned" (Hening, 7:171–231).
3. See, for example, the abstracts of the letter from William Byrd of 21 Oct. 1758 and the letter from John Forbes of the next day.
4. The act was "An Act to amend an act, intituled, An Act for the defence of the frontiers of this colony, and for other purposes therein mentioned" (Hening, 7:251–53).
5. See the twenty-eighth article of the instructions to Loudoun (C.O.5/1367, ff. 103–4) on reasons for passing laws. The first of the two acts referred to here was "An Act to enable the inhabitants of this Colony to discharge their public dues, officers fees, and other tobacco debts, in money, for the ensuing year" (Hening, 7:240–41), which authorized the payment of tobacco debts either in tobacco or in money at the rate of 16s.8d. for every 100 lbs. of tobacco (which is 2d. per lb.). This was the second Two Penny Act, so-called; see Morton, 2:722–24, 751–819, and Brydon, 2:288–320.
6. It is not clear which act Fauquier referred to as having received the royal assent, but it was perhaps the one passed in 1752, "An Act for continuing and amending the act, intituled, An act for amending the staple of tobacco, and preventing frauds in his

majesty's customs" (Hening, 6:222–27), which presumably continued the provision of the amended act (Hening, 6:154–92), in its twentieth head, that no tender of debt payable in tobacco should be accounted lawful unless payment was tendered in inspector's notes, or receipts. The suspending clause was one inserted in an act to suspend and defer the execution of the act until the king's pleasure on the act had been determined: the sixteenth and seventeenth articles of the instructions to Loudoun prescribe the use of the clause (C.O.5/1367, ff. 97–98).

7. The act of the same nature passed in Dinwiddie's time was "An Act to enable the inhabitants of this colony to discharge their Tobacco debts in money, for this present year" (Hening, 6:568–69), passed in 1755. This act and the one Fauquier was trying to justify were both disallowed by an order in council of 10 Aug. 1759, below.

8. The clergy were incensed because their stipends were a fixed amount of tobacco. "An Act for the support of the Clergy; and for the regular collecting and paying the parish levies" (Hening, 6:88–90) of Oct. 1748 set the annual compensation of a clergyman at 16,000 lbs. of tobacco, with cask, and allowance of 4 percent for shrinkage. The effect of the Two Penny Act was to bind the clergy to an exchange of 2d. for 100 lbs. of tobacco, even if the market value of tobacco should rise considerably above that amount. The commissary, Thomas Dawson, refused to call this convention of the clergy, which in fact was called by a group of clergymen headed by the Reverend John Camm; it appears that about thirty-five clergymen, or half of the clergy in Virginia, attended the convention, which chose Camm to go to England to contest the act. John Camm (ca. 1718–1779) was minister of Yorkhampton Parish in York County, and had been professor of divinity of the College of William and Mary until he was dismissed in 1757; he was restored to his professorship in 1764, became president of the college in 1771, commissary in 1772, and a councillor in 1773. The Reverend John Brunskill, Jr., born in Virginia about 1730, was minister of Hamilton Parish, Prince William County, 1754–57, until he was removed by order of the governor and council on the grounds of his parishioners' complaint of his drunkenness, profanity, immorality, neglect of duty, and indecent behavior in church. After his removal, Brunskill was invited by John Camm to preach in his parish of Yorkhampton in York County. The two members of the council before whom Brunskill preached in Camm's church were probably William and Thomas Nelson: they lived in or near Yorktown, where the parish church was, and they had heard the complaint against Brunskill considered in the council meetings of 19 and 20 May 1757.

9. The second of the two acts, passed in the September session of the assembly, which Fauquier singled out for special comment was that cited in n. 4 above; it authorized the emission of not more than £57,000 in paper money. The alarm of British merchants at the emission of paper money, to which Fauquier referred, had been manifested by memorials from the merchants of London and of Bristol, submitted around June 1758; James Abercromby sent a copy of the London merchants' memorial in his letter to Fauquier of 23 June 1758. About three years earlier, Dinwiddie had excused his assent to bills authorizing the emission of paper money on the grounds that the gold and silver coins in the colony had been collected for bills of exchange and sent to New York for the pay of the troops and other expenses (see Dinwiddie's letters of 24 Feb. 1756 to the Board of Trade and of 24 May 1756 to Henry Fox and Lord Halifax in *Dinwiddie* 2:355, 415, 418). On 20 June 1758, John Blair commented in a letter to the Board of Trade (C.O.5/1329, ff. 70–72) that it was hard to find enough gold and silver to pay the comparatively small amount of the quitrents (in the three years 1753–55 running £5,250 to £5,750).

10. The act then in force for regulating the exchange of paper currency and sterling was "An Act to amend an act, intituled, An Act declaring the laws concerning executions, and for the relief of insolvent debtors; and for other purposes therein mentioned," passed in 1755 (Hening, 6:478–83).

11. This letter has not been found.
12. See Fauquier's letter to Lyttelton of 13 Oct. 1758, for a note on the two acts.

From John Pownall

Sir, [Whitehall, 5 January 1759]

I am directed by the Lords Commissioners for Trade and Plantations to send you the inclosed Copies of their Lordships Letters of the 3d of July 1754 and 18 of April 1755 to Mr. Dinwiddie late Lieutenant Governor of Virginia, containing their Lordships directions and Instructions, with respect to the Fee to be taken upon passing Patents for Lands in that Colony,[1] and am, Sir, Your most obedient Servant

John Pownall.

Whitehall / Janry. 5. 1759 / To Francis Fauquier Esqr. Lieutenant Govr. of Virginia.

Copy: C.O.5/1367, f. 172. Fauquier communicated this letter to the council on 9 Apr. 1759.

1. In his letter of 23 Sept. 1758 to the Board of Trade, Fauquier had asked for a copy of the board's letter to Dinwiddie, giving directions in relation to the pistole fee, which, he said, Dinwiddie had not allowed any copy to be made of in Virginia. For more on this fee, see Fauquier's letter to the Board of Trade of 28 June 1758, n. 3.

Enclosure: The Board of Trade to Robert Dinwiddie

Sir, [Whitehall, 3 July 1754]

His Majesty having been pleased, in Consequence of a Report of the Lords of the Committee of Council, to reject the Address of the House of Burgesses of Virginia, complaining of Your Conduct in taking a Fee of a Pistole upon Grants of Land in this Colony, and to direct Us to write to You upon this Occasion, to regulate Your Conduct with respect to Your taking that Fee, and to the method to be observed in Granting Lands for the future,[1] We do, in obedience to His Majesty's Commands, Give it as Our Opinion;

That if the Fee of a Pistole should be suffered to extend to Grants of Fifty Acres, it would be a Great hardship upon the Poorer Sort of Settlers, and may prevent the Settlement of the uninhabited Parts of the Province. We do therefore strictly enjoin you not to take a Pistole, nor any other Fee upon any Grants of a less Quantity than One hundred Acres, or upon Grants of Lands for which application shall be made by any Person in Right of the Number of white Persons they shall have imported, or of which their Family shall consist.

We are also of Opinion, that no Fee whatever should be taken upon sealing Grants of Land in that part of the Colony which lies to the Westward of the Mountains, his Majesty having, from a Consideration of the Great Advantage which will arise from the Settlement of that Country, and of the Difficulties which the Settlers will have to encounter with, thought it adviseable to exempt such Grants from the Payment of Quit Rents and Rights for Ten Years to come; We do therefore forbid you to take any Fee whatever for any Grants of Land of what Quantity soever in those Parts of the Province during that Term.[2]

We cannot omit this Opportunity of taking Notice of your having proposed to the Assembly to establish this Fee by Act, in Manifest Violation of His Majesty's Rights, and of the Powers vested in You by Your Commission and Instructions; We entirely approve however the Proposition in the Bill sent down to the Assembly, That the Proprietors of all Lands, who shall have lodged their Certificates in the Secretaries Office before the 22d of April 1752, shall be intituled to their Patents without the said Fee:[3] and We likewise think, that all Persons, who have got Orders for Land before the 22d of April 1752, though they may not have lodged their Certificates, should likewise be exempted from this Fee.

The taking out Surveys for Lands and neglecting to pass Patents for such Lands, by which His Majesty is defrauded of His Quit Rents, without the Performance of the Conditions of Cultivation, both which take place from the dates of the Patents only, have long been Matter of much Complaint; & therefore every Method ought to be taken to put a Stop to a Practice, which is attended with such Manifest prejudice to His Majesty's Interest and Service; but as it appears clearly from the Laws of the Province, and from the Information which We have received of the method Observed in Granting Lands, that it is in the Governor's Power to prevent such an Abuse; We hope & expect that you will do your Duty in this Particular, even tho' no pecuniary advantage should arise from it.

Another great Irregularity, which Appears to Us to attend the granting Lands in Virginia, is that in general there is no limitation with regard to the Quantity to be granted to any One Person; a cautious Regulation, which has taken place in other Colonies; and therefore We desire, that, in all Grants to be made by you for the future, you do not grant more than One thousand Acres to any one Person.

We have informed Mr. Randolph, that he has vacated his Post of Attorney General by having left the Colony without His Majestys leave of Absence, and will no longer be consider'd by His Majesty as such.[4] if however upon his return to Virginia he shall behave in a decent and proper manner, you are at liberty to reinstate him in the Post of Attorney General, transmitting to Us your Reasons for so doing; which if We approve, We shall prepare a Warrant for restoring him, and lay it before His Majesty for His Royal Signature. This Measure We think may tend to quiet the Minds of the People, and to stop the unjust Clamour that has been raised; And We recommend it the rather, if from Circumstances you shall be of Opinion it can be done with Propriety, as it appears to Us to be at this time particularly necessary for His Majesty's Service, that Harmony and Mutual Confidence should be established between the Governors & the People in all His Majesty's Colonies, but especially in that of Virginia, on the Frontiers of which the French are carrying on such unjustifiable Encroachments. So We bid you heartily farewell, & are &c &c

Dunk Halifax
James Oswald
J. Pitt[5]

Whitehall / July 3: 1754 / To Robert Dinwiddie Esqr. Lieutent. Governor of Virginia.

Copy: C.O.5/1367, ff. 48–51. A copy of this letter was enclosed in the letter of 5 Jan. 1759 from John Pownall to Fauquier.

1. On 28 Feb. 1754 the Privy Council had taken under its consideration the address of the House of Burgesses, which represented that the pistole fee was contrary to the king's instructions, an express violation of the order in council of 9 Sept. 1689 forbidding fees for the use of the great seal of Virginia, unusual and oppressive, and detrimental to the king's interest; the address prayed for relief from the pistole fee, especially because Virginia had provided an ample fund for the support and maintenance of the governor. The address was referred to the Committee of the Council for Plantation Affairs, which recommended on 18 June that the address should be rejected and that the Board of Trade be instructed to write to Dinwiddie to regulate his conduct with regard to the pistole fee; on 21 June an order in council rejected the address and directed the Board of Trade to write to Dinwiddie as had been proposed. See P.C.2/104, pp. 66, 145–46, 161.

2. It appears that in this letter the Board of Trade anticipated the decision to exempt grants of land west of the mountains from payment of rights or quitrents. On 20 June 1754 the Board of Trade submitted to the Privy Council a report recommending approval of the address requesting the exemption, but it was not until 18 July that the Privy Council read and approved the report, and ordered the Board of Trade to prepare an additional instruction ordering the exemption (which was evidently submitted on 6 Aug. and was dated 27 Aug. 1754). See C.O.5/1327, ff. 107–8, 113–14, and C.O.5/1367, pp. 118–22.

3. It is not known why the board ascribed the proposing of the act to Dinwiddie (though it certainly seems likely that he could have proposed it); his letter of 29 Dec.

1753 in which he enclosed a copy of the act (C.O.5/1328, ff. 31A-40) simply states that the council, acting as part of the legislature, drew up the act and sent it to the House of Burgesses. At a meeting of the council on 6 Dec. 1753 Richard Corbin brought in an act entitled "An Act for settling certain differences therein mentioned," which was read, passed, and sent to the burgesses for their concurrence. The act provided that a fee of one pistole should be paid for signing and sealing each patent for land, except that proprietors of lands who had lodged their certificates in the secretary's office before 22 Apr. 1752 would be entitled to their patents without payment of the fee, but upon payment of quitrents due. The House of Burgesses read the bill, had amendments drawn up in a committee of the whole house, but finally rejected the bill on 11 Dec. (see *LJC* 2:1106, and *JHB, 1752–1755, 1756–1758*, pp. 159, 160, 163). The board objected to the act as an infringement on the royal prerogative, inasmuch as it sought the concurrence of the General Assembly in a matter held to be the concern of the sovereign or of the governor and council of Virginia acting as his agents: the governor's commission authorized him to make grants of land, with the advice and consent of the council, on such terms as they should think fit; and the fifty-first article of the instructions to Albemarle (C.O.5/196, p. 280) directed the governor, with the advice and consent of the council, "to regulate all salaries and fees belonging to places or paid upon emergencies."

4. Peyton Randolph (1721–1775) had been appointed king's attorney in Virginia by a warrant of 7 May 1744 (C.O.324/37, ff. 129–30) which required Governor Gooch to issue letters patent under the seal of Virginia, appointing Randolph attorney general of Virginia during the king's pleasure and during Randolph's residence in the colony. On 17 Dec. 1753 the House of Burgesses resolved to appoint Randolph to represent it in Great Britain in its dispute with Dinwiddie over the pistole fee; and it further resolved to ask the king to continue Randolph in his office. On 29 Jan. 1754 Dinwiddie wrote to the Board of Trade that he had appointed George Wythe attorney general in the place of Randolph. On 20 June, Lord Halifax informed Randolph that the king considered Randolph's office was vacated. See *JHB, 1752–1755, 1756–1758*, pp. 168–69; C.O.5/1328, ff. 41–42; and *BTJ* 10:26, 50. (After a while Dinwiddie agreed to reinstate Randolph and requested the appropriate warrant, which probably was issued on or about 13 May 1755; see C.O.5/1328, ff. 124–25, 140–41, 153–53A, 157–57A.)

5. George Dunk (1716–1771), earl of Halifax, had been a member of the Board of Trade, and the president, since 5 Nov. 1748, and continued so until 1761. James Oswald (1715–1769) was appointed to the board on 6 Jan. 1752 and served until 1760; John Pitt (ca. 1706–1787) was appointed to the board on 5 Jan. 1744/45 and served until 1755.

Enclosure: The Board of Trade to Robert Dinwiddie

Sir, [Whitehall, 18 April 1755]

We have received & consider'd your Letter to Us dated the 25th of October last,¹ in which you state a Doubt which had occurred to you with respect to the Orders and directions contained in our Letter of the 3d of July, relative to the Fee to be taken by you upon signing Patents for Lands, and desire our further orders whether you are to demand the

Payment of Quit Rents for those Lands, the Surveys of which had been returned into the Secretary's office, and the orders for which had been obtained previous to the 22d of April 1752, the Date of the Establishment of the Fee.

The Doubt which you state to have arisen is whether the Exemption of the payment of the Fee was to extend to Grants beyond the Mountains in general, which you divide into three Ridges or to those only beyond what is called the Allegany Ridge, with respect to which point We must inform you, that it was plainly our Intention, from the General words of Our Letter tho' not precisely expressed, that those Grants & those only which are exempted from the payment of Rights and Quit Rents by His Majesty's late Order, should also be exempted from the Payment of the Fee, and to whatever District that Order Extends, the Exemption from the Fee must likewise extend.

As to the question whether the Lands the Surveys of which have been returned into the Secretary's office or the Orders for which have been obtained prior to the 22d of April 1752, are liable to the Payment of Quit Rents before the Patents are made out, We are of Opinion, that the Crown will not think it advisable to call upon the Proprietors of them for any Quit Rents prior to the date of the Patents, as it clearly appears to Us, that the Payment of Quit Rents is not a Condition of the Order or Return of the Surveys, but of the Patent only, and not legally payable but within a certain time from the date of it, and if any prejudice arises to His Majesty's Revenue by Persons possessing of Lands without payment of Quit Rents, it must happen either from the Neglect of the proper Officer in making out the Patent immediately upon the return of the Survey, or a defect in the Surveyor's not returning the Survey to the Secretary's Office within a limited time.

If the Mischief arises from the first of these Causes, it will be easily prevented by the Governor and other proper Officers attending carefully to their Duty, and observing to make out and Sign a Patent immediately upon the Return of the Survey, and entring a Docquet of it in the Auditor's Office, that the Land may be immediately carried to the Rent Roll You will therefore take especial care And give positive directions to the proper Officers strictly to observe this Regulation, and upon no pretence whatever to neglect making out and signing the Patents immediately upon the Return of the Survey, and entring a Copy or Docquet of it in the Auditor's & Receiver's Offices.

The Efficacy or Inefficasy of this Regulation depends however entirely upon the other Circumstances which you have not in any of your Letters upon this Subject at all explained to Us, for if the Surveyor is not compelled by some proper Authority to make a return of the Survey to the Secretary's Office within a limited time, and has a discretionary power of doing it when he pleases, the Grantees of Lands may by his fraud or neglect get into possession of Lands to which they would have an equitable Claim without being bound down to the payment of Quit Rents or Terms of Cultivation, because the Survey not being returned no Patent could be made out. If therefore the Defect lyes here, other directions must be given and other Regulations established, but it will be impossible for Us to judge what may be the proper ones untill We are fully informed how this matter stands, and therefore We must desire you to send Us as soon as possible a very explicit and precise account of the Duty and Practice of the Surveyor with regard to the Return of their Surveys. So We bid you heartily farewell, and are Your very loving Friends & humble Servants,

> Dunk Halifax
> J. Grenville
> Fran. Fane
> R. Edgcumbe[2]

Whitehall / April 18: 1755 / Robert Dinwiddie Esqr. Lieutenant Governor of Virginia.

Copy: C.O.5/1367, ff. 65–68. A copy of this letter was enclosed in John Pownall's letter of 5 Jan. 1759 to Fauquier.

1. Dinwiddie's letter is in C.O.5/1328, ff. 124–25, and *Dinwiddie* 1:362–65.
2. James Grenville (1715–1783) was appointed to the board on 26 Feb. 1745/46 and served until 1755; Francis Fane (ca. 1698–1757) was appointed to the board on 20 Nov. 1746 and served until 1756; the Honorable Richard Edgcumbe (1715–1761), who succeeded as second Baron Edgcumbe in Nov. 1758, was appointed to the board on 6 Apr. 1754 and served until 1755.

From John Forbes

[Taffe's Ferry, 11 January 1759]

This letter has not been found. Fauquier communicated it to the council on 23 Feb. 1759, and it is abstracted in *EJC* 6:130–31:

> The Governor communicated to the Board, a Letter from General Forbes, dated Taasses Ferry, Jany. 11th signifying he had received Intelligence that the french Commanders at Presqu' Isle, and Venango, in Conjunction with the French who retreated down the River, in all amounting to about Four Hundred Men, were preparing to attack Pittsburg; that to prevent Accidents, he was obliged to strengthen that Garrison, as likewise Fort Ligonier, to the Amount of Eight Hundred Men be-

twixt them both; and that he was reduced to the Necessity of sending for the Highlanders, and Royal Americans, who are absolutely naked, the Virginia Troops being all gone, and most of the Pensylvanians—desiring this Province may contribute their proper share of Men to the Maintenance of His Majesty's Conquest—and informing that the Pensylvanians have sent their Commissaries with Indian Stores, to the Amount of £800, st. to traffick with the Indians.

Taffe's (or Teaffe's, Teave's) Ferry crossed the Susquehannah River at the point where Harrisburg now stands. Presqu'Isle, or Presque Isle, is a small peninsula in Lake Erie near the present city of Erie in Pennsylvania, the site of a fort built by the French in 1753. Presque Isle was abandoned by the French in 1759. The minutes of the council for 23 Feb. 1759 note that the information in this letter was Forbes's "last Intelligencies before he left Fort Ligonier of the French, and Indians their Followers" (*EJC* 6:130 n. 43).

From the Board of Trade

Sir [Whitehall, 18 January 1759]

We have received your Letters to Us dated June 11th & 28th, July 4th and September 23d 1758, and the publick papers transmitted with them,[1] and are concerned to find that you are of Opinion, that the practice of appointing the Speaker of the House of Burgesses to be Treasurer of the Revenues cannot be set aside without prejudice to His Majesty's Service and obstruction to your Government; We are still of Opinion, that this practice, however warranted by long usage or the acquiescence of the Crown in the Acts which have been pass'd since 1738, for uniting those Offices, is both irregular and unconstitutional, and that a Governor ought not to give his assent to any such Acts for the future, if it can be refused without manifest prejudice to His Majesty's Service.

We are inclined to hope, that the dissatisfaction express'd by yourself and other persons in your Government of the slow progress of His Majesty's Troops under the Command of General Forbes will be found to have been without foundation, and that We shall soon hear of his having taken Fort du Quesne, and recover'd so valuable a part of His Majesty's Rights and Possessions.

It is a great concern to Us to find, that the pernicious and unjustifiable practice of carrying on Trade with the Enemy by means of Flags of Truce, which prevail'd so much in the last War, has again taken place; This and the various other illegal practices, which have been set Up to evade the Laws and Regulations made to prevent the Enemy being supplied with Provisions and other necessaries, require a very serious consideration, to the end that, if possible, some more effectual remedies may be applied to an evil, which has been so long complained of, and which operates so greatly to the dishonour and disadvantage of the State, and to the prejudice of His Majesty's Service.

We are surprized, that We have not received any Letters from you since that of the 23d of September, and the more so, as We find that the printed Journals of the House of Burgesses and other publick transactions of Government, during the Session which began in October last, are in the hands of private persons,[2] and reports prevail, We hope without foundation, that you have assented to another Act for issuing paper Bills of Credit, liable to the same Objections which the Merchants made to that pass'd in 1757.

We cannot but observe to you, that it is very improper and may be of great prejudice to His Majesty's affairs within our department, that this Board should be unacquainted with the publick transactions of Government in any of His Majesty's Colonies in America, the particulars of which transactions are passing up and down through the hands of private persons here. We are, Sir, Your most obedient humble Servants.

James Oswald
Soame Jenyns
W. G. Hamilton
W. Sloper

Whitehall / Jany. 18. 1758 [i.e., 1759] / To Francis Fauquier Esqr. Lieut. Governor of Virginia.

Copy: C.O.5/1367, ff. 174–76. The year date is wrong in the date at the end of the letter but correct in the margin of the entry book.

1. The third letter mentioned was actually dated 24 July 1758. The public papers were those sent with the letter of 28 June, and the duplicates of them sent with the letter of 23 Sept.
2. The board must have had in mind the printed journals of the House of Burgesses for the session of 14 Sept.–12 Oct. 1758 (Evans 8275) and perhaps also the printed journal of the burgesses for the session 9–11 Nov. 1758 (Evans 8276), because no session began in Oct. 1758. See Fauquier's letter to the board of 10 Apr. 1759 for his explanation of how official dispatches from Virginia were in the hands of private persons.

From John Pownall

Sir, [Whitehall, 19 January 1759]

I am directed by the Lords Commissioners for Trade & Plantations, to send you the inclosed Copy of an Order of the Lords of the Committee of Council for Plantation Affairs, approving a Representation of this Board to His Majesty of the 12th of July last, upon the Memorial of the Merchants of London & Bristol, complaining of two Acts pass'd in Virginia in 1748 & 1757, and to acquaint you that an Instruction thereupon to the Governor of Virginia will be prepared and Transmitted to you with all possible dispatch.[1] I am, Sir, Your most obedient humble Servant.

John Pownall

Whitehall / Janry 19. 1759 / To Francis Fauquier Esqr. Lieutenant Govr. of Virginia.

Copy: C.O.5/1367, f. 177. Fauquier communicated this letter to the council on 10 Apr. 1759; see *EJC* 6:135 n. 51.

1. The instruction was that of 9 Feb. 1759, below.

Enclosure: Order in Council

[11 January 1759]

His Majesty having been pleased by His Order in Council of the 28th of July last to referr unto this Committee a Representation from the Lords Commissioners for Trade and Plantations proposing that the Governor of Virginia should be instructed to recommend it in His Majestys Name to the Council and House of Burgesses of that Colony to pass an Act for amending two Acts passed there The one in 1748 entituled "An Act declaring the Law concerning Executions and for Relief of Insolvent Debtors" And the other in 1757 entituled "An Act for granting an Aid to His Majesty for the better protection of this Colony and for other purposes therein mentioned" The Lords of the Committee this day took the said Representation into their Consideration and agreeing in Opinion with the said Lords Commissioners for Trade and Plantations Do therefore hereby Order that the said Lords Commissioners do prepare a Draught of an Instruction for the Governor of Virginia conformable to what is proposed by the said Representation and lay the same before this Committee.

MS: Entry in Privy Council Register, P.C.2/106, p. 320. The date is supplied from the Board of Trade journal for 18 Jan. 1759, where receipt of the order is recorded. A copy of the order was enclosed in Pownall's letter of 19 Jan. 1759 to Fauquier, who sent it to the House of Burgesses on 10 Apr.; the burgesses immediately resolved themselves into a committee of the whole house to consider Pownall's letter, the order in council, and various other correspondence. See *JHB, 1758–1761*, pp. 132–34.

To William Henry Lyttelton

[Williamsburg, ca. 23 January 1759]

This letter has not been found, but it is mentioned in the council journal. The letter enclosed a copy of the speech that Fauquier had made to a delegation of Cherokees on 20 Jan. 1759. See *EJC* 6:127–29 for the text of Fauquier's speech and reference to this letter.

To William Byrd

Sir Williamsburgh Janry 23d 1759

I have received your Letters of the 9th & 29th ulto. and shall endeavour to comply with all your Requests contained in them as far as lies in me. And I hope you will consider the Commission I have enclosed in this Cover to Mr. Menzie[1] as a Specimen of the Readiness with which I shall always be ready to do any Act, that I think can give you pleasure.

By some Expressions in your last Letter you seem to be willing to serve your Country, if She stands in Need of your Service; give me Leave then Sir to hope that an Opportunity has offer'd which will recall you into this Colony. Colonel Washington has resigned his Command of the Virginia Forces (and is married to his agreeable Widow)[2] This Command is intended for you, on Condition the Assembly, when it meets in February will restore the Officers and put the Regiment upon the former Establishment, of which I believe there is now no Doubt, as I have consulted your Friend and mine the Speaker on this Head,[3] and the Gentlemen who were the chief promoters of the Alteration see their Error, and seem willing to retrieve it. But of this, Lieutt. Coll. Mercer who will deliver this to you, can give you a better Account as they are mostly his Friends, so he may better know their Dispositions. I am not without hopes of reinstating him, but this is an Affair in Embryo. Your Acceptance of this Command will I know be very agreeable to the Colony and particularly so to me.

General Amherst has wrote to me to use my Endeavours with the Assembly that they would pay the same number of Men as they paid last Year. Whether they will be prevailed on to raise another Regiment I much doubt; but I firmly believe they will keep up the old one (which I hope I may call yours) on its former footing. If you see the General at New York, I should be obliged to you to have a Conference with him on the Operations of the ensuing Campaign as far as they relate to this

Colony, and let him know, you enter on the Subject at my instance. If he is not far from you I should be glad you would go to him on purpose.

I have mentioned Your Journey into the Cherokee Country in Council, and Coll. Peter Randolph is to draw up a Memorial, and furnish me with Materials, for me to transmit to the Board of Treasury, which you may assure yourself I will faithfully perform.[4]

The little Carpenter is now here, conscious and cast down on Account of his bad Behaviour, and I believe all Differences are accomodated between us, and he seems glad to get off so. We have engaged to send the Goods to open the Trade in Spring.[5]

I should be glad to know your Resolutions as soon as possible, that I may send you the Commission as soon as the Assembly has settled the Affair of the Regiment; tho' I should be much better pleased, if you would give me an Opportunity of presenting it to you in Person, but it shall be done in the way the most agreeable to you, being with great Regard, Sir, Your very Humble Servant

Fran: Fauquier

To the Honble. Wm. Byrd.

ALS: State Historical Society of Wisconsin, Draper Manuscripts 4 ZZ 46.

1. Probably the commission was for Alexander Menzie, who was a lieutenant in the Virginia Regiment under Byrd's command when it was disbanded in 1762.
2. Washington gave up his command at the end of 1758, and on 6 Jan. 1759 he married Martha Dandridge Custis, the widow of Daniel Parke Custis.
3. The speaker of the House of Burgesses was John Robinson.
4. There is no reference in the council journal to Fauquier's bringing up the subject of Byrd's journey into the Cherokee country, which was presumably Byrd's trip to South Carolina and the Cherokee country around Mar. to May 1758 when he was recruiting Indian auxiliaries to support General Forbes's attack on Fort Duquesne. The memorial and materials to be drawn up and furnished by Peter Randolph for submission to the Treasury have not been identified, but they were presumably a claim for compensation and supporting documents. It is possible, though it seems unlikely, that Fauquier referred to another memorial requesting compensation to Byrd and Randolph for their negotiations with the Indians in 1756, for which see Abercromby's letter to Fauquier of 20 July 1758, n. 2. On 15 May 1760 Robert Cholmondeley, the auditor general, reported to the Treasury that he had received its instructions by Mr. Martin's letter of 27 July (apparently 1759), and suggested that £1,000 might be a suitable compensation for Byrd and Randolph (see T.1/401, ff. 203–4).
5. See *EJC* 6:124–30 for the conference with the Cherokees on 19–23 Jan.

From William Pitt

Sir, [Whitehall Janry 23d 1759]

I am now to acquaint You, that the King has been pleased, immediately upon receiving the Account of the Success of His Arms on the River Ohio, to direct the Commander in Chief of His Majesty's Forces in North America, and Brigadier General Forbes,[1] to lose no Time in concerting the properest and speediest Means for compleatly restoring, if possible, the ruined Fort Du Quesne to a defensible and respectable State, or for Erecting another, in the room of it, of sufficient Strength, and Every way adequate to the great Importance of the several Objects of maintaining His Majesty's Subjects in the undisputed Possession of the Ohio; of effectually cutting off all Trade and Communication, this way, between Canada, and the Western and Southern Indians; of protecting the British Colonies from the Incursions, to which They have been exposed since the French built the above Fort, and thereby made Themselves Masters of the Navigation of the Ohio; and of fixing again the several Indian Nations in Their Alliance with, And Dependance upon, His Majesty's Government; And the Province under Your Command is so particularly and nearly interested in the speedy Execution of this great and salutary Work, that It will be Matter of no small Surprize, and must reflect the greatest Blame on their Conduct, should They, in any point, fail to assist, to the utmost, the King's Officers, who shall be employed on this Occasion; I have, therefore, the King's Commands to signify to You His Pleasure, that You should use Your utmost Endeavours with Your Council and Assembly to induce Them to exert every Means in their Power, for Collecting and forwarding the Materials of all Sorts, & the Workmen, which shall be wanted, and which the Commander in Chief in North America, or Brigadier General Forbes, shall require for this Service; And that Your Province do also furnish Every other Assistance of Men, Cattle, Carriages, Provisions, &c &c, That shall be necessary for the Support & Maintenance of the King's Forces, That shall be employed in this essential Work, as well as in all farther Operations to be undertaken, in those parts, the ensuing Campaign. I am, &ca.

W: Pitt.

Copy: C.O.5/214, pp. 113–[16]. Circular addressed to governors of Virginia, Maryland, and Pennsylvania. Endorsed as sent to Admiral Saunders to forward, with a duplicate, by packet on 10 Feb. [1759]. Fauquier communicated this letter to the council on 10 Apr. 1759; see *EJC* 6:135 n. 51.

1. The orders to restore Fort Duquesne or to build another fort to replace it were conveyed in Pitt's letter to Amherst of 23 Jan. 1759 (*Pitt* 2:12–14). The section of Pitt's

letter regarding Fort Duquesne is very much like what he wrote to the governors on that subject. The orders to Forbes have not been traced.

To Jeffery Amherst

Sir Wmsburgh Janry 24th 1759

I recieved your Favour, and Mr. Secretary Pitts Letter notifying his Majesties having appointed you to the Command of his Forces in America,[1] with infinite Pleasure; as it gives me the greatest Reason to hope that a speedy End will be put to the Calamities of War in this Country, when, it is to be conducted by so prudent at the same Time so active a Commander.

One of the Regiments in the pay of this Colony was disbanded before I had the pleasure to receive yours, but you may assure your self that I will use my Endeavours with the Assembly which is to meet on the 22d of February, to keep as great a Number of Forces in pay to serve in Conjunction with the rest of his Majesties Forces, as the Circumstances of the Colony will admit of, and to do all other Acts in their power for the Benefit of his Majesties Service.

There is a Rumour prevails here that We are soon to expect 600 Highlanders, for the Recruiting their Corps here, to be landed in this Colony, if so I could wish General Forbes had Orders to garrison Fort du Quesne with the Forces in the pay of great Brittain, This would give great Satisfaction to the Colonies, and I imagine would forward their Grants for the Service for the ensuing Campaign. The present Garrison is not sufficient to command Respect from the Indians, who have fairly told us they expect a larger Garrison to be kept there to ensure the Country, for if we do not keep that Post, They cannot be our Friends: this is speaking plainer than they usually have done [2]

I shall embrace every Opportunity of carrying on a Correspondence for his Majesties Service, being with the Greatest Esteem, Sir, Your Excellency's most Obedient Humble Servant

Fran: Fauquier

P. S. This I apprehend will be delivered to you by the Honble. Wm. Byrd, who is intended to have the Command of the Forces in the Pay of this Colony, the ensuing Campaign. I have desired him to wait on you to know the plan of Operations for this Year, as far as they concern this Colony, and it is proper for you to communicate. The greater Certainty I can speak with during the sitting of the Assembly which is to meet immediately, The greater Service I am confident I can do to the Common Cause.

F: F:

To Majr. Genl. Amherst

ALS: W.O.34/37, ff. 12–13. Endorsed as received at New York on 25 Feb. [1759]; endorsed also "In answer to mine of the 13th December."

1. These were Amherst's letter of 13 Dec. 1758 and Pitt's letter of 18 Sept. 1758.
2. No indication has been found of which Indian or Indians had so plainly insisted on British (or American) possession of Fort Pitt as a condition of their friendship. It is conceivable that the Little Carpenter had made some such statement during his conversations with Fauquier shortly before the date of this letter.

To John Forbes

Sir   Wmsburgh Janry 24th 1759

I received the Favour of your Letter[1] yesterday which was brought me down by Jenkins. I am extremely sorry to hear you have been so ill and hope rest from the Fatigues of the Campaign will recover your health. I rejoice to hear that some of the Royal Americans and Highlanders are joined to the provincial Troops in the garrisoning Fort du Quesne, as I am sure it will give great Satisfaction to this Colony, and I hope will have a good Effect, in their exerting themselves in his Majesties Service for the ensuing Campaign.

As Coll. Washington's Regiment were so much exposed to the Hardships of the Weather for Want of Cloaths, I have ordered each of them a Blanket to be made up into a Coat to guard them from the Inclemency of the Season, which is the utmost, if not more than, I have a power to do till the Assembly meet in February; at which Time I shall recommend it to them to cloath them entirely, If they continue them in pay beyond the first of May, which is the Time they stand provided for and no longer: But this I hope is not to be doubted. As for the Behaviour of the Virginia Forces in their March downwards, I am heartily sorry for any Irregularity they may have been guilty of, but at the same Time must say it cannot be punish'd for Captn. Field, and the Men who committed these Disorders were of the 2d Regiment whose time of enlisting was expired, and they were no longer under any Martial Law or any Discipline. And I conceive that a Reprimand even, if the particular Aggressors could be found out, would be very imprudent; as such a Step would have bad Effects in the raising Recruits for the ensuing Campaign of which a great Number are wanting.² I don't in the least doubt of your Assiduity, Care and Precaution in securing the Conquests his Majesties Arms have acquired under your Command; and you may assure your self of my most earnest Endeavours to prevail on the Assembly to second you in all your Designs for his Majesties Service, being with the greatest Esteem, Sir, Your most Obedient Humble Servant

Fran: Fauquier

Brigr. Genl. Forbes.

ALS: Scottish Record Office, Dalhousie Muniments GD 45/2/80/4.

1. This was presumably Forbes's letter to Fauquier of 11 Jan. 1759.
2. No other reference to the misbehavior of the Virginia troops on their march southwards, or the disorders they caused, has been discovered.

From William Henry Lyttelton

[26 January 1759]

This letter has not been found, but Fauquier acknowledged the receipt of it in the postscript (of 31 Mar.) to his letter to Lyttelton of 27 Feb. 1759.

From Robert Wood

Sir Whitehall 26th Janry 1759

I am directed by Mr. Secretary Pitt to send You the inclosed Gazette, that You may be informed of the Orders therein contained, with regard to the Mourning for Her Royal Highness the Princess Royal of England & Princess Dowager of Orange.¹ I am &c.

Robt. Wood²

Copy: C.O.324/38, p. 515. Addressed to the governor of New York, but a marginal note indicates that the same letter was sent to the governor of Virginia.

1. Princess Anne (1700–1759), daughter of George II, princess royal, and widow of the late Prince of Orange, died on 12 Jan. 1759.
2. Robert Wood (1717?–1771) was undersecretary of state 1756–63 and 1768–70.

Enclosure: Orders for Mourning

Lord Chamberlain's Office, January 22, 1759.

Orders for the Court's going into Mourning on Sunday next, the 28th Instant, for her late Royal Highness the Princess Dowager of Orange, viz.

The Ladies to wear Black Bombazines,[1] Plain Muslin or Long-Lawn,[2] Crape Hoods, Shamoy[3] Shoes and Gloves, and Crape Fans.

Undress, Dark Norwich Crape.

The Men to wear Black without Buttons at the Sleeves and Pockets, Plain Muslin or Long-Lawn Cravats and Weepers,[4] Shamoy Shoes and Gloves, Crape Hatbands, and Black Swords and Buckles.

Undress, Dark Grey Frocks.[5]

The Lord Marshal's Order for a General
Mourning for her late Royal Highness the
Princess of Orange, January 22, 1759.

In Pursuance of His Majesty's Commands, these are to give publick Notice, that it is expected that all Persons do, upon the present Occasion of the Death of her late Royal Highness the Princess of Orange, put themselves into the deepest Mourning, long Cloaks excepted: The said Mourning to begin upon Sunday next, the 28th Instant.

Effingham, M.[6]

Printed: *Lon. Gaz.*, no. 9863, for 20–23 Jan. 1759. A copy of this issue of the *Gazette* was enclosed in Robert Wood's circular letter of 26 Jan. 1759, to convey the orders in this extract.

1. Bombazine, or bombasine, was twilled or corded material for dresses, made of silk and worsted or of worsted alone. In black the material was much used for mourning dress.
2. "Long-lawn" was evidently some variety of lawn, a kind of fine linen cloth.
3. "Shamoy": chamois, a soft leather.
4. "Weepers" were strips of white linen or muslin worn on the cuffs of men's sleeves as a conventional badge of mourning.
5. These coats had long skirts and were looser and simpler in cut than dress coats.
6. Thomas Howard (1714–1763), earl of Effingham, was deputy earl marshal.

To the Board of Trade

My Lords   Wmsburgh Janry 30th 1759

We have yet learn'd no Particulars to be depended upon in Relation to the French Garrison which abandoned Fort du Quesne: the Indians tell us they are gone to Venango, it is certain they went down the River part in Battoes and part on Foot; but it is said they went up Beaver Creek and then turn'd up the Country.

General Forbes at first left only 200 Men in Garrison there, 100 Pensilvanians and 100 Virginians, for as he wrote me, he had no power to leave any of the Troops in the pay of Great Britain to garrison the Forts; which I was very sorry for, as this Colony was very intent on having all their Troops at home in the Winter; and this I much fear will be a Baulk to their recruiting in the Spring. But since the Indians have informed him that they fear the French from Venango and Presquisle will endeavour to recover the Fort, as the Garrison is so small he has reinforced it with some Highlanders and Royal Americans; so that the Amount of the Whole at that Fort and Loyal Hannon is 800 Men full as many as can be well subsisted in those places.

I must own for my own part I have no such Fears, for by their abandoning this Fort and not staying to defend it, after they found that all their efforts to Obstruct the March of the Kings Troops were ineffectual it looks to me as if their Design was, not to risque their Men to be taken Prisoners or kill'd in the Defence of Forts at a Distance; but to abandon all as we drew near them, and draw their Men down to their principal Settlements to make a stand there once for all.

The Indians have spoke plainer on this Account than they have usually done, and upon so small a Garrison being left have said; We must leave a stronger Garrison to defend the post and protect the Country, or they could not be our Friends; if the French should again become Masters of it, they must again take up the Hatchet against us; that French or English were alike indifferent to them, that we furnish'd them with such Things as they wanted and could not make for themselves, and they must be friends to those who could possess the Country and supply them, and defend them from any Revenge the others might be inclined to take of them. This My Lords is Reason and Truth: tho' from the Mouth of an Indian.

By the Recovery of this Fort, His Majesty is in Possession at present of as fine a Tract of Country by Report as any in the World, and people seem already eager to settle on it. But in Relation to that I hope your Lordships will indulge me in making a few Reflexions. It is supposed that all the Great Grants are actually forfeited,[1] if so, and the Crown should think proper to resume them, I apprehend it will be best not to renew them, for great and extensive Grants are destructive to the well settling and peopling a Colony. This is the Opinion of all the Gentlemen who are themselves concerned in some of these Grants, they acknowledge them to be detrimental; but as they expect some proffit may be made by them they desire to have their Share. This is the Language of all who wish well to their Country. But if the Resumption of these Grants should be thought an impolitic Step for the Crown to take: The Grantees ought at least to be obliged to take up, mark out, and ascertain their Land as soon as possible, and the Land ought to be all contiguous and as near a Square as possible to prevent their running their Lines along the Banks of the Rivers. For want of these Precautions, when persons have come to settle, and have taken up and cleared Lands, built Houses &ct. Their plantations have been claim'd as lying within some great Grant, which are wholly unknown to all the World even the Grantees themselves. Nothing can possibly create a greater Obstruction to the settling a Country, than these Uncertainties and Discouragements.

I thought it my Duty to mention these Circumstances to your Lordships for your mature Consideration and am with the greatest Regard your Lordships most Obedient & devoted Humble Servant

Fran: Fauquier

P.S.

This goes by a Bristol Ship, I am still waiting for a London Ship to carry the Box with the Acts of Assembly and other public Papers.[2] We have been for some Time in daily Expectation of Captn. Clarke in the Ludlow Castle with some Transports,[3] but they are not yet arrived. I likewise hear that I am to be summoned to meet Major General Amherst at Philadelphia,[4] but the Express for that Purpose is not yet come to Hand. I am with the greatest Regard Your Lordships most Obedient Servant

F: F:

Febry. 19

As it is said Captn. Clarke with the Highlanders is gone with the Fleet to the French Islands, the Success of which in Regard to Guardeloupe we have good Advice of,[5] and as there is no prospect of a Ship sailing soon for London, I have sent the Box of public papers by this Ship, under the Care of Mr. Morse who goes in her.[6] The Assembly is just met nothing yet done. I am as above &ct.

F: F:

Febry. 26

The House of Burgesses have yesterday voted a Regiment of 1000 Men compleat, rank and file exclusive of Officers.[7]

March 1st / To the Rt. Hon. the Lords of Trade &ct.

31 January 1759 167

ALS: C.O.5/1329, ff. 109–11. Endorsed as read 23 May 1759.

  1. The grounds for this supposition have not been found.
  2. These public papers were no doubt those which Fauquier had said he was sending with his letter to the board of 5 Jan. 1759.
  3. Capt. Edward Clark was the commander of H.M.S. *Ludlow Castle*.
  4. See Amherst's letter to Fauquier of 11 Feb. 1759.
  5. Captain Clark of the *Ludlow Castle* transported or escorted the second battalion of the Royal Highlanders to join the naval and military operations against French islands in the Caribbean that were carried on during the first half of 1759. On 23 Jan. the British attacked the town of Basse Terre in Guadeloupe and occupied it the next day, but the French continued to resist elsewhere and did not surrender the island until 1 May.
  6. Neither Mr. Morse nor the ship has been identified, though the latter was perhaps the Bristol ship mentioned in the postscript of 19 Feb. 1759. The public papers were presumably those mentioned in Fauquier's letter to the board of 5 Jan. 1759.
  7. On 28 Feb. 1759 the burgesses had resolved to raise money for the recruiting and support of the regiment, but they did not pass the act for the purpose until 12 Apr. 1759. See Pitt's letter to Fauquier of 29 Dec. 1758, n. 1.

From James Abercromby

Jany 31st 1759

In a conference which Mr Secretary Pitt honourd me with, on thursday last on the Affairs of Virginia I was from thence encouraged to apply to His Majesty for an Aid to Virginia in the manner set forth in the Inclosed Memorial[1] and that the Money which may thereupon be granted may not rest in the Treasury as the former Grant still does by Reason that the application thereof is circumscribed to the express Approbation of the Commander in Chief of His Majestys Forces in North America I have taken the liberty to lay before Mr Pitt an Amendment proposed to the Resolves of Parliament in that Case[2] and on any future Grant of Money (vizt) That the Services shall be attested by the Commander in Chief of the Forces *on the Spot* and such attestation to be certifyd to the Secretary of State by the Governor of the Province under the Provincial Seal, and where no Commander in Chief shall be present, the Attestation to come from the Governor, how far this amendment may take place I cannot say but what I have done herein you will please communicate to His Majestys Council from Sir

Gov. Fouquiere.

Copy: Virginia State Library, James Abercromby Letter Book, p. 124. A marginal note seems to read "Per Passengers at Portsmouth," but the whole page is in Abercromby's hand and very hard to decipher. The letter has no salutation or complimentary close.

1. The memorial has not been found.
2. For the resolution of Parliament, see the letter of Abercromby to General Abercromby of 12 Mar. 1758 enclosed in Abercromby's letter to Fauquier of 15 Mar. 1758. No amendment to the resolution has been traced in the journal of the House of Commons, nor has any such amendment proposed by Abercromby to Pitt been found.

Order in Council

[St. James's, 2 February 1759]
At the Court at St. James's the 2d of February 1759
Present
The Kings most Excellent Majesty in Council

Whereas by Commission under the Great Seal of Great Britain, The Governor Council and Assembly of His Majestys Colony of Virginia are Authorized and empowered to make Constitute and Ordain, Laws Statutes and Ordinances for the publick Peace Welfare and good Government of the said Colony; Which Laws, Statutes, and Ordinances are to be as near as conveniently may be agreable to the Laws and Statutes of this Kingdom, and to be transmitted for His Majestys Royal Approbation or Disallowance. In pursuance of which powers An Act was passed in the said Colony in the year 1752, and transmitted, Entituled as follows Vizt.

"An Act for erecting a Light House at Cape Henry"

Which Act together with a Representation from the Lords Commissioners for Trade and Plantations proposing the repeal thereof, having been referred to the Consideration of a Committee of the Lords of His Majestys most Honble Privy Council for Plantation Affairs, The said Lords of the Committee did this day report to His Majesty as their Opinion, That the said Act ought to be repealed. His Majesty taking the same into Consideration, was pleased with the Advice of His Privy Council, to declare His Disallowance of the said Act. And pursuant to His Majestys Royal Pleasure thereupon expressed, the said Act is hereby repealed, declared Void, and of none effect. Whereof the Governor Lieutenant Governor or Commander in Chief, of His Majestys said Colony of Virginia, for the time being, and all others, whom it may concern are to take Notice, and govern themselves accordingly.[1]

A true Copy
W. Sharpe

18 January 1759 169

Copy: C.O.5/1329, ff. 186–87. Endorsed as received on 21 May 1760 and read on 8 July following, being one of a number of copies of orders in council, dated in 1758 and 1759, laid before the Board of Trade on 8 July 1760.

1. Fauquier transmitted this order to the council on 3 Sept. 1759; see *EJC* 6:146.

Enclosure: The Board of Trade to the King

[Whitehall, 18 January 1759]

To the King's most Excellent Majesty.
May it please your Majesty,

We have had under Our Consideration An Act passed in your Majesty's Colony of Virginia in the Year 1752, entituled,

An Act for erecting a Lighthouse at Cape Henry.[1]
and We beg leave humbly to represent to your Majesty thereupon;

That this Act, being of an extraordinary Nature, in as much as the Trade and Shipping of this Kingdom would be affected by the general Duty of Tonnage which it imposes, has been passed with due regard to your Majesty's Instructions relative to such Acts, and accordingly contains a Clause suspending its Execution till it shall receive your Majesty's Approbation.

But there are several Particulars, in which this Act is defective: For it neither expresses any Computation of the Expence of erecting, nor of maintaining the intended Lighthouse; nor does it appropriate the Surplus of the Duty which it imposes for those Purposes. And besides these Defects, it is liable to one Objection, which alone appears to Us to render it unfit to receive your Majesty's Confirmation and Allowance. For the Duty of Tonnage being laid in general on all Ships and Vessels coming into and going out of the Bay of Chesapeak, all Vessels trading to and from Maryland would be comprized in those words, and be liable to that Duty: And thus the Trade and Navigation of that Province would be taxed by the Legislature of Virginia, to whose Authority the Province of Maryland cannot, by the express Exemptions of its Charter, be in any Case liable.

For this Reason We think it necessary humbly to propose, that your Majesty would be pleased to declare your Royal Disallowance of the said Act.

But as it appears to Us, that the erecting and maintaining a Lighthouse on Cape Henry, which is at the Entrance of the said Bay of Chesapeak, may be an Object of great Utility, We have thought it expedient to direct the Agents for the Colonies of Virginia and Maryland, to consult the Merchants and others principally concerned in the Trade and Shipping of those Colonies, to the end that if they shall agree in the Advantages which the Trade and Navigation of each Province will receive from such a Work, proper Measures may be concerted for erecting & maintaining it at the joint Expence of the said Provinces.

Which is most humbly submitted.

Soame Jenyns
W. G. Hamilton
W. Sloper
J. Oswald

Whitehall / Jany. 18. 1759.

Copy: C.O.5/1367, ff. 172–74. Fauquier presented this representation to the council on 3 Sept. 1759; it evidently was sent as an enclosure to the order in council of 2 Feb. 1759. See *EJC* 6:146.

1. See Abercromby's letter to Fauquier of 28 Dec. 1758, and particularly nn. 2 and 3.

From William Pitt

Sir,   Whitehall, Febry 5th 1759

The King having been pleased to appoint Rear Admiral Saunders to be Commander in Chief of all His Majesty's Ships employed, or to be employed, in North America,[1] I am to Signify to you, the King's Pleasure, that you do transmit to Rear Admiral Saunders all Intelligence relative to his Department, in the manner as you was directed to do by my Letters of the 19th February and 30th December 1757,[2] to the former Commander in Chief of His Majesty's Ships; And It is also The King's Pleasure, that you do, on any Application from Admiral Saunders, or the Commander in Chief of the King's Ships, use all legal Methods to supply him with such a Number of Sailors and Workmen from your Province as he shall at any time, require for His Majesty's Service. I am &ca

W. Pitt.

Copy: C.O.5/214, ff. 62–63. Circular addressed to governors in North America. Fauquier communicated this letter to the council on 10 Apr. 1759; see *EJC* 6:135 n. 51.

1. Charles Saunders (1713?–1775) was promoted to vice admiral on 14 Feb. 1759. He was knighted in 1761, named first lord of the Admiralty in 1766, and promoted to admiral in 1770.

2. Pitt's letter of 19 Feb. 1757 was a circular to governors in North America announcing the appointment of Rear Admiral Holburne to command a squadron ordered to North America and directing them to apply to him for naval assistance, to provide naval intelligence to him, and to raise seamen for him at his request. Pitt's letter of 30 Dec. 1757 was a circular to governors in North America for the most part concerned with the replacement of Loudoun by Abercromby; however, it went on to say that the king intended to send a squadron of warships to North America during the ensuing year, and it was his pleasure that governors should transmit naval intelligence to the commander in chief of naval vessels in North America, as they were directed to do in Pitt's letter of 19 Feb., and that they should supply sailors and workmen for the commander in chief at his request (*Pitt* 1:9–10, 135–36).

To George Washington

Sir   Wmsburgh Febry 7th 1759

Captain Stewart was very sure of succeeding in his Wish, as I shall always have pleasure in gratifying you in any thing I dare say you will ever ask of me and in obliging the Gentlemen of the Army.[1] As for the other Affair we will talk of it when we meet. I shall have no Objection.[2] Mrs. Fauquier and my Son[3] are well and join in their Compliments. We all wish you and Mrs. Washington as well as you wish each other, in which perhaps you are not now on a par. I should be glad Captn. Stewart would see the Regiment Station'd as he is second in Command before he leaves it, at least the posts to the Southward.[4] I am Your Very Humble Servant

Fran: Fauquier

ALS: Library of Congress, George Washington Papers, ser. 4. The writing is very faint.

1. Fauquier must have been referring to Robert Stewart's wish to be made an adjutant to the militia. Stewart wrote to Washington on 12 Dec. 1758 asking him to use his influence with the governor to procure the appointment; and in another letter of 16 Jan. 1759 to Washington he indicated the governor had given him a candid, polite, and obliging answer to his wish, although he did not make it clear whether the governor approved the appointment (Library of Congress, Washington Papers).

2. In his letter of 16 Jan. 1759 to Washington, Stewart informed him that on 7 Jan. his appointment as lieutenant in the Royal Americans had been announced. He referred to instances of officers with provincial commissions who obtained inferior commissions in the regular service and were allowed to retain both commissions; he suggested that the influence of Washington and Fauquier might procure the same indulgence for him. This idea of Stewart's was evidently the other affair Fauquier alluded to; Fauquier's letter to Amherst of 11 Mar. 1759 requested that Stewart be allowed to keep both his commissions.

3. Fauquier's wife, Catherine Dalston Fauquier (1710?–1781), and their elder son Francis Fauquier (ca. 1731–ca. 1805) remained in Virginia with the governor until May 1766, when they returned to England.

4. Stewart was second to Lt. Col. Adam Stephen, who succeeded to the command when Washington resigned it. The posts to the southward that Fauquier wanted to see the regiment stationed in were no doubt various ones of the string of fortified places on the Virginia frontier from Hampshire County to Halifax County, discussed in some detail in Koontz, pp. 98–148.

Additional Instruction

[9 February 1759]

Instruction to Our Right Trusty and Right Wellbeloved Cousin John Earl of Loudoun, Our Captain General and Governor in chief of Our Colony and Dominion of Virginia in America; And in his Absence to Our Lieutenant Governor, or Commander in chief of Our said Colony for the time being. Given at Our Court at St. James's the [Ninth] day of [February] 1759, in the thirty second Year of Our Reign.

Whereas by an Act pass'd in Our Colony of Virginia in [the Year] 1749, entituled, *An Act declaring the Law concerning Executions, and for Relief of insolvent Debtors*,[1] it is, among other things, enacted, That "where any Writ of Execution shall, after the Commencement of this Act, sue out upon any Judgment, Decree or Recovery had or to be had or obtained in any Court of Record of the said Colony, for sterling money, the Sheriff or Officer, to whom such Writ shall be directed, shall levy the same in current money at the Rate of 25 Per Cent advance upon the Sterling, for difference of Exchange, and not otherwise."[2] And whereas by one other Act pass'd in Our said Colony in the Year 1757, entituled, *An Act for granting an Aid to His Majesty for the better Protection of this Colony, and for other purposes therein mention'd*,[3] it is, among other things, enacted, That the Paper bills of Credit thereby [to be] issu'd, to the Amount of £80,000, shall during the time limited for their Currency, pass and be received as a lawful Tender in payment of all Debts and Demands whatsoever then already due or [t]hereafter to be contracted:[4] And whereas it hath been humbly represented to Us, that several of the principal Merchants of Our Cities of London and Bristol, in behalf of themselves and others trading to and interested in Our said Colony, have, by their Memorials,[5] humbly set forth their Complaints, that the aboverecited Provisions of the said two Acts are highly prejudicial and injurious to the trading Interest of this Our Kingdom in general, and of themselves in particular, in as much as the first of these Acts establishes the Rate of 25 Per Cent advance upon Sterling Debts, as an Equivalent for the difference of Exchange, altho' such Exchange is (as they allege) now risen to 45 Per Cent; And as the second does, ex post facto, extend to all Debts due before the passing of that Law, and subjects them altho' contracted in Sterling money of fix'd and certain value, to be discharged in paper Bills of a local, uncertain & fluctuating Value; We therefore having taken the Premisses into Our Royal Consideration, do hereby signify to you Our Will and Pleasure, that you do forthwith recommend it earnestly in Our Name to Our Council and the House of Burgesses of Our said Colony to pass an Act for amending the two Acts abovementioned, and that they do thereby provide that all Debts contracted in Sterling money and become due before the commencement of the said Acts respectively, shall be dischargeable in Sterling money only, and that Debts since contracted or hereafter to be contracted between Our loving Subjects of this Kingdom and the Inhabitants of Our said Colony, be made payable in the said Bills of Credit (if the Creditor shall be willing to receive the same, & not otherwise,) not according to their nominal Value, but according to the real difference of Exchange between such paper Bills and Sterling money, at the time of discharging such Debts.

[G. R.]

Copy: C.O. 5/1367, ff. 178–80. The text is that of the undated draft submitted to the Privy Council on 31 Jan. 1759, except for the date and other insertions in brackets, which are taken from another copy in C.O. 324/38, pp. 526–30.

1. This act was passed in 1748; see Hening, 5:526–40.
2. Sec. XXIX of the act (Hening, 5:540) has a couple of inconsiderable verbal differences from the text quoted here.
3. This act is in Hening, 7:69–87.
4. Sec. XXIII of the act (Hening, 7:81) sets the limit of £80,000 on the treasury notes to be issued. Sec. XXIX (p. 85) provides that these notes shall be "a lawful tender in payment of any debt, duty, or demand whatsoever (except for the payment of his majesty's quit-rents) from the time of issuing such notes until the time before specified for the redemption thereof."
5. A copy of the memorial of the London merchants, ca. 21 June 1758, was enclosed in Abercromby's letter to Fauquier of 23 June 1758. The memorial of the Bristol merchants, of about the same date, and to the same effect, is in C.O. 5/1329, f. 57.

James Abercromby to John Blair

Sir   Febry 10th 1759

From a conference which Mr Secretary Pitt honourd me with a few days since I was encouraged to Address the King for an Aid of Money to the Province of Virginia, as you will see by the inclosed Memorial and as the Money heretofore granted by Parliament still rest in the Treasury by Reason that the Application thereof from the Votes of Parliament is circumscribd to the approbation of the Commander in Chief in North America, I have proposed an Amendment to Mr Pitts Consideration which may facilitate the Distribution of that Money and of what may now be granted Viz That the Services, by Forces raised, Forts Erected, Money & Supplys granted by the Province for Military Purposes, within the Meaning of the Parliamentary Grant be Attested by the Commander in Chief of the Forces on the spot or by the Governor in his Absence and so certifyd by the Secretary of State for the Kings Order thereon.[1]

I have now likewise depending before the Treasury a Memorial for Indian Presents to Our new Allies the Ohio & Western Indians the Result of all which shall be communicated to you,[2] in the mean time be pleased to lay these my Proceedings before His Majestys Council and assure them that I have not forgot the Case of an Aid to the Tobacco Duty from the Quit Rents nor that of the Indian Commissioners[3] which Cases have long been before the Treasury and are likely still to continue unattended to amidst the Multeplicity of other Business that engages their full Attention.

Mr. Blair President of Virginia.

Copy: Virginia State Library, James Abercromby Letter Book, p. 126. One marginal note indicates that the letter was sent by Mr. Hanbury's ships, and another says "Inclosd to Governor Fauquier with a few Lines to the same purpose." It is not clear whether Abercromby was sending a copy of the letter for Fauquier's information or simply transmitting it for forwarding to the council. The covering letter from Abercromby has not been found, unless it was the letter to Fauquier of 31 Jan. 1759, held back to be sent with the letter to Blair. This letter to Blair is in Abercromby's hand, and the last fifty words are very hard to decipher.

1. See Abercromby's letter to Fauquier of 31 Jan. 1759 for mention of Abercromby's address to the king on a grant of money to Virginia and the amendment proposed to Pitt.

2. Robert Wood, under secretary of state, referred Abercromby's memorial to the Treasury on 22 Jan. 1759 (C.O.5/1329, ff. 95–98). Abercromby's memorial, dated 20 Jan. 1759, was addressed to Pitt: it represented that the fall of Fort Duquesne had reopened communications with the Ohio and the Indians to the westward of it; that a supply of presents to those Indians would engage them in the British interest; and that a grant of £3,500 for these presents (such as the king had lately made for presents to Indians living to the southward of Virginia) would further the progress of His Majesty's forces in North America.

3. For the aid to the tobacco revenue from the quitrents, see Abercromby's letter to Fauquier of 15 Mar. 1758 and the enclosed memorial. The case of the Indian commissioners must have been the memorial of William Byrd and Peter Randolph requesting compensation, for which see Abercromby's letter to Fauquier of 20 July 1758.

From Jeffery Amherst

Sir   New York 11th Febry 1759

Brigr. Gen. Forbes having represented to me, that nothing could contribute more to the Good of the Service, than a Meeting of the Respective Governors of Virginia, Maryland, Pennsylvania, the Jerseys and New York, in order to treat of, and fall upon Ways and Means of Attaching the Indians more firmly to His Majesty's Interest and Alliance, and to divert them from going over to the Enemy, in case they should be inclined thereto;[1] I Have accordingly pitched on Philadelphia for the place of that Meeting, and only Waited the Arrival of a Packet from England, to Invite You to Assist at it: But the Season being already so far Advanced; the distance of your seat of Government from Philadelphia being so great; And the daily Expectations of the Arrival of such a Packet; (After which I propose to Set out immediately) Induces me to wait no longer, to beg that, if the Affairs of Your Government will admit of your Absence, You will upon Receipt hereof set out for Philadelphia; In which I am the more pressing, as in all probability, I shall be there before You can reach it, and that My other Affairs will not permit me to make any Stay.

I Have Wrote the same Letter to Govr. Sharpe,[2] and hinted to him, that very likely You might Call upon him in your way; if that should be agreeable to You, You will be so good as to give him Notice of it. In hopes of the pleasure of Seeing You soon, I am, &ca.

Governr. Fauquier

Copy: W.O. 34/37, f. 198.

1. In W.O. 34/44, ff. 195–205, there is a series of letters from Forbes to Amherst, written 6 Jan.–7 Feb. 1759, which propose the conference of governors and suggest means of winning the allegiance of the Indians.
2. The copy of this letter to Fauquier has appended at the end an alternative version of the last paragraph which was to be used in the letter to Sharpe. In the Scottish Record Office, Dalhousie Muniments GD 45/2/79/12, is a copy of the letter sent to Sharpe, to which an alternative last paragraph meant for Fauquier is appended.

From Jeffery Amherst

Sir   New York 16th February 1759

I yesterday had the Honour of receiving a Letter from Mr. Secretary Pitt bearing date the 9th of December last, Signifying to me that His

Majesty had judged it expedient to dispatch his Orders to the Several Governors in North America for Levying the Same or a greater Number if possible of Men than they did for the last Campaign;[1] and at the same time enclosed to me Copies of his Circular Letters to the Northern and Southern Governors on that Subject,[2] wherein the Kings directions are so fully Stated that I can have little else to add, than my most earnest Recommendations to You forthwith to use Your utmost endeavours & Influence with the Council and Assembly of Your Province, to induce them to raise with all possible dispatch, within Your Government at least as large a Body of Men, as they did for the last Campaign, and even as many more as the Number of its Inhabitants may Allow; in which I should hope you will prove the more Successfull as I have already prepared you for it, so long ago as by my Letter of the 13th of December last.

As I propose to begin the Operations of the ensuing Campaign, so soon as the Season will permit me, And if possible much earlier than the first of May. I must notwithstanding Mr. Pitts Letter, desire that the Troops of Your Province may be ready by the Tenth of April at farthest.[3]

I must likewise particularly recommend to You the strict and immediate Observance of His Majesty's Directions relative to the Collecting and putting into the best Condition all the Arms issued last Campaign and that have not been returned, which can be any way rendered Serviceable, or that can be found within Your Government, in Order that the same may be employed as far as they will go in this Exigency.

And as most People in North America have Arms of their own, which from their being Accustomed to, And being so much lighter than the Tower Arms,[4] must be more Agreable and proper for them, I do as an Encouragement for their coming provided with them, engage to pay for every one of those they shall so bring, & that may be Spoiled or lost in Actual Service at the Rate of 25s a Firelock,[5] which I understand was Allowed last Campaign. I am Sir &ca.

Copy: C.O.5/54, ff. 108–9. Circular addressed to governors of Pennsylvania, Maryland, and Virginia. Endorsed as received in Amherst's letter of 28 Feb. 1759. The words "at least" and "as they did for the last Campaign, and even as many more," toward the end of the first paragraph, were to be omitted from the letter to Governor Sharpe.

1. Pitt's letter to Amherst is in *Pitt* 1:422–24.
2. Pitt's circular letter to Fauquier is that of 9 Dec. 1758.
3. Pitt's letter of 9 Dec. 1758 to the governors had set the date of 1 May, or as soon thereafter as practicable, as that when the provincial troops should be ready for offensive operations.
4. Amherst probably meant muskets which were tower-proof, that is to say which had been proved or tested in the arsenal at the Tower of London.

5. A firelock was a musket in which the priming charge was ignited by sparks; at this period it referred to a flintlock.

To Arthur Dobbs

[ca. 17 February 1759]

This letter has not been found, but Fauquier mentioned it in his letter of 17 Feb. 1759 to William Denny and stated its subject.

To William Denny

Sir   Williamsburgh Febry 17 1759

I have wrote to his Excellency Governor Dobbs in Relation to John Young alias John or James Gordon who has been apprehended and is now [ ] Philadelphia.[1] I think [ ]s as he is represented to be, ought to be persued and brought to Justice; he made his Escape from a Guard I sent with him and his Brother, to conduct them into Carolina. I therefore think he ought to be detained in Custody, till an Opportunity offers of sending him into Carolina in order to take his Trial, for a Robbery and Murder supposed to be committed by Him and his Brother.[2] I am with the greatest Esteem Honorable Sir your most Obedient Humble Servant

To Governor Denny.

AL: Pennsylvania Historical and Museum Commission, Records of the Provincial Council of Pennsylvania, Executive Correspondence, 1682–1776, no. 2089. The signature has been cut away, so that a portion of the text is missing, for the space of about twenty letters, in each of the two places marked by brackets.

1. According to a report in the *Pa. Gaz.* for 25 Jan. 1759, it was William Young, alias John or James Gordon, who had been taken up on the preceding Tuesday, and committed to the jail in Philadelphia.
2. The brother has not been identified. The report in the *Pa. Gaz.* stated that the robbery and murder took place in North Carolina in Oct. 1758, and it was said that 700 pistoles had been taken.

To William Henry Lyttelton

Sir   Wmsburgh Febry 27th 1759

I recieved your favours of the 7th and 12th of December on the 4th of this month, with your Proceedings with some of the Chiefs of the Cherokee's; This Colony is much obliged to you for the Trouble you have taken in that Affair. General Forbes's Letter which I forwarded to you[1] has I imagine fully informed of the bad Behaviour of the little Carpenter, who has since been here to make up Matters, he has engaged that all past Childish Quarrels shall be forgot; and We are to send up a Quantity of Goods in Spring to trade with them, in Consequence thereof. As his Conduct had been so blameable, his Majesties Council here, did not think it adviseable to be quite so submissive in offering Presents to wipe away the Blood, as they once intended, but sent by Smith the Interpreter, who is gone home with him, a Talk to the Chiefs of their Towns in which We have spoke pretty plain, as you will see by a Copy thereof, which Smith has Orders to convey to you, as soon as he arrives in the Cherokee Towns.[2] I am with the greatest Esteem Your Excellencys most Obedient Humble Servant.

Fran: Fauquier

Please to turn over.

Sir   March 31st 1759

I have this Day received yours of the 26th January by Post.[3] I have waited for an Opportunity of sending this, and inclose it now with a Packet I received from Mr. Secretary Pitt by the Lowestoft Man of War Captn. Dean sent express from Europe with these Dispatches for the Governors and Instructions for the Commander in chief.[4] Governor Dobbs will forward this to you. I am with great Esteem Your most Obedient Humble Servant

Fran: Fauquier

Genl. Forbes is dead but I will forward the Letter to the Commander who is to succeed him.[5]

Governor Lyttelton.

ALS: William L. Clements Library, Lyttelton Papers. Endorsed as received 27 Apr. 1759 by Lieutenant Gray.

   1. Probably a dispatch from Forbes of 26 Nov. 1758, forwarded to Lyttelton in Fauquier's letter of 14 Dec. 1758.
   2. The copy of Fauquier's speech was enclosed in his letter of ca. 23 Jan. 1759 to Lyttelton.
   3. No letter of 26 Jan. 1759 from Lyttelton to Fauquier has been found.
   4. The commanding officer of H.M.S. *Lowestoft* was Capt. Joseph Deane. It is likely that the packet from Pitt which Fauquier forwarded to Lyttelton on 31 Mar. 1759 was one containing Pitt's circular letter to the governors of 9 Dec. 1758, and the dispatches for the governors and instructions for the commander in chief were no doubt Pitt's circulars to the governors and his orders to Amherst, all of 9 Dec. 1758.
   5. It appears that Lyttelton's letter of 26 Jan. 1759 transmitted a letter to be sent on to Forbes, but this enclosed letter has not been identified.

From Horatio Sharpe

[ca. March 1759]

This letter has not been traced, but Fauquier acknowledged it in his letter to Sharpe of 9 Mar. 1759. Sharpe's letter probably invited Fauquier to call on him at Annapolis on his way to Philadelphia. It seems to have enclosed a copy of Amherst's letter to Sharpe, and it forwarded Amherst's letter of 11 Feb. 1759 to Fauquier.

From James Abercromby

[ca. 1 March 1759]

This letter has not been found. Abercromby referred to it and summarized it in his letter of 21 Mar. 1759 to Fauquier.

To Jeffery Amherst

Sir   Wmsburgh March 2d 1759

I yesterday received Your favours of the 11th & 16th ulto. together with a Letter from Mr. Secretary Pitt, all which I shall immediately lay before the Assembly which is now sitting,[1] if they can proceed in the public Business as to levying Men &ct. while I am absent from the Colony, (which is not a determined Point) I shall certainly be at Philadelphia in a short Time, as I propose to go up the Bay; but if no Act can be valid which is transacted in my Absence it will be certainly more for his Majesties Service for me to stay here to expedite the Business, than to postpone it till my Return. Whatever Determinations, his Majesties Council and the House of Burgesses shall come to on this Head shall be immediately communicated to you by Express,[2] If I should not be able to attend you. And You may be assured, that in all Points I shall act on this Occasion in the most effectual Manner I am able for his Majesties Service. I am with the greatest Regard Your Excellency's most Obedient & most Humble Servant

                                     Fran: Fauquier

I was desired to forward the inclosed Letters to you and Governor Pownal by Governor Lyttelton.[3]

To Major Genl. Amherst.

ALS: W.O.34/37, ff. 14–15. Endorsed as received the fourteenth [Mar. 1759] and answered the twenty-second.

1. The letter from Pitt was his circular to governors of 9 Dec. 1758.
2. See n. 2 to Amherst's letter to Fauquier of 11 Feb. 1759 for the opinion of the council and the burgesses on Amherst's invitation to a meeting in Philadelphia.
3. No letter from Lyttelton to Fauquier likely to have enclosed these letters to be forwarded to Amherst and Pownall has been traced.

To William Byrd

Sir   Wmsburgh March 2d 1759

I have some Time since wrote to you in the Name or at least with the Advice of the Council to offer you the Command of the Regiment Coll. Washington resigned,[1] and if on the pressing instances of Mr. Pitt a second Regiment shou'd be raised, you of Course will be Commander in chief of the Forces in the pay of this Colony.

This Letter Lieutt. Coll. Mercer desired to be the Bearer of, which I hope he has long ago sent, (as a handsome rich Widow has detained him in this Colony) and you have received to which I refer you,[2] there was a Commission inclosed for Mr. Menzie whom you recommended to me and you may be assured I shall always have a pleasure in obliging you, being with great Esteem, Sir, Your very Humble Servant.

                                                                        Fran: Fauquier
the Honble. Wm. Byrd.

ALS: New York Public Library, Astor, Lenox and Tilden Foundations, Manuscript Division, Emmet Collection, 6256.

1. See Fauquier's letter to Byrd of 23 Jan. 1759.
2. The letter referred to is the one cited in the preceding note. The handsome, rich widow has not been identified.

To Horatio Sharpe

Sir   [Williamsburg,] March 9th 1759

I am much obliged to you for the Care you took of forwarding Majr. General Amhersts Invitation to meet him at Philadelphia, which I received with your Favour, and Copy of his Letter to you, Yesterday by the Post; I had before received a Duplicate which he sent by Express.[1]

11 March 1759

I am sorry I cannot have the Pleasure of calling on you that we might go together, but as this Assembly is sitting it is judged to be more expedient for his Majesties Service that I should stay in the Colony to expedite the Business, than to postpone it by my Absence. All this you will see more fully by the Papers I herewith inclose to you, all of which I have likewise sent to the General.[2] Major Peachy I apprehend will deliver this to you, in Person at Annapolis if you should not be set forwards before, if you should he will see you at Philadelphia. I am with the greatest Esteem Dear Sir Your most Obedient Humble Servant

Fran: Fauquier

P.S. As a Gentleman from this Colony is going for Maryland before Major Peachy I have sent this by him that you might have the earliest Notice.

To Govr. Sharpe.

ALS: Morristown National Historical Park. The place of writing has been obliterated by a printed label (evidently clipped from a catalogue of some kind) which, however, gives the place of writing as Williamsburg.

1. Amherst's invitation was in his letter to Fauquier of 11 Feb. 1759; Sharpe's covering letter has not been traced. For Amherst's letter to Sharpe, see n. 2 to his letter to Fauquier of 11 Feb. 1759.

2. The papers were Fauquier's address to the House of Burgesses and its reply, which in fact he sent to Amherst two days after this letter to Sharpe. See Fauquier's letter of 11 Mar. 1759 to Amherst.

To Jeffery Amherst

Sir   Wmsburgh March 11th 1759

Your Favours of the 11th & 16th Febry. together with Mr. Secretary Pitts Letter of the 9th December were laid before the House of Burgesses on Tuesday the 6th instant, having been previously communicated to his Majesties Council. I have enclosed to you the Speech I made them on this Occasion; with the Burgesses Address consequent thereupon, and my Answer. The Council were under an Adjournment as an upper House of Legislature, so could take no step in that Capacity.[1]

You will see by the Address that it is not thought expedient I should leave the Colony to be present at the Meeting at Philadelphia which I would with great Pleasure have attended if the Public Business could possibly have been carried on here; but the Assembly must have been prorogued, and reassumed under the President, which would have delayed the raising Men and Money, the expediting which was thought of more Consequence to His Majesties Service, than my Presence at that meeting could possibly be. But as soon as the Resolutions thereof are made known to me I will do my utmost to cooperate with you in every Measure which shall be concluded on for the common Good of the Colonies, and I make no Doubt by the Disposition which appears among all Men but that the Assembly will join in every reasonable Plan or Agreement relative to Trade with the Indians.

Tho' I have not succeeded with the Assembly to raise the same Number of Men as were raised last Year, which I realy believe from the fatigues of the last Campaign would be impracticable (as every Man in this Colony has Land, and none but Negroes are Labourers) yet I hope you are satisfyed that I did all in my Power; and tho' the Address of the House of Burgesses mentions their Inability to support more than 1000 Men, I am not without Hopes that when this Affair is reassumed in that House which it is to be this week, the Number will be encreased to 1500.

The Command of our Forces is offer'd to Coll. Byrd, and tho' I have not his express Answer to that Letter; by other Letters I have received from him, I look upon him to be the Commander in chief of all the Forces in the pay of this Colony for the ensuing Campaign: therefore whatever is proper to be communicated may be safely deposited with him and if he takes the Command will receive and execute such Instructions as you shall give him relating thereto.

I beg of you Sir to be assured that nothing shall be wanting on my part to forward and promote his Majesties Service and the common Cause, by every Measure in my Power, and I will use my Endeavours to get the Men whatever their Number may be, ready to be at the place of Rendezvous as soon as they can be raised and cloath'd which last Article I fear can not be prepared by the Time you mention, but the greatest Expedition shall be used. I am with the greatest Esteem & Regard Your Excellency's most Obedient Humble Servant

Fran: Fauquier

To Majr. Genl. Amherst.

ALS: W.O.34/37, ff. 18–19. Endorsed as received the thirtieth [Mar. 1759] and answered the same day.

1. Fauquier had communicated Amherst's letter of 11 Feb. 1759, which proposed the meeting at Philadelphia, to the council in its executive session on 5 Mar. 1759. Its advice was that he should excuse himself from the meeting, on the grounds that the weighty affairs of his government, and specifically the important business before the General Assembly then in session, would not admit of his absence (see *EJC* 6:132). On the same day, Fauquier made an address in which he mentioned letters from Pitt and Amherst about raising men for the ensuing campaign and referred the invitation from Amherst to the General Assembly for its opinion. On the next day, the House

of Burgesses offered an address to Fauquier in which it referred to Amherst's invitation and advised and earnestly desired Fauquier not to leave the colony at that juncture. On 7 Mar. Fauquier replied to the burgesses that he would not leave the colony (*JHB, 1758–1761*, pp. 77–79, 81–82). Although the council seems to have been in attendance on 5 Mar. to hear Fauquier's address, it had adjourned (in its legislative capacity) on 24 Feb. until 13 Mar. (see *LJC* 3:1207). What Fauquier enclosed in his letter to Amherst was a printed copy of his address to the General Assembly, the answering address of the House of Burgesses, and his reply to the latter address, listed in Bristol as B2085 and B2087; the printed item is W.O. 34/37, f. 20.

To Jeffery Amherst

Sir, Wmsburgh March 11th 1759

I am sollicited by Captn. Robt. Stewart an Officer who has been long, and behaved well in our Service, and who, by the Representations that have been made to me of the whole Tenour of his Conduct, by his late Colonel Mr. Washington would be a Loss to us, if he was to quit the Regiment and not serve us this Campaign; to intercede with you for an Indulgence to him that he may retain both Commissions, and do Duty in our Regiment. I would not ask an unprecedented Thing, but by the paper he has put into my Hands, and which I herewith enclose to you, I find there are many Instances of the like Indulgence.[1] All I can further add is, that I believe all that is said in Relation to him and his Service is strictly true. I would by no means break into any Rule you have prescribed to your self for the good of the Service, but if agreeable to any such you can dispense with such Service, I shall deem it a Favour conferr'd on me who am with the greatest Esteem Your Excellency's most Obedient Humble Servant.

Fran: Fauquier

ALS: W.O.34/37, f. 17.

1. The paper that Fauquier enclosed has not been traced, but it seems to have been a list of instances in which officers holding provincial commissions and an inferior commission in the regular service were allowed to retain both commissions. There is nothing to indicate how such a paper arrived in Fauquier's hands, but it was perhaps brought to him by Washington, who evidently was acting in Stewart's behalf in this business (see Fauquier's letter to Washington of 7 Feb. 1759). Probably Stewart's paper included the examples of Colonel Glazier of the New York Regiment and Colonel Parker of the New Jersey Regiment, both lieutenants in the Royal Americans, whose cases Stewart had cited in his letter of 16 Jan. 1759 to Washington (Hamilton, 3:150–53). Colonel Glazier was presumably Beamsley Glazier, appointed to a lieutenancy in the Royal Americans in 1757, while Colonel Parker must have been John Parker (1729–1762), who had commanded a company in the fourth battalion of the

Royal Americans in 1755–56, then succeeded to command of the New Jersey Regiment.

To Jeffery Amherst

Sir   Wmsburgh March 11th 1759

I very much fear you will think your-self doom'd to be plagued with Letters from me, but I cannot refuse when I think Justice demands my Assistance. I have given Directions that this should not be deliver'd to you, if Brigr. Genl. Forbes's State of Health can permit him to attend to it.[1] The Inclosed is a Narrative of the unfortunate Transaction under Major Grant before Fort du Quesne, designed as a Justification of the Conduct of Major Lewis now a prisoner with the French, against a Charge of Major Grant, who is also a Prisoner. All I can say in Relation to this is, that Major Lewis has served with great Reputation in our Regiment, and his Narrative tallies exactly with all the Accounts I have heard from the Officers who served with him on this Expedition. It is, as you will observe a Letter to Col. Washington,[2] who has applyed to me to take this Step to do Major Lewis Justice, and Coll. Washington's whole Conduct has been such that I cannot help complying with all his Desires which I have always thought to be founded on Reason and Justice. I am with the greatest Esteem Your Excellency's most Obedient Humble Servant.

                                                                    Fran: Fauquier

ALS: W.O.34/37, f. 16.

1. This letter was delivered to Amherst, because Forbes died on 11 Mar. 1759.
2. The enclosed narrative by Andrew Lewis of the defeat of Grant near Fort Duquesne, a letter from him to George Washington, is not with this letter, and no copy of it has been traced. See Washington's letters of 25 and 28 Sept. 1758 to Fauquier on this engagement. Grant's account of the engagement, in a letter of ca. 14 Sept. 1758 to Forbes, blames Lewis for overturning a long-projected scheme and disobeying positive orders, apparently by ordering a withdrawal by the troops under his command; a postscript to Grant's letter states that he had read to Lewis the part of the letter which particularly concerned him, and that Lewis denied he had ordered his men to retire (British Library, Add. Mss. 21652, f. 64, and *Bouquet* 2:499–505).

From Richard Coytmore

                                                    [Fort Prince George, ca. 15 March 1759]

This letter has not been found. Fauquier communicated it to the council on 3 Sept. 1759, and it is abstracted in *EJC* 6:144:

Also a Letter from Lieutenant Coytmore, Commanding Officer at Fort Prince George in the lower Cherokee Nation, informing that two Days after Rd. Smith's Arrival there with his Honor's Talk to those Indians, which was on the 2d of that Month, there was a Meeting of all the lower Towns, when, at Mr. Smith's desire, he read the above Talk to them; that they did not plead being innocent of the Murders they were charg'd with, or mention giving any Satisfaction; that fair Promises of future Amendment, was all he could get from them; but that from their daily Behaviour, and the Informations he has privately received, he is far from thinking they intend to pay the least Regard to these Promises.

The date is a conjecture, but it seems likely that Coytmore wrote his letter to Fauquier about the second week of March, and not improbably when the Little Carpenter wrote his letter of 15 Mar. 1759 from Fort Prince George. On 23 Jan. Fauquier gave a copy of his speech of 20 Jan., directed to the middle and lower settlements of the Cherokee nation, to the Little Carpenter, and at the same time he gave another copy of the speech, enclosed in a letter to Lyttelton, to Richard Smith (see *EJC* 6:127–29). Fauquier's letter of 5 Sept. 1759 to Lyttelton indicates that this speech of Fauquier's is what Coytmore read to the Indians, and that Smith brought this letter from Coytmore to Fauquier on his return to Virginia. It is puzzling that the letter was not communicated to the council until September, for it appears that Smith had returned from delivering Fauquier's message by about the middle of April (on 17 Apr. the council proposed that Smith should be sent to the Cherokees with a message that their trade goods would be dispatched about the end of June) and there were six meetings of the council between 17 Apr. and 3 Sept. It is not clear whether Smith actually carried this message to the Cherokees in April, but he did make a trip to the Cherokee country about the middle of June. Fauquier wrote to Lyttelton on 19 June that Smith was already on his way to warn the Cherokees to expect the trade goods. Smith would have set out on or after 13 June, when the council advised the goods should be forwarded at once, and must have been back in Virginia by about the beginning of August, as is indicated by Fauquier's letter of 5 Sept. to Lyttelton. Perhaps Smith brought the letter on his return from the latter trip.

From the Little Carpenter

[Fort Prince George, 15 March 1759]

This letter (or "talk") has not been found. Fauquier communicated it to the council on 17 Apr. 1759, and it is abstracted in *EJC* 6:135–36:

The Governor communicated to the Board the Talk he had just received from Ottocullocullo, or the Little Carpenter, dated Fort Prince George, March 15th signifying his People are well pleased to hear that all Quarrels were amicably made up, between them and Virginia—promising they shall do no more Mischief on the Frontiers—inclosing a String of white Wampum, to remind his Honor of the Trade promised to them—and desiring that Mr. Smith may be sent to let him know what Time the Goods may be expected.

To Jeffery Amherst

Sir   Wmsburgh March 17th 1759

I hope the Reasons why I could not attend the Meeting at Philadelphia, according to your Invitation, have been delivered to you, and have given you Satisfaction on that Head: and I hope I am doing his Majesty more Service by my remaining in the Colony at this Juncture.

This waits on you in Relation to Captns. Stobo and Vanbraun the two Hostages given by Coll. Washington, for the Delivery of all prisoners and fulfilling all the Articles of the Capitulation signed by him.[1] Monsr. La Force one of the prisoners in Question, taken in the little Meadows when Jumonville was killed,[2] was detained in prison here at the Instance of Stobo himself, who desired to remain as Hostage rather than so useful a Man as La Force was supposed to be to the French at that Time (as he was well acquainted with our back Settlements) should be delivered up. This Letter of Stobo was taken among Bradocks papers.[3] For this gallant Behaviour you must naturally imagine We are desirous in this Colony to release Stobo; and we have accordingly sent La Force to New York to Governor De Lancey, on his parole;[4] in Order to be exchanged for him, which we earnestly desire may be insisted on. There goes with La Force a young Canadian taken two years ago by some of our friendly Cherokee Indians, of whom this Colony purchased him at the Rate of Thirty pounds to save his Life, which was doom'd to destruction;[5] for this Act of Humanity We hope the French will exchange Vanbraun for him, which this Colony intreats you to try to effect; as we have no french prisoner left, of any Kind; all the rest stipulated to be sent home by the Capitulation above mentioned, being long since released.

We dont doubt your Endeavours to succeed in both the Exchanges mention'd, but we particularly desire that La Force may be detained till Stobo releases him. I am With the greatest Regard & Esteem, your Excellency, your most Obedient Humble Servant

Fran: Fauquier

To his Excellency Majr. Genl. Amherst.

ALS: W.O.34/37, ff. 21–22. Endorsed as received the thirty-first [Mar. 1759] and answered the same day.

1. Robert Stobo (1727–ca. 1772) and Jacob Van Braam (born ca. 1727) were handed over to the French as hostages on 4 July 1754, in accordance with the terms of Washington's capitulation at Fort Necessity, which stood at or near the Great Meadows, in Pennsylvania, about 50 mi. southeast of the site of Pittsburgh. See Freeman 1:pass. for an account of the transaction.

2. On 27 May 1754 a party led by Washington attacked a small French patrol under the command of Joseph Coulon de Villiers (1718–1754), sieur de Jumonville, and Jumonville was killed in the skirmish. Michel Pépin, called Laforce, a Canadian scout, was one of Jumonville's party who was captured. The engagement took place at the French camp about 7 mi. northwest of the Great Meadows, and not at the Little Meadows, about 45 mi. to the southeast, in Maryland.

3. Laforce was reputed to have great influence with the Indians, and to be able to converse with them fluently in their own language. The letter that Fauquier mentioned was probably one dated 28 July 1754 which Stobo contrived to send from Fort Duquesne, addressed to the commanding officer in Virginia, according to Stobo's own statement. This letter included a plan of Fort Duquesne and other military intelligence; it was handed over to Maj. Gen. Edward Braddock (1695–1755), commander of British forces in North America, and the French discovered it among Braddock's papers after his defeat near Great Meadows on 9 July 1755 (the text of Stobo's letter, without the plan of Fort Duquesne, is in *P.C. Pa.* 6:161–63; the plan, in facsimile, follows p. 210 of Alberts). This particular letter from Stobo has been confused with another letter from him of 29 July 1754, also from Fort Duquesne, and presumably addressed to the commanding officer in Virginia (*P.C. Pa.* 6:141–43). It refers to the letter of the preceding day and adds some military intelligence, and like the earlier letter makes note of Laforce's value to the French.

4. James De Lancey (1703–1760) was lieutenant governor of New York from 1753 until his death.

5. The young Canadian was probably the French prisoner whom Second Yellow Bird and his party of Cherokees brought to Williamsburg in Mar. 1757. The council recommended that the prisoner should be kept in Virginia if the Cherokees would part with him on reasonable terms, and suggested £20 as a sufficient consideration. See *EJC* 6:31, 34.

From Jeffery Amherst

Sir   New York 18th March 1759

It having become necessary, by the demise of Brigr. Genl. Forbes, that an Officer of Rank and Experience Should without loss of time proceed to Pensylvania to take on him the Command of His Majesty's regular Troops and those to be raised by the Southern Provinces, to Act in Conjunction for the Security and defence of those Provinces, or Otherwise as Opportunities Shall offer or the Exigences may require, I have thought it for the good of His Majesty's Service to Appoint Brigr. Gen. Stanwix[1] to that Command and he does accordingly set out to morrow for Philadelphia to take upon him the Same. I am therefore to request of You, that during Such his Command, You will upon every Emergent occasion Correspond & Cooperate with him in the Same manner as You are enjoined by Mr. Secretary Pitts Letter to do with me,[2] which must prove of great benefit to the publick Service, as from my removal from hence into the back Country, whither I may be called soon, it might prove very prejudicial to the Safety and Security of the Southern Provinces to wait for the Answers to any of the Letters You may have occasion to write to me in relation thereto, and I have accordingly directed Brigr. Genl. Stanwix to Correspond & Cooperate with You in like Manner.

Copy: C.O.5/54, ff. 194–95. Circular to governors of Pennsylvania, Maryland, Virginia, North Carolina, South Carolina, and Georgia. Two paragraphs concerning settlement of accounts and Indian affairs, not included here, were to be sent to Governor Denny only. Endorsed as received in Amherst's letter of 29 Mar. 1759. Fauquier communicated this letter to the council on 10 Apr. 1759; see *EJC* 6:135 n. 51.

1. John Stanwix (1690?–1766).
2. See Pitt's circular letter of 18 Sept. 1758, above.

To Horatio Sharpe

Sir   Wmsburgh March 19th 1759

The Expedition which is requisite to be used, in order to raise Men to compleat our Quota of Men to act in Conjunction with the rest of his Majesties Forces, has encouraged me to give Leave to some of the Officers to try whether they can enlist any in your Colony where they think they have some Acquaintance and Interest.[1] I therefore beg the Favour of you, not only to give them Permission, but to assist them with your Countenance and Protection, for the promoting his Majesties Service, at least so as not to interfere with any Levies your Colony is about to raise for the same Purpose. I am with great Esteem, Your Excellency's most Obedient Humble Servant.

                                                                            Fran: Fauquier
To Governor Sharpe.

ALS: Hall of Records of Maryland, Executive Papers, Folder 130.

1. Fauquier may have had in mind the fact that Amherst, in his circular letter of 16 Feb. 1759, had set 10 Apr. as the date for the Virginia troops to be ready to join him, rather than the date of 1 May suggested in Pitt's circular letter of 9 Dec. 1758. And Fauquier must have been uncertain about the ability of Virginia to raise as many men as had been raised in 1758, because, as he said in his letter of 11 Mar. 1759 to Amherst, the exertions of the recent campaign made recruiting difficult, since all the men (i.e., white men) in Virginia had land and only Negroes were laborers. No indication has been found of which officers Fauquier had authorized to recruit in Maryland, or of whether any officers did attempt to raise recruits in Maryland.

From James Abercromby

Sir   March 21st 1759

I wrote you about 3 weeks since that from some Motions relative to Tobacco made in Parliament I apprehended an Additional Duty might insue, and that thereupon I had applyd to the Merchants with a view to oppose the same;[1] Deputys from the Merchants of Bristol being sent up as was imagined in opposition, but by my information at their first Audience with the Ministers the Bristol Deputys being asked their sentiments declard they had authority to admit of an additional Duty of a penny per pound this being admitted the London Merchants in vain found their opposition, hereupon I attempted an opposition on the part of the Province upon the Reasons copy whereof I lay before you,[2] but after a great deal of trouble to little purpose a general Duty of 5 per cent on Dry goods amongst the rest Tobacco took place, and this on Tobacco is about a penny per pound, the Bristol Deputys I am informd alledge they had reasons to apprehend that a partial Taxation of Tobacco of 2 pence per pound was intended and of two Evils they adopted the least.[3]

In a former letter I told you that Mr Secretary Pitt having recommended to the Treasury my Memorial for Indian Presents I did expect success therein[4] The Memorial being referrd to the Board of Trade that Board Reported to the Treasury thereupon, That as they did not know how far the Measure of Indian Presents might have been taken up by General Forbes with the Government of Virginia, or with the Commander in Chief of the Kings Forces in America, who had upon the application of the Indian Commissioners of the Northern and Southward Districts Authority to make provision for Indian Measures, their Lordships could not give their oppinion on the Case of my Memorial so that it stops at the Treasury upon circumstances not in my Power to remove in time so as to answer Mr Secretary Pitts Views to the Service of the Western Indians.[5]

In the Midst of Parliamentary Business relative to Supplys and other Matters, it is not in my Power tho I have in conjunction with Mr Dinwiddie labord the thing as much as possible to give Motion to my Memorials relative to the Aid from the Quitrents. My Case in behalf of Virginia is not singular others with as much reason complain of Delays which in the end prove a Denial.

I am greatly surprisd to find by General Abercromby that no correspondence had been taken up between your Government & him relative to the Money granted by Parliament I expected to have been informed by him how this Matter stood and from thence to have taken it up with the Treasury I must therefore once more repeat my application to you for Instructions on this head, containing Certificates of the Forces raisd & Maintaind by Your Province the service wherein they were imployd, the Forts built at the Expence of the Province, and the service and Purposes proponed by such Forts, and whatever Military Services you may think within the Meaning of the Kings Message to Parliament copys whereof I have heretofore sent you, In the mean time when I movd for another Aid to Virginia at some time I prepared to the Secretary of State an Amendment to the Resolves of Parliament in that case so as to leave the application of the Money to the Lords of the Treasury without the Intervention of the Commander in Chief upon the proper Certificates being laid before their Lordships of the services perform'd within the meaning of Parliament, All these Matters I have more than once laid before you for Instruction thereon, to which I have no answer hitherto.

You will please however to take notice that by desiring Certificates to be sent to me of your Military Services and Provincial Aids of Money granted that I do not mean to divert you from pursuing your Correspondence with General Abercromby as the Resolves of Parliament direct in this Case my meaning is no more than that I may be prepard to apply to the Treasury in case the Votes of Parliament shall be alterd so as to leave the Apportionment of this Money to the Discretion of the Treasury without the Intervention of the Commander in Chief who probably has no Instructions from home no more than his Predecessors had I am

To the Honble. Gov. Fouquiere.

Copy: Virginia State Library, James Abercromby Letter Book, pp. 128–31. A marginal note suggests the letter was sent by a Mr. Withers. The draft letter is in Abercromby's hand and hard to read.

1. No letter from Abercromby to Fauquier of about 1 Mar. 1759 has been found. His two letters to Virginia of dates in 1759 earlier than 21 Mar. are those of 31 Jan. and 10 Feb.; neither makes any mention of an additional duty and opposition to it by the merchants. No information has been found on Abercromby's application to the merchants, but the journal of the House of Commons throws some light on the "Motions relative to Tobacco made in Parliament": on 15 Feb. 1759 the Commons ordered accounts to be made on tobacco imported into England, with specific reference to imports, exports, duties, allowances, fines and forfeitures, and discounts, and on 19 Feb. another account was ordered to be made of tobacco imports and exports for Scotland. These accounts were submitted on 2 Mar., considered on 7 and 9 Mar.; on 10 Mar. the responsible committee reported that a duty of 12d. in the pound sterling be laid on tobacco and other items imported into the kingdom, in order to raise a supply of money for the king.

2. This enclosure has not been found.

3. The general duty of 5 percent was levied by "An Act for granting to his Majesty a Subsidy of Poundage upon certain Goods and Merchandizes to be imported into this

Kingdom; and an additional Inland Duty on Coffee and Chocolate; and for raising the Sum of six Millions six hundred thousand Pounds, by way of Annuities and a Lottery, to be charged on the said Subsidy and additional Inland Duty," 32 Geo. II, cap. 10 (*Statutes* 8:324–36). The first article of the act authorized an additional duty of 12d. in the pound sterling (which is 5 percent) on the value of tobacco and other named articles imported into Great Britain, to be levied from and after 5 Apr. 1759. Abercromby noted that for tobacco this meant a tax of about 1d. per pound avoirdupois weight; and he seemed to say that the spokesmen for Bristol were inclined to agree to the tax of 12d. in the pound sterling so as to avoid the imposition of a specific tax on tobacco of 2d. per pound avoirdupois.

4. No letter with this information has been found, although Abercromby's letter of 10 Feb. 1759 indicated that his memorial about presents for the Indians had been submitted to the Treasury.

5. Abercromby's memorial, with the letter from Pitt's secretary which referred it to the Treasury, was transmitted to the Board of Trade by Samuel Martin, secretary to the Treasury, in a letter of 20 Feb. 1759. On 1 Mar. the Board of Trade replied that since the king had entrusted the management of Indian affairs to his commander in chief in North America, with two agents to act as his subordinates, it appeared to them that the proper method of offering such a proposal as Abercromby's would have been an application through one of the agents to the commander in chief; since the Board of Trade had no information on what steps the agents might have taken to negotiate with the Indians on the Ohio or to procure a supply of presents for them, the board could not form any judgment on Abercromby's proposal; and, finally, the board considered that if a distribution of presents to the Indians was thought to be expedient, and if no steps had been taken by the commander in chief, or General Forbes, or the government of Virginia, or that of Pennsylvania, to provide such presents, it would no doubt be necessary to send the presents from England. The letter from Martin to the Board of Trade has not been traced, but the board's reply is in C.O.5/1367, ff. 181–83.

From Jeffery Amherst

Sir, New York, 22d March 1759

Lieut. Gray of the Carolina Independent Company[1] returning to his Station, by Land, I take that Opportunity of Acknowledging the Receipt of Your Favor of the 2d Instant, by which I find, it was very uncertain that You could at this time be Spared from Your Seat of Government, and consequently that it was not likely You would be able to come to the Meeting at Philadelphia; Wherefore as my other business requires my Presence here, I, upon that Letter, laid aside all thoughts of going there Myself, but that nothing might be wanting to forward the Services in those Parts, I Sent Brigr. Genl. Stanwix (who set out on Monday last) to Philadelphia, to take upon him the Command of the Troops to the Southward, and to do every thing that may be requisite, either to Act on the Offensive or Defensive, as he shall Judge most for the good of the

Publick, and that no time might be lost therein, I have directed him to Correspond and Cooperate with the Southern Governors, for which purpose I furnished him with my Circular Letter of the 18th Instant to those Several Gentlemen, requesting them to do the like with him; which Letter I doubt not will have reached You before this comes to Your hands. I likewise on Monday last, Sent You Colonel Byrd in order to forward the Raising and Equipping the Men that shall have been Voted by the Dominion of Virginia, that they may be at the Place of Rendezvous without any delay, and I shall wait with impatience to Learn their Numbers and what Provision has been made for them by the Assembly.

Altho' I do not propose to go to Philadelphia yet if it should so happen that You can be there, I shall immediately upon Notice thereof set out to Meet You. I am, with great regard, Sir, Your most Obedient Humble Servant.

To the Honble. Govr. Fauquier.

Copy: C.O.5/54, ff. 253–54. Endorsed as being in Amherst's letter of 29 Mar. 1759. Fauquier communicated this letter to the council on 5 Apr. 1759; see *EJC* 6:133.

1. This was probably Lt. John Gray.

From William Byrd

[Philadelphia, 22 March 1759]

This letter has not been found, but Fauquier communicated it to the council on 3 Apr. 1759, and it is abstracted in *EJC* 6:677–78:

Governor communicated a Letter from Colonel Byrd dated March 22d Philadelphia signifying the General has ordered him up immediately with his Regiment and the Troops of this Province to reinforce Fort Ligonier and to be at hand to sustain the Garrison on the Ohio in case of an attack—that he has ordered Lieutenant Colonel Stephens to march directly up with 300 men and to call in the Rest of the Regiment to Winchester and the South Branch that they may be ready to march at an Hour's Warning, when he finds he can maintain them, which will be as soon as carriages can be provided—that the General has given him an Officer of General Warberton's to act as Brigade major—that he shall leave that Place in three Days to take the Command to the Westward, and by his present Orders is to attack Vennango and Presq'isle—begs whatever number of men shall be rais'd, he'd order them to Winchester forthwith.

The officer whom Amherst had provided as Byrd's brigade major is not identified, but he seems to have been drawn from the Forty-fifth Regiment, under the command of Lt. Gen. Hugh Warburton, and he may have been the Lieutenant Irwin whom Amherst mentioned in his letter of 30 Mar. 1759 to Fauquier.

From William Byrd

[Philadelphia, 25 March 1759]

This letter has not been found, but Fauquier communicated it to the council on 10 Apr. 1759. See *EJC* 6:135 n. 51.

From William Byrd

[Philadelphia, 26 March 1759]

This letter has not been found, but Fauquier communicated it to the council on 21 Apr. 1759, and it is abstracted in *EJC* 6:137:

> Also a Letter from Col. Byrd, dated Philadelphia, March 26th signifying he had employ'd Mr. David Franks to provide the Cloathing for his Regiment according to his Honor's Order—that as he was obliged to advance a Great Deal of Money for that Purpose, he had taken the Liberty of drawing a Bill on him in his Favor for £5000 Pensylvania Currency.

David Franks (1720–1794) was a merchant of Philadelphia who supplied stores and provisions for the British forces.

From John Blagg

[Fort Loudoun, 27 March 1759]

This letter has not been found, but Fauquier communicated it to the council on 3 Apr. 1759. The minutes of the meeting describe this letter as "inclosing a Copy of Colonel Byrd's Instructions to Lieutenant Colonel Stephens or the Commanding Officer of that Garrison which cant be readily complied with as there is not that number of men in the 6 companies at the South Branch, Patterson's that." The text of the minutes breaks off thus, abruptly, and is perhaps garbled; see *EJC* 6:677–78. John Blagg was a captain in the Virginia Regiment. The instructions from Byrd to Stephen that Blagg sent with his letter have not been traced, but they were presumably those mentioned in Byrd's letter of 22 Mar. 1759. Patterson's was probably Patterson's Fort on the south branch of the Potomac River.

From Jeffery Amherst

Sir   New York 28th March 1759

With my dispatches from Mr. Secretary Pitt this Moment received by the Halifax Packet came the enclosed for you,[1] by which you will See, that the King has been pleased to direct me, & Brigr. Genl. Forbes, to lose no time in concerting the properest and Speediest means for compleatly restoring, if possible, the ruined Fort du Quesne to a defensible & respectable State, or for erecting another, in the room of it, of Sufficient Strength, and every way adequate to the great importance of the Several Objects of Maintaining His Majesty's Subjects in the undisputed possession of the Ohio; of effectually cutting off all Trade & Communication this way, between Canada and the Western & Southern Indians; of protecting the British Colonies from the Incursions to which they have been exposed Since the French built the above Fort, and thereby made them selves Masters of the Navigation of the Ohio; & of fixing again the Several Indian Nations in their Alliance with and Dependance upon, His Majesty's Government; for all which wise and good purposes, it is His Majesty's Pleasure that You Should Use Your Utmost endeavours with Your Council & Assembly to induce them to exert every Means in their Power for Collecting and forwarding the Materials of all Sorts, and the workmen, which Shall be wanted, and which the Commander in Chief in North America, or Brigr. Genl. Forbes, Shall require for the Service; and that Your Province do also furnish every other assistance of Men, Cattle, Carriages, Provisions &ca &c that Shall be necessary for the Support and Maintenance of the Kings Forces that Shall be Employed in this essential Work as well as in all farther Operations to be undertaken in those parts the ensuing Campaign.

These directions being so full and Explicit leaves me Nothing further to add to them, than my warmest wishes and hopes that they will meet with a speedy and vigorous Execution as well on the part of Your Province as of those of Maryland & Pensylvania, who are equaly with you so particularly & nearly interested therein & to whom the Same is likewise recommended in the strongest terms.

And as I have already Signified to You that I had appointed Brigr. Genl. Stanwix to Succeed Brigr. Genl. Forbes in the Command to the Southward, and desired of You to Correspond and Cooperate with him on every Matter relative to the Service in those Parts;[2] I am now to request of You, that all the Aid and Assistance required of you by Mr. Secretary Pitts within Letter, in favour of the late Brigr. Forbes, may be granted to Brigr. Stanwix, to enable him in the most Expeditious manner to Execute the before mentioned great and Salutary work, or any other that may be found necessary for the good of the Service; and that You would look, upon whatever he may Ask or require of Your Province during his continuance in that Command, as coming from myself. I am &c.

Copy: C.O.5/54, ff. 196–97. Circular to governors of Virginia, Maryland, and Pennsylvania. Endorsed with the note "In Consequence of Mr. Secretary Pitts Circular Letter to them of the 23d January" and as received in Amherst's letter of 29 Mar. 1759. Fauquier communicated this letter to the council on 10 Apr. 1759; see *EJC* 6:135 n. 51.

1. This was Fauquier's copy of Pitt's circular letter of 23 Jan. 1759 to the governors of Virginia, Maryland, and Pennsylvania. See that letter, and particularly n. 1 on the orders to Amherst.

2. See Amherst's circular of 18 Mar. 1759 for his appointment of Stanwix.

From Jeffery Amherst

Sir   New Yourk 30th March 1759

I am this Moment favour'd with Yours of the 11th Instant, enclosing Your Speech to the House of Burgesses, on Occasion of Mr. Secretary Pitts Letter of the 9th December, and mine of the 11th & 16th ultimo which is so good and so proper a One, that I should have flatter'd myself with a quite different Address from the Burgesses, than that they presented You;[1] for admitting they may be somewhat incapacitated thro' the fatigues of last Campaign, is it not their real Interest, at this present urgent, important & decisive Crisis, rather to Augment than diminish their Numbers of last Year? Since by such an Exertion, they must so much the Earlier bring about a Solid and lasting peace, & Effectually Secure to themselves the quiet and uninterrupted Enjoyment of their Lives & properties, the Advantages of which are so obvious, that I had little thoughts of their not doing their utmost to obtain them; and I am still willing to believe, that in their reassuming this affair, which You mention was to be the Week after the date of Your Letter, they will not only have weighed these Advantages, but also have considered the Obedience they Owe to the recommendations of the best of Kings to raise with all possible Dispatch, at least as large a body of Men, as they did for the last Campaign, and even as many more as the Number of its Inhabitants may allow. And that in conformity thereto, instead of increasing their first Vote to 1500, which you were in hopes of, they will have Augmented it to at least 2000.

From Your Letter of the 2d Instant I foresee that it might not be expedient for His Majesty's Service that You should leave the Colony at this time, and as the preparations I am making for the Operations of the ensuing Campaign also require my presence here, I immediately declined going to Philadelphia, unless it would have been practicable for You to have come there, in which Case I should certainly have met You: of this I acquainted You in mine of the 22d when I likewise inform'd You that I had appointed Brigr. Genl. Stanwix to the Command of the Southward, and beg'd of You to Correspond & Cooperate with him in every thing that could tend to the good of the Service in those parts, which request I now renew, and in Consequence thereof I shall inform him with the Assurance You give me of Your readyness to Cooperate with me in every Measure which shall be concluded on for the Common good of the Colonies, And that You make no doubt by the disposition which appears among all Men, but that the Assembly will Join in any reasonable plan or Agreement relative to the Trade with the Indians; for which I return You most Sincere thanks.

I am very glad to find that the Command of the Virginia Forces is Offer'd to Colo. Byrd; upon a very strong presumption that it would, and a certainty of his accepting the same, I sent him to You about a fortnight ago, in Order to be aiding and assisting to You in the forwarding & Expediting the Levies and to have them properly Equipped & ready to set out for the place of Rendezvous so early as the Season will possibly admit of their taking the field, also immediately to Order a detachment of his Regiment to Fort Ligonier to be distributed according to the disposition which Colo. Bouquet, to whom I had sent directions for that purpose should make of them; which I hear Colo. Byrd has already done. And from your Zeal and his and the Influence you both have in the Colony I make no doubt but You will be able to overcome the little difficulties that might otherwise retard their being ready. I am &ca.

Govr. Fauquier.

Copy: C.O.5/54, ff. 388–89. Endorsed as being a reply to Fauquier's letter of the eleventh [Mar. 1759], and as being in Amherst's letter of 16 Apr. 1759. Fauquier communicated this letter to the council on 21 Apr. 1759; see *EJC* 6:136.

1. The address of the House of Burgesses, presented on 24 Feb. 1759, referred to Amherst's request for additional troops, presented by Fauquier, as something that would increase the great debt already contracted on account of the war; the burgesses flattered themselves that if they fell short of Amherst's expectations it would be the result of their poverty alone (*JHB, 1758–1761*, p. 65).

From Jeffery Amherst

Sir   New York, 30th March 1759

With your publick dispatch 11th Instant I likewise received your two private Letters of the same date. In Answer to that in favor of Lieut.

Stewart, I am sorry to say, that notwithstanding the great Inclination I have to pay all the regard that is due to your recommendation, I cannot at this present time dispense Lieut. Stewart from Joining the Battalion he belongs too, as it is order'd on a Service wide from where Your Troops will be, and where his presence will be Necessary; Nevertheless, if hereafter your Troops are Employed in any Operations wherein I think he can be of use to them I will directly order him to Join them, but till then it is absolutely requisite he should be with his Battalion; not that it is unprecedented for an Officer to be absent from his Corp on other duty, of which there are many Instances and particularly one at this very time, in the Person of Lieut. Irwin, whom Colonel Byrd asked of me as one that he thinks will be of use to him, and which I granted because the Regiment to which that Gentleman belongs is destined this ensuing Campaign for no other Service than Garrison duty, which may admit of the Absence of an Officer.[1] but where Corps are upon actual Service every Officer belonging to them on the Spot and Capable of Service, is expected to be with them. for these reasons, which I am Confindent will have a due weight with you, I trust that you will do me the Justice to believe that it is entirely owing to these Circumstances that I cannot have the Satisfaction of Complying with your request.

I have heard various discourses on the Affair which has occasioned the Narrative you enclosed to me in your other Letter, but as I was at such a distance when it happened, and that I have never sifted into it, I cannot give you my Opinion upon it, but I will take an Opportunity of perusing what you sent me.[2] I am &c.

Govr. Fauquier.

Copy: W.O.34/37, f. 200. Marked "Private."

1. Lieutenant Irwin was probably the officer of the Forty-fifth Regiment, commanded by General Warburton, whom Amherst had provided as Byrd's brigade major. See Byrd's letter of 22 Mar. 1759.
2. Amherst referred to Andrew Lewis's account of Grant's defeat near Fort Duquesne enclosed in Fauquier's second letter (as it appears to be) of 11 Mar. 1759, that in W.O.34/37, f. 16.

To Arthur Dobbs

[31 March 1759]

This letter has not been found. Fauquier mentioned it in his letter to Lyttelton of 7 Apr. 1759, and its date is inferred from that letter and from Fauquier's letter of 5 Sept. 1759 to Lyttelton. This letter of 31 Mar. evidently transmitted dispatches from Pitt to Dobbs and asked Dobbs to forward other dispatches from Pitt to Lyttelton.

To William Henry Lyttelton

[31 March 1759]

This letter has not been found. Fauquier mentioned it in his letters to Lyttelton of 7 Apr. and 5 Sept. 1759; the latter states that this letter of 31 Mar. 1759 referred to a talk with the Cherokees.

From Jeffery Amherst

Sir   New York, March 31st 1759

   Mr. La Force mentioned in yours of the 17th is now upon Long Island, whither he was sent by Govr. De Lancey after having taken his Parole, what you Recommend in Relation to him, and the other two Gentlemen of Virginia, shall be punctually observed upon the very first Occasion that shall offer in Treating for an Exchange of Prisoners,[1] meanwhile I am &ca.

Govr. Fauquier.

Copy: W.O. 34/37, f. 202. Fauquier communicated this letter to the council on 21 Apr. 1759. See *EJC* 6:136.

   1. Stobo managed to escape on 30 Apr. 1759, and he joined the British at Louisburg in the following June; Van Braam was detained in Canada until the surrender of Montreal in Sept. 1760.

From John Stanwix

[Philadelphia, 2 April 1759]

This letter has not been found, but Fauquier communicated it to the council on 10 Apr. 1759, and probably laid it before the burgesses on the same day. It was very probably the letter from Stanwix, enclosing a circular letter of Amherst's, that Fauquier mentioned in the postscript of 10 Apr. to his letter of 8 Apr. 1759 to Amherst. A suggestion of what Stanwix's letter may have said is offered by his letter of 2 Apr. 1759 to Governor Sharpe of Maryland, which enclosed Pitt's circular letter of 23 Jan. 1759 and Amherst's circular letter of 28 Mar. 1759, both of them addressed to the governors of Pennsylvania, Maryland, and Virginia. Stanwix's letter to Sharpe expressed the hope that the forces which Sharpe would raise in Maryland might provide four good companies of rangers. It seems likely that Stanwix wrote to the governors of Pennsylvania, Maryland, and Virginia to ask for rangers or artificers, or both. See *EJC* 6:135 and *JHB, 1758–1761*, p. 123, on the Stanwix letter to Virginia and *Md. Arch.* 56:148–50, for the letter from Stanwix to Maryland and its enclosures.

To Jeffery Amherst

Sir   Wmsburgh April 3d 1759

I have detained Captn. Dean of his Majesties Ship Lowestoffe, who came from Europe express with Orders and Instructions for the Commanders and Governors on the Continent; a few Days, in order to send by Him the Result of the general Assembly in Relation to the Requisitions of his Majesty for the Quota of Troops to be furnished by this Colony. The Burgesses yesterday pass'd a Bill to raise pay and cloath one Regiment of 1000 private Men compleat, which I have power to march out of the Colony to join the rest of his Majesties Forces to act offensively against the Enemy.[1] These shall be raised and order'd to March to the General Rendezvous with the greatest Expedition possible. I used my utmost Endeavours both publickly, by enforcing in three different Speeches the Necessity of complying with his Majesties Demands,[2] and privately by shewing the utility of such Measures to the Members, but I could not obtain another Man. Indeed they have raised a Body of 500, on a different Establishment, to remain at home to protect the Frontiers; But of that Step the only Advantage to his Majesties Cause which I see is; that they will not be to be raised if any great Emergency should hereafter induce the Assembly to be willing to let them march out of the Colony.

I most sincerely wish you Success in all your Operations, and that this Continent may reap all the Advantages they justly expect from your Activity and Prudence and am with great Esteem, Sir, Your most Obedient Humble Servant

                  Fran: Fauquier

To his Excellency Majr. Genl. Amherst.

ALS: W.O.34/37, ff. 23–24. Endorsed as received 14 Apr. and answered the twenty-second [Apr. 1759]. A copy is in C.O.5/54, ff. 390–91, endorsed as being in Amherst's letter of 16 Apr. 1759, and numbered 12.

1. The bill was "An Act for granting an aid to his majesty, for the better protection and defence of this colony, and for other purposes therein mentioned" (Hening, 7:255–65). The main provisions of the act were to bring the strength of the regiment to 1,000 privates, to authorize the expenditure of not more than £28,000 for the purpose, and to enable the governor to send the troops out of the colony or to employ them as the commander in chief directed. It further authorized the raising of an additional 500 men for service only inside the colony. The necessary money was to be raised by a poll tax of 2s. per head in 1765 and in 1766 and one of 4s. per head in 1767, and a duty of 2s. per hogshead on tobacco exported between 20 Oct. 1764 and 20 Oct. 1767; pending the collection of these taxes the treasurer was empowered to issue treasury notes up to the amount of £52,000, these notes to be redeemable on 20 Apr. 1768.

2. Fauquier had urged compliance with the king's demands in his opening address to the General Assembly on 22 Feb. 1759, in his speech to the assembly on 5 Mar. 1759, and in his reply on 7 Mar. 1759 to the burgesses' address of 6 Mar. (*JHB, 1758–1761*, pp. 55–56, 77–78, 81–82).

To William Pitt

Sir   Wmsburgh April 3d 1759

In Obedience to his Majesties Commands notifyed to me in your Letters of the 9th Decr. 23d Janry. last past, both which I immediately laid before the General Assembly[1] which was then and is now sitting I urged in the strongest Terms the complying with every thing which was required of us, but instead of the same Number of Men which was furnished by this Colony for the last Campaign, I could obtain no more than One Regiment of 1000 Private Men compleat, which I will endeavour to keep so all the Campaign. I will use the utmost Expedition possible to get them in Readiness to March to the General Place of Rendezvous.

The Assembly have also raised another Body of 500 Men for the Defence of the Frontiers, of which I see no use for his Majesty's Service, any more than that they will be actually raised and on Foot if any great Emergency should hereafter prevail on the Assembly to let them March to Join his Majesty's Forces.

I have taken the Liberty to enclose my two Speeches to convince his Majesty & his Ministers, that I have done all in my Power, tho' I have not had the Success I wish'd for.[2]

On the Delivery of your last Letter I strongly recommended it to both Houses in a few Words spoke without Notes, which Method I had once before tried & I thought with good Effect.³ I am with the greatest Respect, Sir, Your most Obedient & devoted humble Servant

Fran: Fauquier

P.S. A Bill is ready for my Assent to appoint an Agent who will be furnish'd with proper Documents & power to transact the Affairs of this Colony.⁴

To the Rt. Honble. Mr. Secretary Pitt.

LS: C.O.5/19, f. 74. Marked "Duplicate." The complimentary close and signature are in Fauquier's hand.

1. Pitt's letter of 9 Dec. 1758 was laid before the House of Burgesses on 5 Mar. 1759, apparently (see *JHB, 1758–1761*, pp. 77–78). No record has been found of when Pitt's letter of 23 Jan. 1759 was transmitted to the General Assembly, but it appears that Fauquier communicated it to the council on 10 Apr. 1759 (see *EJC* 6:135 n. 51).

2. No enclosure is present, but Fauquier probably enclosed his address to the General Assembly and his reply to the address of the House of Burgesses, which he had sent to Amherst in his letter of 11 Mar. 1759.

3. Fauquier presumably meant the letter of Pitt's most recently received, for on 26 Mar. 1759 he summoned both houses of the General Assembly to inform them that he had just received Pitt's letter of 29 Dec. 1758, sent express by one of the king's warships, and he recommended the letter to their immediate consideration (see *JHB, 1758–1761*, p. 108). The earlier occasion when Fauquier spoke without notes was probably the proroguing of the session of 9–11 Nov. 1758; see his letter of 14 Apr. 1759 to Pitt.

4. This bill was "An Act for appointing an Agent" (Hening, 7:276–77). The act appointed Edward Montagu of the Middle Temple to act as agent in Great Britain for the colony. He was to be under the direction of a committee of correspondence, and he was appointed for a term of seven years, at a salary of £500 sterling a year.

From Beverley Robinson

[New York, 6 April 1759]

This letter has not been found. Fauquier communicated it to the council on 21 Apr. 1759, and it is abstracted in *EJC* 6:137:

Also a Letter from Mr. Beverley Robinson dated New York April 6th signifying that no Fund being there for maintaining the french Prisoners, that La Force might not be sent back to Virginia, which he thought would not be agreeable to his Honor, he had become answerable for his Maintenance, which will be about two Dollars per Week.

Beverley Robinson (1723–1792), brother of John Robinson who for many years was treasurer of Virginia and speaker of the House of Burgesses, settled in New York when he was in his middle twenties and became a wealthy landowner; he acted as paymaster and commissary for the provincial forces.

To William Henry Lyttelton

Sir   Wmsburgh April 7 1759

As Lieutenant Gray is going for South Carolina, I take the Opportunity of writing to you, to inform that a few Days since I sent an Express to Governor Dobbs of North Carolina with Dispatches from Mr. Secretary Pitt, the Messenger was also charged with Dispatches for you which I desired Governor Dobbs to immediately forward to you.[1] They were brought here by Captn. Dean of the Lowestofte Man of War who was sent from Europe express with orders to leave these Orders to the Governors in his Way to Halifax,[2] where he is to join Admrl. Holmes who is supposed to be already arrived with five Sail from England, to take on him the Command of the Ships which winter'd at Halifax,[3] and then Join Admiral Saunders who was to sail a few Days after Captain Dean with ten Sail of large new Ships of which two carry 90 Guns, to command in chief an Expedition against Quebec which General Wolfe is to command by Land.[4] Capt. Dean left Plymouth the 8th february. I by the same Messenger wrote to you as a private Man which I hope you will duly receive. I am with the greatest Esteem Your Excellency's most Obedient Humble Servant

                                                    Fran: Fauquier

To Governor Lyttelton.

ALS: William L. Clements Library, Lyttelton Papers. Endorsed as received 24 Apr. 1759 by Lieutenant Gray.

1. See Fauquier's letters of 31 Mar. 1759 to Dobbs and Lyttelton.
2. Halifax, on the south coast of Nova Scotia, was founded by the British in 1749 (and named for Lord Halifax, president of the Board of Trade). The town has an excellent harbor, open all the year, and it was the principal naval base for operations against the French in Canada.
3. Rear Adm. Charles Holmes (1711–1761) was third in command of the naval operation against Quebec. He went out from England to Halifax early in 1759 to forward preparations for the campaign.
4. Vice Adm. Charles Saunders, the senior naval commander of the expedition against Quebec, and Maj. Gen. James Wolfe, the senior army commander, sailed from England on 17 Feb. 1759.

To Jeffery Amherst

Sir   Wmsburgh April 8th 1759

I received Your Favour of the 22d of last Month on the 6th instant, I am truly sensible of the Honour You do me in that Letter, but as Your

8 April 1759

Time is precious and the Welfare of the Colonies depends upon it, I shall not think of taking up any part of it, by being the Occasion of your taking the Fatigue of a Journey. If at the End of the Campaign you should think it expedient for the Governors to meet you, in order to adjust any Matters of Treaty with the Indians, or Operations for an ensuing Campaign, I shall with pleasure embrace any Opportunity of cooperating with you for the Service of his Majesty and the Benefit of his Dominions of this Continent. The sooner Your Intentions are then made known the better, that the Congress may be over before the Time of preparing the Forces for the Field if there should be Occasion.

This Colony have given One Regiment 1000 private Men which I shall endeavour to keep always complete if possible during the Campaign; they will be all well and new cloth'd in every particular, and they will be supplyed with Arms in the best Manner We are able to arm them as the Colony is drained of Arms, which We hope for your Interest to have replaced according to Mr. Secretary Pitts promise.

I have not yet received Brigr. General Stanwix's Letter, but shall endeavour to assist him in all his Operations to the best of my Power.[1] Coll. Byrd I have not seen but hear he is gone to Pittsburgh. With the most ardent Wishes for your prosperity both in your public and private Capacity I am with the greatest Esteem Your Excellency's most Obedient Humble Servant

Fran: Fauquier

P.S.

April 10th.

I have this Moment received a Letter of Brigr. Genl. Stanwix with your circular Letter inclosed.[2] I shall take every opportunity of complying with your Request in corresponding and cooperating with that Gentleman in all things which tend to his Majesties Service, and I should be obliged to you to recommend it to him to be frequent in his Correspondence as I find such free Communications greatly tend to dispose the Minds of People to forward the Service. I can with pleasure tell you the House of Burgesses have this day brought in a Bill to add two Companies of 100 Men each to be added to the Regiment as Artificers.[3]

F: F:

To Major General Amherst.

ALS: W.O.34/37, ff. 25–26. Endorsed as received on 20 Apr. and answered the twenty-second [Apr. 1759].

1. Fauquier referred to correspondence from Stanwix that Amherst had directed, as he stated in his letter of 22 Mar. 1759 to Fauquier.

2. This is assumed to be the letter of 2 Apr. 1759 from Stanwix.

3. Fauquier's comment sounds misleading. On 10 Apr. 1759 the House of Burgesses resolved that 200 of the 500 men to be raised for the protection of the frontiers should be employed as artificers and joined to the regiment then in the pay of the colony, and that an additional bounty of £5 be paid to each man joining the companies of artificers; the house ordered the preparation of a bill pursuant to these resolutions (see *JHB, 1758–1761*, pp. 123–24). This bill was passed on 12 Apr. as "An Act to amend the Act, intituled, An Act for granting an Aid to his Majesty, for the better Protection and Defence of this Colony, and for other purposes therein mentioned" (Hening, 7:279–80). The new act also authorized the governor to order the artificer companies to join the Virginia Regiment, whereas the act it amended specifically forbade the 500 men to be incorporated with the Virginia Regiment, or added to the garrison of Pittsburgh, or sent out of the colony on any pretense whatsoever.

To the Board of Trade

My Lords Wmsburgh April 10th 1759

I yesterday received your Favour of the 18th Janry., and am extremely chagrined to find by it that my Conduct here has not given your Lordships all that satisfaction which it is my highest Ambition to endeavour to deserve. I hope your Lordships will excuse me in these Attempts to justify my self.

Just before I left England your Lordships recommended it to me, to disunite the Offices of Treasurer and Speaker if it could be done without Prejudice to his Majesties Service. It was not made an Instruction, because if it had it could not be departed from; and I understood I had a Latitude given me to do as well as I could in this delicate Affair.[1] Upon communicating this Recommendation to many of his Majesties Council, and to his Attorney General, they were all of Opinion that this could not be effected without the most manifest prejudice to his Majesties Service, and that the very attempting it might throw the Country into a Flame: they give me for their Opinion the following Reasons. The Country have uninterruptedly enjoyed this privilege from the first raising Money in the Colony. there is in the printed Book of Laws an Act to appoint a Treasurer so long ago as in the Year 1691 when Mr. Nicholson was Lieutenant Governor.[2] The Treasurer has nothing at all to do with his Majesties Revenue of Quit-Rents, or the 2 shgs. per hhd duty on Tobacco for the Support of Government, both which pass thro' the Receiver General; but has Cognizance only of Money raised by Taxes on themselves for the Service of the Colony. They conceive it to be an old Grudge of the late Lieutenant Governor on Account of the Pistole Affair, and Mr. Dinwiddie has given Cause for this Suspicion, by his publickly writing to his

Friends by Letters which came in with me, that he had procured such an Instruction to be given me, and exulted upon it as a Victory gained over the Speaker. This Fact I have lately learn'd, and that the Eyes of the Country were upon me on my first Arrival here: all anxious for the Fate of their Treasurer. The Gentleman who possesses these places at present and has done from the year 1738 is a Man of Worth, Probity and Honor, the most beloved both in his public and private Character of any Man in the Colony, as these Trusts so long reposed in him plainly evince. let me add my Lords that I believe I owe the Supply I have obtained this Year of Men and Money to the strong Support of himself and his Friends. for I am afraid the Disposition of the House in general was against increasing the Debt of the Colony. The people of this Country are so jealous of their Liberty, and are so reluctant to give up any Point, that tho' they daily see & know the ill Consequences attending their Conduct, yet they cannot be prevail'd on to give any power even to those in whom they most confide.

Under these Circumstances My Lords, I took the Steps of which I gave your Lordships a full and candid Account, and as I thought it my Duty added my opinion plainly and honestly that it could not be done without a manifest Detriment to his Majesties Service. And sorry I am to add (since your Lordships wish it otherwise) that it is still my opinion strengthend by every Day's Experience. But if your Lordships are of a different Sentiment, I have nothing to do, but to obey and follow any Directions your Lordships shall give me on this Head, all of which I will most punctualy observe. And if I should not be permitted to pass another Bill of this Nature,[3] I trust to your Lordships Candour to do the Justice to acknowledge, I apprehend bad Consequences which as a Man of Integrity charged with the Care of his Majesties Affairs I think it incumbent on me to represent to your honourable Board.

As for any Discontent I might express on the slow progress of his Majesties Arms under the Command of the late Brigr. Genl. Forbes, it was purely the Effect of an Apprehension I had, that the Dissatisfaction I had observed might retard the raising Men and Money for this Campaign, which I am convinced, would have been the Consequence, if Success had not crowned our Wishes at last. Of this I fancy your Lordships will be also convinced when you read the Sketch of this Assembly in another Letter on that subject.[4]

In Relation to the Money Bills my Lords I had pass'd two before I received your Lordships Letter, one for the Supplies of last Year, one for this.[5] I had no Scruples on this Head: as I was told before I left England, that the Merchants had drop't all Thoughts of presenting any Memorial in Relation to that Affair, being convinced they are already as well secured as they can be from suffering any Damage from it. And this is still insisted upon by both the Legislative Bodies here. My Letter on that Head I hope your Lordships have, long before this can arrive received and approved.[6] The Colonies Agent will be furnished with a full Answer to the Merchants Memorial.[7] by their private Letters from England they appear now to be satisfyed.

I come now to the last Article in which I own my self very culpable; as it is undoubtedly highly improper, that any person in England should be apprized of acts of Government here, before they are communicated to your Lordships, but I hope for your Indulgence in assigning my Reasons for having acted in this imprudent Manner. When Captn. Legge in the Chesterfield had carried off all the Trade then ready, no Ship bound for London went out of these Ports for a long Time, and I did not think it adviseable to send the Box containing all the public Acts and papers by a Ship bound to any out-Port, till I consigned them to the Care of Mr. Morse who undertook to deliver them at your Office himself.[8] And as my Letters related to the Acts I delayed the sending them till some such Opportunity offer'd, which I waited long for: But no such Neglect shall happen for the future. I must also intreat your Lordships Forgiveness for the Negligence of my Clerk who I find put into the Box the printed duplicate of the Journal of the House of Burgesses instead of the Original.

An Impatience of thinking I am in the least under your Lordships Displeasure, and an earnest Desire to conciliate your good Opinion has made me trespass on your Time, for which I beg your Lordships Excuse being with the highest Regard, My Lords, Your Lordships most Obedient Obliged & devoted Servant

Fran: Fauquier

ALS: C.O.5/1329, ff. 134–36. Endorsed as read 21 June 1759.

1. For the Board of Trade's advice on separating the offices of treasurer and speaker of the House of Burgesses in Virginia, see Fauquier's letter of 11 June 1758 to the board.

2. This was "An act appointing a Treasurer," Hening, 3:92–95.

3. Fauquier must have been referring to "An Act for appointing a Treasurer," passed in the General Assembly of Sept. 1758. (Hening 7:242–43). The act named John Robinson to be treasurer so long as he was speaker of the burgesses, and until the end of the next session of the General Assembly after he should cease to be speaker.

4. Probably Fauquier meant his letter of 23 Sept. 1758 to the board.

5. The money bills were "An Act for the defence of the Frontiers . . .," which Fauquier signed on 12 Oct. 1758, and "An Act for granting an aid to his majesty . . .," which he signed on 5 Apr. 1759 (Hening, 7:171–79, 255–65).

6. Fauquier's letter of 5 Jan. 1759.

7. The answer to the merchants' memorial has not been exactly identified. Fauquier

laid before the burgesses on 10 Apr. 1759 a copy of the Privy Council order of 11 Jan. 1759 on the memorial of the London and Bristol merchants, enclosed in Pownall's letter of 19 Jan. 1759; the order was immediately referred to a committee of the whole house, but the deliberations of the committee are not recorded (see *JHB, 1758–1761*, pp. 123–24). Evidently the committee appointed to supervise the agent, Edward Montagu, did not communicate with him before its letter of 12 Dec. 1759, in which it informed him of his appointment and commented at length on several matters of business, including the dissatisfaction of the merchants of Great Britain with Virginia's emission of treasury notes that were made tender for sterling debts. This letter and the minutes of several meetings of the committee are in *VMHB* 10 (1902–3): 337–53.

8. Mr. Morse was mentioned in the postscript of 26 Feb. 1759 to Fauquier's letter to the board of 30 Jan. 1759. He is not identified, but evidently was sailing in a Bristol ship.

To the Board of Trade

My Lords   Wmsburgh April 14th 1759

    The Assembly have this Day broke up, after having given one Regiment of 1000 private Men exclusive of Officers to join his Majesties Forces under Brigr. Genl. Stanwix appointed to the chief Command in these Parts; and by a second Bill have added two Companies of 100 Men each to act as Artificers, as required by the Letters of Mr. Secretary Pitt, Genls. Amherst and Stanwix. The Command of these Troops is given to the Honble. Coll. Byrd, on the Resignation of Col. Washington, and I will use my utmost power to keep them a real thousand effective Men in the Field and not on Paper only.

    The Difficulties these Bills met with, and the History of their progress thro' the House of Burgesses I shall trouble your Lordships with, as it will give some Insight into the Disposition of the people of this Colony. I opened the Assembly with the Speech which I enclose to your Lordships.[1] In the Burgesses Address you will observe they don't promise a Man, or engage for any Thing but only plead Poverty,[2] however the Speaker & his Friends were very solicitous to get a Vote soon pass'd to raise 1000 Men to obviate any ill Impressions the Address might make on the Commanders of his Majesties Forces. and they at the same Time disbanded four Companies of Rangers of 100 each kept for the protection of the Frontiers.[3]

    On the receiving Letters from Mr. Secretary Pitt and Majr. Genl. Amherst I again call'd them up and in a second Speech recommended vigorous Measures, they answered in the same Tone as before. as your Lordships will see by the enclosed Copies.[4] on the Commitment of the Bill a Motion was made to fill up the Blanks with 1500 and lost by one

Vote. about this Time some of the Frontier Members on breakfasting with me ask'd me what I designed in Relation to the Frontiers, I told them they must look to that, for I would not keep one single Man at home out of the 1000 given. This alarmed them. upon this I sent for the Speaker and told him what had happened, and he immediatly proposed that a Motion should be made in the House, that it should be an instruction to the Committee to receive a Clause for the augmenting the Number of Men.[5] I spoke to some of the warmest against the Augmentation, to desire the House would furnish me with an Answer to the petitions of the Frontier Inhabitants,[6] if they designed them no Protection, by Message, Address or what way they pleased. This Vote was carried by Eight in the House, an Augmentation of 500 was resolved on, but to my great Surprize I found a Tack was made to the Bill, for the appointing an Agent, which had long been a Bone of Contention between the Council and Burgesses. I told some of the chief promoters of this Step, that I would not suffer the Tack, that I had an Instruction to the Contrary, and it should not pass. they answered that they imagined when it came to the point I would not refuse it, but not to give me uneasiness they would try the Council first by an Agents Bill, which they did and the Council pass'd it.[7] As the Augmentation was carried by the coming in of the Frontier Members, they tied it up in such a Manner that it was impossible the Men could be made use of for any purpose but the protection of the Frontiers, the Division was too near to attempt any Alteration, and I took it as it was, considering that at all Events there were 500 Men ready raised and in pay in Case of an Emergency.

On receiving a second very pressing Letter from Mr. Secretary Pitt,[8] I again call'd them and recommended the Letter to them, in a few Words spoken extempore which Step I had observed to make a great Impression on them, when I prorogued the Short Assembly of two Days,[9] but this was to no purpose, so on the 5th April I went to the Capitol and pass'd all the Bills ready for my Assent, that I might immediately set about recruiting. The very Day of my passing this Bill, the Burgesses came to a Vote to send me a Message that I would employ these very 500 Men on an Expedition against the Shawnese, to this Message I returned a very undecisive Answer.[10] But to conclude this long Narrative, on the 9th instant I received Letters from Mr. Secretary Pitt and the Generals requiring Artificers.[11] I sent these Letters to the House of Burgesses and the Speaker seeing a fair Opportunity as several of the other party were gone home, got a Bill ordered in to enable me to send 200 of the 500 to join his Majesties Forces as Artificers which was carried thro' the House without much Opposition.

14 April 1759

I will take up no more of your Lordships Time only to acquaint you that the Money Bill stands upon the same Footing as the former, and the Agents Bill is pretty near the same as that which is at present in force for the Province of South Carolina, The Business and Instructions to the Agent being to be carried on by a Committee of 4 of the Council & 8 of the Burgesses according to Directions received from the general Assembly.[12] I am, my Lords, with the greatest Respect Your Lordships most Obedient Obliged & devoted humble Servant

Fran: Fauquier

To the right Honble. the Lords of Trade & Plantations.

ALS: C.O.5/1329, ff. 121–23. Endorsed as read 19 June 1759.

1. The enclosure (C.O.5/1329, ff. 124–25) was the printed version of Fauquier's speech of 22 Feb. 1759, which Bristol lists as B2084. The text is in *JHB, 1758–1761*, pp. 55–56.

2. The address from the burgesses of 27 Feb. 1759 with Fauquier's answer (C.O.5/1329, f. 127) was enclosed in the printed version that Bristol lists as B2086. The text of the address from the burgesses is in *JHB,1758–1761*, p. 65, but the journal omits Fauquier's brief reply, in which he said he was uneasy at the thought that the burgesses could not prosecute the war with a vigor up to their intentions, but he trusted they would do all they could to support the common cause and secure the country lately recovered.

3. The burgesses resolved on 27 Feb. that the four companies of Rangers then in service should be disbanded immediately; see *JHB, 1758–1761*, p. 69.

4. Fauquier's second speech, of 5 Mar. 1759, and the address from the burgesses of the following day with Fauquier's reply (all in C.O.5/1329, f. 128) were enclosed in the printed versions that Bristol lists as B2085 and B2087; the text is in *JHB, 1758–1761*, pp. 77–78, 79, 81–82.

5. On 21 Mar. it was ordered that it be an instruction to the committee, on the bill for completing the Virginia Regiment, to receive a clause for raising an additional 500 men; see *JHB, 1758–1761*, pp. 103–4.

6. No petitions from the frontier counties of the sort Fauquier must have had in mind have been found.

7. The "tack" was a clause relating to an extraneous matter, appended to a bill (especially a bill of supply) in order to secure the passing of the tack, nowadays called a rider. Fauquier must have meant that the bill for appointing an agent was attached to the bill for augmenting the number of troops. The fifteenth article of the governor's instructions (C.O.5/1367, ff. 97–98) ordered that the governor, so far as possible, should see to it that anything required in a particular matter should be provided for by a distinct law, without including in the same act matters having no proper relation to each other; and that the governor should especially see that no clause or clauses should be inserted in or annexed to any act if they were foreign to what the title of the act suggested. The separate act for appointing an agent was ordered to be drawn up on 17 Mar.; it was presented and got its first reading and second reading on 24 Mar.; it got its third reading and was passed by the burgesses on 27 Mar. and referred to the council; and on 28 Mar. the council agreed to the act, with amendments that the burgesses accepted.

8. Pitt's circular letter of 29 Dec. 1758.

9. The short session of 9–11 Nov. 1758. Fauquier's proroguing speech is in *JHB, 1758–1761*, p. 52.

10. The address from the burgesses asked the governor to use the 500 men, to be raised for protecting the frontiers, in an expedition against the Shawnees if he thought such an expedition practicable and necessary; and it further asked him to provide ammunition and provisions for any volunteers who might join the expedition. On 6 Apr. Fauquier answered "That if he found it, on Enquiry, expedient to undertake an Expedition against the Shawnese, that the Men intended to be stationed on the Frontiers should be employed in that Manner" (*JHB, 1758–1761*, pp. 118–19).

11. Pitt's circular letter of 23 Jan. 1759, Amherst's circular letter of 28 Mar. following, and, presumably, the letter from Stanwix of 2 Apr. 1759.

12. Fauquier presumably had in mind the act passed in South Carolina on 20 May 1755 (Thomas Cooper and David McCord, eds., *The Statutes at Large of South Carolina*, 10 vols. [Columbia, S.C., 1836-41], 4:18-19), by authority of which James Wright had been serving as agent for South Carolina since 19 Nov. 1756. The Virginia committee consisted of William and Thomas Nelson, Philip Grymes, and Peter Randolph, from the council, and of John Robinson, Peyton Randolph, Charles Carter, Richard Bland, Landon Carter, Benjamin Waller, George Wythe, and Robert Carter Nicholas, from the House of Burgesses. All these members of the council, and John Robinson and Peyton Randolph, burgesses from King and Queen County and from Williamsburg respectively, are identified elsewhere. The Charles Carter could be either Charles Carter of Cleve (1707–1764), a burgess from King George County, or Charles Carter of Corotoman and Shirley (1732–1806), a burgess from Lancaster County; it has been assumed that Charles Carter of Cleve was the man named to the committee. The other burgesses on the committee were Richard Bland (1710–1776) of Prince George County; Landon Carter (1710–1778) of Richmond County; Benjamin Waller (1710–1786) of James City County; George Wythe (1726–1806), the burgess for the College of William and Mary; and Robert Carter Nicholas (1715–1780) of York County.

Enclosure: Address to the Assembly

[14 April 1759]

Gentlemen of the Council, Mr. Speaker and Gentlemen of the House of Burgesses.[1]

I cannot dismiss you without expressing the great Satisfaction I have received from the Bill I have this day passed to enable me to send two Companies of Artificers to join the Regiment which is to Act in Conjunction with his Majesty's Forces in offensive Operations against the Enemy: by which Means the Fort at Pittsburgh may be put in a very respectable Condition, either to curb the Indians or put a Stop to any future Encroachments of the French. I did not doubt but that Reason and a just Sense of your true Interest would in the end prevail and overpower, all your Fears of Distress and Poverty.

I am particularly to thank you Gentlemen of the House of Burgesses for the Money you have raised for these purposes, and it shall be my Endeavour by a Careful application of it and a steady observance of what

14 April 1759

you have recommended to me to give you such Conviction of the Sincerity of my Intentions, as will secure to me your future Confidence.

Gentlemen of the Council and of the House of Burgesses.

I sincerely wish this Colony may reap all the Advantages and Benefits expected from an Agent long wish'd for and now appointed by the Act for that purpose. The Act for the encouragement of Arts and Manufactures[2] gives me an Opportunity to recommend to you all in your respective Retirements to encourage and propagate Industry in all its branches, the true, I had almost said the only Source of Riches, Greatness and Happiness. that you may immediately set about this useful Work I think it expedient to prorogue you and you are accordingly prorogued to the first Thursday in August next.

MS: C.O.5/1329, ff. 129–30. Endorsed as received with Fauquier's letter of 14 Apr. 1759 and read 19 June 1759.

1. This is a manuscript copy of Fauquier's speech on 14 Apr. 1759, in which he prorogued the General Assembly.

2. This was "An Act for encouraging Arts and Manufactures" (Hening, 7:288–90). The act named six members of the council and thirteen burgesses to act as trustees of a sum of money not exceeding £1,000 to be supplied by the treasurer from the public funds and laid out in premiums of not more than £20 "for the more speedy and effectual bringing to perfection any art or manufacture of service to the public"; the intention was to encourage many families to settle in Virginia and thus relieve its distressed situation.

Order in Council

[St. James's, 14 April 1759]

At the Court at St: James's the 14 of April 1759

Present

The Kings most Excellent Majesty in Council.

Whereas the Lieutenant Governor and Commander in Chief of His Majestys Colony of Virginia with the Council and Assembly of the said Colony did in August 1754 pass an Act which hath been transmitted in the Words following, Vizt.

> "An Act to dock the Entail of certain Lands whereof Nathaniel West Dandridge[1] Gentleman is seized and for settling other Lands and Slaves of greater Value to the same Uses."

Memd: Here the Act was inserted at length.[2]

Which Act, having been perused and considered by the Lords Commissioners for Trade and Plantations, and by them presented to His Majesty at this Board as fit to be confirmed His Majesty was this day pleased, with the Advice of His Privy Council, to declare His Approbation thereof. And pursuant to His Majestys Royal Pleasure thereupon expressed the said Act is hereby confirmed, finally enacted, and ratified accordingly. Whereof the Governor Lieutenant Govr: or Commander in Chief of His Majestys said Colony of Virginia for the time being, and all others whom it may concern are to take Notice and Govern themselves accordingly.

A true Copy
W: Sharpe

Copy: C.O.5/1329, ff. 190–90A. Evidently certified with the autograph signature of Sharpe. Endorsed as received (at the Board of Trade) 21 May and read 8 July 1760. There is no record of when this order was sent to or received in Virginia.

1. Dandridge (1729–1786) was a justice of the peace and of the quorum (the select group of justices, the presence of at least one of whom was required for the transaction of business) for King William County in 1749. He was a justice of the peace (and of the quorum) for Hanover County in 1753, and again a justice for Hanover County in 1757. He was one of the burgesses for Hanover County from 1756 until 1764, when he was replaced by James Littlepage on the grounds that he had been named coroner of Hanover County; see the journal of the House of Burgesses for the session of Oct. 1764 on Dandridge's complaint of an undue election and the burgesses' dismissal of his complaint as frivolous and vexatious.

2. Hening, 6:428–32.

To William Pitt

Sir Wmsburgh April 16th 1759

I have the Pleasure to acquaint you that two Days before the Assembly was prorogued the House of Burgesses, by a subsequent Bill brought into their House and immediately pass'd, enabled me to march 200 out of the 500 Men mentioned in my Letter of the 3d instant, (a Duplicate of which I have the honour to transmit to you)[1] to join the Forces under the Command of Brigr. Genl. Stanwix as Artificers, agreeable to your Letter of the 23d Janry. in which you require such Assistance from the Colonies. I am with the greatest Respect, Sir, Your most Obedient & devoted humble Servant.

Fran: Fauquier

To the right Honble. Mr. Secretary Pitt.

ALS: C.O.5/19, ff. 86–87. Endorsed as received 5 June [1759].

1. This enclosure was the letter of 3 Apr. 1759 to Pitt, above, the original of which has not been found.

To Horatio Sharpe

Sir   Wmsburgh April 18th 1759

I am informed by Mr. Thomas Walker who was commissary for the Virginia Forces that when Fort Cumberland was evacuated, and the Troops of Maryland took Possession of it there were some Provisions left belonging to this Colony, which by agreement were to be paid for, by Maryland or to be replaced.[1] Mr. Walker is now going for Maryland to settle that Account and I beg the Favour of you to appoint some Body to adjust that affair with him. I am with great Esteem, Sir, Your most Obedient Humble Servant.

Fran: Fauquier

To his Excellency Govr. Sharpe.

ALS: Hall of Records of Maryland, Executive Papers, Folder 132.

1. The Virginia troops evacuated Fort Cumberland in the spring of 1757. The question of these provisions recurs frequently in letters of Dinwiddie, Washington, and others for months after the date of the evacuation. See, for instance, *Dinwiddie*, 2:630 ff. and Fitzpatrick, 2:20 ff.

From Jeffery Amherst

Sir   New York 22d April 1759

Notwithstanding my Apprehensions that the Affairs to the Northward would not permit me to go to Philadelphia; upon finding that they went on Smooth, and that it was Essentially necessary I should be present to settle those to the South, I Seized the very first few Days that Offered, to Repair thither; and was so lucky as to be detained there no longer than a Couple of Days; at my return I was favored with yours of the 3d Instant, a Copy of which I sent to Brigr. General Stanwix, that he might answer the Same,[1] and renew my most Pressing Instances for an Augmentation of Your Numbers which I fully showed you the Necessity of, by my Letter of the 30th March, not received by You on the 10th of this Month, the last date of Yours to me,[2] by the return of my Express, who came in Yesterday; whereby I am sorry to find, that all the Augmentation the House of Burgesses have made, is only two Companies of 100 Men Each, to be added to the Regiment as Artificers, which tho' [I] cannot but Commend, as, if they are properly Chosen, they must be of Great service, yet, I must say, this still falls very short of my Expectations, founded on the Kings Enjunctions & the Exigences of the Service; wherefore I still trust that when my Letter will have been laid before the House, the

Burgesses will have been Convinced of the real Necessity of their Compliance with my Demand and that they will have acted accordingly, all which I soon hope to be informed of thro' Brigr. Stanwix, to whom I shall write in Consequence, and desire him to Correspond with You, as frequently as there may be Occasion for, and I shall likewise Recommend to him, to furnish You with what Number of Arms he shall Judge Necessary to Compleat your Troops, which you will be pleased to Acquaint him with and to apply to him for.[3]

As it is more than probable that at the Close of the Campaign, the Service will require me to Call a Meeting of the Governors, & that You are so kind to Offer to Assist at it, You may depend upon my doing my utmost to have it take place at such a time as may not interfere with Your business of the Colony, of which I shall give You timely notice hereafter.

I am glad to hear Colonel Byrd is gone to Pittsburgh; and with my most sincere thanks for your kind and ardent wishes for my prosperity, I am &ca

Jeff. Amherst

The Honble. Governor Fauquier.

Copy: C.O.5/55, ff. 9–10. Endorsed as being in Amherst's letter of 19 June 1759. The pronoun in brackets was omitted, presumably by accident; the "must" a few words below it is actually spelled "most." Fauquier communicated this letter to the council on 13 June 1759; see *EJC* 6:139.

1. On 16 Apr. 1759 Amherst sent Stanwix a copy of an unidentified letter from Fauquier, probably Fauquier's letter of 3 Apr. to Amherst. Amherst's covering letter of 16 Apr. (W.O.34/45, f. 212) says nothing to suggest that Stanwix should reply to Fauquier, and no answer from Stanwix to Fauquier's letter of 3 Apr. has been identified, although it may have been Stanwix's letter of 28 Apr. 1759.

2. Amherst referred to Fauquier's letter of 8 Apr. 1759, which had a postscript dated 10 Apr.

3. On 23 Apr. Amherst wrote to Stanwix and enclosed a copy of an unidentified letter from Fauquier, probably Fauquier's letter of 8 Apr. 1759 to Amherst, and a copy of his reply. Amherst's covering letter (W.O.34/45, f. 219) to Stanwix says nothing about his corresponding with Fauquier or furnishing arms on Fauquier's application.

From William Henry Lyttelton

[Charles Town, 27 April 1759]

This letter has not been found. Fauquier communicated it to the council on 13 June 1759, and it is abstracted in *EJC* 6:140:

A Letter from Governor Lyttelton, dated Charles-Town April 27th referring his Honor to Mr. Martin, the Bearer, who was appointed Missionary to the Cherokees, for the latest Occurrences there of any Moment.

From John Stanwix

[Philadelphia, 28 April 1759]

This letter has not been found. Fauquier communicated it to the council on 13 June 1759, and it is mentioned in *EJC* 6:139:

> Two letters from Brigadier General Stanwix, dated Philadelphia April 28th and May 30th expressing his Approbation of the Addition of two Companies of Artificers, and his Hopes that some Expedient will be found to compleat the Regiment.

To the Board of Trade

My Lords   Wmsburgh May 9th 1759

Purposing to set forward for Winchester tomorrow in order to see the Troops raised by this Colony, before they march to join the Forces under the Command of Brigadier Genl. Stanwix, I would not omit the Opportunity of writing to your Lordships as I am informed a Liverpool Ship will sail from James River in a few Days.

I have given Orders for the Clerks to make what Dispatch they can, to have the Journals of the Council and Burgesses, together with all the Acts pass'd last Session ready against my Return, that I may have it in my Power to transmit them to your Lordships with the Receiver Generals and Naval Officers Accounts by the first Opportunity which shall offer. The hardships of last Campaign occasioned by Scarcity of provisions and Inclemency of Seasons have a little abated the Military Ardor of the young Men of this Colony, however I hope to find the Body tolerably compleat; a particular Account of which I shall give your Lordships Information of on my Return.

In Consequence of the Letters your Lordships did me the Favour to send me Copies of, in Relation to the Fee of a Pistole on Patents for Lands,[1] an advertisement was published in the Gazette by order of Council giving notice what Lands were exempt from, and what included in that Fee, and warning every one to take out their patents as they would run the risque of having their Lands caveated.[2] This has already produced a very good Effect especially for Lands exempted, as people were afraid to take out patents for fear the Fee should be demanded; I hope his Majesties Quit Rents will be greatly improved, as people begin to be solicitous to take out their patents in Time.

I hope your Lordships are convinced of my good Intentions and Zeal to promote his Majesties Service in every Shape, and satisfied in some

Measure with the Reasons I have assigned for my Conduct in the Letters I did my self the Honor to write to you of the 14th of last Month by the Phaeton Captain Allen.³ My greatest Ambition is to do my Duty and obtain your good Opinion being with the greatest Esteem, My Lords, Your Lordships most Obedient & devoted Servant

Fran: Fauquier

The Rt. Honble. the Lords of Trade &ct.

ALS: C.O.5/1329, ff. 137–38. Endorsed as read 18 July 1759.

1. The board's letters to Dinwiddie of 3 July 1754 and 18 Apr. 1755, which Pownall transmitted to Fauquier with his letter of 5 Jan. 1759.

2. On 9 Apr. 1759, when Fauquier communicated to the council Pownall's letter and the two letters to Dinwiddie, the journal of the council has this entry: "Which Letters being read, it was the Advice of the Council, and accordingly order'd, that it be notified in the Virginia Gazette what Patents are subject to the Fee of a Pistole; and that if Patents lying in the Secretary's Office, for which such Fee is due, are not sued out within six Months from this Time, the said Lands shall be liable to be caveated; and that hereafter, no Certificates for Lands will be received into the Secretary's Office without such Fee, where the same is due." The minutes of the council (from which the journal entry for this date was written in its final form) say of the lands which the journal describes as "liable to be caveated" that "the same will be forfeited, and esteemd King's Lands" (*EJC* 6:134). No issue of the *Virginia Gazette* with the advertisement has been found, and no copy of the advertisement is known.

3. Neither the *Phaeton* nor Captain Allen has been identified, but they are probably the ship and the Capt. Samuel Allyne, of Norfolk or Hampton, concerned in the mutiny or piracy that is the subject of Fauquier's letter of 26 Dec. 1761 to the Admiralty and its enclosures.

From Horatio Sharpe

Sir [18 May 1759]

In a Letter which I have just now received from General Stanwix he desires me to forward to You the inclosed Letters & to beg the favour of You to forward those of them that are not addressed to Yourself. At the same time I do myself the honour to acknowledge the Receit of Your Letter by Mr. Walker¹ in Compliance with which I have wrote to Dr. Ross² who had the Care of Victualling our Troops at Fort Cumberland & have desired him to account with Mr. Walker for the Provisions that were left there when the Virginia Troops evacuated that post in April 1757 & which were afterwards served out to the Maryland Provincials & I hope these Gentlemen will settle the Affair to the Satisfaction of all Parties.

To Governor Fauquier the 18th May 1759.

Copy: Hall of Records of Maryland, Governor's Letter Book, III.
1. Fauquier's letter of 18 Apr. 1759.
2. Dr. David Ross was commissary for the Maryland troops.

From Samuel Davies

[Hanover, 30 May 1759]

This letter has not been found. Fauquier communicated it to the council on 13 June 1759, and it is abstracted in *EJC* 6:140:

Also two Letters from Mr. Davies, dated Hanover May 30th and June 9th, the one signifying that the Society for managing the Indian Missions and Schools, have lately received Mr. Richardson's Journal; and communicating according to their Order to his Honor some Particulars of Consequence therein contained, respecting the Temper and Disposition of the Cherokees; adding if his Honor pleases to see the said Journal, his Commands shall be obey'd.

The other signifying he had desired Mr. Martin, in the Name of the Society, to request his Honor, to order the Interpreter who is in the Pay of Virginia, to assist the Missionary occasionally when he is not engaged in the public Service.

Mr. Richardson's journal is now in the collections of the New York Public Library, and parts of it were published in Samuel C. Williams, "An Account of the Presbyterian Mission to the Cherokees, 1757–1759," *THM*, 2d ser., 1(1931): 125–38. The published excerpts contain several comments on the hostility of the Cherokees toward the British colonists, particularly on account of the way the Little Carpenter and his party had been treated after the surrender of Fort Duquesne. The interpreter in the pay of Virginia was no doubt Richard Smith, who was well acquainted with the Cherokees; on several occasions Richardson's journal noted the difficulty of communicating with the Indians except through an interpreter, especially because the Indians sometimes refused to speak English even when they knew how to.

From John Stanwix

[Philadelphia, 30 May 1759]

This letter has not been found. Fauquier communicated it to the council on 13 June 1759, along with another letter from Stanwix of 28 Apr., and the two letters are mentioned in a brief abstract in *EJC* 6:139. See the letter of 28 Apr. 1759 from Stanwix.

From William Byrd

[Winchester, 4 June 1759]

This letter has not been found. Fauquier communicated it to the council on 13 June 1759, and it is abstracted in *EJC* 6:140:

A Letter from Col. Byrd, dated Winchester June 4th informing that Fort Cumberland is in Danger, the Indians appearing before it every Day—that he had sent Captain McKenzie there with Fifty Men—that several of Capt. Waggoner's Men have been killed at Pittsburg lately—that the Posts are in a miserable Situation above, for Want both of Men and Provisions—that the Regiment is at a low Ebb from the Losses they have sustained, the Small-Pox and Meazles amongst them, and great Desertion—desiring a Commission to hold a General Court-Martial, some blank military Commissions, and a Sum of Money for Contingent Charges.

Capt. Robert McKenzie was evidently serving under Byrd at Winchester. Capt. Thomas Waggener had been left in command of a detachment of men at Fort Duquesne after its evacuation by the French.

From William Henry Lyttelton

[Charles Town, 7 June 1759]

This letter has not been found. Fauquier communicated it to the council on 3 Sept. 1759, and it is abstracted in *EJC* 6:144:

A Letter from Governor Lyttelton dated Charles Town June 7th signifying he had received Advices that Nineteen Persons had been scalped on the Yadkin and Catawba Rivers by a Party of the Cherokee Indians; that he had sent Remonstrances thereon to the Head-Men of that Nation, but has not yet received their Answer.

Perhaps Lyttelton was communicating several reports of 4 and 5 May 1759 that he had received; they notified him that on 25 and 26 Apr. the Cherokees had killed and scalped fourteen persons on the Yadkin River, the Catawba River, and Fourth Creek; and that on 29 Apr. the Cherokees had killed and scalped a man named Mull, his wife, his son, and eight children of a man named Hannah, all on the Catawba River, as well as two unnamed families on the Yadkin River. It is not unlikely that the several reports refer to the same incidents. The reports are in *S.C. Records*, pp. 485–87.

To the Board of Trade

My Lords   Wmsburgh June 9th 1759

I have the Honour to transmit to your Lordships the Acts of the last general Assembly,[1] the Journals of both Houses,[2] the Accounts of the

9 June 1759

Receiver general and Naval Officers,³ by this Conveyance, which is the first Opportunity I had since they have been delivered to me. I hope the Merchants of great Britain are fully satisfied of the Care that is taken of their Interest, by the Laws of this Colony; and that all their Objections to the Money Bills as they stand, are entirely removed; if not, I have the Assurances of the chief people here that they will be ready to secure them by any subsequent Bill, in the Manner they desire: it being their Intentions that all Sterling Debts due to them should be fully satisfyed and paid.

I returned from Winchester on the 5th instant, and found the Regiment not so complete as I wish'd, the Men enter very unwillingly, it does not at present amount to quite 800. But as the recruiting is continued and the Body is daily encreasing, I am in hopes that by the Time General Stanwix wants them to join him, they will be tolerably complete. He is now at Philadelphia settling the Accounts of Waggonage of last Campaign, left unsettled by the late General Forbes. The want of regular payments to the planters for their Waggons, is the great and only Reason both in this Colony and Pensilvania, of the Difficulty of getting provisions to the respective posts. Provisions can be got, but Carriage for them meets with great Difficulties, which I hope will be overcome by the General's Care in providing for the payments in a regular Manner.

The Men raised by this Colony are in general healthy active likely young fellows, who I hope will support the Reputation the Regiment gained in the Campaign of last Year. they are new clothed and well appointed that they may be serviceable to his Majesty and the common Cause is the ardent Wish of, My Lords, Your Lordships most Obedient Obliged & devoted humble Servant

Fran: Fauquier

The Rt. Honble. the Lords of Trade &ct.

ALS: C.O.5/1329, ff. 143–44. Endorsed as read 14 Nov. 1759, and, it seems as enclosing four papers and some acts.

1. The thirty-four acts passed in the General Assembly of Feb. 1759; manuscript copies are in C.O.5/1329, ff. 1–75, and the text is in Hening, 7:255–330.
2. The journals of the session of 22 Feb.–14 Apr. 1759. The journal of the House of Burgesses was evidently that in C.O.5/1434, ff. 128–226, while the journal of the council in assembly was apparently either the copy in C.O.5/1429, ff. 204–19, or that in C.O.5/1431, ff. 56–70.
3. The "accounts of the Receiver General" seem to have comprised only the account of the revenue of 2s. per hogshead for 25 Oct. 1758–25 Apr. 1759, the copy in C.O.5/1329, ff. 145–45A; see app. C. for 1759. The Board of Trade journal describes the naval officers' returns as those for the several districts for 29 Sept. 1758–5 Apr. 1759; the returns sent have not been identified, but they may have included various returns from Port Accomack for 10 Oct. 1758–5 Apr. 1759 (C.O.5/1447, ff. 96–97); from the

Lower James for 29 Sept. 1758–25 Apr. 1759 (C.O.5/1447, ff. 76, 79, and C.O.5/1448, f. 5); from the Upper James for 10 Oct. 1758–5 Apr. 1759 (C.O.5/1447, ff. 98, 101, or perhaps C.O.5/1448, f. 18); from Rappahannock for 29 Sept. 1758–25 Apr. 1759 (C.O.5/1447, ff. 93–94); and from South Potomack for 10 Oct. 1758–5 Apr. 1759 (C.O.5/1447, f. 88, C.O.5/1448, f. 8).

To William Henry Lyttelton

Sir Willmsburgh June 19th 1759

I received your Favour of the 27th of April by Mr. Martin, whose Account of the Cherokee's has given us great pleasure here, as We were under some apprehensions from them on Account of some Murders supposed to be committed by them in North Carolina.[1] But as they are in the Temper represented by Mr. Martin, We have determined to send off the Trade as promised them directly; and Smith the Interpreter is actualy set out to give them Information thereof that they may prepare for the Reception of the Goods, with a Talk from me and a String of white Wampum.[2] The Draught of the Talk is with Colonel Peter Randolph, otherwise I would have sent you a Copy of it, but that, and the Conversation you and I had with the Little Carpenter as Mr. Martin tells me correspond entirely.[3]

I have sent you five Receipts from Mr. Grymes his Majesties Receiver general for £55.8.0 this Currency which is all that was charged to your Account for that Express, We thinking it but just to take part of the Expence on our Selves as we made use of the Man as far as New York.[4]

I have also enclosed to you a Copy of my Essay according to your Request.[5] You do me much Honour in thinking it worth your Acceptance, but in this as well as every thing else I shall always be glad to comply with your Desires being with great Esteem, Sir, Your Excellency's most Obedient humble Servant

Fran: Fauquier

To Governor Lyttelton.

ALS: William L. Clements Library, Lyttelton Papers. Endorsed as received 16 Aug. 1759, and with the notation "Letter from the Lt. Govr. of Virginia & Receits for Monies paid by me in pursuance of Mr. Secy. Pitts *Secret* Letters which Monies I have been reimbursed by the Treasury of Great Britain."

1. It is likely that Fauquier referred to the incidents which Lyttelton reported in his letter of 7 June 1759, for both the Yadkin River and the Catawba River are in the west central part of North Carolina.
2. In the conference of 19, 20, and 23 Jan. 1759, Fauquier had told the Cherokees

that a quantity of trade goods would be sent to them in the spring. On 17 Apr., when Fauquier had communicated to the council the message of 15 Mar. from the Little Carpenter, they advised that Smith the interpreter should be sent to inform the Cherokees that the goods would be sent about the end of June, and Smith evidently carried out this mission in the latter part of April or the early part of May. On 13 June, Fauquier informed the council of what Martin had told him about the Cherokees, and they advised that the trade goods then in the colony intended for the Cherokees should be sent to them at once. See *EJC* 6:124–30, 135–36, 140.

3. The contents of Fauquier's message to the Cherokees and of Lyttelton's conversation with the Little Carpenter have not been found, but Fauquier seemed to say they were exactly like what he had told the Little Carpenter during the conferences in January.

4. See Fauquier's letters of 27 July 1758 to William Prentis and of 5 Oct. 1758 to Lyttelton on this transaction.

5. This is assumed to be Fauquier's essay on taxation, which Lyttelton mentioned in his letter of 12 Dec. 1758.

Enclosure: Philip Grymes to William Henry Lyttelton

Virginia June 13th 1759

Received from his Excelency William Henry Littleton the Sum of Fifty five Pounds eight Shillings Current Money of this Colony, it being for so much advanced to Thomas Withers on Account of the Province of South Carolina for Payment of an Express to Admiral Boscawen at Louisbourg 1st Receipt.

Philip Grymes

DS: William L. Clements Library, Lyttelton Papers. Enclosed in Fauquier's letter of 19 June 1759 to Governor Lyttelton. The enclosure consists of two sheets of five copies of the receipt numbered 1st, 2d, 3d, 4th, and 5th Receipt; only the first of these is transcribed above. The receipts are all in a clerk's hand, evidently, but signed by Philip Grymes.

To the Board of Trade

My Lords   Wmsburgh June 23d 1759

I do my self the Honour to transmit to your Lordships, by the Spotswood Captn. Seaton for Bristol a Duplicate of my Letter of the 14th of April, and also of a Letter of the 9th instant which your Lordships will receive by the Jenny Captn. Crawfurd who will sail on this s'en night for London, by whom I shall send all the public Acts and Papers.[1] I am extremely sorry I can not send these sooner, but I cannot get them out of the Offices for Want of Clerks who can write the engrossing hand. They are not now all finish'd and deliver'd to me. I propose for the future as an Expedient in some Measure to remove this Difficulty, to send your Lordships the principal Acts as soon as the Session is over by themselves, and let them be followed by the Journals and other Acts of less Consequence: if this Method will be agreeable to your Lordships.

Captn. Elphinston in his Majesties Ship Eurus arrived in Hampton Road on the 20th with three Transports under Convoy containing three Hundred Highlanders Recruits for Montgomery's and Frasers Battalions.[2] They expected I had received Instructions in Relation to their future Destination, but as I have received no Instructions or Information on this Head, I find my self at a Loss to provide for the Men and Officers whom I have ordered to follow their own Instructions and disembark the Men for whom I will do all in my Power both as to Accomodations and Refreshments of fresh provisions after their long passage. I have dispatch'd a Messenger to Brigr. Genl. Stanwix at Philadelphia to know how I shall dispose of the Men; I expect his Return in about eight Days from this Date; and have detained Captn. Elphinston and the Transports till I receive his Answer, for if he would have them immediately join him there, the Transports can carry them, and Captn. Elphinston Convoy them into Delaware River in his Way to join Admiral Saunders as his Orders are: and I have wrote to Mr. Saunders my Reasons for detaining him these few days.[3]

Captn. Elphinston has brought in with him two Rhode Island-Men, supposed to be concerned in the same illicit Trade as the Vessel brought in here by Captn. Legge and condemned here last year.[4] These Captains have, I am informed, burnt many of their papers, so the Event of the Seizure is uncertain. I have the Honour to be with the greatest Regard, My Lords, Your Lordships most Obedient humble Servant.

Fran: Fauquier

To the Rt. Honble. the Lords of Trade &ct.

ALS: C.O.5/1329, ff. 146–47. Endorsed as read 14 Nov. 1759.

1. The captain of the *Spotswood* was Charles Seaton, but Captain Crawfurd of the *Jenny* has not been more exactly identified.

2. Capt. John Elphinstone was in command of H.M.S. *Eurus*, a twenty-gun frigate. The *Pa. Gaz.* for 28 June 1759 reported that the Virginia fleet had arrived from the River Clyde, in Scotland, under the convoy of the *Eurus*, along with transports carrying 400 Highlanders. Archibald Montgomerie (1726–1796) was the lieutenant colonel in command of the Seventy-seventh Regiment of Foot, and Simon Fraser

(1726–1782) was the colonel commanding the Seventy-eighth Regiment, or Fraser's Highlanders.

3. No trace has been found of the messages to Stanwix and Saunders, or of any replies from them. The *Pa. Gaz.* for 19 July 1759, however, reported that three transports with Highlanders had arrived at New York a few days before, from Virginia, so it appears that they were not disembarked in the Delaware River.

4. The *Pa. Gaz.* for 28 June 1759 described the two vessels that the *Eurus* captured as a brig and a schooner, from Monte Cristi in what is now the Dominican Republic, and belonging to New York and Rhode Island. See Fauquier's letter of 23 Sept. 1758 for Legge's capture.

To the Earl of Loudoun

My Lord   Wmsburgh July 13th 1759

I should have done my self the Honor to have wrote to your Lordship long before this, but that I waited for your Answer to [the] Letter I addressed to you of the 20 of November last, in which I set the Affair in a clear Light in Regard to the proffits of this place. That Letter, I have just had the Misfortune to hear has never reach'd you, as the Ship by which I sent it, is said to be taken by the French and carried into Morlaix.[1] I have herewith sent your Lordship a Copy of that very Letter, as I cannot express my self more fully on the Subject, and it is still quite equal to me whether your Lordship and I come to a settled Agreement, or whether your Lordship appoints an Agent here, to whom I shall pay half of the Proffits agreeably to the Royal Instructions.

There is a Case which has actualy now happened which will shew your Lordship that I cannot in Equity be bound to a certain Time in my Remittances on an Agreement for by a Defficiency in the Duties on Tobacco laid for the Support of Government here; The last half years Salary due the 25th of April is not yet paid; and as long as the Warr continues I apprehend there may be always an Arrear.[2] for this Reason my Lord I can be no further bound as to the Times of Remittance, but by the first London Ship that shall sail after the payment of the Salary. The Colony has made Applications to the Board of Treasury for an Aid out of his Majesties Revenue of Quit-Rents to make good this Deficiency, as the Tobacco Duty has often heretofore gone in Aid of the Quit-Rents. It is not impossible but I may hereafter sollicit your Lordship to join with me to back this application, as our Interests are so nearly concerned.

My Brother who will deliver you these Letters has full powers from me to settle with your Lordship. He has an Account of my whole Receipts from the 5th June 1758 the Day on which I landed and was sworn in to office to the last December inclusive. I am with great Regard, My Lord, Your Lordship's most Obedient humble Servant.

Fran: Fauquier

To the Earl of Loudoun.

ALS: The Huntington Library, San Marino, Calif., HM, Loudoun Papers, LO 6121. Endorsed as received 12 Sept. 1759. The word in brackets was omitted.

1. Morlaix is a French seaport on an inlet of the English Channel, 33 mi. northeast of Brest, in Brittany.

2. Fauquier had signed a warrant for his half year's salary of £1,000 on 5 May; the salary was probably unpaid because of the deficit in the revenue of 2s. per hogshead. With the governor's salary included, the account showed a deficit of £2,193.1.3 for the half year ending 25 Apr. 1759, and it continued to show a deficit until the half year ending 25 Oct. 1761.

To the Board of Trade

My Lords　　　　　　　　　　　　　　Wmsburgh July 14th 1759

I have had the Honor to receive an Instruction from his Majesty, in Relation to the Securing the Merchants of great Britain in the recovery of sterling Debts due to them, from any Loss they may Sustain on Account of the paper Currency of this Colony, which I shall earnestly recommend to the Assembly on their Meeting:[1] and which I apprehend will meet with no Difficulty of any sort; as I am sure it is the Desire and Design of the Legislature to give the Merchants full Security in their Property here. This they supposed was effectualy done by the Laws now in force, and I cannot help thinking that if the Merchants had paid due Attention to their present Situation in Regard thereto they would have been of that Opinion themselves.

The Colony would be in a perfect State of Tranquility if the Conduct of the Clergy was as temperate as it ought to be.[2] Their Provision is of such a Nature and on such a footing that I fear there will be constant Animosities between the Clergy and Laity in every Scarce Year of Tobacco. If the Clergy were to receive their full Quota of Tobacco in a Year when the planter makes small Crops, Their Gains would encrease in proportion to the Distresses of the planter: Then the Laity would murmur. If the Legislature set a price to ease the Country in Distress, then

14 July 1759

the Clergy murmur. The Situation is very different in England; where by means of Tythes,³ the Clergy have a certain proportion of the Crop be it great or small, and the price makes amends to both Parson and Farmer, in scarce Years. This Law at which the Clergy are so incensed, is a general Law respecting all payments in Tobacco of whatever Nature they may be: and all were content but themselves. I am confident if the Clergy had applyed to the Legislature, which they ought to have done, They would have had a better price, tho' a price would have been set.

Our Quota of Troops under the Honble. Coll. Byrd, are moved from Winchester in order to join Major General Stanwix. The 1200 given by the Assembly are now about 1000 effective Men, so unwillingly do Men enlist. But in Order to do every thing in my power I have directed Coll. Byrd to buy up the Convicts Two Ship Loads of which are come into our Rivers, who he says are as good as any fresh Recruits when got into the Field. I have promised Mr. Stanwix to make our Body complete, and if it is possible to be done, I will do it. I am with the greatest Respect, My Lords, Your Lordships most Obliged and devoted Servant

Fran: Fauquier

P.S. All the public Acts and papers went by the Jenny Captn. Crawfurd who sail'd the 3d instant I did myself the Honor to write to your Lordships by the Spotswood Captn. Seaton the 26th ulto. By a Letter I have this moment seen from Mr. Jas. Buchanan's house to the Honble. Willm. Nelson,⁴ I hear the Merchants are satisfied, their Dissatisfaction, as they acknowledge in that Letter and I suspected arose from their Ignorance of the Laws here in force.

F: F:

July 18th. / To the Rt. Honble. the Lords of Trade &ct.

ALS: C.O.5/1329, ff. 148–49. Endorsed as read 14 Nov. 1759.

1. The instruction was that of 9 Feb. 1759. Fauquier communicated this instruction to the council in its executive session on 3 Sept. 1759, and it advised him that the requirements of the instruction had already been provided for and it was therefore not necessary for him to call the assembly, although he should lay the instruction before the assembly when it did meet. On 1 Nov. 1759, in his opening address to the General Assembly, Fauquier acquainted it that he had received the instruction and recommended that it should reconsider the interests of British merchants in recovering their sterling debts and, if the merchants' interests were not already fully secured, provide full and ample security for them. See *EJC* 6:145–46; *JHB, 1758–1761*, p. 134.

2. See Fauquier's letter of 5 Jan. 1759 on the dissatisfaction of the clergy.

3. Tithes were payments of one tenth of the annual produce of (for instance) agriculture, given for the support of the clergy.

4. Probably the letter came from someone in the firm of James & Robert Buchanan of Glasgow, tobacco merchants.

From the Lords of the Admiralty

[20 July 1759]

We send you herewith an act pass'd the last Session of Parliament, Intitled an act to explain and amend an act made in the Twenty Ninth Year of His present Majesty, intituled an Act for the Encouragement of Seamen and the more speedy and Effectual Manning His Majestys Navy; and for the better prevention of Piracies and Robberies by Crews of Private Ships of War.[1] You are hereby requir'd and directed very carefully to observe every part thereof that may relate to you. Given under our Hands the 20 of July 1759.

      Anson. G Hay. Gilbt. Elliot[2]

To the Vice Admiralty Court of Virginia, and the Vice Admiral or his Deputy or Judge of the said Court or his Deputy, now and for the time being.[3]

Copy: Adm.2/1056, pp. 158–59. Circular. The model is the letter to Jamaica, and the address above is altered as appropriate. The letter to Virginia, according to a list of addresses, was sent by the *Mercury*. Above the text of the circular is "By &ca." perhaps in place of a set preamble; after the address is "By &ca J.C.," perhaps for a form of attestation. The letter as sent to the colonies has not been found.

 1. The act enclosed was 32 Geo. II, cap. 25 (*Statutes* 8:364–69); the act which this act amended and explained was 29 Geo. II, cap. 34 (*Statutes* 7:708–16). The act of 32 Geo. II repealed that part of the earlier act which directed the Admiralty to grant commissions to privateers and substituted other directions to the same effect; it went on to give detailed instructions for granting commissions and regulations for the handling of captured ships; with specific reference to the plantations in America, the act forbade all officers of courts of admiralty or vice admiralty to have any interest whatsoever in privateers, or to act, directly or indirectly, as proctors or advocates in any business of privateers before the courts in which they functioned. The act was to continue only during the current war with France.

 2. Lord Anson was in his second term as first lord of the Admiralty, 1757–62. George Hay (1715–1778) was a member of the Admiralty Board 1756–65; Gilbert Elliot (1722–1777) was a member of the board 1756–57 and 1757–61.

 3. The vice-admiralty court had cognizance of violations of the laws of trade and quarantine and other maritime causes. Officials of the court were a judge commissioned by the Admiralty and a judge advocate, a register, and a marshal, all appointed by the governor, who held a commission from the Admiralty as vice admiral of Virginia. Loudoun's commission as vice admiral is in H.C.A.50/11, ff. 10–16, 106.

From James Abercromby

Sir   Craven Street 26th July 1759

By Mr. President Blairs to me of the 30th May and by yours to Mr. Pownal,[1] I find you have assented to an Act relative to the Agency, which you have been made believe was agreeable to that for South Carolina, which is not the Case: Mr. Blair at the same time informs me that you used your Endeavours with the Assembly to nominate me, but their Prejudice to the Affair of the Pistole Fee stood in my Way; I am much obliged to you for your Endeavours to serve me in this Respect, but I am much better satisfied to continue Agent under the Authority of the Governor & Council as before (for Mr. Blair tells me that now they have two Agents) than under that of a Committee of Assembly, and if the Act stands its Ground, which may be much questioned if it is according to the Bill heretofore rejected, I shall for my own part have no kind of Objection to cooperate where the Governor or Council shall think proper to direct my Concurrence with Mr Montague as Agent for the Assembly,[2] and in this light, I wish the Act may stand in favour of an Agent for the Assembly, and it appears to me to be the most likely Means to establish this Act to give it this Construction leaving the Duty of the Agent for the Governor & Council to such Matters of State, and of Revenue coming under the Cognizance of the Governor and Council alone.

I am greatly concerned however to find by Mr Blair's, that some Motion had been talked of in Consequence of this Nomination of an Agent for the Assembly, for laying me totally aside as Agent for the Governor & Council, it being in the present Instance my own Case, may take off the Force of my Arguments with you, but upon the Face of the Proposition, the Assembly having, by the Concurrence of the Governor & Council, obtained what they have long aimed at, an Agent of their own Nomination, acting under their authority, whereas the Agent appointed by the Governor & Council did the whole Business of the Province under the Direction of the Governor & Council, and accordingly I find, from the Records in Office here, the Establishment of the Agent to have been in Virginia ever since 1680[3], why then shall they, the Assembly aim at laying aside the Agent for Government, who receives neither Pay nor Authority from them? or, why shall the Governor & Council on the other hand, throw Matters merely relative to Government & the Kings Revenue, into the hands of a Committee of Assembly, or one acting under their Direction: Nothing can be more repugnant to the System of Government at home, it is therefore extreamly prudent in you to consider the Impropriety of corresponding in matters of Government with an Agent under the Direction of a Committee of Assembly.

My Letters to Mr. Presidt. Blair will inform you more particularly of the several Matters now in hand concerning the Publick,[4] I have therefore little more to trouble you with at present, but to beg your Protection against factious Measures, and to continue in the Service under the Authority of the Governor & Council as before this Act.

I hope at last to get the 50000 issued; the Case is, by Reference from the Treasury directing the Agents to get Lord Loudons Approbation of our several Claims, Copys of my Claim for Virginia and of all Papers relative thereto I have transmitted to the President,[5] And in this Case, whatever turn the Agency may hereafter take, I expect, on the part of the Government of Virginia the same Emoluments as other Agents have on this Money.[6]

The News Papers sent you will shew you the Situation of Affairs abroad, Nothing but a Superiority of Military Skill on the Side of the King of Prussia & Prince Ferdinand, and the Bravery of their Troops, can surmount the Superiority of Numbers of their Enemy.[7] Complements to your Lady & Family concludes me always very sincerely Sir &ca.

Governor Fauquiere.

Copy: Virginia State Library, James Abercromby Letter Book, pp. 173–74. In a clerk's hand.

1. It is likely that Abercromby meant Fauquier's letter of 14 Apr. 1759 to the Board of Trade, which Pownall would have dealt with.
2. Edward Montagu (ca. 1715–1798), the second son of James Montagu, of Lackham in Wiltshire, was admitted to the Middle Temple on 3 May 1737 and to Gray's Inn on 4 May 1773. By 1773 he was a master in chancery, and in 1776 he was elected treasurer of Gray's Inn. Montagu was appointed agent for Virginia (especially for the House of Burgesses) by the act of assembly passed in the session of Feb. 1759, and he acted as agent until about June 1770.
3. It is not clear why Abercromby used this date: there was an agent of some sort for Virginia during most years from 1624 until 1690 (except for the years 1676–88), and a regular agent from 1691 onwards.
4. Abercromby presumably referred to letters he had written to Blair since 21 Mar. 1759, the date of his last letter to Fauquier before this one. In the interval, Abercromby had written to Blair about public business on 30 Mar., 3, 11, and 20 May, 25 and 30 June, and 25 July (pp. 134–36, 146–51, 161–64, and 169–72 of Abercromby's letter book). The topics were the opinions of the Board of Trade and of British merchants on payment of debts by paper money; the Reverend Mr. Camm's remonstrance to the Board of Trade against the Two Penny Act; Virginia's claims on grants of £50,000 and £200,000 to compensate the colonies for their defense expenditures; and an application for a transfer of funds from the quitrents to make up a deficit in the revenue of 2s. per hogshead on tobacco. In his letter of 25 July Abercromby probably referred to his representation to the Treasury dated, in his hand, 23 July 1759 (T.1/389, f. 107), a renewal or reminder of his request for a repayment to the account of tobacco revenue of money diverted to the quitrent account.
5. The papers relative to the share of the £50,000 seem to have consisted of Abercromby's memorial to the Treasury concerning Virginia's claim on that grant, enclosed in his letter of 20 May; an additional copy of the memorial, enclosed in his letter of 25 June; and something, enclosed and ambiguously mentioned in his letter of 25 July,

which could have been either another statement of Virginia's claim on the £50,000 or perhaps a communication from the Treasury referring that claim to Loudoun. The memorial to the Treasury was probably the one in T.1/372, f. 132, signed by Abercromby and James Wright, the agent for South Carolina, which stated the shares of the £50,000 appropriate for Virginia and the Carolinas, with Virginia's share set at £30,815.10.7. Whatever was sent with the letter of 25 July remains unidentified.

6. Abercromby's commission on Virginia's share of the £50,000 should be 2½ percent, or about £600, according to his comment to Richard Corbin in a letter of 29 June 1759 (pp. 152–57 of his letter book).

7. The newspapers are not identified. King Frederick II, operating in eastern Germany, was considerably outnumbered by the Russians and Austrians, and the Russians were advancing into Brandenburg. Ferdinand, duke of Brunswick, commander in chief of allied forces in western Germany, had 43,000 British and Hanoverian troops to oppose 60,000 Frenchmen; he was defeated near Frankfurt in mid–April, and early in July the French seized Minden and threatened Hanover.

From Jeffery Amherst

Sir,   Camp before Tienderoga 27th July 1759.[1]

On Saturday morning last I Embarked with the Army at Lake George; the next day Landed without Opposition & proceeded to the Saw Mills, and took Post on the Commanding Grounds,[2] meeting only a trifling Opposition from the Enemy; We lay on Our Arms all Night, and early on the 23d We Continued our March to this Ground, which I took possession of in the forenoon, the Enemy having Abandonned the Lines without Destroying them, first having Carried off their Effects, as well as Sent away the greatest part of their Troops; As soon as I was Set down before the Place, and after having Reconnoitred it, I Ordered the Trenches to be Opened, and Batteries to be made, which were finished last Night, and were to have Opened at Break of day, but the Enemy did not think proper to Wait till then, having about ten of the Clock Yesterday Evening, blown up a part of the Fort, and made their Escape all to about 20 Deserters. Our Loss, considering the Fire We Sustained, is Inconsiderable; We have only Two Officers killed, Vizt. Colonel Townshend, Deputy Adjutant General, & Ensign Harrison of Late Forbes's.[3]

I Take the Earliest Opportunity of Acquainting You with this, and of Assuring You that I am, with great Regard, Sir, &ca.

Copy: W.O. 34/36, f. 167. Circular letter to governors on the continent from Louisburg to Georgia inclusive. Fauquier communicated this letter to the council on 3 Sept. 1759, and it is abstracted in *EJC* 6:146.

1. Tienderoga is a variant form of Ticonderoga.
2. Amherst embarked on Sat. 21 July 1759. See Lawrence Gipson's account of

Abercromby's unsuccessful attack on Ticonderoga in Gipson, 7:221–31, and pp. 361–64 for a brief account of Amherst's capture of the fort.

3. The Hon. Roger Townshend (ca. 1732–1759) was killed by a cannonball on 25 July. Ensign Harrison, elsewhere identified as of General Forbes's Regiment (the Seventeenth), was reported killed in a letter of 26 July from Lake George.

To the Board of Trade

My Lords,   Wmsburgh Augst 2d 1759

   I have nothing of importance to add to my Letter of the 14th ulto. which I did myself the Honor to write by the Randolph Captn. Walker.[1] I do not know what Success we have had in the purchase of Convicts to complete our Quota, having had no Return since. Colonel Byrd is march'd with the Men he had to sustain Fort Bedford (Rays-Town) Fort Legonier (Loyal Hannon) so to keep the Communication open with Pittsburgh.[2] The Enemy has appeared before Fort Legonier but were repulsed with the Loss of one Officer kill'd and three private Men wounded. I apprehend they came with a Design to carry off any Cattle they might find without the Fort, but finding none they retired without attacking the Post. It is said that the French have a body of 2000 including Canadians and Indians at their Forts of Presquisle, Machault or Fort le Boeuf, and Venango,[3] and that they have plenty of provisions. As I apprehend the last part of the Intelligence must be false, I don't give much Credit to the other parts of it. Mr. Stanwix will have between 3 and 4000 real Effective Men under his Command as I imagine; whether he designs to keep upon the Defensive to secure the posts we are in possession of, or to act offensively to get possession of the French Forts between the Mountains and the Lakes; I cannot say having not heard from him for some Time. If it was consistent with his Orders I could wish he was a little more Communicative of his plan of Operations; as such Intelligences keep the military Spirit of the Colony which will begin to want all such Supports.

   When I last heard of him he was on his Way from Philadelphia to the general Rendezvous,[4] I shall expect an Express from him on his Arrival there as all our posts have been alarmed. I am with the greatest Respect, My Lords, Your Lordships most Obedient Obliged and devoted Servant
                                                                                Fran: Fauquier

To the Rt. Honble. the Lords of Trade &ct.

ALS: C.O.5/1329, ff. 150–51. Endorsed as read 14 Nov. 1759.

1. Capt. Robert Walker was master of the *Randolph*, a ship of 180 tons, with a crew of fifteen, built in the River Thames in 1753 and registered in London on 20 Oct. 1758.

2. Fort Bedford was built in 1758 in southwest central Pennsylvania where the town of Bedford now stands, about 100 mi., or a little less, to the southeast of Pittsburgh. Fort Ligonier was about halfway between Fort Bedford and Pittsburgh. Pittsburgh itself was the site of Fort Pitt, begun in Sept. 1759 and completed in 1761.

3. The fort at Presque Isle was built by the French in 1753 at or near the peninsula in Lake Erie where the city of Erie, Pa., now stands. Fort Le Boeuf was built in 1753 on Leboeuf Creek, where Waterford, Pa., is now, about 15 mi. south and east of Presque Isle. Fort Machault was built around 1754 at Venango, now Franklin, where French Creek joins the Allegheny River, about 40 mi. south and east of Waterford.

4. The most recent letter from Stanwix to Fauquier was apparently that of 30 May 1759, from Philadelphia.

From Jeffery Amherst

Sir, Camp at Crown Point[1] 8th Augst 1759

On the 27th Ultimo, I had the pleasure of Communicating to You, that the Enemy had, on the Evening before, abandonned the Fort at Tienderoga; to which I have now the further Satisfaction to Add, that they have likewise withdrawn themselves from this place, after having also attempted to blow up the Fort,[2] in which they have Succeeded only in part, and that I am in possession of the Ground ever since the 4th where I propose building such a Strong Hold as shall most effectually Cover and secure all this Country.

The Night of my Arrival here I received Letters from Sir William Johnson with the Additional good News of the Success of His Majesty's Arms at Niagara, which Surrender'd, by Capitulation, on the 25th to Sir William, upon whom the Command has devolved by the demise of Poor Brigr. General Prideaux, killed in the Trenches on the Night of the 20th.[3] The Garrison consisting of 607 Men being Prisoners of War and now on their March to New York, together with 17 Officers and 160 Men more, part of a Corps of 1200 Assembled at Detroit, Venango, & Presqu'Isle, under the Command of Messrs. Aubry & Delignery,[4] for Raising the Siege, but Sir William Johnson having Intelligence of their Approach, provided so properly for their Reception, that on the Morning of the 24th, when they meant to March Strait to the Fort, they met with such an Opposition as they little Expected, being entirely Routed, with the

Loss of all their Officers, and a great Number of their Men killed, whilst the Loss on our Side is inconsiderable.

This Signal Success, added to the other Advantages, seems an happy presage of the Entire Reduction of Canada this Campaign, or at least of Circumscribing the Enemy within such Narrow Bounds as will ever after deprive them of the Power of Exercising any more Encroachments, on which I hope I shall have the Satisfaction of Congratulating You, as I now do on these late great Events, and am, with great Regard, &ca.

Copy: W.O.34/36, f. 169. Circular to governors.

1. Crown Point is on Lake Champlain about 7 mi. north of Ticonderoga.
2. Fort St. Frédéric was built by the French in 1731. The French who had retreated from Ticonderoga fell back on the fort at Crown Point and then blew it up on 31 July.
3. John Prideaux (1718–1759), colonel of the Fifty-fifth Foot and appointed brigadier general in America, was in command of the expedition against Fort Niagara until he was killed by the untimely explosion of a British mortar shell.
4. Charles Aubry (1726–1770) was first an army officer and later, it appears, a naval officer; he was in command of the party that defeated Grant before Duquesne in 1758. Aubry was wounded at Niagara and captured by the Iroquois but was retrieved and cared for by the English. François-Marie Le Marchand, sieur de Ligneris (1703–1760), was a captain in the French forces, the last commandant of Fort Duquesne and later commandant of Fort Machault. He was captured and died a prisoner of the English at Fort Niagara.

Order in Council

[Kensington, 10 August 1759]
At the Court at Kensington the 10th August 1759
Present
The Kings most Excellent Majesty in Council.

Whereas by Commission under the Great Seal of Great Britain, the Governor Council and Assembly of His Majestys Colony of Virginia, are authorized and empowered to make constitute and Ordain Laws Statutes and Ordinances for the Publick Peace Welfare and good Government of the said Province; Which Laws Statutes and Ordinances, are to be, as near as conveniently may be, agreable to the Laws and Statutes of this Kingdom, and to be transmitted for His Majestys Royal Approbation or Disallowance. And Whereas in pursuance of the said Powers Four Acts have been passed in the said Colony in the Years 1753, 1755, and 1758, and transmitted, Entituled as follow, Vizt.

"An Act for paying the Ministers of the Parishes of Frederick in the County of Frederick and of Augusta in the County of Augusta, and of Hampshire in the County of Hampshire, one hundred pounds annually instead of the Sallaries now Allowed,"[1]

passed in 1753

"An Act for enabling the Inhabitants of the Countys of Princess Anne and Norfolk to pay their publick dues in Money,"[2]

passed in 1755.

"An Act to enable the Inhabitants of this Colony to discharge their Tobacco Debts in Money for this present Year"[3]

Passed in 1755

"An Act to enable the Inhabitants of this Colony to discharge their publick dues, Officers Fees, and other Tobacco Debts in Money for the ensuing Year"[4]

Passed in 17[5]8

Which Acts, together with a Report made by the Lords Commissioners for Trade and Plantations thereupon, having been referred to the Consideration of a Committee of the Lords of His Majestys most Honourable Privy Council for Plantation Affairs, The said Lords of the Committee did this day report as their Opinion to His Majesty, that the said Acts ought to be Disallowed. His Majesty taking the same into Consideration, was pleased, with the Advice of His Privy Council, to declare His Disallowance of the said Acts. And pursuant to His Majestys Royal Pleasure thereupon expressed, the said Acts are hereby Disallowed, declared Void, and of none Effect. Whereof the Governor Lieutenant Governor or Commander in Chief of His Majestys said Colony of Virginia for the time being, and all others whom it may concern, are to take Notice and Govern themselves accordingly.[5]

A true Copy
W: Sharpe

Copy: C.O.5/1329, ff. 191–92. Evidently certified with the autograph signature of Sharpe. Endorsed as received (at the Board of Trade) 21 May and read 8 July 1760.

1. Passed in the session of May 1753 (Hening, 6:369–70).
2. Passed in the session of May 1755 (Hening, 6:502).
3. This was the first Two Penny Act, passed in the session of Oct. 1755 (Hening, 6:568–69).
4. This was the second Two Penny Act, passed in the session of Sept. 1758 (Hening, 7:240–41). The date of passage of the act is incorrectly written as 1748 in the manuscript.
5. Fauquier informed the General Assembly of the receipt of this order in his address on 6 Oct. 1760 (JHB, 1758–1761, p. 184).

From Jeffery Amherst

Sir,   Camp at Crown Point 14th August 1759

Yesterday I received from the War Office Sundry Copies of the Cartel Concluded & Agreed upon between our Court & that of France for the Exchange & Ransom of Prisoners,[1] of which I here Enclose You One, and am, &ca.

Copy: C.O.34/36, f. 170. Circular to governors.

1. The cartel that Amherst enclosed must have been a copy of the treaty signed at Sluys, in Flanders, on 6 Feb. 1759. The text was printed in London in 1759, and reprinted in the same year in Philadelphia by W. Dunlap (Sabin 96550, Evans 8348) as *Traité et Conventions, pour les Malades, Blessés, et Prisonniers de Guerre des Troupes de Terre, de Sa Majesté très Chrétienne, et de Sa Majesté Britannique. A Treaty and Convention for the Sick, Wounded, and Prisoners of War, of the Land Forces, of His Majesty the King of Great-Britain, and of His Most Christian Majesty.* The thirty-three numbered articles of the treaty provide for the exchange or ransom of all prisoners of war within one month of the signing of the treaty, and for subsequent exchanges or ransoms; set the values in money of officers; and prescribe the details of procedure. An unnumbered separate article provides for the immediate appointment of commissaries to regulate the sums of money to be paid by the two sides.

From William Byrd

Sir   [Fort Ligonier, 15 August 1759]

I have the pleasure to congratulate you on the Evacuation of Venango Presquisle & Le Beuf, which Forts the Enemy burnt and abandoned six days ago.[1] By our Ohio Indians we learn the Cherokees have actually declared War against the English & have been soliciting them to join them.[2] It will be necessary to keep a good look out on our Frontier.

The Remaining Part of our Campaign will be employ'd in establishing strong Posts on the Ohio, from whence I shall by every Opportunity advise you of every thing worth communicating. I am with the highest Respect, Sir, Your most Obedient Humble Servant

                                                          W: Byrd

Fort Ligonier Augt. 15th 1759.
An Express arrived just now with the above Account from Pittsburgh which is not to be doubted.

Copy: C.O.5/1329, f. 172. Marked as a copy. Endorsed as being in Fauquier's letter of 30 Aug. 1759 and as received 26 Nov. and read 12 Dec. 1759. Fauquier communicated this letter to the council on 3 Sept. 1759, and it is abstracted in *EJC* 6:146.

1. It is not clear just when the three French forts were evacuated, although contemporary French records show that Fort Machault was evacuated and burned on 6 Aug. Byrd's report apparently derives from the same source as that in the *Pa. Gaz.* for 30 Aug. 1759, which said that on 13 Aug. three Indians had arrived at Pittsburgh with the news that the French had burned their forts at Venango, Presque Isle, and Le Boeuf and gone to Detroit.

2. The Cherokees had not yet gone to war against the English. Perhaps the solicitation from the Cherokees that the Ohio Indians reported was the message to some northern Indians from Old Hop, mentioned by Richard Coytmore in his letter of 3 Aug. to Governor Lyttelton, enclosed in Lyttelton's letter of 15 Aug. 1759 to Fauquier.

From William Henry Lyttelton

[15 August 1759]

This letter has not been found. Fauquier communicated it to the council on 3 Sept. 1759, and it is abstracted in *EJC* 6:144–45:

Also another Letter from Governor Lyttelton, dated Augt. 15th acquainting his Honor with the Measures he had taken in Consequence of a Letter from Lieutt. Coytmore, dated Augt. 3d (an Extract whereof he inclosed, advising, "that at a late Meeting between the Heads of the Cherokees, and four Creeks, two of which were Headmen, but of different Towns, who came on the 28th of July, with a Messenger sent to renew their Friendship and Alliance, the Cherokees being persuaded by the Creeks that the French had a Regard for them, and could amply supply them with every Necessary, came to a Resolution to join with them against the English,") and recommending it to him to stop the Trade intended from hence with the Cherokees, until it appears what Turn our Affairs will take with those People.

The enclosure in Lyttelton's letter probably was the same as (or part of) the following enclosure, which was in his letter of 1 Sept. 1759 to the Board of Trade.

Enclosure: Richard Coytmore to William Henry Lyttelton

Sir, [Fort Prince George, 3 August 1759]

Altho' I wrote to your Excellency ten days ago by James Holmes,[1] I think it my Duty to acquaint you of several Particulars, that have since happen'd, exactly answerable to the Information I mention'd receiving.

On the 28th ult. the Messenger sent by these People to renew their Friendship and Alliance with the Creek Nation return'd with four Creeks; two of which were Head-Men, but of different Towns, one coming from near the Albama Fort;[2] and I was inform'd, that that very Day there was to be a private Meeting of all these Lower Towns at Keohee.[3] As I imagin'd they would not talk so free, was I to send a White Person to the Town-House, with much Difficulty I persuaded a young Indian Fellow to go, and bring me all the News. Accordingly after the Meeting he return'd, & was some Time before he car'd to tell any thing; but at last inform'd me, as follows;

"That being all met, the Heads of the Cherokees told the Creeks, they were welcome to their Town, and that they were all ready to hear the Talk they had brought with them from their Nation; that they might speak freely, as whatever they said would not be discover'd as there were no Women in the Town-House; and at the same Time strictly charging the young Men not to discover what they heard even to their Wives, declaring that the first, that was found to divulge it, should die. On this the Creeks produced some white & a great many black Beads, telling them, that they had lately come from the Albama Fort; that the French, who profess'd a great Regard for the Cherokees, as well as their Nation, had now a large Supply of Goods; that just before they set off, two Boats of Ammunition arrived there; that they gave them vast Quantities of Liquor; and lastly that they had frequent Talks with them. That the Creeks believed, that the French had a Regard for them, and that they were determined, if their Brothers, the Cherokees, would join them, to break out a War with the English. At this the others desired to have two Days to consult among themselves, saying that they must first send over the Hills, before they could give a positive Answer. To which the Creeks replied, that at the same Time, that they set off for these Parts, another Messenger set off for Chotee[4] with the same Proposals."

Accordingly in two Days they met. I prevaild on the same young Fellow to go again, & bring me the answer they sent;

"Being all met, after the strictest Charge (as before) for no one to divulge what was said, Wohatchee[5] in the Name of all these lower Towns sent some Beads, and the following Talk; We have heard our Brothers, the Creeks', Talk; We have long been in Friendship with the English, but it now seems, as if they wanted to desert us, as we have scarce Goods enough come among us to cover us from the Cold; and as you are the same Sort of People as ourselves, & our Brothers, we do not imagine you would deceive us, by telling us, the French can supply us amply with every necessary; We will therefore join you against the English, conditionaly; that you will first kill all the White People belonging to the English in your Nation. The Creek Messenger then produced a red Pipe, & some Tobacco, which he said were sent to these People by the French.

It was graciously received by the Head beloved Man of Keohee; he then told them, he had received their Answer to the Proposals he made, & hop'd they would not deceive them, but assist them; and that they might depend, that soon after he and the Messenger, that went to Chotee got home to their Nation, they would kill all their Traders &c. and on that immediately send in a Warrior to acquaint them with it."

I asked the young Fellow what Quantity of Ammunition they had in these Towns; he said, Not much; but that they intended, as soon as the Creeks had kill'd the People in their Nation to come to me, & tell me of it, desiring some Powder & Ball to assist us and defend themselves against the Creeks; that when they got it they were to begin with their Villainy; the Time fix'd for this is the Fall. However as he inform'd me that a large Party of Creeks with all the Middle Settlements are to come to see the Green-Corn Dance at Keohee in 25 Days,[6] I shall be upon my Guard during their Stay.

Old Hop sent some Time ago a Messenger to some Northern Nation, who is expected about the Fall with a Party of that Nation; also a Body of the Upper Creeks, with a few French, are to come by the Way of Coosawatahee[7] to assist the Over-Hill-Towns in cutting off Fort Loudoun.

There is not one of the Indians know that I am the least in the Secret; nor does any white Person even in their Towns (except Mr. Beamer)[8] know of any [of] their Consultation. Mr. Beamor acquainted me with the whole Story, Word for Word, as I had it from the young Fellow; and told me that the Person, that inform'd him of it gave him the strictest Charge not to tell it again to any white Person or Indian, for (as my Informer likewise told me) he said he risqued his Life by mentioning it.

About six Days ago three young Fellows belonging to Toxaway (one of these Lower Towns) set off to War against the Back Settlements, either of Virginia, or North Carolina.

Not an Indian of the least Distinction has been in the Fort these several Days; and most of them declare openly, that they have done with the White People!

Copy: C.O.5/376, ff. 117–18. Headed "Extract of a Letter to his Excellency Governor Lyttelton from Lieutenant Coytmore, dated Fort Prince George, Augt. 3d 1759." The word in brackets is supplied to complete the sense. Endorsed as received in Lyttelton's letter (to the Board of Trade) of 1 Sept. 1759 and as received 26 Nov. and read 12 Dec. 1759. Lyttelton's letter to the board has not been found. Probably this is the extract enclosed in Lyttelton's letter of 15 Aug. 1759 to Fauquier.

1. This was probably the wagonmaster James Holmes who was active ca. 1759–64 in the transportation of furs for the South Carolina Cherokee trade.

2. Fort Toulouse, built by the French in 1716 on the east bank of the Coosa River about 4 mi. above its junction with the Tallapoosa River, was completely rebuilt in 1751. Its site, in southeast central Alabama (a little to the north of Montgomery), was near the settlements of the Creek nation.

3. This is a variant form of Keowee, principal Cherokee town of the region, next to Fort Prince George.

4. Chotee was a Cherokee town on the Little Tennessee River, a short distance upstream from Fort Loudoun.

5. Wohatchee, a Cherokee, was a headman of Keowee.

6. This Green-Corn Dance, commonly called busk, was a solemn annual festival of the Creeks, described as one of the most remarkable ceremonial institutions of the American Indians. See Frederick Webb Hodge, ed., *Handbook of American Indians North of Mexico* (Washington, D.C., 1912), pt. 1, pp. 176–78.

7. Coosawatahee, or Cusawatee, was an important Cherokee settlement on the lower Coosawatee River, in what is now Gordon County, Ga.

8. James Beamer was an Indian trader at Estatoe.

To Jeffery Amherst

Sir   Wmsburgh Augst 18th 1759

I beg leave to congratulate you on the repeated Successes of his Majesties Forces under your Command.

By what you have already done; and by the Withdrawing of the French Garrisons from Venango and the adjacent Forts, which I hope will leave but little for Mr. Stanwix to do; I have conceived great Hopes that the Enemy will be drove out of this part of the Continent, by the end of this Campaign.

If this should fortunately be the Case, this Colony will be disposed to ease the Country by saving every Expence possible; and reducing the Troops in their pay. the Time they stand at present provided for is to the first of December next and no longer. I have summoned the Assembly to meet on the 13th of November, in order to give them Time to provide further for them if it should be necessary.

I thought it much for His Majesties Service to give you this Information; desiring, that if you have any Reasons to urge why they should be continued longer in pay, you would be pleased to favour me with them, before the Meeting of the Assembly, that I may communicate them at that Time, or at least during the Session which I apprehend will be very short, as I have call'd them together for this purpose only, it is not imagined that they will proceed upon the Country Business.

I most sincerely wish you a Continuation of your prosperity and the

Reputation you so justly acquire thereby, being with the greatest Esteem, Sir, Your Excellency's most devoted and obedient humble Servant

Fran: Fauquier

To Major Genl. Amherst.

ALS: W.O. 34/37, f. 27.

From William Byrd

[Fort Ligonier, 23 August 1759]

This letter has not been found. Fauquier communicated it to the council on 3 Sept. 1759, and it is abstracted in *EJC* 6:146:

The second Letter signifying he shall proceed to Pittsburg, as soon as a sufficient Quantity of Provisions can be got up, and recommending Mr. Finnie to his Honor's Notice for his good Conduct in opening the Communication to Pittsburg by General Braddock's Road, in which Service he was at great Expence.

Mr. Finnie was Alexander Finnie, whose petition requesting an allowance for his expenses and trouble in clearing Braddock's Road was presented to the House of Burgesses on 7 Nov. 1759. For the contents of the petition, some particulars of the clearing operation, and the resolution of the General Assembly to allow Finnie £100 for his services, see *JHB, 1758–1761*, pp. 139, 143, 147, 152. This Alexander Finnie has not been exactly identified. He may have been the man who was adjutant of the middle district of Virginia and died at his plantation of Porto Bello, in York County, about the beginning of May 1769; or he may have been the man who was apparently an innkeeper in Williamsburg and in 1755 advertised his intention to go to the Ohio River country.

From Henry Bouquet

Sir   Fort Bedford 25th August 1759

General Stanwix being gone to Pittsburgh I give my Self the Honour to write to you upon a Subject in which delay could be prejudiciable.

The Concourse of Indians is very great at Pittsburgh, where they bring a large quantity of Skins to trade with us; But the difficulty of Carriage and the danger of the Communication Some time ago have prevented The Commissioners for Indian Trade[1] and the Merchants in Pennsylvania from Sending a Sufficient Assortment of Goods to answer the demands of Indians.

The Communication between Virginia and the Ohio being now opened by Braddocks Road cleared by Mr. Finnie, It would be Advantageous for your Province to Share in the Trade with the Indians, and Send as Soon as possible Goods to Pittsburgh.

If you think proper to open that Trade, I will take the Liberty to recommend to your Protection, Mr. Finnie, who by opening the Trade with great Industry and diligence deserves Some Encouragement: He offers under Your approbation to forward Speedily a Quantity of Goods to Pittsburgh, where The General will fix the Prices upon just & equal Terms between The Provinces & the Indians.

Besides the Profits that can be expected from a well regulated Trade upon the Ohio: it seems to be the most Effectual way of fixing these wavering Tribes in Our Interest, and prevent leaving them any reason to regrett the French, who used to Supply them largely.

And to render the Communication from Virginia Still easier The General has Ordered a Road to be cleared to the mouth of Red Stone Creek and to build there a little Stockaded Post with Storehouses: This will reduce much the land Carriage, in making use of The Mononghehela.[2]

Colo. Burd of the Pennsylvania Regiment march on Monday next with 200 Men of his Battalion for that purpose and we hope that So many Communications will Encourage the Country people to Send their Product to The Army; and enable us to Subsist that Multitude of Indians, preying upon us; used to be fed by the French, they have planted no Corn, and have no other dependance to live than our Provisions. It is to be hoped that they will by degrees return to their former peaceable Way of living, Plant Corn & Hunt, But in the present Circumstances we are Obliged to humour them tho' the Weight is almost intolerable. I have the honour to be with great respect, Sir, Your most obedient and most Humble Servant.

Governor Fouquier.

Copy: British Library, Add. Mss. 21652, ff. 155–56. Endorsed as "Copy of a Letter from Colonel Bouquet To Fouquier." Fauquier communicated this letter to the council on 3 Sept. 1759, and it is abstracted in *EJC* 6:146.

1. In its session of Jan. 1758, the Pennsylvania assembly had passed "An Act for preventing Abuses in the Indian Trade . . ." (pp. 381–90 of the session acts, Evans 8225) which appointed nine commissioners to supervise the trade. The commissioners set up three stores: one was at Fort Allen, built in 1756 on the Lehigh River, on the site of Weissport in the middle of eastern Pennsylvania; another was at Fort Augusta, built in 1756 near the junction of the north and west branches of the Susquehanna

River, on the site of Sunbury and about 60 mi. west of Fort Allen; and the third was at Pittsburgh, around 170 mi. southwest of Fort Augusta.

2. Fort Burd, or as it was usually called, Redstone Old Fort, was built late in 1759 on the Monongahela River at or near the mouth of Redstone Creek, where Brownsville is now, and about 30 mi. to the south of Pittsburgh.

Order in Council

[Kensington, 29 August 1759]

At the Court at Kensington the 29th of August 1759
Present
The Kings most Excellent Majesty in Council.

Whereas the Lieutenant Governor of His Majestys Colony of Virginia, with the Council and Assembly of the said Colony, did, in 1757, pass An Act, which hath been transmitted in the words following, Vizt.

"An Act to impower Armistead Churchill[1] Gentleman to sell and dispose of certain intailed Lands."

Memd: Here the Act was inserted at length[2]

Which Act, having been perused and considered by the Lords Commissioners for Trade and Plantations, and by them presented to His Majesty at this Board as fit to be confirmed. His Majesty was this day pleased, with the advice of His Privy Council to declare his Approbation thereof. And pursuant to His Majestys pleasure thereupon expressed, the said Act is hereby confirmed finally Enacted and ratified accordingly. Whereof the Govr: Lieut Govr: or Commander in Chief of His Majestys said Colony for the time being and all others whom it may concern are to take Notice and govern themselves accordingly.[3]

A true Copy
W: Sharpe

Copy: C.O.5/1329, f. 193. Evidently certified with the autograph signature of Sharpe. Endorsed as received (at the Board of Trade) 21 May and read 8 July 1760.

1. Armistead Churchill (1704–1763?) of Middlesex County was a justice of the peace, colonel in the militia, and collector for the Rappahannock River district.

2. The aim of the act (Hening, 7:157–59) was to make provision for Churchill's younger children; he had five sons and six daughters then alive. The meaning of the note found here and some other orders, that the act in question was at this point inserted at length, is open to question. Obviously the act was not inserted in the Privy Council registers, where the notes occur, and there is no indication that the act was inserted in the copy of the order sent to the persons concerned. Possibly the note marks the point at which the act was read aloud during the proceedings of the Privy Council, and in that case the note should be disregarded in copies of orders.

3. There is no record of when this order was sent to or received in Virginia.

To the Board of Trade

My Lords   Wmsburgh Augst 30th 1759

   A Ship which sails for Glascow to morrow, very fortunately gives me an Opportunity of transmitting to your Lordships the Copy of a Letter I received by Express last night from Colonel Byrd;[1] on the Subject of which I congratulate your Lordships. By the evacuation of these Forts, the Reduction of Niagara, and the Success of General Amherst on Lake Champlain, the whole Country between the Sea and the Lakes is clear; of which I hope we shall long keep the uninterrupted Possession. I have not heard from Brigr. Genl. Stanwix for some time, and do not know where he is at present.

   As to the Information Mr. Byrd received from his Indians in Relation to the Cherokee War, I have the greatest Reason to believe the Affair is amicably adjusted between them and us, in the accomodating which Govr. Lyttelton has been very active. Two Deputies from that Nation were down with me some Time since Strings of white Wampum were exchanged, an Oblivion was promised reciprocally of all Skirmishes and Blood shed which pass'd last year, and assurances given that if any Murder was committed the Aggressor should be given up; in Consequence of which We sent up a pretty large Cargo of Goods which they sollicited for their Trade, and at the same Time threaten'd them, that if they fail'd in their Engagements we would fall on them with all our Force. The Success of this Convoy sent into their Country we do not yet know but if after this, they breathe nothing but War, they will be more treacherous than even Indians usualy are.[2]

   As the Operations on this Side seem to be over by the Surrender of these last Forts, I am apprehensive the Assembly (which I have call'd to meet on the 13 of November, but which probably will not then sit to go through the Country Business) will be for reducing their Expences as much and as soon as possible. I will endeavour to keep the Forces on foot till I have the Honor to be informed of his Majesties pleasure. The sooner that is communicated to me, the greater Confidence I can speak to the Assembly, and the more effectual Service I can do his Majesty and the common Cause. I have the Honor to be with the greatest Respect, My Lords, Your Lordships most Obedient & devoted humble Servant

                                                             Fran: Fauquier

To the Rt. Honble. the Lords of Trade &ct.

ALS: C.O.5/1329, ff. 170–71. Endorsed as received 26 Nov. and read 12 Dec. 1759, and (apparently) as enclosing one paper.

1. Byrd's letter of 15 Aug. 1759 to Fauquier.
2. Fauquier's summary of relations with the Cherokees refers to the deputation of two Cherokees who returned with Smith the interpreter, mentioned in Fauquier's letter of 5 Sept. 1759 to Lyttelton. The trade goods were sent off to the Cherokees about the middle of June, it appears, since on 19 June Fauquier wrote to Lyttelton that Smith the interpreter had already set out to tell the Cherokees the goods were on the way.

To William Henry Lyttelton

Sir, Wmsburgh Sepr 5th 1759

All your Favours (viz) of the 27th April by Mr. Martin, of the 7th June by Post, and of the 15th August by Express have come duly to hand. Your Activity in Relation to the Indian Affairs is very acceptable to this Colony, which will always endeavour to cooperate with you in every thing which may tend to the Advantage of his Majesties Subjects in these Colonies.

In my Letter which I sent express with some Dispatches from Mr. Secretary Pitt on the 31st of March, I referrd you to a Talk which By the Advice of his Majesty's Council was sent by the Little Carpenter to the Chiefs of the Cherokee Nation a Copy of which I ordered Mr. Smith the Interpreter to send to you.[1] On Smiths return from that Country he brought with him a Letter to me from Lt. Coytmore commanding Officer at fort Prince George, giving me an Account of the Behaviour of the Indians on hearing that Talk; and expressing his Doubts of their future Behaviour.[2] Along with Smith came down two Cherokee Deputies (viz) the Yellow Bird, and young Atossita with the Answer of their Nation and a String of white Wampum. They were both much afraid of coming for fear We should take Revenge on them for the Behaviour of their young Warriours, and were much shock'd at my first Refusal of my Hand on their offering to shake Hands as usual.[3]

After several assurances that they were deputed from their Nation as friends and brothers I gave them my Hand. They then told me that their Nation were very sorry for the Behaviour of their Young Men; that the Murders in Carolina lately committed,[4] were not done with the Consent of the Nation but that the Young Men could not be stop'd from taking Revenge for some Murders committed on their Relations in Bedford (and by the bye I am much afraid one Action of some of our people in Bedford was attended with most shocking and treacherous Circumstances).[5] And they promised that if we could forget all that was pass'd no such Thing should happen for the future and if we would send the Goods we should live as Sons of the same Father for ever, and produced a String of white Wampum with one black at one of the Ends. After many Doubts and many Reproaches to them I returned this Answer. That on Condition that if any Murder should hereafter be done by their People the Murderer should be immediately given up to us, and relying on their peacable Intentions for the future as they had so solemnly promised; I would trust them once more, would forget all Injuries, receive them as friends, and send up the Goods: But I added that they might assure their Nation, that on the first Cause of Complaint against them, The White People would never trust them more, nor be again deceived, but would unite their whole Forces, to take such ample Revenge of them as they had never yet seen or felt from any People. Upon these Terms we agreed. They then desired as a Token of it I would take the black bead from the End of the String of white Wampum which they gave me and throw it away before their Face, which I accordingly did, to their very great apparent Joy. I then added that to show the Justice and good faith of the white people; I would send up some Goods which had been taken from some of their people in Bedford, which I had taken into my Custody to keep for the right owners thereof, that their chief men might find out to whom they belongd and return them to the Owners.[6] I then ordered them Coats &ct. and dismiss'd them most singularly satisfied. Smith went back with them to protect them from Insults in passing thro' our back Settlements. Notwithstanding the Intelligence received by Lt. Coytmore; I am of Opinion that when these Deputies return home, and the Cherokees find the French can not supply them, Things will take another Turn in that Country. in the mean time I have sent to stop our Goods setting out till Smiths Return on the Receipt of your Letter.[7] The Deputies set out for home on the 12th August and were in a great Hurry to go home by a Certain Day, by which I judge the Nation waited the Event of this Embassy before they designed to proceed to Action.

 Thus Sir I have fully informed you of our Transactions with the Cherokees, that you may be Master of the whole affair in the prosecuting of which We shall be happy to go hand in hand with a Gentleman of your known Probity and prudence, which Qualities demand of me to say that with the highest Esteem I am, Sir, Your Excellency's most Obedient humble Servant

Fran: Fauquier

P.S. I have just heard that the £50,000 voted by Parliament some time since for our Colonies is proportioned and will be soon remitted.

Sepr. 14

As this Letter has been unavoidably delayed, I have thought it adviseable to order Mr. Smith to send from fort Prince George to your Excellency to inform you of his Arrival there, to communicate his Instructions, and to wait there till he receives your Directions how to proceed, that We may go hand in hand in this delicate affair. Our Goods will halt at Salisbury in North Carolina,[8] till he has your Determination whether they may proceed with Safety or return into Virginia.

F: F:

To his Excellency Gov. Lyttelton.

ALS: William L. Clements Library, Lyttelton Papers.

1. This is the message which Fauquier enclosed in his letter of ca. 23 Jan. 1759 to Lyttelton.
2. See the abstract of Coytmore's letter to Fauquier of ca. 15 Mar. 1759, and the discussion of the date when Smith delivered the letter.
3. It is impossible to identify the two Cherokees with certainty. The Yellow Bird was possibly a headman of Oustate, or Oustastee, or Oustatoe, one of the Lower Towns; the young man Atossita was perhaps one of the several Cherokees named Otasite. The Indians must have come with Smith when he returned to Virginia about the beginning of August. See the abstract of the letter of ca. 15 Mar. 1759 from Richard Coytmore and the discussion of it.
4. These were no doubt the killings that Lyttelton mentioned in his letter of 7 June 1759 to Fauquier.
5. He referred to the killings of Cherokees in May 1758, presumably; see his letter of 16 June 1758 to Lyttelton.
6. See Captain Winn's letter to Fauquier of ca. Oct. 1758, on the disposition of booty taken from the Cherokees.
7. On 3 Sept. the council advised Fauquier to direct Charles Turnbull, who was entrusted with the goods for the Cherokees, not to forward them until he had further instructions. Turnbull was a merchant of Petersburg, and evidently a supplier of Indian goods.
8. Salisbury is in western central North Carolina, about 30 mi. southwest of Winston-Salem. It was founded in 1751.

To Henry Bouquet

Sir   Wmsburgh Sepr 11th 1759

Your Favour of the 25th Augst. was delivered to me on the 2d instant. This Colony has certainly great Obligations to Genl. Stanwix for the Advantages he has procured to it by opening the Roads to Pittsburgh, & I sincerely hope his Army will immediately and daily receive the Benefit he expects, by being well supplyed with provisions from our back Settlements.

I am truly sensible of Mr. Finnies Merit, in the Share he had in executing the Generals Orders, and have recommended it in the Manner I think I ought, to his Majesties Council, and shall be ready to do the Same to the Assembly.

As for the Trade with the Indians, it is open with us and not confined, and I hope the Merchants will for their own Sakes, as well as that of the Colony be expeditious in sending up all the Goods they can procure, to furnish the Indians with in Return for their Skins. But tho' the Trade is open, yet there is a Committee appointed by Act of Assembly to trade with the Indians on the Stock of the public, to the Amount of any Sum not exceeding £5000.¹ And as I am of Opinion, with you, that the putting the Trade on a proper Footing with the Indians, is a proper Step to keep their Friendship, I shall recommend it to this Committee to employ good part of this Money in the Trade with the Indians on the Ohio, the first Time a Number of them are in Town,² for they are not put under my Orders to summon them to meet on any Occasion. I most sincerely congratulate you on the uninterrupted Successes of his Majesty's Arms this Campaign for which under God we are obliged to the prudent Conduct of those to whom his Majesty has wisely entrusted the Command of his Troops. I am with great Regard, Sir, Your Very Humble Servant

Fran: Fauquier

To Colonel Bouquet.

ALS: British Library, Add. Mss. 21644, ff. 379–80. Endorsed as received 23 Oct. [1759].

1. The act was one passed in the session of Apr. 1758, entitled "An Act for establishing a trade with the Indians in alliance with his majesty" (Hening, 7:116–18). The act appointed five trustees and directors to manage and carry on trade with the Indians, specifically in skins and furs, for a period of five years from the passing of the act. The trusees were to be called the Trustees of the Indian Factory of Virginia.
2. If the five trustees named in the act were still in office, Fauquier would have expected to see all of them when the General Assembly met. Peter Randolph, one of the council, had been a burgess for Henrico County and presumably still lived there; Richard Bland was a burgess for Prince George County, and Thomas Walker was a burgess for Hampshire County. The two other trustees were William Randolph (d. 1761), burgess for Henrico County, and Archibald Cary (1721–1787), burgess for Chesterfield County.

To Richard Smith

[Williamsburg, 14 September 1759]

Copy of Mr. Smith's Instructions

You are to proceed to Petersburgh,¹ & there take up the two Cherokee Indians deputies,² & Conduct them into the Cherokee Country, with all

14 September 1759 247

the Speed you can. When you arrive there you are to go immediately to Fort Prince George & deliver the Letter sent by you to Mr. Coitmore the Commanding Officer there.³ You are by this means, by the two Indians that go with you, or by any Other Means in your Power to find out if possible the true spirit & Intention of the Cherokees, you are to explain yourself to the Chiefs fully, letting them know that we on our parts are ready to fulfill all our Engagements to them, that the progress of the Goods promisd is Only Retaind by Information we have received of their Treacherous designs. That if they have a mind to be Enemies to the White People they will find the White People as ready as themselves to go to War: & as Powerful Enemies as Faithfull Friends.

You are on your Arrival at Fort Prince George to Inform Govr. Lyttelton thereof whom I have also Apprized of my having sent you. You are to remain at Fort Prince George or at least in the Cherokee Country till you have an Answer from his Excellency how to proceed. in Consequence of the result of all these Measures you are to Order the goods to proceed from Salisbury in North Carolina & where I have Orderd them to halt or to return back to Petersburgh in Virginia as Shall be found most expedient & safe by his Excellency & Mr. Coitmore on the Reception you shall meet with. & lastly you are to Omit no Oppertunity in your power to inform either Govr. Lyttelton or myself of all your proceedings with the Cherokees.

Given at Williamsburgh this 14th day of Septemr. An. Dom. 1759
Signd / Francis Fauquier.

Copy: William L. Clements Library, Lyttelton Papers.

1. Petersburg, in Dinwiddie County in southeast Virginia on the Appomattox River at the head of navigation, was laid out as a town in 1748; there had been a white settlement on the site since 1646, and an Indian village even earlier.
2. These must have been the Yellow Bird and Atossita, although (according to Fauquier's letter of 5 Sept. 1759 to Lyttelton) they had set out for home on 12 Aug. and were in a great hurry to be at home. Since Petersburg is only about 40 mi. west of Williamsburg, the Cherokees must have been delayed.
3. If this was a letter from Fauquier to Coytmore (as it seems to have been), it has not been traced. However, Fauquier may have been referring to his letter of 5 Sept. 1759 to Lyttelton, which was to be handed over to Coytmore for forwarding to Lyttelton. See Fauquier's letter of 21 Oct. 1759 to Lyttelton.

From Jeffery Amherst

Sir, Camp at Crown Point, 14th Sepr 1759
In Acknowledging the Receipt of Your favor of the 18th Ultimo, I must likewise beg leave to tender You my most sincere thanks for Your

kind Congratulations, on the Success of His Majesty's Arms, which I have no Doubt, but will be productive of the hopes You have Conceived; At the Same time, altho' no one can be more Inclined than myself to Ease the Country of every Expence possible, Yet I Cannot, for their own Interest, think of Diminishing it untill Such time as they may be perfectly secure of their not being called upon again so soon, of which, if they now Continue to Exert themselves, there is certainly not the least prospect; how long therefore it may be Necessary to keep the Virginia Regiment in pay, beyond the first of December, depends entirely on Brigr. General Stanwix's Operations, Wherefore that You may be the more timely Informed of what You Desire to know on that head, I shall transmit a Copy of Your Letter to Mr. Stanwix, and Desire him to Answer it; And whatever he may Request of You by that Answer, I must beg of You to look upon as an Application from Myself, to be recommended to the Assembly in the same light: I am nevertheless greatly oblidged to You for this Early notice, and am with real truth & Esteem, Sir, &ca.

Jeff: Amherst

Honble. Govr. Fauquier.

Copy: C.O.5/56, ff. 98–99. Endorsed as being in Amherst's letter of 22 Oct. 1759.

To Jeffery Amherst

Sir Wmsburgh Sepr 16th 1759

I have the Honour to transmitt to you a Pacquet I received from his Excellency Governor Lyttelton to be forwarded to you.[1]

I with Pleasure acknowledge the Receipt of your Favours of the 8 & 14th ulto. and heartily congratulate you on the repeated Success of his Majesty's Arms under your Conduct and Command which has put this and the neighbouring Colonies, I may say the whole Continent in a State of Security to which they have been long Strangers. That your Country may have the Sentiments of your Services which we entertain is the earnest Wish of all his Majesty's Subjects here. I am with the highest Regard and Esteem, Sir, Your Excellency's most Obedient humble Servant

Fran: Fauquier

To his Excellency Majr. Genl. Amherst.

ALS: W.O.34/37, f. 28.

1. The packet is not identified. It probably was brought by the express who delivered Lyttelton's letter of 15 Aug. 1759 to Fauquier.

Additional Instruction

[Kensington, 21 September 1759]

Additional Instruction to Our Trusty and Wellbeloved Francis Fauquier Esqr. Lieutenant Governor of Our Colony and Dominion of Virginia; And, in his Absence to the President of Our Council and Commander in chief of Our said Colony for the time being. Given at Our Court at Kensington the [21st] day of [September] 1759, in the thirty third Year of Our Reign.

Whereas by the 16th Article of Our Royal Instructions to Our Captain General and Governor in Chief of Our Colony of Virginia and in his Absence to you Our Lieutenant Governor thereof, it is amongst other things declared to be Our Royal Will and Pleasure that Our Commander in chief of Our said Colony for the time being, shall not give his Assent to any Act, that shall be enacted for a less time than two Years, except in the Cases in Our said Instructions thereafter mentioned: And further that he shall not give his Assent to any Act for repealing any other Law pass'd within Our said Colony, whether the same has or has not received the Royal Approbation of Us or Our Royal Predecessors, unless a Clause be inserted in such Act, suspending and deferring the Execution thereof, untill Our Pleasure shall be known concerning the same.[1] And whereas notwithstanding the said Directions in Our said Instruction contain'd, several Acts have of late Years been pass'd without any such Clause of suspension in Our Colony of Virginia, (and particularly one in October 1758, entituled *An Act to enable the Inhabitants of this Colony to discharge their publick Dues, Officers Fees, and other Tobacco debts in money for the ensuing Year,*) whereby an Act which was pass'd in Our said Colony in 1748,[2] and received our Royal Allowance and Ratification in 1751, has been either partially repeal'd for particular parts of Our said Colony, or occasionally set aside throughout the whole Colony, in contradiction to Our said Instruction and to the great and manifest Injury of Our loving Subjects the Clergy of Our said Colony and the Merchants of London trading thither; For which Reasons We have thought fit by Our Order in Council dated the [10th] of August 1759 to declare Our Royal Disallowance of the said several Acts: We do therefore strictly command and require you for the future, upon pain of Our highest Displeasure and of being recall'd from the Government of Our said Colony, punctually to observe and obey the several Directions contained in the 16th Article of Our said Instructions, relative to the passing of Laws in Our said Colony of Virginia.[3]

[G. R.]

Copy: C.O.5/1367, ff. 192–94. This is the text of the instruction as submitted for approval. Matter in brackets is taken from the copy in C.O.324/39, pp. 14–16, of the instruction as sent, which is generally an inferior text.

1. See C.O.5/1368, f. 47, for the sixteenth article of the instructions.
2. This was "An Act for the support of the Clergy; and for the regular collecting and paying the parish levies" (Hening, 6:88–90), setting the annual compensation of a clergyman at a fixed quantity of tobacco. See Fauquier's letter of 5 Jan. 1759 to the Board of Trade for comment on these various acts.
3. Fauquier mentioned this additional instruction in his address to the General Assembly on 6 Oct. 1760: he stated his determination to adhere strictly to all the king's instructions and recommended very earnestly to the assembly that all bills offered to him for his assent should conform in every particular to his instructions, which, he added, he would always be ready to communicate to them (*JHB, 1758–1761*, pp. 184–85).

To James Abercromby

[29 September 1759]

This letter has not been found, but Abercromby's reply of 22 Dec. 1759 indicates that it concerned the act for appointing an agent.

From Adam Stephen

[ca. October 1759]

This letter has not been found, but in his letter of 24 Oct. 1759 to Stephen, Fauquier acknowledged receipt of a letter from Stephen which was perhaps written about October.

From William Henry Lyttelton

[1 October 1759]

This letter has not been found, but Fauquier acknowledged it in his letter of 21 Oct. 1759 to Lyttelton. It was evidently a warning of commotions among the Cherokees and a request for Virginia's assistance in putting down these troubles, which caused Fauquier to call the General Assembly to meet on 1 Nov.; see his address to the assembly in *JHB, 1758–1761*, pp. 133–34.

From John Stanwix

Sir   Pittsburgh 4th October 1759

I had the Favour of Your letter from General Amherst, dated 14th September, inclosing me a Coppy of your letter to Him,[1] in regard to the Continuance of The Regiment, in the Pay of the Dominion of Virginia, and recommends it to me, to give you my thoughts on this Head. After the General himself has so very Judiciously said that he cannot think of diminishing this Regiment even for their Own Interest, until such Time as they may be perfectly secure of their not being called upon again and I am so thoroughly in the Generals Opinion, that I think reducing this fine Regiment before a General Peace, or a more settled Tranquility, would be the most dangerous, & distructive measure, that can possibly be pursued at this Time, as well for the General Interest of This Continent, as the particular Interest of The Dominion so exposed on every side. It is True I am endeavouring to Build a Strong & Respectable Fort here in Order to Secure (agreeable to my Instructions) His Majestys Countrys to The Southward but from Numberless disappointments too Tedious to Relate, was Obliged to begin this so late,[2] which will make it Impossible to Carry the Works into Such Execution so earnestly to be wish'd for but am hopefull to be able to Build good Barracks for such a Number of Men as will be necessary for its defence and hope to be so Successfull this Fall to Form (thro Numberless difficultys) a Sufficient Magazine of Provisions for their Support for Six Months, from the First of January, having Open'd every Passable Avenue to This Place, for that Purpose, and the more incomplete the Works the more Men it will require to defend this very Important Post. I am, Sir, Your most Obedient & most Humble Servant

                                                      John Stanwix

Governour Fouquier

Copy: W.O.34/45, f. 105.

1. The text sounds garbled, but Stanwix must have been referring to a copy of Fauquier's letter of 18 Aug. 1759 to Amherst, sent by Amherst to Stanwix on 14 Sept.
2. The construction of Fort Pitt had begun on 10 Sept.

From Jeffery Amherst

Sir,   Camp at Crown Point 7th October 1759

I am to Return You my most Sincere thanks for Your very oblidging favor of the 16th Ultimo Which Came to my hands Yesterday; as also for the Packett it Enclosed from Governor Lyttelton, for Whom I beg leave to trouble You with another, to be forwarded by the very first safe Conveyance, Excuse this freedom and believe me to be with a very sincere regard, Sir, &ca.

The Honble. Govr. Fauquier.

Copy: W.O.34/37, f. 205

To the Board of Trade

My Lords   Wmsburgh Octr 13th 1759

By the Conveyance of his Majesty's Ship Lynn commanded by Captn. Walter Stirling I transmit to your Lordships the Duplicates of the Journals of the Council and of the House of Burgesses, of the Acts of last Session, of the Receiver generals Account of the 2 sh Duty, and of the Accounts of the Naval Officers all which were sent by the Jenny, Crawford which sailed on the 3d July: and also of all other public Accounts which have been deliverd to me since.[1]

By the Act of Assembly which raised and provided for the pay of the 1500 Men for the Service of this Campaign, they stand provided for till the first of December next and no longer. I have therefore summoned the Assembly to meet on the 13th of November (as soon as conveniently could be after the general Court)[2] that they may come to some Resolutions as to the further providing for the Men. And as I am apprehensive that the Colony will be disposed to ease themselves as much as possible from the great Expences they have been at (the Enemy being now driven from our Frontiers) have wrote to both Major Genl. Amherst, and Brigr. Genl. Stanwix, that nothing might be wanting on my part to forward his Majesty's Service, to inform them of my Opinion; and to desire them to furnish me with their Reasons for keeping up the whole or any part of the Men, before the Assembly meets; that I may use them as Motives to the Assembly to continue the Men for a longer time.[3] From the present Turn and Temper of the people, I sincerely hope, that no public Acts relative to the Affairs of the Clergy will arrive before this Assembly is up which probably will not be long, unless retarded by that unfortunate Affair. for unfortunate I fear it will be.

At the last General Court in April one Mr. Baylis & others, were convicted of a Trespass assault and Battery on the person of Mr. Peyton and were fined: Mr. Baylis in the sum of Ten pounds, the others in smaller Sums. This assault was committed, and both parties resident in the Northern Neck.[4] Mr. President Blair who is also deputy auditor repeated to me part of a Letter from Colonel Henry Lee Lieutenant of the County to this Effect, that Lord Fairfax had remitted the Fines,[5] laying a Claim to all Fines arising in the northern Neck, by Virtue of his Grant. I asked Mr. Blair whether he proposed to mention in his Answer his having communicated this to me; he said, yes. I then said, I admit no such Claim of Lord Fairfax, and if the Sheriff neglects to levy the Fines be it at his peril.[6] I have since heard no more of this Affair. as it came to me in a loose irregular Manner I gave a verbal Answer only: But if hereafter it should come regularly before me, I will take the Advice of his Majesty's Council, and some Resolutions will undoubtedly be taken thereon which I will transmit to your Lordships by the first Opportunity.

The Crop of Tobacco was actualy so small last Year, by which so great a Deficiency is fallen on the Revenue arising from the 2 sh Duty (as will plainly appear by the Receiver-general's Accounts)[7] that altho' there is another half year due on the 25th of this Month, there is one half of the salary usualy paid on the 25th of April, still due to me. I am with the greatest Respect, My Lords, Your Lordships most Obedient Obliged & devoted Servant

Fran: Fauquier

To the Rt. Honble. the Lords Commissioners for Trade &ct.

ALS: C.O.5/1329, ff. 173–74. Endorsed as read 12 Dec. 1759.

1. See Fauquier's letter of 9 June 1759 to the Board of Trade for the public papers sent to them by the *Jenny*. Perhaps he referred to some unidentified naval officers' returns as duplicates of all other public accounts that had been delivered to him since the departure of the *Jenny*, for he had not yet received the account of quitrents for 1758 or the account of 2s. per hogshead for 25 Apr.–25 Oct. 1759.

2. The General Court convened on 10 Oct. and sat for twenty-four days, excluding Sundays, unless its business should happen to be finished in time for an earlier adjournment. Its term could thus have extended from Wednesday 10 Oct. through Tuesday 6 Nov.

3. See Fauquier's letter of 18 Aug. 1759 to Amherst, Amherst's reply of 14 Sept., and Stanwix's letter of 4 Oct. to Fauquier. No letter from Fauquier to Stanwix on this subject has been traced, and Fauquier may have been referring to the copy of his letter that Amherst sent to Stanwix.

4. There are no General Court records of this case and no particulars of it have been uncovered. Mr. Baylis was perhaps John Baylis of Prince William County, burgess for the county 1761–65, colonel of the county militia (and perhaps justice of the peace for the county and vestryman of Dettingen Parish), who was killed on 4 Sept. 1765 in a duel with Cuthbert Bullitt. Mr. Peyton may have been Henry Peyton, burgess for Prince William County 1756–61, justice of the peace (and perhaps also a vestryman of Dettingen Parish); however, there were a number of men named Peyton, and of some consequence, who were active in the Northern Neck at this period, so that identification is very tentative.

5. Thomas Fairfax (1693–1781), sixth Baron Fairfax of Cameron, was the proprietor of the Northern Neck.

6. The sheriff of Prince William County in 1759 seems to have been John Frog.

7. The account of 2s. per hogshead for 25 Apr.–25 Oct. 1758 showed a deficit of £893.17.3, and the account of 25 Oct. 1758–25 Apr. 1759 showed a deficit of £2,193.1.3.

To John Clevland

[13 October 1759]

This letter has not been found, but Clevland acknowledged the receipt of it in his letter of 12 Mar. 1760 to Fauquier and described it as saying Fauquier had issued four of the five Mediterranean passes left with him by Dinwiddie and desired a further supply of the passes. A Mediterranean pass was one which guaranteed protection against the Algerine pirates; it was issued by the Admiralty under treaty arrangements with the Barbary States.

From William Henry Lyttelton

[16 October 1759]

This letter has not been found, but Fauquier acknowledged receipt of it in his letter of 11 Nov. 1759 to Lyttelton. It was perhaps the letter that Fauquier sent to the House of Burgesses on 9 Nov. 1759, although it may have been a letter or letters, not identified, from Lyttelton and concerning commotions among the Cherokees, which Fauquier laid before the burgesses on 1 Nov. See *JHB, 1758–1761*, pp. 133, 134, 142.

To William Henry Lyttelton

Sir   Wmsburgh Octr 21st 1759

In Consequence of your Favour of the 1st instant, which I received by the Express who returns with this, I immediately call'd a Council,[1] and by their Advice have summoned the Assembly to meet on Thursday the 1st of November. Whatever Resolutions they may come to I shall immediately communicate to you, that we may all jointly concur to suppress the Insolence, and correct the Treachery of our neighbouring Savages. I should be glad to be informed of your Plan of Operations against them, and in what Manner we can on our Parts be most effectualy assisting.

The greatest Difficulty as it appears to me will be the providing for the Men, at so great a Distance in the Winter Season.

I must say, I am yet not quite out of hopes that on the Return of the two Cherokees with whom Smith the Interpreter is gone back: Things may take a more favourable Turn. They left Petersburgh on the 16 or 17 Sept. to make the best of their Way to Lieutenant Coytmore at fort Prince George. the Goods I have so long promised the Cherokee's I have ordered to stop at Salisbury in No. Carolina, and have given Smith Instructions to send an Express immediately to your Excellency with a Letter from me to inform you of our proceedings and with a Copy of his Instructions: and to wait at fort Prince George till he receives your Directions how to proceed. All this, I hope, has duly reach'd you before this, tho' you could not be informed of it, at the Time you wrote. This Government has given them all possible Demonstrations of Friendship and Fidelity; and if some of our Inhabitants have misbehaved they must thank themselves for it, having provoked them to it by their own Misconduct. Tho' I must own some of our back Settlers are by no means defensible.

There is a Report here brought by a Ship from the Northward, that the French Army under Quebec being reduced to almost Famine, have attacked Genl. Wolfe, that a most bloody Conflict and Carnage ensued, in which both Mr. Wolfe, and Monsr. Moncalm fell; but that we are in possession of the Ruins of Quebec.[2] This is not authentic, but is related with so many Circumstances, that I can't help giving some Credit to it. I am with the greatest Esteem, Sir, Your Excellency's most Obedient humble Servant

Fran: Fauquier

To Goverr. Lyttelton

ALS: William L. Clements Library, Lyttelton Papers.

1. There is no record of an executive session of the council between 3 Sept. and 1 Nov. in 1759.
2. On 13 Sept. 1759 the British launched their assault upon Quebec, the capital of New France, and both General Wolfe and the marquis de Montcalm (1712–1759), the French commander, received fatal wounds during the battle. The city was surrendered on 18 Sept.

From Jeffery Amherst

Sir, Camp at Crown Point 22d Octor 1759

It being necessary, the better to Ensure the Acquisitions of the Campaign in these Parts, as well as to penetrate into the heart of Canada, by Lake Champlain, first to take or destroy the Four Armed Vessels which the Enemy had upon it, and which gave them a Superiority over our Boats and Batteaus; I accordingly Caused Vessels to Be built for that purpose, which having been finished and Arrived here the 11th Instant, I Set out the very Evening of that day with a Detachment of the Army, & proceeded with the whole in Search of the Enemys Vessels, three of which Ours came up with, and drove into a Bay, where the Enemy themselves, sunk and ran them on Shore; The fate of the Fourth is not yet known;[1] but whether or not she be taken or destroyed, We are now not the less Masters of the Lake, and had the Weather permitted, nothing could have prevented the Attempt of penetrating into Canada, but the Winds, whilst I was out, have proved so obstinately Contrary, and the Season already so far advanced, that I have been Compelled to return to this Place, where I Arrived, with my Detachment, Yesterday afternoon. I am, with great Regard, &ca.

Copy: W.O. 34/36, f. 72. Circular to governors.

1. The four French vessels were a schooner and three xebecs (small three-masted vessels), all heavily armed with cannon easily capable of sinking the whaleboats and bateaux that made up Amherst's waterborne transport. The vessels Amherst had built were a brigantine and a large raft with sails, capable of mounting six 24-lb. cannon. The British captured the three French xebecs, but the schooner escaped them. See Gipson, 3:364–67.

To Adam Stephen

Sir Wmsburgh Octr 24th 1759

As I am always glad to hear of any thing which concerns our Troops, I take this Opportunity to acknowledge the Receipt of your Letter.[1] Our Affairs are in a prosperous Situation and our Enemy, I suppose, master'd all over the Continent, which must necessarily bring in all the Indians. I hope our Conduct towards these will be such as to convince them of the Advantage they will reap by changing Sides. As it is agreeable to you I congratulate you on being relieved from the post which you protected with so much honour to yourself and Advantage to the Colony,[2] and am Sir Your very Humble Servant

Fran: Fauquier

To Lieutt. Coll. Stephen

ALS: Maine Historical Society Library, Fogg Autograph Collection.

1. This was perhaps a letter written about Oct. 1759.
2. Stephen had been the commanding officer at Fort Ligonier.

From Jeffery Amherst

Sir, Camp at Crown Point, 25th October 1759

This will be delivered to You by Mr. Stobo, who, tho' You may not be personally Acquainted with, You will soon have knowledge of from the Gentlemen in Your Government; he came to me about Sixteen days ago, from Major General Wolfe, who had given him some Dispatches for me, but unfortunately, twelve Leagues off Hallifax, he was taken by a Pirate, and obliged to fling his Papers overboard, so that I know not what General Wolfe said in his behalf, but as I am Certain, he has been of great Use to him,[1] I am Confident he came well recommended, but as I have it not in my power, at present, to do any thing for that Gentleman, I must beg leave to recommend him to Your particular Notice and favor, and if any thing can be done for him in Your Government, I must beg Your Interest to procure it him, as I on my part, when I have an Opportunity, shall be very glad to reward his Zeal and Services. I am, with the greatest Regard, Sir, &ca.

Honble. Govr. Fauquier.

Copy: W.O.34/37, f. 206. This letter was laid before the House of Burgesses on 19 Nov. 1759. See *JHB, 1758–1761*, p. 150. The house voted a reward of £1,000 and its thanks to Stobo.

1. In what way Stobo was of great use to Wolfe has not been determined. It has been asserted (by Stobo among others) that Stobo informed Wolfe of the best way for attacking Quebec, while others have denied the claim. It is no doubt true that Stobo provided intelligence of French strength in Quebec, where he had been a prisoner for the best part of five years and much of the time had great freedom of movement. And it is obvious that he was entrusted with dispatches from Wolfe to Amherst. See Alberts, pp. 238–63, for Stobo's providing of intelligence and for the circumstances of his capture by pirates.

From William Henry Lyttelton

[Charles Town, 25 October 1759]

This letter has not been found. Fauquier communicated it to the council on 12 Dec. 1759, and it is abstracted in *EJC* 6:151:

His Honor also communicated a Letter from Governor Lyttelton, dated Charles-Town the 25th of Octor, promising, if Matters are brought to a successful Issue, in the Cherokee Nation, to take the first Opportunity of acquainting those who remain with the Goods at Salisbury therewith.

From William Byrd

[Pittsburgh, 29 October 1759]

Two letters from Byrd written from Pittsburgh on 29 Oct. 1759 are mentioned in *EJC* 6:151. No abstracts are given, and neither letter has been found.

From Adam Stephen

Sir   Camp at Pittsburgh Octr 29th 1759

   I received the honour of your Letter, and would have been under the greatest Obligation for your Sentiments on the Indian Trade.[1] There are proper Regulations wanting to make it usefull and profitable for us, and a manner is wanting to make it agreable and Easy to the Indians. The Pensylvanians engross it at present and are pushing all possible measures to keep it in their Hands.

   About twenty Tuns of Skin & Furr have been bought at this place within these three months. The Pensylvanians say the post is within their Limits, and accordingly have made an Act of Assembly for enhancing the Trade.[2] This does not Affect Virginia whilst the General Commands, but were one of the Pensylvania Officers to Command, They would be obliged to act according to their Orders from that Province.[3] The determination is of importance to us who first engaged in Virginia Service; as we are entituled to a Considerable Quantity of Land by Virtue of Governor Dinwiddie's Proclamation approved of by his Majesty and I would be glad to know the Sense of your Honor and Council on that Head.[4]

   Two Officers are just returned from presquisle with an Account of the Country, Communication & the Situation of the French Posts.[5]

   It is about Seventy miles to Venango. It has been a Small Stocade, about 400 yards below the mouth of French Creek which is there about 100 yds. over. There are about 50 houses 12 feet by 16 Standing the Vestige of as many burnt A fine Saw Mill Stands in good Order.

   From that about 46 miles to Le Beuf, very bad ground, a Barren Country for 30 Miles—about nine Miles mere Swamp—The Situation of the Post very pleasant and Commodious.

   From Le Beuf to Presquisle about 18 miles the Road well made; it is one Continued bridge through a Swamp the Whole Way The Situation of Presquisle was upon the Bank of Lake Erie, poor Soil, & piney Land about. That Post and Le Beuf was a Stocade with four Bastions, built only for the Communication. I have the Honour to be, Sir, Your most obedient Humble Servant.

                                                                     A.S.

Copy: C.O.5/1330, ff. 26-27. Endorsed as received with Fauquier's letter of 1 Dec. 1759. Headed "Copy of a letter from Lt. Coll. Stephen." Fauquier communicated this letter to the council on 12 Dec. 1759, and it is mentioned in *EJC* 6:151.

1. It is possible, but rather unlikely, that Stephen referred to Fauquier's letter of 24 Oct. 1759 to him. Lois Mulkearn (pp. xxxi, 446) suggests that this letter of Stephen's is the reply to a letter from Fauquier, sent to Stephen in response to John Mercer's letter to Fauquier; Mulkearn dates Mercer's letter as ca. Sept. 1759 or in the period of 25 July to mid-Oct. 1759, but this editor dates it as ca. Nov. 1759. This letter of 29 Oct. from Stephen apparently did not arrive in Williamsburg until some date in the period 20 Nov.–1 Dec.: presumably Fauquier did not receive it in time to communicate it to the council at its meeting on 20 Nov., but he did communicate it at the next meeting of the council, on 12 Dec., and in the meantime he had enclosed a copy of it in his letter of 1 Dec. to the Board of Trade.

2. For the boundaries of Pennsylvania, see Boyd Crumrine, "The Boundary Controversy between Pennsylvania and Virginia, 1748–1785," *Annals of the Carnegie Museum* 1 (Pittsburgh, 1902): 505–24, and Charles O. Paullin, *Atlas of the Historical Geography of the United States* (Washington, D.C., and New York, 1932), pp. 77–78 and plate 97G. It appears that no one gave any special attention to settling the western boundary of Pennsylvania until Virginia began to grant land and build forts in a region where claims of Pennsylvania and Virginia were in conflict. Stephen probably referred to the act passed in the session of Jan. 1758, for which see Bouquet's letter of 25 Aug. 1759 to Fauquier, n. 1. However, in its session of Feb. 1759, the Pennsylvania assembly had passed "A Supplement to an Act, intituled 'An Act for preventing Abuses in the Indian Trade . . .' " (pp. 460–63 of the session acts, Evans 8454), which increased the amount of money at the disposition of the commissioners.

3. Stephen must have been referring to General Stanwix as commanding officer at Pittsburgh, rather than as commanding officer of the southern district of North America.

4. By "determination" Stephen evidently meant the settling of the Pennsylvania-Virginia boundary. Having been in the service of Virginia since the spring of 1754, he felt himself entitled to the benefits of Dinwiddie's proclamation of 19 Feb. 1754 (*EJC* 5:499–500), which promised that persons who volunteered to erect and support a fort on the Ohio River at the Monongahela fork would receive (in addition to their pay) grants of land from a tract of 200,000 acres of the king's lands on the east side of the Ohio, in Virginia, of which one half was to be contiguous to the fort and the remainder on or near the Ohio River. The council journal contains no advice on Stephen's letter, but Fauquier's opinion is stated in his letter of 1 Dec. 1759 to the Board of Trade that transmitted a copy of the letter from Stephen.

5. The two officers were Capt. William Patterson and Lt. Thomas Hutchins; for mention of their trip, see William Hunter, *Forts on the Pennsylvania Frontier, 1753–1758* (Harrisburg, Pa., 1960), p. 97.

From John Mercer

Honoble Sir [ca. November 1759]

As I am one of the Ohio Company,[1] I was a good deal alarmed by Colo. Stephen's Information that the Pennsylvanians and other foreigners were about to survey large quantities of Land upon the Ohio, within this Government.[2] I think I may venture to say that Company had not only a prior Claim in Virtue of his Majesties Instruction but that the Considerations therein mentioned were public and valuable ones.[3] And that they first at their own Expence made such discoveries of those parts as could be depended on, cleared the public Roads, took Possession and were about to build a fort and Warehouses for carrying on their Trade where Pittsburg now stands are facts cannot be controverted, yet when this Government thought proper to pitch on that place to build a Fort for the public defence and to issue a Proclamation promising two hundred thousand Acres of Land (one hundred thousand of which were to be contiguous to the Fort) as an Encouragement to the Officers and Soldiers who should voluntarily inlist to repel the French Encroachments it is notorious that the Company readily submitted, desiring only such reasonable tracts of Land at proper Stages and convenient distances along the Road they had been at the Charge of clearing as should be judged necessary for building Storehouses and securing their Carriages employed in transporting Goods from their Storehouse at Wills creek to a proper place on the Monongahela where they proposed to build their boats. These were adjudged by the principal Officers and persons concerned to be not only reasonable but greatly advantageous to the Proprietors of the adjoining Lands, and such was the general opinion at that time of the great Utility of the Company's Undertaking, that, the Earl of Granville, Lord Baltimore and Mr. Penn (according to Mr. Hanburys information)[4] assured him they should have what quantities of Land they desired for securing their Settlements and extending their trade within their respective Proprietaries on the same terms they had procured the Grant from his Majesty.

I am sensible the Company has been charged with delay in not having surveyed their Lands long since but it is too tedious a Subject to enter upon their Vindication however I think I may venture to affirm they did everything in their power, and if so it is certain they cannot be justly blamed. They did indeed at length procure a Commission for Mr. Gist to Survey their Lands but he scarce got it before Hostilities began and he unfortunately died this last Summer or I imagine he would have made a considerable progress in it this last Fall.[5] as I was afterwards informed that my Son was applying for a Commission I thought whether he obtained it or not I might depend upon him for timely notice when and to whom the Commission would be granted.[6] but having heard nothing from him on that head and not dreaming that the Company had any other Competitors than the Officers and Soldiers claiming under the Proclamation, with whom I made no doubt everything would be easily and amicably settled, I made myself very easy till Colo. Stephen acquainted me that no Commission is yet granted to any Person in this Colony, and that he expects before any is, great tracts will be surveyed, and, among them, those very Lands engaged by the Proclamation and others absolutely necessary to carry on the Indian trade, and this for Persons who I doubt will prove very bad Neighbours and take every measure in their power to exclude us from that Trade and every other Advantage they can deprive us of, I therefore presume your Honour will take such measures as you shall judge necessary to prevent such an Encroachment and that you will not suffer any Lands to be surveyed or taken up in those parts, before the People of this Colony have their just Claims first satisfied.

I have not yet seen the last Act of Assembly past in Pensylvania relating to the Indian Trade but from a Letter of Capt. Trents to Colo. Lomax,[7] it is a most insolent attempt to engross to themselves that whole Trade on the Ohio, notwithstanding that whole river is without their province and within this Colony, Yet This they may effectually compass if they can secure those Lands they propose to survey which may properly be called the Key of the Ohio, as through these Lands are all the Roads and Passes both from North and South that lead to that River, The Consequences of which would be so fatal to this Colony that I greatly dread it and fear they depend on some other Interest than their own. Should they first seise the Possession however unjust their claim, it would be very troublesome to remove them, though in the end it should be effected, so that a timely Prevention can alone answer all good Purposes.

I have not time to enumerate the many disadvantages this Colony must suffer by such a Loss I must therefore beg leave to refer your Honour to Colo. Stephen who is so well acquainted with those parts that it would be a piece of presumption in me to undertake to do it, would my time permit as he can do it so much better. Honble. Sir Your most obedient Servant

J Mercer

To the Honble. Fras. Fauquier Esqr. His Majesties Lieut. Govr. & Commander in Chief of Virginia.

LS: Darlington Memorial Library, University of Pittsburgh, George Mercer Papers. Printed in Mulkearn, pp. 93–95, where the text of the letter is stated to be in the hand of Richard Rogers, John Mercer's clerk, while the complimentary close, signature, and some endorsements are in Mercer's own hand. The letter was written after 25 July 1759, the date of the death of Christopher Gist, which Mercer mentioned; and it probably was written before the middle of December, since Mercer indicated that he did not know whether his son had procured a surveyor's commission, although on 10 Dec. George Mercer was appointed surveyor of lands on the Ohio. Mercer's phrase "this last Fall" suggests that his letter was written late in the year, perhaps even as late as December; a date of ca. November seems to be a reasonable conjecture. One endorsement is simply "Copy to Governor about surveying Ohio." The other endorsement reads "The Information I received from Colo. Stephen was that the Philadelphians under Bouquets Protection (who it was said) was concerned with them were surveying about Pittsburg after they had by Acts of Assembly engrossed the trade to themselves & Bouquet had presumed by Proclamation to threaten the rest of his Majesties Subjects with Courtmartial Law for which he deserved to be hanged himself by the same Law." Lois Mulkearn suggests that this latter endorsement was added around the end of 1761, since Bouquet's proclamation which it mentioned was one of 30 Oct. 1761.

1. The Ohio Company of Virginia, organized 1747–49, was a group of influential men of Virginia, Maryland, and London who aimed at a share of the trade with the western Indians and at the development of the Ohio Valley; the company received a grant of 500,000 acres, approximately bounded by the Ohio River, the crest of the Appalachians, and the Great Kanawha River, which is to say most of West Virginia, parts of Maryland and Virginia, and the southwest corner of Pennsylvania. A useful account of the company is found in James. John Mercer (1704–1768) of Stafford County, Va., was made a member of the company in May 1751 and acted as secretary from that date on.

2. There is no record of when or how Stephen's information was conveyed to Mercer. Lois Mulkearn (p. 446) suggests that they had a conversation in the spring of 1759, while Stephen was in Virginia. However, Stephen could have written to Mercer, as he wrote to Fauquier, and it seems remarkable that Mercer would have waited for six months or so to voice his alarm to Fauquier.

3. A draft of the additional instruction to Governor Gooch, of 23 Feb. 1749, is in C.O.5/1366, ff. 217–20; the draft was approved by an order in council of 16 Mar. 1749, and the instruction was presumably sent to Gooch on or shortly after that date. Evidently Governor Gooch communicated the order to the council in Virginia on 12 July 1749, for the substance of the order is set out in the council journal for that day (*EJC* 5:295–96).

4. John Hanbury (1700–1758), a London merchant, was one of the members of the Ohio Company of Virginia and the principal of the petitioners for the grant of land approved by the order in council of Mar. 1759. John Carteret (1690–1763), earl of Granville, was the remaining proprietor of lands in North Carolina after the other proprietors had sold their rights to the crown; Frederick Calvert (1731–1771), sixth Baron Baltimore, was proprietor of Maryland; Thomas Penn (1702–1775) was one of the proprietors of Pennsylvania.

5. Christopher Gist, an explorer and topographer, evidently acted as surveyor for the Ohio Company, although there is no record of his official appointment (see Mulkearn, p. 610 n. 511).

6. Col. George Mercer was appointed surveyor on 10 Dec. 1759.

7. See Stephen's letter of 29 Oct. 1759 to Fauquier, n. 2, for the act of the Pennsylvania assembly. William Trent (1715–1787?), an Indian trader and land speculator, was appointed factor for the Ohio Company late in 1752; Lunsford Lomax (1705–1772) of Caroline County, burgess for the county 1742–56, became a member of the Ohio Company in 1752, having bought Lawrence Washington's holdings in the company. The letter from Trent to Lomax has not been identified.

To John Stanwix

[ca. 1 November 1759]

This letter has not been found, but that it was sent is implied in Fauquier's letter of 24 Nov. 1759 to Stanwix; presumably Fauquier sent the letter on or about 1 Nov., the day when he delivered the speech to the General Assembly of which (according to his letter of 24 Nov. to Stanwix) he enclosed a copy.

From Arthur Dobbs

[ca. 1 November 1759]

This letter has not been found, but Fauquier sent it to the House of Burgesses on 9 Nov. 1759. On 1 Nov. he had already laid before the burgesses a letter or letters, not identified, from Dobbs concerning commotions among the Cherokees. See *JHB, 1758–1761*, pp. 133, 134, 142.

To Jeffery Amherst

Sir,   Wmsburgh Novr 10th 1759

    I inclose under Cover with this, two Pacquets which I have at different Times received from his Excellency Governor Lyttelton to be forwarded to you; and I will take Care to send yours to him by an Express which will set out to morrow morning for Charles Town. The House of Burgesses came to a Resolution two days since to keep up the Regiment in the pay of this Colony till May next, before which Time the General Assembly will meet again. A Bill is now in its progress thro' that House for this Purpose.[1] I call'd them to meet on the 1st instant instead of the 13th on Account of some Advices I received from Govr. Lyttelton of Disturbances being to be feared from the Cherokee Indians.

    I congratulate you on the glorious Success of His Majesty's Arms during this Campaign. I am concerned it is allayed by the Loss of so brave an Officer as General Wolfe.

    We all pray for your Preservation in which I am not backward, being with the greatest Esteem, Sir, Your Excellencys most Obedient humble Servant.

                                                  Fran: Fauquier

To his Excellency Genl. Amherst.

ALS: W.O.34/37, f. 29. An extract, consisting of the first paragraph of this letter, and endorsed as received in Amherst's letter of 9 Jan. 1760, is in C.O.5/57, ff. 16–17.

1. On 8 Nov. 1759 the House of Burgesses agreed to two resolutions concerning the retention of the regiment; the first was that the regiment should be continued in the service of the colony until 1 May 1760, and the second was that a sum not exceeding £10,000 should be raised to defray the expenses of the regiment until that date. On 9 Nov. the burgesses agreed to a resolution that the sum of £10,000 for meeting the expenses of the regiment should be raised by a tax of 2s. on every hogshead of tobacco exported from the colony in 1768 and 1769, and they ordered a bill to be brought in pursuant to that resolution. See *JHB, 1758–1761*, pp. 141–42.

To William Henry Lyttelton

Sir   Wmsburgh Novr 11th 1759

I have detain'd Michael Kellenson who brought me your Favour of the 16th ulto.[1] in order to be able to inform you of the Disposition of this Colony in Relation to the Cherokee Indians.

I laid your Letters and Orders before the Assembly which I had summoned to meet on the 1st instant in order to consider these Affairs.[2] the House of Burgesses immediately came to a Resolution to keep up the Regiment which is in the Pay of this Colony. On the Receipt of your Dispatch by Wood I also sent that Letter to the House[3] and a Bill is now in its progress thro' that House to appoint the Disposition and pay of the Troops. I propose to keep Wood here till that Bill is committed, and I able to give your Excellency more certain Advice. The Council have desired me to join their Thanks with my own for the Care and Precaution you have taken about the Goods designed by this Colony to trade with those Indians.

When I am informed in what place and manner you think I shall be able to give you most assistance, in Case the Cherokees do not embrace the party of Peace, you may depend on my applying the Force the Colony puts in my Hands in the Manner you shall think most serviceable being with the greatest Esteem, Sir, Your Excellencys most Obedient humble Servant

                                     Fran: Fauquier

I forward you a Packet I received from Major Genl. Amherst.
To Govr. Lyttelton.

ALS: William L. Clements Library, Lyttelton Papers.

1. Lyttelton's letter of 16 Oct. 1759 has not been found. Fauquier may have written the messenger's name as Keltenson, and he was probably referring to Michael Kalteisen, a wagoner engaged in the Cherokee country at about this time.

2. Fauquier referred to letters from Lyttelton in his address to the General Assembly on 1 Nov. and delivered what were probably the same letters to the speaker of the House of Burgesses on that day. See *JHB, 1758–1761*, pp. 133–34.

3. John Wood was a courier, or an express. The letter he brought was probably the one that Fauquier transmitted to the speaker on 9 Nov. See *JHB, 1758–1761*, p. 142.

From the Board of Trade

Sir,   1759. Novr. 13th

It having pleased Almighty God to give signal Success to His Majesty's Arms, both by Sea and Land, particularly by the Defeat of the French Army in Canada, and the taking of Quebec; and His Majesty having thought fit, in Acknowledgment of so great Blessings, to appoint a day of Publick Thanksgiving for the same throughout Great Britain; We herewith inclose to you His Majesty's Royal Proclamation for that purpose; and it being His Majesty's Pleasure, that the like Publick Thanksgiving should be solemnized in all His Majesty's Colonies in America, which are so particularly interested in these happy Events; We do hereby signify to you His Majesty's Commands, that you do, as soon as possible after the Receipt hereof, appoint a proper day for that purpose, to be observed throughout the Province under your Government,[1] with such Solemnities as are suitable to so great an Occasion. We are, Sir, Your most Obedient humble Servants,

                                                   Dunk Halifax
                                                 James Oswald
                                                 Soame Jenyns
                                                 W. G. Hamilton

Copy: C.O.324/16, pp. 171–72. Circular to all royal governors in North America.

1. Fauquier communicated this letter to the council on 4 Mar. 1760. Tuesday 8 Apr. following was proposed and appointed for the public thanksgiving in Virginia, and it was ordered that a proclamation should be issued immediately for that purpose; the Virginia proclamation has not been found. See *EJC* 6:155.

Enclosure: Proclamation

                                                            [23 October 1759]

By the King, A Proclamation, For a Publick Thanksgiving.
George R.

We do most devoutly and thankfully acknowledge the great Goodness and Mercy of Almighty God, who hath afforded Us His Protection and Assistance in the just War, in which, for the common Safety of Our Realms, and for disappointing the boundless Ambition of France, We are now engaged; and hath given such signal Successes to Our Arms both by Sea and Land; particularly by the Defeat of the French Army in Canada, and the taking of Quebec; and who hath most seasonably granted us at this Time an uncommonly plentiful Harvest: And therefore duly considering that such great and publick Blessings do call for publick and solemn Acknowledgements, We have thought fit, by and with the Advice of Our Privy Council, to issue this Our Royal Proclamation, hereby appointing and commanding, that a General Thanksgiving to Almighty God, for these His Mercies, be observed throughout Our Kingdom of England, Dominion of Wales, and Town of Berwick upon Tweed, upon Thursday the Twenty-Ninth Day of November next. And for the better and more Religious and orderly Solemnizing the same, We have given Directions to the most Reverend the Arch Bishops, and the Right Reverend the Bishops of England, to compose a Form of Prayer suitable to this Occasion, to be used in all Churches and Chapels, and other Places of Publick Worship, and to take Care for the Timely dispersing thereof throughout their respective Dioceses. And we do strictly Charge and Command, that the said Publick Day of Thanksgiving be religiously observed by all Our loving Subjects, as they tender the Favour of Almighty God, and upon Pain of suffering such Punishment as We may justly inflict upon all such as shall contemn or neglect the Performance of so religious and necessary a Duty. Given at Our Court at Kensington, the Twenty-Third Day of October, 1759, in the Thirty-Third Year of our Reign.

God save the King.

Printed: *Lon. Gaz.*, no. 9942, for 23–27 Oct. 1759. A marginal note on the copy of the letter of transmittal states that a printed copy of the proclamation was enclosed but does not indicate whether the text was that of the proclamation above or that of another of the same date calling for a thanksgiving in Scotland.

From Jeffery Amherst

Sir, Camp at Crown Point 16th Novemr 1759

Enclosed is the Copy of a Letter and Account I Received Yesterday, by a flag of truce from Mr. Van Braam at Montreal,[1] as they speak for them selves, I have only at the request of that Gentleman, and agreable to the promise I made him in Answer, to transmit them to You.

I likewise send You a Letter, Which came by the same Opportunity for Mr. Stobo.[2]

Ensign Stewart of His Majesty's 17th Regiment, late Brigr. Genl. Forbes's,[3] being of Opinion, that he could raise some Recruits in Virginia, I have given him a beating order for that Purpose, with Which he is set out and will wait upon You; and I must beg the favor of You to give him all the Countenance & Protection he may stand in need of in that Service. I am, Sir &ca.

Honble. Govr. Fauquier.

Copy: W.O.34/37, f. 207.

1. See the letter of 9 Nov. 1759 from Van Braam to Amherst that follows. Van Braam had been a hostage or prisoner in the hands of the French since the capitulation of Fort Necessity in July 1754, and he was kept in custody in Quebec and then in Montreal from the fall of 1754 until the British took Montreal in Sept. 1760. See Alberts for Van Braam's career.
2. The letter to Stobo has not been identified; he was on his way to Williamburg, carrying Amherst's letter of 25 Oct. 1759 to Fauquier.
3. Ensign Stewart has not been further identified.

Enclosure: Jacob Van Braam to Jeffery Amherst

Sir.   Montreall the 9e 9ber 1759

I humbly beg leave to address your Excellency, Concerning my Scituation (Which is not the least distressfull the War has produced) in hopes it may Gain that attention, Which for these five years, I have in Vain laboured to find.

The cause of my detention here is too well known to repeat it; & unless your Excellencys humanity interferes, it is likely to continue untill the end of the War; which will deprive me of all hopes, not only of advancement, but of even an establishement in a Service I wished to pursue.

I dare not presume to ask favours of your Excellency, who can best Judge What is most proper to be done for my releif; I only humbly entreat, that I may not be entirely forgot; & that the confinement & difficulties I have allready met with here, may plead in my behalf, & prevent my becoming a Sacrefice to a Country I Strongly desire to Serve.

I hope to be excused the liberty I take in transmetting an account of my debts in Canada, & of my Appointments from the Regement I belong to;[1] Which I beg leave to do, with the presumtion that they will be the more readily attended to in Virginia, by passing thro' your Excellencys hands, than by any remonstrance from me; & that his Excellency the Governor of that Colony, will be pleased to Give Such orders, as will enable me to discharge them. I have the honour to be with the Greatest respect. Your Excellencys most obedient humble Servent.

J: V: Braam

An Account of my Appointments Which are due to me from the Regiment in Virginia.[2]

As a Liutt from the 28e janua. 1754 till the 8e of may at 4 Sh: a day.	£ 20.
As an Adjud: from the first of Aprill, till the 8e of may, at 3 Sh: a day.	5.11.
As a Capt: from the 8e May 1754 till the 8e 9ber 1759 at 8 Sh: a day.	803.
	£828.11.

Which 828£ 11 Sh. Verginia Currenties reduced into french Livres amounts to	L 15345	11
An Account of my debts in Canada.[3]		
by bils drawn upon Coll: Schuyler.	L 6490	
To Generall Duquéne	4000	
To Mess. Roscheblame	960	
	L 11450	

ALS: W.O.34/78, ff. 141–42. A copy of this letter was enclosed in Amherst's letter of 16 Nov. 1759 to Fauquier. It was no doubt this letter from Van Braam which Fauquier delivered to the House of Burgesses on 7 Mar. 1760, and which led to the resolution of the House of Burgesses on 10 Mar. 1760 that Van Braam should be allowed the sum of £828.11.0 for his pay as a captain in the service of Virginia from the time that he became a hostage. See *JHB, 1758–1761*, pp. 162–66.

1. This was the Virginia Regiment raised in 1754.
2. Van Braam used "appointments" in the now obsolete sense of the pay attached to an office. There is evidently no surviving record of exactly when Van Braam became a lieutenant or when he got his promotions. However, he seems to have submitted an accurate account of what pay was owed to him in the various ranks, for the House of Burgesses resolved on 10 Mar. 1760 to allow payment of £828.11 to Van Braam.
3. Col. Peter Schuyler, commander of the Jersey Blues, was a prisoner in Canada at the same time as Van Braam; he loaned money to his fellow prisoners, entertained them, and negotiated exchanges. General Duquéne was probably the marquis Duquesne, the governor of New France. The last name in Van Braam's list is clearly Roscheblame, but what precedes it is doubtful, except for the initial letter; no Messrs. Roscheblame have been identified.

From the Board of Trade

Sir, [Whitehall, 20 November 1759]

We have had under Our Consideration the Act pass'd by you in September 1758 for appointing a Treasurer, and are so fully convinced of the irregularity and impropriety of annexing the Office of Treasurer to the person of the Speaker by an express Clause in the Act contrary to the former practice and custom of the Colony, that We should certainly have immediately laid it before His Majesty for His Majesty's disapprobation, but as you have in your Letter to Us of the 10th of April last, insisted in such strong terms that a stop cannot be put to this practise at this time without manifest detriment to His Majesty's Service, We have for the present waved coming to any other resolution upon the Case, except that of repeating to you our Sentiments and Opinion of the bad Consequence of such an irregular practice that being fully apprized thereof you may in proper time govern yourself Accordingly. We are, Sir, Your most obedient humble Servants,

Dunk Halifax
James Oswald
Soame Jenyns
W. G. Hamilton
W. Sloper

Whitehall / Novr. 20. 1759.
To Francis Fauquier Esqr. Lieut. Governor of Virginia.

Copy: C.O.5/1367, f. 198.

To William Henry Lyttelton

Sir Wmsburgh Novr 22d 1759

I have detained John Wood your Express till the general Assembly broke up in hopes I might be able to give you a Satisfactory Account of their Proceedings.[1] But whether they were infected by the Example of your Colony; or whether they were convinced that the Cherokee Indians would be more politic than to declare War; they have not furnished me with means to give you any tolerable degree of Assistance, and I have no more Reason to be satisfied with them than you had with yours.

They have not impowerd me to march the 300 Men now on our Southern Borders, out of the Colony; but have kept them in pay till the 1st of

February only, by which Time they expect I shall be able to bring down part of the Regiment now at Pittsburgh to relieve them and protect the Frontiers in that Part. These Men, when they arrive there, I can march to your assistance if they should be wanted. They have impower'd me to leave 400 Men at Pittsburgh, and if more are detained there on any pretence or by any Power whatever, they are not to be deemed to be in the Pay of the Colony. these are provided for but to the first of May.[2] Notwithstanding these Restrictions, I am of Opinion that General Stanwix rather than part with the Men, will take them into British pay: if so, I shall not have a Man either to protect the Frontiers or assist you. But you may depend upon my using every effort in my power to give you what little Assistance I can, in Case of Need; but I hope the Indians will be ready to comply with your Terms of Peace, as they will now probably have heard of all our Advantages over the French.

These Proceedings of the Assembly have the more surprized me, as there seem'd to be a great Spirit of Revenge against the Cherokee Indians for all their Robberies and Outrages, stir'd up among the Inhabitants of this Colony.

I heartily wish I had been able to have given you better News, being with the highest Esteem, Sir, Your Excellencys most Obedient humble Servant

Fran: Fauquier

To Govr. Lyttelton.

ALS: William L. Clements Library, Lyttelton Papers.

1. Fauquier prorogued the General Assembly on 21 Nov. 1759.
2. The measures that Fauquier mentioned here were incorporated in "An Act for granting the sum of ten thousand pounds, for the further protection of this colony" (Hening, 7:331–37).

To William Byrd

[ca. 24 November 1759]

This letter has not been found, but that it was sent is deduced from Fauquier's remark to Stanwix, in a letter of 24 Nov. 1759, that he was by the same express sending orders to Byrd to conduct himself in accordance with the assembly's act for the protection of the colony, passed a few days before.

To John Stanwix

Sir, Williamsburgh Novr 24th 1759

I am very Sorry I am Obliged to Inform You that the General Assembly, which broke up last Wednesday, by an Act they have passed this Sessions, have not given me a power to be so Assisting to His Majesty's Forces, under Your Command, in the Erecting & protecting the Works now Carrying on at Pittsburgh as I Could Wish; The two Companies of Artificers are to be immediately Disbanded; and of the Regiment I am not to leave above 400 Men at Pittsburgh; the rest I am to March Southward to protect the South West Frontiers to Relieve Colo. Peachy,[1] whose Corps is to be Disbanded by the First of February; If more than 400 are detained at Pittsburgh, the Act provides that all above are not to be deemed to be in the Pay of the Colony; but are Understood to be Paid by the Power that detains them.

I Hope You are fully Convinced, that I did all in my power to recommend more Vigorous Measures in my Speech, a Copy of which I sent You in my last;[2] and by the Copy which I Send You enclosed of what I said to them on the dismissing them; You will See I am far from being Satisfied with their Proceedings,[3] which I can't help thinking extremely Imprudent, but their Plea is Poverty, and an Inability to do more.

I Have Sent Colo. Byrd Orders,[4] by this Express, for him to Conduct himself agreably to the aforesaid Act, which I well believe he will Communicate to You, and Consult You thereon, that Everything may be Conducted with a perfect Harmony to the Service of His Majesty, and the Annoyance of our Enemy. I am, with the greatest Regard, Sir, &ca.

 Fran: Fauquier

General Stanwix.

Copy: C.O.5/57, ff. 140–41. The copy is marked as being a duplicate and endorsed as sent in Stanwix's letter to Amherst of 12 Jan. 1760, as received in Amherst's letter of 17 Feb. 1760.

1. Lt. Col. William Peachey was in command of the frontier battalion in Augusta County.
2. This was evidently a letter of about 1 Nov. 1759.
3. In his speech proroguing the General Assembly on 21 Nov. (*JHB, 1758–1761*, p. 153), Fauquier expressed his regret that the assembly had not made more ample provision for their own protection but promised that he would use the forces entrusted to him for the construction at Fort Pitt, for assistance to Lyttelton, and for protecting the frontiers of Virginia; and he hoped that if he failed in any of these undertakings, the assembly would be honest enough to blame the scantiness of the resources they had given him.
4. The communication to Byrd has not been found.

To Jeffery Amherst

Sir   Wmsburgh Novr 25th 1759

I received your Favour by Captain Stobo, and immediately sent it to the House of Burgesses who were then sitting and were to break up the next Day,[1] and recommended him to the Care of the Speaker and his old Friend Coll. Washington. The Consequence of this Message from me, you will see by the Resolution the House came to that Day: a Copy of which I send you printed in our Gazette.[2] They even went farther and sent a Message of Address to me to desire I would prefer Captn. Stobo whenever I had an Opportunity.[3] This I had promised him of my own Accord, and shall with Pleasure fulfill it; but as preferments here will be very moderate, I hope you won't forget a Man of his Merit.

Give me Leave now Sir to congratulate you on the Mark of Approbation his Majesty has been pleased to give to your Services by appointing you Governor in chief of this Colony.[4] Which Reward of true Merit gives great Satisfaction to all Ranks of people here.

I hope this may induce you to travel southward this Winter to see your Government & to settle with me, that I may have an Opportunity of showing you what Part I take in this Instance of his Majesties Justice and Favor.

I don't doubt but it will be acceptable to you to be informed of the Value of the Government:[5] of which I will candidly make you Master as far as I am able. By his Majestys Instructions the Salary and all Emoluments are to be divided equally between us. I have given my Brother in London Power to have agreed with Lord Loudoun to remit him £1500 Sterling on the Exchange in London by ½ Yearly Payments. I will frankly acknowledge I do not take this to be full half of the Value, but if I am to negotiate and endorse Bills of Exchange and take the Chance of their being protested I think I ought to have the Turn of the Racket in my Favor, especialy as it would save his Lordship the Expence of an Agent here, to whom I am willing to pay the full and exact Moiety here as I receive it, if his Lordship should have chosen that Method. I likewise would have engaged that if hereafter the Income should turn out better than it now appears to me, I would raise it to 1500 Guineas, but further I was sure I could not go. I by no means intend to hurry on an agreement: but that you may judge yourself of the reasonableness of the proposal, when I see you here which I hope you will have Leisure to do, I will show you my Book of the Whole Receipt since my Arrival in the Colony. I dare affirm we shall have no Difference, because I think I can affirm that we are both fair Candid Men, who mean to take no little Advantages of each other. By a Letter I received last Week from my Brother, Mr. Calcroft Ld. Loudouns Agent would have agree'd for 1500 Guineas but my Brother could not make such an absolute Agreement.⁶

To conceal no part of this Affair from you I must tell you that my Predecessor Govr. Dinwiddie paid £1665 on this Account. Sir Wm. Gooch paid Ld. Orkney £1300 only; when he went to England, Mr. Lee the then President agreed to pay him 20 sh. per Day as long as he could keep the Government vacant, or during their joint Lives if he could procure the Government for him. Ld. Albermarle succeeded Ld. Orkney: and when Mr. Dinwiddie was appointed Lieutenant Governor demanded the £365 to be added to the £1300 because he said Mr. Lee who did the Business found he could afford to pay so much, and added if he would not take it on those Terms Mr. Lee would. Mr. Dinwiddie who fear'd Ld. Albermarle's Interest closed the Bargain on those Terms: much in his own wrong. I believe I have said above, all Emoluments, but I must except 40 a year for Stationery and 20 a year to pay my Gardener, allowed to me personally in the Article of Contingent Expences of Government: there is also a Sort of Quit Rent paid by some Tenants of Lands formerly set apart for the Governors Service, paid in Corn: always supposed to belong absolutely to the resident Commander in chief, as the Lands were designed originaly to raise Stock for the Governors Table.⁷ I mention these Trifles to show you I am quite above-board, and intend to conceal nothing from your Knowledge.

The Assembly broke up on the 21st instant, and tired, or as they say incapacitated to do more, have curtailed the Men left with Brigr. Genl. Stanwix at Pittsburgh to 400, and these to the 1st of May only. I am with the greatest Esteem, Sir, Your Excellency's most Obedient humble Servant

Fran: Fauquier

To Majr. Genl. Amherst.

ALS: W.O.34/37, ff. 30–31. Endorsed as received 24 Dec. and answered 27 Dec. 1759. An extract, consisting of the last paragraph of this letter, is in C.O.5/57, ff. 20–21, endorsed as received in Amherst's letter of 9 Jan. 1760.

1. Stobo delivered Amherst's letter of 25 Oct. 1759, which Fauquier sent to the House of Burgesses on 19 Nov. See *JHB, 1758–1761*, pp. 150–51, for the transmittal of the letter and its consequences.

2. Fauquier meant a resolution of the House of Burgesses to present to Stobo a formal message of thanks and of congratulations on his safe and happy return to Virginia, agreed to on 19 Nov. soon after Amherst's letter was read. Fauquier must have enclosed the *Va. Gaz.* for 23 Nov. 1759, which has not survived; but the resolution and Stobo's reply on 20 Nov. to the message are printed in the *Va. Gaz.* for 30 Nov. 1759.

3. The burgesses resolved on 19 Nov. to present an address to Fauquier asking him

to grant his special care and favor to Stobo and promote him in the service of the colony; this resolution is in the *Va. Gaz.* for 30 Nov. 1759. The burgesses went considerably further than this message to Fauquier: on 19 Nov. their first resolution after the reading of Amherst's letter was to give Stobo a reward of £1,000 for his zeal and the hardships he had suffered; the council agreed to the resolution on the same day, and Fauquier assented to it the following day.

4. The appointment of Amherst to be captain general and governor in chief of Virginia, as of 12 Sept. 1759, was announced in the *Lon. Gaz.*, no. 9930, for 11–15 Sept.

5. See Fauquier's letters of 10 Sept. and 20 Nov. 1758 for much the same statement of financial arrangements made by Fauquier's predecessors.

6. The letter from William Fauquier has not been found. John Calcraft (1726–1772) was for many years engaged in military finances, including the private business of senior officers. He was agent for Amherst as well as for Loudoun.

7. No further information has been found on the allowances to the governor of £40 a year for stationery and £20 a year for his gardener, evidently included in the items of contingent charges against the revenue of 2s. per hogshead; none of the accounts of contingent charges, which as a rule were submitted to the governor and council shortly before the submission of the account of 2s. per hogshead, has been found. The lands set aside for the governor's benefit were perhaps the palace farm of 364 acres, north of the Governor's Palace, and perhaps other tracts of land near Jamestown or Williamsburg. Records of the situation and extent of public lands at various periods are scarce and confusing, and no information at all on these quitrents paid in corn has been found.

Warrant for David Bowman

George R. [St. James's, 26 November 1759]
Trusty & Welbeloved We greet you well Whereas We are well satisfied of the Loyalty, Integrity & ability of Our Trusty & Welbeloved David Bowman, Gent[1] We have thought fit hereby to authorize & require you forthwith to cause Letters Patent to be passed under Our Seal of Our Colony & Dominion of Virginia,[2] for constituting & appointing him the said David Bowman Clerk of the Naval or Navy Office of the Eastern Shore of Our said Colony & Dominion To have hold exercise & enjoy the same to him the said David Bowman by himself or his sufficient Deputy or Deputies during Our Pleasure, together with all and singular the Fees, Rights, Privileges, Perquisit's and Advantages, to the said Office or Place belonging or appertaining, With a Proviso that nothing in the said Letters Patent contain'd, shall extend or be construed to extend to the Prejudice or Disadvantage of the Office of Our High Admiral of Great Britain or of Our Admiralty of Our foreign Plantations, for the time being or any the Rights, Privileges Jurisdictions, Powers & Authorities, to the same in any wise appertaining, And you are also to take effectual Care that a Clause be inserted in the said Letters Patent revoking

& annulling all former Appointments to the said Office of Clerk of the Naval or Navy Office of the Eastern Shore of Our said Colony, whither the same have been made by Us or by any acting under Our Authority, And for so doing this shall be your Warrant, Given at Our Court at St. James's the 26 Day of November 1759 in the Thirty Third Year of Our Reign,

By His Majesty's Command
W Pitt

Copy: C.O. 324/39, pp. 17–18. The copy has no address. Another copy of this warrant, dated 6 Dec. 1759, is in C.O. 324/51, pp. 187–88. The earlier date is correct: see n. 2 below.

1. Little is known of David Bowman, except that he was reappointed to this post in Mar. 1761 and was submitting his returns as late as 1774; it is possible that he held the post until the Revolution, or even until Isaac Smith was appointed as naval officer for Accomack in 1777. Bowman may have been the David Bowman whose will was recorded in Accomack in 1786.

2. There is no record of when Fauquier received this warrant, but on 14 Mar. 1760 he informed Pitt that he had issued Bowman's patent, in obedience to the king's warrant of 26 Nov. 1759.

From William Peachey

[Augusta Court House, 28 November 1759]

This letter has not been found. Fauquier communicated it to the council on 12 Dec. 1759, along with another letter from Peachey of 4 Dec. There is an abstract of the letter or letters in *EJC* 6:151:

Also two Letters from Lt. Col. Peachey, dated Augusta Court-House, the one Novemr. 28th, the other, Decemr. 4th signifying he apprehends no Danger or Disturbance from the Enemy at present on the Frontiers; and recommending, when the Men under his Command shall be discharged, to allow them to draw Six or Eight Days Provision to carry them Home, and to pay them as long.

To the Board of Trade

My Lords,   Williamsburgh Decr 1st 1759

I inclose to your Lordships a Copy of a Letter I have just received from Lt. Colonel Stephen; which as it contains some minute particulars of Points of Consequence I have chose to communicate to your right Honble. Board in the words of the Writer.[1] By it you may observe my Lords, that the Affair of the Indian Furr Trade; if not prevented, may again prove a bone of Contention between this Colony and Pensylvania. The surest Way to stop any ill Consequences that may arise from such a Contention, appears to me to be to settle the Determination of the Boundary Line of Pensylvania which is to run 5 Degrees due west from Newcastle.[2] We say from Messrs. Fry & Jefferson's Authority that this Distance terminates 15 or 20 Miles short of Pittsburgh.[3] The Pensylvanians act, as if it did not; upon what Authority they proceed I am as yet intirely ignorant.

I hope your Lordships will be of Opinion that this should be settled by Commissioners either appointed by your right Honble. Board immediately or mediately by Instructions sent to the Governors of the respective Provinces to appoint such Commissioners. The first Method seems least liable to create Disputes, as the Lands between the Mountains and the Ohio are now cleared of the Enemy, people seem to be very desirous to settle on the fine fertile Lands, lying on the Waters which fall into the Ohio, and so into the Mississipi and are generaly call'd by the general Name of Lands on the Waters of the Mississipi, but to the well future settling of these Lands, there are some Points which seem to require Consideration. By Proclamation from Mr. Dinwiddie all Officers and Private Men who have served in those Parts have a Right to a Certain proportion of those Lands, to which they are daily laying claim. It is also to be considered whether the Crown will renew the two Great Grants.[4] If they should be renewed, whether the Grantees should be at Liberty to take up Lands within their Grants, in as small parcels as they please; by which means they have it in their power to Skim all the fine Lands on the Waters and leave the uplands unpatented, whether they should not be obliged not to exceed a certain price for a Certain Term of Years, to their under Patentees.

Your Lordships may be fully convinced that I think these things of Consequence, and that I speak my Sentiments with Sincerity, when I inform you that my Son is taken in Partner into one of the great Grants.[5] But I hope that or any other Consideration in which my Interest shall be concerned, will never make me prostitute my Opinion to your right Honble. Board, whenever I think his Majesty's & my Country's Interest at Stake.

It seems to be the general Opinion of all the Speculative Gentlemen here, that It will be more adviseable to make a Seperate Government of all the Lands between the Mountains and the Waters;[6] the Reasons they assign are these which are Specious enough.[7] It will require a Constitution of a more Military form, than this Colony I believe can ever be prevailed upon to enter into, in order to protect these out Settlers from Insults & Incursions of the Indians. The Militia Laws now in force in this Colony would be ineffectual to secure them, and from a Jealousy of the Liberty of the Subject, I apprehend the General Assembly would never be brought to put them under such Restraints as are necessary to make a Militia serviceable. I attempted an Amendment of those Laws on my first arrival, without Success:[8] The Establishment of the Clergy in this Colony is thought to be of such a Nature, as to be an obstacle to the coming in of protestant Foreigners, from whom we are to hope the greatest Accession of people who must have a Minister of their own to maintain besides paying their Quota to a public Levy for the Support of a parochial Minister of the establish'd Church.

I thought it my Duty my Lords to throw out these Hints for your Lordships Consideration, to do therein as you shall judge most expedient, whenever it may please his Majesty in his most honourable Privy Council, to take the Matters relative to the patenting and Settling these Lands into Consideration.

The Assembly broke upon the 21st Novr. after having pass'd an Act to keep up the Regiment till the first of may next, and to disband the 500 Men before that time; vizt. 200 immediately and 300 on the first of february, and an Act to prevent Frauds on Negro Duties. I shall transmit those Acts and some few of a private Nature by the first Opportunity I can find. I have wrote to Brigr. Genl. Stanwix to inform him of these Transactions and to desire he will be particular in the Service for which he will require the Men to be kept longer in pay if necessary; otherwise I fear the Colony will be for droping them at the Time prescribed.

I shall write more particularly on the aforesaid Acts when I send them to your Lordships with the other public papers of Government. I am, my Lords, with the greatest Respect Your Lordships most Obedient and devoted Servant

Fran: Fauquier

To the Rt. Honble. the Lords Commissioners for Trade &ct.

LS: C.O.5/1330, ff. 24–25. Marked as a triplicate, with the latter part of the complimentary close and the signature in Fauquier's hand; endorsed as read 19 Nov. 1760.

1. The enclosure was a copy of Adam Stephen's letter of 29 Oct.
2. Fauquier mistook the relevance of New Castle (now in Delaware) to the boundaries of Pennsylvania. The southern boundary of Pennsylvania, according to the charter granted by Charles II in 1681, was to run along the fortieth parallel of north latitude, its eastern end being the point of its intersection with a circle of 12-mi. radius with New Castle at its center (although in fact the fortieth parallel passes about 13 mi. north of such a circle). It was the northern boundary of Pennsylvania that was to extend for five degrees, running west from the Delaware River.

3. It is not clear what authority Fauquier refers to. Joshua Fry (ca. 1700–1754) and Peter Jefferson (1708–1757) prepared a map of Virginia and Maryland with parts of New Jersey, Pennsylvania, and North Carolina (1751) which was first published about 1754 or 1755. Versions of the map assumed to have been published in 1755 place the neighborhood of Pittsburgh at a point which is inside Pennsylvania, if one reckons (as Fauquier did) the western boundary of the province to be five degrees west of New Castle, but which is outside the province if one reckons that western boundary to be five degrees west of Philadelphia.

4. These were probably the grant of 800,000 acres to the Loyal Land Company made in 1748 and the grant of 500,000 acres made to the Ohio Company in 1749.

5. Francis Fauquier, junior, may have been a partner in one of the two companies just mentioned, or in the Greenbrier Company, which received a grant of 100,000 acres in 1745.

6. This idea had been proposed in 1755 by Lewis Evans (ca. 1700–1756), the geographer, in the analysis accompanying his general map of the British colonies in America, printed in Philadelphia by Benjamin Franklin and D. Hall (Evans 7411): the analysis suggested that the king might "be pleased to appoint a Colony to be made in Ohio, with a separate Governor, and an equitable Form of Government, a full Liberty of Conscience, and the same secured by Charter."

7. Fauquier evidently agreed with the arguments advanced in favor of a separate government in the western lands, and he must in that case have used the word "specious" in an obsolete sense of "sound" or "convincing," without the suggestion of falseness that the word now carries.

8. In his first address to the General Assembly, on 14 Sept. 1758, Fauquier earnestly recommended a revisal of the militia law, which was "An Act for the better regulating and disciplining the Militia," passed in the session of Apr. 1757 (Hening, 7:93–106). On 19 Sept. the burgesses resolved that the act should be amended, but on 27 Sept. the bill to amend the act was presented, read, and rejected. See *JHB, 1758–1761*, pp. 4–5, 12, 14, 25.

To John Stanwix

Sir, Williamsburgh Decr 1st [1759]

I was entirely Ignorant of Your Disposition of the Troops of this Colony, and of the Garrison You proposed to keep in Pittsburgh, when I Wrote to You on the 24th Ultimo, in which I gave You a full Account of the Provision the General Assembly had made for all the Men in the Pay of the Colony. By that Letter You will see that I am Obliged to disband the Artificers immediately, If You think it adviseable to detain them on the British Establishment, I Suppose it is as much in Your power, as to have detained any of the Regiment; or if more are necessary to be sent to Supply their Place, I beg You will let Colo. Byrd know Your Desires as soon as possible; and You may be Assured, I will do all that is in my power to do, to promote His Majesty's Service. I Apprehend at the next Meeting of the Assembly, it will be very difficult to persuade them to Continue the Men in Pay beyond the first of May, unless there should

Appear an absolute necessity for so doing, therefore if You should have Occasion for them, I beg the favor of You to be very Explicit with me, as to the Numbers You will want, and the particular Service on which You will Stand in need of their Assistance. I would not press this, if I did not know His Majesty's Service requires it, for without such Authority I shall despair of keeping a Man. I should be glad to be Apprised of this sometime before March, for the Assembly need not meet unless it is to Continue the Men in Pay. I am, with the greatest Regard, Sir, &ca.

Fran: Fauquier

General Stanwix.

Copy: C.O.5/57, ff. 142–43. The copy is marked as being a duplicate and is wrongly dated 1 Dec. 1760. It is endorsed as sent in Stanwix's letter to Amherst of 12 Jan. 1760 and as received in Amherst's letter of 17 Feb. 1760.

From John Stanwix

[1 December 1759]

This letter has not been found, but Fauquier acknowledged it in his letter of 24 Dec. 1759 to Stanwix; Stanwix referred to it in his letter of 6 Jan. 1760 to Fauquier and indicated it had informed Fauquier that the Virginia Regiment, under the command of Colonel Byrd, was marching to Winchester, to be more immediately under Fauquier's command and available for the needs of Virginia or the other southern colonies.

From William Peachey

[Augusta Court House, 4 December 1759]

This letter has not been found. Fauquier communicated it to the council on 12 Dec. 1759, along with another letter from Peachey of 28 Nov. See the letter of 28 Nov. 1759 from Peachey for an abstract of the letters.

From John Stanwix

[5 December 1759]

This letter has not been found, but Fauquier acknowledged receipt of it in his letter of 24 Dec. 1759 to Stanwix.

From John St. Clair

[Trenton, 8 December 1759]

This letter has not been found. Fauquier communicated it to the council on 21 Feb. 1760, and it is abstracted in *EJC* 6:154:

Also a Letter from Sir John St. Clair, dated Trenton, Decemr. 8th promising as soon as he is able to send the Account stated between this Government and the Crown, in the meantime sending his Honor the Order for the Ballance due to the Colony, which Colo. Hunter will pay at Sight, amounting to £912.4d. Sterling, after deducting Major Stewart's Demand.

Presumably Colonel Hunter was John Hunter, acting as an agent for military supplies and accounts. The order for £912.0.4 that Hunter was to pay has not been traced, and nothing is known of the demand by Major Stewart, perhaps one by Robert Stewart of the Virginia Regiment for expenses incurred during the Forbes expedition.

From Lord Colville

[Halifax Harbor, 9 December 1759]

This letter has not been found. Fauquier communicated it to the council on 21 Feb. 1760, and it is abstracted in *EJC* 6:155:

Also a Letter from Lord Colvill, dated Hallifax Harbour Decemr 9th informing that he had writ an Order for Capt Faulknor of the Mercury, then at Boston, to repair without Loss of Time to Virginia, to take under Convoy all the homeward bound Trade, and see them safe to the Downs.

The council ordered that a notice of the convoy be published in the *Virginia Gazette*. Alexander Colville (1717–1770), seventh Baron Colville of Culross, was at this date a captain in the Royal Navy, and for a short time from Oct. 1759 he was the commanding officer in American waters. Captain Jonathan Faulknor (d. 1795) of H.M.S. *Mercury* did not convoy the Virginia fleet on this occasion: he sailed for Virginia on 7 Jan. 1760 to carry out Colville's orders, but bad weather drove him to Barbados, whence he sailed for England on 14 Feb.

Memorial to the Treasury

[ca. 12 December 1759]

The memorial has not been found, but it is assumed that it was drawn up about 12 Dec. 1759, when the council considered a number of letters from James

Abercromby, and on the question of a grant of money from Parliament, "They further advised that a Memorial be drawn to the Lords of the Treasury, praying them to direct that the Sum which shall be apportioned to Virginia may be paid to Mr. Abercrombie, upon his giving Security to remit the same to such Person, and in such Manner as his Majesty shall be pleased to order" (*EJC* 6:151–52). Abercromby's letter of 1 June 1760 indicates that the memorial was submitted in the name of the lieutenant governor and council.

To James Abercromby

[14 December 1759]

This letter has not been found, but Abercromby acknowledged receipt of duplicates of the letter in his letters of 1 June and 1 Oct. 1760 to Fauquier. In his letter of 1 June, Abercromby stated that he had received with Fauquier's letter the memorial (of ca. 12 Dec. 1759) from Fauquier and the council to the Treasury regarding payment of Virginia's share of the grants from Parliament.

To the Board of Trade

My Lords   Wmsburgh December 17th 1759

    In consequence of some Letters I received from Governor Lyttelton to give me Notice of some Commotions among the Cherokee Indians which seem'd to threaten Mischief to this & the Neighbouring Colonies; I call'd the general Assembly to meet on the first of November instead of the 13th the Day to which they stood prorogued, at their Meeting I laid these Letters and Informations before them, as also the Letters I had received from Generals Amherst and Stanwix in answer to those I wrote to them to know their Sentiments about the keeping up our Forces, of which I gave your Lordships an Account in my Letter of the 13th Octr. and I recommended these services to them in the manner your Lordships will see in the Journals herewith sent you.[1] They fell short of my expectations and indeed of common Prudence in providing for these Exigences, for they disbanded the two Companies of Artificers on the first of Decr. the other three Companies on the South West Frontiers under Lt. Coll. Peachey They have provided for till the first of Febry. when they are to be relieved by Part of Coll. Byrds Regiment; but they have not untied my Hands, as to marching them out of the Colony to the Assistance of

Govr. Lyttelton, if he should want them. As to the Regiment I have a power to leave 400 with Genl. Stanwix and I am to march the rest to occupy the posts where Coll. Peachey's Men now are; these are provided to the first of May and no longer, all which particulars your Lordships will observe in the act herewith sent.[2] My speech at the dismissing the Assembly will shew your Lordships that I was far from being satisfyed with what they had done. I am of Opinion that Govr. Lyttelton will not want our Assistance as he is gone up into the Cherokee Country with a Little Army to demand or rather command Peace, which the Indians in their present situation unsupported by the French will scarcely be hardy enough to refuse him.[3]

But if he should have wanted us, it looks like Madness to have obliged me to march Men 600 Miles in Winter, and not give me power to make use of those which were near at hand, and which I had privately order'd down there on purpose to be ready. In providing for all these Men, the Assembly have endeavour'd to avoid the Emission of new paper Currency Notes,[4] by empowering their Treasurer to receive the whole or any part of the £50,000 voted by Parliament, for the Southern Colonies, which shall be paid unto his Hands by the person appointed by his Majesty to receive the same from his Royal Treasury, and thereout to pay for the Subsistance of these Men any Sum not exceeding £10,000. I have wrote to Mr. Stanwix to desire he would be explicit as to the Service he expects and requires from our Troops for the ensuing Campaign; otherwise I fear by the turn of the Members they will be for disbanding the whole Corps on the first of May. If I should receive any account of more Money Voted by the British Parliament, or a proportionable Remittance of the Money already voted agreably to the Affectionate Messages of his Majesty in Behalf of the Colonies; it would be a means of keeping up the Spirits of the Assembly which seems to groan under the Expence they have been at.

Your Lordships will receive in the Box an Act entituled "An Act to oblige persons bringing Slaves into this Colony from Maryland, Carolina, and the West Indies, for their own use to pay a Duty." The Intent of this Act is to prevent Frauds daily put in practice to evade an Act which has long been in force in this Colony; but which appeared to me to be so contradictory to the 26th Instruction, that I call'd a Council, produced the Instruction, shew'd my objection and desired their Opinion, as the persons appointed by his Majesty to be a Council of State to me, whether I could and ought to pass this Act, I told them that I was clear in my Opinion that I ought not, and did believe they would be so too, but that if contrary to my Expectations they should advise me to pass it, I desired they would give me their Reasons in writing; that I might Transmit them to your Lordships which they Accordingly did, and which I have enclosed under Cover with this. Out of Eight of the Council then present, there was but one against my passing the Act.[5]

It may be necessary to explain the progress of this Act which will make an odd appearance in the Journals. In order to prevent the fraud complain'd of, two Methods were thought of, one was by a Bill of this Nature, the other by a Bill to lessen the Duty one half,[6] a Bill was brought in which lay'd the Duty at 7£ per head, which pass'd the Burgesses, when it came before the Council, I told some of the Gentlemen I should have objections to the Bill; they gave me to understand that I need not be uneasy for that they should throw it out which they accordingly did.[7] Upon this a Bill was Order'd into the House of Burgesses to lower the Duty one half. Several Members were gone out of Town, the Favourers of the former Bill, call'd this a piece of Jockey ship and in their turn Jockyed the promoters of this second Bill by offering an Amendment, This Amendment introduced the first Bill with the Alteration of laying the Duty at 20 pr. Cent instead of 7£ pr. head. The Council to my Surprize pass'd this Bill so alter'd,[8] and to my greater Surprize still, advised me to pass it also. I hope your Lordships will not condemn my proceedings herein, for I have the greatest ambition to obtain your approbation being with the highest Respect, My Lords, Your Lordships most Obedient & obliged humble Servant

Fran: Fauquier

To the right Honble. the Lords of Trade &ct.

LS: C.O.5/1329, ff. 176–77. Marked as a duplicate, and with the latter part of the complimentary close and the signature in Fauquier's hand. Endorsed as read 8 May 1760 and as containing no enclosures.

1. The journals must have been those of the General Assembly of Nov. 1759, but there is no indication that they accompanied any copy of this letter. There is a manuscript copy of the journal of the council in assembly for the session of Nov. 1759 in C.O.5/1429, ff. 157–64, but the time and manner of its transmittal are unknown. No manuscript copy of the journal of the House of Burgesses for that session has been found. Fauquier may have sent a copy of the printed version (Evans 8512), although it was his practice to offer excuses for sending a printed journal.

2. The act was "An Act . . . for the further protection of this colony" (Hening, 7:331–37).

3. For an account of Lyttelton's expedition into Cherokee country in Oct. 1759, see Alden, pp. 83–88.

4. The item of paper money provoked a formal protest against the act just cited from two members of the council, Philip Ludwell and Philip Ludwell Lee. They objected succinctly to the act as failing to protect the frontiers against the Cherokees; and they objected to it in some detail as contravening the instruction against making paper money legal tender for payment of sterling debts and as having no provision for

the destruction of any paper money authorized by the act after it had served its purpose. See *LJC* 3:1227.

5. The act is in Hening, 7:338–40. The instruction cited forbade the governor's assenting to any law imposing duties upon Negroes imported into Virginia to be paid by the importer (C.O.5/1368, ff. 52–53). The council session took place on 20 Nov., and the council's advice (no doubt what Fauquier enclosed) is in the journal entry under that date: the council considered the act acceptable because it levied a duty to be paid not by the importer but by the buyer, like several other acts that neither the Board of Trade nor the king's ministers had objected to; and the council considered the act necessary to prevent Virginians from going into Maryland or North Carolina to buy slaves whom they brought home (as they asserted) for their own use, thus avoiding duties. The members of the council present were John Blair, William and Thomas Nelson, Philip Grymes, Peter Randolph, Philip Ludwell, Philip Ludwell Lee, and John Tayloe. There is no hint as to which one opposed the passing of the act. See *EJC* 6:149–50.

6. Presumably Fauquier meant a bill which imposed a duty restricted to slaves imported from Carolina, Maryland, and the West Indies, as distinguished from a bill which imposed a duty, amounting to one half of current duties, on all slaves imported into the colony from any other place. The total of existing duties on imported slaves was 20 percent: a basic duty of 5 percent until Apr. 1767, an additional duty of 5 percent until Feb. 1760, and an additional duty of 10 percent until July 1765; see the acts in Hening, 6:217–22, 353–54, 417–20, 468–70 and 7:69–86 and 281.

7. On 8 Nov. 1759 the House of Burgesses ordered the preparation of a bill "To oblige the Importers of Negroes for their own Use to pay a Duty," which was presented, read, committed to a committee of the whole house, and amended and on 15 Nov. was passed and sent to the council for its concurrence as "An Act to amend the several Acts laying a Duty on Slaves imported into this Colony"; the council rejected the act on the same day. See *JHB, 1758–1761,* pp. 141, 143, 144, 146, 148, and *LJC* 3:1225–26.

8. On 16 Nov., the day after the council had rejected the act mentioned in n. 7 above, the House of Burgesses ordered the preparation of a bill "For lessening the Duty on Slaves imported," which was presented and read twice that day, then ordered to be committed to a committee of the whole house. On 17 Nov. the bill was considered in that committee and amended, presumably by the amendment Fauquier describes. On 19 Nov. the burgesses passed and sent to the council for its concurrence "An Act to oblige the Persons bringing Slaves into this Colony from Carolina, Maryland, and the West Indies, for their own Use, to pay a Duty," which the council read and passed the same day. See *JHB, 1758–1761,* pp. 148–50; *LJC* 3:1228.

From Jeffery Amherst

Sir, New York 21st December 1759

I was on my road from Crown Point to this Place When I Received Your favor of the 10th Ultimo, with the two packetts Enclosed from Govr. Lyttelton, Which I have Answered by His Majesty's Ship the Scarborough,[1] Which is to Sail on Sunday next, and herewith I take the liberty of transmitting to You Duplicates of Said Answers, to be forwarded by the first Opportunity that Shall Offer, as likewise a Duplicate of my Letter to Govr. Ellis,[2] to be sent in the Same manner; And at the Same time that I return You my most Sincere thanks for Your care of those from Govr. Lyttelton, and my former one to him, I must beg Your pardon for the additional trouble I now give You.

Nothing could give me more pleasure, than to learn that the house of Burgesses, were come to a Resolution to keep up the Regiment in the pay of the Colony of Virginia till May next, as long before that, we shall be Informed by His Majesty's Minister, Whether their Service will be any longer requisite, and that if it is, this is an Earnest of the House of Burgesses further Zeal for the good of the Common Cause.

I hope Mr. Lyttelton's Expedition will have had a Successfull Issue, and that he will not have had any Occasion for other Troops than those of the Province of South Carolina. I am, with great Regard, Sir, &ca.

Honble. Govr. Fauquier.

Copy: W.O.34/37, f. 208. Another copy, C.O.5/57, f. 18, is endorsed as sent in Amherst's letter of 7 Jan. 1760. Fauquier communicated this letter to the council on 21 Feb. 1760, and it is abstracted in *EJC* 6:154.

1. H.M.S. *Scarborough*, a ship of twenty-four guns commanded by Capt. John Stott, had been part of the naval force in the expedition against Quebec.
2. Henry Ellis (1721–1806) was governor of Georgia 1757–60.

From James Abercromby

Sir   Decr 22d 1759

I have your Favour of 29th Septr. relating to the Agency Law, which at length is come to the Office, from whence I have a Copy thereof and find no Variation therein from the Bill heretofore rejected but in the Name and Salary to the Agent thereby nominated.[1] The Presidents Letter to me of the 30th of May confirmed me in my Opinion that I was not superseded by Virtue of this Act, for he expressly tells me that no Step had been taken in Council to lay me quite aside, for that now they had two Agents and my Salary as usual had been paid to him,[2] however that I might act with the greater Propriety in the Several Provincial Affairs under my Solicitation, it became necessary for me to take the Opinion of the Attorney General Copy whereof I send you as the same is entered in the Several Offices here,[3] and as the Act does not Affect the special Authority of the Governor and Council, or that of the Agent acting under their immediate Authority, the Act now in Question shall stand or fall upon the Propriety or Impropriety thereof without any further Interposition on my part, and under this Explanation thereof I sincerely wish you may escape Censure, which I am afraid must have attended this Act, had an Opposition been taken to it on Argument before the Council in Consequence of the Attorney Generals Opinion thereon.[4] It seems strange that the House of Burgesses should have thrown the Affairs of the Province into the hands of a Person who has never appeared, I have made all the Enquiry possible after Mr. Montague, but no such Person is to be heard of in the Temple or elsewhere; about ten Years since there was in the Temple one of that Name, who about that time retired to the Country from Business, whether dead or alive, I have not been able to learn.[5]

Under all these Difficulties that have been thrown in the way of my Service, I am very much obliged to you in particular for being so explicit in testifying your Opinion, and adhering thereto, on my Right in the Case of Virginia to whatever Emoluments may hereafter become due to the Agents on the Money granted by Parliament to the American Provinces. It had been cruelly hard and unjust to have found myself deprived, and more especially in the Case of the £50,000 of such Emoluments, since that Money was absolutely obtained through my Means in the first Instance taken up by me alone and solicited with different Administrations since 1756, and finally accomplished thro' Mr. Secretary Pitt's good Offices to me; And in Testimony thereof I have his Recommendation to the Treasury as the proper Person to receive it for the Use of the Province and I make no Doubt of having the Kings Warrant accordingly for the Proportion of the £50000 which by the Words of the Act of Parliament is to be paid to such Person, or Persons, and in such Manner as His Majesty shall direct, and had it not been for the unaccountable Delay given us on the part of Loudon, whose Approbation, of our Services in the Case of the 50,000 becomes necessary, the money had been long since issued to the Agents.

In the mean time the Provincial Proportions of the 200,000 are adjusted and accordingly I have in my hands the Kings Warrant for £20,546,[6] which is the Proportion given to Virginia but as the Warrant to the Exchequer does direct that this Money shall be issued to such Person or Persons, who is, are, or shall be, duly Authorized for, and on the Behalf of the said Provinces, a Doubt arises amongst several Agents who have not special Powers, how far their General Powers as Agents and not particularly named in the Warrant, will Authorize them to receive this Money; a little time will determine this Point Should a Special Power be deem'd necessary it may be done by order of the Governor & Council under the Provincial Seal, and in order to avoid all kind of Umbrage to the Assembly, for Justification of the Governor and Council and of myself, I desire that I may in the Power or Instruction given me to receive this 20,546 be required to give proper Security in the Exchequer for Accounting for this Money to such Uses & Purposes of Government as the Legislature in Virginia shall direct.

I have taken Notice to Genl. Abercromby that he had not acknowledged the Receipt of your Letters, he says he did receive them but as he was immediately called home, he did not incline to open a Correspondence on Business which had given you an additional Trouble, hopes therefore, with his Complements to be forgiven.

The News Papers will shew you our Publick Affairs here & abroad, & with Compliments to your Lady and Family I always am Sir &c

J. A.

Gov. Fauquiere.

Copy: Virginia State Library, James Abercromby Letter Book, pp. 184–87. Possibly in a clerk's hand. A marginal note indicates that the letter was sent by Mr. Hyndman's ship on 28 Jan. 1760.

1. Abercromby had procured, evidently at the office of the Board of Trade, a copy of "An Act for appointing an Agent" (Hening, 7:276–77), "the Agency Law" that the General Assembly passed in the session of Feb. 1759 and the Board of Trade had read as recently as 14 Nov. The rejected bill with which Abercromby compared that act was "An Act for appointing an Agent," passed by the House of Burgesses in the assembly session of Sept. 1758 but rejected by the council. No text of the rejected act has been found, but Abercromby had seen a copy of it, as he said in his letter of 28 Dec. 1758 to Fauquier.

2. Blair's letter of 30 May has not been found, but Abercromby submitted an extract from it (C.O.5/1329, f. 166) to the Board of Trade. The extract has only this to say about Abercromby's tenure of the agency: "So at present we have two Agents, but the last on such a Footing, that the Governor, I find, thinks he cannot conveniently correspond with him."

3. See the opinion of the attorney general that follows. There is no indication of how and when Abercromby solicited the opinion of the attorney general on the agency act, but it seems likely that he did so at about the same time that he presented a memorial to the Board of Trade, read on 21 Nov., in which he represented that the executive in Virginia was relatively independent of the assembly and had always appointed the agent for the colony, who was paid from the revenue of 2s. per hogshead on tobacco; that a new agent had been appointed by an act assented to by the governor although it had no suspending clause, a violation of instructions; and that the assembly had rejected his bill of £196.7.0 for services rendered, including negotiations for Virginia's share of money awarded by Parliament. The memorial requested, finally, that the Board of Trade should advise the king either to assume the direct appointment of an agent or to order the governor and council to continue Abercromby in his office, with an appropriate salary and expenses. The memorial and various papers attached are in C.O.5/1329, ff. 152–69.

4. Abercromby was not careful to avoid a suggestion of censure. In addition to his observation already noted, that Fauquier had disregarded his instructions in assenting to the act appointing an agent, Abercromby appended to his memorial an extract of a letter to Dinwiddie of 22 Mar. 1759 from Philip Ludwell (C.O.5/1329, f. 164) which begins "You need not be surprized that the Governor has dispensed with his Instructions, if you knew the great Services that are expected from the Subserviency of that Gentleman and all his Connections," and goes on to say that Ludwell alone (of the council, presumably) had opposed the act appointing an agent, but in vain, for Peter Randolph had assured the burgesses that Fauquier had promised to pass the act if the council approved it. The suggestion of argument on the act arising from the attorney general's opinion on it refers to the Privy Council in England.

5. See Abercromby's letter of 26 July 1759 for an earlier comment on Montagu. It is true that little information can be found on Montagu's activities in the years between about 1742 and 1759, but he was hardly a nonentity, being a member of a rather distinguished family and apparently a competent lawyer.

6. By the act of 33 Geo. II, cap. 18, Parliament voted £200,000 "to enable his Majesty to give a proper Compensation to the respective Provinces in North America, for the Expences incurred by them in the Levying, Cloathing and Pay of the Troops raised by the same, according as the active Vigour and strenuous Efforts of the respective Provinces shall be thought by his Majesty to merit." The act was "An Act for enabling his Majesty to raise the Sum of one Million for the Uses and Purposes therein mentioned; and for further appropriating certain Supplies granted in this Session of Parliament" (*Statutes* 8:447–54). On 30 Mar. 1759 Abercromby submitted to the Treasury a return of troops raised in the North American colonies for 1758, and on 19 June following he submitted a claim for Virginia's share of the £200,000 for expenses incurred in levying, clothing, and paying troops raised for 1758; the total claimed was £52,000 Virginia currency, or £41,600 sterling (T.1/388, pp. 83–85, 172).

Enclosure: Opinion of the Attorney General

[24 December 1759]

Q 1st   Whether the Act as it now stands can be legally construed without express Words therein to supersede the Solicitor or Agent appointed by and acting as aforesaid under the Authority of the Governor and Council &ca.

Ansr.   I am clearly of Opinion that this Act of Assembly does not supersede the ancient Agent; For he being the King's proper Officer, paid out of his Revenue, and employed about his Affairs, under the Directions of the Governor and Council cannot be laid aside by Implication, and swallowed by another Officer, who as far as I see is the Servant of the Assembly in Opposition to the Crown.

Q 2d   Whether the Solicitor or Agent appointed by the Govr. & Council, and acting under such their first Establishment, corroborated as aforesaid by the President's Letters, wrote since Passing of the Act, is not well justified in Pursuing the Negociations recommended in the usual Manner to his Care as well before as since the Act, and thereupon justly Entitled to all Salary and Perquisites incident to his Office 'till such time as the Govr. & Council shall think fit to signify to him his Dismission from their Service by Letter or otherwise.

Ansr. Clearly this Agent is well empowered to transact all Business committed to his Charge by the Governor & Council, and 'till he is removed, will be Entitled to the Salary & Perquisites of his Office.

Q 3d In the Case of Virginia, where no Money is raised by the Assembly for Paying the ancient usual Agent appointed by the Govr. and Council, the One acting therein as the King's Representative and the other giving their Advice and Approbation, as his Council or Adviser, and not in their Legislative Capacity, and the Agent so appointed by them being paid out of the King's particular Revenue with other Officers of Government, May not the King interpose in this Case, and in what Way, to prevent the Governor and Council giving up the Appointment of this Office to the Legislature, or his Pay being absorbed by the Agent appointed by the Assembly or abolished in his Favour.

Ansr. If the Governor lays aside this Agent and concurs with the Assembly, in Intrusting their Agent [with] all the Colony Business, He will in my Opinion behave improperly, and become liable to the Censure of the Crown: The Method of doing this must be by Complaint to the Council, but perhaps before any Step of that Sort is taken, the Law in Question may come before that Board, and possibly may not receive the Sanction of the Crown.

Decr. 24th 1759
(Signd) C Pratt[1]

Copy: T.1/389, ff. 30–31. The word in brackets was incorrectly written as "will." A copy of this opinion was enclosed in Abercromby's letter of 22 Dec. 1759. It is not clear why the enclosure bears a later date than the covering letter.

1. Charles Pratt (1714–1794), created Baron Camden in 1765 and Earl Camden in 1786, was attorney general from July 1757 until Jan. 1762.

To John Stanwix

Sir   Williamsburgh Decemr 24th 1759

I received your favours of the 1st & 5th inst. yesterday & in return beg you wou'd accept of my thanks in the name of the Colony for the great care you have taken of us in sending back the chief part of the Regiment under Coll. Byrd, and for the indefatigable pains you have been at in opening & Securing the Communications between Pittsburgh & the Centre of this Colony. I shall with the greatest pleasure make this known to the General Assembly at their next Meeting.

When I first arrived here, Captain Trent applyed for the Payment of the Money he now Claims.[1] I laid his claim before His Majesty's Councill, who did not enter into it, supposing there was no just demand from Capt. Trent against the Country. the Reasons they gave I was not Master of, as the whole Affair was transacted before I had any Conections with this Colony; neither do I at present recollect them. Some time since he desired Coll. Byrd to transmitt me his account & papers, who requested I wou'd interest myself in the Payment of what I find Capt. Trent calls due & the Councill do not. I again communicated this to the Councill, who again refused to take it up, Saying to the best of my Remembrance that *that* Affair was finished, however when I have the pleasure of Communicating your letter to the Council at their next meeting, I imagine they will give some more decisive answer to this Point of which I will most certainly inform you.

I will forthwith forward your Letter to Governor Lyttelton from whom I have not heard since the letters I laid before the General Assembly. I am with the greatest Regard, Sir, Your most Obedient Humble Servant

Signd / Frans. Fauquier

To Majr. Genl. Stanwix.

Copy: W.O.34/45, f. 122.

1. Captain Trent is not exactly identified, but it is likely that he was William Trent, commissioned in the Virginia service in 1754 by Dinwiddie. There is no reference to Trent's claim in the journals of the council either before or after the date of this letter. The connection of Stanwix and Byrd with the claim suggests that it may have involved Trent's military service, but the claim has not been traced. Perhaps the claim was the account of William Trent with the government of Virginia, 8 Apr. 1754, now in the Colonial Papers at the Virginia State Library, which includes charges of carriage of powder, lead, and flints to the Ohio River; deer and bear skins and wampum; and a gun, pistols, a coat, and shirts, all of them presents to the Indians (see *VSP* 1:249).

From Jeffery Amherst

Sir, New York 27th December 1759

It is with the greatest Satisfaction, that I learn by Your favor of 25th Ultimo, the Sense, the House of Burgesses have of Capt. Stobo's Signal Zeal for His King, and the Dominion of Virginia, Which the handsome provision they have made for his past Services, by the Resolution they have Come to Sufficiently Evinces, and I make no doubt but You will, Whenever You have an Opportunity, with pleasure preferr him altho' it had not been Recommended to You by the House for my part I shall not forget him, if ever it lays in my way.

On the other hand, I am Sorry to find, that the Assembly have since Your former Letter, altered the good Resolution they had come to, of keeping up the Regiment in the pay of the Colony till May next, and that now they have Curtailed it to 400 men, and those to the 1st of May only I hope this will not be Attended, with any bad Consequences by having Interfered with Brigr. General Stanwix's Measures.

I am now Sir, to return You my most Sincere thanks, for Your kind Congratulations on the distinguishing Mark of my Royal Master's gracious Approbation of my feeble Endeavors, to Discharge the trust he has been pleased to repose in me; Mr. Secretary Pitt did indeed Signify it to me,[1] but as the Board of Trade has not Yet mentioned it, I deferred Acquainting You therewith, till the arrival of the Patent,[2] Which I daily Expect by Colonel Amherst,[3] or my Aid de Camp and so soon as it Comes to my hands I shall transmit it to You with my request of having the Same published in the Dominion, which I shall think myself very happy to Visit, When the Service will permit of it, particularly as it will give me an Opportunity of kissing your hands, and Assuring You that I am with the greatest regard, Sir, &ca.

Honble. Govr. Fauquier.

Copy: W.O.34/37, f. 209. An extract, consisting of the second paragraph above from the first comma, is in C.O.5/57, f. 22, endorsed as being in Amherst's letter of 9 Jan. 1760. Fauquier communicated this letter to the council on 21 Feb. 1760, and it is abstracted in *EJC* 6:154.

1. Pitt wrote to Amherst on 29 Sept. 1759 to inform him that the king had appointed him to be governor of Virginia and that his commission was passing under the Great Seal and would be sent to him by the Board of Trade as soon as it was ready.
2. The commission arrived on the *Earl of Leicester* packet on 13 Feb. 1760.
3. William Amherst (1732–1781) was General Amherst's younger brother.

From William Henry Lyttelton

[Fort Prince George, 27 December 1759]

This letter has not been found. Fauquier communicated it to the council on 21 Feb. 1760. It is mentioned in *EJC* 6:153 as transmitting a copy of the treaty that

Lyttelton had concluded on 26 Dec. 1759 with the Cherokees. It is assumed to have been one of the letters Fauquier mentioned in his address to the assembly on 4 Mar. 1760 and transmitted to the House of Burgesses on the same day; see *JHB, 1758–1761*, pp. 157–58. Lyttelton sent a copy of his treaty with the Cherokees as an enclosure in his letter of 27 Dec. 1759 to Amherst (W.O.34/35, ff. 136–37); the text of the enclosure follows.

Enclosure: Treaty with the Cherokees

[Fort Prince George, 26 December 1759]

Treaty of Peace and Friendship Concluded by His Excellency William Henry Lyttelton Esqr. Captain Genl. and Governour in Chief of His Majesty's Province of South Carolina with Attakullakulla (or the little Carpenter) Deputy of the whole Cherokee Nation and other Headmen and Warriors thereof, at Fort Prince George the twenty Sixth day of December 1759.[1]

Article I   There Shall be a firm Peace and friendship between all his Majesty's Subjects of this Province & the Nation of Indians called the Cherokees, and the said Cherokees shall Preserve Peace with all his Majesty's Subjects whatsoever.

II   The Articles of friendship & Commerce Concluded by the Lords Commissioners for Trade and Plantations with the Deputy of the Cherokee Nation by his Majesty's Command at Whitehall the 7th day of September 1730 Shall be Strictly Observ'd for the Time to Come.[2]

III   Whereas the Cherokee Indians have at Sundry times & Places since the 19th day of November 1758,[3] Slain divers of his Majesty's good Subjects of this Province and his Excellency the Governour having demanded that Satisfaction should be given for the same according to the Tenor of the said Articles of friendship and Commerce abovementioned; in Consequence whereof two Cherokee Indians of the Number of those who have been Guilty of Perpretating the said Murders have already been Delivered up to be put to Death, or otherwise Dispos'd of, as his Excellency shall Direct. It is hereby Stipulated and agreed, that twenty two other Cherokee Indians Guilty of the said Murders, shall as soon as Possible after the Conclusion of this Present Treaty in like manner be deliver'd up to Such Persons as his Excellency the Governor or the Commander in Chief of this Province, for the Time being Shall appoint to Receive them, to be put to Death, or Otherwise dispos'd of, as the said Governour, or Commander in Chief shall Direct.

IV The Cherokee Indians whose Names are hereinafter mentioned, Viz. Chinohé, Ousanatah, Tallichama, Tallitahé, Quarrasattahé, Connasoratah, Katactoi, Otassité of Watoga, Ousanoletah of Jore, Ousanoletah of Cowitche, Chisquatalone, Skiagusta of Sticoe, Sannaoesté, Whoatehé, Woeyah, Oucah, Chisanah, Nicholehé, Tony, Totaiah hoi, Skaliloske, Chistu, Shall remain as Hostages for the Due Performance of the foregoing Article in the Custody of such Persons as his Excellency the Governour shall Please to Nominate for that Purpose and when any of the Cherokee Indians, Guilty of the said Murders shall have been deliver'd up, as is Express'd in the said Article, an equal Number of the said Hostages, shall forthwith be set at Liberty.

V Immediately after the Conclusion of this Present Treaty the Licensd Traders from this Government, and all the Persons Employ'd by them shall have leave from his Excellency the Governor to Return to their Respective Places of abode in the Cherokee Nation, and to Carry on their Trade with the Cherokee Indians in the usual Manner according to Law.

VI During the Continuance of the Present War between his most Sacred Majesty & the French King, if any Frenchman shall Presume to Come into the Cherokee Nation, the Cherokees shall use their utmost Endeavors to put him to Death, as one of his Majesty's Enemies; or if taken alive they Shall deliver him up to his Excellency the Governor or the Commander in Chief of this Province, for the Time being, to be dispos'd of as he shall direct. And if any Person whatsoever Either White man or Indian shall at any Time bring any Messages from the French into the Cherokee Nation, or hold any Discourses there in favour of the French, or tending to Set the English and Cherokees at Variance and interrupt the Peace and friendship Established by this Present Treaty, the Cherokees shall use their utmost Endeavours to apprehend such Person or Persons, and Detain him, or them, untill they shall have given Notice thereof to his Excellency the Governor or the Commander in Chief for the Time being and have received his Directions therein.

> Given under my Hand and Seal at Fort Prince George in the Province of South Carolina this 26th day of December 1759, And in the thirty third Year of his Majesty's Reign.

By his Excellency's Command

                                        Willm Henry Lyttelton   LS

Wm Drayton Secy.[4]

We whose Names are underwritten do agree to all and every of these Articles, and do engage for Ourselves and for our Nation that the same shall be well & faithfully Performed. In Testimony whereof we have hereunto set our Hands and Seals the day and Year abovementioned.

Attakullakulla	LS	Katagusta	LS
Oconostota	LS	Oconeca	LS
Otassité	LS	Kilcannokeh	LS[5]

Witness
H: Hyrne Adjt. Genl.[6]
  Joseph Axson ⎫
  Thomas Forster ⎬ sworn Interpreters[7]
A true Copy.
  Wm: Drayton, Secretary.

Copy: W.O.34/35, ff.138–39. Endorsed as enclosed in Lyttelton's letter of 27 Dec. (to Amherst) and as received 16 Mar. 1760. The final attestation and signature are presumably Drayton's autograph.

  1. For the circumstances leading up to this treaty, and the signing of it, see Alden, p. 87.
  2. On this treaty, see Crane, pp. 298–302.
  3. It is not clear why this date was specified.
  4. William Drayton (1732–1790) was evidently accompanying Lyttelton as an aide-de-camp or secretary. He was later a jurist, chief justice of East Florida 1763–77.
  5. Of these Indians, Attakullakulla (the Little Carpenter) was the plenipotentiary of the Cherokee nation, and Oconostata was the Great Warrior of Chotee; Katagusta was perhaps a brother of Oconostata, known as the Prince of Chotee. It is impossible to identify the other Cherokees.
  6. Maj. Henry Hyrne, formerly of the provincial forces, was acting as adjutant on Lyttelton's expedition.
  7. Joseph Axson (sometimes called Axton or Axon) and Thomas Foster, as his name is usually spelled, were often engaged in the service of South Carolina as interpreters or Indian agents.

1759: Appendix A

The Account of his Majestys Revenue of 2/ Per Hogshead &c Arising within this colony of Virginia from the 25th of April to the 25th of October 1758.[1]

The Receiver General doth Charge himself with the Receipt of the said Revenue as follows[2]

To the Account of the Upper District of James River	£1261.10.10
The Account of the Lower District of James River	346.12. 9
The Account of the District of York River	1037.13.10
The Account of the District of Rappahannock River	1242.10. 1
The Account of the District of South Potomack	497. 8. 5
The Account of the Port of Accomack	
The Account of Sundry Rights of Land sold	129.14. 8
The Account of Fines and Forfeitures	7.11. 3
So that the whole Receipt amounts to	£4523. 1.10
And there will remain due to the Receiver General to Ballance this Account[3]	893.17. 3
	£5416.19. 1

The Receiver General doth Discharge himself by the Payment of the following Sums

By Ballance of the last Account[4]	£ 986. 1.11
By a Warrant for half a Years Salary to the Governor	1000.—.—
By a Warrant for Ditto to the Gentlemen of the Council	600.—.—
By a Warrant to the Judges & other Officers of a Court of Oyer & Terminer[5]	100.—.—
By a Warrant to the Honble. & Reverend Robert Cholmondeley Auditor of the Plantations for half a Years Salary[6]	50.—.—
By a Warrant to James Abercrombie Esqr. Sollicitor of the Virginia Affairs for Ditto	100.—.—
By a Warrant to Peyton Randolph Esqr. his Majestys Attorney General for Ditto	35.—.—
By a Warrant to Nathaniel Walthoe Esqr. Clerk of the Council for Ditto	50.—.—
By a Warrant to the Adjutants for half a Years Salary[7]	120.—.—
By a Warrant to Joseph Davenport Armourer for Ditto	6.—.—
By a Warrant to the Gunners of the Batteries for Ditto	12.10.—

By a Warrant to the Ministers attending one General Court & Assembly[8]	18.—.—
By a Warrant for Repairs done to the Governors House	162.15. 2
By a Warrant for Contingent Charges[9]	1707. 7. 3
By Allowance to the Receiver General of ½ Per Cent on £3386.3.5 for Negotiating the same in Bills of Exchange in London[10]	16.18. 7
By Allowance to the Auditor[11] at 5 Per Cent on £4523.1.10	226. 3. 1
By Allowance to the Receiver General[12] on the same Sum	226. 3. 1
	£5416.19. 1

Philip Grymes Recr. Genl.

I have Examined the within Account of his Majestys Revenue Commencing the 25th of April 1758 and ending the 25th of October 1758 and have Compared every Article with its proper Voucher produced by Philip Grymes Esqr. Receiver General and find the same truly stated, and that there is due to the said Receiver General for Ballance thereof Eight hundred ninety three Pounds seventeen Shillings & three Pence Sterling

John Blair D. Audr.

November 6th 1758
The within Account Compared & Examined by John Blair Esqr. Deputy Auditor was produced to me in Council and sworn to by Philip Grymes Esqr. Receiver General.

Fran: Fauquier

MS: C.O.5/1329, ff. 104–5. Autograph signatures of Grymes, Blair, and Fauquier. Endorsed as received 12 May and read 23 May 1759. Evidently enclosed in Fauquier's letter of 5 Jan. 1759 to the Board of Trade, though not so endorsed.

    1. The revenue of 2s. per hogshead was one of the royal revenues arising in Virginia. The revenue derives its name from a tax of 2s. laid on each hogshead of tobacco exported from Virginia. The other and minor components of the revenue were a tax of 15d. per ton on shipping (port duty or ship money); a tax of 6d. per head on each person not a mariner imported into Virginia (head or poll money); the proceeds of the sale of land rights at 5s. for fifty acres; and the fines and forfeitures imposed for a variety of breaches of the laws. As a rule, most of the revenue was spent for the support of the provincial government. A useful account of the revenue is given in Flippin.
    2. The statement of receipts gives the total amount collected in each district for the tobacco duty, port tax, and poll tax, but the receipts from sale of rights and fines and forfeitures are for the whole colony. It appears that the reported total of receipts in surviving accounts, certainly until 1767 and probably throughout the rest of the colonial period, was inaccurate, because masters of ships received an allowance of 10 percent of the export tax on tobacco, while the naval officers received a commission

of 10 percent, usually, of that tax, the shipping tax, and the head tax. No mention of the allowance to masters of ships has been found in accounts of the revenue, while the commission to the naval officers was not reported after the account for Oct. 1715–Apr. 1716: thus a considerable part of actual receipts, perhaps at times nearly 20 percent, was not reported after Apr. 1716. The history of these payments to masters of ships and to naval officers is not altogether clear. By an act of the session of Oct. 1710, "An act for raising a Public Revenue for the better support of the Government of her Majesty's Colony and Dominion of Virginia" (Hening, 3:490–95), a salary of not more than 10 percent was allowed to collectors from the duties on tobacco exports, tonnage, and passengers, and an abatement of not more than 10 percent of those duties was allowed to masters of ships. In *The Present State of Virginia, and the College*, written in 1697, Henry Hartwell, James Blair, and Edward Chilton had already noted that an allowance of 10 percent was paid from the 2s. per hogshead revenue to masters of ships and vessels to encourage them to return true accounts, and that the same amount was paid to the collectors. The act of 1710 cited above superseded an act of the session of June 1680 with much the same title (Hening, 2:466–69) which authorized unspecified salaries to collectors and an allowance of not more than 10 percent to masters of ships and others who rendered true accounts. The earliest surviving returns of the 2s. per hogshead revenue, in the first years of the eighteenth century, show payments of 10 percent or more or less to naval officers, who had by that time replaced collectors as recipients of the commission on duties, but evidently the amount had been fixed at 10 percent by the time of its last appearance in the accounts. The payments to masters of ships and the naval officers were still being made as late as 1767, when Richard Corbin referred to them in a memorandum on the 2s. per hogshead revenue, enclosed in Fauquier's letter of 20 May 1767 to Shelburne.

3. Philip Grymes, of the council, was also the receiver general, holding the office jointly with John Roberts, an absentee official. The amount due to him to balance this account was the excess of expenditure over receipts for the period of the account.

4. This was the amount by which expenditures had exceeded receipts in the preceding account, for 25 Oct. 1757–25 Apr. 1758.

5. The payment of £600 to the council is thought to have been divided at this period among the members on the basis of their attendance at executive meetings of the council and at sessions of the General Court, but the manner of division is undetermined. The way in which the £100 for service at the courts of oyer and terminer was divided is also conjectural: the judges were presumably members of the council, but how they divided their share of the money is not known. The "other Officers" of the court are not known, but they were perhaps some of those connected with the General Court: the attorney general, the clerk of the General Court, the sheriff of York County (and perhaps his undersheriffs), the court cryer, the tipstaff, and the minister or chaplain.

6. Robert Cholmondeley (ca. 1727–1804), a clergyman and a son of the earl of Cholmondeley, was appointed surveyor and auditor general of His Majesty's revenues in America in 1757.

7. The adjutants were the supervisors of militia for the four districts into which the colony was divided in 1752: the frontier district of Frederick, Augusta, Halifax, Lunenburg, and Albemarle, or the western part of the colony; the Eastern Shore and Northern Neck, or the Eastern Shore and the counties north of the Rappahannock River and east of the Blue Ridge; the middle district (or Middle Neck), the counties between the Rappahannock and the James River west to the frontier counties; and the southern district, counties south of the James and west to the frontier counties. The identity of the adjutants who drew the salaries represented here is not certain, but they were perhaps George Washington for the Northern Neck and Eastern Shore or his deputy and successor Colin Campbell (d. 1780) of Northumberland Co.; George

Muse (d. 1791?) of Westmoreland Co. for the middle district or his deputy and successor Alexander Finnie; and Francis Thornton (ca. 1704–1795) for the southern district. Since the adjutants were paid £100 a year in Virginia currency, or £80 sterling, the amount in this account indicates that only three adjutants were being paid a half year's salary; other accounts suggest that between Oct. 1756 and Oct. 1762 there were never more than three adjutants drawing salaries. The other quasi-military salaries here are for the armorer who maintained the arms kept in the Governor's House or the magazine in Williamsburg; and (presumably) the gunners of Fort George at the mouth of the James River on Point Comfort and of the two batteries near York and Gloucester on the two sides of the York River.

8. Only one minister has been identified as serving the General Assembly at this period. He was William Yates (1720–1764), minister of Abingdon Parish in Gloucester County ca. 1750–59, of Bruton Parish in James City County 1759–64, and president of the College of William and Mary 1761–64. Yates was appointed chaplain to the House of Burgesses on 25 Mar. 1756 and continued in office thereafter, his last appointment being made on 12 Jan. 1764. It is supposed that the chaplain of the House of Burgesses preached regularly before the council when it sat as a court, visited condemned prisoners, and attended them to the gallows; but other clergymen may have shared these duties.

9. The contingent expenses were probably (as they clearly were in earlier accounts) for occasional charges such as presents to the Indians, guns, gunpowder, postage, and courier service, as a rule; however, Fauquier noted in his letter of 25 Nov. 1759 to Amherst that he received yearly allowances of £40 for stationery and £20 for a gardener as part of the "Contingent Expences of Government."

10. It has not been possible to identify the sum negotiated in bills of exchange.

11. John Blair, president of the council, was in fact deputy auditor, appointed 1728, and used that style in his certification of accounts. He and the receiver general each received a commission of 5 percent of the total receipts. Blair's letter of 27 Sept. 1768 to Lord Hillsborough (C.O. 5/1346, ff. 96–100) pointed out that for more than sixty years the deputy auditors in Virginia had taken the commission of 5 percent and had remitted 2½ percent to the auditor general in England.

12. No details of the financial arrangement between Roberts and Grymes have been found, but probably Grymes remitted some part of his commission to Roberts.

1759: Appendix B

The Account of his Majestys Revenue of Quitrents &c arising within this Colony of Virginia for the Year 1757.[1]

The Receiver General doth Charge himself with the Receipt of the said Revenue as follows

To Ballance of the last Account[2]	£12092. 3. 2
To the Quitrents of the Northern Neck[3] for the Year 1757	6.13. 4
To the Account of Compositions for Escheated Lands	

Quitrents for the Year 1757

Counties Names	Number of Acres paid for	Paid in Money	Sheriffs Allowances	Amount
Amelia	370000	£370.—.—	£37.—.—	£333.—.—
Augusta	300000	£300.—.—	£30.—.—	270.—.—
Albemarle	440000	£440.—.—	£44.—.—	396.—.—
Accomack	233379	£233. 7. 7	£23. 6. 9	210.—.10
Brunswick	170000	£170.—.—	£17.—.—	153.—.—
Bedford	110000	£110.—.—	£11.—.—	99.—.—
Caroline	240000	£240.—.—	£24.—.—	216.—.—
Charles City	90000	£ 90.—.—	£ 9.—.—	81.—.—
Cumberland	200000	£200.—.—	£20.—.—	180.—.—
Chesterfield	248604	£248.12. 1	£24.17. 2	223.14.11
Dinwiddie	170000	£170.—.—	£17.—.—	153.—.—
Elizabeth City	20000	£ 20.—.—	£ 2.—.—	18.—.—
Essex	144821	£144.16. 5	£14. 9. 7	130. 6.10
Gloucester	120000	£120.—.—	£12.—.—	108.—.—
Goochland	140000	£140.—.—	£14.—.—	126.—.—
Hanover	140000	£140.—.—	£14.—.—	126.—.—
Henrico	130000	£130.—.—	£13.—.—	117.—.—
Hallifax				
James City	70000	£ 70.—.—	£ 7.—.—	63.—.—
Isle of Wight				
King William	110000	£110.—.—	£11.—.—	99.—.—
King & Queen	180000	£180.—.—	£18.—.—	162.—.—
Louisa				
Lunenburgh				
Middlesex	75350	£ 75. 7.—	£ 7.10. 8	67.16. 4
Nansemond	164274	£164. 5. 6	£16. 8. 6	147.17.—
Norfolk	130000	£130.—.—	£13.—.—	117.—.—
Northampton	104297	£104. 6.—	£10. 8. 7	93.17. 5
New Kent	50000	£ 50.—.—	£ 5.—.—	45.—.—
Orange				
Prince George	150000	£150.—.—	£15.—.—	135.—.—
Princess Ann	80000	£ 80.—.—	£ 8.—.—	72.—.—

Quitrents for the Year 1757					
Counties Names	Number of Acres paid for	Paid in Money	Sheriffs Allowances	Amount	
Prince Edward	172871	£172.17. 5	£17. 5. 8	155.11. 9	
Spotsylvania	241448	£241. 8.11	£24. 2.11	217. 6.—	
Surry	130000	£130.—.—	£13.—.—	117.—.—	
Southampton	230000	£230.—.—	£23.—.—	207.—.—	
Sussex	227023	£227.—. 5	£22.14.—	204. 6. 5	
Warwick	39000	£ 39.—.—	£ 3.18.—	35. 2.—	
York	40000	£ 40.—.—	£ 4.—.—	36.—.—	4914.19. 6
					£17013.16.

			Brought Over	£17013.16.—

Arrears of Quitrents paid in the Year 1757					
Counties Names	Acres paid	Paid in Money	Sheriffs Allowances	Amount	
Augusta 1755	27409	£ 27. 8. 2	£ 2.14.10	£ 24.13. 4	
Ditto 1754	50446	£ 50. 8.11	£ 5.—.11	45. 8.—	
Brunswick	319148	£319. 2.10	£31.18. 3	287. 4. 7	
Ditto 1755	80735	£ 80.14. 8	£ 8. 1. 5	72.13. 3	
Bedford	56051	£ 56. 1.—	£ 5.12. 1	50. 8.11	
Caroline	236687	£236.13. 9	£23.13. 4	213.—. 5	
Chesterfeild	2470	£ 2. 9. 5	£ 4.11	2. 4. 6	
Dinwiddie	210000	£210.—.—	£21.—.—	189.—.—	
Goochland	43139	£ 43. 2. 9	£ 4. 6. 3	38.16. 6	
Ditto 1755	58991	£ 58.19.10	£ 5.17.11	53. 1.11	
Hanover	119859	£119.17. 2	£11.19. 8	107.17. 6	
Hallifax	105000	£105.—.—	£10.10.—	94.10.—	
King & Queen	38552	£ 38.11.—	£ 3.17. 1	34.13.11	
Nansemond	12046	£ 12.—.11	£ 1. 4. 1	10.16.10	
Norfolk	26896	£ 26.17.11	£ 2.13. 9	24. 4. 2	
New Kent 1755	5494	£ 5. 9.10	£ 11.—	4.18.10	
Ditto 1754	5494	£ 5. 9.10	£ 11.—	4.18.10	
Middlesex	365	£ 7. 3	£ . 8	6. 7	
Orange	210000	£210.—.—	£21.—.—	189.—.—	
Ditto 1751	134904	£134.18. 1	£13. 9.10	121. 8. 3	
Prince George	36909	£ 36.18. 2	£ 3.13. 9	33. 4. 5	
Prince Edward	1187	£ 1. 3. 9	£ 2. 4	1. 1. 5	
Ditto	10034	£ 10.—. 8	£ 1.—.—	9.—. 8	
Spotsylvania	3708	£ 3.14. 2	£ 7. 5	3. 6. 9	
Southampton	106665	£106.13. 4	£10.13. 4	96.—.—	
Warwick	5362	£ 5. 7. 3	£ 10. 8	4.16. 7	
York	29783	£ 29.15. 8	£ 2.19. 7	£ 26.16. 1	
Received of Sundry Persons in several Counties			31.18. 6	1775.10. 9
					£18789. 6. 9

Appendix B for 1759

The Receiver General doth Discharge himself

By paid to the Honble. & Reverend Robert Cholmondeley on his Majestys Warrant one Years Allowance ending the 25th of October 1758	£ 150.—.—	
By paid to Mr. Commissary Dawson on his Majestys Warrant one Years Salary ending the 25th of October 1758	100.—.—	
By two Warrants to the Attorney General for one Years Salary ending the 25th of October 1758	70.—.—	
By his Majestys Warrant dated at St. James's the 27th day of February 1758 for paying to James West Esqr. or to his Assigns[4]	5540.—.—	
By allowance of ½ Per Cent for Negotiating the Bills of Exchange in London[5]	33. 9. 8	
By Allowance to the Auditor at 5 Per Cent on £6697.3.7	334.17. 2	
By Allowance to the Receiver General on the same Sum	334.17. 2	
So that the Sum Disburst amounts to	6563. 4.—	
And there will remain due to Ballance this Account	£12226. 2. 9	
	£18789. 6. 9	

     Philip Grymes Recr. Genl.

I have Examined the within Account of his Majestys Revenue of Quit-rents for the Year 1757 & have Compared every Article with its Proper Voucher produced by Philip Grymes Esqr. Receiver General & find the Charge thereof amounting to Eighteen thousand seven hundred eighty nine Pounds six Shillings & nine Pence, and the Discharge to Six thousand five hundred sixty three Pounds four Shillings both truly Stated So that there is due to his Majestys Revenue for Ballance of this Account Twelve thousand two hundred twenty Six Pounds two Shillings and nine Pence Sterling

           John Blair D. Audr.

November 11th 1758.
The within Account Compared & Examined by John Blair Esqr. Deputy Auditor was produced to me in Council and sworn to by Philip Grymes Esqr. Receiver Genl.

            Fran: Fauquier

MS: C.O.5/1329, ff. 106–8. Autograph signatures of Grymes, Blair, and Fauquier. Endorsed as received 12 May and read 23 May 1759. Evidently enclosed in Fauquier's letter of 5 Jan. 1759 to the Board of Trade, though not so endorsed.

1. The revenue of quitrents was, like the revenue of 2s. per hogshead, a royal revenue. It consisted of an annual rent of 1s. for every fifty acres of land; an annual token payment of quitrents for the Northern Neck propriety; and an irregular and usually rather small collection of fees of 2s. per acre for escheated land, or land which had reverted to the crown. Except for the customary commissions to officials concerned with the collection and handling the revenue and some payments of salary to officials, the revenue of quitrents was remitted to England for the use of the crown. A comprehensive study of quitrents is in Beverly W. Bond, Jr., *The Quit-Rent System in the American Colonies* (New Haven, 1919), with chap. 8 on the quitrents in Virginia. Flippin's *Royal Government* discusses the financial system and administration in Virginia, and specifically the quitrents, in chap. 6.

2. The quitrent return for 1756 is missing, but this balance was evidently the excess of receipts over disbursements in the 1756 account.

3. The Northern Neck proprietary, the Fairfax grant, was the region between the Rappahannock and Potomac rivers, bounded on the west by a line running northwest from the headwaters of the Rapidan River to the western boundary of Maryland; at this time the proprietor was Thomas Fairfax, Baron Fairfax of Cameron. The sum of £6.13.4 was fixed as the annual payment for the grant by the patent of 18 Sept. 1649 from Charles II. For an account of the proprietary, see Freeman, 1: app. 1, pp. 447–513.

4. This appears to be a remittance to the Treasury, for James West (1704–1772) was joint secretary of the Treasury 1746–62.

5. The allowance of £33.9.8 (presumably to the receiver) is 0.5 percent of £6,697.3.7, the total of receipts collected in 1757 and the sum on which the commissions of 5 percent to the auditor and receiver were based.

1759: Appendix C

The Account of his Majestys Revenue of 2/ per hogshead &c Arising within this Colony of Virginia from the 25th of October 1758 to the 25th of April 1759.

The Receiver General doth Charge himself with the Receipt of the said Revenue as follows

To the Account of the Upper District of James River	£ 391. 1. 1
The Account of the Lower District of James River	434.16. 9
The Account of the District of York River	124. 3.—
The Account of the District of Rappahanock River	129.17. 4
The Account of the District of South Potomack	264.16. 6
The Account of the Port of Accomack	
The Account of Sundry Rights of Land sold	220.—. 8
The Account of Fines and Forfeitures	
So that the whole Receipt amounts to	£1564.15. 4
And there will remain due to the Receiver General to Ballance this Account	2193. 1. 3
	£3757.16. 7

The Receiver General doth Discharge himself By payment of the following Sums

By Ballance of the last Account[1]	£ 893.17. 3
By a Warrant for half a Years Salary to the Governor	1000.—.—
By a Warrant for Ditto to the Gentlemen of the Council	600.—.—
By a Warrant to the Judges & other Officers of a Court of Oyer & Terminer	100.—.—
By a Warrant to the Honble. & Reverend Robert Cholmondeley Auditor of the Plantations for half a Years Salary	50.—.—
By a Warrant to James Abercrombie Esqr. Sollicitor of the Virginia Affairs for Ditto	100.—.—
By a Warrant to Peyton Randolph Esqr. his Majestys Attorney General for Ditto	35.—.—
By a Warrant to Nathl. Walthoe Esqr. Clerk of the Council for Ditto	50.—.—
By a Warrant to the Adjutants for half a Years Salary	120.—.—
By a Warrant to Joseph Davenport Armourer for Ditto	6.—.—
By a Warrant to the Gunners of the Batteries for Ditto	12.10.—

By a Warrant to the Ministers Attending one General Court & Assembly	24.—.—
By a Warrant for Repairs done to the Governors House	164. 9. 5
By a Warrant for Contingent Charges	441.—. 6
By a Warrant to the Receiver General of half Per Cent on £899.5.5 for Negotiating the same in Bills of Exchange in London[2]	4. 9.11
By Allowance to the Auditor at 5 Per Cent on £1564.15.4	78. 4. 9
By Allowance to the Receiver General on the same Sum	78. 4. 9
	£3757.16. 7

Philip Grymes Recr. Genl.

I have Examined the within Account of his Majestys Revenue Commencing the 25th of October 1758 and ending the 25th of April 1759 & have Compared every Article with its proper Voucher Produced by Philip Grymes Esqr. Receiver General and find the same truly Stated and that there is due to the said Receiver General for Ballance thereof Two thousand one hundred & ninety three Pounds one Shilling & three Pence Sterling

John Blair D. Audr.

May 5th 1759.
The within Account Compared and Examined by John Blair Esqr. Deputy Auditor was produced to me in Council and sworn to by Philip Grymes Esqr. Receiver General

Fran: Fauquier

MS: C.O.5/1329, ff. 145–45A. Autograph signatures of Grymes, Blair, and Fauquier. Endorsed as read 14 Nov. 1759. Presumably enclosed in Fauquier's letter of 9 June 1759 to the Board of Trade, though not so endorsed.

1. This balance is the amount by which expenditures exceeded receipts in the preceding account, for 25 Apr.–25 Oct. 1758.
2. It has not been possible to identify the sum negotiated in bills of exchange.

1760

Petition of James Pittillo

[ca. 1760]

To The Honourable the Governour in Councill
James Pittillo[1] humbly Petitions
Whereas your Petitioner Entred a Caveat & Summonses against Thomas and John Leath, Heirs of John Ledbetter Decd. of the County of Prince George, and they not appearing, your Petitioner Obtained a Certificate from the Councill Board Dated the 15th Day of June 1745 for to have a Pattent for the Land, 400 Acres more or less,[2] But Collo. Bolling the Surveyor [now] Strenously sets himself in Opposition Right or wrong against your Petitioner, in favour of all Delinquents of this kind, and has kept the Rights and Survey of the Said Land in his own Possesion about 15 Years,[3] to the Damage of his Majestys Revenue in Defrauding him of the Quitrents, and the Said Leaths themselves haveing refused the Land, Notwithstanding the Surveyor wo'd not Show your Petitioner the Records which ought to be the true Test in these Matters, and Refused him a Coppey of the Survey, nor a Plott of the Land, tho your Petitioner offered him Payment for it, But allways Defames your Petitioner for following that imployment, Saying that he does not aprove nor will he Encourage any Such Proceedings, It being the Right hand & Eye to him, being himself an old Defaultant, as well as an Abetor and Protector of all those that your Petitioner has any Concernment with about Laps land. Therefore humbly Prays your Honours to take it to Consideration,[4] That your Petitioner may have Justice done him in the Premises, According to the Rules in Such Cases prescribed by the Government

And he shall Pray

MS: Virginia State Library, Colonial Papers, Folder 51, no. 8. Endorsed as Pittillo's petition against Col. Robert Bolling and dated ca. 1760. The dating may be questioned, since the specific date in the text is a year late, and the ensuing period is only loosely stated. The word in brackets replaces what is "how" in the manuscript.

1. The petitioner was probably a James Pittillo (Patillo, Petillo) of Bristol Parish in Prince George County, who got a grant of 1,000 acres in the county as early as 1727 and over a period reaching to about 1750 was a party to various caveats, petitions, and grants involving lands usually in Prince George County but occasionally in Brunswick

or Lunenburg. It seems impossible to be sure which of these pieces of business involved this James and which involved his son James (born 1725), who in 1758 was allowed to retain 600 acres which the elder James had recovered from one Thomas Williams.

2. On 15 June 1744 (not 1745) the governor and council ordered that a patent be granted to James Petillo for 400 acres lying on both sides of Warwick Swamp in Prince George County, he having entered a caveat against Thomas and John Leath for that tract.

3. There seems to be a confusion of two persons here. Robert Bolling (1686–1749) of Prince George County was surveyor for the county as early as 1714 and as late as 1741, and perhaps until his death in 1749; but Pittillo seems to refer to a Robert Bolling still alive about 1760, presumably Robert Bolling (1730–1775) of Bollingbrook, at Petersburg, a colonel of militia and the son of Robert Bolling the surveyor for Prince George.

4. This petition is not mentioned in the council journal, and there is no evidence that it was considered.

To Beverley Robinson

[ca. January 1760]

This letter has not been found, but Fauquier mentioned it in his letter of 17 Jan. 1760 to Amherst and indicated that the letter to Robinson asked him to inform Amherst and Governor De Lancey that if M. Laforce was not of use in obtaining the release of Van Braam, the colony of Virginia desired to have Laforce released to save the expense of keeping him.

From John Stanwix

Sir, Pittsburgh the 6th Janry 1760

The same Express brought me both Your Favors of the 24th November & the 1st of December but since You must have received my Letter of the 1st of December wherein I Inform You of the March of the Virginia Regiment under the Command of Colonel Byrd to Winchester, to be more immediately under Your Command, for such Services as might be necessary for Your own, or any Other of Your Southern Provinces, 'till it will be absolutely necessary for a greater Number of them to be here, to Assist in Carrying on the Works in the Spring, and defending as Occasion may Require. As the Southern Indians (I was Early Inform'd) began to be very troublesome, kept as few here of Your Regiment as possible, no more than 250 with this Post, Redstone Creek, the two Crossings of the Yohio Geny[1] & Fort Cumberland; but as the Pensylvanians have broke all their Troops to 150, Officers Included, without giving me the least Notice in time, have not been a little distressed to Garrison the Other Communication, having sent down Four Companies of the First Battalion of Royal Americans to Lancaster,[2] they being Eat out with the Scurvy, having been here and on this Communication since the beginning of General Forbes's Campaign; This Quarter, which I proposed as a Quarter of Refreshment for them till Spring, cannot now be Allowed them, having been Obliged to remarch a large Detachment of them to Fort Bedford & Juniata[3]—I am really of Opinion that the Assembly let the necessity be almost what it will, don't propose for the future, to keep more than 150 Men in their Pay of Pensylvania, which will Garrison their Old Frontiers, Fort Loudoun, Fort Littleton & Fort Augusta.[4] I think it will not be in General Amherst's Power to part with any more Regulars, than the First Battalion of the Royal Americans, for the Service of this Post, which Shews You how absolutely necessary it will be to keep up Your Virginia Regiment at 1000 Men during the War, so that what may safely be Spared from the Service of Your own Frontiers may be so necessarily Employed in Carrying on the Works here, and keeping up Your own Communication from Redstone Creek to Fort Cumberland without this, 'tis my Opinion, nothing can be truly Established here in proper time, so absolutely Necessary for the protection of all His Majesty's Southern Provinces.

I Have had a Fitt of the Gout, which has kept me here beyond the time proposed Staying at this Post; hope to be able to get down to New York Early next Month, by which time I Imagine the Operations for the next Campaign will be Settled, and of Course General Amherst will Acquaint You, as likewise all the Other Southern Governors what Assistance His Majesty Expects from them. I am with very great Respect, Sir, &ca.

John Stanwix

Honble. Govr. Fauquier.

Copy: C.O. 5/57, ff. 144–45. Marked as a copy and duplicate; endorsed as being in Stanwix's letter to Amherst of 12 Jan. 1760. Fauquier communicated this letter to the council on 21 Feb. 1760; it is abstracted in *EJC* 6:154. It is assumed to be one of the letters he mentioned in his address to the assembly on 4 Mar. 1760 and transmitted to the House of Burgesses on the same day. See *JHB, 1758–1761*, pp. 157–58.

1. The two crossings on the Youghiogheny were the Great Crossing, which was just north of the present Pennsylvania-Maryland boundary and about 24 mi. southwest of Somerset, Pa., and Stewart's Crossing, about 20 mi. northwest of the Great Crossing.
2. Lancaster is in southeastern Pennsylvania, about 200 mi. to the southeast of Pittsburgh.
3. Fort Bedford was built on or near the stream that was then called Juniata Creek and is now known as Raystown Branch, one of the branches of the Juniata River.

4. Fort Lyttelton, built in 1755, stood about 10 mi. north of Fort Loudoun. Fort Augusta was built at the site of the present town of Sunbury, at the forks of the Susquehanna River, in 1756 and was the most impressive Pennsylvania fort of the time; it was around 90 mi. northeast of Fort Loudoun, and about 170 mi. northwest from Pittsburgh.

From William Pitt

Sir,   Whitehall Janry 7th 1760

His Majesty having Nothing so much at Heart, as to improve the Great and Important Advantages gained the last Campaign, in North America, and, not doubting that all His Faithfull and Brave Subjects there, will continue most chearfully to cooperate with; and second to the utmost, the large Expence & extraordinary Succours, supplied by this Kingdom, for their Preservation and future Security; And His Majesty considering that the several Provinces from Pensylvania inclusive, to the Southward, are well able, with proper Encouragements to furnish a Body of several Thousand Men, to join the King's Forces in those Parts, for some Offensive Operations against the Enemy; And His Majesty not judging it expedient to limit the Zeal & Ardor of any of His Provinces, by making a Repartition of the Forces to be raised by Each, respectively, for this most important Service, I am commanded to signify to You the King's Pleasure,[1] that You do forthwith use Your utmost Endeavours & Influence with the Council & Assembly of Your Province to induce them to raise, with all possible Dispatch, within Your Government, at least as large a Body of Men, as they did for the last Campaign, and even as many more as the Number, and Situation of It's Inhabitants may allow, And forming the same into Regiments, as far as shall be found convenient, that You do direct them to hold themselves in readiness, as early as may be, to march to the Rendezvous, at such Place or Places as may be named for that Purpose, by the Commander in Chief of His Majesty's Forces in America, or by the Officer who shall be appointed to command the King's Forces in those Parts, in order to proceed from thence, in Conjunction with a Body of His Majesty's British Forces, and under the Supreme Command of the Officer to be appointed as above, so as to be in a Situation to begin, by the First of May, if possible, or as soon after as shall be any way practicable, such Offensive Operations, as shall be judged, by the Commander of His Majesty's Forces in those Parts, most expedient for annoying the Enemy; And the better to facilitate this important Service, the King is pleased to leave it to You to issue Commissions to such Gentlemen of Your Province, as You shall judge, from their Weight & Credit with the People & their Zeal for the Publick Service, may be best disposed & enabled to quicken & effectuate the speedy Levying of the greatest Number of Men; In the Disposition of which Commissions, I am persuaded You will have Nothing in View, but the Good of the King's Service & a due Subordination of the whole, when joined, to His Majesty's Commander. And all Officers of the Provincial Forces, as high as Colonels inclusive, are to have Rank according to their several respective Commissions, agreable to the Regulations, contained in His Majesty's Warrant of the 30th of December 1757.

The King is further pleased to furnish all the Men, so raised as above, with Arms, Ammunition & Tents, as well as to order Provisions to be issued to the same, by His Majesty's Commissaries, in the same Proportion and Manner, as is done to the Rest of the King's Forces: And a sufficient Train of Artillery will also be provided at His Majesty's Expence for the Operations of the Campaign: The whole therefore that the King expects & requires from the several Provinces, is, the Levying, Cloathing & Pay of the Men, And, on these Heads also, that no Encouragement may be wanting to the fullest Exertion of Your Force; His Majesty is farther most Graciously pleased to permit me to acquaint You, that strong Recommendations will be made to Parliament in their Session next Year to grant a proper Compensation for such Expences as above, according as the active Vigour, & strenuous Efforts of the respective Provinces shall justly appear to merit.

It is His Majesty's Pleasure, that You do, with particular Diligence, immediately collect, & put into the best Condition all the Arms issued last Campaign, which can be any ways rendered Serviceable, or that can be found within Your Government, in order that the same may be employed, as far as they will go in this Exigency. I am, at the same Time, to acquaint You, that a reasonable Supply of Arms will be sent from England to replace such as may have been lost, or have become unfit for future Service.

I am further to inform You, that similar Orders are sent by this Conveyance, to [Pensylvania, Maryland,] North Carolina & South Carolina.

The Northern Governments are also directed to raise Men in the same Manner, to be employed in such Offensive Operations, as the Circumstances & Situation of the Enemy's Possessions in those Parts may point out, which, it is hoped, will oblige them so to divide their Attention & Forces, as will render the several Attempts more easy & successfull.

It is unnecessary to add any Thing to animate Your Zeal in the Execution of His Majesty's Orders on this great Occasion, where the future

Safety and Welfare of America, and of Your own Province in particular are so nearly concerned; And the King doubts not, from Your known Fidelity and Attachment, that You will employ Yourself, with the utmost Application, & Dispatch, in this promising, & decisive Crisis. I am &ca.

W: Pitt

Copy: C.O.5/214, pp. 271–[280]. Circular addressed to the governors of Pennsylvania, Maryland, Virginia, North Carolina, and South Carolina. This particular version was that intended for Pennsylvania, and the alteration proper for Virginia is indicated in brackets. Endorsed as sent "by a Sloop." This was enclosed in Amherst's letter to Fauquier of 21 Feb. 1760, below. Fauquier communicated both letters to the council on 4 Mar.; see *EJC* 6:155. The two letters are assumed to have been among those Fauquier transmitted to the House of Burgesses on 4 Mar. 1760; see *JHB, 1758–1761*, p. 158.

1. See the very similar circular letter of 9 Dec. 1758 from Pitt to the governors of the southern colonies.

To Jeffery Amherst

Sir   Wmsburgh Janry 17th 1760

I have received your Favour of the 10th November last[1] with the Copy of Mr. Vanbraams Letter and Account which I will certainly lay before the Assembly on their Meeting in March, when there is no Doubt but they will order the payment of his Due; which I cannot of my Self do, as the Regiment's full pay is drawn every Month exclusive of his and Major Stobo's Arrears. I have wrote to Mr. Robinson of New York requesting him to acquaint you and Governor Delancy that if you cannot make any Use of Monsr. LaForce (the last of the Prisoners which were to be delivered up by Col. Washingtons Capitulation, and for the Release of whom Major Stobo and Mr. Van Braam were given in Hostage) in order to set the last Mentioned Gentleman at Liberty, the Colony were desirous to set him at Large in order to be eased of the Expence of Maintaining him.

I have given Mr. Stewart leave to beat up for Recruits here, for the Regiment you mention and shall give him all the protection in my power, as I have his Majesty's Service so much at Heart.

I have received some distant Intimation that I am to expect the pleasure of seeing you here. I hope it is true, as We may then have an Opportunity of settling all affairs both of a public and a private Nature between us, and as it will give me the Satisfaction of beginning an Acquaintance with a person of your Worth and Merit.

This Letter will be deliverd to you by Major Stobo, for whom I am engaged to do all that I can, but as you are sensible very little can be done in the Colonies, I hope you will not leave his Services to his Country on that dependance wholy, but will think of him your-self and recommend him to the Ministry at home.

I observe Mr. Van Braam makes his Account for single Pay. Major Stobo has made up his for double, which he says is always allowed to Hostages; as I am ignorant of these Affairs, I should be obliged to you for your Sentiments thereon, and am with the greatest Esteem Sir Your most Obedient humble Servant

Fran: Fauquier

To his Excy. Majr. Genl. Amherst

ALS: W.O.34/37, f. 32. A copy of this letter which omits the third paragraph above is in C.O.5/57, ff. 130–31; it is a copy and a duplicate, endorsed as received in Amherst's letter of 17 Feb. 1760.

1. Amherst's letter was dated 16 Nov. 1759.

From Robert Stobo

[ca. February 1760]

This letter has not been identified. Fauquier transmitted it to the House of Burgesses on 7 Mar. 1760; see *JHB, 1758–1761*, p. 162. It seems likely that the letter was written during Feb. 1760 from New York; Stobo arrived there from Virginia on 7 Feb. and sailed for England on 19 Feb.

From William Henry Lyttelton

[Charles Town, 2 February 1760]

This letter has not been found. Fauquier communicated it to the council on 21 Feb. 1760, and it is abstracted in *EJC* 6:153–54:

Also another Letter from him, dated Charles-Town Feby. 2d informing that since the Treaty of Peace concluded with those Indians, they have renewed their Hostilities, and slain a considerable Number of his Majesty's Subjects trading in their Towns, and that he has strong grounds to apprehend they will very speedily make Incursions in that, and the neighbouring Provinces—inclosing a Copy of a Letter to him from Lieutenant Coytmore, dated Fort Prince George giving a particular Relation of the late Behaviour of the said Indians—intreating his Honor to send a Reinforcement of Men and Provisions to Fort Loudoun as soon as possible, to secure that Post from falling into the Hands of the

Indians—adding that he had dispatched an Express to Salisbury in No. Carolina with a Letter to the Store keeper of the Indian-trading-Goods lodged there, belonging to this Province, a Copy of which was inclosed.

Probably this was one of the letters Fauquier mentioned in his address to the assembly on 4 Mar. and transmitted to the House of Burgesses the same day; see *JHB, 1758–1761*, pp. 157–58. The letter from Coytmore to Lyttelton that Lyttelton enclosed is assumed to be the letter of 23 Jan. 1760, which follows. The letter from Lyttelton to the storekeeper at Salisbury has not been traced. However, a letter of 10 Feb. 1760 from Richard Smith (presumably the interpreter and Indian agent) to Lyttelton acknowledged Lyttelton's letter of 2 Feb. 1760 that ordered Smith not to proceed with the Indian trade goods belonging to Virginia, and Lyttelton's letter to the storekeeper also was probably meant to prevent forwarding of the goods. Smith's letter is in *S.C. Records*, p. 496.

Enclosure: Richard Coytmore to William Henry Lyttelton

Sir,   Fort Prince George, January 23d.1760.

Before I Endeavour to give Your Excellency an Account of the Situation of this Fort, I should Apologize for the Incorrectness Your Excellency will meet with in the following, but time is so precious I will it will make an Excuse for me, for it will not allow me to Write otherwise than from a daily Journal, for the Veracity and Exactness of which I can bring all the Officers and Garrison to Vouch.

Jany:13th. 1760. Mr. Elliott, who Carried off Letters for Fort Loudoun returned, having been no further than Cowee in the middle Settlements; He sent the packet by One James McCormick, who is not since heard of; Mr. Elliott thinking it proper to Inform me of the News in the Middle Settlements, returned, and Acquainted me that the Hywassee People in the Valley had killed a White Man (John Kelly); that the Middle Settlements and Valley were much Chagreen'd at the Confinement of their People, and were then preparing Victualls, &ca, to come down to try every method to redeem them, if not by fair means by force.[1]

The Same day. One Thompson, A Hireling of Mr. Beamers, came to me with a Message from the Young Warriour of Estatoe, that in three days he would come down, and bring three or four Murderers to deliver up, to redeem some of the Hostages.[2]

17th. Cornelius Doarthy, James Baldridge, Henry Lucas,[3] and other White Men being at Keowee, came to the River Bank, but could not pass, the water being very high, but Informed me that they were all desired by some Indian Women to make their Escape directly; that they (the Women) were well Informed, that that Night, or Early in the next morning, the Estatoe & Other Towns People up the River, were determined to Come in a Body to kill the White Men, first at Keowee, than at Mr. Elliotts, and then to try what they could do at the Fort. I had the Garrison under Arms, and told the Indian Hostages that I had heard of the Designs of the People up the River, that I should nevertheless Use them well, as usual, 'till such time their Countrymen begun any Mischief, but that if One of my Garrison was hurt by them, I would put every One of them to the Sword directly, this seemed to terrify them, and they sent off immediately the Slave Catcher of Stecoe[4] to Estatoe to prevent Mischief. Jany. 18th The Messenger returned, having met a Runner from the Young Warriour, and Informed me, that he was ordered to tell me that the next day, the Young Warriour would be at the Fort, with three or four of the Murderers according to his promise, that he would send Mr. Beamer's Son Thomas[5] before.

19th Isaac Atwood & Thomas Hayley Arrived at Keowee, having made their Escape a few Nights before from Hywassee, & brought Information that all the People of Great Tellicoe over the Hills,[6] were then at Hywassee on their way to this Fort; that the Hywassee People told them, as they had begun, and had in conjunction with those of Nottallee, killed a White Man (John Kelly) they were desirous that they (the Tellicoe People) should go & kill Atwood & Hadley,[7] who being informed of it made off; They further said that the Setticoe people were on their March for this Fort over the Twenty four Mountains;[8] Just afterwards came Thos. Beamer & William Thompson, & Informed me that the Young Warriour & several Indians were near the Fort, with some of the Murderers according to his promise; As I had been so lucky as to have had some hints before of their Designs, I took every precaution to guard against any Stratagem they might Endeavor to practice. I Enquired how many were in Company with the Young Warriour, and was told by Thomas Beaver[9] (who had just left them) Twenty five Men, beside some Women, but soon appearing on the Hill were counted by several of the Soldiers, to the Number of an Hundred & odd. Jacob Shortman Soldier, in particular counted One Hundred & fifteen Men. It rained very hard, and Every One had a Blanket, or Match Coat over their heads; I Ordered all the Soldiers to Stay in their Barracks with their Arms ready; I sent outward, I was ready to hear the Young Warriour talk, and Begg'd that he, & three or four of the Heads of them (together with the Murderers) would come into the Fort; he first refused unless all were admitted; but afterwards Consented, on which ordering them to be admitted, I observed more pushing into the Fort (as they were all on the Parade) than I Judged proper, and therefore had the Gates Shut, having let in the Young Warrior & Twelve Others; As I had some doubt of their honesty, I strictly observed them, and it was no difficulty to find out that Each of them had under their Blankets, Either a Tomhawk, Pistol, or Knife, a small Hatchet I myself saw and several were seen by Men of the Garrison. The Young Warriour gave me, and received from me a good Talk, and behaved to all outward Appearance in a friendly manner; he went out to fetch the Murderers but soon returned with Several frivolous Excuses, but without the Villains, We parted however friendly. Soon after came a Soldier (John Rowlin) from Mr. Elliott's house, where he left Mr. Elliott and Thirteen Other White Men, and said that just as he came off, about Fifty Indians, Each with a Hatchet [or] Pipe Tommahawks. That day in the Croud, when the Young Warrior went out, two of the Hostages (Tullatahee of Toque & the Yellow Bird of Watogo) Escaped.[10]

Sunday 20th. Several Indians were observed at daybreak lurking on the Hills, & continued so all day: About Sunrise a Woman, who had lain that Night at the New Town up Crow Creek (or Keohee Plantations)[11] came to the Fort, and gave the following Intelligence to the Hostages, who came & Communicated it to me, Vizt. That the Young Warriour came down to the Fort, the day before, with all his People, intending (as he imagined all would be admitted into the Fort, & were every One Secretly Armed) to fall on the People of the Garrison when in, with their Hatchetts &ca, being very wet Weather. That at the same time, about Fifty went off to Mr. Elliotts; That the Young Warriour finding his Scheme against the Fort prove abortive went there, that they then killed Mr. Elliott & Nine Other White Men, took two Prisoners (Morris Glynn & John Winbourn)[12] and Carried them to the New Town, where She, the Woman, just left them. That they had plundered his House & Store, & were dividing the Goods. That Mr. Beamer & all his family were Unhurt & would remain so, as they professed a great regard for them. I Beg'd Round O of Stecoe[13] (who Continues voluntarily with his Sons in the Fort) to go to Mr. Elliotts and See how things were there, but the Water being very high prevented him.

Monday 21st. Round O (by my desire) went up the Creek to find how Everything was, in the meantime, three of the Soldiers being Cutting some fire Wood, in sight of the Fort, were fired at, and One Shot in the Wrist with a Swan Short, the Indian who shot him, & two Others who were Lurking near ran off directly. Soon after Round O came with the following Account, that when he left the Fort in the morning, he met Six

Young Indian Fellows, that he Asked them where they were going, they replied to the Fort for White Scalps by the Young Warriour's Orders, he Confirmed the Account given by the Woman, & Saw the two Prisoners; he further said that they were all up the Creek drinking Rum, that they had between Twenty & Thirty Keggs, & all Elliott's Goods. About Eight o'Clock at Night, some Indians were seen by the Centrys lurking about the Outhouses & Hogpen, but on firing some Shot from the Fort, I believe they soon dispersed.

Tuesday 22d. Had all the Outhouses pulled down, & put together for the Use of the Fort as Firewood, & killed some Hoggs. Indians seen Skulking about all day. Round O was sent to Call Tiftoe of Keowee over the River, but could not get over, the Water yet being very high. Tiftoe sent me word that his Town was quiet, that only three or four Young Fellows were with the rest, but that he could not help it.

Wednesday 23d. Henry Lucas came early in the morning to the Riverside at Keohee and hollowed for a Horse. I Ordered ten Men with their Arms to fetch him over, two Shot were fired at them from the Hills, but did no hurt. Lucas said that since the 19th he had lain in a Cornhouse day & Night, and was fed at Midnight by his Woman, who kept him there till a proper time should offer for him to Escape. That he learnt from her, that One of the White Men at Elliotts (Maurice Morris)[14] had got off. About twelve o'Clock We were informed by an Indian across the River that Twelve were killed (if so None Escaped) That they had divided the Prisoners, given One to Toxaway, and were to send the Other off tomorrow to the Valley. This day Tiftoe hoisted an English Flag on his House, & Sent me Word not to blame him.

This, Sir, is the present Condition We are in, Surrounded and Shut up (like Birds in a Cage) both day & Night, could any Person Venture to go, I have not a Horse near, nor can any One go an hundred Yards to hunt One; Whether this will reach You or not, tis impossible to Say; the Bearers of this are two Women that belong to the Fort, and have been before of great Service, they are threatened as much as Us, but offered their Service to me to Carry this. I Enclose it to Mr. Goudy[15] who I have desired to forward it with all Speed; I have also desired him to procure the Bearers two Horses & a Guide, as they intend to go quite to Town; If they are found out or met by any of their People they unavoidably die; they Set off this Night, I had made large Promises to them, & Assured them that on their Arrival in Town, Your Excellency will See they want for Nothing, as they leave all their Cloaths behind. Should this happen to reach Your Excellency, it is the last I have any possibility of Sending,[16] nor can I Expect to hear from You without You send us a strong Reinforcement, or rather Relief. I have Provisions enough for some Months, so can manage pretty well, but should Carolina think us not worth taking Notice of, I shall (but Your Excellency may depend upon it not while I have a Single Bag of Flour left) Endeavor to march my men safe off. Your Excellency, I am certain from what I Write, will Judge how Matters are, & I must beg leave to Assure You, that nothing on my side, that I can do, shall be wanting for the good of the Service & Safety of the Garrison. I am very uneasy about Fort Loudoun, I have not heard from there since Your Excellency came up here. This very moment the whole Gang of Villains are paraded with Drum beating & Colours flying, on the top of the Hill. I remain with great Respect Your Excellency's Obliged & most Obedient humble Servant

Richd. Coytmore
Commandant of Fort Prince George

Copy: C.O. 5/57, ff. 313–15. Endorsed as enclosed in Lyttelton's letter of 2 Feb. 1760 to Amherst and as enclosed in Amherst's letter of 8 Mar. 1760. Coytmore's dates for his journal entries, in the margin of the copy, have been moved in to the body of the text. The word in brackets replaces "of" in the manuscript, but a verb is missing from this part of the sentence.

1. John Elliott was an Indian trader of Keowee, killed by the Cherokees in the latter part of 1760. On his mission to Fort Loudoun he turned back at Cowee, a Middle Cherokee town at the mouth of Cowee Creek on the Tennessee River, in what is now Macon County, N.C., a short distance north of the South Carolina line; Cowee was roughly 30 mi. west of Fort Prince George and 70 mi. southeast of Fort Loudoun. The James McCormick who carried the letters on from Cowee is not further identified. Elliott reported that John Kelly, an Indian trader and interpreter, had been killed and that the Cherokees were planning to come to rescue the twenty-two Cherokees being held in Fort Prince George as hostages for the surrender of the Cherokees supposed to have murdered some white people.

2. James Beamer was a trader at Estatoe, and his hireling or servant Thompson was presumably the William Thompson mentioned later in the letter under date of 19 Jan.

3. Doharty, as his name was commonly spelled, was an Indian trader at Hywassee; Baldridge was an Indian trader at Settico; Lucas had been a servant to various Indian traders, and was perhaps by this time a trader himself.

4. Stecoe was a Middle Cherokee town, to the west of Fort Prince George.

5. James Beamer's son Thomas was probably the half-breed guide and interpreter.

6. Atwood was an Indian trader of Hywassee; Hayley was perhaps the Thomas Healy who had been a soldier in Fort Prince George about 1756; Great Tellico was an Overhill Cherokee town, on the Tellico Plains by the Tellico River, in what is now Monroe County, Tenn.

7. Nottallee was a Valley Cherokee town; Hadley must have been the Hayley mentioned in the preceding note.

8. Settico was an Overhill Cherokee town. The Twenty-four Mountains have not been identified but were probably some part of the Blue Ridge or the Appalachians.

9. This was probably the Thomas Beamer already mentioned.

10. The two hostages were from Toqua, an Overhill Cherokee town on the Little Tennessee River near the mouth of Toco Creek, in what is now Monroe County,

Tenn.; and from Watoga, one of two Middle Cherokee towns of that name: one a settlement at Watauga Old Fields, at or near Elizabethton on the Watauga River in what is now Carter County, Tenn., and the other a settlement on Watauga Creek, a branch of the Little Tennessee River, below Franklin in what is now Macon County, N.C.

11. The New Town must have been New Keowee, on the headwaters of Twelve-mile Creek in what is now Pickens County, S.C., and a few miles to the east of Fort Prince George.

12. These men were probably Morris Gwin or Gwynn, a messenger or carrier, and John Winburn, perhaps an Indian trader.

13. Round O was chief of the town of Stecoe and the recognized leader of a group of Middle Cherokee towns.

14. Maurice Morris appears to have been a courier.

15. This was evidently Robert Goudy, one of the principal Indian traders among the Overhill Cherokees.

16. Coytmore was shot by the Cherokees on 16 Feb. and died about a week later.

To William Henry Lyttelton

Sir   Wmsburgh Febry 4th 1760

Inclosed with this I have the pleasure to forward to you, a Letter I received from Major General Stanwix. As I had no particular Business to communicate to you since my Letter of the 22d Novr. nor any Men to send to reinforce you I have deferred writing till I could hear from you in Relation to the accomodating all Matters with the Cherokee Indians, but hearing of a Gentleman going into Carolina on his own Affairs I have taken the Opportunity of writing by him, to congratulate you on the Success of your Negotiations with that Nation, the Authentic Account of which I am in daily Expectations of hearing from your self. This Colony are much obliged for your Conduct in this Affair, and can not think of your leaving the Government of a neighbouring Colony without regretting your Loss.[1]

Give me Leave to congratulate you on this Instance of his Majesty's Approbation of your Conduct, and be assured that whatever is for your Advantage will at all Times give pleasure to Sir Your Excellencys most Obedient humble Servant

                                              Fran: Fauquier

To Governor Lyttelton.

ALS: William L. Clements Library, Lyttelton Papers.

1. On 27 Nov. 1759 the king in council had approved the recommendation of the Board of Trade that Lyttelton should be appointed governor of Jamaica. The Clements Library records indicate that the letter forwarded was that of 5 Dec. 1759 from Stanwix to Lyttelton.

From Peter Wyche

[5 February 1760]

This letter has not been found, but Fauquier acknowledged it in his letter of 22 Apr. 1760 to Wyche. An endorsement on Fauquier's letter of 22 Apr. indicates that Wyche's letter communicated the ideas of the Society of Arts about planting varieties of grapes in America.

The Society of Arts (since 1908 the Royal Society of Arts) was founded in 1754 with the aim of encouraging the arts, manufactures, and commerce. Peter Wyche (d. 1763) was elected to the society in 1755 and took a prominent part in the society's work for the development of the North American colonies and in the promotion of scientific agriculture in England and elsewhere. Fauquier was elected to membership in the society on 15 Feb. 1758 as a corresponding member, a category of membership including men distinguished in various capacities, or men who had rendered services to the society, who for the most part were foreigners or resident abroad.

From Jeffery Amherst

Sir   New York 9th February 1760

Two days ago, Arrived Major Stobo, & delivered me Your favor of 17th Ultimo, Which I take the Opportunity of Acknowledging, by a Messenger Colonel Byrd is going to Dispatch to You.

The Major certainly is very deserving, nothing could give me greater pleasure, than to learn what the Dominion of Virginia had done for him, and I shall be glad myself to have it in my power to serve him, but I cannot think his Voyage to England will be of any use to him, for I Dare Venture to say, the Ministry will send him back to me; however since he seems so strongly enclined to go, I will not dissuade him from it, nor shall he want for my recommendation.

From what the Assembly have done for Mr. Stobo there is no matter of Doubt but they will be equally Considerate of Mr. Vanbraam's situation, particularly so, as he is so Ingenuous, as to Charge only his simple pay, for tho' he is certainly, of right, Entitled to no more, Yet under his Circumstances I really think, he should be allowed Something more; and this as far as depends on me, shall be as short a Charge upon the Government as possible, having kept Mor. La Force for that very purpose, nay I even sent him back, for he had got as far as Saratoga in his way home,¹ When I was informed Whom he was and as I knew, We should get Mr. Van Braam the sooner by keeping La Force I accordingly had him returned to his Quarters Where he is maintained as all the other french Prisoners agreable to the Cartel I transmitted You a Copy of last Summer.²

I am obliged to You for the protection you promise Mr. Stewart, and with that, and his Diligence, doubt not of his Success.

There are now two Packets due, so that I am still in the dark, with regard to the Operations, if any, of the Ensueing Campaign, so soon as I receive His Majesty's Commands I shall do myself the pleasure to Communicate them to You, Meanwhile I am to thank You for Your very civil wishes for our meeting, Which would be no less agreable to me, since it would procure me the favorable Opportunity of Assuring You in person of the great regard with Which I am, Sir, &ca.

Honble. Govr. Fauquier.

Copy: W.O.34/37, f. 210. Another copy, in C.O. 5/57, f. 132, is endorsed as being in Amherst's letter of 17 Feb. 1760.

1. Laforce was sent from Virginia to New York at some time around or before the middle of Mar. 1759, and by the end of that month he was being held on Long Island. Evidently he was released at some date in 1759 to go home and had got as far north in New York as Saratoga (about 175 mi. north of Long Island) when Amherst had him returned to his quarters; no details of this episode have been traced.

2. The treaty regulating the exchange of prisoners was enclosed in Amherst's letter of 14 Aug. 1759 to Fauquier. This treaty provided for the exchange or ransom within thirty days after 6 Feb. 1759, and at intervals thereafter, of all prisoners "made during the present War," which Great Britain had declared on 18 May 1756 and France on 9 June 1756. It appears that therefore the provisions of the treaty did not apply to prisoners taken as early as Laforce and Van Braam. Laforce became a prisoner in May 1754 and was evidently still a prisoner when Amherst's letter of 9 Feb. 1760 was written; the date of his release has not been ascertained, but he had arrived in Montreal before the end of Oct. 1760. Van Braam was a hostage from July 1754 until he was released upon the capture of Montreal in Sept. 1760.

From William Byrd

[New York, 11 February 1760]

This letter has not been found. Fauquier communicated it to the council on 4 Mar. 1760, and it is mentioned in *EJC* 6:155 as recommending that the Virginia Regiment should be continued until Christmas 1760. Probably this was one of the letters Fauquier mentioned in his address to the assembly on 4 Mar. and transmitted to the House of Burgesses the same day; see *JHB, 1758–1761*, pp. 157–58.

From Jeffery Amherst

Sir, New York 14th February 1760

Yester Evening arrived the Earl of Leicester Packet, & by her I am honoured with a Letter from Mr. Secretary Pitt of the 11th December last and altho' he does not Send me His Majesty's Commands, for the Operations of the Ensuing Campaign, Yet he directs me to make all the necessary preparations for pushing the War with the utmost Vigour, as early in the Year as the Season will permit, & thereby Compleat the great work, so Successfully begun of Rendring His Majesty entire Master of Canada.[1]

In order therefore to Enable me to fullfill these Instructions I must renew to You my most earnest Solicitations, for Your moving Your Assembly to make immediate Provision for the Same or a greater Number, if possible, of men than they did for the last Campaign, and to have them in such immediate readiness, that When I inform You of my Intentions to take the field, Which shall be as early as possible, I may be certain of the Motion & Junction, of all the Forces at the times & Places, Which I Shall hereafter Acquaint You with,[2] Which I shall be able to do more particularly, upon the arrival of Colo. Amherst, Whom I expect out soon, with the King's ulterior Commands for the ensuing Operations. I am, with great regard, Sir, &ca

Jeff: Amherst

Copy: C.O.5/57, f. 100. Circular addressed to governors of New Hampshire, Massachusetts, Connecticut, Rhode Island, New York, New Jersey, Pennsylvania, Maryland, and Virginia. Marked as copy and duplicate and endorsed as being in Amherst's letter of 17 Feb. 1760.

1. Pitt's letter of 11 Dec. 1759 to Amherst is in *Pitt* 2:216–18. The summary of Pitts instructions to Amherst is quoted almost verbatim from the letter. The rest of the letter conveyed the king's qualified satisfaction with the recent campaign and reported the British victory at Quiberon Bay; it warned Amherst that he should not allow tentative negotiations for a general peace to slacken preparations for the forthcoming campaign and should try to prevent rumors of those negotiations from influencing the provincial councils and assemblies to relax their efforts in the war.

2. This letter is assumed to be one of those which Fauquier mentioned in his address to the assembly on 4 Mar. 1760 and transmitted to the House of Burgesses on the same day: the burden of the address was the need to keep the Virginia Regiment in service (*JHB, 1758–1761*, pp. 157–58).

From James Abercromby

Feby 15th 1760

Having presented the Warrant for 20546.0.0 for payment at the Exchequer by way of Loan at 4 & ½ Interest till paid as by the Warrant is directed out of the Supply for 1759 I was told that the Rules of the Exchequer require Special Powers in money matters & that such must be under the Seal a Resolve of Governor & Council will do, but desire security may be given in the Exchequer by me to the King for the use of the Legislature of Virginia to account accordingly.[1]

The Proportion of 50,000 as aprovd of by Ld. Loudoun & for which my Memorial is now before the Treasury for payment by Mr Pitts Recomendation is 32814.19.0¼ some difficulty may attend the Manner of Ld. Loudouns Certificat which becomes the greater from the great Scarcity of Money to answer the Exigencys of Government at home, but I hope to get over these difficultys[2] I am not sure but it may become necessary for me to apply for further Supplys this Session I shall act according as I feel the Disposition of the Ministry for other Colonys I have but just time to send this by a Ship in the Downs[3] the 20546.0 may be payable in May I am Gentlemen Yours

Copy: Virginia State Library, James Abercromby Letter Book, p. 190. The letter is addressed in the margin to the Council of Virginia, but another marginal note indicates that the same letter was sent to Governor Fauquier. It is not clear whether the note means that a copy was sent to Fauquier or that substantially the same letter with appropriate changes in the salutation and the complimentary close was sent to him. Further notes indicate that whatever was sent to Fauquier went to Mr. Hanbury's on 21 Feb. 1760 and then went by Bristol soon after. And, finally, a note indicates that a duplicate of the attorney general's opinion was enclosed. It is likely that this opinion was that which Abercromby had already sent to Fauquier in his letter of 22 Dec. 1759, but the note does not make it clear whether the duplicate of the opinion went with the letter to the council only or with that to Fauquier as well. The letter is in Abercromby's hand, with numerous abbreviations, and is very hard to decipher.

1. In his address to the assembly on 19 May 1760, Fauquier referred to Abercromby's letter and identified this £20,546 as part of the £200,000 granted by Parliament for the use of the colonies in general for services performed in 1758 (*JHB, 1758–1761*, pp. 171–72).

2. In the address just cited, Fauquier identified this sum of £32,814.19.0¼ as a share of the £50,000 granted by Parliament in 1756 for the use of the southern colonies. In fact, the grant was approved in 1757.

3. The Downs is the roadstead off Deal in Kent, in the south of England.

From Jeffery Amherst

Sir,   New York 15th February 1760

By the Arrival of the Earl of Leicester Packet Which has brought me His Majesty's Patent, Creating me Governor of the Dominion of Virginia,[1] I have it now in my power to Answer more particularly, Your favor of 25th November last already Acknowledged.

But before I proceed on the Subject Matter of the Contents I am to inform You that I now, by Express Send You the Original Patent under the Great Seal,[2] in order to have it proclaimed throughout the Dominion in the usual and requisite forms, Which You will be so good as to Cause to be done without delay, as the Bearer is to Remain with You untill he can bring it me back. I need not therefore Recommend Dispatch to You.

With regard to the Offer You make me, I will dwell upon it as little as possible, not to take up too much of Your time, and in order thereto I shall here transcribe the Paragraph of a Letter I have received from England upon that Subject vizt.

"Mr. Dinwiddie says, the Government has produced £4000 Some Years, but always Whilst he had it, a Sum Sufficient to make it Answer to the Lieutenant Governor paying by Compromise £1665 a Year and leave Something handsome for him, Mr. Blair kept to this Bargain."[3]

Notwithstanding this, Sir, as I am Desirous to be free from all Agencys, if You will give me proper Security for the payment of £1500, a Year, Clear of all Deductions and by half Yearly payments in London, I shall Wave all other Considerations in Your behalf, and I shall Accordingly wait Your Answer by the Return of my Express. I am &ca.

Honble. Lt. Govr. Fauquier.

Copy: W.O.34/37, f. 211. Marked "Private."

1. For Amherst's commission, dated 25 Sept. 1759, see the enrolled copy in C.66/3665, no. 8. It is in all essentials the same as the commission to Loudoun, for which see nn. 1 and 4 on the commission of 10 Feb. 1758 to Fauquier.

2. Amherst's commission was in the form of letters patent under the Great Seal, the seal used for the authentication of documents of the highest importance issued in the name of the sovereign.

3. Amherst quoted from a letter of 29 Sept. to him from his agent, John Calcraft (W.O.34/99, ff. 47–48). That letter, with other correspondence regarding Amherst's salary as governor of Virginia, is included in Beverley McAnear, ed., "The Income of the Royal Governors of Virginia," *Journal of Southern History* 16 (1950): 196–211.

From Jeffery Amherst

Sir,   New York 21st February 1760

With His Majesty's Commands for the Reduction of all Canada, received last Night,[1] I likewise had the Copy of Mr. Secretary Pitt's Circular Letter to the Northern and Southern Governors of the 7th January last, the Original of which goes Enclosed, and whereby You will See, that His Majesty having Nothing so much at heart, as to Improve the great & Important Advantages gained the last Campaign in North America, and, not doubting that all His Faithfull & Brave Subjects there, will Continue most Chearfully to Co-operate with, and Second to the utmost, the large Expence & Extraordinary Succours, Supplied by the Kingdom of Great Britain, for their Preservation and future Security; And His Majesty Considering that the Several Provinces, from Pensylvania Inclusive, to the Southward, are well able, with proper Encouragements, to furnish a Body of Several Thousand Men, to Join the King's Forces in those Parts, for some Offensive Operations against the Enemy; And His Majesty not Judging it Expedient to limit the Zeal & Ardor of any of His Provinces, by making a repartition of the Forces to be Raised by Each respectively, for this most Important Service; He (Mr. Secretary Pitt) is Commanded to Signify to You the King's Pleasure that You do forthwith Use Your utmost Endeavors and Influence, with the Council & Assembly of Your Province[2] to Induce them to raise with all possible dispatch, within Your Government, at least as large a Body of Men as they did for the last Campaign, and even as many more as the Number and Situation of its Inhabitants may Allow; and forming the same into Regiments, as far as shall be found convenient; That You do direct them to hold themselves in readiness, as Early as may be, to March to the Rendezvous, at such Place, or Places, as may be Named for that purpose, by the Commander in Chief of His Majesty's Forces in America, or by the Officer who shall be Appointed to Command the King's Forces in those Parts, in order to proceed from thence, in Conjunction with a Body of His

Majesty's British Forces, and under the Supreme Command of the Officer to be Appointed as above, so as to be in a Situation to begin, by the First of May, if possible, or, as soon after as shall be any way practicable, such Offensive Operations as shall be Judged, by the Commander of His Majesty's Forces in those Parts, most Expedient for Annoying the Enemy.

As the King's directions, on the foregoing Subject, are so fully Stated in the above Abstract, I have only to Request that You would Exert Your utmost Endeavors to encite & Encourage Your Assembly to the full and due Execution of the King's Commands, in a matter so Essential to the future Welfare and prosperity of the Several Provinces, and the Success of the Ensueing, decisive and (it is greatly hoped) last Campaign in North America; which desireable Ends cannot be better Attained than by Commencing the Operations as Early as shall be practicable; And that Nothing may be left undone that it is possible for me to Attempt in the Execution of His Majesty's Commands, I must be Urgent with You to Quicken & Expedite the Levies of Your Province, so that they may be Assembled at the Rendezvous which I shall hereafter appoint, by the Tenth of April next, at furthest.

I Have also in Command from His Majesty to recommend to You the Collecting & putting into a proper Condition, all the Arms which can be anywise render'd Serviceable, or that can be found within Your Government, in order that the Same may be Employed as far as they will go in this Exigency: As a further Reason for which I referr You to my Letter of the 16th February 1759, and now Offer You the Same Encouragement I did then, Vizt. That for Every One of such Arms as any of Your Men shall bring with them, and that may be Spoiled, or Lost, in Actual Service, I will pay at the rate of Twenty Five Shillings a Firelock.

From this Encouragement, and Your known Fidelity and Attachment to His Majesty, I have no doubt of Your Exerting Yourself to the Utmost, on this great Occasion, where the future Safety and Welfare of America, and of Your own Province in particular, are so nearly Concerned. I am, with great Regard, Sir, Your most Obedient Humble Servant.

Jeff: Amherst

Copy: C.O.5/57, ff. 115–16. Circular addressed to the governors of Pennsylvania, Maryland, Virginia, North Carolina, and South Carolina and endorsed as being in Amherst's letter of 9 Mar. 1760.

1. The king's orders to Amherst were conveyed in a letter from Pitt to Amherst dated 7 Jan. 1760, *Pitt* 2:237–42.
2. Fauquier communicated this letter to the council in executive session on 4 Mar.

1760, and it is abstracted in *EJC* 6:155. The letter is assumed to be one of those he mentioned in his address to the General Assembly on 4 Mar. 1760 and transmitted to the House of Burgesses on the same day; see *JHB, 1758–1761*, p. 158.

To Jeffery Amherst

Sir   Wmsburgh Febry 23d 1760

I have now before me your two Favours of the 21st and 27th of December last, which I take this Opportunity of acknowledging the Receipt of. The inclosed packet for you I received from Govr. Lyttelton in which I presume he has informed you of the fresh Treachery of the Cherokee Indians. This Event may probably be an Inducement to the general Assembly which meets on Tuesday the 4th of March to continue the Regiment beyond the 1st of May, which without this Circumstance I am of Opinion would not have been the Case. If any thing could have prevailed on this Colony, to be at the Expence of keeping any Men longer in pay, it would have been the requiring a certain Number for a determinate Time, to finish the Works at Pittsburgh.

As for the Regiment being reduced to 400 Your Excellency misunderstood me,[1] the Regiment was kept up, but I was restrained from leaving more than 400 there, the Rest being to be employed in the Defence of the Southwest Frontiers.

I rejoice at thinking there is any possibility of my having the pleasure of kissing your Hands here. I shall wait with Impatience for the next Return of the Northern post which I expect to arrive to morrow s'ennight, by which I hope to receive your patent as Governor of this Colony.

Whatever Resolutions the general Assembly may come to, in Regard to the Men in their pay; shall be immediately communicated to you, being with the greatest Esteem Sir Your Excellency's most Obedient humble Servant

                                                     Fran: Fauquier

To his Excelcy. Majr. Genl. Amherst.

ALS: W.O.34/37, f. 33. A copy of this letter which omits the third paragraph above is in C.O.5/58, ff. 113–14, endorsed as received in Amherst's letter of 28 Apr. 1760.

1. See the second paragraph of Amherst's letter of 27 Dec. 1759 for his regret that the assembly of Virginia had reduced the regiment to 400 men.

From William Byrd

[ca. March 1760]

This letter has not been identified. Fauquier transmitted it to the House of Burgesses on 7 Mar. 1760; see *JHB, 1758–1761*, p. 162.

Proclamation

[ca. 5 March 1760]

On 4 Mar. 1760 the council, in compliance with the Board of Trade's letter of 13 Nov. 1759, ordered that Tuesday 8 Apr. should be appointed a day of public thanksgiving for the success of His Majesty's arms, and particularly for the defeat of the French army in Canada and the taking of Quebec; see *EJC* 6:155. No copy of the proclamation has been found, and the date is a conjecture.

Proclamation

[ca. 5 March 1760]

The minutes of the council for 4 Mar. 1760 contain this entry: "Ordered That a Proclamation issue for apprehending Thomas Baber, offering £20 Reward for taking him" (*EJC* 6:155). Nothing more is known of the proclamation and its purpose. No copy has been found, and the date is a conjecture.

To Jeffery Amherst

Sir   Wmsburgh Mar 5th 1760

I am much obliged to you for your great assiduity in sending down Expresses with Mr. Secretary Pitts and your own Letters, They all arrived Time enough for me, to lay them before the general Assembly on their meeting Yesterday, and to recommend them by the Speech a Copy of which I Send You enclosed.[1]

I have the further Satisfaction to inform you, that I flatter my self with the Hopes of their producing some good Effect; for till now, I had dispaired of keeping together any body of Men whatever. The Event is still doubtfull; but you may depend on my immediately communicating to you and Mr. Stanwix whatever Resolutions the Assembly may come to, that you may be apprized of what Assistance you are to expect from this Colony. I am with the greatest Regard Sir Your Excellencys most Obedient humble Servant

Fran: Fauquier

To his Excellcy. Majr. Genl. Amherst.
P.S. I have this moment heard the Committee have resolved to keep up the Regiment. I hope the House will approve.[2]

ALS: W.O. 34/37, f. 36. A copy of this letter is in C.O. 5/58, ff. 117–18, endorsed as received in Amherst's letter of 28 Apr. 1760.

1. Fauquier's speech to the General Assembly on 4 Mar. 1760 (*JHB, 1758–1761*, pp. 158–59) announced that his intention in calling the assembly together was to ascertain what it meant to do about the regiment, which he was bound to disband on 1 May unless the assembly gave further assistance; in support of the expedience of keeping up the regiment Fauquier cited letters from Amherst, Stanwix, Lyttelton, and Byrd, and he reminded the assembly that Great Britain had reimbursed the colonies for some part of their expenditures on defense; he assured the assembly that his recommendation of additional expenses was in the interest of the colony's honor and safety. After announcing the appointment of Amherst as governor of Virginia, Fauquier closed with mention of letters just received from Pitt and Amherst that signified the king's commands for him to urge the General Assembly to exert itself vigorously in support of the forthcoming campaign.

2. On 5 Mar. 1760 the House of Burgesses resolved itself into a committee to consider Fauquier's speech and the letters to which he referred. The committee offered resolutions that the regiment in the pay of the colony should be continued in service until 1 Nov. 1760; that 300 men of that regiment should be further continued in service from 1 Nov. 1760 to 1 Apr. 1761 if the governor or commander in chief should think it necessary; and that a sum not exceeding £20,000 should be raised for the pay and maintenance of the regiment until 1 Apr. 1761. The House of Burgesses heard and agreed to these three resolutions, still on 5 Mar. 1760.

To Jeffery Amherst

Sir   Wmsburgh Mar 5th 1760

I have the pleasure to inform you that I laid your Patent before the Council yesterday, when it was read, and recorded in the Journals of the Council: which is all the publication it can receive in this Colony.[1] The patents of all your Predecessors are kept in the Council Office which has always been the practice; because it is the only Instrument which declares the power vested in me; my own Appointment being only a sign manual empowering me to act with all the power vested in the Governor and Commander in chief.[2] However if you have any particular Reasons why you chuse to have it in your own possession, it can be registred in the Office, and the Original sent back to you: which shall be immediately done on your signifying such a Desire. It has always been usual for the Governor to have a Commission of Vice Admiral from the Admiralty Office which if not already done it may be proper for you to apply for. Lord Loudouns Commission being what I now must act under, that remaining in Force, not being revoked by your patent under the Great Seal.[3]

Your Manner of acting in Relation to the Agreement is exactly agreeable to the Character you are so happy as to injoy in your public or private Capacity. If you please then to order an Instrument with what Security you think proper for my paying you £1500 a Year on the Exchange of London by half Yearly payments, to be remitted by Bills of Exchange at 60 Days sight (the Common Usance here) by the first Ship which shall sail after the General Courts in April and October; which are the Times the Salary is paid; I will immediately execute it. At the same Time you will let me know whether I shall remitt the Bills I receive here and endorsed by my self to your Banker, or whether I shall draw on my Brother in London who transacts my Affairs, or give him Orders to pay it constantly as he receives the Remittances from me. either Way will be entirely equal to me.

Your generous Manner of agreeing to the £1500, shall not be an Obstruction to my paying it in Guineas,[4] if I should hereafter find the Government at all approach to the Sum Mr. Dinwiddie mentions. hitherto I have not found it so, perhaps *I* never shall.

My whole Receipt has been as follows

from the 5th June 1758 to Decr. 31st 1758   £ 900. 4. 8 Sterling
from 1 Janry. 1759 to Decr. 31st   1759   2437. 12. 6
from the 5th June 1758 to Decr. 31   1758   £ 315. 9. 6 Currency
from 1 Janry. 1759 to Decr. 31   1759   1032. 0. 0

The Exchange has been some times at £135, some times at £140 Currency for Sterling.[5]

My Brother will pay Mr. Calcraft at the Rate of £1500 to the 25 Sepr. the Date of your patent, from the Time the proffits become due to you.[6] There is now a little advantage arising from the Confiscation of one of Governor Denny's Flags of Truce.[7] tho' this is trifling it may happen if the War should continue that something of much greater Value may fall to our Share, therefore I don't mean to include these in our Agreement, but I propose to pay you your Moiety thereof, be it more or less.

5 March 1760

As there is now an Arrear from the Government of one half year due to us, I should be glad to be indulged in being permitted on such Occasions to be one half Year under another,[8] assuring you on the Honour with which Gentlemen ought to act in all their Concerns, and with which I trust We always shall act, that I will never make use of the Indulgence without an absolute Necessity. I am with the sincerest Regard and Esteem Sir Your most Obedient & most humble Servant

Fran: Fauquier

ALS: W.O.34/37, ff. 34–35. Marked "Private." Endorsed as received 29 Mar. 1760 and answered 1 Apr.

1. Fauquier produced the commission in the executive session of the council on 4 Mar. 1760, and on the same day, in his opening address to the General Assembly, he announced that he had received the commission. See *EJC* 6:155 and *JHB, 1758–1761*, p. 158.

2. A sign manual was a document signed at the top with the monarch's signature and at the bottom with the monarch's cipher or the countersignature of a secretary of state. Oftentimes the document also bore the signet, the monarch's seal, and it was referred to as a signet and sign manual.

3. For Amherst's commission as vice admiral, dated 6 Oct. 1759, see H.C.A.50/11, ff. 10–16, 126. It was essentially the same as that granted to Loudoun, for which see n. 2 to John Clevland's letter of 14 Mar. 1758 to Fauquier.

4. Fauquier meant that if his income justified it, he would pay Amherst 1,500 guineas, or £1,575, rather than £1,500. In his letter of 25 Nov. 1759 he told Amherst he had been willing to make such an arrangement with Loudoun.

5. Presumably the sterling account for 1758 means that from his half year's salary of £1,000, for which he signed the warrant on 6 Nov. 1758, Fauquier paid £218.11.7 for President Blair's salary as acting governor up to 5 June 1758 when Fauquier assumed office and retained a balance of £781.8.5, so that he must have taken in £118.16.3 sterling in fees or other incidentals by the end of 1758. The sterling account for 1759 appears to show that in addition to the two payments of a half year's salary of £1,000 each, for which he signed the warrants on 5 May and 6 Nov. 1759, Fauquier collected £437.12.6 sterling in fees or other incidentals during 1759. The two accounts of currency, or Virginia money, probably represent only fees or other incidentals. The reason why Fauquier mentioned the rates of exchange for sterling and currency is not clear: he may have wanted to justify his estimate of the annual income of the governorship as £3,000 (and Amherst's share as £1,500) by showing that his income for about seven months of 1758 was approximately £1,130 sterling, and for the twelve months of 1759 about £3,190.

6. This seems to suggest that the first payment of Amherst's share of the governor's income should be for the period from some date not yet settled up to 25 Sept. following. Calcraft had informed Amherst that some lieutenant governors of Virginia were said to have held they were not obliged to pay the governor his share of the income for any time before his commission was published in Virginia: under this arrangement Amherst would have had no share of the income for the period 25 Sept. 1759–4 Mar. 1760. However, the agreement made between Calcraft and William Fauquier in the summer of 1760 evidently assumed 25 Sept. 1759 as the date from which Amherst's share of income should be reckoned. See the Amherst-Calcraft correspondence cited in n. 3 to Amherst's letter of 15 Feb. 1760.

7. The flag of truce was probably a merchant ship licensed by William Denny of

Pennsylvania to transport prisoners of war to the French West Indies, captured with illicit cargo to or from those islands, and libeled and condemned in the admiralty court in Virginia. No details of the matter have been found, but the money realized from the confiscated ships or cargoes was commonly shared by the crown, the governor, and the captor.

8. Fauquier may have meant to say that the salary was paid at the end of the half year to which it applied, rather than in advance, for the salary up to 25 Oct. 1759 had been paid (as Fauquier informed Amherst in his letter of 8 May 1760) and the salary for the next half year was not due until 25 Apr. 1760.

To John Stanwix

[8 March 1760]

This letter has not been found, but Fauquier mentioned it in his letter of 22 Mar. 1760 to Stanwix and indicated it notified Stanwix that the General Assembly had voted to maintain the Virginia Regiment for the summer.

From John Clevland

Sir   12 March 1760

I received your Letter of the 13 of October last representing that you had received five Mediterranean Passes left by the late Governor Dinwiddie four of which you had issued and desiring a further supply may be sent to you, in return to which I now send you by Captain Hooper of the ship Polly[1] a box containing a dozen Passes with the like number of Certificates, Oaths and Bonds as usual;[2] and when Opportunity Offers I am to desire you will Please to send a Register of all the Passes you have issued and at the same time a Bill of Exchange for the amount thereof I am &ca.

J. C

Francis Fauquier Esqr. Governnor Virginia

Copy: Adm.2/1321,p. 519.

1. The ship *Polly*, of London, commanded by Thomas Hooper was owned by John Reeves of Stockton. She was entered in York River on 21 June 1760.

2. These were perhaps printed forms for the bonds that obligated ship captains to obey the laws regulating shipping of enumerated commodities, articles originating in the British colonies that could be exported to certain destinations only; the certificates attesting that such bonds had been executed; and the oaths taken by owners of ships that their vessels had been certificated and registered according to law. See Charles M. Andrews, *The Colonial Period of American History* (New Haven, 1938), 4: passim.

13 March 1760

To the Board of Trade

My Lords,[1]   Wmsburgh Mar 13th 1760

I have the pleasure to inform your Lordships that the Assembly which I had summoned to meet on the 4th instant that I might have Time to give his Majesty's Commander in chief early Notice of the Intentions of this Colony in Relation to the Regiment; broke up on the 11th: and to my unspeakable Satisfaction unanimously resolved to continue the Regiment in pay.[2] This Step gave me the more pleasure as it was entirely unexpected, for by the whole Tenour of the Discourse of the Burgesses, even those who had most strenuously supported the granting Supplies of his Majesty; I had Reason to expect the Regiment was designed to be dropt. What occasioned this sudden alteration of Sentiments, so different from those I represented to your Lordships in my Letter of the 17th December, I cannot determine. I have heard they altered their Minds on their meeting one another in Town, before they met in the House.

In my Letter of the 1st December to your Lordships I did my self the Honor to represent to you the Necessity, as it appear'd to me, of settling the Boundary Line of the Province of Pensylvania and mentioned several other Particulars relative to the settling the Lands on the Ohio. I must beg Leave to repeat my Sollicitations on that Head & to express my earnest Desire that I may be favour'd with an Instruction from his Majesty directing me how I am to conduct my self on this Occasion. Fresh Difficulties arise daily. The Officers who have served in this War, are very pressing to have the Lands near Fort du Quesne or Pittsburgh surveyed, that they may be possessed of them, agreeably to the proclamation of Mr. Dinwiddie as they urge an equitable Right to them by their Service and the Dangers which they have exposed themselves to the Recovery of them. They further urge that if we do not grant them, Pensylvania will, and then by the Common Usage, the Grantees Right will be confirmed, in whatever Colony the Lands may lie, and to whomsoever the Quit Rents may be payable.

The Objections to these Claims are as follows. It is uncertain in which Colony the Lands claim'd lie. It is confidently said, that by a Treaty which General Forbes made with the Indians when he took possession of Pittsburgh, it was agreed that the Lands in Question should not be settled by White people; and that this Treaty has been since confirmed and enlarged by General Stanwix. That the Indians insisted that we should only build Forts to protect ourselves and them from the French, but should not make Plantations in that Country as it would take away their hunting Country and drive them too far back. Whether these points are so or not we are not certain, as we have not received a Copy of either Treaty:[3] But the Fact is, the Indians scalp every White Man they catch on the Western Side the Ohio.

Upon these Considerations his Majesty's Council here, have not run into the granting these Lands with that precipitation which the Gentlemen of the Army have wish'd; fearing that by so doing they might irritate the Indians and promote a Defection of them from our Interest.

The two great Points in View, in driving the French from this Country, was, I conceive, to stop the Communication between Canada and New Orleans on this Side the Lakes, and to get possession of the fertile Lands on the Ohio. How far we ought in Prudence to proceed on the Latter at present, I submit to your Lordships superior Knowledge and Judgment.

If it should be your Lordships Opinion, and his Majesty's pleasure, that we should not proceed in the making these Grants; I hope your Lordships will think it adviseable, and accordingly enjoin the proprietary's Agents, not to make any such Grants on their part; for if the Lands are to be settled, the Gentlemen who now claim under the proclamation seem to have purchased their Prior Right by the Hazard of their Lives.

I have wrote to General Stanwix for Copies of these Treaties,[4] that we may have all the Materials requisite for our Conducting ourselves properly.

I have had the Honor to receive two Letters from your right honble. Board by the last New-York Mail which arrived; viz of the 13th & 20th Novr. last. In Obedience to his Majesty's Commands notifyed in the first, I have issued out a proclamation to return Thanks to Almighty God for the signal Successes with which he has vouchsafed to bless his Majesty's Arms, on Tuesday the 8th of April.

In Relation to that of Novr. 20th I am extremely happy that my Reasons in Relation to the Treasurership found such Weight with your Lordships, as to induce you to postpone the pushing that Affair; which I am confident would have been attended with bad Consequences to his Majesty's Service in the present Situation of Affairs; which is the Object I have always uppermost in my Thoughts; chiefly at Heart in all my Transactions. If Your Lordships compare the Act I pass'd with others of the same Nature pass'd by Governors Dinwiddie and Gooch I am humbly of Opinion you will find nothing particular in the Act of 1758 pass'd by me. I have myself examined the Act appointing a Treasurer pass'd in 1748 by Sir Wm. Gooch, those pass'd in 1752, and 1756 by Governor Dinwiddie,[5] all of which are expressed in the same Terms, as to the Office of Treasurer continuing as long as he shall be Speaker, and to the End of the next Session of Assembly; which is the Paragraph I apprehend your Lordships hint at. I am told that every Act of this Sort from the Year 1741 have been constantly copied from one to the following, but of this I am not certain, as I have not examined them; as they have been long expired they are not printed in the Book of Laws reprinted at the revisal in 1748.[6]

As soon as I can get the Acts and Journals of this short Session copied from the respective Offices, I will transmit them to your Lordships with the Duplicates of the papers I sent by the Deliverance Captn. White in December.[7] I am with the greatest Respect My Lords Your Lordships most Obedient & obliged humble Servant

Fran: Fauquier

To the right honble. the Lords Commissioners of Trade.

ALS: C.O.5/1329, ff. 178–80. Endorsed as read 8 May 1760.

1. A commission of 14 Jan. 1760 had changed the membership of the Board of Trade. James Oswald and Richard Rigby were left out of the new commission, while Edward Eliot (1727–1804) and Edward Bacon (1713–1786) were appointed to the board.

2. On 5 Mar. 1760 the House of Burgesses agreed to a resolution to keep the regiment in pay, and on 11 Mar. Fauquier assented to the consequent act of assembly, "An Act for granting the sum of twenty thousand pounds, for the further security and protection of this colony" (Hening, 7:347–53).

3. What Fauquier described as a treaty which Forbes made with the Indians after he had taken possession of Fort Duquesne is likely to have been the conference with the Delaware chiefs held at Pittsburgh 4–5 Dec. 1758, which Forbes had called for but could not attend, so that Bouquet presided. Or, conceivably, Fauquier may have had in mind a conference at Philadelphia on 8–9 Feb. 1759 between Indians of several tribes and Richard Peters, secretary of Pennsylvania, acting for Forbes who was too ill to receive the Indians. The mention of confirmation and enlargement of the Forbes treaty by Stanwix seems to refer to a meeting held at Philadelphia in Apr. 1759 between Amherst, Stanwix, Gov. William Denny of Pennsylvania, Gov. James De Lancey of New York, and Gov. Francis Bernard of New Jersey and various chiefs of the Indians living at the heads of the Ohio. The records of these several conferences do not indicate that the Indians raised any of the points which Fauquier stated. However, at the meeting in Dec. 1758, Bouquet, speaking for Forbes, told the Indians that the English had not come to take possession of the Indians' hunting country in a hostile manner; at the meeting in Feb. 1759, Forbes, by a written message, assured the Indians that the English had not come to take the Indians' lands from them and had no intention of making settlements in the hunting country beyond the Alleghenies, unless the Indians should desire them to build warehouses for carrying on a fair and just trade; and, finally, after the meeting in Apr. 1759, Denny reported to the Delawares that the English meant to force the French from all the country along the Ohio, with no intention of settling those lands themselves, although the king had commanded them to build a fort on or near the ruins of Fort Duquesne, in order to protect the Indians. For the proceedings of the meetings in Dec. 1758 and Apr. 1759, see *Pa. Arch.* [1], 3:571–74, 622–24; and for proceedings of the meeting in Feb. 1759, see *P.C. Pa.* 8:263–71.

4. See Fauquier's letter of 22 Mar. 1760 to Stanwix.

5. These were "An Act for appointing a treasurer, and other purposes therein

mentioned," Oct. 1748, "An Act for appointing a Treasurer," Feb. 1752, and "An Act for appointing a Treasurer," Mar. 1756 (Hening, 6:195–96, 248–50, 7:33–35).

6. The latest act for appointing a treasurer before those Fauquier had already mentioned was "An Act, for appointing a Treasurer," May 1742 (Hening, 5:173–74). No act for this purpose was passed in 1741. The successive acts are not simply repetitions of the act of May 1742 (that of Oct. 1748 being especially different from the others), but they are very much alike in their essentials. The collection of laws mentioned is probably the one printed by William Hunter at Williamsburg in 1752 (Evans 6941).

7. The acts and journals were those of the General Assembly session of 4–11 Mar. 1760. The duplicates would be duplicates of papers sent with Fauquier's letter of 17 Dec. 1759 to the board; the *Deliverance*, of Virginia, owned by James Mills and commanded by William Whyte, was cleared from Rappahannock River on 28 Dec. 1759, bound for London.

To William Pitt

Sir   Wmsburgh Mar 14 1760

In Obedience to his Majesty's Commands notifyed to me in the Letter I had the Honour to receive from you, the very Night before the general Assembly met,[1] I recommended the Measures directed in it, and laid your Letter before the Assembly: and I have the pleasure to acquaint you that the Assembly unanimously agreed to keep up the Regiment now on Foot. Of this I have apprized Major Generals Amherst & Stanwix.[2]

I have also ordered the Patent under the Seal of this Colony to be made out, appointing Mr. David Bowman to be naval Officer of the District of the Eastern Shore, as ordered by his Majestys Sign Manual bearing Date the 26th Day of Novr. 1759. I am with the greatest Respect Sir Your most Obedient and devoted humble Servant

                                                            Fran: Fauquier

The right Honble. Wm. Pitt.

ALS: C.O.5/19, ff. 227–28. Endorsed as received 25 Apr.

1. Pitt's letter of 7 Jan. 1760.
2. See Fauquier's letters of 5 Mar. 1760 to Amherst and of 8 Mar. 1760 to Stanwix.

From Jeffery Amherst

Sir,   New York 17th March 1760

Yesterday I was favored with Your Letter of the 23d Ultimo together with the Dispatch from Govr. Lyttelton, the Duplicates of which, I have already sometime since Answered, & in Consequence of later Intelligence, and at his Solicitations I have Embarked, a Body of His Majesty's Troops for the protection of South Carolina and the punishment of the Cherokee Indians,[1] for their late perfidious breach of Faith.

I am sorry that this event only should Induce the Assembly of Virginia to continue the Regiment in pay, beyond the first of May as their Assistance is absolutely necessary for other Service, than the finishing the Works at Pittsburgh, my Intention being to open a Communication between that place and Niagara, for unless we have such a one, and that we are entire Masters of Lake Erie, our business to the Southward is not near done; and as Virginia cannot but be Sensible, of the Security & Advantages that must result to them from such a Communication, & possession of Lake Erie, I cannot think they would be so blind to their own Interests, as not to Contribute to their utmost, towards obtaining both; besides they would not now, at the Eve of Enjoying the Advantages, already obtained by the Success of last Campaign relax in their late Zeal for the good of the Publick Cause, & from a noncompliance with the King's requisition,[2] Which I transmitted You from Mr. Secretary Pitt on the 21st of February, forfeit His Majesty's good opinion.

Colonel Byrd cleared up to me, that part of Your former Letter relative to the Reduction of the Regiment, Which I was very glad to find not to be as I had understood it. I am, with great regard, Sir &ca.

Honble. Govr. Fauquier.

Copy: W.O.34/37, f. 212. Another copy is in C.O.5/58, ff. 115–16, endorsed as being in Amherst's letter of 28 Apr. 1760.

1. Amherst ordered 1,312 men from the First and Seventy-seventh regiments to the aid of South Carolina, under the command of Lt. Col. Archibald Montgomerie, commandant of the Seventy-seventh Regiment.
2. In Pitt's letter of 7 Jan. 1760.

From Samuel Martin

[19 March 1760]

This letter has not been found, but it was presumably enclosed in Abercromby's letter of 20 Mar. 1760. Fauquier communicated it to the council on 25 June 1760, and it is abstracted in *EJC* 6:165:

The Governour was likewise pleas'd to communicate to the Board a Letter dated the 19th of March from Mr. Martin Secretary to the Board of Treasury signifying it was their Lordships pleasure to issue the proportion of the £50,000 alotted to Virginia to the person acting as Agent for the Colony, tho' he does not appear to be authorised to receive the same, on his giving proper security for the payment thereof to such person or Persons as shall be impowered to receive the same for the Use of the Colony: And that they desire his Honour will use his endeavours that proper persons may be impowered to receive such Monies, as the Parliament may hereafter think fit to grant for the service of this Colony.

From James Abercromby

March 20th 1760

Herewith I have the honour to transmit to you a letter from the Treasury,[1] which they inform me signefys to you that it is their pleasure to Issue the Proportions of the 50,000 to the respective Agents acting for these Provinces for the use of the said Provinces on their giving proper Security for the due payment thereof to such Person or Persons as shall be Impowerd to receive the same for the use of the said Province;[2] at the same time desiring you to use your Endeavours that proper Powers may be transmitted to receive such Monies as Parliament may hereafter Grant this agrees with what I have heretofore suggested to you and to the Council, and which becomes necessary, in the Case of the Proportion of the 200000 heretofore alloted for Virginia according to the Claim given in by me on the part of Virginia, and for which I have his Majestys Warrant for payment of £20546: but my name not being expressd in said Warrant and my general Powers of Agency not coming up to the Rules of the Exchequer in Money Matters, the Warrant must remain with me til I have proper Powers from the Province for receiving the same as my letter of the 15th Feby signefyd to you and to the Council.[3]

In that letter I likewise acquainted you, that I should apply to the Administration for further Supplys and from the Treasury letter to you it would appear that the Ministry had in view a further Supply for Services performed by the several Colonies in 1759, and how to asertain those of Virginia I can form no other Judgement than from the Supplys for Military Services that may be met with in the Journals and Provincial Acts transmitted to the Plantation Office.

As The Lords of the Treasury have not as yet finally asertaind the respective Sums payable to the Provinces in consequence of Lord Loudons approbation I cannot precisely tell you the Virginia proportion that I am to receive but as it stands on my Claim it amounts to 32814.19.0¼ for Virginia, to North Carolina 7789.1.1¾ South Carolina 9941.19.10 which together make 50000.0.0.[4]

The utmost efforts are making for a Vigorouse Campain, at the same time their seems to be some tendency towards Negociation for Accommodation, on the part of some of the Powers at War, and chiefly on the part of France, With Complements to your Lady & Family, I am with truth Sir

Gov. Fouquier.

Copy: Virginia State Library, James Abercromby Letter Book, pp. 195–96. A marginal note indicates that the letter was sent to the Admiralty to go by the Virginia convoy and that it enclosed the attorney general's opinion (presumably that of 24 Dec. 1759, already sent to Fauquier with Abercromby's letter of 22 Dec. 1759) and Mr. Pownall's attestation of Abercromby's credentials (not identified). A further note states that receipt of the letter was acknowledged in Fauquier's letter of 22 June.

1. Evidently the letter of 19 Mar. 1760 from Samuel Martin.
2. James Wright was still acting as agent for South Carolina, though he was very soon appointed lieutenant governor of Georgia. The agent for the governor and council of North Carolina 1759–64 was Samuel Smith, a merchant and attorney of London, who for a while acted as solicitor for Governor Dobbs of North Carolina.
3. This letter of 20 Mar. was communicated to the council on 25 June 1760; see *EJC* 6:165–66. Fauquier's reply was presumably a letter of ca. 25 June 1760.
4. The sum of these three amounts is £50,546.

To John Stanwix

Sir   Wmsburgh Mar 22d 1760

In my Letter of the 8th instant I informed you that the Assembly had voted the Regiment should be kept up for this summer. It is to be kept upon the Foot it now stands, the Strength of which by the last Return was 762. I am by the Act obliged to keep 300 at home for the Defence of the Frontiers; and all the rest I shall give Orders to Colonel Byrd to have in Readiness at Winchester, to march to the place of Rendezvous at the Day you shall order.

As the Gentlemen who have served in the Pay of this Colony have applyed to me in Council for Grants of the Lands, to which they claim a Right by proclamation of the late Lieutenant Governor; I must beg the Favour of you to procure me Copies of the Treaty made with the Indians by Brigr. General Forbes when he took possession of Pittsburgh, and of the Confirmation of it entered into by your self. For we cannot proceed to order such Grants till we know by Authority, what Right we have, consistent with those Treaties and Agreements: otherwise we may inadvertently draw in a Quarrel with the Indians, and alienate them from our Interest. I must likewise entreat you to use your Interest with the proprietarys Agent of Pensylvania, to stop them from doing, what we are so cautious of doing our selves; for fear of bad Consequences.

This will be delivered to you by Lieutenant Price a young Gentleman who has long served in our Regiment with Reputation, the Son of a Member of our general Assembly.[1] give me Leave to recommend him to you, and to assure you I shall at all times be ready to return any Civilities you shall think proper to shew him to any Friend of yours, being with the greatest Regard Sir Your most Obedient humble Servant

Fran: Fauquier

To Majr. Genl. Stanwix.

ALS: Library of Congress, Peter Force Papers, ser. VIII D, Vernon-Wager Papers, vol. 18, Papers of Robert Monckton, ff. 47089–90.

1. Leonard Price was an ensign in the Virginia Regiment as early as 1755 and was promoted to lieutenant in 1757; about the middle of 1760 he was appointed adjutant to the force raised for the relief of Fort Loudoun in Tennessee. Lieutenant Price's father was Thomas Price, one of the burgesses from Middlesex County.

From Thomas Pownall

[24 March 1760]

This letter has not been found. Fauquier communicated it to the council on 6 May 1760, and it is abstracted in *EJC* 6:157:

> The Governor was pleased to communicate to the Board a Letter from Governor Pownal dated March 24th requesting his Assistance towards relieving the Sufferers by the late dreadful Fire at Boston.

The council advised that the commissary prepare a brief suitable to the occasion to be read in all the churches in the colony. Pownall's proclamation of 24 Mar. 1760, in which he solicited contributions to relieve the distress of those who had suffered from the fire at Boston, noted that the fire had broken out on 20 Mar. and within a few hours had burned 174 dwelling houses and as many warehouses, shops, and other buildings, along with the furniture and goods they contained, leaving 220 families homeless and destroying property to the value of £100,000 sterling. A facsimile of the broadside is in Worthington Chauncey Ford, ed., *Broadsides, Ballads &c. Printed in Massachusetts 1639–1800* (Boston, 1922), facing p. 165.

From Abraham Maury

[Halifax County, 28 March 1760]

This letter has not been found. Fauquier communicated it to the council on 10 Apr. 1760, and it is abstracted in *EJC* 6:156:

> The Governor communicated a Letter he received last Week from Col. Maury dated Halifax County March 28th signifying that on the 26th of the said Month he was advised by an Express from Capt. William Satterwhite, living on Smith River, that the Indians had fallen upon the People settled at and near the Confluence of the Dan and Mayo, and taken and killed many Persons; informing what he had done and intended to do thereupon, till he received his Honor's Instructions.

It is assumed that Colonel Maury was Abraham Maury of Halifax County, a colonel in the militia. William Satterwhite, evidently a captain in the militia, lived on what is now called Smiths River, at that time in Halifax County but now in Henry County, which it crosses from the northwest to the southeast. The Indians had attacked settlers at or near what is now Madison, in Rockingham County, N.C., about 10 mi. south of the Virginia line.

From William Byrd

[Philadelphia, 30 March 1760]

This letter has not been found. Fauquier communicated it to the council on 10 Apr. 1760, and it is abstracted in *EJC* 6:156:

> The Governor also communicated a Letter from Col. Byrd, dated Philadelphia March 30th signifying he proposes being at Winchester on the 6th of April, and that he has Orders from General Amherst, to hold the Regiment in Readiness to march on the earliest Notice from him.

From Jeffery Amherst

Sir,   New York 31st March 1760

As the time mentioned in my Circular Letter of the 21st February for Assembling the Troops requested by His Majesty, from the Southern Provinces draws nigh, and that I then Acquainted You, I should Inform You of the place of Rendezvous, I should Appoint; I am, agreable thereto to give You Notice, that I have wrote to Major General Stanwix, to fix on such places as he shall think most proper and Convenient, for that purpose and that he do give You notice thereof; You will accordingly order the Troops of Your Province, or such part thereof as he Shall desire, to the place or places of Rendezvous, Which he Shall appoint, and to Cause them to be there on the days he Shall fix. I am, with great regard, Sir &ca

Jeff: Amherst

Copy: C.O.5/58, ff. 137–38. Circular addressed to the governors of Maryland, Pennsylvania, and Virginia (with a postscript addressed to Governor Sharpe, acknowledging a recent letter and hoping for news of what the Maryland assembly had done). Endorsed as being in Amherst's letter of 28 Apr. 1760.

To Andrew Lewis

[ca. April 1760]

This letter has not been found, but it is evident from *EJC* 6:156 that it conveyed orders to send eighty men, with officers, into Halifax County. See Maury's letter to Fauquier of 28 Mar. 1760 and Fauquier's reply of ca. April.

To Abraham Maury

[ca. April 1760]

This letter has not been found, but it answered Maury's letter of 28 Mar. 1760 and its contents are indicated in *EJC* 6:156:

His Honor acquainted the Council, that upon Receipt of the said Letter, he dispatched his Orders to Major Lewis to send Eighty Men immediately with proper Officers into Halifax to be stationed in the most advantageous Manner for protecting the Inhabitants there; which he judged more eligible than raising the Militia of the adjacent Counties; that he at the same time signified this to Col. Maury, telling him he might provide for the Subsistence of these Men upon the terms of his former Contract; and desired their Opinion if any more effectual Aid should be sent to the People in those Parts.

Maury's former contract was evidently the one into which he and the governor had entered in Nov. 1758, by the terms of which Maury was bound to supply the militia and rangers in the king's service in the counties of Bedford and Halifax until 1 May 1759. In March 1761 the House of Burgesses heard a petition from Maury which gave a brief account of the contract and requested compensation for the losses Maury had sustained in discharging the contract. See *JHB, 1758–1761*, p. 204.

From Thomas Bullitt

[ca. April 1760]

This letter has not been found. Fauquier communicated it to the council on 10 Apr. 1760, and it is abstracted in *EJC* 6:156–57:

> Also a Letter from Capt. Bullett, informing that several Soldiers belonging to the Virginia Regiment had overstaid their Furloughs, and may probably not return from an Apprehension of Punishment for such a Breach of Duty.

Thomas Bullitt (1730–1778), born in Stafford County, was an ensign in the Virginia Regiment in 1755, when he was promoted to lieutenant, and captain lieutenant in 1758, when he was promoted to captain.

From Jeffery Amherst

Sir, New York 1st April 1760

Altho' Your Letter bears date the 5th Ultimo, it did not reach my hands 'till the 29th of same Month, which is uncommonly long, considering it Came by my return Express, but he pleads the Impracticability of Crossing the Bays, and that he was detained twelve days at One of them; It is certain however, that Letters from You to Colonel Byrd, of a Subsequent date,[1] have been in Town these Eight days past, and that, in Consequence thereof, he Set out for Philadelphia on the 26th.

It gives me pleasure to find that Mr. Secretary Pitt, and my Letters, came so opportunely, since without them, You despaired of keeping together any Body of Men whatever; and I am in daily Expectations of receiving the Confirmation of Your hopes that the House have Approved of the Resolves of the Committee to keep up the Regiment; Upon the Strength of which, and the time drawing very near for the Assembling of the Troops, I Yesterday Wrote to M. General Stanwix at Philadelphia, to fix the Places of Rendezvous, & the days on which he would Chuse to have them there; desiring him, at the Same time, to give Notice thereof to the respective Governors, for whom I Enclosed him my Circular Letter, requesting their Compliance with his Requisition, which I here Renew, with the within Duplicate thereof.[2] I am, with great Regard, Sir, &ca.

Honble. Lt. Govr. Fauquier

Copy: W.O.34/37, f. 214. An extract, consisting of the second paragraph above, is in C.O.5/58, f. 119, endorsed as being in Amherst's letter of 28 Apr. 1760.

1. These letters have not been found.
2. Presumably Amherst enclosed a duplicate of his circular letter of 31 Mar. 1760.

From Jeffery Amherst

Sir, New York 1st April 1760

I Have already Acknowledged the Receipt of Your Public Letter of the 5th Ultimo, I am now to own Your Private one of the same date, and to thank You for what You have done in regard to my Patent; which I did not know it was Customary to Lodge in the Councill Office, or I should not have desired You to return it; however since it must remain in the Office, I shall be Obliged to You for an Attested Copy of it, for my Use: It must be a mistake not to have sent a Commission for me of Vice Admiral,[1] I shall Write for One, and Cause it to be transmitted to You directly from England.

Your disinterested Report of the Revenues of the Government, and the Method You propose for securing to me the Fifteen Hundred Pounds Sterling, a Year, I Asked of You, are so satisfactory to me, that for Your greater Ease, I shall leave the Whole to be settled, upon the Conditions You mention, between the Gentlemen, Your Brother and my Agent Mr. Calcraft; Wherefore You will be so good as to Write to the first, and I, on my part, will transmitt to the Latter, such part of Your Letter, as will be necessary for him to Come to a proper Settlement; and in my Instructions to him, I shall have a particular Regard to what You mention, in relation to when there are any, as at present, Arrears due by the Government, upon which Occasions, I very readily Agree to Your desire, of being One half Year under Another. I am, with the greatest Regard, Sir, &ca.

Honble. Lt. Govr. Fauquier

Copy: W.O.34/37, f. 213. Marked "Private."

1. For the commission of a vice admiral, see John Clevland to Fauquier, 14 Mar. 1758.

To Jeffery Amherst

Sir Wmsburgh April 5th 1760

In my Letter of the 5th March, I informed you of the Resolution of the House of Burgesses to keep up the Regiment. An Act has since pass'd

5 April 1760   343

for that Purpose, to provide for it till the first of November next upon the footing of the last Return which was 761 private Men. 300 of these I am obliged to keep on the South-West Frontiers for the Defence thereof; the rest are at Liberty to act in Conjunction with his Majestys Forces, as ordered by the Commander in chief, of all which I have apprized Major General Stanwix.

I have the further pleasure to acquaint you that the House of Burgesses, on my laying your Letter with Mr. Van Braams Account before them, voted him his Arrears of Pay as Captain, for which he may draw as he pleases:[1] and I have the greatest Reason to believe that, upon a future Application he will experience the Readiness of the general Assembly to recompense all their Officers, whose Merit and Sufferings, claim their Regard.

The Addresses of both Council and Burgesses fully express the Satisfaction they receive from his Majesty's having appointed you to be their Governor.[2] I am with the greatest Esteem Sir Your Excellency's most Obedient humble Servant

Fran: Fauquier

To his Exc. Majr. Genl. Amherst.

ALS: W.O.34/37, f. 37. An extract, consisting of the first paragraph of the letter above, is in C.O.5/58, ff. 121–22; it is endorsed as being in Amherst's letter of 28 Apr. 1760.

1. See Amherst's letter to Fauquier of 16 Nov. 1759, enclosing Van Braam's letter and account of 9 Nov. 1759.

2. On 5 Mar. 1760 the council in assembly agreed to an address to Fauquier which included an expression of its "great Satisfaction on his Majesty's Appointment of his Excellency General Amherst to be Governor in Chief of this Colony" (*LJC* 3:1234). The next day the House of Burgesses agreed to an address to Fauquier which included this sentence: "The Appointment of Major-General Amherst to be Governor and Commander in Chief of this Colony, cannot but give us great Satisfaction, since the Valor and Conduct of that able Commander, have long made him dear to us" (*JHB, 1758–1761*, p. 160).

Order in Council

[5 April 1760]

Upon reading a Report from the Right Honourable the Lords of the Committee of Council for hearing Appeals from the Plantations dated the 26th of last Month in the following Words Vizt:

Your Majesty having been pleased by Your Order in Council of the 16th of last

Month, to referr unto this Committee, the humble Petition of Thos. Edmundson and John Edmundson of the County of Essex in Your Majestys Colony of Virginia Merchants, humbly praying that they may be admitted to bring a Cross Appeal to Your Majesty in Council from two Decrees made in the General Court in Chancery in Virginia on the 10th of April, and 2d of October 1758 in favour of William Tabb, Humphry Toy Tabb, and Martha Tabb, in a Cause depending there relating to the Division of the Slaves and Personal Estate of Sarah Allaman deceased. The Lords of the Committee, in Obedience to your Majestys said Order of Reference, this day took the said Petition into Consideration, and heard the Petitioners by their Council thereupon, and do agree humbly to report to Your Majesty as their Oppinion that the Petitioners should be admitted to bring their Cross Appeal to your Majesty in Council from the said Decrees made in the General Court in Chancery in Virginia, on the 10th of April and 2d of October 1758, upon entering into the Usual Security here for prosecuting the same to Effect within a Year and a Day and abiding the Determination of Your Majesty in Council thereupon.

His Majesty this day took the said Report into Consideration and was Pleased with the advice of His Privy Council to approve thereof, and to Order as it is hereby Ordered that the said Thos. Edmundson and John Edmundson be admitted to bring their Cross Appeal to His Majesty in Council from the said Decrees made in the General Court of Chancery in Virginia on the 10th of April and 2d of October upon entering into the usual Security here for prosecuting the same to Effect within a Year and a day and Abiding the Determination of His Majesty in Council thereupon and paying such Costs as shall be awarded by His Majesty in Council in Case that said Appeal be dismissed. Whereof the Governor, Lieut. Governor or Commander in Chief of His Majestys said Colony of Virginia for the time being, and all others whom it may concern, are to take Notice and Govern themselves accordingly.

MS: P.C.2/107, pp. 310–30. Date of Privy Council session supplied. For a summary of this case and reference to related documents, see Smith, pp. 506–8.

Order in Council

[5 April 1760]

Whereas the Lieutenant Governor of his Majestys Colony of Virginia with the Council and Assembly of the said Colony Did in 1759 pass an Act which hath been Transmitted in the words following Vizt.

An Act to dock the Intail of certain Lands whereof Turnstal Banks is seized and for setling other Lands and certain Slaves therein mentioned of greater Value to the same uses.¹

Memd. Here the Act was inserted at length.

Which Act having been perused and considered by the Lords Commissioners for Trade and Plantations and by them presented to his Majesty at this Board as fit to be confirmed. His Majesty was this Day pleased with the Advice of his Privy Council to declare his Approbation hereof And pursuant to his Majestys Royal Pleasure thereupon expressed the said Act is hereby confirmed finally Enacted and ratified accordingly whereof the Governor Lieutenant Governor or Commander in Chief of his Majestys said Colony of Virginia for the Time being and all others whom it may concern are to take Notice and govern themselves accordingly.²

MS: P.C.2/107, p. 333. Date of Privy Council session supplied.

1. The act (Hening, 7:293–96) enabled Tunstal Banks to break the entail on the residue of a parcel of about 1,200 acres, called Mantapike, in St. Stephen's Parish, King and Queen County, and to replace it by a thousand acres in St. David's Parish, King William County, and seventeen named slaves (or the survivors) with their children.

2. This order was produced in the meeting of the council of Virginia on 15 Dec. 1769 and ordered to be recorded in the secretary's office; see *EJC* 6:339.

Proclamation

[ca. 11 April 1760]

On 10 Apr. 1760 the council considered a letter from Captain Bullitt reporting that several soldiers of the Virginia Regiment had overstayed their furloughs and probably would not return to duty because they apprehended punishment. The council thereupon ordered that a proclamation issue to promise pardon to all such soldiers who joined the regiment at Winchester by 10 May. See *EJC* 6:156–57. No copy of the proclamation has been found, and the date is a conjecture.

To Horatio Sharpe

Sir Wmsburgh April 12th 1760

This will be delivered to you by Mr. Fox who is going into Maryland with a Hue & Cry from me to look after a Mulatto Slave belonging to Colonel Bernard Moore of this Colony,¹ who has received Intelligence of his being now on Board some Ship in Maryland. If any Orders from you to the Justices of your Colony should be necessary to secure him I take the Liberty to beg your Assistance, or if the Expences should exceed his Stock of mony, I will be answerable for any Sum, you will draw upon me for in favour of Mr. Fox. Colonel Moore being a Gentleman of Note in this Colony for whom I have a great personal Regard. I am with great Esteem, Sir, Your Excellency's most obedient humble Servant.

Fran: Fauquier

P.S. When you write to Dr. Gregory Sharpe, I should be much obliged to you to enquire what is become of Sir Isaac Newtons papers relating to the History of the two first Centuries of Christianity. I am solicitous about their Fate.[2]

ALS: Hall of Records of Maryland, Executive Papers, Folder 141.

1. Mr. Fox has not been identified. Bernard Moore, of King William County, was a justice of the peace, colonel of militia, and one of the burgesses from his county in the assemblies of 1744–58 and 1761–72.
2. The papers that Fauquier mentioned cannot be identified satisfactorily with any of Newton's theological or chronological writings, and no explanation of Fauquier's interest in the papers has been discovered, beyond his statement (in a letter of 28 July 1760 to Horatio Sharpe) that he and Dr. Gregory Sharpe had often talked about Newton's papers.

From William Bull

[12 April 1760]

This letter has not been found. Fauquier communicated it to the council on 7 May 1760, and it is abstracted in *EJC* 6:158:

His Honor communicated to the Board a Letter from the Honble William Bull Esqr. Lieutenant-Governor of South-Carolina, dated April 12th advising that the War is certainly become general with all the Cherokees on this Side of the Mountains—acquainting what their Assembly has done—and what Numbers the Army to be employed under Col. Montgomery against the Cherokees will consist of.

From James Abercromby

Sir   April 14th 1760

In my last I informed you of my Intention to apply with the rest of the American Agents for a further Supply from Parliament, which being done, a Vote is accordingly passed for £200,000 to the several Provinces for *Levying Pay* and *Cloathing* of Troops in 1759.[1] Having no particular Instructions thereon I must have Recourse to the Acts & Journals in the

Plantation Office for Vouchers to support our Claim to the due Proportion thereof from the Treasury, which being done, it will rest with you and the Council to send me proper Powers to receive this Money as well as that for which I have the King's Warrant as heretofore told you.

This with many other Negociations of late give ample Proof that the Affairs of Virginia are altogether in my hands without the least Interposition, or so much as the Appearance of any other Person on the Part of the Province.

You may easily conceive how much you & the [Council] had been blamed by the Administration here, and how m[uch the] Province had been injured by throwing your Affairs, co[ncerned] as they are with National Measures, and with the gen[eral] Preservation of His Majesty's Dominions into so precarious [a] Channel as that depending on the Operation of the Agency Law which is attended with so many Objections, and rendered moreover precarious from the Uncertainty of a Gentleman in Mr. Montague's Situation in Life, taking upon him the Charge of such Business, many had been the Inconveniencies to the Publick, and great the Prejudice to your Administration had I not stood my Ground in the Management of your Publick Affairs, & therein Conducted myself with due Consistency to the King's Service, and to that of the Province as you will see by the Attorney General's Opinion, by the Testimony of the Board of Trade & by Mr. Secretary Pitts Letter in my Favour Copy whereof I ommitted to send you in my last Letter, Standing on such Ground I hope the Assembly will not press the Operation of the Agency Law in any Respect to my Prejudice, whose Cause the Attorney General plainly points out to be the Case of Government, and must be treated accordingly. So soon as I have received the Proportion of the 50,000, I shall notify the same to you for your Instructions as to the Application thereof to the Use of the Legislature agreable to my Security given for so doing. I am &ca.

J.A.

Gov. Fauquiere.

Copy: Virginia State Library, James Abercromby Letter Book, pp. 203–3A. In a clerk's hand. A piece is torn from the outer edge of the leaf, and what is assumed to be the missing text is supplied, in brackets.

1. On 31 Mar. 1760 a committee of the whole House of Commons resolved: "That a Sum, not exceeding Two hundred thousand Pounds, be granted to his Majesty, upon Account, to enable his Majesty to give a proper Compensation to the respective Provinces in North America, for the Expences incurred by them, in the Levying, Clothing and Pay, of the Troops raised by the same, according as the active Vigour and strenuous Efforts of the respective Provinces shall be thought by his Majesty to merit."

From Jeffery Amherst

Sir   New York 20th April 1760

I Learn with pleasure, by Your Letter of the 5th Instant, that an Act has passed for keeping up the Regiment of Virginia, but I must own I should have been much more pleased, for the honor of the Assembly, as well as the Public good, that they had resolved to Compleat the Regiment to its Original Numbers, & that they had not Limitted its Service to the first of November; First, by reason of the great Drawback You mention of 300 which You are obliged to keep on the South West Frontiers; And next, because We are not Certain (tho' I am hopefull) their Service can be dispensed with at that period; but I am less Embarrassed at the former of these Resolves, because, as I mentioned to You in my last Letter, having sent a sufficient Body of Troops to Carolina to punish the perfidiousness of the Cherokees,[1] I have not the least Doubt, but You will soon be freed of all Apprehensions from those Quarters, and that those Three Hundred Men abovementioned, will be at Liberty to Join their Corps to Act in Conjunction with them.

I Beg You would tender my thanks to the House of Burgesses for what they have done, at my Instance, in favor of Mr. Van Braam, who, by the first Opportunity, shall be Acquainted therewith.

I must also Recommend to You, my most Sincere Acknowledgements to the Council & Burgesses for the Satisfaction they are pleased to Express, in their Addresses, at His Majesty's having Appointed me their Governor. I am, with great Regard, Sir, &ca.

Honble. Lt. Govr. Fauquier.

Copy: W.O.34/37, f. 215. An extract, consisting of the first paragraph above, is in C.O.5/58, ff. 123–24; it is endorsed as being in Amherst's letter of 28 Apr. 1760.

1. Amherst mentioned the dispatch of troops to South Carolina in his letter of 17 Mar. 1760 to Fauquier.

To Peter Wyche

Dear Sir,   Williamsburgh 22d Apll 1760.

I immediately on the Receipt of your Letter of the 5th of Feby. communicated the Contents of it & of Mr. Box's Letter to Dr. Garden of Carolina & to Colonell Ludwell who was then in Town, & who assured me he would write to you himself by this Ship, & inform you that he is certain he never had the true Cephalonian & Zant Corinth Grape, & the Disappointment he received after he had been promised it by a Gentleman inhabiting one of those Islands.[1] Colonell Ludwell as well as Several other ingenious Curious Gentlemen in this Colony are Intent on trying all Experiments which promise mutual Advantage to this & their Mother Country. An Act of Assembly has lately passed here to give Premiums for the Encouragement of all new Products, & a Committee is appointed to regulate this Affair & correspond with your Society in England.[2] As soon as Colonel Charles Carter the Chairman of this Committee comes to Town,[3] I will give him these Letters which will infuse new Life to your Schemes, under the Advice & Direction of your Board he is the properest Man to try Experiments, particularly in the Products of the Earth, Industrious & very Intent on What he is about, & may be depended upon. He is a Man of Parts as you will find by the Correspondence which my Shewing him your Letters will I am sure produce between Your Society & him. The Multiplicity of Affairs in Which I am engaged during the Continuance of War, & the great Attendance I am forced to give & hear the Business of Others will I am affraid render me incapable of forwarding your laudable Designs for the good of the Whole any otherwise than being the Channell of Correspondence Which Office I believe I can perform better than any Body here, as I can better inform You, Who will be the proper Persons to employ in any particular Pursuit; but I beg of you to assure your Society that in every Shape in my Power I shall always be ready to serve them, therefore desire they would not be scrupulous about Writing to me on any Occasions in Which They think I can promote their good Intentions.

Copy: Royal Society of Arts, Guard Book, vol. 4, no. 141. Headed: "Part of a Letter wrote to Peter Wyche Esq: from his Excellency Francis Fauquier Esq: Governor of Virginia in answer to What the Society desired might be done in America relative to the Planting the Zant & Cephalonian Grapes in those Parts." After the extract is a note that the letter was received by Mr. Wyche on 13 June 1760 and communicated to the society on 17 June 1760; the latter date may be 16 or 18 June, since the photocopy of the original is not clear.

1. George Box served the Society of Arts from Jan. 1756 until his retirement in 1779; he was secretary or assistant secretary for the whole period, and collector for some time until 1771. Dr. Alexander Garden (ca. 1730–1791), a naturalist and physician, who emigrated to South Carolina about 1753 and remained there until he was banished as a loyalist, was the first colonial corresponding member of the society. He was elected in Mar. 1755 and at once began a brisk correspondence with the society on the cultivation of vines, a machine for pounding rice, and other topics; it is likely that the letter to Garden from Box concerned currants, a subject on which the society wrote to Garden in late January 1760. Philip Ludwell did write to the society, on 21 Apr. 1760, about the "true Curran Grape of Zant" and other matters (society's Guard Book, vol. 4, no. 140).

2. This was "An Act for encouraging Arts and Manufactures," passed in the session of Feb. 1759; see Fauquier's address to the assembly, enclosed in his letter of 14 Apr. 1759 to the Board of Trade.

3. Col. Charles Carter (1707–1764) of Cleve, in King George County, was a member of the House of Burgesses for his county from 1736 until his death. For an extended account of Carter's dealings with the society, see Robert Leroy Hilldrup, "A Campaign to Promote the Prosperity of Colonial Virginia," *VMHB* 67 (1959):410–28.

From Arthur Dobbs

[24 April 1760]

This letter has not been found. Fauquier communicated it to the council on 7 May 1760, and it is abstracted in *EJC* 6:158:

> Also a Letter from Governor Dobbs dated April 24th signifying that their Assembly met that Day, he hopes, with a Disposition of raising what Troops they can, to act against the Cherokees.

This is evidently the letter which Fauquier transmitted to the House of Burgesses on 19 May 1760; see *JHB, 1758–1761*, p. 172.

From Jeffery Amherst

Sir,   New York 28th April 1760

Major General Stanwix having obtained His Majesty's Leave to go home, and he intending shortly to set out for England, I have given the Command of the Forces, that are now, and shall serve during the Ensueing Campaign, in the Southern District, to the Honble. Brig. General Monckton,[1] Who is on his Departure for Philadelphia and will take upon him the said Command, whenever M. Genl. Stanwix quits that place; I have therefore now to beg of You, that so soon as the Brigadier will have informed You of his Acting in that Capacity, You will Correspond, and Co-operate with him, in the same manner as You have done with M. Genl. Stanwix, and that You will give him all the Aid and Assistance he may, from time to time, require of You, for the good of the Service. I am, with great regard, Sir, &ca.

                                                                        Jeff: Amherst

Copy: C.O.5/58, ff. 100–101. Circular addressed to the governors of Pennsylvania, Maryland, Virginia, North Carolina, South Carolina, and Georgia. Endorsed as being in Amherst's letter of 19 May 1760.

1. Robert Monckton (1726–1782) was the second son of Viscount Galway.

May 1760

From William Bull

[Charles Town, 28 April 1760]

This letter has not been found. Fauquier communicated it to the council on 8 May 1760, and it is abstracted in *EJC* 6:159:

> His Honor was pleased to communicate a Letter from Governor Bull, dated Charles Town Aprll 28th signifying the Necessity of an immediate Relief from this Government to the Garrison at Fort Loudoun in the Cherokee Country, all Communication being cut off with South-Carolina; and desiring to know by Express what he proposes to do on the approaching Extremity.

Fauquier mentioned this letter in his address to the General Assembly on 19 May 1760 and transmitted it to the House of Burgesses the same day; see *JHB, 1758–1761*, pp. 171–72.

From Thomas Walker

[29 April 1760]

This letter has not been found. Fauquier communicated it to the council on 6 May 1760, and it is abstracted in *EJC* 6:157:

> His Honor also communicated a Letter from Mr. Commissary Walker, dated April 29th signifying it is not in his Power to victual Troops in the Manner they have been victualed for 6d. per Day during the Months of May, June, and July.

The council advised that 8d. per day should be allowed to Walker for those months.

To William Bull

[ca. May 1760]

This letter has not been found, but Fauquier told the assembly on 19 May 1760 that he had written it, no doubt in reply to Bull's letter of 28 Apr. 1760. See *JHB, 1758–1761*, p. 171.

To Arthur Dobbs

[ca. May 1760]

This letter has not been found, but Fauquier told the assembly on 19 May 1760 that he had written it, apparently in reply to Dobbs's letter of 24 Apr. 1760; see *JHB, 1758–1761*, p. 171.

To John Stanwix

[ca. 3 May 1760]

This letter has not been found, but Fauquier remarked in his letter of 3 May 1760 to Amherst that he was writing a few lines to Stanwix by the same conveyance, probably to inform him that the Virginia troops would be ready for his orders.

To Jeffery Amherst

Sir   Wmsburgh May 3d 1760

Since I had the pleasure of writing you, I must acknowledge the Receipt of your Favours of 31st March, of 1st and 20th instant. Tho I have nothing material to communicate to you I would not omit the Opportunity of Col. Hunter,[1] to assure you that nothing shall be wanting on my Part to assist his Majesty's Forces with every Man I can legally send to join them, but the extreme Caution of (I believe) all the Assemblys on this Continent leave little in the power of their Governors. I shall take Care that our little Corps shall be ready to obey Mr. Stanwix's Orders to whom I write a few Lines by this Conveyance. I am with the greatest Esteem Sir Your most Obedient humble Servant

                                                                            Fran: Fauquier

To Majr. Genl. Amherst.

ALS: W.O.34/37, f. 38. A copy is in C.O.5/58, ff. 57–58, endorsed as received in Amherst's letter of 21 June 1760.

1. This was probably Col. John Hunter of Elizabeth City County.

To James Hamilton

Sir   Williamsburgh May 7th 1760

My Predecesser Mr. Dinwiddie, by Authority of his Majesty Notifyed by one of his principal Secretary's of State; issued a proclamation to encourage persons to engage in the Services then proposed to be carried on against Fort du Quesne, and other French Settlements on the Waters of the Ohio. In this proclamation he promised a grant of 200,000 Acres of Land on the east Side of that River, to be apportioned to the Officers and private Men who should voluntarily enter into that Service, 100,000 of which were to be contiguous to Pittsburgh or Fort du Quesne, the other 100,000 on some other part of that River.

In consequence of this promise by Authority, The Officers and Men who served on the Ohio have laid in their Claims to me in Council, to have these Lands immediately granted to them, which they say they have merited at the Hazards of their Health and Lives.[1]

But some Difficulties arising, from the Bounds of your Colony not being settled, and from the treaties which it is said Genl. Forbes made and Genl. Stanwix has since confirmed with the Indians inhabiting that Country (but which I have not yet seen), This Colony has done nothing in that Affair.

I have also to inform you that about three Months since I wrote to the right Honble. the Board of Trade and Plantations: in which Letter I informed them of these Claims; and of the Difficulties which attended our granting these Lands; desiring at the same Time that Commissioners might be appointed by the Crown to settle the Extent of your Line which is to run 5 Degrees due West from Delaware Bay in the Latitude of 40 North: and that the proprietors of Pensylvania or Maryland might be restrained from Making any Grants of Lands, which from our Scrupulous Observance of Treaties &ct. we did not think proper to make our selves, till his Majesty's pleasure was known thereon on which Head I desired I might have Instructions as soon as conveniently could be.[2]

By advice of his Majesty's Council, on these Consideration's I have postponed the Making of any Grants of the Lands in Question, till I receive Directions from Home relative thereto.[3] And that a perfect Harmony and Unanimity may at all times subsist between the Sister Colonies of the same Common Mother on which the Safety and Security of all depend, I have to request you that you on your parts, would, as we have on ours postpone the granting those Lands till such Instructions arrive which shall be immediately made known to you. And if you shall already have made any such Grants, I beg the Favour of you to inform me thereof, as to the Quantity, the Situation and the Names of the Grantees. I am with the greatest Regard Sir Your very humble Servant

Fran: Fauquier

To Govr. Hamilton[4]

LS: C.O.5/1330, ff. 6–7. Copy with the latter part of the complimentary close and the signature in Fauquier's hand. Endorsed as received with Fauquier's letter of 12 May 1760 and read 19 Nov. 1760.

1. There is no record in the council journals that any claims for the lands offered by Dinwiddie's proclamation of 19 Feb. 1754 had been submitted to the governor and council during Fauquier's administration or that the council had advised Fauquier to postpone any grants of those lands.

2. Fauquier refers to passages from his letters to the Board of Trade of 1 Dec. 1759 and 13 Mar. 1760.

3. See n. 1 above.

4. James Hamilton (ca. 1710–1783) was lieutenant governor of Pennsylvania 1748–54 and 1759–63.

From Robert Monckton

Sir: Philadelphia, the 7th May, 1760

Being appointed by Major General Amherst to The Command of the Forces that are to Serve in the Southern District of North America, I am to acquaint you of my Arrival here, and of Major General Stanwix (who remains here some Days to Settle His Accounts) having given up the Command to me.

As the Service the Forces of the Southern Provinces are to be Employed in, requires the utmost Dispatch, I have not the least doubt but the Troops of your Province will Rendezvous at the Time (or as soon after as can be) & places appointed by Major General Stanwix.

I shall be happy, Sir, in concurring with you in any Steps for the Advancement of His Majesty's Service. I am, Sir, Your most obedient, and most humble Servant,

Robt. Monckton

Printed: *Pa. Arch.* [1], 3:732–33. In his letter of 24 May 1760 to Monckton, Fauquier acknowledged a letter announcing Monckton's appointment to command in the southern colonies; it is assumed that Fauquier received a copy of a circular letter, identical (except for the address) with that above, sent to Governor Hamilton of Pennsylvania. No manuscript copy of the letter has been traced.

To Jeffery Amherst

Sir   Wmsburgh May 8th 1760

Having already answered your public Letter, I take the Opportunity of giving an Answer to your private one of the 1st of April of which I have already sent a Copy to my Brother for his Agreement with Mr.

Calcraft. The Government have paid me to the 25th of October last past, and left the Arrear of one half year to the 25th April still unpaid.¹ I shall remit £750 to my Brother by a Ship which will sail the beginning of next Week, by which he will be enabled to clear off Lord Loudoun to the 25th September, and to pay what is due to you to the 25 October. If any payments should be made to me during the running half year, I will remitt them to him for your Use having no Occasion for them here.

I have given Orders for an attested Copy to be taken of your Commission which I shall take Care to transmit to you: and have signifyed your Thanks to the Council: I shall do the same to the Speaker of the House of Burgesses when they meet, which I have summoned them to do immediately in hopes they will enable me to Succour Fort Loudoun in the upper Cherokee Country. I am with the greatest Esteem Sir Your Excellency's most Obedient humble Servant

Fran: Fauquier

To Majr. Genl. Amherst.

ALS: W.O.34/37, f. 39. Marked "Private."

1. On 7 May 1760 Fauquier had signed a warrant for payment of the governor's salary for the half year to 25 Apr. 1760 (see *EJC* 6:158). It is possible that actual payment of the salary was deferred, for receipts on the account of 2s. per hogshead for the period 25 Oct. 1759–25 Apr. 1760 were only about half the amount of disbursements, and were in fact not quite enough to discharge the debit carried over from the preceding account; see app. C for 1760.

From James Abercromby

Sir   May 10th 1760

It is by Chance I hear of an Opportunity in the Downs to inform you that on the 8th Inst. the £50,000 so long depending was then issued to the Respective Agents, the Proportion for Virginia to me, amounting to £32268.19 as per Account inclosed,¹ I know of no farther Charges on your Government except Mr. Sharps Bill,² which I reckon to be about £50, but I choose, rather than keep the Account open for this Article, to ascertain the Ballance as it now stands, which Ballance, by the Bonds given by the Agents (Copy whereof I send you)³ you will please to observe is to be paid to such Persons as the Governor Council and Assembly shall direct to receive the same, I am therefore to wait their Orders accordingly. Of all the Solicitations I ever was engaged in, this has proved the most tedious and troublesome, owing greatly to the Difficultys and Delay given us by a certain Noble Lord,[4] whose Approbation to our Claim became Necessary. Mr. Montague in Consequence of a Letter I had wrote him some time since, has been in Town and as he seems inclinable to act under the Agency Law I have thereupon informed him, that I shall very readily concurr with him for the Publick Service, reserving to myself the Liberty Nevertheless of acting alone where particular Instructions from the Governor and Council shall require it. Be pleased to Communicate this with the inclosed to the Council. & beleve me to be very sincerly Sir your most obedient Servant

J.A.

Gov. Fauquiere.

Copy: Virginia State Library, James Abercromby Letter Book, p. 204. A marginal note apparently reads "Original per Bristol per Mr Hanburys care Duplicate per Passenger from London per Mr Wrights Convoy Triplicate to the Virginia Coffee House in July." Fauquier must have communicated this letter to the council on 16 Sept. 1760, although it is not cited by date. See *EJC* 6:169. It is probably one of the letters Fauquier mentioned in his address to the assembly on 6 Oct. and sent to the House of Burgesses the same day; see *JHB, 1758–1761*, pp. 184–85.

1. This amount is £546 less than that which Abercromby had stated in his letters of 15 Feb. and 20 Mar. 1760. Nothing has been found to explain the reduction in Virginia's share of the grant, but see the error of £546 in Abercromby's addition in his letter of 20 Mar. 1760.
2. Mr. Sharp has not been identified, but he was perhaps Joshua Sharpe, a solicitor of Lincoln's Inn often engaged in suits and other business involving colonials and the colonies; and this Joshua Sharpe was probably the brother of Gov. Horatio Sharpe of Maryland.
3. Abercromby must have sent copies of bonds given by himself, by James Wright the agent for South Carolina, and by Samuel Smith the agent for North Carolina. No form of the bonds has been found.
4. The earl of Loudoun.

Enclosure: Agent's Account

[ca. 8 May 1760]

James Abercromby Esqr. doth Charge himself with the Money received from the Exchequer being the Proportion due to the Province of Virginia out of the 50,000 granted by Parliament in 1757 to Virginia North & South Carolina Vizt.

1760		
May 8th	Received on Account of Virginia	£32268.19.—
	Whereof He discharges himself as follows Vizt.	
Jany. 29th	To Lord Loudoun's Secretary &ca on Receiving His Lordships Approbation on the Virginia Claim	1.14. 6
May 6th	Paid Mr. Tomkins & Messengers at the Treasury Fees on the Warrant &ca[1]	21.—.—
	Paid Mr. Jennins at the Auditor of the Exchequers Office Fees &ca.[2]	39.15.—
	Paid at the Pell Office Fees &ca[3]	17.11.—
	Paid Do. at the Tellers Office[4]	80. 2. 6
	Paid for the Sign Manual[5]	14.—
	By Commission or Agency at the usual Rate of 2½ Per Cent on the £32268.19	806.14.—
	By Mr. Abercromby's Salary from 25 April 1759 to Do. 1760, retained out of this Money, and to be allowed, and made good to this Money by the Governor's Warrant on the Tobacco Duty at £200 Per Annum[6]	200.—.—
	By Money due to Mr. Abercromby from the Government of Virginia for Fees at Offices paid by him & not repaid (the said Disbursements being made at sundry times from 1753 to 25 April 1760) by the Province[7]	88.19.—
	By Expences of Travelling (Horse hire included) being 4 Days to Ld. Loudoun's House, in order to Settle Matters with his Lordship[8]	5. 5.—
	Paid Mr. Francis for Bond of Security &ca[9]	3. 3.—
	Paid Fees to Council &ca in Mr Camms Case[10]	13.13.—
	Discharge	£ 1278.11. 0
	Ballance due to Virginia	£30990. 8.—
		£32268.19. 0

Copy: Virginia State Library, James Abercromby Letter Book, p. 205b. Enclosed in Abercromby's letter of 10 May 1760 to Fauquier.

1. Thomas Tompkins was under clerk at the Treasury 1742–76. Probably he was the Treasury official who originated the warrant for payment of Virginia's share of the grant from Parliament.

2. Mr. Jennins probably was the official in the office of the auditor of the Exchequer who entered the Virginia warrant upon its arrival from the Treasury.

3. The warrant passed (though perhaps not directly) from the auditor of the Exchequer to the clerk of the pells (which were the parchment records of receipt and disbursement kept at the Exchequer).

4. The warrant was endorsed by the clerk of the pells and passed on to the teller, who made the payment directed by the warrant.

5. Perhaps the Virginia warrant was drawn up in the form of a royal sign manual.

6. No record has been found of an agreement whereby Abercromby was to withhold his salary and expenses from this grant. The warrant for his salary of £100 from 25 Apr. to 25 Oct. 1759 had been signed on 6 Nov. 1759, but probably the salary had not been paid because there was a large deficit in the 2s. per hogshead account; Abercromby no doubt assumed that payment of his salary for 25 Oct. 1759–25 Apr. 1760 (the warrant for which had been signed on 7 May 1760) would likewise be delayed.

7. The relation between this account and an earlier account for £196.7.0 submitted by Abercromby is puzzling, since it appears that nothing had been paid on the earlier account; see Abercromby's letter of 28 Dec. 1758 to Fauquier, n. 4.

8. Loudoun's house was presumably Loudoun Castle, in Ayrshire, about 20 mi. southwest of Glasgow. Abercromby's residence in Scotland was at Brucefield in Clackmannanshire, about 27 mi. northeast of Glasgow. It is likely that Abercromby traveled from Brucefield to Loudoun's house, for he could hardly have done the trip of over 300 mi. from London within four days.

9. Mr. Francis has not been identified, but he may have been the Thomas Francis who was assistant solicitor to the Treasury 1750–81 and seems also to have had a private practice.

10. After John Camm was dismissed from his appointment of professor of divinity at the College of William and Mary, he procured a mandamus (dated 4 Nov. 1758) directing the governor or visitors of the college to reinstate him or show cause at the General Court. On 10 Oct. 1759 the General Court quashed the writ, and Camm appealed to the Privy Council to reverse the judgment. Presumably the counsel to whom Abercromby paid fees were Charles Yorke (1722–1770), who was solicitor general 1756–61, and Alexander Forrester (ca. 1711–1787); both barristers were counsel for the respondents when the Privy Council heard Camm's appeal in 1763.

To the Board of Trade

My Lords   Wmsburgh May 12th 1760

I inclose in this Box to your right Honble. Board the Acts of the last Session of Assembly which broke up the 11th of March, the Journals of the Council and Burgesses, The Minutes of the Council since the Departure of the late Lieutenant Governor, The Accounts of the Receiver General, and of the Naval Officers.[1] With the Duplicates of the Acts and

12 May 1760 359

Journals of the former Session.² I hope your Lordships will not accuse me of remisness in the Discharge of my Duty, for I cannot get the Acts and Journals sooner out of the respective Offices.

The Cherokees having immediately broke the Peace made with them by Governor Lyttelton before his Departure, and having taken up Arms throughout all their Towns; Mr. Bull has applyed to this Colony for assistance, particularly for Succour for the Garrison of Fort Loudoun in the upper Cherokee Country.

As I was not in a Capacity to send them any Relief by the powers vested in me by the general assembly I have by and with the advice of his Majesty's Council call'd the assembly to meet again on Monday the 19th instant, the Result of which I will give your Lordships the earliest Information of.

The affair of granting the Lands on the Ohio grows every Day of more Importance; for which Reason, I crave your Lordships Excuse for again mentioning that affair, and for begging Leave to refer your Lordships to my Letters of the 1st December & 13th March on this Subject. I have wrote fully to Governor Hamilton upon these Matters, a Copy of which Letter I inclose to your Lordships.³ I am with the highest Regard and Respect My Lords Your Lordships most Obedient Obliged and devoted Servant

Fran: Fauquier

To the Rt. Honble. the Lords of Trade &ct.

ALS: C.O. 5/1330, ff. 4A–5. Endorsed as read 19 Nov. 1760.

1. The acts of the session of 4–11 Mar. 1760 (Hening, 7:347–56) were presumably the manuscript copies in C.O. 5/1399, ff. 76–81, but conceivably the printed version, Evans 8754. The journal of the council in assembly for that session was evidently the manuscript in C.O.5/1429, ff. 229–33, and the corresponding journal of the burgesses the manuscript in C.O.4/1429, ff. 220–28 (or conceivably the printed version, Evans 8757). The executive journal of the council was that for the period 2 Jan. 1758–8 May 1760, probably the manuscript in C.O.5/1429, ff. 165–203. The accounts were apparently the accounts of the revenue of 2s. per hogshead for 25 Oct. 1758–25 Apr. 1759 (C.O.5/1330, ff. 12–12A, a duplicate of one already sent in Fauquier's letter of 9 June 1759 to the Board of Trade), for 25 Apr.–25 Oct. 1759 (C.O.5/1330, ff. 13–14), and for 25 Oct. 1759–25 Apr. 1760 (C.O.5/1330, ff. 15–16) and the quitrent account for 1758 (C.O.5/1330, ff. 10–11). See apps. A-C for 1760 for these last three accounts. The Board of Trade journal indicates that the naval officers' returns were these, all in C.O.5/1448: for York River, 24 June–25 Dec. 1759 (f. 6); for Upper James, 10 Oct. 1759–5 Apr. 1760 (ff. 40 and 37); for Hampton, 29 Sept. 1759–25 Mar. 1760 (ff. 3, 23), and the separate return of 25 Oct. 1759–25 Apr. 1760 for Portugal, Madeira, and the West Indies (f. 4); for South Potomack, 10 Oct. 1759–5 Apr. 1760 (ff. 9,26).

2. The former session was that of 1–21 Nov. 1759, the journals of which Fauquier had sent to the Board of Trade with his letter of 17 Dec. 1759. See n. 1 to that letter; probably the journal of the council in assembly in C.O.5/1429, ff. 157–64, went with

this letter of 12 May 1760. The Board of Trade journal does not indicate that the six acts passed in the session of 1–21 Nov. 1759 (Hening, 7:331–45) accompanied either Fauquier's letter of 17 Dec. 1759 or this letter of 12 May 1760, but there is a printed version of the acts (Evans 8510) in C.O.5/1399, ff. 75–78, which may have come with either letter.
   3. The letter of 7 May 1760 to Hamilton.

To the Treasury

My Lords   Wmsburgh May 12th 1760

   I herewith transmitt to Your Lordships The Accounts of his Majesty's Receiver General both as to the Receipt of the Quit Rents due to his Majesty and the Duty of 2 shgs. Pr. Hhd on Tobacco exported for the Support of Government here, in the last of which Your Lordships will observe an increasing Deficiency. I am with the greatest Respect My Lords Your Lordships most Obedient & devoted humble Servant

                                                                    Fran: Fauquier

To the Rt. Honble. the Lords Commissioners of Treasury

ALS: C.O.5/1330, ff. 8–9. Endorsed as read 19 Nov. 1760 and, apparently, as having enclosures. It is not clear why this letter is in the files of the Board of Trade. It may have covered a set of accounts duplicating those sent in the letter of the same date to the Board of Trade: Art. 34 of the instructions to Loudoun and Amherst directed that copies of an account of the royal revenues be sent every half year to the Treasury and to the Board of Trade (C.O.5/1367, ff. 106–7).

To Jeffery Amherst

Sir   Wmsburgh May 18th 1760

   Mr. Turner[1] has left this City some Time since, and as I am informed, is gone for New York to pay his Respects to you there. As I thought this Letter from you to him might contain some thing of Consequence, I have thought it adviseable to return it to you, not knowing when I should have the pleasure of seeing Mr. Turner again. I hope this Step I have taken will be attended with no bad Consequences either to you or Mr. Turner. I am with the greatest Esteem Sir Your Excellency's most Obedient humble Servant

                                                                  Fran: Fauquier

To his Excellency Majr. Gen. Amherst.

ALS: W.O.34/37, f. 40.
   1. This was perhaps George Turner, an Indian agent.

From Robert Monckton

[Philadelphia, 18 May 1760]

This letter has not been found. Fauquier communicated it to the council on 11 June 1760, along with another letter of 19 May from Monckton, and the two letters are abstracted in *EJC* 6:159–60:

> The Governour was pleased to communicate to the Board two Letters from General Moncton dated Philadelphia May 18th and 19th signifying he shall send an Order to Colo. Byrd to March to Pittsburg with that part of the Virginia Regiment destin'd to serve under him; that he is sorry the Incursions of the Indians should require the keeping three hundred of that Regiment on our southern Frontiers; that he is of opinion no Lands West of the Allegany Mountain should as yet be granted to any Person.

From Robert Monckton

[Philadelphia, 19 May 1760]

This letter has not been found: see Monckton's letter of 18 May 1760 to Fauquier for an abstract.

To William Byrd

[ca. 20 May 1760]

This letter has not been found, but Fauquier's letter of 24 May 1760 to Monckton stated that he had summoned Byrd to take command of the Cherokee expedition. These orders to Byrd were presumably sent about 20 May 1760, or just as soon as the House of Burgesses had resolved to raise men and money for the relief of Fort Loudoun.

Order in Council

[20 May 1760]

Whereas the Lieutenant Governor of His Majestys Colony of Virginia with the Council and Assembly of the said Colony, did in October 1758, and April 1759 pass three Acts which have been transmitted, Entitled as follows: Vizt.

An Act for vesting certain Lands therein mentioned in Philip Johnson Gentleman adding the same to the City of Williamsburg and for other Purposes therein mentioned.[1]

Passed in October 1758

An Act for vesting certain Lands in the County of Hanover in Philip Whitehead Claiborne Gentleman in Fee simple and for other Purposes therein mentioned.[2]

Passed in April 1759

An Act to enable the Executors of the Will of John Spotswood Esqr. to pay the Debts and Legacies due from the Estate of Major General Alexander Spotswood and for other Purposes therein mentioned.[3]

Passed in April 1759

And Whereas the said Acts together with a Representation from the Lords Commissioners for Trade and Plantations proposing the Repeal thereof having been referred to the Consideration of a Committee of his Majestys most Honourable Privy Council for Plantation Affairs the said Lords of the Committee did this Day report as their Opinion to his Majesty that the said Acts ought to be repealed. His Majesty taking the same into Consideration was pleased with the Advice of His Privy Council to declare his Disallowance of the said Acts and pursuant to his Majestys Royal Pleasure thereupon Expressed the said Acts are hereby repealed, declared void, and of none Effect, Whereof the Governor Lieutenant Governor, or Commander in Chief of his Majestys said Colony of Virginia for the time being and all others, whom it may concern, are to take Notice and Govern themselves accordingly.[4]

Copy: P.C.2/107, pp. 386–87. The date is supplied from the heading of the day's proceedings in the Privy Council registers. The order was enclosed in the Board of Trade's letter of 13 June 1760 to Fauquier.

1. This act (Hening, 7:247–48), passed in the session of Sept. 1758, vested in Philip Johnson a tract of about seventeen acres south of Williamsburg, held in trust for him, which Johnson desired to have added to the city, and exchanged for that tract an adjoining tract of forty-three acres to be held in trust for him. Philip Johnson was one of the burgesses for King and Queen County 1752–58.

2. This act (Hening, 7:296–97), passed in the session of Feb. 1759, exchanged a tract of 605 acres in King William County, owned by Claiborne, for two tracts of land amounting to about 1,200 acres in Hanover County, which had been devised to his wife Elizabeth. Philip Whitehead Claiborne (d. 1772) of Liberty Hall in King William County was one of the burgesses for that county in 1771.

3. This act (Hening, 7:323–30), passed in the session of Feb. 1759, authorized the disposing of Alexander Spotswood's land, ironworks, and slaves in Spotsylvania County and his land in Orange and Culpeper counties to meet various charges on the estate. John Spotswood (ca. 1725–1756) was a colonel of militia and in the period 1749–56 a burgess for Orange, then Culpeper, and finally Spotsylvania. His father, Alexander Spotswood (1676–1740), was lieutenant governor of Virginia 1710–22.

4. Fauquier produced this order at the council meeting of 16 Sept. 1760 and mentioned it in his address to the General Assembly on 6 Oct. 1760. See *EJC* 6:170 and *JHB, 1758–1761*, p. 184.

Order in Council

[20 May 1760]

Whereas by the 18th Article of his Majestys Instructions to the Governor of the Colony of Virginia and in his Absence, to the Lieutenant Governor thereof, he is required and enjoyned to take care that no private Act whereby the Property of any private person may be affected be past in which there is not a Saving of the Right of his Majesty his Hiers and Successors, all Bodies politick and Corporate and of all other Persons except such as are mentioned in the said Act and those claiming by from or under them, nor without a Clause suspending the Execution thereof untill the same shall have received his Majestys Royal Approbation. And he is likewise directed not to give his Assent to any private Act untill proof be made before him in Council (and Entered in the Council Books) that publick Notification was made of the Parties intention to apply for such Act in the several parish Churches where the Premises in Question lie, for three Sundays at least successively before such Act was brought into the Assembly And that a Certificate thereof under the said Governors Hand should be transmitted with and annexed to every such Private Act signifying that the same was passed thro' all the Forms above mentioned.[1]

And Whereas notwithstanding the aforesaid Instruction it appears that the present Lieutenant Governor of that Colony has presumed to give his Assent to three private Acts, affecting the Rights and Propertys of his Majestys Subjects without paying the least Regard to any one of the Regulations contained in the said Instruction so necessary to be observed in the Passing all Acts of such a Nature and Tendency Which are intitled as follows, Vizt.

An Act for vesting certain Lands therein mentioned in Philip Johnson Gentleman adding the same to the City of Williamsburg and for other Purposes therein mentioned.

Passed in October 1758.

An Act for vesting certain Lands in the County of Hanover in Philip Whitehead Claiborne Gentleman, in Fee simple and for other Purposes therein mentioned.

Passed in April 1759.

An Act to enable the Executors of the Will of John Spotswood Esquire to pay the Debts and Legacies due from the Estate of Major General Alexander Spotswood, and for other Purposes therein mentioned.
Passed in April 1759.

His Majesty having taken the same into Consideration was this Day pleased by his Order made at this Board, to declare his Disallowance of all the said Acts. And his Majesty doth hereby signify his Dissatisfaction at the Proceedings of the said Lieutenant Governor in Giving his Assent to the said Acts And for preventing the like for the future his Majesty Doth with the Advice of his Privy Council hereby require and Command that the Governor, Lieutenant Governor, or Commander in Chief of the said Colony for the Time being Do strictly and punctually observe and obey the several Regulations contained in his Majestys afore recited Instruction upon pain of his Majestys highest Displeasure and of being recalled from the Government of the said Colony. And altho his Majesty has judged it necessary to repeal the said Acts aforementioned, Yet his Majesty is hereby graciously pleased to permit and allow the Legislature of Virginia to reenact the Laws, provided the same be done in due conformity to his Majestys afore recited Instructions Whereof the Governor, Lieutenant Governor, or Commander in Chief of his Majestys said Colony of Virginia for the time being, and all others whom it may concern are to take notice and Govern themselves accordingly.[2]

Copy: P.C.2/107, pp. 387–88. The date is supplied from the heading of the day's proceedings in the Privy Council registers. The order was enclosed in the Board of Trade's letter of 13 June 1760 to Fauquier.

1. Except for verbal differences of no importance, this paragraph is identical with the eighteenth article of the instructions (C.O.5/1367, ff. 98–99).

2. Fauquier produced this order at the council meeting of 16 Sept. 1760 and mentioned it in his address to the General Assembly on 6 Oct. 1760. See *EJC* 6:170 and *JHB, 1758–1761*, p. 184.

To County Lieutenants

[ca. 24 May 1760]

This letter, which Fauquier produced at the council meeting on 24 May 1760, has not been found. It seems likely that it was the circular letter which Fauquier mentioned in his letter of 24 June 1760 to William Preston, a circular informing certain county lieutenants that Fauquier did not intend to call out any militia during that year.

To William Bull

Sir,   Williamsburgh, May 24: 1760.

I have the pleasure to inform you that the General Assembly which I summoned to meet on the receipt of your Letters, and which broke up this day, have passed an Act to raise Thirty two thousand pounds for the levying and providing for Seven hundred Men to be added to the three hundred now on our South West Frontiers, till the first day of December next, in order if possible to relieve Fort Loudoun, or to act otherwise offensively or defensively against the Cherokee Indians as shall be judged most expedient.[1]

With this force of One thousand Men as soon as raised, I am desirous to attempt the relief of the above named Fort, even provided I should not be joined by any Troops of North Carolina, But by all Accounts I have received of the condition of that Garrison, I fear it will be impracticable to arrive there in time to save it from falling into the Enemys Hands; If this should unhappily be the case, I shall keep these Men together, till I hear from you, in what other manner they can be serviceable to the Common Cause. And I hope you, and Colonel Montgomery[2] will settle some regular plan of Operations, that we may all make the best use in our power of the Force that is in our Hands; If I should not receive such information from you in a reasonable time, I shall think it my Duty to disband the Men, to ease this Colony of the prodigious Expence they are at. I can't doubt but their exerting themselves as they have on this Occasion, after being engaged in a long expensive War, will meet with due Honor from your Colony, who will not send so many Provincial Troops into the Field against the Cherokees as we shall do:

I have further to inform You, that if possible we shall endeavor to send provisions for twelve Months for the Two hundred Men in the Garrison, a particular and distinct Account of which, with the Carriage and other Expences will be kept by our Commissaries, which we expect should be repaid by your Colony, or the Crown; I hope to hear very soon from You And am with the greatest respect. Sir, Your most obedient humble Servant,

                                                          Francis Fauquier

Copy: Ballindalloch, Banffshire, Scotland, Ballindalloch Castle Muniments, Bundle 561. A copy sent to Colonel Grant, presumably. Fauquier produced the letter at the council meeting on 24 May 1760; see *EJC* 6:160 n. 57.

1. The General Assembly of 19–24 May 1760 (summoned specifically on account of the request for aid from South Carolina) passed "An Act for raising the sum of

thirty-two thousand pounds, for the relief of the garrison of Fort Loudoun in the Cherokee country" (Hening, 7:357–63).

2. Lt. Col. Archibald Montgomerie commanded the regular troops sent against the Cherokees.

To Robert Monckton

Sir   Wmsburgh May 24th 1760

I hereby acknowledge the Receipt of your Favour of the 7th instant, and take this Opportunity of congratulating you on your Appointment to the Command of his Majesty's Troops in these parts; and to assure you that I shall take every Opportunity of corresponding with you for his Majesty's Service, which will be attended with a particular Satisfaction, as I had long the pleasure of an Acquaintance with Ld. Galloway.[1]

By the Act of Assembly which provided for the Continuance and pay of the Virginia Regiment I was not at Liberty to recruit it to the complete Number of 1000 Men, but was obliged to keep it at the Number of the then last Return which was 760, out of which I was also obliged to keep 300 Men at home to guard our South West Frontiers, so that the Number left to act with his Majesty's Troops was only 460, of all which I informed Major Generals Amherst and Stanwix. I have given Orders for the Regiment to be recruited to that Number that I may if possible assist his Majesty with every Man the Law will permit me to do.

Lieutt. Governor Bull of South Carolina has call'd upon this Colony for assistance against the Cherokee Indians who have declared War against the White People: upon which Occasion I have with the Advice of his Majestys Council call'd Colonel Byrd to Command a Body of Men raising for this Service, who is well acquainted with the Cherokee Country having been through most parts of it. the Command of that part of our Troops which will serve under you devolves on Lieutenant Colonel Stephen a brave and experienced Officer, who has serv'd in our Troops from our first raising them.

I some time since wrote to General Stanwix for Copies of the Treaties made with the Ohio Indians by Mr. Forbes and confirmed by himself; I must beg the Favour of you to speak to Colonel Bouquet who was the Negotiator of that affair, that I may be furnished with them, as I cannot proceed to grant any Lands on the Ohio till I am apprized what Agreements were made with those Indians. I am with the greatest Regard Sir Your most Obedient humble Servant

Fran: Fauquier

To Brigr. Genl. Monckton

ALS: Library of Congress, Peter Force Papers, ser. VIII D, Vernon-Wager Papers, vol. 18, Papers of Robert Monckton, ff. 47091–92.

1. Probably Fauquier refers to General Monckton's father, John Monckton (1695–1751), who was created first Viscount Galway in 1727; but he may mean William Monckton (1725?–1772), the second viscount and General Monckton's brother.

To Horatio Sharpe

Sir   Wmsburgh May 26th 1760

The Revd. Mr. Burnaby a very ingenious and well behaved young Clergyman for whom I have a great Regard, having a Mind to see as much of this Continent as he can, before he departs for England, will pass thro' Annapolis, and do himself the Honor to wait on you for your Commands.[1] I shall be much obliged to you to show him all Sorts of Civilities and Countenance, for the short Time he proposes to stay in your Colony. and am with great Esteem Sir Your most Obedient Humble Servant

Fran: Fauquier

To Governor Sharpe.

ALS: Historical Society of Pennsylvania.

1. According to his *Travels through the Middle Settlements in North America in the Years 1759 and 1760: With Observations upon the State of the Colonies* (London, 1775), Andrew Burnaby (1743?–1812) arrived in Virginia on 4 July 1759 and left Williamsburg on 26 May 1760 on his way to Maryland; he arrived at Annapolis on 12 June and left the next day. Fauquier's letters to Sharpe of 14 June and 28 July 1760 suggest that Burnaby carried this letter himself, but nothing has been found to indicate that he delivered it.

From James Hamilton

[Philadelphia, 27 May 1760]

This letter has not been found. Fauquier communicated it to the council on 11 June 1760, and it is abstracted in *EJC* 6:161:

Also a Letter from Governour Hamilton, dated Philadelphia May 27th signifying that the Proprietors of Pensylvania have no thoughts of granting the Lands promised by Mr Dinwiddie's Proclamation to the Officers and Men who served on the Ohio, until his Majesty's pleasure respecting it shall be known.

From Jeffery Amherst

Sir,   Albany 28th May 1760

Altho' I have Nothing to trouble You with I cannot let the Post go without thanking You for Your Letter of the 3d Instant, received three days ago, and of Assuring You that I am fully persuaded that Nothing will have been wanting on Your part to Assist His Majesty's Forces with every Man You could legally send to Join them; I Could Wish the Assembly Entertained the same Zeal for the King, and the good of His Service, & then the Numbers they have Voted would have been Equal to their Abilities; which they now are certainly short of; I am however much Obliged to You for the Assurances You give me, of Your Care that Your little Corps would be ready to Obey Mr. Stanwix's Orders, & that You had Wrote to him thereupon.

I must not Omit Acknowledging the Receipt of Your private Letter of the 8th Instant, which came to my hands at the same time with the Other. I am, with great Regard, Sir &ca.

Honble. Lt. Govr. Fauquier.

Copy: W.O.34/37, f. 216. Another copy, lacking the second paragraph, is in C.O.5/58, ff. 59–60, endorsed as being in Amherst's letter of 21 June 1760.

From Arthur Dobbs

[28 May 1760]

This letter has not been found. Fauquier communicated it to the council on 11 June 1760, and it is abstracted in *EJC* 6:161:

> Also a Letter from Governour Dobbs dated the 28th of May, informing that their Assembly have had two Sessions without giving any supply to the Crown.

From William Byrd

[Winchester, 29 May 1760]

This letter has not been found. Fauquier communicated it to the council on 11 June 1760, and it is abstracted in *EJC* 6:161:

> The Governour was likewise pleased to communicate, a letter from Colo. Byrd dated Winchester May the 29th—requesting that he may be excused from taking the Command of the Troops raised for the Cherokee Expedition, and to desire the Opinion and Advice of the Council thereupon.

From William Bull

[Charles Town, 31 May 1760]

This letter has not been found. Fauquier communicated it to the council on 25 June 1760, and it is abstracted in *EJC* 6:164:

His Honour communicated to the Board a Letter from Governour Bull dated Charles Town May the 31st—informing of the hostile Commotions and Outrages of the Upper Creeks—that he shall leave nothing unattempted to effect an accomodation, which if not soon done, the lower Creeks will undoubtedly fall into the same Conduct of acting against us—Of the number of Indians to the West under the influence of the French at Missisippi—that he has ordered the Militia to be in readiness to take the Field on the first Orders—that he expects the Army will reach Keowee by the 4th of June at farthest—that by advices from Fort Loudoun of the 16th and 17th of May he learns Captain Demeri could hold out no longer than a Month.

The Creek Indians of what is now Alabama and Georgia were divided into the Upper Creeks, who lived for the most part in the valleys of the Coosa and Oakfuskie rivers, and the Lower Creeks, whose towns were scattered along the valleys of the Chattahoochee and Flint rivers. In mid-May 1760 the tribesmen of Oakfuskie, one of the principal Upper Creek towns, killed the English traders among them, and other towns of the Upper Creeks followed their example. The army to which Bull referred was the force sent by Amherst under the command of Lt. Col. Archibald Montgomerie. Capt. Paul Demeré of the Independent Regulars was the commanding officer at Fort Loudoun.

From Landon Carter

[ca. June 1760]

This letter has not been found, but Fauquier acknowledged it in his letter of 30 June 1760 to Carter and indicated that Carter's letter enclosed a bill for £50 sterling for the relief of sufferers from the fire in Boston.

From William Preston

[ca. June 1760]

This letter has not been found, but Fauquier acknowledged it in his letter of 24 June 1760 to Preston, which indicates that Preston's letter transmitted a petition from inhabitants of Augusta County for a force of militia to protect them against the Indians.

From Horatio Sharpe

[ca. June 1760]

This letter has not been found, but it was referred to, and returned, in Fauquier's letter of 14 June 1760 to Sharpe. It appears that the letter returned to Sharpe was his reply to Fauquier's letter of 12 Apr. 1760, which Fauquier has confused with his letter of 26 May 1760 to Sharpe.

From James Abercromby

Sir   June 1st 1760

A few days ago I had Duplicate of your Letter of 14th Decr. the original no doubt gone to France or otherwise lost, and with your letter I had the Memorial from you and the Council to the Treasury for paying to me the Virginia Proportion of the 50000 & the 200000 the first being already paid as heretofore I informd you, I shall now apply for the Last, and the Security requir'd will no doubt be of the same nature as that before given, and Your Directions concerning the Disposition of the money must be accordingly transmitted to me, whether I am to be drawn upon by Bills or to remit the same in Specie, in whatever Manner it is to be done, by the Condition of my Bond to the Crown you will please to observe that the joint concurrence of the Governor Council and Assembly is necessary in such directions to acquit me so as to get my Bond up and properly discharged.

I find on enquiry at the Plantation Office[1] that the Acts amongst others the Negro Act recommended to my attention are miscarryd,[2] Mr President Blairs letter to me containing Instructions from the Council relative to my Conduct as Agent being likewise miscarryd,[3] and it is probable so has the Committee of Correspondence letter to Mr Montague,[4] however as to what relates to the Service of the Province, my letter to you of the 10th May will let you see that I had taken up the very system of Conduct with regard to the Agency as what is now pointed to me by you and the Council and you may be assurd of my Concurrence accordingly with Mr Montague who I believe is now doing Regimental Duty at Winchester Incampment.[5]

It will however become necessary since your former letters to me have miscarryd to transmit Copys of your Reasons for passing the Negro Act and also for Mr President Blair to furnish me with Copys of his former letter containing the Councils Instructions to me for my future Conduct.

I shall not fail to communicate to your Brother from time to time what may personally concern you.

The Armys of the contending Powers being in the Field some Capital blow is now expected which may decide as to Peace or War, in the mean time the arrival of and the Negociations of the Spanish Ambassador since his Arrival gives us hitherto no public notification of either[6] I am

Gov. Fouquier.

Copy: Virginia State Library, James Abercromby Letter Book, pp. 209-10. Probably a draft, as it contains numerous deletions and insertions. A note in the margin indicates that a duplicate was sent by Mr. Wright's convoy. Fauquier communicated this letter to the council on 16 Sept. 1760; see *EJC* 6:169-70. It is probably one of the letters Fauquier mentioned in his address to the assembly on 6 Oct. 1760 and sent to the House of Burgesses the same day; see *JHB, 1758-1761*, pp. 184-85.

1. The office of the Board of Trade.
2. Abercromby must have been referring to some or all of the acts passed in the assembly session of 1-21 Nov. 1759, presumably sent with Fauquier's letter of 17 Dec. 1759 to the Board of Trade. The Negro Act was the act imposing a duty on imported slaves, which Fauquier certainly enclosed in his letter of 17 Dec. to the board.
3. This was probably a letter of ca. 12 Dec. 1759 from Blair to Abercromby in reply to Abercromby's letters of 20 May, 25 June, 30 June, 25 July, and 3 Aug., abstracted along with the reply which the council advised in *EJC* 6:151-52.
4. This was probably a letter of ca. 14 Nov. 1759 in which the Committee of Correspondence, in compliance with an order of the burgesses of 14 Nov. 1759, directed Montagu that if any appeal should be made from Virginia to England relative to the second Two Penny Act, he should do whatever he could, including the retaining of proper counsel, to support the proceedings of the Virginia vestries acting under authority of that act (*JHB,1758-1761*, p. 146).
5. Winchester is the cathedral city in Hampshire, about 65 mi. southwest of London and near Salisbury Plain, much used for military maneuvers.
6. The count de Fuentes, the new Spanish ambassador, arrived in London on 24 May 1760 and presented his letters of credence to the king on 27 May. It does not appear that he had undertaken any negotiations by the first of June, although he had paid several visits of courtesy to the Prince of Wales and other members of the royal family.

To the Board of Trade

My Lords,   Wmsburgh June 2d 1760

The Assembly which I had summoned to meet on the 19th ulto., of which I gave your Lordships advice in my Letter to your right Honble. Board of the 13th[1] sat six Days, and provided for the raising and paying 700 Men till the 1st of Decr. to be joined to the 300 already stationed on the south west Frontiers, to attempt the Relief of Fort Loudoun, or to be otherwise employed as Lieut. Govr. Bull shall advise. These Men are now raising and as I hear the Recruits enter very fast. This Act, with two other Acts of course, I shall transmit to your Lordships as soon as engross'd.[2]

At the End of the Supply Bill the House of Burgesses added a Clause to encrease the Duty arising by the Importation of Slaves, by reducing it to ten Pr. Ct. instead of Twenty,[3] which was the Method I most approved in the late Act relative thereto of which I wrote your Lordships a full Account in my Letter of the 17th of Decr. sent by the Deliverance Captn. Whyte, who I hope is safely arrived tho' we have not heard of her. She carried the Box of public papers and Acts.

The Incertitude of the proceedings of the general Assembly of this Colony, has struck me on many Occasions and seems to be so inherent in the Nature of the Members, as to be characteristic of the people. This Act was pass'd this Sessions in the lower house but by a single Voice, on Account of this Clause, and it is apprehended will occasion a Battle in the next Session whenever the Assembly meets again: for the Contest on this Occasion is between the old Settlers who have bred great Quantity of Slaves, and would make a Monopoly of them by a Duty which they hope would amount to a prohibition; and the rising Generation who want Slaves, and don't care to pay the Monopolists for them at the price they have lately bore which was exceedingly high. These Reasons your Lordships may guess, are not urged in the Arguments on either Side; but I believe are the true Foundation of the Squabble.

But setting this Act aside, the Uncertainty of all public Measures is in nothing more apparent than in their immediate disbanding Men, who by seeing some Service are become useful, upon the least relaxation from their fears of an Enemy; and as immediately raising first raw Men at a great Bounty; as soon as their passions are again alarmed. Whoever charges them with acting upon a premeditated concerted plan, don't know them: for they mean honestly, but are Expedient Mongers in the highest Degree, even to their own Cost daily. I am confident the assembly could have kept two Regiments in constant pay since my arrival in the Colony at a much less Expence than the Methods they have persued have occasioned. I am My Lords with the greatest Respect Your Lordships most Obedient and devoted Servant

Fran: Fauquier

To the Lords Commissioners of Trade &ct.

ALS: C.O.5/1330, ff. 17–18. Endorsed as read 19 Nov. 1760.

1. His letter of 12 May 1760.
2. He referred to the act for the relief of Fort Loudoun and two other acts which were "of course," or customary and routine, one to continue the acts for preventing mutiny and desertion and the other to pay the burgesses their wages, both of which acts were reenacted repeatedly as necessary; see Hening, 7:364–67.
3. The last two clauses of the supply bill, or the act for the relief of Fort Loudoun, repealed that clause of an act passed in the session of May 1755 which laid an additional duty of 10 percent on all slaves imported into Virginia. The act of May 1755 was "An Act to explain an act, intituled, An Act for raising the sum of twenty thousand pounds, for the protection of his majesty's subjects, against the insults and encroachments of the French; and for other purposes therein mentioned" (Hening, 6:461–68). The reason given for repealing the additional duty was that it was a burden on the fair purchaser, an obstacle to settlement of lands, the source of frauds, and ineffectual inasmuch as it prevented the importation of slaves and thereby lessened the revenue from duties on them.

From Arthur Dobbs

[Brunswick, 8 June 1760]

This letter has not been found. Fauquier communicated it to the council on 25 June 1760, and it is abstracted in *EJC* 6:164–65:

Also a Letter from Governour Dobbs dated Brunswick June the 8th—signifying that upon advice that the upper Creeks have by the instigation of the French broke into open War with Georgia and South Carolina, he had summon'd the Council to meet him there, and believes they will advise him upon that Emergency to summon the Assembly to meet at Wilmington as soon as possible, to see if the present danger will not induce them to raise Men and assist the neighbouring Provinces, and that he shall cooperate with this Government or South Carolina, if any force can be raised in time to be of Service.

Dobbs probably wrote from his residence near Brunswick, N.C., a town on the west bank of the Cape Fear River a short distance above its mouth. He expected the council would advise him to call a meeting of the assembly at Wilmington, the port town about 15 mi. above Brunswick on the Cape Fear River.

Proclamation

[ca. 12 June 1760]

On 11 June 1760 Fauquier informed the council that he proposed, with their approval, to issue a proclamation calling a halt to recruitment for the expedition against the Cherokees until he had a return of the men already enlisted; requiring an immediate return of recruits; and ordering the recruits to be marched to the places of rendezvous. It is not clear whether the proclamation also declared

Fauquier's intention to transfer sixty surplus recruits to the Virginia Regiment if they agreed to serve. See *EJC* 6:161–62. No copy of the proclamation has been found, and the date is a conjecture.

To William Byrd

[ca. 12 June 1760]

This letter has not been found, but it is assumed that it was sent in reply to Byrd's letter of 29 May 1760, in which he asked to be excused from the command of the expedition against the Cherokees. The advice of the council regarding Byrd's request is reported in *EJC* 6:161:

The Council were of Opinion that Colo. Byrd was indispensably obliged, while in the Government to pay obedience to the Governours Commands; and advised his Honour to give him peremptory Orders to return, if he has not joined the Regulars, and in case he has, that his Honour would write to General Moncton, acquainting him how necessary Mr. Byrd's presence here will be at this juncture, and desiring he would order him back; they further advised his Honour to signify to Colo. Byrd that this Board was surprised and concern'd to learn that the three hundred Men appointed for the Protection of the Southern Frontiers were not yet compleated according to the directions of the Act of Assembly.

Probably this letter to Byrd was written at the same time as Fauquier's letter of 12 June 1760 to Monckton.

To Robert Monckton

Sir Wmsburgh June 12th 1760

I am very sorry the Situation of Affairs in this Colony in Relation to the Rupture between the Carolina's and the Cherokee Indians in which we have been solicited to give all the Assistance we are able, should make it absolutely necessary for me to recall Mr. Byrd to take upon him the Command of the Expedition we are projecting to assist Colonel Montgomery. As he is march'd from Winchester, it is possible he may have join'd you; if so, I beg the Favour of you to give him Leave to return into this Colony, for this Business of Importance, and I make no Doubt, but you will find Lt. Colonel Stephen in every Respect equal to the Command of the few Men I am impower'd by Acts of Assembly to join to his

Majesty's Forces under your Command for this Campaign. I will use my utmost Endeavours by recovering the Sick and recruiting for the lost Men to give you every Man the Law will let me, being with the greatest Esteem Sir Your most Obedient humble Servant

Fran: Fauquier

To the Honble. Brigr. Genl. Monckton

ALS: Library of Congress, Peter Force Papers, ser. VIII D, Vernon-Wager Papers, vol. 18, Papers of Robert Monckton, ff. 47093–94. Endorsed as received at Bedford on the twenty-third [June 1760].

From the Board of Trade

Sir [Whitehall, 13 June 1760]

We have received your Letter of the 13 of March, inclosing a Duplicate of one of the 17 of December 1759 the original of which, with the Box of publick papers referr'd to therein, has not been receiv'd, so that we are altogether unable to give you our Sentiments & Opinion upon the Act for imposing a Duty upon Slaves payable by the Importer, not having before us, either the Act itself, or the Reasons which induced the Council to Advise the passing it; We cannot however help observing to you, that your Conduct in this transaction appears to us to have been influenced, as far as we can judge from your own state of the Case, by a Misapprehension or misconstruction of Your Instruction of a very dangerous and pernicious tendency and Consequence. The Cases, in which the Advice and Consent of the Council are required in any Acts of Government; are precisely mark'd out in the Instructions; in all other Cases of Dutys enjoined by these Instructions, the Governor alone is accountable for his own Conduct, and if it should ever be Admitted, that the Advice and Opinion of the Council can dissolve the Governor from the Obligation he is under of Obeying those Instructions, by which the negative voice in the passing of Laws is limited and restrain'd; the Interest of the Crown and the Mother Country must depend solely for Security upon the uncertain Wills, Interests and Inclinations of the Members of the Council; and what the Consequences of such a System would be, are too obvious to mention.

Having thus given you our Opinion at large upon the general Error which You seem to have fallen into in respect to the Obligation You apprehend Yourself under of taking and following, the Advice of Your

Council, tho' contrary to your own Judgment, We will not seek to aggravate the Concern you will necessarily feel for having Acted under this Error, by any remarks upon the particular Case to which it has been apply'd, hoping that what We have said, together with the just Displeasure of the Crown, signify'd in the inclosed Orders in Council, in the Case of some private Laws passed by you in October 1758 and April 1759,[1] together with the Opinion given by us in the inclosed representation upon those Laws and upon which Opinion the Orders were founded, will awaken you to a more serious Attention to Your Duty, in the Observance of those necessary Regulations which have been prescribed by the Governor's Instructions with respect to the passing Laws either of a publick or private Nature.

All the other publick Laws passed by you in April 1759 are as yet before Our Counsel for his Opinion, except that for appointing an Agent, which has been under our Consideration, and inclosed We send you Our Counsel's Opinion upon it.[2] We entirely agree with him, that those parts of the Act which give a power to the Committee of Correspondence to remove the Agent at pleasure and put in another, reporting their proceedings to the House of Representatives only; are very irregular and Improper: But as the General plan and other parts of the Act appear to Us to be just and reasonable, We shall not lay it before His Majesty for his Disapprobation; But we desire You will take the first Opportunity of recommending to the Council and House of Burgesses to prepare another Bill for the same purpose not liable to these Objections, signifying to them at the same time, that unless that be done We shall think it incumbent upon us to Advise His Majesty to repeal the present Law.

We come now to Your Letter of the 13 of March last which relates principally, to the Difficulties you state yourself to be under from the pressing Sollicitation of Officers and others for Grants of Lands upon the Ohio: As We have not received your Letter of the 1st of December We cannot guess upon what Grounds and Motives it was, that You then urged the Necessity of Settling those Lands; nor is it necessary for us at this time to enter into any general Consideration either of the policy or propriety of those measures which were taken for encouraging their Settlement previous to the present War; it will be sufficient for us to say, that no Contest then existed with any foreign power in reference to the Dominion of the Country, nor was it then understood to be part of Lands claim'd by Indians as their hunting Grounds; these Questions have since involved us in a very bloody and dangerous War, the Event of which, in Reference to the French, is still in the hands of Providence, and the Hostilities and Barbarities of the Indians seem to have subsided solely upon Our having engaged, as well by the Treaty of Easton as other subsequent Transactions, not to Settle upon their hunting Grounds: In this Situation therefore it appears to us, that the attempting to make any Settlement upon those Lands would be a Measure of the most dangerous Tendency; That it would be an open Violation of our late solemn Engagements with the Indians, and infallibly provoke them again to take up the Hatchet against us and desolate Our Frontiers; That, Independent of this unsurmountable Objection, the Impropriety of encouraging Settlements upon Lands, the Dominion and possession of which remain yet to be decided by the Sword, is so obvious, that we are at a loss to guess at the Motive which could induce you to encourage such a proposition; for as to your Apprehension, that, if Virginia does not settle these Lands, Pensylvania will, there is not the least Ground for it, the proprietaries having, by the Treaty of Easton, solemnly relinquished to the Indians all the Land to the Westward of the great Mountains, and Engaged not to make any Settlement upon it.

This matter appearing therefore to Us in this light, We think it Adviseable and for His Majesty's Service, that no further Steps whatever should be taken for Settling any Lands upon the waters of the Ohio, untill His Majesty's further pleasure be known. We are, Sir, Your most Obedient Humble Servants,

       W. Sloper Dunk Halifax
       Ed. Bacon Soame Jenyns

Whitehall / June 13th 1760
To Francis Fauquier Esqr. Lieut. Governor of Virginia

Copy: C.O.5/1367, ff. 202–5.

1. The two orders in council of 20 May 1760.
2. The counsel was Sir Mathew Lamb (1705–1768), who acted as legal adviser to the Board of Trade from 1746 until his death.

Enclosure: The Board of Trade to the King

[Whitehall, 16 May 1760]

To the King's most Excellent Majesty
May it please your Majesty,

We have had under our Consideration three Acts pass'd in Your Majesty's Colony of Virginia, in Octr. 1758 & April 1759 entituled,

>   An Act for Vesting certain Lands therein Mentioned in Philip Johnson Gent: adding the same to the City of Williamsburg and for other purposes therein Mentioned.
>
>   pass'd Octr: 11 1758.
>
>   An Act for vesting certain lands in the County of Hanover in Philip Whitehead Claiborne, Gentleman in Fee simple, and for other purposes therein Mentioned
>
>   pass'd in April 1759.
>
>   An Act to enable the Executors of the Will of John Spotswood Esqr: to pay the Debts and Legacies due from the Estate of Major General Alexander Spotswood, And for other purposes therein Mentioned.
>
>   pass'd April 1759.

Whereupon We beg Leave humbly to represent to Your Majesty,

That Altho' these Acts are in the Nature and by the provisions of them, Acts Affecting the Rights and property of Your Majesty's Subjects, We find nevertheless that they have been pass'd by the Legislature of Virginia without regard to any one of those Regulations, which Your Majesty's Governor of Virginia (in Common with the Governors of the other Colonys in America) is required, by the 18th Article of Your Majesty's Instructions, to observe in the passing of all Acts of such a Nature and tendency, For in these Acts there is no Certificate of any previous Notification, in the parish Church, of the Intention of the Respective parties to Apply for such Act; Nor any Proof (which has sometimes been Admitted instead of the said Certificate) of the Consent of the Several persons interested in them respectively; There is no saving of the Right of Your Majesty, or of any Body Politick or Corporate, or of any private persons not Mentioned in these Acts; Neither is there any Clause suspending their Effect, untill the Receipt of Your Majesty's Royal Approbation. These Regulations so essential to the Security Not only of the Rights and property of Your Majesty's Subjects but also that just Right of Your Majesty are coeval with the Constitution of the British Colonys, and being founded upon that principle of equity and Justice which has invariably taken place and been observed in all of them, of Allowing Appeals to Your Majesty in Council in all Cases Affecting private property, they do in our humble Opinion form an essential part of that Constitution and Cannot be set Aside without subverting a Fundamental principle of it, Wisely framed for the Security and protection of Your Majesty's Subjects, in whatever may affect their private rights and Interests and therefore We are humbly of Opinion, that not only Your Majesty's Displeasure should be Signified to the Lieutenant Governor, for having given his assent to these Laws, but that the Laws themselves should be repealed,

15 May 1760

with permission however to the Legislature to re-enact them provided it be done in due Conformity to Your Majesty's Instructions.

                        Which is most humbly Submitted
                Dunk Halifax   W. G. Hamilton
                T: Pelham   W. Sloper
                Soame Jenyns

Whitehall / May th 16 1760

Copy: C.O.5/1367, ff. 200–202. A copy of the representation was enclosed in the Board of Trade's letter of 13 June 1760 to Fauquier.

Enclosure: Mathew Lamb to the Board of Trade

                                [Lincoln's Inn, 15 May 1760]
            To the Right Honoble the Lords
              Commissioners for Trade & Plantations

My Lords

In Pursuance of Your Lordships Commands Signified to me By Mr Pownall's Letter wherein You are pleased to Desire my Opinion in Point of Law upon the following Act Passed in Virginia in April 1759 I have Perused and Considered the same (vizt.)

    An Act for Appointing an Agent

This is the first Act that has been passed by the Legislature of this Province appointing an Agent. There has been usually an Agent to solicit the Affairs Relating to this Province, appointed and paid by the Governor and Council; But as the Legislature have thought fit by this Act to appoint an Agent for the Province, I have no Objection thereto in that Respect, as they have the same Right so to do, as the other Provinces have, and which they have usually done, provided the same was consistent with, and did preserve the Powers that belong to the different Branches of the Legislature. This Act is to continue for seven years from the time it was Passed, which differs from other Acts whereby Agents are appointed, which are usually for One year, and so are Renewed by Acts yearly, and the Treasurer of this Province is Directed to pay to the Agent out of the Publick Money, a Salary of Five Hundred Pounds Sterling a year. Upon this I lay no great Stress as there is a Power of Removing such Agent, if thought necessary. But my Objection to this Act is, as to the manner and to the power by which he is to be Removed. He is by the Act appointed by the whole Legislature to be Agent for the Province for that Time, and a Committee is appointed to Correspond with him and to transmit to him such Matters and things as shall be comitted to their Charge by *the General Assembly*, and they are Directed to lay their Correspondence before *the General Assembly* when required, And if any of the Committee of Correspondence shall act contrary to the Directions in the Act, they are made Liable to the Censure of *the General Assembly*. So far the General Assembly have preserved some Power to themselves, relating to the Committee of Correspondence. But in the Proviso, they have given up their Power as to the Agent, Intirely into the Hands of the Committee, and to the Assembly alone (that is the House of Burgesses only) for the Comittee or the major Part of them are Impowered to Remove the Agent, Laying their Reasons before *the Assembly only*. And in Case of his Removal Death or Refusing to Act they are to appoint some other Person in his Room to be Agent to be approved of by the *Succeeding Assembly*. Therefore by this Act, the Governour and Council have put it into the Power of *the Committee of Correspondence and the Assembly alone*, Immediately after to Remove such Agent and to appoint another, and so to continue for the Term of Seven years, without any Controul or Approbation on their Part I am therefore of Opinion, that the Governour and Council have Departed by this Act for a Term of years, with that Share of the Power and Controul which they ought to have, in the appointing of a Province Agent, and that as he is appointed by Act of the whole Legislature, in Case of his Removal Death or Refusing to Act, that another Agent should be appointed in his Stead by the same Act of the whole Legislature, and not by any Single Part of it, or any Committee of Persons named, And for these Reasons I am of Opinion this Act should not be Confirmed, and am My Lords Your Lordships Most Obedient Humble Servant

Mat Lamb

Lincolns Inn / 15th May 1760.

LS: C.O.5/1329, ff. 181–82. Endorsed as received 16 May and read 19 May 1760. A copy of this letter was enclosed in the Board of Trade's letter of 13 June 1760 to Fauquier.

To Horatio Sharpe

Sir Wmsburgh June 14th 1760

The Letter[1] inclosed with this was brought me by Lieut. Colonel Mercer as you see it, who said it was given to him in a Hurry. As I am confident the Letter was designed for some other person I having never wrote to you on the Date mention'd by you, nor having the least knowledge of the Gentleman who is the Subject of it, I have returned it to you to prevent any Disappointment which might happen on your supposing you had sent your Letter as you design'd. The only Thing that stagger'd me was, I have mention'd those papers of Sir Isaac Newton, in a Letter I have taken the Liberty to write to you by the Revd. Mr. Burnaby begging the Favour of you to show him Countenance as he passes thro', your province in his Way to England. I am with great Esteem, Sir, Your most obedient humble Servant.

               Fran: Fauquier

To Governor Sharpe.

ALS: Hall of Records of Maryland, Executive Papers, Folder 142.

1. This must have been Sharpe's letter of ca. June 1760, answering Fauquier's letter of 12 Apr. to Sharpe.

To James Abercromby

[22 June 1760]

This letter has not been found, but a note beside the copy of Abercromby's letter of 20 Mar. 1760 to Fauquier indicates that it was acknowledged in Fauquier's letter of 22 June; and Abercromby's letter of 19 Jan. 1761 to Fauquier acknowledged receipt of a duplicate of Fauquier's letter of 22 June to him. But see Fauquier's letter of ca. 25 June 1760 to Abercromby.

To William Preston

Sr.   Williamsburgh June 24th 1760

I received yours by Mr. Hamilton with the pet[ition of] several Inhabitants of Augusta;[1] but can do noth[ing] therein, for I will not take upon me to put the Colony to the great and useless Expence of a Militia to ease a few people of their ill-grounded Fears.

I say ill-grounded, for it is very apparent to every thinking Man that they can never be in so great Security from Incursions from Indians, as when the Indians have a War to carry on in their own Country. It was upon this Consideration that with the Privity and Advice of his Majesty's Coun[cil] I wrote the circular Letter to Colonel Bu[chanan] and the neighbouring County Lieutenants that [I] should have no Militia out this Year. Whi[ch] was thought a wise Measure and approved of by every [Me]mber of the House of Burgesses to whom I com[munica]ted the Contents of my Letter.[2] It is a Shame [for] Men to talk of deserting a Country and their growing Crops, because 10 or 11 Indians have been seen thereabouts, but I have long seen it is not in the power of Man to rid the Augusta people of their unreasonable Fears, and there is no keeping them easy without a Militia; of which they have long enjoyed the Sweets, and therefore will not for the future, I suppose; be easy without them. However the Council shall see the Letter and the petition, and [if they] think proper to enter into the Expence [with] all my Heart, but I will not take upon me [to] do it, in full Opposition to my own Opinion. I am Sir Your Humble Servant

Fran: Fauquier

To Colonel Preston.

ALS: State Historical Society of Wisconsin, Draper Manuscripts 2 QQ 28–29. Addressed in a second hand, and franked in what is seemingly a third hand. Three holes in the letter have caused a loss of text; brackets indicate conjectural readings by the editor.

1. William Preston (1729–1783), to whom this letter was addressed, was evidently at this time colonel in command of the militia of Augusta County. Mr. Hamilton was probably John Hamilton, a provision merchant who kept a store at Dunkard Bottom on the New River. No trace has been found of the petition.

2. The circular letter to Colonel Buchanan (evidently Col. John Buchanan, county lieutenant of Augusta County since 1758) and other county lieutenants was very possibly that of ca. 24 May 1760. Fauquier had the opportunity to communicate the letter to members of the House of Burgesses met for the session of the General Assembly of 19–24 May 1760.

To James Abercromby

[ca. 25 June 1760]

This letter has not been found. Abercromby's letter book (Virginia State Library, p. 196) has a note that his letter of 20 Mar. 1760 to Fauquier had been acknowledged by Fauquier's letter of 22 June; and Abercromby's letter of 1 Oct. 1760 acknowledged a letter of 22 June from Fauquier. However, it is likely that

Abercromby mistook the date of Fauquier's letter, or that Fauquier had misdated it, and that it was written about 25 June 1760. On 25 June 1760 the council considered Abercromby's letter of 20 Mar. and advised that a copy of its proceedings of 12 Dec. 1759, regarding a memorial to the Treasury, and a full power of attorney for receiving Virginia's share of the two grants from Parliament should be sent to Abercromby. Abercromby's letter of 1 Oct. 1760 suggests that Fauquier's letter of 22 or 25 June 1760 enclosed copies of the memorial and the power of attorney; a duplicate of Fauquier's letter to him of 14 Dec. 1759; a copy of the council's advice of 20 Nov. 1759 regarding passage of the act for imposing a duty on slaves imported; a copy of Fauquier's letter to Samuel Martin (of ca. 25 June 1760?); and a letter to the Board of Trade, not identified, but presumably from Fauquier.

To Samuel Martin

[ca. 25 June 1760]

This letter has not been found, but James Abercromby's letter of 1 Oct. 1760 to Fauquier acknowledges receipt of Fauquier's letter of 22 June (assumed to be that of ca. 25 June) with several enclosures, one of them being a copy of Fauquier's letter to Samuel Martin. This is taken to be the reply to Martin's letter of 19 Mar. 1760, written about 25 June 1760, when the council advised that another copy of its memorial (asking that money apportioned to Virginia should be paid to Abercromby), agreed on at its meeting of 12 Dec. 1759, should be sent to the Treasury. See *EJC* 6:151–52, 165.

To the Board of Trade

My Lords, Wmsburgh June 30th 1760

By the Fleet which arrived here the 20th instant I had the Honor to receive an Order from his Majesty in Council to repeal four Acts of Assembly. The Repeal of which I shall proclaim in the next Gazette.[1] His Majesty's royal Instruction to me to enforce former Instructions relative to the passing Laws was deliver'd to me at the same time to which I shall pay all due Obedience on all Occasions.[2]

The Manner in which this Order and Instruction were deliver'd to me, appeared to me so unusual and extraordinary, that I hope your Lordships will excuse my relating the Circumstances to your right honble. Board.

The Copies of these papers have been in the Colony above these six Months, they were sent to Mr. Camm's Friends, and have been communicated to many. I then thought that the sending Copies of his Majesty's royal Orders and Instructions, before they were made known to his Governor to whom they are directed was a Step unprecedented, of pernicious Consequence, and a high Insult on Majesty.[3]

On the 20th instant Mr. Camm landed in this Colony and immediately went down to Hampton to meet and consult with his particular Friends.[4] On the 27th He came to me accompanyed by two of them,[5] and delivered to me his Majesty's royal Order in Council and Instruction, both open, dirty, and worn out at the Edges and Folds. Seeing they were of an old Date, I ask'd him where they had been till this Time. He answer'd in his Custody. I ask'd him if they were deliver'd to him open and without Cover. His answer was, they were.

The Order in Council carried all the Marks of its not being the original Order designed to be sent to me, but a Copy obtained by Mr. Paris Sollicitor to the Convention of the Clergy,[6] it being so indorsed on the back. But as it came accompanyed with his Majestys Instruction which had all the Appearance of being the original Instruction under his Majesty's Sign manual: for Fear of being negligent in my Duty and Obedience to his Majesty's Pleasure; I have acted upon it, in the same manner as if I was fully convinced it was authentic.

This is so unlike the Manner in which I received the Orders and Instructions with which I have already been honoured; which have come directly from your right honble. Board or from one of his Majesty's principal Secretaries of State, that I am at a Loss what to think about it. As I have received no Letter or advice from your Lordships on this Head, tho' it is long since your Lordships had the Act, and my Reasons for giving my assent to it;[7] I cannot entertain the least Thought that your Lordships meant to cast a Slurr upon me, and lessen me in the Eyes of the Gentlemen in the Colony, as it must of course do, if it is so understood. There is an universal Surprize at this proceeding of Mr. Camm which He and his Friends publish with Triumph. Besides, as Mr. Camm has on all Occasions studiously affected to treat me with great Indignity, I must imagine that this was an Act merely his own, to keep up the same Spirit.

This Transaction makes the greater Impression on the Gentlemen of the Colony, because when Mr. Attorney Randolph went to England about the Pistole Affair He ask'd whether he might carry his Majesty's Instructions to Mr. Dinwiddie, and was answer'd that the Board would send his Majesty's Instructions to his Majesty's Governor. A Copy of them was refused him, but the Instructions were read over to him. And no Copy was in the Colony when I came into it.

As it is my Duty to support the Dignity of his Majesty's Crown, and Authority, I thought it incumbent on me to be circumstantial in the Relation of this Affair, that if your Lordships should think Mr. Camm's proceedings derogatory to the Honor of his Majesty and his Lieutenant Governor, I may receive your Directions how I shall conduct my Self in this Affair.

The Men are raised for the Assistance of Carolina against the Cherokee Indians, and I hope will be ready to march as soon as I hear from Lt. Gov. Bull and Colonel Montgomery, in what Manner we can most effectually serve them; to whom I have wrote to this purpose.

I inclose to your Lordships a Copy of a Letter sent by Captn. Petersham the 9th instant,[8] and am with the greatest Respect, My Lords Your Lordships most Obedient Obliged & devoted Servant

Fran: Fauquier

To the right Honble. the Lords of Trade.

ALS: C.O.5/1330, ff. 19–21. Endorsed as received 4 Nov. 1760 and read the nineteenth [Nov. 1760].

1. The order in council was that of 10 Aug. 1760. It is uncertain when it was published, since no issues of the *Virginia Gazette* for 1760 are known.

2. The additional instruction was that of 21 Sept. 1759.

3. Nothing seems to be known about who may have received copies of the order and instruction or to whom their contents may have been communicated. It does not appear that Fauquier made any complaint about the airing of these documents before the date of this letter.

4. Hampton is a port city on the Chesapeake Bay, formerly the county seat of Elizabeth City County, which has now been incorporated in the city of Hampton. Camm went to Hampton to visit his friend Thomas Warrington (d. 1770), minister of Elizabeth City Parish, in Elizabeth City County, from about 1756 until his death.

5. Camm was accompanied by Warrington and by William Robinson (1717–1768), minister of Stratton-Major Parish in King and Queen County from 1744 until his death. Robinson wrote his own account of this encounter with Fauquier to bishops of London in his letter of 20 Nov. 1760 and an undated letter of late 1762 (Perry, 1:463–70, 473–86).

6. This was probably Ferdinand John Paris, the Mr. Paris described in the journal of the Board of Trade as solicitor for the agent to the clergy in Virginia.

7. Fauquier sent the act of Sept. 1758, the second Two Penny Act, with his letter of 5 Jan. 1759 to the Board of Trade, which included his reasons for assenting to the act; the board read Fauquier's letter on 23 May 1759.

8. This may have been Fauquier's letter of 2 June 1760 to the board; Captain Petersham has not been identified, but was presumably the captain of a merchant vessel.

To Landon Carter

Sir Wmsburgh June 30th 1760

I this Day received your Bill for £50 Sterling for th[e] Relief of the Sufferers by Fire in the Town of Boston a noble Instance of your Benevolence to Mankind in general. Your Letter which accompanied it fully shews your Sence of Feeling for those more closely connected to you.

Your Modesty must not be offended if you should see your Benefaction in print, for as I propose to print in the Gazettes occasio[n]ally the Collections I recei[v]e of the Parishes, that M[is]takes may be rectifyed if any should happen [by] the persons sent to me with the Money; I should not do Justice to you or to the Cause of the distressed if I was to with-hold so illustrious an Example.

I long to see you in print as the Conversation on the Subject of the Clergy is revived by the Arrival of Mr. Camm.[1] He treated me as usual with Indignity, and in Return I forbad him my House. Mr. Giberne[2] will have a full Account of the Transaction by ye[ster]da[ys] post, which I suppose by the Means of Col. Charles[3] you may amuse your self with, if it will afford you any Relief from the melancholy Thoughts constantly attending a humane Master of a sick Family. I am Sir Your very humble Servant

Fran: Fauquier

To Col. La[ndon] Carter

ALS: Colonial Williamsburg Foundation. The letter is worn at edges and folds with some loss of text; conjectural readings are in brackets.

1. In 1759 Landon Carter had written a pamphlet, *A Letter to the Right Reverend Father in God, the Lord B . . . p of L . . . n* (Bristol B2016); the pamphlet was a criticism of the bishop of London's letter of 14 June 1759 to the Board of Trade, which described the Two Penny Act as treason (C.O. 5/1329, ff. 131–33A; printed in Perry, 1:461–63).
2. Isaac William Giberne is thought to have settled in Lunenburg Parish, Richmond County, at some time in 1760. He was minister of the parish from about 1762 until 1795 or later.
3. This was probably Col. Charles Carter (1707–1764), Landon Carter's brother, whose estate of Cleve was only a few miles from Landon Carter's Sabine Hall.

From William Bull

[ca. July 1760]

This letter has not been found. Fauquier communicated it to the council on 8 July 1760, and it is mentioned in *EJC* 6:166 as reporting Colonel Montgomerie's progress and success in the Cherokee country.

From William Byrd

[ca. July 1760]

This letter has not been found. It may have been dated in June; Fauquier communicated it to the council on 8 July 1760, and it is mentioned in *EJC* 6:166 as reporting that recruiting for the Cherokee expedition was completed, but the men needed arms.

From John Chiswell

[ca. July 1760]

This letter has not been found. Fauquier communicated it to the council on 8 July 1760, and it is mentioned in *EJC* 6:166 as giving Colonel Chiswell's report that many stands of arms had lately been imported for the militia of King and Queen, Gloucester, and James City counties. It is assumed that Colonel Chiswell was Col. John Chiswell, of James City County.

From Horatio Sharpe

[ca. July 1760]

This letter has not been found but is assumed to have been written in reply to Fauquier's letter of 14 June 1760 to Sharpe.

From James Abercromby

Sir   July 3d 1760

I am now to acquaint you & the Council that I have received Payment at the Exchequer of the Sum of £20546 Sterling being the Proportion due to Virginia out of £200,000 granted last Session of Parliament and, for this purpose, I was obliged to obtain the King's special Sign Manual, as the Memorial of the Governor & Council to the Lords of the Treasury in this Case, not being authenticated under the Provincial Seal, was not held Sufficient Authority. The Ballance being as by the inclosed Account, £19,901.1.4, is subject, as the former Money, to the Order of Governor Council & Assembly.

In Mr. Montague's Absence, with his Regiment at the Incampment at Winchester I have given in our Claim for a due Share of the £200000, granted this last Session in proportion to 1400 Men clothed and paid by the Province for last Year, which Number, including 400 Rangers by Major Stub's[1] Information I ventured to give in, the Publick Journals being taken by the Enemy or otherwis lost, from thence I could form no Document of the Number of Troops. If I am Short, as there is no Disposition of the Treasury to make Partition of this Money, their long Adjournment taking Place, this Matter may lay over 'till towards the Meeting of Parliament, so that you will have time to set me to Rights, and at the same time to transmit proper Powers to receive the Money, and as Mr Montague and I are now acting conjunctly, I submit it to you, that the Power under the Provincial Seal be accordingly directed to us jointly, being signed by the Governor President of the Council and Speaker, which will at once obviate all Obstruction at the Treasury & Exchequer on the Receipt of the Money.

The Board of Trade are now Adjourned for their long Vaccation: the Treasury do the same towards the End of the Month, from thence will ensue a Stagnation to all Bussiness for some time, except Military Operations. Last Mail brought us an Account of a severe Blow on the Confines of Silesia given by Genl. Laudoun with his Austrian Army to Genl. Fauquet & Prussians,[2] another such will probably enable the Austrians & Russians to give Laws of Peace to the King of Prussia, who must at last give Way to Superiority of Numbers, which all our Money cannot make up to him, with Regard therefore to Us, a General or Separate Peace must in all Probability be produced by the present Operations in Germany I am Sir &ca.

J.A.

Governor Fauquier.

Copy: Virginia State Library, James Abercromby Letter Book, p. 213. Marginal notes indicate that the original went by Mr. Wright's convoy (which sailed about 20 July), the duplicate by the New York packet, and the triplicate by the *Randal* (the *Randolph*), Captain Walker. Fauquier communicated this letter to the council on 16 Sept. 1760, and it is abstracted in *EJC* 6:169–70. It is probably one of the letters Fauquier mentioned in his address to the assembly on 6 Oct. 1760 and sent to the House of Burgesses the same day; see *JHB, 1758–1761*, pp. 184–85.

1. Major Stub was probably Major Stobo, who spent the last ten days of March and the first three weeks or so of April 1760 in London.

2. On 23 June 1760 the Austrian general Baron von Laudon defeated the Prussians under Baron de La Motte-Fouqué in an engagement at what was then Landeshut in Lower Silesia, and is now Kamienna Góra, in southwestern Poland.

Enclosure: Agent's Account

[ca. 3 July 1760]

James Abercromby Esqr. charges himself with the Receipt of £20546 Sterling July 3d 1760 the Proportion alloted to Virginia out of the £200000 Sterling granted to the American Colonies in 1759 for their Respective Services

	£ sh d	
1760 July 3d		
To Cash received at the Exchequer on Account of Virginia		20546.—.—
Discharges himself thereof as follows Vizt.		
By the usual Commission thereon at 2½ Per Cent	513.13.—	
By Fees paid at the Treasury to Mr Tompkins on the two Warrants from the King and the Treasury Warrants, and for Several Orders	35.14.—	
By paid the Messengers at the Treasury	2. 2.—	
By Fees paid to Mr. Jennings & others in the Auditor of the Exchequer's Office	27.17.—	
By Fees paid at the Pell Office	11.11.—	
By Fees paid at the Tellers Office on Do.	50.18. 8	
By paid Mr Francis for Bond	3. 3.—	644.18. 8
Ballance due to Virginia is		£19901. 1. 4
		£20546.—.—

Copy: Virginia State Library, James Abercromby Letter Book, p. 214. This account was enclosed in Abercromby's letter of 3 July 1760 to Fauquier.

From William Byrd

[Augusta Court House, 4 July 1760]

This letter has not been found. Fauquier communicated it to the council on 23 July 1760, and it is abstracted in *EJC* 6:166–67:

The Governour was pleas'd to communicate to the Council, and to desire their Opinion and Advice upon, two Letters from Colo. Byrd, the first dated Augusta Court House July 4th signifying his arrival there the day before, and that he shall proceed on Sunday, to the Army—that upon examining the Commissary's Returns of what was provided for the expedition, he finds every Article, except Provisions, vastly deficient—inclosing a List of every thing they now have in readiness, and also of such Articles as they can't move without, which he has ordered to be provided forthwith; and that he shall get every thing forwarded according to the best of his ability.

Byrd dated his letter from the place now known as Staunton, the county seat of Augusta County. The second letter was that of 11 July 1760.

To Commanding Officers

[ca. 8 July 1760]

This letter has not been found. It is assumed to have been written to the commanding officers of King and Queen, Gloucester, and James City counties, directing them to buy and collect arms for an expedition against the Cherokees. See *EJC* 6:166 for Colonel Chiswell's letter on the subject and the council's advice about a reply.

To the Board of Trade

My Lords   Wmsburgh July 11th 1760

Under Cover with this I inclose to your Lordships a Triplicate of a Letter I wrote to your right honble. Board on the 1st of December last with a Copy of a Letter from Lt. Col. Stephen to me referred to in it. My Reason for sending this is my apprehension that the Duplicates were both lost: one being sent in my Box of public papers to your right honble. Board, by the Deliverance Captn. White who we know was lost on the Coast of France. The other I sent by post to New York, and fear it went by the General Wall packet which was Taken & ransom'd, but all the papers thrown overboard.[1] I am with the greatest Respect My Lords Your Lordships most Obedient & devoted Servant

                                                Fran: Fauquier.

To the Lords Commissioners for Trade &ct.

ALS: C.O.5/1330, ff. 22–23. Endorsed with note "Originals not received" and as read 19 Nov. 1760.

1. Fauquier probably meant that he had sent the original of his letter of 1 Dec. 1759, with a copy of Stephen's letter to him of 29 Oct. 1759, by the *Deliverance*,

Captain White, when she sailed from Virginia on 28 Dec. 1759; and that around or after the middle of March he had sent duplicates of those two letters by post to New York to be forwarded; see Fauquier's letters of 13 Mar. and 2 June 1760 to the Board of Trade.

From William Byrd

[Camp at Bryan's, 11 July 1760]

This letter has not been found. Fauquier communicated it to the council on 23 July 1760, and it is abstracted in *EJC* 6:167:

the 2d dated Camp at Bryan's July the 11th signifying he thinks it will be necessary to have small Posts all the way out to the Big-Island on Holton's River at 25 Miles distance, sending the distances inclosed and the proper places for such Posts—is of opinion a respectable Fort should be built at the Big-Island, from whence the Cherokees might easily be humbled in the Spring—desires his Honour's Instructions, should the Cherokees intimidated at the preparations carried on against them sue for Peace, whether he is to grant it them, and on what Terms? If he finds by any means the Garrison at Fort Loudoun holds out when he gets to Holston's River, and should think they might be brought off by a strong scouting Party, and a forced March when the whole Army could not be marched to their relief with Provisions to support them for any considerable Time, whether he may attempt to bring off his Majesty's Troops, and abandon the Fort? adding he shall be at a Loss for an Interpreter should he take any Prisoners, or any Flags of Truce should come in—inclosing a Return of his Strength—also a return of the Men recruited by the different Officers.

Byrd probably dated his letter from the homestead of William Bryan at the Great Spring, a couple of miles southwest of the present Salem, in Roanoke County. The list of posts that Byrd proposed was possibly much the same as that enclosed in Fauquier's letter of 30 Apr. 1761 to Amherst, according to which the first post was to be at Dunkard Bottom, 40 mi. from Bryan's; the second at Sayer's Mill, 24 mi. from Dunkard Bottom; the third at Davis's, 26 mi. from Sayer's Mill; the fourth at Stalnaker's, 25 mi. from Davis's; the fifth at Half Way Spring, 25 mi. from Stalnaker's; and the last at the Big Island (or Long Island), 25 mi. from Half Way Spring. A fort on the Long Island, at the present city of Kingsport in Tennessee, near the point where the several branches of the Holston River come together, would have been well placed to command the Cherokee villages to the southward. The places mentioned in this list are hard to fix precisely, but it is probable that they can be located as follows in the counties of today: Dunkard Bottom was on the west side of New River in the neighborhood of the present Dublin, in Pulaski County; Sayer's Mill was Alexander Sayers's mill on Reed or Reedy Creek, in central Wythe County; Davis's was the homestead of James Davis near the head of the middle fork of Holston River, in central Smyth County; Stalnaker's was the homestead of Samuel Stalnaker on the Holston near the present-day Chilhowie, in western Smyth County; and Half Way Spring was presumably a point somewhere in the southwestern part of Washington County.

To William Byrd

[24 July 1760]

This letter has not been found, but Fauquier mentioned it in his letter of 1 July 1761 to Byrd, and it is assumed to have been written in answer to Byrd's letters of 4 and 11 July 1760 and in accordance with the council's advice, stated in *EJC* 6:167–68:

> Upon which it was the advice of the Council that his Honour would Order Colo. Byrd to proceed with all possible Expedition to the relief of Fort Loudoun, with what is already provided for his March without any View to a future Campaign—and signifie to him there is no necessity of erecting any more Forts than one at Big Island, and that a Stockaded Fort to secure the Provisions will be sufficient, unless it should be likewise necessary to establish some small Post near Stalnaker's. In relation to any Offers of Peace from the Cherokee's, they are of Opinion that, as we act only in the Capacity of Auxiliaries, all such Proposals, and the Deputy's who bring them, should be referred to Governour Bull, and Mr. Montgomery, but that Mr Byrd may Act in concert with them.
>
> As to bringing off the Garrison they advise that his Honour would direct him to take all possible methods to inform Captain Demeri of his Approach, and endeavour to learn from him in what manner he can be most serviceable to him, to acquaint him he comes to his relief, to assist him to maintain the Fort to the last Extremity; or in case he should by a superior Force, or by a scarcity of Provision be obliged to abandon it to secure his retreat—they also advised that his Honour would order one of the Smith's to attend Mr Byrd as Interpreter.

The Smiths whom the council mentioned were no doubt Richard Smith, who often acted for the colony as interpreter and agent, and his brother Abraham, also an interpreter and a trader.

From William Bull

[Charles Town, S.C., 26 July 1760]

This letter has not been found. Fauquier communicated it to the council on 10 Oct. 1760, and it is described in *EJC* 6:172 as reporting Colonel Montgomerie's reply to a letter from Bull, who had asked Montgomerie "To continue there for the Protection of that Province, till the Storm that threatens it, is blown over, or at least delay his Embarkation." The council advised Fauquier to send the letter to the House of Burgesses, and he did so the same day; see *JHB, 1758–1761*, p. 190.

To [Richard Bland]

Sir[1] [Williamsburg, 28 July 1760]

The first account of the Collections for the sufferers of Boston was sent to the press in haste & was indeed not distinct. It has since then been mended, as by this time you probably have seen, & I hope in such a manner that your generous contribution will be no longer liable to the mistake which I confess there was too much room for before.

The particulars that passed at your court I read with concern and indignation, as well as the others about the same person, & with abundance of hearty wishes for some easy method of remedying abuses so mischievous & so scandalous.[2]

Rowe's foolish affair has not been told you exactly as it happened. The matter is too idle, and too long to trouble you with a full account of.[3] I have always been sensible that too many of the clergy were sufficiently ignorant of their real interest to engage in such suits as those you mention, tho I hope there are not a few that from reasons of superior kind will decline to take a step that is so likely to be followed by disagreable consequences.[4]

The Present you have been kind enough to desire the printer to make me will be most acceptable. I acknowledge to you freely that I have become so much a Virginian as to be very impatient to see our defence managed by so able an advocate.[5]

You will cease to wonder at the shortness of my letter when I have told you that it is the indifferent state of my health which obliges me to employ the hand of another to assure you that I am Sir Your very humble Servant

Fran: Fauquier

Wmsburg 28th July 1760.

LS: University of Virginia, Tracy W. McGregor Library. The letter has no superscription or address.

1. The contents of the letter are taken to identify the recipient as Richard Bland, as the notes will indicate. Bland (1710–1776) was a member of the House of Burgesses for Prince George County from 1742 till 1775.

2. Bland was named one of the justices of the peace for Prince George County on or about 2 Oct. 1744 and remained in office until 1771 or later. Nothing is known of the events in court which Fauquier refers to, and the person referred to has not been identified.

3. The Reverend Jacob Rowe, born about 1730, was licensed for Virginia in 1758 and on 14 June of that year took office as professor of morality, or master of the philosophy school, at the College of William and Mary. In Sept. 1758 Rowe was accused of making scandalous and malicious utterances about the House of Burgesses and was taken into custody, but was released upon making an apology and paying some fees. In April and May 1760, Rowe was examined by the visitors of the college on charges of drunkenness, profanity, and insubordination; Fauquier, as rector, admonished Rowe severely, and Rowe promised to mend his ways. Richard Bland had been named a visitor about 1758, but it appears that he was not present at the meetings when Rowe's behavior was under consideration. See *JHB, 1758–1761*, pp. 16–18, and Lambeth Palace Library, Fulham Palace Papers, XIII, 284–87, for particulars of Rowe's difficulties with the burgesses, and the minutes of the college visitors.

4. The suits concerned are not identified, but it is likely that they were suits brought by the Virginia clergy for payments of salary in consequence of the Two Penny Act; Bland was the author of the act and its champion.

5. The present must have been a copy of Bland's pamphlet *A Letter to the Clergy of Virginia, in which the Conduct of the General Assembly is Vindicated against the Reflexions contained in a Letter to the Lords of Trade and Plantations, from the Lord-Bishop of London* (Williamsburg: William Hunter, 1760; Evans 8551); Bland dated his *Letter* 20 Mar. 1760, so that it was presumably already printed, or at least in the printer's hands.

To Horatio Sharpe

Sir   Wmsburgh July 28th 1760

I have absolutely nothing left me to do but to ask your Pardon. Knowing nothing of Mr. Fox or even his name but as told me for that Purpose, I had quite forgot the whole Affair: and looking in my Copy Book of Letters I found no Copy of that Date (not thinking it of Consequence enough to copy) which together occasioned my last Letter. I well remember'd the having mention'd Sir Isaac's papers, being a Subject the Doctor and I had often talk'd over; and thought it must be in the Letter I sent by Mr. Burnaby not finding it among my other Letters in my Copy Book,[1]

If you will excuse this great piece of Impertinence, I have been guilty of, you will much oblige. Sir, Your most Obedient humble Servant.

                                                           Fran: Fauquier

To his Excellcy Govr Sharpe.

ALS: Hall of Records of Maryland, Executive Papers, Folder 143.

1. This letter appears to be Fauquier's reply to an untraced letter ca. July from Sharpe answering Fauquier's letter of 14 June 1760. See Fauquier's letters of 12 Apr. and 24 May 1760 to Sharpe and Sharpe's reply of ca. June 1760 for the earlier pieces of this confusing exchange.

From Jeffery Amherst

Sir,   Camp at Oswego 28th July 1760

Having received my Patent of Vice Admiral of the Dominion of Virginia (and Caused a Copy thereof to be taken which remains with me) I herewith transmit You the same,[1] that You may be so good as to Cause it to be Published in like manner as You did that of Governor, the Copy of which I shall be glad to Receive, whenever it is transcribed.

By this same Opportunity I must Return You my thanks for Your Favor of the 18th May, returning the Letter directed to Mr. Turner.

I Was in hopes, I should have had the pleasure of Acquainting You with our having taken the Vessells the French have on this Lake,[2] of which there was the greatest Appearance a few days ago, but they have Unluckily Escaped Us, and got down the River St. Lawrence, for which place I am preparing to set out shortly on my Way to Montreal,[3] from whence I flatter Myself to Communicate to You the Success of His Majesty's Arms, I am, with great Regard, Sir, &ca.

Honble. Lt. Govr. Fauquier.

Copy: W.O.34/37, f. 217. Marked "Private."

1. For Amherst's commission as vice admiral of Virginia, dated 6 Oct. 1759, see H.C.A.50/11, ff. 10–16, 106, 126.
2. Amherst's camp at Oswego was on Lake Ontario, and the French vessels on that lake were the *Outaouaise* and the *Iroquoise*.
3. Amherst left Oswego on 10 Aug. to cross Lake Ontario and on 15 Aug. moved down the St. Lawrence toward Montreal, the objective of the campaign of 1760.

From William Byrd

[Camp at Campbell's, August 1760]

This letter has not been found. Fauquier communicated it to the council on 16 Sept. 1760, and it is mentioned in *EJC* 6:169. The abstract given there does not differentiate between the contents of this letter and those of Byrd's letter of ca. 20 Aug. 1760 from Sayer's Mill; see the second letter for the abstract. It is possible that other letters than these two were written by Byrd to Fauquier during August. Byrd probably dated his letter from James Campbell's homestead in the neighborhood later called Fort Lewis, in the western part of Roanoke County.

From Cadwallader Colden

Sir   New York August 4th 1760

On Wensday last our late worthy Governor Mr. De Lancey departed this life.[1] He was not apprehensive of any danger when he was seised in the morning with a pain in his breast, and tho' a Physician was afterwards sent for, he expir'd before any releife could be applied: In this gentleman his Majesty has lost a most able and faithfull Servant, and, I may add the Provinces in general a sincere friend.

The Administration by virtue of his Majesties Commission devolving on me,[2] as eldest Councelor, it is expedient I should inform the Governors of his Majesties other Colonies of this Event; least any interruption might be given to a correspondence between them which I am sensible must be necessary at all times, but more especially at present, to promote the kings service and to preserve Union and Harmony among the several provinces, so essential to their common welfare. I assure myself of establishing & keeping up an intercourse with you on all occasions conducive to those ends. And it will give me a singular satisfaction if by my present situation, I should have in my power to serve your [Honour] or any of your Friends. I am &c &c &c

To the Honble Francis Fauquier Governor of Virginia.

Copy: New-York Historical Society, Cadwallader Colden Papers. Circular to governors. In the transcript above, "your Honour" in the last paragraph replaces "your Excellency" of the letter-book copy, which is underlined and was presumably meant to be replaced as necessary by the form of address used to lieutenant governors.

1. James De Lancey (1703–1760) was lieutenant governor of New York.
2. Cadwallader Colden (1688–1776), senior member or president of the council of New York, became acting governor on the death of the lieutenant governor; he received a commission as lieutenant governor in 1761 and held his office until he died.

From William Byrd

[Sayer's Mill, ca. 20 August 1760]

This letter has not been found. Fauquier communicated it to the council on 16 Sept. 1760, and it is abstracted in *EJC* 6:169:

His Honour communicated to the Council, and desired their advice upon, several Letters from Colo. Byrd of last Month, the first dated from Camp at Campbells the last at Sayer's Mill informing of his present situation, the Disposition of the Troops under his Command, and the steps he had taken towards the relieving Fort Loudoun; inclosing a letter he had just received from Governor Bull, and a Copy of Captain Demeri's letter, with the resolution of the Officers, and the Capitulation for the surrender of Fort Loudoun to the Cherokees.

It is not certain how many letters from Byrd are represented in this abstract. See the note on Byrd's letter of August 1760 from Campbell's. The letters from Bull and Demeré have not been found. The resolution of the officers has not been traced, but it was presumably an account of the council of war held on 6 Aug. 1760, at which the officers of Fort Loudoun decided to ask the Cherokees for terms of peace. The capitulation was that of 7 Aug. 1760, a copy of which follows.

Enclosure: Articles of Capitulation

[7 August 1760]

Copy On the 7th August Captain John Stuart set out to Chotie, accompanied by Lt. Jas. Adamson,[1] & some Indians where the following terms were Stipulated. Articles of Capitulation agreed upon, and assented to by Captain Paul Demere Commanding His Majesty's Forces at Fort Loudoun, and the Head Men and Warriors of the Over Hill Cherokee Towns.

1st That the Garrison of Fort Loudoun, march out with their Arms and Drums, each Soldier having as much Powder and Ball as their Officers shall think necessary for the March, and what Baggage he may choose to carry.

2d That the Garrison be permitted to March for Virginia, or Fort Prince George, as the Commanding Officer shall think proper unmolested, and that a Number of Indians be appointed to escort them, and to hunt for Provisions on the March.

3d That such Soldiers as are lame, or by Sickness disabled from Marching, be received into the Indian Towns, and kindly used untill they recover, and then to be returned to Fort Prince George.

4th That the Indians do provide the Garrison with as many Horses as they can conveniently for their March, agreeing with the Soldiers or Officers for payment.

5th That the Fort, Great Guns Powder, Ball, and spare Arms be deliver'd to the Indians, without any Fraud on the Day appointed for the March of the Troops.

Signed. / Paul Demere.   Cunni [Mark] Catogue[2]
                                      his Mark.
                                      his
                       Oucannastote[3] [Mark]
                                      Mark.

Copy: C.O.5/1330, f. 3. Endorsed as received with Fauquier's letter of 17 Sept. 1760, and as received 10 Nov. and read 11 Nov. 1760.

1. Adamson had been a lieutenant in the South Carolina provincial force since 1756.
2. Conocotocko (or Kanagataucko), whose name is spelled in a number of ways, was also known as Standing Turkey. He was one of the chiefs of Chotee, and about the beginning of 1760 he was chosen "emperor" of the Cherokees.
3. Oconostota, also known as Great Warrior, was another of the chiefs of Chotee and at this time was the leader of the Overhill Cherokees.

From Robert Monckton

Sir,   Fort Pitt August the 21st 1760

As it cannot be Expected, that General Amherst will be able to spare any of the Regular Troops now with him for the Winter Garrisons of the Posts in this Department, which are now Considerably Encreased, & the Number of Troops greatly lessened.

I think it my duty, Sir, to give You the Earliest Notice, that it will be absolutely necessary for the Support of His Majesty's Rights on Lake Erie and the River Ohio; That at least 300, of the Troops, now here should be Continued the Winter.

This Sir, is so Essential a Service, that I cannot in the least doubt, but You will use Your utmost Endeavors with Your Council & Assembly to Induce them to Comply with this so necessary a requisition.[1] I have the honour to be, Sir, &ca.

                                                                Robert Monckton
To Govr. Hamilton Govr. Fauquier & Govr. Sharpe

Copy: C.O. 5/59, f. 157. Endorsed as enclosed in Monckton's letter of 23 Aug. 1760 to Amherst and as sent in Amherst's letter of 7 Nov. 1760. The text of the copy, with variations as indicated for Virginia, would have the second paragraph continue and conclude with the words "with Officers & Non Commission'd Officers in Proportion, Should be immediately re-enlisted for this Service." Probably these words were meant to be included only in the letter to Pennsylvania.

1. Fauquier communicated this letter to the council on 16 Sept. 1760; the abstract in the council journal states Monckton's request as being "that at least three hundred of Virginia Troops now there should be continued for the Winter" (*EJC* 6:170). Fauquier reported the assembly's response to Monckton's request in his letter of 17 Oct. 1760 to Monckton.

To Jeffery Amherst

Sir   Wmsburgh Augst 22d 1760

I have this moment received your Dispatch containing your Commission of Vice Admiral of this Colony, which I will enter on the Minutes of the first Council and lodge it in the Council Office,[1] as I did your Commission of Governor and Commander in chief; an attested Copy of which I will send you by the first Opportunity.

I am sorry the French Vessels have for the present escaped you but I assure you I expect every thing from your Troops commanded as they are.

I am afraid So. Carolina is in great Distress. I know no particulars having received no Express from Lt. Govr. Bull for a long time, which I am surprized at, as he seemed to depend much on our cooperating with Col. Montgomery. I am with the greatest Esteem Sir Your Excellencys most obedient humble Servant

Fran: Fauquier

To Majr. Genl. Amherst.

ALS: W.O.34/37, f. 41. Marked "Private."

1. Fauquier produced Amherst's commission as vice admiral at the council meeting on 16 Sept. 1760. See *EJC* 6:168.

From William Pitt

Sir   Whitehall 23d Augt 1760

The Commanders of His Majesty's Forces & Fleets in North America, and the West Indies, having transmitted repeated & certain Intelligence of an illegal & most pernicious Trade, carried on by the King's Subjects in North America, & the West Indies, as well to the French Islands, as to the French Settlements on the Continent of America & particularly to the Rivers Mobile & Mississippi, by which the Enemy is, to the greatest Reproach & Detriment of Government, supplyed with Provisions, and other Necessaries, whereby they are, principally, if not alone, enabled to sustain & protract this long and expensive War, & it farther appearing that large Sums in Bullion are, also, sent, by the Kings Subjects, to the above Places, in return whereof Commodities are taken, which interfere with the Produce of the British Colonies Themselves, in open Contempt of the Authority of the Mother Country, as well as to the most manifest Prejudice of the Manufactures & Trade of Great Britain: In Order, therefore, to put the most speedy & effectual Stop to such flagitious Practices so utterly subversive of all Law, & so highly repugnant to the Honor & Wellbeing of this Kingdom, It is His Majesty's express Will & Pleasure, that You do, forthwith, make the strictest & most diligent Enquiry into the State of this dangerous and ignominious Trade, and that You do use every Means in your Power, to detect & discover Persons concerned either as Principals, or Accessories therein, and that You do take every Step, authorized by Law, to bring all such heinous Offenders to the most exemplary and condign Punishment: And You will as soon as may be, & from time to time, transmit to Me, for the King's Information, full &

particular Accounts of the Progress You shall have made in the Execution of these His Majesty's Commands, to which the King expects that You do pay the most exact Obedience: And You are farther to use your utmost Endeavors to trace out & investigate the various Artifices & Evasions, by which the Dealers in this iniquitous Intercourse, find Means to cover their criminal Proceedings, & to elude the Law, in order that from such Lights due & timely Consideration may be had what farther Provisions shall be necessary to restrain an Evil of such extensive & pernicious Consequences. I am &c.

                                                                              W: Pitt

Copy: C.O.5/215, pp. 283–[87?]. Circular addressed to governors in North America and the West Indies.

Petition of St. Andrew's Parish

[ca. 25 August 1760]

To the Honorable Francis Fauquier Esqr. his Majesty's Lieutenant Governour and Commander in Chief of the Colony and Dominion of Virginia.

The Petition of the Church Wardens and Vestry of the Parish of Saint Andrew humbly shew. That this Vestry being applied to [by] the Reverend Mr. Patrick Lunan[1] and since such application by the Reverend Mr. Gronow Owen[2] who had your Honour's Letter of Recommendation Directed to us and they being intire Strangers to us. We therefore have agreed with the said Gentlemen to take them both upon Trial until the tenth Day of November next. And taking it into Consideration that your Honour may in the mean Time make Presentation into the Parish of such Minister as your Honour shall please. We therefore humbly Petition your Honour That in your Clemency you'l suffer us to make trial of those Gentlemen and at the expiration of such Time choose for ourselves.[3] And your Petitioners as in Duty bound shall ever pray &c.

                        Edward Goodrich
                        Robert Briggs   } Ch: Wardens[4]

Copy: Virginia State Library, Vestry Book of St. Andrew's Parish, Brunswick County, p. 44. The date given is that of the meeting of the vestry at which the petition was approved; the word in brackets was apparently omitted in error.

1. Patrick Lunan was licensed for Virginia 23 Dec. 1758 and had the king's bounty for Virginia 29 Jan. 1760.

2. Gronow, or Goronwy, Owen (ca. 1742–1770) was licensed for Virginia 21 Oct. 1757 and in 1758–59 was master of the grammar school at the College of William and Mary.

3. It is assumed that both Lunan and Owen served the parish in 1760. Lunan became minister of the Upper Parish of Nansemond County at some date in 1760 and served there until 1764. On pp. 45–46 of the St. Andrew's Parish Vestry Book, in the minutes of the vestry meeting of 22 June 1761, is recorded the reading of a presentation from Fauquier inducting Owen into the parish of St. Andrew, where he served until 1769.

4. Edward Goodrich and Robert Briggs were commissioned justices of the peace for Brunswick County in 1749. Goodrich was elected one of the burgesses for Brunswick County in 1755, and reelected in 1758, but was replaced when he became sheriff of the county in 1759.

From Jeffery Amherst

Sir,   River St. Lawrence below the Isle Royale[1] 26th August 1760

On the 10th Instant, I Embarked the Army, and proceeded with the Same, across Lake Ontario into this River, Where on the 16th in the Evening, off Oswegatchie[2] the Advanced Guard descried one of the Enemy's Vessels but it being Soon after duskish, Nothing could be Effected that Night, tho' we tryed as much as possible to Attack her: At Day break on the 17th our Row Galleys Engaged her, & by seven in the morning She Struck: Her Name was the Ottawawa, mounting ten twelve pounders, and one hundred Men Officers Included, besides Monsr. de La Broqueri,[3] Who Commanded her: in the Engagement we had only one Man killed, & another wounded; And the Enemy thirteen of both.

The Army which the preceding Night had Encamped on the Pointe du Baril,[4] then moved down to Oswegatchie, a very good Indian Settlement with a Blockhouse Fort but Abandoned; the Enemy being posted on an Island, between four & five Miles further down the River, Where they were reported to be very Strongly fortified; both Shores were reconnoitred during the night, and early the next Morning, and the Engineers having reported to me the Situation of the Coasts & Islands nearest the Fort; immediately on the return of the Engineers on the 18th a part of the Army passed down on each Coast, and after Some Opposition by a smart Cannonading, the Fort was Compleatly invested, so that none of its Garrison could make its Escape: the four following days were employed in raising my Batteries, Which being finished on the Morning of the 23d in Concert with our Shipping, I began to fire on the Fort, Which lasted till Yesterday afternoon, When the French beat a Parley, desiring to know What terms Should be granted them: My Answer was, that the

Garrison should be Prisoners of War; that every thing in and depending on the Fort, should be delivered in its present State; and that I gave them only ten Minutes to Accept of, or dissent from these Proposals; They Accordingly Yielded to these Conditions, and I have the Satisfaction to Inform You, that His Majesty's Troops are now in possession of Fort Levis.

Our loss upon this Occasion has been very inconsiderable; that of the Enemy (Whose Garrison Consisted of about three hundred Men) about twelve killed and Forty wounded; Mor. Pouchot[5] the Same Gentleman that was last Year taken at Niagara Commanded them. I am, with great regard, Sir, &ca.

Jeff: Amherst

Copy: C.O.5/59, ff. 106–7. Circular addressed to governors on the continent from Cape Breton to Georgia, inclusive. Endorsed as being in Amherst's letter of 26 Aug. 1760. Following the text above are two paragraphs: one for the president of the council of New York recommends a reassuring proclamation to the inhabitants along the Mohawk River; the other, for the aforesaid president and for the governor of New Jersey, states arrangements for disposing of French prisoners.

1. The Isle Royale, in the upper St. Lawrence, later called Chimney Island, was the site of Fort Lévis, the chief defense of the upper river.
2. The Oswegatchie River in northern New York flows into the St. Lawrence at what is now Ogdensburg. At about that point, not far above the Isle Royale, the French built the post called Fort La Galette, which had by this time been deserted for some months.
3. Not much is known of this man beyond his military service. He was perhaps Joseph de la Broquerie, a Canadian born in 1732.
4. The Pointe du Baril was on the St. Lawrence, a few miles from Fort La Galette and nearer to Lake Ontario.
5. The Chevalier Pierre de Pouchot, captain in the Régiment de Béarn, later wrote the *Mémoires sur la dernière guerre* (1781), a study of the Seven Years' War.

To Cadwallader Colden

Sir   Wmsburgh Augst 31st 1760

I am very sensible of the Loss your Colony must sustain in their late Worthy Governor; but at the same Time think they are very happy in being so well compensated for it as they are, by the Administration of their Affairs devolving on a Gentleman who has on many Occasions shown his Ability to undertake them.

You may assure your self that I shall embrace every Opportunity of cultivating a Correspondence with you to the advancement of the Interest of the Colonies, and the promoting his Majesty's Service. I am with great Regard, Sir, Your most obedient humble Servant.

Fran: Fauquier

To the Honble Cad. Colden.

ALS: New-York Historical Society, Cadwallader Colden Papers.

To the Board of Trade

My Lords,   Wmsburgh Septr 1st 1760

I take the opportunity of a Bristol [ship] which is just ready to sail, to acknowledge the Receipt of your Favour of the 13th June which I received on the 30th ulto. together with the Copy of the Representation of your right honorable Board to His Majesty in Relation to three Acts of Assembly passd by me in the Years 1758 and 1759; his Majesty's Order's in Council, and Repeal of the said Acts in Consequence thereof; and the Report of Sir Matthew Lamb, concerning the Agents Act.

Give me Leave My Lords to make an acknowledgement of the Obligations I have to your Lordships for the Tenderness you show me in not aggravating the deep Concern I feel my self under, for having inadvertently fallen into so many Errors as I find I have done, in Respect to the giving my assent to Acts which have pass'd the other two Branches of the Legislature. But I hope My Lords to set my Actions in such a point of View, as to take off, in great Measure at least, the unfavorable Opinion your Lordships entertain of them at present.

As to the three particular Acts in Question; upon the Receipt of his Majesty's Repeal thereof, I enquired of Mr. Waller the Clerk of the General Court, an old and leading Member in the House of Burgesses;[1] who is frequently employed in drawing the Acts, and actualy drew one of these three, what was the Reason that the saving and suspending Clauses were left out in these three Acts; whereas I must own that in examining into all the private Acts pass'd since the Revisal of the Laws in 1748 I could not find one single Instance of their being omitted. His answer was, that in these Acts, as in all others, He had followed the established practice and Custom of their House; which was this. That in all Acts to dock Entails, and in case of Infants, where the parties in possession cannot alienate the premises without an Act for that purpose; the saving and suspending Clauses are never omitted. But that, where the parties in possession had an undoubted Right in themselves to alienate and convey the Lands upon a proper Application to a Court of Judicature (which was the Case in all these Acts) and only applyed for an Act of Assembly to expedite the sale and make it clear and indisputable hereafter; they were never inserted. But my Lords to confess a plain Truth which shall always be the Measure of my Conduct to your right honorable Board; I fairly own, that upon a presumption that all such acts were prepared according to Form, in the lower House; and the Rights of his Majesty were properly taken Care of when the Bills came before the Council; I gave my Assent to them without ever examining them, or paying any Attention to them. But as I have incurred his Majesty's Displeasure by doing so, Your Lordships may be assured I will be more circumspect for the Future.

The Box of public papers and Acts, among which was the Negro Act, was ship'd on Board the Deliverance, Capt. White who was lost on the Coast of France, the Duplicates of these Acts went by the Jacob and Joanna Capt. Clarkson who sailed the latter End of May,[2] who I hope is safely arrived and that your Lordships are in possession of the Acts of that Session.

I am truly sensible that a Governor or Commander in chief is not to ask the Advice of the Council assigned him by his Majesty, whether he shall obey the Instructions of his Majesty: but in Regard to this Act[3] it was attended with some particular Circumstances which induced me to take that Step from which I thought I ought not afterwards to recede. The Act did not lay any new Duty; if it had, I should most certainly have refused it without taking Advice upon it: but it only provided against a Fraud daily practised to avoid a Duty, originally laid and by other subsequent Acts continued long before I arrived in the Colony. But the Act, in express Terms (which could not be avoided, to give it, its intended Force and Effect) contradicted the Instruction; in this Situation and under these Circumstances I applyed to the Council for their Advice what I should do, who, all but one, were unanimous that the Sense and Spirit was by no means broke in upon as no new Duty was imposed by the Act; as your Lordships will find by their Reasons inserted in the Minutes of the Council, and by a Duplicate I sent as soon as I heard of the Loss of the Deliverance. I have been unfortunate for duplicates of all these papers were sent by the New York packet which was taken by the French and Ransomed; but the papers were all thrown overboard and lost. However there is now an End of this Affair, as in the next Sessions this Act was repealed and the Duty lowered from twenty to ten pr. Cent, to answer the same purpose as was intended by the former act; viz. to increase the Money coming into the Treasury from the said Duty.

In Relation to the Agent's Act I am fully convinced that it was not the

1 September 1760

Design of any part of the Legislature to give the Committee of Correspondence any powers for which they should not be accountable to the General Assembly; so that the alteration desired by Your Lordships will not as I apprehend meet with the least Difficulty. Whether the word General was left out by mistake; or whether the common Acceptation of the Words, Assembly and general Assembly having the same Import have occasioned this, I know not, but your lordships may depend on my rectifying this in the next Session. I hope your Lordships will indulge me in the Explanation of the Steps leading to this Agents Act. When my predecessor the honble. Mr. Dinwiddie had a Dispute in this Colony about the Pistole Fee, the Burgesses lamented their not having an agent at home to represent affairs of this Nature to his Majesty and your right honble. Board, supposing naturaly enough that Mr. Abercrombie who was paid by the Governor & Council out of the 2 sh. Duty would not solicit that or any other affair against the Governor: so they sent home an Agent on purpose at a great Expence. From that Time they have been very intent on an Agents Act, which in Mr. Dinwiddies Time they could never obtain. So intent were they on this Affair that they attempted to tack it to the Money Bill, in the second session after my arrival; which I told them I would certainly refuse under such Conditions, as I hoped never to make my self liable to any complaint. I could not see the ill Consequence of letting them have an Agent upon their raising Money on themselves to pay him. Thus the Agents Bill was prepared and pass'd. Notwithstanding this appointment of an Agent by Act of Assembly, Mr. Abercrombie is still continued as Agent to me and the Council to transact all Business relating to the royal Revenues and such other Affairs as are immediately under our Cognizance only. He has Instructions to cooperate with the other Agent in all Matters for the Behoof and Benefit of the Colony.

As I have already mentioned to your Lordships my having lately sent Duplicates or Triplicates of the Letters lost your Lordships will see by my Letter of the first of December that I am very far from being urgent in having the Lands on the Ohio settled. I have been pressed thereto my self but am so far from pressing it that I have incurred the Displeasure of the Officers who are Claimants under the late Governor's proclamation, and have been charged with Breach of his Engagement by that proclamation; for having obstructed their having Surveys and patents for those Lands, and for having wrote to Governor Hamilton to desire he would desist from making any such grants till his Majesty's pleasure therein should be known. This I did because I found some of our Officers designed to apply to the proprietarys Office in Pennsylvania for Grants of the said Lands, as they apprehended the Grants would be made good, in whichever Colony the Lands granted should be found to lie. The Lands the Officers (who were on the Spot and had Time to examine) had fixed their Eyes on were many of them in Pensylvania, and many on the western Side the Ohio; which made me apply for a Copy of the Agreements or Treaties made with the Indians by the late General Forbes and General Stanwix, but which I have never got Sight of. I am extremely well pleased that your Lordships Sentiments on this Head concur with and confirm mine, as I hope it will make the Claimants more easy under my Refusal to make them the Grants they required.

I hope my Lords I have now cleared my self to your Lordships Satisfaction, from the least Symptom of Inclination to disobey my Royal Masters Instructions. If I at all know my own Heart, there is not the least wish of that Sort lurking in it. Perhaps I have let Circumstances weigh too much with me; if that is the Case I will be hereafter more cautious.

If your Lordships have ever favoured me with any Letter on the Subject of the Act relating to the Clergy, I have never received it; nor any Instructions, Orders of Council or other papers, excepting those deliver'd by the Revd. Mr. Camm on the 27th June, in the extraordinary Manner which I notifyed to your Lordships in my Letter of the 30th of that Month. I am with the greatest Respect & Esteem My Lords Your Lordships most Obedient Obliged & devoted Servant

Fran: Fauquier

To the right Honble. the Lords of Trade.

ALS: C.O.5/1330, ff. 28–31. Endorsed as received 1 Dec. and read 2 Dec. 1760. The word in brackets is supplied to complete the sense.

1. Benjamin Waller (1710–1786), an attorney, was one of the burgesses for James City County 1744–61.
2. The *Jacob and Joanna*, John Clarkson master, was entered in York River from Maryland on 15 Jan. 1760, but there is no record of her clearance. The vessel was a brig of 300 tons, built and registered in Maryland in 1759 and owned by Jacob Giles.
3. The Negro Act.

To James Abercromby

[2 September 1760]

This letter has not been found, but Abercromby acknowledged it in his letter of 1 Dec. 1760 to Fauquier.

From Jeffery Amherst

Sir, Camp of Montreal 9th September 1760

In mine of the 26th ultimo I acquainted You with the progress of the Army, after their Departure from Oswego, and with the Success of His Majesty's Arms against Fort Levis, now Fort William Augustus, where I remained no longer than was requisite, to make such preparations as I Judged Essentially necessary for the Passage of the Army down the River, which took me up till the 30th.

In the Morning of the following day, I sat out, and proceeded from Station to Station to our present ground, where we arrived on the 6th in the Evening; after having in the Passage Sustained a Loss of Eighty Eight men Drowned; twenty Nine Batteaus of Regiments; Seventeen of Artillery with some Artillery and Stores; Seventeen Whaleboats, and one Row Galley Staved, Occasiond by the Violence of the Current, and the rapids being full of broken Waves.

The Inhabitants of the Settlements I passed thro', in my way hither, having Abandoned their Houses, & run into the Woods, I sent after them; Some were taken, and others came in of their own Accord; I had them disarmed, and Caused the Oath of Allegiance to be tendered to them, Which they readily took; And I Accordingly put them in quiet possession of their habitations, with Which treatment they seemed no less surprised than happy.

The Troops being formed, and the Light Artillery brought up; the Army lay on their Arms the Night of the 6th.

On the 7th in the Morning two Officers came to an Advanced Post, with a Letter from the Marquis de Vaudreuil,[1] referring me to What one of them, Colonel Bouquinville,[2] had to say. The Conversation ended, with a Cessation of Arms, till twelve o'Clock When the Proposals were brought in: Soon after I returned them with the terms I was willing to grant; Which both the Marquis de Vaudreuil & Monsr. de Levis the French General,[3] were very Strenuous to have Softened; this Occasioned Sundry Letters to pass between Us, during the day as well as the Night (When the Army again lay on their Arms) but as I would not on any Account deviate in the least from my original Conditions, and Insisted on an immediate and Catagorical Answer; Monsr. de Vaudreuil Soon after day break, Notified to me that he had determined to Accept of them, and two Setts of them, were accordingly Signed by him and me, and Exchanged Yesterday, When Colo. Haldimand[4] with the Grenadiers and Light Infantry of the Army took possession of one of the Gates of the Town, and is this day to proceed in fullfilling the Articles of the Capitulation by Which the French Troops are all to lay down their Arms; are not to Serve during the Continuance of the present War; And are to be sent back to Old France as are also the Governors, and principal Officers of the Legislature of the Whole Country, Which I have now the Satisfaction to Inform You, is entirely Yielded to the Dominion of His Majesty, on Which Interesting & happy Event, I most Sincerely Congratulate You.

Governor Murray,[5] with the Troops from Quebec landed below the Town on Sunday last, & Colonel Haviland with his Corps[6] (that took Possession of the Isle au Noix, Abandoned by the Enemy on the 28th) Arrived Yesterday at the South Shore, opposite to my Camp. I am, with great regard, Sir, &ca

Jeff: Amherst

Copy: C.O.5/59, ff. 143–44. Circular addressed to governors on the continent from Cape Breton to Georgia, inclusive. Endorsed as being in Amherst's letter of 4 Oct. 1760. Writing is very faint on f. 143 verso. Fauquier communicated this letter to the council on 6 Oct. 1760.

1. This letter from the governor of Canada, requesting a truce, was brought to Amherst's camp at Lachine, on the western end of the island of Montreal.
2. Louis-Antoine de Bougainville (1729–1811) had served in Canada since 1756. He was promoted to colonel in 1759 and in 1760 was in command of the defenses of the Isle aux Noix, at the northern end of Lake Champlain.
3. François Gaston de Lévis (1720–1787) succeeded Montcalm in command.
4. Frederick Haldimand (1718–1791) was a colonel in the Royal American Regiment.
5. James Murray (ca. 1719–1794) of the Royal Americans was one of the three brigadiers under Wolfe in the expedition against Quebec. He apparently acted as governor of Quebec from about the time of its surrender, but his commission was not ordered until the end of Oct. 1760.
6. William Haviland (1718–1784) was lieutenant colonel in command of the force of about 3,400 men moving against Montreal from Crown Point.

To Robert Monckton

Sir   Wmsburgh Sepr 10th 1760

I have received your Favour of the 21st of August from Pittsbourgh, which I will certainly lay before the general Assembly which is to meet on the 6th of next Month, and earnestly recommend it to them to comply with your Request for His Majesty's Service, which I think so reasonable that I hope it will be come into without any Difficulty.

I procured a Boat to carry your Message up the Bay to Annapolis and expect his Return every Hour.¹ I am Sir with great Regard Your most Obedient humble Servant

Fran: Fauquier

To Brigr. Genl. Monckton

ALS: Library of Congress, Peter Force Papers, ser. VIII D, Vernon-Wager Papers, vol. 18, Papers of Robert Monckton, f. 47097. Endorsed as received 25 Sept.

1. No doubt the messenger was delivering Sharpe's copy of Monckton's letter of 21 Aug.

From William Byrd

[Sayer's Mill, 10 September 1760]

This letter has not been found. Fauquier communicated it to the council on 16 Sept. 1760; it is noted in *EJC* 6:169 as enclosing Lewis's letter from Spring Hill of 9 Sept. 1760, which follows.

Enclosure: Andrew Lewis to William Byrd

Sir, [Spring Hill,¹ 9 September 1760]

The seventh in the Evening I received your Orders by Drepar,² I was Incamped on Holston's River a little above the Great Iseland, the 8th we met with Captain Stewart,³ his Servant and an old Docter⁴ Conducted by the Little Carpinter his Brother⁵ two Young Felows & three Wenches.⁶

Fort Loudoun Being given up to the Indians with all the Ammunition &ct. the Indians were to Escort the Garrison Safe to Fort Prince George. the Garrison had not marched above 15 Miles before they were fired on by a large party of Indians. all the Officers Kill'd (Except Captain Stewart) and about 25 of the private. the others they have made prisoners and Dispersed through the Nation.

The Little Carpinter has given Every thing he could Command for Captain Stewart, and came of under pretence of Hunting for 6 Days.⁷

If the Weather prove good I shall see you in 5 or 6 Day's I am &ct.

Copy: C.O.5/377, ff. 3–4. Headed "Copy of a Letter from Major Lewis to the Honble. Colo. Byrd," endorsed as received with Lieutenant Governor Bull's letter of 9 Sept. 1760, and as received 10 Nov. and read 11 Nov. 1760. The date is supplied from the reference to the letter in *EJC* 6:169. A copy of this letter was enclosed in Byrd's letter to Fauquier of 10 Sept. 1760.

1. Spring Hill has not been identified, but it was evidently on or near one of the branches of the Holston River.
2. Possibly this was John Draper, of Augusta County, a member of Byrd's command.
3. John Stuart (1718–1799), later the agent for Indian affairs in the southern district, had been appointed a captain to command one of two South Carolina provincial companies raised to serve under Demeré.
4. Perhaps the old doctor was someone named Johnson. A report in the *S.C. Gaz.* for 4–11 Oct. 1760 says that the Little Carpenter had brought to Lewis four white people: Stuart, his servant, William Shorey the interpreter, and someone named Johnson.
5. Probably his brother Willinawa or a brother named Killaque; possibly the two names belonged to the same man.
6. The report in the *S.C. Gaz.* for 4–11 Oct. 1760 says there were two Indian women with the Little Carpenter, one of them his wife.
7. See Alden, pp. 115 ff. for the surrender of Fort Loudoun and its consequences. In the British Library, Add. Mss. 14036, ff. 8, 10, are two manuscript maps, one of the southern Indian district, dated 1764, and the other of the Cherokee country, by John Stuart and undated, both of which show the route of escape taken by Stuart and his party.

To William Bull

[ca. 16 September 1760]

This letter has not been found. As a result of Byrd's letter of 10 Sept. 1760, above, the council on 16 Sept. advised Fauquier to write to Bull as indicated in *EJC* 6:169:

The Council having considered this unhappy Incident, advised his Honour to send the above Orders to Colo. Byrd, and write to Governour Bull requesting that he would as soon as possible acquaint him what Resolutions South Carolina shall come to in this dangerous Emergency, that he may communicate the same to our Assembly; and that he and Governour Dobbs would concurr with him in representing to General Amherst the perilous Situation of the Southern Provinces, and intreating in the most pressing Terms an effectual and speedy Aid against an Enemy too Powerful for their united Strength.

To William Byrd

[ca. 16 September 1760]

This letter has not been found. It is assumed to have been written in reply to Byrd's letters of August and 10 Sept. 1760, and in accordance with the council's advice, stated in *EJC* 6:169:

Upon which the Council advised his Honour to order Colo. Byrd to Continue where he is, until he shall learn the consequences of the said Treaty, or proceed to take a more advanced Post, if he can do it with security, to construct a Fort on the most commodious spot thereabouts, and act upon the whole as he shall judge most conducive to the service in General and the protection of this Colony in particular.

To the Board of Trade

My Lords,   Wmsburgh Septer 17th 1760

   I yesterday received the disagreeable News, of the Garrison of Loudoun Fort in the Cherokee Country being treacherously and barbarously murdered, or taken, in their March down to Fort Prince George, at Keowee in the lower Settlements agreeable to a Capitulation made by Captain Demeré Commandant in the Fort with the Head Warriors of the Indians: a Copy of which I herewith inclose to your Lordships, who in all probability will have received an Account thereof before this will reach your Lordships.

   After the Retreat of Colonel Montgomery from the lower Cherokee Country who had 2000 Men under his Command the Majority of which were Regulars; it was not thought adviseable to let Colonel Byrd with 1000 Men mostly new levies march into the Enemy Country with our Convoy of Provisions which we had purchased for the Relief of the Garrison; when there was no Diversion in the lower Towns, and the united Force of the whole Nation was at Liberty to Oppose our throwing in the Succours intended. It was very fortunate and providential that we were so late for it would have been absolutely impossible for Mr. Byrd to have been at the Fort by the Time Captn. Demeré signed the Capitulation, and if he had been advanced far into the Enemy's Country, in all probability our whole Convoy had been lost; and the provisions we designed for our Friends had fallen to the Lot of our Enemies. Tho' I must at the same Time own, that the many unforeseen Delays in arming and providing for our Men, gave me great uneasiness when they happened. This must have happened for as far as I can learn no attempt was made to give Mr. Byrd who was on his March the least Intelligence of this Step of the Commandant who has lost his Life at the Head of his Garrison on his March tho' escorted by Indians. I suppose it was utterly impracticable to keep open a communication in those parts.

   If this warr grows serious it will be impossible for the Carolina's to defend themselves without assistance from Mr. Amherst, I dare say this Colony would do all in their power; their Interest is at Stake; but I am of Opinion, the Security and Safety of part of his Majesty's Colony's cannot be procured by provincial Troops only.

I wrote to your Lordships on the 1st instant (in answer to your Favour of the 13th June) by the Spotswood, Seton, for Bristol,[1] and am with the greatest Respect My Lords Your Lordships most Obedient Obliged & devoted Servant

Fran: Fauquier

The right honble. the Lords of Trade &ct.

ALS: C.O.5/1330, ff. 1–2. Endorsed as received 10 Nov. and read 11 Nov. 1760. A copy of the letter is in C.O.5/7, ff. 223–25, endorsed as being in the Board of Trade's letter of 11 Nov.; perhaps it was a copy made for the secretary of state.

1. The *Spotswood*, Charles Seton master, was a vessel of 150 tons owned by Thomas Knox of Bristol. She was entered in York River on 8 May 1760, but the date of her clearance has not been found. These are probably the same ship and master that Fauquier had previously used for sending correspondence.

From William Byrd

[Camp at Sayer's, 19 September 1760]

This letter has not been found. Fauquier communicated it to the council on 6 Oct. 1760, and it is abstracted in *EJC* 6:171:

His Honour also communicated a Letter from Colonel Byrd, dated Camp at Sayer's September the 19th signifying that Major Lewis return'd the Sunday before and brought in the little Carpenter and three more Indians, Captain Steuart and three more Prisoners, besides two Squaws—that he is convinced by the conferences he has had with the Carpenter, that he is well inclined—informing of the designs which he learnt from him, the Enemy had against Fort Prince George—also that the Cherokees are in General desirous of Peace, in consequence of which he has sent a Letter (of which a copy was inclosed) to the Warriours by one of the Indians, and the Carpenter has sent to summon all the Chiefs to meet him at Chotte at the New Moon of October—that by him, who goes in a few Days, he shall send them his Terms of Peace, a Copy whereof was inclosed, that the Carpenter was to be back at all Events by the full Moon of October, and promises, if they accept the offers of Peace, to bring in the Heads of each Town, all our Prisoners, and the Offenders; if not, to bring in his own Friends, and as many of our People as he can—desiring to know his Honour's pleasure on what he has done, and proposed further to do herein—if he is to proceed in his scheme, requests that Indian Goods, mention'd in an Invoice, may be sent forthwith.

This is evidently the letter Fauquier referred to in his address to the assembly on 6 Oct. 1760 and transmitted to the House of Burgesses the next day; see *JHB, 1758–1761*, pp. 183–84, 186. Byrd's letter to the Cherokees and his terms of peace are printed next, but the invoice of Indian goods evidently enclosed in his letter to Fauquier has not been traced.

16 September 1760

Enclosure: William Byrd to the Cherokees

[Camp on the Kanawha, 16 September 1760]
To the Standing-Turkey, Ocunnastotah, and the Rest of the Head-Warriors of the Cherokee Nation.

My good brother the Little-Carpenter, has delivered me capt. Stuart, and three others of my countrymen; who have informed me of your treacherous behaviour to the garrison of fort Loudoun, and have told me of the many English prisoners now in your nation, which I am determined to chastise you for, unless you immediately deliver them all up to me; for Virginians and Carolinians are the same people. As you know I always wished your nation well and never told you a lie in all my talks with you. I will now tell you my situation; and what you may expect from me, if you persist in your own obstinacy to bring destruction on yourselves, your women and children. I am now encamped on the waters of Kanawa, with a powerful army of Virginians; and can have as many more men as I please; and as many Indians as I want, from the Ohio and Sir William Johnson, now we have drove the French out of Canada and their forts to the Northward. I am building forts all the way, and propose soon to be in your nation; when I will not leave one Indian alive, one town standing, or one grain of corn, in all your country, if I do not find all the white people well when I go there. I tell you this truth, because I am not afraid of you; and wish for nothing more than to fight with you, if you still desire war; for my men have beat all the Indians to the Northward, and are not to be frightened by your yells. But, as I once loved you like my brothers, and still wish to see you happy, hear what I have to say to you, and think on your own miserable situation. King George's armies have drove the French from the Northern parts of America, and the Indians there are now begging for peace. We have nothing to do now, but drive the French from the Southward: Then what will become of you? Who will supply you with goods to keep yourselves and your families warm? Who will let you have ammunition to kill deer; or knives, or salt, or any necessaries of life? Our people know the way into your nation: They are as numerous as the fish in the sea; and will go every fall into your towns, and kill you if they find you; and if they cannot find you (because you run away) they will destroy your corn in your granaries, and will build forts in your hunting grounds: and at last drive you into the South-Sea. Think of these things, Cherokees, and think of all my straight talks, and believe what I now say; for, 'tis for your own good. Call in all your warriors directly; come down, and talk with me, and bring me in your prisoners; and you shall be safe and go home when you please; and I will be your friend and brother again, and will procure you a good peace. Tom will tell you how I used him;[1] and the Little-Carpenter will be with you as soon as he has refreshed himself with me; and they will all tell you what I say is true. If you have a mind for a peace, come in directly; and depend upon it, I will not detain you, but let you go when you have a mind: You shall meet with good usage, and not a hair of your heads shall be hurt, for I do not want to destroy your people: Send in a runner before you, and the path shall be clear. Be sure to have a good interpreter, that he may tell you all I say: I would send you Dick Smith, but I do not know how you would use him.

> Given under my hand, at the camp on the waters of Kanawa, September the 16th, 1760.
> William Byrd, commanding an army of Virginians.

P.S. If you refuse my offer now, my guns shall talk of war, and not of peace.

Printed: *S.C. Gaz.*, no. 1368, for 11–18 Oct. 1760. A copy of this letter was presumably enclosed in Byrd's letter of 19 Sept. 1760 to Fauquier.

1. Tom was apparently the Indian who delivered Byrd's letter to the Cherokees and who was identified by a report in the *S.C. Gaz.* for 11–18 Oct. 1760 as one of the young fellows who had accompanied the Little Carpenter.

Enclosure: Articles of Peace

[17 September 1760]

Articles of Peace proposed to the Cherokees Septr. 17th 1760

1st. That they shall, before the Full Moon in October, deliver up such Offenders as I shall demand.

2d. That they shall, by the same time, deliver up to me all the English Prisoners that are already in their Nation; or that may be brought in by any of their Warriors hearafter.

3d. That they shall deliver up Fort Loudoun as it now stands, with all the Cannon, Ball, Coehorns[1] & Shells in their possession, to whatever Troops the General is pleased to send there.

4th. That they shall agree the General, or the Governor of Carolina shall build what Forts they please in their Nation, for the protection of the Traders.

5th. That they never shall admit a French Man in their Country.
6th. That the Little Carpenter shall be acknowledg'd Governor of the Nation, & that he shall be obeyed as such.

In Consideration of their Performance of the above Articles, I have engaged to procure them his Majesty's Pardon, for their Rebellion. 2dly. I have engaged to return them all the Prisoners [we have] of their Nation, as soon as they can be brought up, after the Delivery of ours. And lastly to send Traders among them in the next Spring.

DS: W.O. 34/37, ff. 54–55. A copy of these articles was enclosed in Byrd's letter of 19 Sept. 1760 to Fauquier. The copy above is evidently a clerk's copy with Byrd's autograph signature, but it may be a Byrd holograph. It is endorsed by Fauquier "Copy of the Articles of Peace proposed by Colonel Byrd, and sent by the little Carpenter Sepr. 17th 1760," and it is endorsed in another hand as enclosed in Fauquier's letter to Amherst of 16 Mar. 1761. Another copy, in C.O. 5/61, ff. 20–21, evidently enclosed in Amherst's letter of 4 May 1761 to the War Office, provides the words in brackets, which are garbled in the copy transcribed here.

1. A coehorn (or cohorn), or coehorn mortar, was a small mortar for throwing grenades.

From William Bull

[Charleston, S.C., 21 September 1760]

This letter has not been found. Fauquier communicated it to the council on 10 Oct. 1760, and it is abstracted in *EJC* 6:172:

The second dated September the 21st informing of the State of Fort Prince George—that his first Endeavour's shall be to give that Fort a temporary Relief—that the Assembly has provided pay for a Regiment of one thousand Men for six Months—that this Corps with the rangers and royals will form a Body of about two Thousand Men—requesting that his Honour would join with him in recommending some vigorous Steps to the Government of North Carolina, and acquaint him as soon as possible with the result of our Determinations.

The council advised Fauquier to send this letter to the House of Burgesses, and he did so the same day; see *JHB, 1758–1761*, p. 190.

From William Byrd

[24 September 1760]

This letter has not been found. Fauquier communicated it to the council on 6 Oct. 1760, and it is mentioned in *EJC* 6:171 as "requesting to know if the regiment is to be compleated, and how the Detachment is to be disposed of this

Winter, and recommending Mr. Christian to have the Cloathing of the Regiment." Mr. Christian was Israel Christian, a merchant of Augusta County and one of the burgesses for the county 1758–65.

From James Abercromby

Sir London Octr 1st 1760

A few days ago I was favoured with yours of the 22d June inclosing Duplicate of that of the 14th Decemr., also a Copy of Reasons given by the Council for your Passing the Negro Act, together with Copy of Minutes of Council of 12th Decr. confirming my Authority as Agent, with a Power of Attorney to receive the Money granted by Parliament, likewise Copy of your Letter to Mr Martin and One to the Lords of Trade, which I have delivered accordingly.

Duplicates of the Acts of Assembly (the Originals whereof are lost) not being come to the Office, the Negro Duty Act, & others passd at the same time, cannot be taken up, In the mean time I have considered the Reasons for giving your Assent to the Negro Duty Act, they appear to me very strong, and to which may be added, that in other Colonies, under like Instructions with yours, Dutys payable by the Importer of Negro's have been imposed by Provincial Acts without Blame, and whether imported by Land or by Water does not alter the Principles of the Case.

It gives me great Pleasure that the Plan agreed upon twixt Mr. Montague & myself for our Conduct in Negociating the Affairs of Virginia, as stated to you & to the Council by my Letters of the 10th of May last, is approved of, and thereupon by next Ships I hope to receive Duplicates of the Presidents Letters, the Originals whereof have miscarried. Had the Power of Attorney now come, arrived (which probably wou'd have been the Case, had not the Ship been Lost or taken) before the Controversy took Place upon the Agency Law, I might, as you observe, have shewn the Country could have got the Money from home by ours & the Councils Authority alone: As the Case now stands, Altho' by Mr. Secretary Pitts Interposition with the Treasury their Lordships determined the Matter in my Favour from my personal Services therein, yet they laid me as well as Others under an Obligation for the Disposal thereof as the Governor Council & Assembly shall direct: Of all which Circumstances relative to this Money, my Letters to you and to the Council of the 10th of May, inclosing the particular Accounts of the Money, two days after Receiving the Dividend, will inform you, Original of which Letters, that no time might be lost on my part, was transmitted by a Ship from Bristol, the first that offered for Virginia, Duplicate by a Ship from hence, Triplicate by Virginia Ships in July under Govr. Wright's Convoy.[1] By which said Ships my Letters of the 3d July (having that day received the Second Dividend) informed you and the Council of the Same, & inclosed my Accounts thereof. Duplicates of said Letters of 3d July were sent by the New York Pacquet, & Triplicates by the Randal, Capt. Walker,[2] & so it rests with the Legislature to order the Disposal of the Ballance of this Money, agreeable to the Security given by me to His Majesty in the Exchequer, whether by Bills drawn on me or by remitting it in Specie I cannot take upon me to direct. It will no doubt occur to the people of Business in both Houses that by Bills of Exchange Freight & Insurance will be saved, besides the high Price of Silver & Gold in time of War.

In whatever manner the Legislature, whether by Act of Assembly, or by a joint Resolution under the Seal of the Province, shall direct Payment of the Ballance, I am ready to Comply therewith. From the Nature of my Security, Copy thereof heretofore sent, you will observe that I cannot comply (however willing I am so to do) with your & the Councils Advice in paying Mr. Dinnwiddies Demand.[3]

Next Week, or the Week thereafter, the Treasury Board meets, I shall then renew my Solicitations for Aid out of the Quitrents. The Auditor Generals Report thereon is Strongly in our Favour.[4] I send you Copy of Mr Montagues Letter to me, from the Camp,[5] by which you will see his Disposition to Concur with me in the Publick Service of the Province, and believe me to be very Sincerly Sir &ca.

Governor Fauquier.

Copy: Virginia State Library, James Abercromby Letter Book, pp. 214–16. A marginal note indicates that the letter was sent by the *Charming Jeany,* Captain Todd.

1. Presumably this was the convoy in which James Wright, appointed lieutenant governor of South Carolina in the spring of 1760, had sailed to that colony.
2. This was properly the *Randolph,* Capt. Robert Walker.
3. Nothing appears to be known of what Fauquier and the council had advised Abercromby to do with regard to Dinwiddie's demand, or of what his demand was. Presumably Dinwiddie had asked for some part of Virginia's share of the grant of £200,000 as compensation for services rendered or expenses incurred by himself on behalf of the colony, and Fauquier and the council had advised Abercromby to pay what Dinwiddie had asked.
4. See T.1/400, ff. 230–33, for the auditor general's letter of 18 Feb. 1760 to the Treasury. It made a favorable report on Virginia's request that the revenue of 2s. per hogshead on tobacco should be paid £3,079.4.3 from the quitrents.
5. Montagu's letter has not been found.

To Jeffery Amherst

Sir   Wmsburgh Octr 5th 1760

    Amidst the Hurry of Business which I am sensible you must be engaged in, give me Leave so far to intrude, as to acknowledge the Receipt of your Letters of the 26th Augst. and 9th Septr. and to express my Sense of the Services you have done this Continent, The pleasure you must have given his Majesty, and the Honor you have acquired your self. You had long convinced your Enemies as well as Friends, of your Valour and Prudence, you have now convinced both of your great Humanity, a Quality as much more noble, as it is more amiable and valuable than either of the other. You have taught your Enemies to love you as well as to fear you.

    Our Assembly meets to morrow. Whether your Successes will incline them, to ease themselves of the Expence of giving Mr. Monckton the 300 Men he desires, Time must show. I shall lay his Letter before them.[1]

    The Cherokee Affairs look as if you would receive a Joint Application from the two Carolinas and our selves for further Assistance to reduce them, tho' Colonel Byrd has sent the little Carpenter into the Country to try to procure peace. I most sincerely wish it had been the policy of these Colonies to treat Indians with that Justice and Humanity you show to them. This and this alone, (if any thing can do it) must make them our Friends. White, Red, or Black; polished or unpolished Men are Men. I am with the highest Esteem and Regard, Sir Your Excellency's most Obedient humble Servant

                                                                 Fran: Fauquier

To Majr. Genl. Amherst

ALS: W.O.34/37, ff. 42–43. Endorsed as received 26 Oct. [1760].

  1. Monckton's letter of 21 Aug. 1760.

From Robert Monckton

                                                        [16 October 1760]

This letter has not been found, but Fauquier acknowledged it in his letter of 27 Oct. 1760 to Monckton, which suggests that Monckton's letter requested the assistance of Virginia troops, presumably to man some military posts.

17 October 1760

To Adam Stephen

[ca. 17 October 1760]

This letter has not been found, but Fauquier wrote in his letter of 17 Oct. 1760 to Monckton that he had sent his orders to Stephen by the same express. The orders were presumably those which Fauquier mentioned in his address to the General Assembly on 20 Oct. 1760, when he said he had recalled Stephen from Monckton's command and ordered him to march his corps southward immediately to join Byrd (*JHB, 1758–1761*, p. 197).

To William Byrd

[17 October 1760]

This letter has not been found, but Fauquier mentioned it in his letter of 1 July 1761 to Byrd, in which he indicated that this letter of 17 Oct. (and an earlier letter of 24 July) to Byrd informed him that Virginia did not consider itself a principal in the war with the Cherokees and that questions of a peace should be referred to Governor Bull. This letter of 17 Oct. is no doubt what Fauquier showed to the council on 16 Oct. 1760 as his reply to Byrd's letters of 19 and 24 Sept. 1760; a mention of the letter in *EJC* 6:172 indicates it gave instructions to Byrd.

To Robert Monckton

Sir   Wmsburgh Octr 17th 1760

I laid your Letter before the general Assembly which is now sitting and recommended their giving you the 300 Men you required, in my Speech to them;[1] but as you had not then heard of the glorious period put to the War, by General Amhersts having reduced all Canada to his Majesty's Obedience: and as there is an urgent Necessity for the Service of all our Men to guard our Southwest Frontiers from the Inroads of the Cherokee Indians; they have pass'd a Bill by which I am required to recall all our Force to the Northward to join the rest of the Regiment under the Honble. Col. Byrd to the Southward. And as is usual in all Bills of this Nature, it enacts that if the Men are detained they are not to be deemed to be in the pay of this Colony.[2]

I hope this Measure so necessary for our own protection will not be detrimental to his Majesty's Service and the good of the general Cause as

Mr. Amherst will now have Men sufficient to garrison all posts that it shall be thought expedient to maintain.

I have sent my Orders to Lieutenant Colonel Stephen by this Express. I am with great Esteem Sir Your most Obedient humble Servant

Fran: Fauquier

To the Honble. Brigr. Genl. Monckton

ALS: Library of Congress, Peter Force Papers, ser. VIII D, Vernon-Wager Papers, vol. 18, Papers of Robert Monckton, f. 47101. Endorsed as received at Fort Bedford the thirtieth [Oct. 1760]. A copy is in C.O.5/60, ff. 111-12, endorsed as sent to Amherst in Stanwix's letter of 30 Oct. 1760 and received in Amherst's letter of 7 Jan. 1761.

1. Fauquier mentioned Monckton's letter of 21 Aug. to the General Assembly in his address on 6 Oct. 1760, and he transmitted it to the House of Burgesses on the same day; see *JHB, 1758–1761*, pp. 184–85.

2. The act was "An Act for recruiting and further continuing the old regiment in the service of this colony, and for other purposes therein mentioned" (Hening, 7:369–72).

From John Pownall

Sir,   [Whitehall, 18 October 1760]

I am directed by the Lords Commissioners for Trade and Plantations to desire you will transmitt to their Lordships three or four Sets of the last printed Edition of the Laws passed in the Province under your Government with the publick seal affixed to each Set. I am Sir, Your most Obedient & most humble Servant,

John Pownall

Whitehall / Octr. 18, 1760

Copy: C.O.324/16, p. 182. Circular addressed to governors in America.

To Robert Monckton

Sir   Wmsburgh Octr 27th 1760

I received your Favour of the 16th instant, yesterday. by mine of the [17 October] you will find that the Assembly have not put it in my power to comply with your Request, which I, in my own Opinion, should think expedient, as there are so many posts to maintain till all things are finaly settled.

Lest you should think I was deficient in the recommending the Measure to the general Assembly; I have enclosed to you a Copy of what I said to them on their meeting.[1]

The absolute Necessity of having a pretty considerable Force on the South West Frontiers to repell the Incursions of the Cherokee Indians, was the Motive that induced them to assemble all the Men in our pay, in that Quarter. I am with the greatest Esteem Sir Your most Obedient humble Servant

Fran: Fauquier

To Brigr. Genl. Monckton

ALS: Library of Congress, Peter Force Papers, ser. VIII D, Vernon-Wager Papers, vol. 18, Papers of Robert Monckton, f. 47103. Endorsed as received 18 Nov. [1760]. Fauquier left a blank space where he meant to write a date, and the date in brackets is that of the letter he must have meant to cite.

1. The enclosure has not been found. It may have been the whole of Fauquier's address to the General Assembly, or it may have been the first three paragraphs, which stated that money raised for the support of the regiment was insufficient and that Monckton had asked for 300 men from Virginia to garrison posts taken from the French; it noted that Amherst's victory made anything but garrison duty unnecessary; and it asked whether the assembly would refuse to provide pay for a few men, after the bounties it had received from Parliament. And perhaps the enclosure included Fauquier's expression of hope that the House of Burgesses would cheerfully give the little he had asked and would raise that little in the way easiest for the colony.

From Robert Monckton

[27 October 1760]

This letter has not been found, but Fauquier acknowledged receipt of it in his letter to Monckton of 12 Nov. 1760.

To William Pitt

Sir   Wmsburgh Octr 28th 1760

In Obedience to his Majesty's Commands, signifyed to me in your Letter of the 23d August which I had the Honor to receive yesterday, I shall immediately proceed to lay before you all the Information I am Master of in Relation to the Subject Matter of it.

It will not be in my Power to give you as full Intelligence of these Affairs as you may receive from some others of his Majesty's Colonies:

for I conceive this Trade has been chiefly carried on, by the Means of Flags of Truce: of which I have never been prevailed upon to grant one, on any Consideration whatever; tho' I have been tempted by large Offers, and my Compassion has been endeavoured to be wrought upon, by pitiful Stories of Relations lying in French Dungeons for want of such Flags. In order to avoid this infamous practice, I have sent the French prisoners ordered here by Lord Colvill, on board the Tobacco Ships to England, putting two or three on board a Ship as the masters wanted Hands.[1]

There is an open Trade carried on to Monte-Christo which I imagine is wholy a French Trade, for Bullion is the chief if not only Commodity exported, which is a Commodity the Spaniards cannot want. But this Trade is not very considerable, occasioned as I conceive by the Want of Bullion to export: and not equaly profitable to the Trade carried on to French ports immediately; as I was given to understand I might have 400 Guineas if I would license a Flag of Truce.

There is an illicit Trade carried on, but not I believe to any great Degree, which is the exportation of Corn to neutral ports: it is done in this Manner. The Vessel is cleared out for Gibraltar, and then under pretence of being drove by stress of Weather into Madeira or some of the western Isles.[2] The Governors lay their hands on the Cargo, and from a Plea of Want in the Islands oblige the Master to sell the Cargo, for which a large price is given.

This is the whole of what has hitherto come to my Knowledge of Things of this Nature, and is I presume the whole of what is now practised in this Colony; which I firmly believe to stand as clear of charges of this Kind as any of his Majesty's Colonys. If hereafter I shall be able to trace out any farther Steps by which I can give his Majesty or his Ministry any fresh Light into such Transactions, which I shall make it my Study to enquire into, I will lay it before You, as his Majesty requires me to do. I am with the highest Esteem and Respect Sir Your most Obedient and most humble Servant

Fran: Fauquier

P.S. I have just now been informed by the Surveyor general[3] that, more Ships clear for Scotland than Gibraltar, in the Corn Trade.

F:F:

To the right Honble. Mr. Secretary Pitt.

ALS: C.O.5/19, ff. 294–95. Endorsed as received 10 Mar. [1761].

1. No information on these prisoners ordered to Virginia by Lord Colville has been uncovered. It seems likely that they were sailors.
2. The British colony of Gibraltar is about 275 mi. southeast of Lisbon. Madeira is the principal island of the Madeira archipelago, in the north Atlantic about 600 mi.

southwest of Lisbon, and the Azores, "the western Isles," are in the north Atlantic about 1,000 mi. west of Lisbon. Both groups of islands belonged to Portugal and consequently were neutral. Fauquier's meaning is clear enough, but he must have omitted a verb from the last clause.

3. Peter Randolph was surveyor general of His Majesty's customs in the southern district of America.

From John Pownall

Sir, [Whitehall, 29 October 1760]
In consequence of the melancholy Event of the King's Death on the 25th instant, I am directed by the Lords Commissioners for Trade and Plantations, to take the Opportunity by the packet of acquainting you, that the necessary Forms for proclaiming his present Majesty in the Colonies, together with Warrants for using the old Seals, Proclamations for continuing Officers in their Employments, Orders for Alteration of the Liturgy &c &c are preparing with all possible Dispatch, & will be transmitted to yourself and the rest of the Governors and Commanders in Chief of His Majesty's Colonies in America in a few Days. I am, Sir, Your most Obedient humble Servant,

John Pownall
Secry.

1760 / October 29th

Copy: C.O.324/17, pp. 24–25. Circular addressed to governors in America.

From Robert Monckton

[Fort Bedford, 30 October 1760]
This letter has not been found. Fauquier acknowledged receipt of it in his letter to Monckton of 12 Nov. 1760 and communicated it to the council the same day. It is abstracted in *EJC* 6:174:

The Governour Communicated a Letter from Brigadier General Moncton dated Fort Bedford October the 30th signifying he is under a necessity of sending Orders to the Commanding Officer at Fort Pitt and to Lieutenant Colo. Stephen for the Virginia Troops to remain where they now are until he can hear from General Amherst, as the Garrisons can't be kept without them.

To James Abercromby

[31 October 1760]

This letter has not been found, but Abercromby's letter of 19 Jan. 1761 to Fauquier acknowledged receipt of a duplicate of Fauquier's letter of 31 Oct. 1760 to him.

From the Board of Trade

Sir, [Whitehall, 31 October 1760]

Inclosed you will receive an Order from the Lords of His Majesty's most Honorable Privy Council, notifying to you the Death of Our late gracious Sovereign Lord King George of ever blessed Memory; and directing you to proclaim the high and mighty Prince George Prince of Wales King of Great Britain, France and Ireland, and of all the Dominions thereunto belonging &c. Defender of the Faith &c. We do therefore earnestly recommend to you, that you do proceed without loss of Time to the Execution of these Orders, and that His Majesty be accordingly proclaimed in the most solemn Manner and most proper Parts of your Government; and You are to return to Us a speedy Account of your Proceedings herein.[1]

Inclosed you will also find His Majesty's Warrant, authorizing you to make Use of the old Seal of the Province until a new one can be prepared together with four printed Copies of His Majesty's Proclamation continuing all Officers in the Plantations civil and military in their respective Employments, till His Majesty's Pleasure shall be further signified; which Proclamation you will take Care to make publick in such manner that all His Majesty's Subjects may be fully apprized of His Majesty's Pleasure in this Respect.[2]

Under the same Cover We likewise transmit to you an Instruction sign'd by his Majesty, containing His Majesty's Direction for an Alteration in the Prayers for the Royal Family, to which you will not fail to pay a due Obedience.[3] We are, Sir, Your most Obedient humble Servants,

Dunk Halifax
W. G. Hamilton
Andrew Stone
W: Sloper

1760 / October 31st

Copy: C.O.324/17, pp. 29–32. Circular addressed to governors in America. Marginal notes indicate passages to be omitted from some letters, though not the one to Virginia.

1. Fauquier communicated this letter to the council on 11 Feb. 1761, when it was ordered that George III should be proclaimed king the following day. See *EJC* 6:177–80 for the council's record of the various procedures resulting from the accession of George III, and Fauquier's letter of 17 Feb. 1761 for his report on how these orders transmitted by the Board of Trade were carried out.

2. The proclamation continuing all officers in their employment was ordered to be published in the *Virginia Gazette*, but no issue containing the proclamation has been found. See *EJC* 6:179.

3. It was ordered that the order in council regarding prayers for the royal family should be communicated to all the clergy in the colony. See *EJC* 6:179.

Enclosure: From the Privy Council

[Leicester House, 31 October 1760]

After Our hearty Commendations. It having pleased Almighty God to take to His Mercy, out of this troublesome Life, Our late Sovereign Lord King George the Second of blessed and Glorious Memory, and thereupon His Royal Majesty King George the Third being here proclaimed. We have thought fit to signifie the same unto you, with directions, that You do with the Assistance of the Council and numbers of the Principal [Inhabitants & Planters of Virginia] forthwith Proclaim His Most Sacred Majesty King George the Third according to the Form here inclosed, with the Solemnities and Ceremonies requisite on the like occasions. And you are likewise to publish and proclaim a Proclamation for continuing the Officers in His Majesty's Plantations till His Majesty's pleasure shall be further signified; Which Proclamation will be transmitted to You by the Lords Commissioners for Trade and Plantations. And so not doubting of Your ready compliance herein, We bid You heartily farewell. From the Council Chamber at Liecester house this 31st day of October 1760.

Your Loving Friends,[1]

Gower	Tho. Cant.
Cornwallis	Granville, P.
Falmouth	Temple, C. P. S.
Delawarr	Bedford
T. Robinson	Denbigh
R. Nugent	Halifax

Copy: P.C.2/108, pp. 30–31. The copy entered in the Privy Council register was the form sent to Hudson's Bay, and variations for other colonies are not clearly indicated.

The words in brackets are probably what stood in the version sent to Virginia with the letter of 31 Oct. 1760 from the Board of Trade to governors in America.

1. The privy councillors who signed this order were: Granville Leveson-Gower (1721–1803), second Earl Gower; Charles Cornwallis (1700–1762), first Earl Cornwallis; Hugh Boscawen (1707–1782), second Viscount Falmouth; John West (1693–1766), seventh Baron Delawarr; Sir Thomas Robinson, Bart. (1695–1770); Robert Nugent (1702–1788); Thomas Secker (1693–1768), archbishop of Canterbury; John Carteret (1690–1763), first Earl Granville, president of the council; Richard Temple Grenville-Temple (1711–1779), first Earl Temple, lord privy seal; John Russell (1710–1771), fourth duke of Bedford; Basil Feilding (1719–1800), sixth earl of Denbigh; and George Montagu Dunk (1716–1771), second earl of Halifax.

Enclosure: Proclamation of George III

[29 October 1760]

Whereas it hath pleased Almighty God to call to his Mercy Our late Sovereign Lord King George the Second of blessed and glorious Memory, by whose Decease the Imperial Crown of Great Britain, France and Ireland, as also the supreme Dominion and Sovereign Right of the [Colony and Dominion of Virginia] are solely and rightfully come to the High and Mighty Prince George Prince of Wales; We therefore the [Lieutenant Governor and Council, with Numbers of the principal Inhabitants & Planters of this Colony and Dominion] Do now hereby with one full Voice and Consent of Tongue & Heart publish and proclaim, that the High and Mighty Prince George Prince of Wales is, now by the Death of Our late Sovereign of happy and glorious Memory, become our only lawfull and rightfull Liege Lord George the Third, by the Grace of God King of Great Britain, France and Ireland, Defender of the Faith, Supreme Lord of [the said Colony & Dominion of Virginia] and all other His late Majesty's Territories and Dominions in America; To whom We do acknowledge all Faith & constant Obedience with all hearty and humble Affection, Beseeching God, by whom Kings and Queens do reign, to bless the Royal King George the Third with long and happy Years to reign over Us.

Given at[   ]

God save the King.

Copy: C.O. 324/17, pp. 5–7, 15. The date, from a marginal note, is that on which the Board of Trade read the order in council directing the preparation of proclamations for the several colonies, as well as the date on which the board submitted the proclamation for approval. The words in brackets fill in blanks left in the proclamation and meant to be filled by those indicated as proper for each colony; the wording for Virginia is on p. 15. Enclosed in the Board of Trade's circular of 31 Oct. 1760 to governors in America.

27 October 1760

Enclosure: Warrant for Use of Seal

George R. [Saville House, 28 October 1760]

Our Will and Pleasure is, and We do hereby authorize and impower you to make use of the Publick Seal made Use of within Our [Colony and Dominion of Virginia] in America, during the Lifetime of Our dearest Grandfather the late deceased King, for sealing all Things whatsoever that are used to be sealed therewith, untill another Seal shall be prepared and transmitted to Our said [Colony and Dominion] duly authorized by Us. And for so doing this shall be your Warrant. Given at Our Court at Saville House the 28th Day of October 1760 in the first Year of Our Reign.

By His Majesty's Command
W: Pitt

Copy: C.O.324/17, p. 2. The warrant was sent to royal governors in America, this entry-book copy being addressed to Nova Scotia; the style of the colony, in brackets, is modeled on that indicated for inclusion in the proclamation of George III. Enclosed in the Board of Trade's circular of 31 Oct. 1760 to governors in America.

Enclosure: Proclamation

[27 October 1760]

By the King
A Proclamation
Declaring His Majesty's Pleasure for continuing the Officers
in His Majesty's Plantations 'till His Majesty's Pleasure
shall be further signified

George R

Whereas by an Act of Parliament made in the First Year of the late Queen Anne, of Blessed Memory, intituled, "An Act for the Security of Her Majesty's Person and Government, and of the Succession to the Crown of Great Britain in the Protestant Line," it was enacted (amongst other Things) That no Office, Place, or Employment, Civil or Military, within any of her said late Majesty's Plantations, should become void by reason of the Demise or Death of her said late Majesty, her heirs, or Successors, Kings or Queens of this Realm; but that the person and persons in any of the Offices, Places, or Employments aforesaid, should continue in their respective Offices, Places and Employments, for the Space of Six

Months next after such Death or Demise, unless sooner removed and discharged by the next in Succession to whom the Crown of this Realm should come, remain, and be, according to the several Acts of Parliament for limiting and settling the Succession of the Crown, as by the said recited Act may appear:[1] And in regard it may happen, that Our Pleasure may not, within the said Time, be declared, touching the said Offices, Places and Employments, in Our foreign Plantations, which will, at the End of the said Six Months, become void; We, for preventing the Inconveniences that may happen thereby, in Our Princely Wisdom and Care of the State (reserving to Our Judgement hereafter the Reformation and Redress of any Abuses in the Execution of any such Offices, Places, and Employments, upon due Knowledge and Examination thereof) have thought fit, with the Advice of Our Privy Council, to issue this Our Royal Proclamation, and do hereby order, signify, and declare, That all Persons that, at the Time of the Decease of Our late Royal Grandfather King George the Second, of Glorious Memory, were duly and lawfully possessed of, or invested in, any Office, Place, or Employment, Civil or Military, in any of Our Plantations, and which have not been since removed from such their Offices, Places, or Employments, shall be, and shall hold themselves continued in the said Offices, Places, and Employments as formerly they held and enjoyed the same, until Our Pleasure be further known, or other Provision be made, pursuant to the Commissions and Instructions of Our late Royal Grandfather, to his Governors and Officers of the Plantations aforesaid; and that in the mean time, for the preservation of the Peace, and necessary proceedings in Matters of Justice, and for the Safety and Service of the State, all the said Persons, of whatsoever Degree or Condition, do not fail every one severally, according to his Place, Office, or Charge, to proceed in the Performance and Execution of all Duties therunto belonging, as formerly appertained unto them, during the Life of Our said Royal Grandfather: And further, We do hereby will and command all and singular Our Subjects in the said Plantations, of what Estate or Degree they, or any of them, be, to be aiding, helping, and assisting, at the Commandment of the said Officers, in the performance and Execution of the said Offices and Places, as they tender Our Displeasure, and will answer the contrary at their utmost Perils. Given at Our Court at Saville House, the Twenty seventh Day of October, One thousand seven hundred and Sixty, in the First Year of Our Reign.

Copy: P.C.2/108, pp. 11–12. Printed copies of this proclamation were enclosed in the Board of Trade's circular letter of 31 Oct. 1760 to governors in America.

1. The reference ought to be to "An Act for the Security of her Majesty's Person and Government, and of the Succession to the Crown of Great Britain in the Protestant Line," 6 Anne, cap. 7 (*Statutes* 4:276–81). The act was passed in 1707 to make changes in previous laws, necessitated by the union of England and Scotland: its eighth article provided for the continuing of officers in the plantations.

Enclosure: Additional Instruction

[Leicester House, 31 October 1760]

Additional Instruction to Our [Trusty & well beloved Jeffery Amherst Esquire] Our Captain General & Governor [in] Chief in and over Our [Colony and Dominion of Virginia] in America; And in his Absence to Our Lieutenant Governor or Commander in Chief of the said [Colony and Dominion] for the time being; Given at Our Court at Leicester House the [31st] of October 1760 in the first Year of Our Reign.

Whereas We have been pleased by Our Order in Council of the 27th of October instant, (a Copy whereof is hereunto annexed) to declare Our Pleasure, that in all the Prayers, Litanies and Collects for the Royal Family, instead of the Words (*their Royal Highnesses George Prince of Wales, the princess Dowager of Wales, the Duke, the Princesses and all the Royal Family*) there should be inserted, (*Her Royal Highness the Princess Dowager of Wales & all the Royal Family;*) Our Will and Pleasure therefore is, that in all the Prayers, Litanies and Collects for the Royal Family, to be used within Our [Colony and Dominion of Virginia] under your Government, instead of the Words *their Royal Highnesses George Prince of Wales, the Princess Dowager of Wales, the Duke, the Princesses and all the Royal Family*, there be inserted *Her Royal Highness the Princess Dowager of Wales and all the Royal Family*. And for the better Notice hereof in our said [Colony and Dominion], It is Our further Will & Pleasure, that you cause the same to be forthwith published in the several parish Churches & other Places of divine Worship within the said [Colony and Dominion], and that you take Care that Obedience be paid thereto accordingly.

Copy: C.O.324/17, pp. 26–30. The instruction was sent to all royal governors in America, as an enclosure in the Board of Trade's circular of 31 Oct. 1760. The entry-book copy is addressed to Nova Scotia, and bracketed words in the text above represent changes appropriate in the instruction to Virginia, except for "in" omitted by mistake. The journal of the Virginia council (*EJC* 6:178) confuses the order in council that follows and this additional instruction to which the order was annexed, dating the order 31 Oct. That was evidently the date of the additional instruction as it was sent out, and it has been inserted in brackets to replace 30 Oct., the date of submission, in the entry-book text above.

Enclosure: Order in Council

[27 October 1760]

Whereas by the late Act of Uniformity which establisheth the Liturgy, and enacts, That no Form or Order of Common Prayers be openly used, other than what is prescribed and appointed to be used in and by the said Book, it is notwithstanding provided That in all those Prayers Litanys and Collects which do any wise relate to the King, Queen, or Royal Progeny, the Names be altered and changed from time to time and fitted to the present Occasion according to Direction of lawful Authority.[1] His Majesty was pleased this day in Council to declare His Royal Will and Pleasure, That in all the Prayers Liturgies and Collects for the Royal Family instead of the Words [Their Royal Highnesses George Prince of Wales, the Princess Dowager of Wales, The Duke, The Princesses and all the Royal Family] be inserted [Her Royal Highness the Princess Dowager of Wales and all the Royal Family]. And His Majesty doth strictly charge and Command That no Edition of the Common Prayer be henceforth printed but with this Amendment and that in the mean time 'till Copies of such Edition may be had all Parsons, Vicars and Curates within this Realm do (for the preventing of Mistakes) with the Pen, correct and amend all such Prayers in their Church Books, according to the aforegoing Direction; And for the better Notice hereof, That this Order be forthwith Printed and published, and sent to the several Parishes; And that the Right Reverend the Bishops do take Care that Obedience be paid to the same accordingly.

Copy: P.C.2/108, pp. 8–9. Brackets and parentheses are as in the manuscript. A copy of this order was annexed to the additional instruction of 31 Oct. 1760 ordering the changes in prayers.

1. This probably refers to "An Act for the Uniformity of Publick Prayers, and Administration of Sacraments, and other Rites and Ceremonies: And for establishing the Form of Making, Ordaining and Consecrating Bishops, Priests and Deacons in the Church of England," 13 and 14 Car. II, cap. 4 (*Statutes* 3:224–30). The seventeenth article prescribes use of the Book of Common Prayer only, and the twenty-fifth article authorizes changes in references to members of the royal family.

To Edward Montagu

[ca. November 1760]

This letter has not been found, but it is referred to in a letter of 5 Nov. 1760 from the Virginia Committee of Correspondence to Edward Montagu (*VMHB* 11[1903–4]:12–13):

The Governor having inform'd the Committee that he has wrote to you, desiring you to join Mr. Abercrombie in removing any ill Impressions the Ministry may have of him, on his giving his Assent to several Laws, which have been judged to be contrary to his Majesty's Instructions, & consequently repeal'd by his Royal Proclamation, we earnestly recommend it to you to contribute every thing in your Power to wipe off any Odium he may be under, or any Aspersion thrown on him for passing those Acts.

From William Byrd

[Camp at Sayer's, 3 November 1760]

This letter has not been found. Fauquier communicated it to the council on 12 Nov. 1760, and it is abstracted in *EJC* 6:174:

His Honour also communicated a Letter from Colo. Byrd dated Camp at Sayer's November the 3d signifying the little Carpenter returned to that place on Saturday with thirty two Cherokees, and delivered up to him ten more of Captain Demeri's Company—that the Indians have agreed to suspend all Hostilities till the New Moon in March when they promise to come in to that Post on his Terms, provided the Army proceeds no further this Fall, and their Party returns safe—that he shall dismiss the savages as soon as the Goods come up—that he shall endeavour to station the Troops in such a manner as will best protect the Frontier.

To James Abercromby

[6 November 1760]

This letter has not been found, but Abercromby referred to it in his letter of 14 Jan. 1761 to Fauquier as being a letter from Fauquier, the president of the council, and the speaker of the General Assembly and indicated that it concerned Abercromby's authority to handle money credited to Virginia from the two grants authorized by Parliament. This letter of 6 Nov. was evidently the reply to Abercromby's letters of 1 June and 3 July 1760 to Fauquier, which Fauquier communicated to the council on 16 Sept. 1760. The council advised that consideration of the letters should be deferred until the meeting of the assembly; Fauquier referred to Abercromby's letters in his address to the General Assembly when it convened on 6 Oct., and transmitted them to the House of Burgesses. On 8 Oct. the burgesses resolved that proper persons should be appointed to receive money granted to Virginia by Parliament; on 15 Oct. the burgesses passed "An Act for appointing persons to receive the money granted, or to be granted, by the parliament of Great-Britain, to his majesty, for the use of this colony," which was accepted by the council, and assented to by Fauquier on 20 Oct. Probably the letter of 6 Nov. to Abercromby reported the actions of the

General Assembly. See *EJC* 6:169–70; *JHB, 1758–1761*, pp. 184, 187, 194, 196; Hening, 7:372–75.

To Jeffery Amherst

Sir   Wmsburgh Novr. 7th 1760

I take the opportunity of a Sloop which is going to New-York to enclose to you an attested Copy of the Commission appointing your Excellency Governor & Commander in chief of this Colony, which the Colony in general and I in particular hope you will visit before you leave this Continent.

The Income arising from the perquisites of this Government has greatly exceeded that of last Year, and I have the pleasure to advise you that all Arrears are paid, so that I shall give my Brother Directions to pay Mr. Calcraft to the 25th of last Month, for which purpose I shall remit the Bills next week, by a Ship which will then sail for London. Whether the Increase of my Receipts is owing to the Badness of the last Year, or the extraordinary Goodness of this, I am not yet certain; but I should suppose that both Causes concur to make this Difference. As I made my Calculation of what I thought I could afford to pay on the Exchange of London without subjecting you to any Disappointment whatever, on the Receipts of the Year and half of which preceded our Agreement; I think my self in honor obliged to pay the 1500 Guineas, since you so generously took my Word without any examination & came to an Agreement on my own Representation of the State of the Revenue. All I meant by an Agreement was that I then thought I could not oblige my self to pay more than £1500 without suffering, for by the then Appearances, I had Reason to form such a Judgment. I have accordingly given Orders to my Brother to make the payment in Guineas; and also to pay the Value of £47 Currency Exchange at 140, for your Share of a Confiscation not included in the Agreement. If the Articles are signed between Mr. Calcraft and him, they are not yet arrived here. If the Income should be a constant increasing one I shall think my self bound as an honest Man to let you know it, and do you Justice. hard would it be, if you who do Justice to your Enemies should not receive it from your Friends! Such permit me to call my self as I am with a sincere Esteem Sir, Your Excellency's most Obedient humble Servant

                                                           Fran: Fauquier

To Majr. Genl. Amherst.

ALS: Kent Archives Office, Maidstone, England, U 1350 052/1. Marked "Private."

To Robert Monckton

Sir   Wmsburgh Novr 12th 1760

I have received your Favours of the 27th and 30th ulto. and by mine of the 27th Octr. you will find that it is not in my Power to do any thing towards Garrisoning the Posts, or assisting you with any of our men to forward his Majesty's Service for which I have the greatest Zeal. However if our Men are absolutely necessary, there is one Expedient which you may take hold of, tho' I cannot; that is, your employing the Men for the Time they now stand provided for, and putting them on the British pay. The Expence will be but small to the Crown of great Britain, tho' at the same time I must acknowledge, it may be a Step, neither Mr. Amherst or you may chuse to take. The Assembly is up and no Liberty is left me of doing otherwise: and even in this Case I shall beg the Favour of you to apply to Mr. Amherst that they may be relieved in February,[1] at farthest, for by the last Letters from the Honble. Col. Byrd, the Cherokee's have entered into a sort of Suspension of Hostilities till the full Moon in March; and if they should then be renewed, this Colony would be in the utmost Distress and exposed to great Danger's for want of these Men.

All these Affairs I leave to your Consideration, and am with the greatest Esteem Sir Your most Obedient humble Servant

Fran: Fauquier

To the Honble. Brigr. Genl. Monckton

ALS: Library of Congress, Peter Force Papers, ser. VIII D, Vernon-Wager Papers, vol. 18, Papers of Robert Monckton, ff. 47105–6. Endorsed as received the twenty-ninth [Nov. 1760].

1. The General Assembly was adjourned on 20 Oct. 1760 until 11 Dec. However, on the day this letter was written Fauquier had referred Monckton's letter of 30 Oct. to the council, whose advice was to inform Monckton "that if he will take upon himself to detain the Virginia Troops, they must be put on British Pay; but in that case it is expected he will apply to General Amherst that they may be remanded back to us by February next as it is probable we shall want their Aid towards repelling Hostilities which the southern Indians may renew against us" (*EJC* 6:174).

To William Byrd

[13 November 1760]

No letter of this date from Fauquier to Byrd has been found, and perhaps none was written: it is likely that Fauquier's letter of 10 Dec. 1760 to Byrd, mentioning "mine of 13 and 14 November," referred to one letter written on those two days.

To William Byrd

[14 November 1760]

This letter has not been found, but Fauquier mentioned it in his letters of 10 Dec. 1760 and 1 July 1761 to Byrd. According to the latter, in the letter of 14 Nov. Fauquier made it very clear that the General Assembly wanted all money spent on the Virginia Regiment to be expended in Virginia; and he mentioned that the demurrage on payment of Byrd's draft to Mr. Cunningham was designed as a check. It is likely that Mr. Cunningham was William Cunningham, the merchant of Falmouth who furnished food and supplies for the Virginia troops.

From William Bull

[16 November 1760]

This letter has not been found. Fauquier communicated it to the council on 11 Dec. 1760, and it is abstracted in *EJC* 6:176:

Also a Letter from Governour Bull dated November the 16th signifying they do not proceed with the Levies for their Provincial Regiment with the success he expected, that the latter end of August he sent to General Amherst a representation of the state of their Affairs relative to the Cherokees, and requested earnestly some Assistance, to which he received an Answer the 14th of October promising, if those Barbarians should break out into fresh Hostilities all the Assistance he could give, and for that purpose should have some Reinforcement at Hand to send him upon the first certain Intelligence of the necessity they may have for them, that on the 19th of October he again acquainted the General of their Perilous situation, and that they must rely on his Excellency for Succours—that as soon as he receives an Account from the General of the number of Troops he shall destine for their service he will immediately inform his Honour thereof by Express.

From William Byrd

[Camp at Bryan's, 22 November 1760]

This letter has not been found. Fauquier communicated it to the council on 11 Dec. 1760, and it is abstracted in *EJC* 6:175–76:

The Governour communicated two Letters from Colo. Byrd, the first dated Camp at Bryan's Novr. 22d signifying his having that Day paid and discharged the new Levies, and the manner in which he had disposed of the five Companies of the Old Regiment—that they have had little success in recruiting in Camp—that he has ordered out several Officers on that service—that the Indians are gone home well satisfied—that he shall proceed to Winchester next Day; and hopes his Honour will have no objection to his going from thence to New York, where his private Business calls him this Winter, as he begs to be excused from serving the Colony any longer in a military Capacity.

To James Abercromby

[23 November 1760]

This letter has not been found, but Abercromby acknowledged it in his letter of 19 Jan. 1761 to Fauquier and indicated that the letter of 23 Nov. enclosed duplicates of Fauquier's earlier letters of 22 June and 31 Oct. and made some comment on an address sent to Edward Montagu (and perhaps transmitted a copy of the address itself, although Abercromby's reference is ambiguous). The address must have been the address and representation to the king, stating the reasons for the assembly's passage of acts lately disallowed, which was signed by the president of the council and the speaker of the House of Burgesses, and delivered to the Committee of Correspondence for transmittal to Montagu, who was to present it to the king. See *JHB, 1758–1761*, pp. 188, 196. Copies of the address and representation, referred by the Privy Council to the Board of Trade, are in C.O.5/1330, ff. 50–56. The address, dated 20 Oct. 1760, expresses apprehension of the king's displeasure which has been indicated by his disallowance of several acts lately passed by the General Assembly; the members of the assembly presume to offer their reasons for passing those acts and hope to erase any impression that they tried to encroach on the king's prerogative. The representation, also dated 20 Oct. 1760, offers a detailed review of Virginia laws regarding payment of levies and fees and distraining and sale of the property of delinquents, and particularly of the acts to enable inhabitants of the colony to discharge their debts in money. In summary, the representation begs the king to allow the governor's assent to necessary acts of less than two years' duration and to acts altering or repealing other acts that have not received the king's approval, relate only to Virginia, and do not affect the king's prerogative or the trade of Great Britain.

From Arthur Dobbs

[25 November 1760]

This letter has not been found. Fauquier communicated it to the council on 11 Dec. 1760, and it is abstracted in *EJC* 6:176:

His Honour was likewise pleased to communicate a Letter from Governour Dobbs dated the 25th of November informing he cannot yet give any assurance of a supply from his province, that as soon as the fate of a Bill for that purpose depending is determined, he shall give him Notice of it—and desiring his Honour to forward a Letter to General Amherst, wherein he has pressed him to send an immediate Aid to quell the Cherokees.

From the Board of Trade

Sir, [Whitehall, 28 November 1760]

In Your Letter to Us, dated the 30th of June last, You take notice of the irregular manner, in which the Order of Council, repealing the Laws complained of by the Clergy of Virginia, and His Majesty's Instruction to You upon that Occasion, were delivered to you; in answer to which it is necessary for us to acquaint you, that Orders in Council and Instructions, (tho' the Draughts of the Latter be usually prepared by us, yet) being finally executed in the Council Office and the Office of the Secretary of State; We apprehend they are in all Cases, where they are founded upon the Application of Parties, delivered from those Offices (upon proper Application) to the Partys, in whose favour Judgment is given. We are, Sir, Your most Obedient humble Servants,

Dunk Halifax
Soame Jenyns
Wm. Sloper

Whitehall / Novr. 28th 1760 / To Francis Fauquier Esqr. Lieut. Governor of Virginia.

Copy: C.O.5/1368, f. 1.

From James Abercromby

London Decr 1st [1760]

I am favoured with yours of 2d Septr. by which I find other letters are a missing, I hinted in former letters by what means I became circumscribd in regard to the Public money chiefly owing to Lord Loudouns delay which gave time for the Contest about the different Agents, tho properly speaking the Authority quasi Agent was out of the Case yet it furnishd Mr Montague with the pretence of interfering by the Assemblys Authority but to this moment he has received no Instructions of any kind so that he remains with his Regiment at Wells, by Copy of your letter to the Board of Trade I find their Lordships on Sir Mathew Lambs Report do find the Agency Law defective and have thereupon proposed an Amendment as no opposition is to be given to that Law it probably may be agreed to when properly amended, I wish however it may not occasionally prove a thorn in the side of the Governor & Council.

The Event of the Kings death and thereupon the various Negociations

1 December 1760

for supporting the Possessors of Offices in their own Offices will probably divert their Attention from those in Office in America, but whatever ill will might have been shewn to some of your Measures more particularly those relative to the Clergy Act, and on the back thereof the Repeal of some other Acts I have no reason to think the seeds of Discontent to your Administration have taken deep root.

However to speak the language of a friend you cannot after such Alarm given to the Different Boards by former Steps, be hereafter too much upon your guard against giving too great a Way to the Assembly where your Instructions are at stake; I sincerly do not know that you have one Enemy here from public or private Motives, and you may rest satisfyd thereof so far as my Judgment may be depended on nor do I think so much stress as to the Indignity you mention is to be laid on the manner in which the Kings Instructions in Mr Camms Case came to you, there is nothing more common in Cases before the King & Council, than for the Attorney to the party to get the Instruction which is in Fact the final Judgment of the Council Board put into his hands on paying the Fees for the same, I have done it on several Occasions, Mr Camm has no reason to boast of this being given him in Contempt to you, the Partys concerned have always a right to serve such Instructions on the Party, against whom Judgment goes, and such Instructions are not to be lookd on as the Kings privat Rule of Government but rather as Judicial sentences, to which the Partys have right to make use of, this being the case you need not give yourself much trouble to sift into the matter.

[I have always found more affected Secrecy at the Plantation Office than in any other of the Public Offices, and the reason seems to be that they are only the Channel through which Matters of Government pass, and in few Instances can take upon them to act independently of Superior Officers, and in my privat opinion could not properly have called upon the Council Office for the Instruction in Camms Case.]

You may be assurd that I shall continue to be attentive to what may concern you personally & consult from time to time with your Brother, when the exigency of the Case requires our so doing I am &c

PS tell him to send letters in small Packets to avoid Postage, that the next Parliament letters are to come free to me being a Member.[1]
Gov. Faquier.

Copy: Virginia State Library, James Abercromby Letter Book, pp. 225-27. In Abercromby's hand, with numerous insertions and deletions, and probably a draft, the postscript being a memorandum for Abercromby or his amanuensis; the paragraph in brackets is crossed through as if for deletion, but is retained here on account of its interest. The whole letter is extremely hard to make out. A marginal note indicates that the letter was to be sent by Captain Carlisle "if not gone."

1. Although the Parliament of 1754 was not dissolved until 20 Mar. 1761, Abercromby evidently was sure of being elected to the succeeding Parliament, and in fact he was elected member for Clackmannanshire in Scotland on 10 Apr. 1761, apparently unopposed.

From William Byrd

[Winchester, 3 December 1760]

This letter has not been found. Fauquier communicated it to the council on 11 Dec. 1760, and it is abstracted in *EJC* 6:176:

The second, dated Winchester Decembr. the 3d signifying that he shall make all the despatch he can to attend in Williamsburg at the next sessions of Assembly—is sorry he has given so little satisfaction in his Command, and therefore resigns his Commission.

To Jeffery Amherst

Sir　　　　　　　　　　　　　　　　　　　Wmsburgh Decr 5th 1760

I take the Liberty to trouble you in Behalf of several of the Inhabitants of this Colony, for Debts due to them from the Crown.

I have always understood (for it was a Transaction which pass'd before my Arrival in the Colony) that when the Cherokee Indians were sent for to join his Majesty's Forces under General Forbes, it was agreed that if the Colony would subsist them at their Expence in their passage thro' it; The presents and all other subsequent Charges were to be paid for by the Crown. That the Colony understand it so, is evident by their never having paid these Demands, and the poor Men to their great Detriment are still out of their Money. These Accounts were once laid before Sir John St. Clair, but I suppose it was at a Time when the Inhabitants of this Colony were not in Favour, and he did nothing in the Affair. If the paying of these Demands is not inconsistent with your Instructions and Powers, I beg Leave to interest my self in Behalf of these Sufferers, and to recommend them to your protection.[1]

Lieutenant Colonel Mercer[2] a young Gentleman who has served with Reputation in the Troops of this Colony and who has been very active in the performance of any Duty which he thought might forward his Majesty's Service will wait on you with this, and is abler to give you more full Information of all these Affairs than I am.

6 December 1760

In order to do all the Justice in my power it is necessary I should inform you that Mr. Welder the Clerk, and Messrs. Watts and Smith the Interpreters have received Money from this Colony for Services performed by them, of which I have given Mr. Mercer Advice.[3] I am with the greatest Esteem Sir Your Excellencys most obedient Servant.

Fran: Fauquier

His Excy. Majr. Genl. Amherst.

ALS: W.O. 34/37, f. 44.

1. The persons who had debts due to them from the crown have not been identified, but they were probably people who had supplied presents for the Cherokees recruited at Loudoun's request, such as Charles Turnbull, whose letter of 14 May 1758 concerning goods for the Indians was considered by the council on 19 May 1758. The council advised that Turnbull should be referred to General Forbes for payment, since Loudoun had sent for the Indians and required nothing from Virginia except provisions for the Indians during their march across Virginia to Winchester. No record of accounts for these Indian goods has been traced.
2. George Mercer.
3. Samuel Welder was clerk to Christopher Gist, deputy agent for Indian affairs, from 14 June 1758 until 14 June 1759, and perhaps before and after that period as well. John Watts (d. 1770) and Richard Smith were doubtless the interpreters in question. What payment had been made to Welder, Watts, and Smith is not known; on 25 May 1763 the council considered and disallowed Welder's account for salary for the year noted above, and for a horse, and accounts from Watts and Smith for pay as interpreters for an unspecified period.

To the Board of Trade

My Lords   Wmsburgh Decr 6th 1760

Under cover with this I send to your Lordships, Duplicates of my late Letters, and a Triplicate of my Letter of the 30th June, the Original and Duplicate of which I have heard are both lost; one in the Resolution, Hogg, the other in the Russel, Crawfurd, taken by the French.[1]

There is a Doubt arisen here, whether in the Letter I had the Honor to receive from your Lordships of the 13 June, Your Lordships meant to include the Lands on Green Bryar, New River, or Kanhawa River,[2] as Lands not to be patented. These Rivers have been tolerably seated for some time but the Settlers have abandoned their plantations on account of the late Disturbances, but are now returning, and applications are making for new patents. The Lands I particularly wrote about are two or three hundred Miles to the Northwards of these Lands; but as your Lordships Words are general I have understood them in the most general Sense as including all Lands on Waters running into the Ohio and have refused to grant patents for these Lands. If I have been mistaken in your Lordships Sentiments I hope you will soon favour me with an Explanation of them.

I was some time since honoured with a Letter from Mr. Secretary Pitt, signifying his Majesty's pleasure that I should inform his Council of any Clandestine Trade carried on in this Colony, to the Benefit of his Majesty's Enemies and the Detriment of his Subjects, to which I have given a full Answer, 1st that such Trade has been chiefly carried on by Means of Flags of Truce, of which I have not been prevailed on to grant one, tho' great Temptations have been thrown in my Way. 2dly that there is an open Trade carried on to Monte Christo, which I conceive to be wholy a French Trade. and 3rdly that the Act prohibiting the Exportation of Grain to neutral ports is evaded, by Ships clearing out for Scotland or Gibraltar and then pretending to be blown into the Madeiras or some of the Western Isles by Stress of Weather; the Governor lays his Hands on the Cargo and obliges the Captains to dispose of it, at a great price.

The Assembly in a short Session began in October have pass'd an Act to keep up 1000 Men this Winter to be ready to assist the Carolina's against the Cherokees in the Spring, in Case the Negotiations for peace now on Foot do not come to a happy Issue. But I fear we shall not be able to bring them to Reason without the Assistance of some Regulars from Mr. Amherst. I could not prorogue this Assembly on Account of the Expiration of the Tobacco Law; and as their sitting at the Time of the General Court is attended with many and great Inconveniences, instead of proroguing them I have ordered them to adjourn themselves that their meeting in Spring may be a Continuation of the same Session.[3]

The Acts, Accounts, and all public papers I have now out of the respective Offices ready to be transmitted to your Lordships by the first Ship which sails for London.

We have had the Misfortune to lose Mr. Commissary Dawson, a Gentleman of great Worth, Probity and many other Virtues; by whose Death there is a Vacancy in the Council.[4] According to my Instructions I send your Lordships the Names of three Gentlemen,[5] all Men of property and much respected in this Country, and every Way Qualifyed for the Honor of succeeding the late Mr. Dawson as Councilor. Their Merit is so great that I cannot give either the preference, but as I am particularly circumstanced at present I leave it to your Lordships Consideration whether Conveniency ought to take place. By my Instructions I am ordered not to act with less than five of the Council unless in Cases of great Emergency when I may act with three.[6] By the Death of Mr. Dawson, and the Absence of Colonel Ludwell,[7] there are but three of the Council within Call in Cases which require Dispatch (viz) Mr. President Blair and the two Mr. Nelson's. I have found by Experience that the Gentlemen at a Distance who have great Rivers to cross, cannot be expected to attend Councils except at stated Times as assemblies and General Courts; as the Gentlemen who live near can etc. it is for this Reason that I have picked out a Gentleman who lives within three miles of me. And I hope your Lordships will always consider this Conveniency, in your Recommendations to his Majesty that I may constantly have five Gentlemen near at hand to consult with in Cases which require Dispatch. I think the Service of the Government demands it.

The Gentlemen I now name to your Lordships, are Mr. John Page who lives in Gloucester, Col. Presly Thornton who lives in Northumberland and Col. Lewis Burwell who lives in this Neck 3 Miles from Williamsburgh.[8] I am with the greatest Respect My Lords Your Lordships most Obedient & devoted Servant

Fran: Fauquier

To the right Honble. the Lords of Trade &ct.

ALS: C.O.5/1330, ff. 32–34. Endorsed as read 5 Feb. 1761.

1. Fauquier presumably sent duplicates of his letters of 1 and 17 Sept. 1760 to the board. The *Resolution*, Capt. Francis Hogg, was a ship of 300 tons owned by John Trapnell & Co. The *Russel*, Capt. Archibald Crawfurd, was a ship of 230 tons owned by John Wilkinson & Co. Both ships were cleared out of the Upper James district on 19 July 1760, bound for their home port of London.

2. The Greenbrier River, formed by the junction of two streams in Pocahontas County, W.Va., flows southwest to join the New River, which flows from northwestern North Carolina across Virginia into West Virginia. At Gauley Bridge, in south central West Virginia, the Gauley River and the New River join to form the Kanawha River, which flows northwest to Point Pleasant, where it empties into the Ohio River.

3. On 20 Oct. Fauquier adjourned to 11 Dec. the General Assembly session begun on 6 Oct., in order to avoid sitting during the session of the General Court which normally began on 10 Oct. The tobacco law in question was "An act for continuing and amending the act, intituled, An act for amending the staple of tobacco, and preventing frauds in his majesty's customs" (Hening, 6:222–27) passed in the General Assembly of Feb. 1752, and to continue in force until 20 Oct. 1760 or until the end of the next session of assembly.

4. The Reverend Thomas Dawson, commissary of the bishop of London, died on 29 Nov. 1760.

5. See the seventh article of the instructions, in C.O.5/1367, ff. 92–93.

6. See the sixth article of the instructions, in C.O.5/1367, f. 92.

7. Philip Ludwell went to England sometime after the end of the Mar. 1760 session of the General Assembly, prorogued on 11 Mar., and presumably before the May session of the assembly which began on 19 May, and remained in England until his death on 25 Mar. 1767.

8. These were John Page (ca. 1720–1774) of North End, on the North River in what was then Gloucester County, but is now Mathews County; Presley Thornton (1721–1769) of Northumberland House in Northumberland County; and Lewis Burwell (d. 1784) of Kingsmill in James City County, a member of the House of Burgesses for his county 1758–74.

To William Byrd

Sir   Wmsburgh Decr 10th 1760

I have received your Commission and Letter of Resignation by the Hands of Mr. Rutherford[1] and as I have not yet had an Opportunity of communicating it to the Gentlemen of the Council, I can say nothing more to it, than that I am sorry you have so understood Matters as to give you Cause to think you have Reason to take this hasty and ill-considered Step.

When I had the Pleasure of seeing you at Winchester,[2] if you recollect Sir the first opening of Intimacy and Confidence between us was my advising you against another Resignation which I thought as inconsiderate. I then had Success in my Counsels, and tho' my Correspondence by Letters has not been attended with the same good Fortune as my Conversation then was (which I have always attributed to your Minds being poisoned by the Advice of young and hasty Counsellors in my Absence) yet I can with Confidence say all my Advice whether of a public or a private Nature was sincerely meant to do you Honor and Service. And I have the Satisfaction to think that when more Years have roll'd over your Head, and the Influence of Passions of all Kinds subside and give Way to the Dictates of cool Reflection you will see and acknowledge, that tho' a new Acquaintance, I have acted the Part of an old Friend.

Your Letter from Bryants Camp in answer to mine of the 13 & 14 November by Mr. Allen is not yet come to hand.[3]

I have the Pleasure to inform you that on the late melancholy Occasion of the Commissary's Death Mr. John Page is nominated for a Councillor without your Resignation to make Room for him. His own Merit and your Desire were sufficient Motives to me.

In your last Paragraph you seem to take a final Leave of all Correspondence, perhaps you did not mean it so; whether you did or not, I with great Sincerity of Heart wish you well and happy wherever you are, and am Sir Your very humble Servant

                                                                Fran: Fauquier

To the Honble. Wm. Byrd

ALS: Virginia Historical Society.

1. The letter of resignation was presumably that of 3 Dec. 1760. The bearer may have been Thomas Rutherford, who served as deputy to Dr. Thomas Walker in supplying provisions to the Virginia troops.
2. This was evidently in May or June 1759, during Fauquier's visit to Winchester.
3. Fauquier evidently referred to Byrd's letter of 22 Nov. 1760, but it is not clear how many letters of his own it answered: probably he meant that he had written one letter on 13 and 14 Nov. Mr. Allen has not been identified.

To Jeffery Amherst

Sir   Wmsburgh Decr 15th 1760

I have received very pressing Letters from Govr. Dobbs of North, and Govr. Bull of South Carolina, that I would join with them in Application to you for Assistance from some of his Majesty's Troops under your Command to subdue and quell the Cherokee Indians.[1] I am of Opinion that if a peace is not made with them, provincial Troops alone cannot effectualy finish this Affair to the Advantage and Honor of his Majesty's Colonies.

The plan proposed between those Gentlemen and my self is, that an Attack should be made by the South Carolinians assisted by some Regulars from You on the Lower Towns; and by Us, assisted likewise in the same Manner, on the upper Towns at one and the same Time, to divide their Force as much as possible.[2] By the best Information I can obtain, it is probable that if both parties of the Cherokees retire into their middle Towns, they can long elude the Force of our Arms by the Impracticability of the Country; but in that Case they must abandon all their upper and lower Towns and Crops, to the Mercy of their Enemies; and they must very soon be reduced to the greatest Extremities for want of Necessaries.

I have great Reason to hope that the general Assembly which meets in the first Week in March, will continue the old Regiment of 1000 Men through the Summer to undertake the foregoing plan of Operations, or any other you may Judge more effectual which I entirely submit to Your superior Abilities.

If it is consistent with your Excellency's Instructions to give us Assistance, or to let me know what that Assistance can be; such Assurances from you will be a great Inducement to the Assembly to exert themselves; they hope for it as they have persever'd to the last in Assisting his Majesty's Forces at a very great Expence. If you will permitt me to ask for a certain Number of Men, I am clear in my Opinion that two thin Battalions, or at least one entire Complete one will be necessary to be join'd to our Regiment to effect our part of the Work. The Road from our back Settlements to the upper Towns, is so plain and good, and the Country so practicable that Waggons may pass all the Way, as I am informed. I have mentioned the least Number possible, because I would not be thought too presuming, but more men would make the Work more certain. I am with the highest Esteem, Sir Your Excellency's most Obedient Humble Servant

Fran: Fauquier

To his Excelcy. Majr. Genl. Amherst.

ALS: W.O.34/37, f. 45. A copy of this letter (but with "Provisions" as the last word in the second paragraph) is in C.O.5/61, ff. 171–72, endorsed as received in Amherst's letter of 27 Feb. 1761.

1. It is likely that Fauquier referred to the letter from Dobbs of 25 Nov. 1760 and the letter from Bull of 16 Nov., although the abstracts of those letters do not indicate any suggestion that Fauquier should ask Amherst for regular troops.
2. It is not clear how or when this plan was formulated.

To the Board of Trade

My Lords   Williamsburgh Decr 15th 1760

I transmit to your Lordships in this Box the Acts pass'd in the short Session of Assembly held in May on Account of the Dangers from the Cherokee Indians; and the Acts pass'd in the beginning of the present Session which adjourned in order to preserve the Tobacco Law in Force till the Expiration of the Session; the Journals of the Council and House of Burgesses; the Accounts of the Receiver General both in regard to the Quit Rents and 2 shg. Duty; and the Naval Officers Accounts, together with Duplicates of Accounts formerly sent.[1] It was thought improper to send part of the Journals of the present Session as it is possible some alterations may be made, when the General Assembly meets on the 5th of March according to their present Adjournment.

I am informed by the Judge of the Admiralty Court[2] here that he has received Directions from that Board to transmit an Account of the proceedings on all Captures of Spanish Vessels brought under his Jurisdiction; on a Complaint from the Ambassador from the Court of Spain now in London. If I may judge of other Colonies by this, the Complaint is not groundless for I granted a Letter of Marque to Mr. Sprowle a Merchant

15 December 1760

of Norfolk, for a Privateer[3] who sent in here as Prizes two Spanish Coasting Vessels, one of which Mr. Sprowle did not think proper to libel in the Court, but discharged the Captain without making him any Satisfaction; the other he libell'd, the Vessel was cleared, but by means of an Appeal hanging over the Captains head, he has refused to make him any Satisfaction also, who fell sick and died in the Country. His conduct has appear'd to me in so scandalous a Light, that I should have put his bond in Suit (given for the performance of all things required by his Instructions) if I had thought a Suit could have been maintained without a Complaint regularly lodged.

I wrote to your Lordships a few days since by the three Sisters Captn. Gordon bound to Glascow,[4] a Duplicate of which Letter, and of this I shall send by a Bristol Ship which is to Sail in a Week. I am with the greatest Respect My Lords Your Lordships most Obedient & obliged humble Servant

Fran: Fauquier

To the right Honble. the Lords of Trade &ct.

ALS: C.O.5/1330, ff. 35–36. A duplicate, endorsed as read 5 Feb. 1761.

1. The acts transmitted were the three passed in the session of 19–24 May 1760 and the three passed in the period 6–20 Oct. 1760 (Hening, 7:357–67, 369–77). No manuscript copy of the acts of May is now in the Public Record Office, but there are copies of the printed acts (Evans 8755) in C.O.5/1390, ff. 73–75 and C.O.5/1396, ff. 211–13. There is a manuscript copy of the acts of Oct. in C.O.5/1399, ff. 82–87, and copies of the printed acts (Evans 8756) are in C.O.5/1390, ff. 76–79 and C.O.5/1396, ff. 214–17. The journals transmitted were evidently those of the May session of the assembly. No copy of these journals is in the Public Record Office; at least one printed copy of the journal of the House of Burgesses (Evans 8758) is known, but the journal of the council in assembly has never been found. The accounts transmitted were presumably that of quitrents for 1759 and that of the 2s. per hogshead revenue for 25 Apr.–25 Oct. 1760, both of them approved 12 Nov. 1760; copies of these accounts in C.O.5/1330, ff. 83–84, 85–86, the only ones known, were transmitted much later, in Sept. 1761. The naval officers' returns were perhaps some for the period from about Apr. 1759 up into Oct. 1760; and the duplicate accounts were probably duplicates of the naval officers' returns for the period Sept. 1758–Apr. 1759 that Fauquier had sent with his letter of 9 June 1759 to the Board of Trade.

2. The commission of Peyton Randolph, the attorney general, as judge of vice admiralty for Virginia, dated 21 Nov. 1744, is registered in H.C.A.50/10, f. 211, and his later commission from George III, dated 25 July 1761, is in H.C.A.50/11, f. 152.

3. A letter of marque was a license for fitting out an armed vessel for capturing merchant shipping of an enemy, and this letter was probably granted to Andrew Sproule or Sprowle. The name of privateer was given both to the person holding the letter of marque and to the ship which he had fitted out.

4. The ship *Three Sisters*, Capt. Robert Gordon, was a vessel of 180 tons, registered in Boston and owned by Robert Gordon, Samuel McCall & Sons. She was cleared outwards from the port of Rappahannock on 12 Dec. 1760, bound for Glasgow.

From William Pitt

Sir   Whitehall Decr 17th 1760

His Majesty having nothing so much at Heart, as by the most vigorous Prosecution of the War, to reduce the Enemy to the Necessity of accepting a Peace on Terms of Glory & Advantage to His Majesty's Crown, and beneficial, in particular, to his Subjects in America; and as nothing can so effectually contribute to that Great and essential Object, as the King's being enabled to employ, as immediately as may be, such Part of the Regular Forces in North America, as may be adequate to some Great and Important Enterprize against the Enemy; I am commanded to signify to you the King's Pleasure, that, in order the better to provide for the full and entire Security of His Majesty's Dominions in North America, & particularly of the Possession of His Majesty's Conquests there, during the Absence of such Part of the regular Forces, you do forthwith use your utmost Endeavours, and Influence, with the Council and Assembly of your Province, to induce them to raise, with all possible Dispatch, within your Government, As large a Body of Men, as the Number & Situation of It's Inhabitants may allow; Your Province having been extremely wanting to the King's Service, in this respect, last Year. And forming the same into Regiments, as far as shall be found convenient, that you do direct Them to hold Themselves in readiness, and particularly as much earlier, than former Years, as may be, to march to such Place, or Places, in North America, as His Majesty's Commander in Chief there, or the Officer who shall be appointed to command The King's Forces in those Parts, shall appoint, in order to be employed there under the supreme Command of His Majesty's said Commander in Chief, or of the Officer to be appointed as above, in such Manner as, from the Circumstances, & Situation, of the Enemy's Posts, & the State, & Disposition, of the Indian Nations, on that Side, He may judge most conducive for the King's Service; And the better to facilitate this important Service, The King is pleased to leave it to you to issue Commissions to such Gentlemen in your Province, as you shall judge, from their Weight and Credit with the People, and their Zeal for the Publick Service, may be best disposed, and enabled, to quicken and effectuate the speedy levying of the greatest Number of Men; In the Disposition of which Commissions, I am persuaded, you will have nothing in View, but the Good of the King's Service, & a due Subordination of the whole to His Majesty's Commander; And all Officers of the Provincial Forces, as high as Colonels inclusive, are to have Rank, according to their several respective Commissions, agreable to the Regulations contained in His late Majesty's Warrant of the 30th of December 1757, which is renewed by His present Majesty.

The King is further pleased to furnish all the Men, so raised as above, with Arms, Ammunition, and Tents, as well as to order Provisions to be issued to the same, by His Majesty's Commissaries, in the same Proportion, & Manner, as is done to the rest of the King's Forces: The whole therefore, that The King expects, and requires, from the several Provinces, is, the Levying, Cloathing, and Pay of the Men; and on these Heads also, that no Encouragement may be wanting to the fullest Exertion of your Force, His Majesty is farther most graciously pleased to permit me to acquaint you, that strong Recommendations will be made to Parliament, in their Session next Year, to grant a proper Compensation for such Expences as above, according as the active Vigour, and strenuous Efforts of the respective Provinces shall justly appear to merit.

It is His Majesty's Pleasure, that you do, with particular Diligence, immediately collect, & put into the best Condition, all the Arms, issued last Campaign, which can be, any ways, rendered Serviceable, or that can be found within your Government, in order that the same may be again employed for His Majesty's Service.

I am further to inform you, that similar Orders are sent, by this Conveyance to [Pensylvania, Maryland,] North Carolina, & South Carolina. The Northern Governments are also directed to raise Men in the same Manner, to be employed, as His Majesty's Commander in Chief shall judge most Conducive for the King's Service in North America.

It is unnecessary to add any Thing to animate your Zeal in the Execution of His Majesty's Orders in this important Conjuncture, which is finally to fix the future Safety and Welfare of America and of your own Province in particular; And the King doubts not, from your known Fidelity and Attachment, that you will employ yourself with the utmost Application and Dispatch, in this promising & decisive Crisis. I am &ca
W: Pitt

Copy: C.O. 5/214, pp. 373–[81?]. Circular addressed to the governors of Pennsylvania, Maryland, Virginia, North Carolina, and South Carolina. This copy was intended for Pennsylvania, and brackets indicate the alterations proper for Virginia; marginal notes indicate different versions of the number of men to be raised and the reference to compensation from Parliament; the text above incorporates the changes indicated for Virginia. This is probably one of the letters which Fauquier sent to the House of Burgesses on 8 Apr. 1761; see *JHB, 1758–1761*, p. 253.

From Robert Monckton

[Philadelphia, 18 December 1760]

This letter has not been found. Fauquier communicated it to the council on 5 Mar. 1761, and it is abstracted in *EJC* 6:182:

A Letter from Brigr. General Moncton dated Philadelphia December the 18th informing he has sent Orders for such of the Virginians as can be immediately spared to March to Winchester and that the remainder will follow as soon as he can get a part of Colo. Vaughan's regiment up to relieve them.

Colonel Vaughan was the Honorable John Vaughan (ca. 1737–1795), lieutenant colonel commandant of the Ninety-fourth Regiment, or Royal Welsh Volunteers, which he had raised and brought to North America.

From James Abercromby

Decr 25th 1760

Within these few days Several Bills drawn by you, Mr Blair President, and Mr Robinson Speaker to the account of the £32268.19 allotted by his Majesty to Virginia out of the 50000 granted in 1757 to North South Carolina and Virginia have been presented to me for Acceptance; whereupon a difficulty does arise for the Bills so drawn do not expressly set forth that the Persons who Sign such Bills are Authorisd by the Legislature (viz) the Governor Council and Assembly to draw Bills nor is the Value received in Virginia said to be for the Use of the Province and as the Rules prescribd by the Treasury and as my Security given to the Crown several Copys whereof were sent you do require that the Money shall be paid to such persons as are or shall be authorisd by the Governor Council and Assembly to receive the same Such Authority then not appearing from the Tenor of the Bills nor from any letter of Advice from you, or from the Council or Assembly and neither Act of Assembly nor Journals appearing in the Plantation Office to signefy the Authority of the Legislature to you & those Gentlemen for drawing Such Bills; under this difficulty for my justification and that of my Securitys I must lay the Bills before the Treasury for their pleasure thereon, and unless their Lordships shall peremptorily *order me to suspend payment* I am resolvd to pay them, and to Trust to your being properly Authorisd and if not that you will procure the Authority of the Legislature to justify your drawing such Bills which you will please to transmit to me under the Provincial Seal that I may pass my Accounts at the Treasury, and my Security be dischargd. No Motive but that of discharging myself of this Money and at the same time the desire I have to keep Matters quiet and to avoid bringing you and those Gentlemen under any difficulty or reproach here or in Virginia for not keeping expressly up to the Terms prescribd for payment of this Money Such then being my Motives for departing from the express Condition of my Bond I do not doubt but that you will without loss of time take the proper Measures if not already done with the Council & Assembly to Indempnify me and my Securitys for paying your Bills, the Treasury being under Adjournment for 10 days I shall take the first opportunity on their meeting to lay the Bills before them, and in the mean time I have signefyd the same to the Merchants in whose hands such Bills are I am always Sir

Gov. Fouquiere.

Copy: Virginia State Library, James Abercromby Letter Book, pp. 223–24. Evidently a draft, as it has a number of deletions and insertions; it is in Abercromby's hand, and hard to decipher. A marginal note indicates that the letter went by Captain Carlisle to Mr. Hyndman.

From Jeffery Amherst

Sir, New York 28th December 1760

Since my Return to this Town, I have been favored with Your Letter of the 7th Ultimo, Enclosing a Copy of the Commission Appointing me Governor of the Colony of Virginia, for both Which I should long eere this have returned You my most sincere thanks, but that I have been much occuppied, in the Assembling & Embarking for South Carolina, a body of Troops, intended, and (in Conjunction with the Provincial Forces, Which Lt. Govr. Bull Informed me were to be furnished by the two Carolinas & Virginia) I trust every way Capable most effectually to Chastise the Cherokee Indians.

This Body consists in two Battalions of Independents, lately Arrived from England, of each 440 Men Officers Included:[1] two Compleat light Infantry Companies of Monckton's & Whitmore's;[2] two hat Companies of said Regiments likewise Compleat,[3] and a few Mohawk Indians; besides the four Companys of the Royal, that were already in Carolina;[4] the Whole under the Command of Lieut. Colonel Grant An Experienced Officer, Who has had great share in Colonel Montgomery's late Operations, against those barbarian savages;[5] so that if he meets with that Chearfull aid and Assistance from the Southern Provinces, Which the Exigency requires, and it is so much their Interest to grant, I have no Doubt but he will soon reduce those Savages to reason, & Compell them to a good and lasting peace, without Which he is to shew them no Mercy.

I cannot sufficiently Acknowledge Your Generous & disinterested Proceedings, with regard to the Income, arising from the perquisites of the Government; And am much Obliged to You for the Remittances, Which You proposed to make in my behalf to Mr. Calcraft, Whom I shall Acquaint therewith by the first packett, that if he has not already entered into Agreement with the Gentleman Your Brother, the same may take place for our mutual satisfaction. I ever am with the greatest Esteem, Sir, &ca.

Honble. Lt. Govr. Fauquier.

Copy: W.O.34/37, f. 218. Marked "Private." Fauquier communicated this letter to the council on 5 Mar. 1761, it appears, although it was private; see *EJC* 6:182.

1. Independent companies of infantry were those not belonging to regiments; each of the two battalions of independents mentioned appears to have consisted of about ten companies.

2. A light infantry company was one of the two picked companies of an infantry regiment (the other being the grenadier company). Men of the light infantry were typically of light but vigorous physique and good marksmen and were often used for scouting or skirmishing; they carried muskets lighter than those used in most infantry companies. Monckton's regiment was the Seventeenth Foot, of which he had been appointed colonel late in Oct. 1760. Whitmore's regiment was the Twenty-second Foot, named for Edward Whitmore (d. 1762), its colonel.

3. Hat companies were the ordinary companies of an infantry regiment, so called because they wore cocked hats, while the grenadiers and light infantry wore caps.

4. The Royals were the First Foot, the regiment that had provided some of the men sent to South Carolina in Mar. 1760 under Montgomerie's command.

5. James Grant, previously a major in the Highland Regiment, was appointed lieutenant colonel of the Fortieth Foot in 1760; he was second in command to Montgomerie in the expedition against the Cherokees in Mar. 1760.

1760: Appendix A

The Account of his Majestys Revenue of Quitrents &c arising within this Colony of Virginia for the Year 1758

The Receiver General doth Charge himself with the Receipt of the said Revenue as follows

To Ballance of the last Account[1]	£12226. 2. 9
To the Quitrents of the Northern Neck for the Year 1758	6.13. 4
To the Account of Compositions for Escheated Lands	3.11. 8

Quitrents for the Year 1758			
Counties Names	Number of Acres paid for	Paid in Money	Sheriffs Allowances	Amount
Amelia	350000	£350	£35	£315
Augusta	260000	£260	£26	234
Albemarle	597605	£597.12. 1	£59.15. 2	537.16.11
Accomack	233713	£233.14. 3	£23. 7. 5	210. 6.10
Brunswick	240000	£240	£24	216
Bedford	100000	£100	£10	90
Caroline	200000	£200	£20	180
Charles City				
Cumberland	300000	£300	£30	270
Chesterfield	251453	£251. 9	£25. 2.10	226. 6. 2
Dinwiddie	250000	£250	£25	225
Elizabeth City	35317	£ 35. 6. 4	£ 3.10. 7	31.15. 9
Essex	144690	£144.13.10	£14. 9. 4	130. 4. 6
Gloucester				
Goochland	148155	£148. 3. 1	£14.16. 3	133. 6.10
Hanover	253782	£253.15. 8	£25. 7. 7	228. 8. 1
Henrico	110000	£110	£11	99
Hallifax				
James City	50000	£ 50	£ 5	45
Isle of Wight	130000	£130	£13	117
King William	80000	£ 80	£ 8	72
King & Queen	110000	£110	£11	99
Louisa				
Lunenburgh	35000	£ 35	£ 3.10	31.10
Middlesex	75385	£ 75. 7. 8	£ 7.10. 9	67.16.11
Nansemond	140000	£140	£14	126
Norfolk				
Northampton	104051	£104. 1	£10. 8. 1	93.12.11
New Kent	50000	£ 50	£ 5	45
Orange				

Quitrents for the Year 1758					
Counties Names	Number of Acres paid for	Paid in Money	Sheriffs Allowances	Amount	
Prince George	130000	£130	£13	117	
Princess Anne	120000	£120	£12	108	
Prince Edward	160000	£160	£16	144	
Spotsylvania	237708	£237.14. 2	£23.15. 5	213.18. 9	
Surry	90000	£ 90	£ 9	81	
Southampton	236421	£236. 8. 5	£23.12.10	212.15. 7	
Sussex	220000	£220	£22	198	
Warwick	41478	£ 41. 9. 6	£ 4. 2.11	37. 6. 7	
York	69713	£ 69.14. 3	£ 6.19. 5	62.14.10	4999.—. 8
					£17235. 8. 5

Brought Over £17235. 8. 5

Arrears of Quitrents paid in the Year 1758.					
Counties Names	Number of Acres paid for	Paid in Money	Sheriffs Allowances	Amount	
Amelia	11799	£ 11.16	£ 1. 3. 7	£ 10.12. 5	
Augusta	100000	£100	£10	90	
Ditto 1756	100312	£100. 6. 3	£10. 7	90. 5. 8	
Albemarle	29283	£ 29. 5. 8	£ 2.18. 6	26. 7. 2	
Ditto	151371	£151. 7. 5	£15. 2. 9	136. 4. 8	
Bedford	32536	£ 32.10. 9	£ 3. 5. 1	29. 5. 8	
Charles City	9191	£ 9. 3.10	£ 18. 4	8. 5. 6	
Ditto 1756	13382	£ 13. 7. 8	£ 1. 6. 9	12. 11	
Cumberland	80000	£ 80	£ 8	72	
Chesterfield	4166	£ 4. 3. 4	£ 8. 4	3.15	
Elizabeth City	13818	£ 13.16. 4	£ 1. 7. 7	12. 8. 9	
Hanover	1546	£ 1.10.11	£ 3. 1	1. 7.10	
Ditto	114551	£114.11	£11. 9. 1	103. 1.11	
Hallifax	45000	£ 45	£ 4.10	40.10	
James City	18482	£ 18. 9. 8	£ 1.17	16.12. 8	
Isle of Wight	130000	£130	£13	117	
King William	34713	£ 34.14. 3	£ 3. 9. 5	31. 4.10	
Ditto 1756	16928	£ 16.18. 7	£ 1.13.10	15. 4. 9	
King & Queen	8110	£ 8. 2. 2	£ 16. 2	7. 6	
Louisa	335291	£335. 5.10	£33.10. 7	301.15. 3	
Ditto 1756	134733	£134.14. 8	£13. 9. 5	121. 5. 3	
Lunenburgh	190000	£190	£19	171	

Appendix A for 1760

Arrears of Quitrents paid in the Year 1758.				
Counties Names	Number of Acres paid for	Paid in Money	Sheriffs Allowances	Amount
Orange	170000	£170	£17	153
Spotsylvania	5089	£ 5. 1. 9	£ 10. 2	4.11. 7
Surry	1081	£ 1. 1. 7	£ 2. 2	19. 5
Southampton	5618	£ 5.12. 4	£ 11. 2	5. 1. 2
Warwick	562	£ 11. 3	£ 1. 1	10. 2
York	1900	£ 1.18	£ 3. 9	1.14. 3
Ditto	30083	£ 30. 1. 8	£ 3. 2	27. 1. 6

                                                                                        1610.12. 4

Received of Sundry Persons in Several Counties   31.10.

                                                                                        £18877.10. 9

The Receiver General doth Discharge himself

By paid to the Honble & Reverend Robert Cholmondeley on his Majestys Warrant one Years Allowance ending the 25th of October 1759	£ 150
By paid to Mr. Commissary Dawson on his Majestys Warrant one Years Salary ending the 25th of October 1759	100
By two Warrants to the Attorney General for one Years Salary ending the 25th of October 1759	70
By his Majestys Warrant dated at St. James's the 7th day of April 1759 for paying to James West Esqr. or his Assigns	6360
By Allowance of ½ Per Cent for negotiating the Bills of Exchange in London[2]	33. 4. 7
By Allowance to the Auditor at 5 Per Cent on £6651.8	332.11. 5
By Allowance to the Receiver General the same Sum	332.11. 5
So that the Sum Disburst amounts to	£ 7378. 7. 5
And there will remain due to Ballance this Account	11499. 3. 4
	£18877.10. 9

                            Philip Grymes Recr. Genl.

I have Examined the within Account of his Majestys Revenue of Quitrents for the year 1758 and have compared every Article with its proper Voucher produced by Philip Grymes Esqr. his Majestys Receiver General and find the Charge thereof amounting to eighteen thousand eight hundred seventy seven Pounds ten Shillings & nine Pence and the Discharge to seven thousand three hundred seventy eight Pounds seven Shillings and five Pence both truly stated so that there is due to his Majestys Revenue for Ballance of this Account eleven thousand four hundred ninety nine Pounds three Shillings & four Pence Sterling

John Blair D. Audr.

Novr. 19th 1759

The within Account compared & Examined by John Blair Esqr. Deputy Auditor was produced to me in Council & Sworn to by Philip Grymes Esqr. Recr. Genl.

Fran: Fauquier

MS: C.O.5/1330, ff.10–11. Autograph signatures of Grymes, Blair, and Fauquier. Endorsed as read 19 Nov. 1760. Presumably enclosed in Fauquier's letter of 12 May 1760 to the Board of Trade.

1. This is the amount by which receipts exceeded expenditures in the 1757 quitrent account.
2. The allowance, presumably to the receiver, for negotiating bills of exchange is about sixpence less than 0.5 percent of £6,651.8.0, the total collection in 1758.

1760: Appendix B

The Account of his Majestys Revenue of 2/ per Hogshead &c Arising within this Colony of Virginia from the 25th April 1759 to the 25th of October 1759.

The Receiver Genl. doth Charge himself with the Receipt of the said Revenue as follows

To the Account of the Upper District of James River	£ 449. 8. 8
The Account of the Lower District of James River	309.12.11
The Account of the District of York River	293. 6.—
The Account of the District of Rappahannock River	687.—. 3
The Account of the District of South Potomack	279.12.—
The Account of the Port of Accomack	45.18.—
The Account of Sundry Rights of Land sold	196. 9. 4
The Account of Fines & Forfeitures	25.12.—
So that the whole Receipt amounts to	£2286.19. 2
And there will remain due to the Recr. General to Ballance this Account	2641. 2. 6
	£4928. 1. 8

The Receiver Genl. doth Discharge himself By the Payment of the following Sums

By Ballance of the last Account[1]	£2193. 1. 3
By a Warrant for half a Years Salary to the Governor	1000.—.—
By a Warrant for Ditto to the Gentlemen of the Council	600.—.—
By a Warrant to the Judges & other Officers of a Court of Oyer & Terminer	100.—.—
By a Warrant to the Honble. & Reverend Robert Cholmondeley Auditor of the Plantations for half a Years Salary	50.—.—
By a Warrant to James Abercrombie Esqr. Sollicitor of the Virginia Affairs for Ditto	100.—.—
By a Warrant to Peyton Randolph Esqr. his Majestys Attorney Genl. for Ditto	35.—.—
By a Warrant to Nathl. Walthoe Esqr. Clerk of the Council for Ditto	50.—.—
By a Warrant to the Adjutants for half a Years Salary	120.—.—
By a Warrant to Joseph Davenport Armourer for Do.	6.—.—

By a Warrant to the Gunners of the Batteries for Do.	12.10.—
By a Warrant to the Ministers attending one General Court	12.—.—
By a Warrant for Repairs done to the Governors House	69.—.10
By a Warrant for Contingent Charges	342. 1.—
By Allowance to the Receiver General of ½ Per Cent on £1947.17.4 for Negotiating the same in Bills of Exchange in London[2]	9.14. 9
By Allowance to the Auditor of 5 Per Cent on £2286.19.2	114. 6.11
By Allowance to the Receiver General on the same Sum	114. 6.11
	£4928. 1. 8

Philip Grymes Recr. Genl.

I have Examined the within Account of his Majestys Revenue Commencing the 25th of April & ending the 25th of October 1759 & have Compared every Article with its proper Voucher produced by Philip Grymes Esqr. Receiver General & find the same truly stated & that there is due to the said Receiver General for Ballance thereof two thousand six Hundred forty one Pounds two Shillings & six Pence Sterling

John Blair D. Audr.

Novr. 6th 1759
The within Account Compared & Examined by John Blair Esqr. Deputy Auditor was produced to me in Council & sworn to by Philip Grymes Esqr. Receiver General

Fran: Fauquier

MS: C.O.5/1330, ff. 13–14. Autograph signatures of Grymes, Blair, and Fauquier. Endorsed as read 19 Nov. 1760. Presumably enclosed in Fauquier's letter of 12 May 1760 to the Board of Trade.

1. This balance is the amount by which expenditures exceeded receipts in the preceding account, for 25 Oct. 1758–25 Apr. 1759.
2. It has not been possible to identify the sum negotiated in bills of exchange.

1760: Appendix C

The Account of his Majesty's Revenue of 2/ per Hogshead &c Arising within this Colony of Virginia from the 25th of October 1759 to the 25th of April 1760.

The Receiver General doth Charge himself with the Receipt of the said Revenue as follows

To the Account of the Upper District of James River	£1068.—. 1
The Account of the Lower District of James River	329. 2. 8
The Account of the District of York River	384. 5. 6
The Account of the District of Rappahanock River	359. 3.11
The Account of the District of South Potomack	115.19.11
The Account of the Port of Accomack	
The Account of Sundry Rights of Land sold	196. 9. 4
The Account of Fines & Forfeitures	4. 6. 5
So that the whole Receipt amounts to	£2457. 7.10
And there will remain due to the Receiver General to Ballance this Account	2853.14. 4
	£5311. 2. 2

The Receiver General doth Discharge himself By the Payment of the following Sums.

By Ballance of the last Account[1]	£2641. 2. 6
By a Warrant for half a Years Salary to the Governor	1000.—.—
By A Warrant for Ditto to the Gentlemen of the Council	600.—.—
By a Warrant to the Judges & other Officers of a Court of Oyer & Terminer	100.—.—
By a Warrant to the Honble. & Reverend Robert Cholmondeley Auditor of the Plantations for half a Years Salary	50.—.—
By a Warrant to James Abercrombie Esqr. Sollicitor of the Virginia Affairs for Ditto	100.—.—
By A Warrant to Peyton Randolph Esqr. his Majesty's Attorney Genl. for do.	35.—.—
By a Warrant to Nathl. Walthoe Esqr. Clerk of the Council for Ditto	50.—.—
By a Warrant to the Adjutants for half a Years Salary	120.—.—
By a Warrant to Joseph Davenport Armourer for Ditto	6.—.—

By a Warrant to the Gunners of the Batteries for Ditto	12.10.—
By a Warrant to the Ministers attending one General Court & Assembly	14.—.—
By a Warrant for Repairs done to the Governors House	45.13. 5
By a Warrant for Contingent Charges	280.12. 7
By allowance to the Receiver General of ½ Per Cent on £2088.1.10 for Negotiating the same in Bills of Exchange in London[2]	10. 8.10
By allowance to the Auditor at 5 Per Cent on £2457.7.10	122.17. 5
By allowance to the Receiver General on the same Sum	122.17. 5
	£5311. 2. 2

Philip Grymes Recr. Genl.

I have Examined the within Account of his Majesties Revenue Commencing the 25th of October 1759 & ending the 25th of April 1760 and have compared every Article with its Proper Voucher produced by Philip Grymes Esqr. Receiver General & find the same truly stated and that there is due to the said Receiver General for Ballance thereof two thousand eight hundred fifty three Pounds fourteen Shillings & four pence Sterling.

John Blair D. Audr.

May 7th 1760
The within Account compared & Examined by Jno. Blair Esqr. Deputy Auditor was produced to me in Council & sworn to by Philip Grymes Esqr. Receiver General

Fran: Fauquier

MS: C.O.5/1330, ff. 15–16. Autograph signatures of Grymes, Blair, and Fauquier. Endorsed as read 19 Nov. 1760. Presumably enclosed in Fauquier's letter of 12 May 1760 to the Board of Trade.

1. This balance is the amount by which expenditures exceeded receipts in the preceding account, for 25 Apr.–25 Oct. 1759.
2. It has not been possible to identify the sum negotiated in bills of exchange.

LIBRARY OF DAVIDSON COLLEGE